PLAYS AND PLAYWRIGHTS

2010

edited and with an introduction by

Martin Denton

This collection copyright © 2010 by The New York Theatre Experience, Inc.

Introduction copyright © 2010 by Martin Denton

All rights reserved. Except for brief passages quoted in newspaper, magazine, radio, or television reviews, no part of this book may be reproduced in any form or by any means, electronic or mechanical, including photocopying or recording, or by any information storage and retrieval system, without permission in writing from the publisher.

CAUTION: These plays are fully protected, in whole, in part, or in any form, under the copyright laws of the United States of America and of all countries covered by the International Copyright Union (including the Dominion of Canada and the rest of the British Commonwealth), and of all countries covered by the Pan-American Copyright Convention and the Universal Copyright Convention, and of all countries with which the United States has reciprocal copyright relations, and are subject to royalty. All performance rights, including professional, amateur, stock, motion picture, radio, television, recitation, and public reading are strictly reserved. Please refer to Permissions, beginning on page i, for information concerning such inquiries.

Published by The New York Theatre Experience, Inc.
P.O. Box 1606, Murray Hill Station, New York, NY 10156
www.nyte.org
email: info@nyte.org

ISBN-13: 978-0-9794852-3-7
ISSN 1546-1319

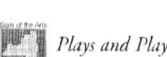

Plays and Playwrights 2010 is made possible, in part, with public funds from the New York State Council on the Arts, a state agency.

Plays and Playwrights 2010 is made possible, in part, with public funds from the New York City Department of Cultural Affairs.

Plays and Playwrights 2010 is made possible, in part, by support from the Peg Santvoord Foundation.

Book and cover designed by Nita Congress

PERMISSIONS

The Invitation copyright © 2008 by Brian Parks. Amateurs and professionals are hereby warned that *The Invitation* is fully protected by copyright law and is subject to royalty. All rights in all current and future media are strictly reserved. No part of this work may be used for any purpose without the written consent of the author. All inquiries concerning production, publication, reprinting, or use of this work in any form should be addressed to the author in care of The New York Theatre Experience, Inc., P.O. Box 1606, Murray Hill Station, New York, NY 10156; by email: info@nyte.org; or by emailing the author directly: bparks3000@yahoo.com.

Flip Side copyright © 2008 by Ellen Maddow. Amateurs and professionals are hereby warned that *Flip Side* is fully protected by copyright law and is subject to royalty. All rights in all current and future media are strictly reserved. No part of this work may be used for any purpose without the written consent of the author. All inquiries concerning production, publication, reprinting, or use of this work in any form should be addressed to the author in care of The New York Theatre Experience, Inc., P.O. Box 1606, Murray Hill Station, New York, NY 10156; by email: info@nyte.org; or by contacting the author directly: Ellen Maddow, c/o The Talking Band, P.O. Box 293, Prince Station, New York, NY 10012.

Any Day Now copyright © 2009 by Nat Cassidy. Amateurs and professionals are hereby warned that *Any Day Now* is fully protected by copyright law and is subject to royalty. All rights in all current and future media are strictly reserved. No part of this work may be used for any purpose without the written consent of the author. All inquiries concerning production, publication, reprinting, or use of this work in any form should be addressed to the author in care of The New York Theatre Experience, Inc., P.O. Box 1606, Murray Hill Station, New York, NY 10156; by email: info@nyte.org.

The Spin Cycle copyright © 2009 by Jerrod Bogard. Amateurs and professionals are hereby warned that the plays *Copper Green*, *Hedge*, *Just Your Average G.I. Joe*, *First Base Coach*, and *Jerome Via Satellite* are fully protected by copyright law and are subject to royalty. All rights in all current and future media are strictly reserved. No part of these works may be used for any purpose without the written consent of the author. All inquiries concerning production, publication, reprinting, or use of this work in any form should be addressed to the author in care of The New York Theatre Experience, Inc., P.O. Box 1606, Murray Hill Station, New York, NY 10156; by email: info@nyte.org.

Suspicious Package: Rx copyright © 2009 by Gyda Arber and Aaron Baker. Amateurs and professionals are hereby warned that *Suspicious Package: Rx* is fully protected by copyright law and is subject to royalty. All rights in all current and future media are strictly reserved. No part of this work may be used for any purpose without the written consent of the authors. All inquiries concerning production, publication, reprinting, or use of this work in any form should be addressed to the authors in care of The New York Theatre Experience, Inc., P.O. Box 1606, Murray Hill Station, New York, NY 10156; by email: info@nyte.org.

Our Country copyright © 2009 by Tony Asaro and Dan Collins. Amateurs and professionals are hereby warned that *Our Country* is fully protected by copyright law and is subject to royalty. All rights in all current and future media are strictly reserved. No part of this work may be used for any purpose without the written consent of the authors. All inquiries concerning production, publication, reprinting, or use of this work in any form should be addressed to the authors at their website: www.ourcountrytoo.com; or by email: info@ourcountrytoo.com.

Maddy: A Modern-Day Medea copyright © 2009 by Will Le Vasseur. Amateurs and professionals are hereby warned that *Maddy: A Modern-Day Medea* is fully protected by copyright law and is subject to royalty. All rights in all current and future media are strictly reserved. No part of this work may be used for any purpose without the written consent of the author. All inquiries concerning production, publication, reprinting, or use of this work in any form should be addressed to the author in care of The New York Theatre Experience, Inc., P.O. Box 1606, Murray Hill Station, New York, NY 10156; by email: info@nyte.org.

Al's Business Cards copyright © 2009 by Josh Koenigsberg. Amateurs and professionals are hereby warned that *Al's Business Cards* is fully protected by copyright law and is subject to royalty. All rights in all current and future media are strictly reserved. No part of this work may be used for any purpose without the written consent of the author. All inquiries concerning production, publication, reprinting, or use of this work in any form should be addressed to the author: At Play c/o The eXchange, 310 West 72nd Street, Suite 5c, New York, NY 10023; by email: info@atplayproductions.com.

The Songs of Robert copyright © 1998, 2009 by John Crutchfield. Amateurs and professionals are hereby warned that *The Songs of Robert* is fully protected by copyright law and is subject to royalty. All rights in all current and future media are strictly reserved. No part of this work may be used for any purpose without the written consent of the author. The author maintains right to first refusal to perform in all future productions of *The Songs of Robert*. All inquiries concerning production, publication, reprinting, or use of this work in any form should be addressed to the author in care of The New York Theatre Experience, Inc., P.O. Box 1606, Murray Hill Station, New York, NY 10156; by email: info@nyte.org.

MilkMilkLemonade copyright © 2009 by Joshua Conkel. Amateurs and professionals are hereby warned that *MilkMilkLemonade* is fully protected by copyright law and is subject to royalty. All rights in all current and future media are strictly reserved. No part of this work may be used for any purpose without the written consent of the author. To obtain stock and amateur performance rights, please contact: Playscripts, Inc., 450 Seventh Avenue, Suite 809, New York, NY 10123; www.playscripts.com; 1-866-NEW-PLAY (639-7529).

TABLE OF CONTENTS

PERMISSIONS i

FOREWORD vii
   Leslie Bramm

ACKNOWLEDGMENTS ix

INTRODUCTION 1
   Martin Denton

THE INVITATION 13
   Brian Parks

FLIP SIDE 57
   Ellen Maddow

ANY DAY NOW 93
   Nat Cassidy

THE SPIN CYCLE 165
   Jerrod Bogard

SUSPICIOUS PACKAGE: Rx 203
   Gyda Arber and Aaron Baker

OUR COUNTRY 251
    Tony Asaro and Dan Collins

MADDY: A MODERN-DAY MEDEA 277
    Will Le Vasseur

AL'S BUSINESS CARDS 297
    Josh Koenigsberg

THE SONGS OF ROBERT 325
    John Crutchfield

MILKMILKLEMONADE 351
    Joshua Conkel

FOREWORD

Leslie Bramm

I overheard the following conversation at a writer's lab. Work was being done on the first nine pages of a new full-length play. The playwright fidgeted. Twisted the corner of his notebook. Chewed on his pen cap. It's easy to understand his nervous excitement. This was the first time this nascent nine pages had ever been read out loud. It was exhilarating. Anything could happen. The actors gave it a great reading, the playwright was jotting notes, I was curious to hear the feedback. A few moments of awkward silence followed, before one of the actors chimed in—

ACTOR: Your stuff reminds of me Dwight…

PLAYWRIGHT: You mean, from *The Office*?

The whole table started to laugh, except me. I haven't owned a television in years and found myself on the fringes of an inside joke.

ACTOR: It's like when he goes… *(Insert clever line from sitcom.)*

PLAYWRIGHT: Yeah, or like when… *(Insert another clever line which they reenact together.)*

The playwright had found a common language in which to communicate his theatrical idea. The language of television.

Aristotle says theatre is the celebration of the idea. Nowhere does the idea reign more sublime than in the indie theater movement. From the indie theater movement comes the work that's bold enough to reflect our present culture back to itself. From the indie theater movement comes work that speaks of peace and demands a sense of justice. And, in the indie theater movement, the idea is still necessary.

Of the obstacles our theatre faces, from a lack of funding to an apathetic world, none compares to television, which not only keeps people at home and disconnected, but also subverts what our very audience expects from those of us who make theatre.

For over ten years now, Martin Denton and The New York Theatre Experience have found a way to keep the *idea* alive and vital. The ten plays in this anthology represent some new and passionate voices. Read these plays. See what's on these writers' minds. See what you can learn from them. Let them entertain you. Keep encouraging these ideas.

*Leslie Bramm is the author of fourteen plays. His work has been produced, workshopped, and/or developed by Three Crows Theatre, The Present Company, Penobscot Theatre, Actors Theatre of Louisville, Emerging Artists Theatre Company, Nicu's Spoon, the Edward Albee Last Frontier Conference, and Reverie Productions, to name a few. Bramm is the recipient of a Stanley Drama Award (*Oswald's Backyard*), a Paul T. Nolan Award (*Islands of Repair*), and a Tennessee Williams Literary Award (*Big Ball*). He is published by JAC Publications, Smith and Kraus, Brooklyn Publishers, One Act Play Depot, and The New York Theatre Experience. He is a member of The Pool, The League of Independent Theater, and The Dramatists Guild.*

ACKNOWLEDGMENTS

Plays and Playwrights 2010 is the eleventh in our annual series of anthologies. As we enter a second decade of publishing these volumes, it's a happy fact that their creation remains a labor of love for all involved, and for that I am especially grateful.

There are many collaborators who need to be mentioned for their contributions to this book. Obviously the most crucial are the playwrights themselves, who have agreed to let me present their work to readers. To Gyda Arber and Aaron Baker, Tony Asaro and Dan Collins, Jerrod Bogard, Nat Cassidy, Joshua Conkel, John Crutchfield, Josh Koenigsberg, Will Le Vasseur, Ellen Maddow, and Brian Parks: it has been a pleasure to work with you; thank you for being part of this volume.

I am also indebted to the people who helped guide me to these plays, and who, in some cases, introduced me to these playwright: Michael Gardner and Robert Honeywell of The Brick Theater; Katie Rosin, Glory Bowen, Frank Calo, and Amber Gallery of the Planet Connections Theatre Festivity; Kristin Skye Hoffmann of Wide Eyed Productions, Michael Martinez, and Carlo Riveccio and Christy Benanti of Shortened Attention Span; Sara Jeanne Asselin and Montserrat Mendez; Erez Ziv and Emily Owens of Horse Trade Theater Group; Elena K. Holy and Ron Lasko of the New York International Fringe Festival; Sam Rudy, Dale Heller, and Bob Lasko; Emily Otto; and John Clancy.

The creation of this book is almost entirely the work of Nita Congress, our tireless and dedicated copy editor and designer. Without her, that would be no *Plays and Playwrights* anthologies.

Rochelle Denton, who is the managing director of NYTE, does all the behind-the-scenes work to make our books a reality: everything from coordinating with our printer to overseeing all of our marketing and distribution activities (which she does in a very hands-on way: it's not uncommon to see her packing orders at midnight!) to running the nytesmallpress website and our online storefront. NYTE's publishing program is very much her baby, and the indie theater world is indisputably the better for her contributions. *Plays and Playwrights 2010* is dedicated to her.

Martin Denton
March 1, 2010

INTRODUCTION

Martin Denton

In September 2008, when *The Invitation* (chronologically the earliest of the ten plays in this volume) debuted, America was a few weeks away from an election that most of us believed would be the most important of our lives, one that proved historic and, many hoped, transformational.

In September 2009, when *MilkMilkLemonade*, the last of this collection's plays, appeared, too little had changed, and what had—the economic outlook, mostly—was for the worse. How did we get here? How might we pull ourselves out of the rut we seem so stuck in?

Drama really can supply some of the answer. Because the production of indie theater doesn't generally require the enormous outlays of time and money that commercial Broadway shows or most film or TV work need in order to be put before the public, the elapsed time from conception to presentation is often relatively brief; in this way, the best indie theater can be a reliable barometer of the national mood in ways that other performance media can't muster.

The ten plays brought together here reflect the American mood, for better and worse, in 2008 and 2009. Brian Parks's *The Invitation* and Joshua Conkel's *MilkMilkLemonade* take vitriolic swipes at, respectively, the cult of greed and the so-called family values that threaten to cripple our capacity to move forward as a nation. Ellen Maddow's *Flip Side*, Nat Cassidy's *Any Day Now*, and Josh Koenigsberg's *Al's Business Cards* offer more gentle glances at the culture wars, while John Crutchfield's lyrical *The Songs of Robert* reminds us of the core values Americans supposedly share. Jerrod Bogard's *The Spin Cycle* focuses sharply on the aftermath of the conflict in Iraq, while Tony Asaro and Dan Collins's musical, *Our Country*, probes the continuing problem of institutionalized homophobia. Will Le Vasseur's *Maddy: A Modern-Day Medea* and Gyda Arber's *Suspicious Package: Rx* transform theatrical tradition in very different ways to comment on how we experience art and how we interact with our environment.

I'm proud and excited to bring these works together for readers to enjoy and appreciate. I hope that these plays will stimulate the imagination sufficiently to inspire new productions; these are all eminently actable and directable works that deserve long life beyond their original productions in New York City during 2008 and 2009.

✍ ✍ ✍ ✍ ✍

Ah, the dinner party—reliable setting for many a sophisticated and/or scathing examination of societal mores. You know the kind of thing: elegantly dressed and coiffed folk seated on expensive-looking furniture, surrounded by beautiful objects and sipping exclusive wines from exquisite crystal, all the while engaging in snappy repartee about this and that, conversation filled with wit and undertone. This is just what happens in Brian Parks's *The Invitation*...until it isn't. In this impassionedly vitriolic dark satire, Parks has a field day making fun of America's cultural and social elite. And he's not handling them with kid gloves; no, the gloves are definitely off as Parks moves in for the kill. I won't tell you what happens to make this dinner party quite unlike any other I've seen depicted on stage, but it gets right to the heart of the sick cults of entitlement and greed that made the first decade of the twenty-first century into a new Gilded Age here in America.

Of course, it all begins innocently enough. Dave and Marian are hosting their friends John and Sarah (another married couple) and Steph for a dinner celebrating Steph's birthday. They've just finished another of Marian's amazing dinners (something with lamb) and are savoring some fine wine as they chat about this and that. Dave is in publishing, John's a high-powered attorney, and Steph is an equally high-powered advertising exec. Sarah does good works at a foundation she runs. And Marian is a very opinionated socialite:

> MARIAN: I agree. Vegetarianism—it's just sort of retarded.
>
> SARAH: "Retarded" is not a word one uses these days.
>
> MARIAN: I'm sorry. "Mongoloid," then.
>
> DAVID: Marian—
>
> MARIAN: *(Happily coining term.)* "Neo-Cretinism."
>
> SARAH: Now, now—

MARIAN: Then let them choose their own word.

SARAH: Fine.

MARIAN: Just don't ask them to spell it!

The banter flies fast and furious—this is the kind of dialogue of which Parks is a master—and as it does, we discover that Dave and Marian are a sort of latter-day George and Martha (à la Albee's *Who's Afraid of Virginia Woolf?*). Things are bound to explode, and they do. The second half of the play succeeds in making us pay lots of attention to Parks's ideas, which feel subversive and dangerous and enormously important and prescient.

The Invitation was impeccably directed by frequent Parks collaborator John Clancy, and David Calvitto (Dave), Paul Urcioli (John), Leslie Farrell (Steph), Katie Honaker (Marian), and Eva van Dok (Sarah)—all veterans of previous Clancy and/or Parks productions—offered flawless performances in the original production. The comedy here is frothy in places, and mordant and lethal in others. It's designed to deliver jolts, to shake up its audience—and it does.

✠ ✠ ✠ ✠ ✠

Flip Side is a whimsical, wise, theatrical meditation on longing and its close siblings greed, envy, and entitlement. Ellen Maddow's script is full of profound and gloriously elegantly poetry that I am glad to capture here in this book so that it may be properly savored.

Flip Side takes place in two worlds. In "Side A" we are in Drizzle Plaza, a place of missed connections and missed opportunities, of stifling grimness and sameness that stymies most of its denizens. In "Side B" we go to The Waterfalls, which is more or less (as the play's title suggests) the flip side of Drizzle Plaza; here everything moves to a relentless, frenetic beat, and there's too much, rather than too little, to do.

What the people of Drizzle Plaza and The Waterfallls have in common is a desire for something more, and most of them spend their time literally or figuratively pressing their noses against the glass divide that separates the two universes.

A clash of cultures is imminent. The catalyst for it is an innocent-seeming flirtation between Alan Flynnalyn of Drizzle Plaza and Sylvia Waterfall. They went to high school together decades ago, and have found each other online in an alumni chatroom. Alan's wife Marilyn eventually becomes furious at being brushed aside by her husband in favor of his new cyberbuddy, and so she packs a suitcase full of treacherous household objects and journeys to The

Waterfalls in search of her nemesis and revenge. When the barrier between the two worlds is breached, though, havoc is wrought and then a kind of understanding is achieved by folks from both sides.

Though *Flip Side* offers us many storylines to follow, it is the reunion of Alan and Sylvia that anchors the piece. Their rediscovery of one another in cyberspace—necessarily platonic and rooted inescapably in nostalgia—exemplifies the deep, ineffable, unquenchable longings that everyone in *Flip Side* experiences.

There's genuine profundity in this play, which was brilliantly augmented by Paul Zimet's playful direction. His production for The Talking Band was full of surprises and featured perhaps the most effective use of computer video (some of it right on the MacBook screen!) that I've ever encountered on stage.

The two "Sides" of Maddow's play are states of mind; the boundary between them is mental rather than physical. We've all lived in Drizzle Plaza or The Waterfalls sometime during our lives; perhaps we've lived in both at the same time. As soon as we erect that barrier between the two, we make it insurmountable; this is a play about balance and moderation—in our needs and wants as well as our daily habits—which makes it surprisingly resonant in this hectic age of ours.

✦ ✦ ✦ ✦ ✦

Any Day Now takes place in the kitchen of the Colby home in New London, Connecticut. The play opens with Mom and Dad—Pen (short for Penelope) and Adam—on stage; she's making chicken salad for dinner and he's seated quietly at the table. The elder daughter, Beverly, arrives; it's clear that Beverly is a bit of a control freak and that her relations with her parents are strained, but she's ready to help out with what she immediately recognizes as a crisis. Shortly thereafter, younger daughter April turns up. The sisters do not get along. Pen confides in April warmly, leaving Beverly to ask complainingly why nobody confides in her. April's husband Josh is here also, and it turns out that the two of them are about to get a divorce. And Beverly's husband David arrives, with news that their daughter Jackie is being expelled from college because she was caught dealing drugs.

It does not take long for the scene to reach a cacophonous crescendo. This could be the family in *August: Osage County* or any number of contemporary dysfunctional family dramedies.

But there is one significant difference that I haven't mentioned yet. Dad is dead. In fact, he's a zombie, staring out dead-eyed from his seat at the kitchen table.

INTRODUCTION

Any Day Now frequently feels neatly off-kilter, with the audience never quite sure whether to laugh or to gasp. Playwright Nat Cassidy packages his supernatural theme with such naturalistic aplomb that he evokes David Lynch, particularly the very first episode of *Twin Peaks*, where you were trying to decipher the creator's intent while increasingly jaw-dropping weirdness unfolded before your eyes.

Cassidy also packs into his play discussion of various religions' beliefs about resurrection of the dead and the relationship of that phenomenon to the apocalypse; there's also some political material that feels like a reaction to Sarah Palin and, more generally, our national mood post-9/11.

Cassidy directed the original production at Manhattan Theatre Source, sustaining the heightened, off-balance naturalism beautifully throughout. The cast featured Elyse Mirto, who would go on to win a New York Innovative Theatre Award for her performance as April, and Arthur Aulisi, who is now the actor with the most frequent appearances in the *Plays and Playwrights* series (he was in plays featured in our 2005, 2006, and 2009 volumes).

Any Day Now, only Cassidy's second full-length play, portends a promising theatre career for this talented and intelligent young artist.

✔ ✔ ✔ ✔ ✔

The Spin Cycle, a program of five plays, is an impressive showcase of playwright Jerrod Bogard's range. And as conceived by Bogard and his collaborators at Wide Eyed Productions and Shortened Attention Span, it proved a sterling example of how to successfully mount an evening of short plays.

Bogard is clearly concerned about the state of the world, especially the war in Iraq; three of the five plays deal directly or indirectly with that conflict and how it has affected Americans. At the center of *The Spin Cycle* is a remarkable one-man play called *Just Your Average G.I. Joe* (which Bogard himself performed in *The Spin Cycle*, under the sharp direction of Kristin Skye Hoffmann); it takes place in a bar somewhere in the American South, and introduces us to a young soldier just returned from Iraq, who is explaining to some unseen person or persons that being in the army is just like any other job. This fellow doth protest too much: the more he tries to convince us that he likes his work, the more we begin to suspect otherwise. *Just Your Average G.I. Joe* is fascinating because it's so ambivalent—there have always been people who justify and even glorify war, but can they really look us in the eye as they make their arguments?

Copper Green, which opens the evening, takes place on the Staten Island Ferry, where a dad from the American Heartland uses this moment to try to explain what his older son is fighting for in Iraq. *The Spin Cycle* concludes with *Jerome Via Satellite*, which may be the strongest and most potent play of this quintet. It's about an American soldier named Jerome in Iraq who is going to appear on a cable talk show (called "The Spin Cycle") to receive birthday greetings from his family back home in the States. The places where Bogard takes this familiar concept are surprising and jolting; the play juxtaposes crassness, indifference, courage, and love in a harrowing and resonant manner.

Nestled among this socially conscious fare are two much lighter works: *Hedge*, about two young women in Hollywood hiding out from the paparazzi, and *First Base Coach*, the funniest play of *The Spin Cycle*, featuring an eleven-year old girl and nine-year-old boy who are testing out hypotheses about just exactly what it means to get to first base in a relationship.

The Spin Cycle is tightly knit together with video transitions featuring the same talk show host character who is integral to *Jerome Via Satellite*, a smart choice that gives the evening cohesion and unity.

✦ ✦ ✦ ✦ ✦

The immersive theatre experience known as *Suspicious Package: Rx*—the work of Gyda Arber, Aaron Baker, and a host of artistic collaborators—is enormous fun. It casts each of its audience members in a role in a short comedy of suspense and intrigue that carried them (in the original production) from the front door of The Brick Theater to locales all around the lively Williamsburg block surrounding the venue. It's sort of like a video/adventure game with live actors (who are the audience members).

There are six characters in *Suspicious Package: Rx*: a doctor, a corporate executive, a chemist, a colonel in the U.S. army, a secretary, and a computer whiz. There are also six audience members/participants at each performance of *Suspicious Package: Rx*, each cast in one of the roles I just named. A short, informative orientation (conducted, during the Brick engagement, with charm and aplomb by Arber) goes a long way toward relieving audience anxiety about interactive theatre. Each participant then receives a hat or similar prop that identifies his/her character. They also receive an iPod, customized for their role, which serves as their guide to the next forty-five minutes or so: as you'll see in the play's script, it contains instructions about where to go and what to do and also the dialogue that each participant will speak when he or she meets up with a counterpart in one of the play's many scenes. The iPod also contains video and audio clips that provide the back story for the participant's character. By the end of the show, the six audience members/participants wind up together, with the mystery each of them has been wrapped up in satisfactorily resolved.

Arber, Baker, and their confederates have found a way to make the *Suspicious Package* franchise ("Rx" was preceded by a premiere edition in 2008) entirely fresh, and have crafted a one-of-kind immersive event that's tightly scripted and timed down to the millisecond. *Suspicious Package: Rx* is a great deal of fun to take part in. It's also extremely well written—the adventure that unfolds is gripping and interesting and even a little bit timely in a *Twilight Zone*-y way. And, significantly, it is authentically innovative—a multimedia theatre experience that exploits new technology in a way quite unlike anything that's come before.

✍ ✍ ✍ ✍ ✍

Our Country, a musical by Tony Asaro (music and lyrics; original concept) and Dan Collins (book) about a country singer's rise, fall, and turnaround, is a top-notch entertainment. It concerns Tommy Dautry, who confesses to us in the opening musical number "Lord, Lord, Lord, How the Mighty Fall," that he has recently been arrested for "lewd conduct" with an undercover cop. Once a rising star in the country music scene, Tommy is now a has-been and a joke, rejected by the industry and fans who once adored him.

He then narrates for us his life story, from his roots in a small town in the Bible Belt where he and his pal Duane become the center of a local band. Though Duane is a fundamentalist Christian and Tommy is an ambivalent, closeted young gay man, the two fall in love, and the song that Tommy writes for Duane, "Honestly," becomes their ticket to Nashville and a recording contract. A romantic night together leads to a close shave that prompts Tommy to abandon Duane and play it "straight." He becomes a star, with a string of hit records. But he's empty inside because of the double life he believes he must lead to sustain his success.

Our Country travels some well-trodden territory, albeit with a gay twist that makes it timely and gives it a certain gravitas. What makes this show special is the material: I wish you could hear Asaro's toe-tapping, infectious music; at least we can share here the smart, witty, and often quite moving book and lyrics.

There are great theatre songs in the mix: "Not Like That At All," for example, is a jubilant celebration of first love and first success that pushes the show forward brilliantly in its early scenes. "Sicka

Singin' 'Bout Girls" is about exactly what the title says, and proves to be a great turning point in the story. The eleven o'clock number, "When Music Mattered," is Tommy's heart-felt summation of what he's learned in the play. And the finale, the title song "Our Country," is a rousing anthem that should get adopted by anti-Proposition 8 folks pronto.

In a bow to economy, the authors have structured their show shrewdly: the band members interact with Tommy throughout the show, essentially playing all of the other characters in what is otherwise pretty much a one-man musical. In the original production at the Planet Connections Theatre Festivity, that one man was Justin Utley, a newcomer to the NYC theatre scene, who sang and acted the role of Tommy with unwavering presence and enormous charm. *Our Country* feels like it could be a breakout hit on the order of *Rent* or *Jersey Boys*, though on a smaller scale: it has more heart, more melody, and more musical theatre craftsmanship than most of the new shows on Broadway right now.

✔ ✔ ✔ ✔ ✔

Twenty-five hundred years after the fact, it's difficult to imagine the impact that the great Greek tragedies might have had on their audiences. Fundamental human emotions transcend time, but fundamental belief systems often do not; the connections to a pantheon of gods, to nature, and to the mercurial hand of destiny parse very differently for us than they must have for our ancestors sitting on a hillside watching a play like Euripides' *Medea*.

So I was immediately fascinated and excited by Will Le Vasseur's remarkable new play, *Maddy—A Modern Day Medea*. This taut, smart, and very intense one-act captures what's at the heart of this legend in a thrillingly contemporary and accessible way. The story and themes have never made more sense to me.

Maddy shifts the famous story of Medea from ancient Corinth to the Corinthian Trailer Park in a small town somewhere in the American Heartland. Here resides the title character, who is very much both protagonist and heroine in this rendering. At the beginning of the play, a man named Alan is speaking with Maddy; their conversation ends with him telling her she has until sundown to make her decision. Soon we start to understand what is at stake for her: her husband, Billy-Jae, is going to marry the daughter of the richest man in town this afternoon, and he wants to bring their two sons to live with him. Maddy asks her neighbor Flo whether she, in a similar circumstance, would seek retribution against the husband who is leaving her high and dry, a husband whom she still loves and for whom she gave up almost everything important in her life till now. Flo admits that if there were no obstacles to doing so, she would certainly take revenge. Who would not?

If you know how *Medea* plays out, then you can guess what will happen here, but there are nonetheless several surprises, the most important of which is that Maddy is a being from an advanced civilization. This transposition accounts for the otherworldliness of Medea, who was supposedly a sorceress or witch, after all; it also gets right to the point of this scary myth, which is that one should not tamper with destiny or nature or the elements—whatever you call the greater powers-that-be around and above us. The climax of the play is thrilling and the ending not quite what you'd expect.

Le Vasseur himself directed the premiere at the tiny Spoon Theatre in midtown Manhattan. One of his smartest ideas is to limit the onstage cast to just five (with some offstage recorded voices); the children and Billy-Jae's intended bride are never seen, which is economical in terms of stagecraft as well as indie theater production.

❧ ❧ ❧ ❧ ❧

> But that's when I realized that *this is* the way the world works, y'know? You, you sneeze and a person dies. You leave your book on the bus, and a war breaks out! I mean if one thing leads to another, how can you *do* anything? How can you get up in the morning, say hi to someone, eat a meal? I move my hand this way and somewhere a kid starts crying! So *of course* life is monotonous!

This little bit of philosophy is the center of Josh Koenigsberg's delightful *Al's Business Cards*. Interestingly, the play is a comedy—a very funny one, in fact; sort of what would happen if *La Ronde* were a farce and not about sex—and so the philosophizing is very much incidental to the warm-hearted good spirits that pervade this charmer.

The chain of events that propels *Al's Business Cards* begins on a film set in New Jersey, where two of the assistant gaffers, Al and Barry, are munching on snacks during a break. Al says to Barry, "I tell you I got business cards?…They say 'Al Gurvis, Professional Gaffing Assistant.'" Barry thinks this seems pretty silly. Why didn't Al write "Electrician" on the cards? But Al is undaunted in his plans to move ahead in the business world. Except that the cards delivered to Al don't arrive as scheduled. Instead, Al's cards say "Eileen Lee, Executive Realtor" on them. The printer made a mistake. Al calls Eileen instead of the printer to try to arrange a swap, and the game, as they say, is on.

What follows is a succession of scenes built on misbegotten ideas and misapprehensions that escalate and involve—in addition to Al, Barry, and Eileen—Daniel, who is Eileen's estranged husband, and Jose Alvarez, a private detective working for Daniel to help him discredit Eileen at their divorce hearing. The story spirals quickly into inspired craziness; real estate, gaffing, gassers, the Mets, a pair of suits from Men's Wearhouse, and Alcoholics Anonymous all somehow figure prominently.

Koenigsberg's characters are badly flawed and goofy as all get-out, but he has written them with so much affection that we love them and root for them, warts and all. Along the way, they offer some potent commentary on the shallow manner in which we judge each other (especially based on names, skintones, and the like) and, as already mentioned, on what Rowan and Martin used to call the Fickle Finger of Fate.

✔ ✔ ✔ ✔ ✔

If Robert were
A dog, he'd purr

That's just one small, delightful example of the poetry that floods *The Songs of Robert*, John Crutchfield's gorgeous solo show. Told in song, poetry, and monologue—all brimming with remarkable language that evokes breathtaking image after breathtaking image—this play is the story of a young man on the brink of everything, filled with the ineffable longing of first love and the lonesomeness that comes from not fitting in and not being properly understood.

Robert is a senior in high school in a small town in southern Appalachia; it's the mid-1980s, in the final spring before his graduation. The events of *The Songs of Robert* mostly revolve around how he has not yet asked the dark-haired girl he is infatuated with to go to the prom with him. But the places that this extraordinary play takes us are boundless and deep.

The story is told by a dozen different characters. Young Robert—looking forward to leaving his North Carolina home for art school at a New England university—is one of these voices; others include his father, who loves and tries to comprehend the son whose interests are so different from his own; his high school English teacher, Mrs. Anderson, who leads a thrilling discussion of *The Catcher in the Rye* that resonates with Robert's own circumstance; his little sister Jennie, a cheerleader; and his guidance counselor. I think my favorite among the characters is Coach Sloe, a P.E. teacher with a poet's soul. (I also enjoyed meeting Lurlene, the school bus driver—once encountered she's not easily forgotten, believe me.)

Two of the characters are from beyond the realm of family and school. Juan-Jorge Jesus is Robert's inexplicably Hispanic guardian angel (not in Robert's fantasy, apparently, but an actual guardian angel—I love that the world of the play encompasses this). And Ol' Preacha is described as "a wandering bluesman of uncertain age and origin," a minstrel who puts his hat out for tips at the top of the show and intermittently returns to sing most of the songs in *The Songs of Robert*, heart-tugging blues that reflect the anxious and questing spirit of our young hero even as the things they tell about are miles and years beyond anything he's experienced thus far.

Juan-Jorge and Ol' Preacha are the wisest characters in this wise show; everyone in it is big-hearted and humane, though, and all delightfully transcend archetypes, because Crutchfield's writing make them achingly real. The words soar in almost every moment, reflecting Robert's desires. The play moves around its various narrators in a more or less chronological fashion until an end comes that I certainly wasn't expecting, one that's perfect in its inevitability and simplicity.

✔ ✔ ✔ ✔ ✔

Not to overstate how well-written *MilkMilkLemonade* is, but it feels like something Edward Albee might have written for a pair of ten-year-old protagonists. Mind you, Joshua Conkel, author of this darkly comic new play, is not Albee; not yet: but he has a unique and remarkable voice and his concerns aren't all that different from what was being investigated in plays like *The American Dream* and *The Sandbox* fifty years ago: namely, the festering, melancholy rot that's eating away at the American spirit.

MilkMilkLemonade takes place on a farm near a place called Mall Town, USA, somewhere in the middle of our country—"now-ish," according to the script. This farm is owned by Nanna, a hardworking and hard-luck middle-aged lady who is dying of lung cancer and wheels around a portable oxygen unit, from which she wheezingly inhales between puffs on an omnipresent cigarette. (Subtlety is not the name of the game here.) Nanna raises chickens on her farm, and today the birds are due to go into the "machine," where they will be (allegedly) mercifully slaughtered and processed into sellable chicken parts.

The only other person on the farm is Emory, her ten-year-old grandson. Emory is, as the playwright himself puts it, a "sissy boy." He wants to leave the farm and go to the City where he instinctively knows he will find other boys like himself. He dreams of winning a TV reality show. Nanna doesn't really get Emory, and at the beginning of the play she tries to instill some of her values in her wayward grandson: he needs to stop playing with dolls and stop acting like a girl. Maybe he should play with that little boy next door, Elliot, who likes to set fires on his parents' lawn.

Elliot turns out to be as big a misfit as Emory, only lacking the self-knowledge and confidence that keep Emory afloat. The two are a sad pair of youngsters, victims of the stasis they find themselves in and the provincial attitudes of the grown-ups who are rearing them. With them, Conkel makes important observations about the state of our union.

I almost forgot to mention that Emory's only other friend is a talking chicken named Linda.

Conkel's play is bitterly funny and broadly satiric, a modern surrealist drama where a lady in a black leotard translates Linda's clucking into English and characters are prone to burst into song or dance numbers at pretty much any time. Its antic, absurdist ambience keeps us enough removed from the story so that its emotional center isn't unbearably sad and also helps focus us on the troubling way we Americans deal with issues like sexuality, identity, and self-actualization.

THE INVITATION

Brian Parks

BRIAN PARKS was born in 1962 in Ann Arbor, Michigan, and grew up in suburban Detroit. His interest in theatre began in high school. "The first play that I actually enjoyed was Tom Stoppard's *Rosencrantz and Guildenstern Are Dead*, which I saw at the Hillberry Studio Theater at Wayne State University in Detroit," he says. "That set something off in me…" Parks graduated from Brown University with an AB in American civilization; more recently he attained an MFA in English/playwriting from Brooklyn College. Parks's produced plays include *Out of the Way* (1989, Studio Eremos, San Francisco), *Americana Absurdum* (1997, New York International Fringe Festival, with later productions at the Edinburgh Fringe Festival and London's Menier Chocolate Factory Theatre), *Goner* (1999, The Present Company Theatorium, with later productions at the Edinburgh Fringe Festival and the Kraine Theatre), *Suspicious Package* (2004, HERE Arts Center); and *American Poodle: Splayfoot* (2007, Edinburgh Fringe Festival, with later productions at the Adelaide Fringe Festival and Riverside Studios, London). *Americana Absurdum* won the award for Best Writing at FringeNYC and a Fringe First citation in Edinburgh. *The Invitation* has been translated into German (as *Einladung zum Abendessen*) by John and Peter von Düffel and has been presented in Heidelberg and Berlin. Parks is currently working on a new play entitled *Imperial Fizz* with a planned premiere at the Edinburgh Fringe in 2010. He resides in Brooklyn.

The Invitation was first presented by Wordmonger at the Ohio Theatre on September 5, 2008, with the following cast and credits:

David .... David Calvitto
John .... Paul Urcioli
Marian .... Katie Honaker
Sarah .... Eva van Dok
Steph .... Leslie Farrell

Directed by: John Clancy
Stage Manager: Caroline Patterson
Sets and Costumes: Rose A. C. Howard
Lights: Eric Southern

Special thanks to Leslie Farrell, Ed Parks, Chris Sorensen, Mac Wellman, Adam Saucy, Robert Lyons, Vanessa Sparling, Ron Lasko, Ruth McCann, and Shiho Miyazawa.

CHARACTERS

DAVID: Co-host of the dinner party. Married to Marian. David is a successful book publishing editor. He is engaged and energetic, but with a creeping bitterness.

MARIAN: Co-host of the dinner party. Married to David. She is always upbeat, self-assured, and cheerful, no matter what she is saying or doing.

SARAH: A dinner party guest. Works for a charitable foundation. Married to John, she is thoughtful and a little bit earnest.

JOHN: A dinner party guest. A highly successful lawyer, but a down-to-earth, gregarious, friendly man. He is married to Sarah.

STEPH: A dinner party guest. An advertising executive. A little bit of a cynic, but not negative.

SET

The dining room of the fashionable city apartment of Marian and David. The apartment entrance door is upstage right, a closet door is near it, and there is a hallway to the kitchen stage left. An unseen downstage wall and window are occasionally indicated by the actors. A dinner table sits center stage.

Stage directions have intentionally been kept to a minimum, to best allow the director to pursue his or her own vision of the production.

SCENE ONE

In the darkness, the sound of the "Peasants March" from Tchaikovsky's Eugene Onegin. It's playing very loudly. It plays, and at the very end a WOMAN's voice is heard shouting.

MARIAN: *SHUT IT UP!*

(*The music stops, and lights come up abruptly on DAVID and MARIAN's apartment. A dinner party is ongoing. DAVID stands next to the stereo. SARAH, JOHN, STEPH, and MARIAN are at the table. It is a birthday dinner for STEPH. The characters are all nicely dressed. The main course is close to finishing, a bit of food remains on the table, including some wine bottles and bread baskets. No one is drunk, but there's a boisterous mood fueled by lots of very nice wine.*)

MARIAN: *(About the music.)* That's enough loud Russian peasantry!

STEPH: How Tsarist of you!

MARIAN: I like to hear my guests.

SARAH: *(Referring to music.)* I *love* that section.

MARIAN: I like to hear their different thoughts.

JOHN: Does gossip count as thought?

MARIAN: Their new stories. That opera—play it *a hundred times* and the story never changes.

DAVID: It's a *classic*—it's beautiful.

STEPH: Like *my* story never changes.

DAVID: You're beautiful, too.

STEPH: As long as I'm not a classic yet.

SARAH: We told you, Steph, someone *new* will come along.

DAVID: And we'll all enjoy loud Tchaikovsky together.

JOHN: At the opera house.

MARIAN: We'll bring picnic baskets!

JOHN: And chianti. A cheap one to match the sentimentality onstage.

SARAH: Lovely!

MARIAN: Just no oysters.

SARAH: Why?

MARIAN: Oysters are like eating someone else's phlegm.

STEPH: *(Indicating food.)* When does lamb become mutton?

MARIAN: In the hands of an Irish chef.

DAVID: Can "Irish" and "chef" be used in the same sentence?

JOHN: When its permanent teeth develop.

STEPH: The same time my relationships turn to mutton.

DAVID: Now, now—

STEPH: At least I'm catching up on movies. Last night I rented a Rodan film.

SARAH: My favorite sculptor!

STEPH: The Japanese monster. Does that make me pitiful?

JOHN: Pity's okay. It's condescending, but at least someone's paying attention.

DAVID: *(To JOHN, while pointing at stereo.)* Tchaikovsky went to law school, too.

JOHN: But had the good sense to *abandon* the bar.

DAVID: "Good sense" is a separate question. Closet homosexual. Tried covering it by marrying one of his students, who was not only female but a *nymphomaniac*. After two months, he tried committing suicide by jumping in a river. His brother dragged him out.

MARIAN: *(Waving at the stereo music.)* To years later ruin our birthday dinner for Stephanie.

DAVID: He once called Brahms a "presumptuous mediocrity."

SARAH: Words that *cannot* be applied to this dinner.

JOHN: Agreed!

STEPH: It was fantastic, Marian.

MARIAN: Only the best for your special occasion.

JOHN: I was starving—I could have eaten all the kittens at the county fair.

MARIAN: *(To SARAH.)* What was that fish you made us at your place?

SARAH: Sea bass.

MARIAN: No—it tasted more bottom-feeder.

SARAH: I may have overcooked.

MARIAN: Or undershopped! Anyway, I chose lamb for tonight. Thought you all deserved something further up the food chain.

DAVID: But condor seemed a stretch.

JOHN: And impossible to match the wine.

STEPH: *(Pointing to her plate.)* What was the—

MARIAN: Cilantro. It tastes like metal, but in a good way.

DAVID: *(To JOHN.)* Finish your story.

JOHN: Right, right. So the judge motions us up, then asks me and plaintiff's counsel to fill him in on the parts of the trial he *napped* through. That he was having trouble differentiating our counterclaims and the *dreams* he'd had. He was pretty sure about the cases we'd cited, but didn't know why we'd argued them dressed as Hamiltonian federalists.

STEPH: You're making this up.

JOHN: These judges have *lifetime* appointments. Tenures that frequently outlast the lifetimes of their corpus callosums. *(Points to his head.)*

DAVID: Couldn't you complain to someone?

JOHN: Why? I was winning the case.

MARIAN: *(To table.)* More anything?

SARAH: Oh, I'm fine.

JOHN: Full up.

STEPH: My aunt went senile overnight. One day she was fine, then—*click*—spent the rest of her life in the attic looking for Amelia Earhart.

MARIAN: Maybe Amelia *is* in an attic somewhere, just no one's thought to look there.

DAVID: Sarah, you haven't said a word all night about the foundation.

JOHN: She's being modest.

SARAH: John—

STEPH: Modest?

DAVID: What, what?

STEPH: No secrets!

JOHN: Cough it up.

SARAH: Well, it's not quite official, but the foundation is about to give over ten million dollars to autistic kids.

MARIAN: Not that they'd notice.

DAVID: That's tremendous—

MARIAN: Unless it was ten million dollars' worth of loud noises!

STEPH: That's great, Sarah.

DAVID: Fantastic.

SARAH: Next they're organizing a capital campaign for the zoo. They're building settings closer to the animals' natural habitats.

JOHN: Each will feature its own corrupt African regime.

DAVID: A toast to Sarah's success!

(DAVID raises glass but MARIAN speaks, cutting him off.)

MARIAN: Penguins and elephants I understand, but what's a dog's *natural* habitat at this point in evolution?

JOHN: Duck blind.

SARAH: Sofa.

STEPH: Nature's a puzzle.

MARIAN: That's why they invented supermarkets—they figure it all out for you.

JOHN: Gonorrhea and Mount Everest—nature's a little schizophrenic.

STEPH: Hurricanes I like.

MARIAN: Massive storms wiping out whole beach communities?

STEPH: That's why I like them.

JOHN: There's good nature and there's bad nature.

SARAH: Leopards.

JOHN: That's good nature.

STEPH: Not if you're the impala watching his gnawed-off leg dragged across the veldt.

SARAH: Quasars.

MARIAN: I personally have no use for them.

JOHN: Fault lines.

STEPH: San Francisco is overrated.

MARIAN: Gouda!

SARAH: Good nature!

DAVID: Joyce called cheese "corpse of milk."

MARIAN: What did he call name-dropping?

SARAH: Nitrogen.

JOHN: Who argues about nitrogen?

SARAH: Cholera.

DAVID: It's what finally killed Tchaikovsky.

MARIAN: Put it in the "good" column.

SARAH: Yeast.

STEPH: Depends on where it's growing.

DAVID: It's all a bit relative.

SARAH: But electricity, what is that?

JOHN: A vast, almost supernatural force that makes my razor work.

DAVID: Massively agitated ions.

SARAH: Our bodies are full of electricity.

JOHN: *(Pointing to bottle.)* Wine, please—

STEPH: It's how we operate. We're our own little power stations.

SARAH: Ghosts are electricity, I think.

JOHN: That Confederate soldier in our basement?

SARAH: An electrical field. Frozen.

DAVID: Does it whistle Dixie?

JOHN: *(Shaking head "No.")* Bakes pecan pie.

DAVID: I don't believe in them.

JOHN: You would if you smelled his recipe.

SARAH: I do.

DAVID: They're nothing but projected *fear*.

SARAH: They're *something* real.

STEPH: If ghosts existed, they'd be *everywhere*. They'd be constantly sticking their noses into things.

JOHN: Maybe ghosts *are* everywhere, but they're just being polite about it.

DAVID: It's a *mythology*.

SARAH: I think they're a kind of static electricity, trapped by the architecture. A great burst of energy given off by sudden trauma.

MARIAN: Like the sight of David stepping from the shower.

STEPH: But not sentient?

SARAH: Who knows.

MARIAN: You'd think ghosts would be a little friendlier, what with all the time on their see-through hands. Why go around frightening people when you could play Scrabble with them instead?

JOHN: Or charades.

MARIAN: If I were a ghost, I'd be *brilliant* at parlor games.

STEPH: *(To SARAH.)* Then animals would have to have ghosts too. But you never hear much about the ghosts of, say, old pets.

JOHN: She's got a point.

STEPH: If animals had ghosts, think what a *spookhouse* the butcher shop would be.

MARIAN: Excellent thought! I'll use that one next time some vegetarian shakes their pale, undernourished finger at me. They're a tiresome breed! Nature is full of animals eating other animals—why stop humans from doing it too, especially since we have the best kitchen appliances? Lions eat zebras. Barracudas eat mackerel. I mean, what's the official vegetarian position on *venus flytraps?*

JOHN: If meat were wrong, it wouldn't taste so good.

MARIAN: And be much better at running away.

STEPH: Cutting into a nice steak is nature's way of saying "Job well done!"

MARIAN: I agree. Vegetarianism—it's just sort of retarded.

SARAH: "Retarded" is not a word one uses these days.

MARIAN: I'm sorry. "Mongoloid," then.

DAVID: Marian—

MARIAN: *(Happily coining term.)* "Neo-Cretinism."

SARAH: Now, now—

MARIAN: Then let them choose their own word.

SARAH: Fine.

MARIAN: Just don't ask them to spell it!

SARAH: It's a disability.

MARIAN: *(To OTHERS.)* My, how the retarded do enjoy a good drool.

SARAH: But Marian—

MARIAN: The family down on the eighth floor has a retarded boy. The first children were fine, then—*bing!*—out popped a kid with the mental acuity of a scone. Then they had another kid, a "makeup" child. Now there was a roll of the dice! One is bad enough, but two retarded kids—it's like you're trying to staff a school cafeteria.

DAVID: *(To OTHERS.)* The family handles him well.

MARIAN: Retarded people are depressing.

SARAH: They can be inspiring.

MARIAN: They can be *per*spiring.

SARAH: It's not their fault, Marian.

MARIAN: Well—

SARAH: What?

MARIAN: I think some of them play it up.

SARAH: Whatever for?

MARIAN: For the free group trips to the zoo.

SARAH: They're people, too. Society has a responsibility.

MARIAN: Yes, it's sweet of us to care.

JOHN: *(Intentionally changing the topic.)* We're going on a trip!

DAVID: *(With some relief.)* Excellent, guys!

SARAH: Yes... Well, now that I've finished the foundation project, we're rewarding ourselves by taking two months off to travel.

DAVID: Job well done!

STEPH: Where to?

SARAH: South America.

JOHN: Always wanted to go. It's going to be a *huge* trip.

DAVID: The bigger the better!

STEPH: South America seems so far away, but you could *walk* there if you really wanted to.

MARIAN: What's to see in South America?

SARAH: Machu Picchu.

JOHN: The boulevards of Buenos Aires.

STEPH: Insects the size of canned hams.

JOHN: The firm has given me the okay to take the time.

SARAH: It's been a dream of both of ours forever.

DAVID: A toast to that then!

(DAVID raises his glass but is again cut off by MARIAN.)

MARIAN: Aren't you afraid of disease? David's friend what's-his-face—

DAVID: Dennis.

MARIAN: Went down the Amazon on a cruise. Fell overboard. They hauled him out, but three days later he couldn't move his arms or speak.

STEPH: River virus.

DAVID: *(Moves away from table in irritation at MARIAN.)* He's better now.

MARIAN: Mostly.

DAVID: Arms are fine.

MARIAN: But he hasn't got his adverbs back.

STEPH: Doesn't surprise me.

DAVID: Oh, c'mon Steph.

STEPH: I prefer to stay here and let the tourists come to *me*. Instead of spending all that money to go see strange people, I'd rather hang here and be the exotic local color *myself*.

SARAH: But the adventure—

STEPH: Adventure is problematic. Ask those dead mountain climbers they carve out of the ice eighty years later with their fur hoods and "Vote Hoover" buttons.

MARIAN: That's why I like London—no avalanches.

DAVID: If you don't count the puking drunks.

JOHN: Westminster Abbey is tremendous.

STEPH: The famous people buried there.

DAVID: Chaucer.

SARAH: Dickens.

STEPH: To his dismay.

DAVID: Isaac Newton.

JOHN: England is a good country for dead people.

SARAH: The British just seem more civilized.

DAVID: Island races—can't be trusted.

STEPH: Monarchy—that's a bit childish of them.

JOHN: Rather true.

STEPH: In the fourteenth century you had to kill somebody to be king. Storm a citadel. Drop arsenic in a wine goblet. You had to *earn* it. Now you go to fancy schools and dribble beer on your Eton suit, then party for thirty years till dad or mums pops off. Then they hose you down, plop you in the Coronation Chair, and BOOM!—your face is on the money and crowds of poor people throw flowers at you for no legitimate reason whatsoever.

MARIAN: I like their castles. The fox-hunt tapestries and secret passages.

JOHN: We'll find you one in this country.

STEPH: *(Indicating the candleholders on the table.)* Your candleholders would fit in perfectly.

MARIAN: The latest for my collection.

DAVID: She has hundreds in storage.

MARIAN: Louis Quatorze. Victorian. A candelabra owned by the Kennedys. Steer clear of menorahs, though—you never know when someone's going to come along and wipe out the Jews, destroying your resale market.

(An awkward pause.)

SARAH: I wish I had a hobby.

STEPH: *(Suggesting.)* Stamps!

JOHN: Butterflies.

MARIAN: Bring a net to Brazil with you.

DAVID: Ships in a bottle.

SARAH: All been done.

STEPH: *Quilts* in a bottle.

JOHN: I like wine in a bottle.

SARAH: You like wine *out of* a bottle.

JOHN: The time-tested respite after a week of dealing with chief executive officers. South America might not be far enough away. They're big, puckered anuses in tailored suits.

SARAH: They can, however, afford his law firm's hourlies.

MARIAN: Someone has to run things.

STEPH: Yes! Without bosses, the workers would get too much accomplished.

DAVID: He's right about CEOs. My publishing house chief has never read a book, just balance sheets. If he ever stumbled across a parenthetical aside, he'd think it was a debit.

MARIAN: Now, now—

DAVID: It's true!

MARIAN: David just resents his success.

DAVID: At what? Debasing a noble profession?

MARIAN: Oops! Here we go again.

SARAH: I'm sure even Guttenberg kept a balance sheet, Dave.

DAVID: I'm not denying the need for profit. I'm challenging the religion of profit *maximization*. The rationale that a corporation owes a *maximal profit* to its shareholders. *Greed* turned into *moral duty*. No! Not at the expense of what made the trade worthy. The self-help and bodice-ripping business memoirs—fine. I'm not allergic to cash cows if they get people to turn off the fucking TV. But that's all it is now! Literature, history—virtually *wiped* from the catalogue.

SARAH: You've made a pretty good living off those pop bestsellers.

DAVID: I have an unfortunate recipe for success—the more a book repels me, the more I know it's going to sell. Dave's Law of Inverse Tripe. I'm sure Pascal had a better term for it.

MARIAN: Can you tell they've refused to publish David's novel?

JOHN and SARAH: *What?!*

STEPH: Your own publishing house?

DAVID: *(Irritated by revelation.)* Marian—

SARAH: Geez, Dave!

JOHN: Why didn't you mention this earlier?

DAVID: It's okay—

STEPH: How can they do that?

MARIAN: Apparently novels are supposed to be entertaining.

STEPH: That's ridiculous they won't publish one of their own editor's books!

JOHN: Even if it's *crap*, they still owe you!

MARIAN: I kept telling him, don't write so arty. You can practically smell the garret and absinthe coming off the page.

SARAH: *(To DAVID.)* You worked on that forever.

DAVID: Ten years less one minor nervous breakdown.

MARIAN: Why write a book you know nobody's going to read? It's cowardly.

STEPH: I'd buy it!

DAVID: Thank you.

MARIAN: Besides, David's novel would have translation problems.

JOHN: How so?

MARIAN: It would never translate into *money*.

SARAH: But if it captured an uncharted part of the human spirit—

MARIAN: The bitter book editor part?

JOHN: Tell them if they publish it, I'll negotiate the film rights for free.

MARIAN: Ah, now movies are a different matter! Make a movie, we can all go to the premiere and hobnob with *real* stars, not those French writers David likes to drag home as party guests. They're a smoking, grumpy lot—chased down by the paparazzi in their minds but nary a flashbulb when they leave the house. Who was that Paris guy last week?

DAVID: Delois.

MARIAN: An ink-stained wretch, but it was *me* doing the retching.

DAVID: *(To OTHERS.)* His book won *Le Monde*'s Grand Prix. He's a radical ontologist. Believes that because of cyberspace, true *corporeal* identity has ceased to exist.

MARIAN: He certainly made our *liquor* cease to exist.

DAVID: That because of the Internet and technology, our digital selves are now the *actual* beings accomplishing everything.

SARAH: Don't think I buy his thesis.

DAVID: Neither do I! But it's an idea. Something to gain pleasure and possible *insight* from thinking about.

MARIAN: David *loves* ideas.

JOHN: Ideas are okay.

MARIAN: They're excuses for *not getting things done*. If professors and psychiatrists really want to help the world, they'd trash *ideas* and teach everyone to make *lists*.

SARAH: So just can philosophy.

MARIAN: Into a landfill, with the coffee grounds and headless prostitutes.

SARAH: Anti-intellectualism has a long history of getting cultures into trouble. Think of the book burnings.

DAVID: *(Sarcastically.)* On a nice winter night, all bundled up with some nice Irish coffee, what's to complain about?

MARIAN: A book burning is just a more social version of what a book critic does! Someone's always destroying someone else's novel in the *Sunday Book Review*. But do the same thing in the town square with a bunch of friends and you're evil incarnate. And think of all the books that publishers like David have destroyed by *never printing them in the first place*. One group destroys books with gasoline, the other with rejection letters on nicely folded corporate stationery.

DAVID: A lovely analysis.

MARIAN: He tried to burn his own book!

SARAH: What?

JOHN: Dave!

DAVID: In drunken despair one night, I tossed it in the microwave.

STEPH: And?

DAVID: It got warm.

SARAH: Well, I'm glad it survived.

MARIAN: Alas.

JOHN: Literature *matters*.

MARIAN: Literature is just a small group of people who've talked each other into believing what they do is important. It'd be endearing if they weren't adults. Look at garage sales—all rusty bicycles and moldy paperbacks. Flooded basement—*that's* the smell of literature.

SARAH: *(To JOHN.)* Tell them your product idea.

JOHN: It's nothing.

SARAH: An air freshener.

STEPH: Been done.

JOHN: I know.

SARAH: Tell them.

JOHN: You know how they have those spray cans of new car smell? Same idea, but mine sprays the smell of *new dollar bills*. Like stacks of them straight from the mint. Spray it around before an important business meeting or whenever you're feeling down about yourself.

SARAH: The product will be called "Nouveau Riche."

DAVID: Money only masks odors.

MARIAN: *(To OTHERS.)* David's a little testy this evening. He's been feeling nervous these days.

DAVID: Please, Marian—

MARIAN: It's insecurity, I think.

DAVID: *(Challenging.)* About what?

MARIAN: Aging. David's not wearing it well. *(To DAVID.)* Your youth is gone, dear—just accept it. *(Points to the downstage "mirror.")* Inspect the mirror. It fled in alarm one day, leaving the heavy crusty parts it couldn't take along.

DAVID: *(To OTHERS.)* I feel fine.

MARIAN: If he only looked fine!

DAVID: Thank you very much—

MARIAN: The waves of time have rather eroded David's coast.

STEPH: I think he's still handsome.

MARIAN: That act of charity is not tax deductible.

JOHN: Happens to us all, Dave.

MARIAN: The eyesight retreating—

DAVID: I'm not that old—

MARIAN: His "before" photo is a daguerreotype!

DAVID: I'm a little seasoned.

MARIAN: Women used to be interested in David, attractive women even. Flirting with him at parties. Some weeping into their pillows at night, the more desperate stopping by his office with unexpected lunch invitations, then staring longingly over their cobb salad into young David's eyes. But that was a different era, wasn't it, dear? What with everyone worrying about the Kaiser's next move.

DAVID: *(To OTHERS.)* Marian has misplaced her charm this evening.

MARIAN: *(To OTHERS.)* Apologies.

DAVID: Or garroted it.

(Awkward pause, then STEPH speaks.)

STEPH: I still can't believe your own publishing house wouldn't print your novel.

JOHN: Fuck 'em.

DAVID: Vernacular I longed to deploy.

JOHN: In fact, fuck 'em twice.

DAVID: Quality—*art*—is no longer even an issue. And people wonder why the culture's become what it is. Always plenty of arguments against publishing something beautiful or profound, but never any against the celebrity crap.

SARAH: Can't you fight it, for everyone's sake?

DAVID: Why keep battling for an industry that's doing its inevitable counterclockwise swirl down the toilet? I should just retire, step out of the fight.

JOHN: "Give me a staff of honor for mine age, but not a sword to rule the world"!

SARAH: Oh, Lord, who quotes *Titus Andronicus*?

DAVID: That's not it. It's "a scepter to control the world."

STEPH: If you're going to be pompous, at least quote a better play!

JOHN: "A sword to rule the world"—"Scepter to control" has the wrong meter.

DAVID: I can settle this! *(Jumps up to fetch a big Shakespeare volume off the shelf.)*

MARIAN: *(Distressed.)* No, no, no!

JOHN: He's *the Bard*, for chrissakes—he's not going to screw up the meter.

MARIAN: Please stand back from the Shakespeare collection!

DAVID: *(Leafing through.)* Titus, Titus, Titus.

JOHN: I'll bet you one free lawsuit!

MARIAN: Argh!

(Having watched this quote-searching a million irritating times, MARIAN puts her fingers in her ears and starts humming "London Bridge Is Falling Down" to drown out the conversation.)

DAVID: *(Turning pages.)* "And then run mad—stark mad."

SARAH: *Winter's Tale*!

DAVID: *(Turning pages and reading.)* "The tempter or the tempted, who sins most?"

JOHN: That's *Measure for Cressida*.

DAVID: *(Turning pages.)* "Welcome dread fury, to my woeful house—"

SARAH: There you go.

DAVID: Arms turned to stumps.

JOHN: Back a bit.

DAVID: *(Turning pages.)* Tawny slaves. Blood-drinking pits. Hounds on limbs. *Staffs!* Here we go. From Señor Titus himself: "Give me a staff of honor for mine age, but not a *scepter to control the world*."

JOHN: Fuck me.

STEPH: A boring choice.

DAVID: Doesn't end up that way.

JOHN: I blame Yale!

SARAH: You went to Dartmouth.

JOHN: If Yale had accepted me, I'd have gotten that right.

DAVID: *(Loudly to MARIAN.)* You can stop with the crumbling European infrastructure. The Shakespeare danger has receded.

MARIAN: *(Sitting back up.)* Thank God—pentameter gives me migraines.

STEPH: I like the bit with the pie.

MARIAN: If you ever do marry, Stephanie, please do not wed a reader. Pick a sportsman or the owner of a large, smoking factory.

STEPH: If ever.

MARIAN: I'm sure *someday* it will happen.

STEPH: I hope.

MARIAN: There's got to be *someone* out there, dear. A dashing, handsome man with too much time on his hands.

STEPH: We'll see—

MARIAN: Though you do have the makings of a very colorful spinster.

JOHN: I like that play, even though people make fun of it.

MARIAN: Why do people quote Shakespeare as if he were the Bible? He made all that stuff up.

JOHN: He's a genius!

SARAH: Indeed!

MARIAN: He cannot be applied *practically* to reality.

DAVID: I'll take the First Folio over the Bible any day—Shakespeare's jokes are intentional.

MARIAN: Oh, let's not anger Jesus this *one* evening.

DAVID: But that's when he's most entertaining! Stomping his sandals and going all flush in his Nazarean face.

MARIAN: God's ways are mysterious.

DAVID: If Jesus were God, he'd have been a *much better carpenter*. People would still be collecting his coffee tables.

MARIAN: I don't think you should insult religion.

STEPH: What *better* thing to insult?

DAVID: *(Raising his wineglass in an another attempted toast.)* To agnosti—

MARIAN: It's wrong.

DAVID: John, how much money do you make?

JOHN: Not enough.

DAVID: No, really.

JOHN: Whatever I can talk people out of.

DAVID: An *actual* number.

JOHN: If I say, I'll lose my aura of mystery.

DAVID: Steph—what's the burn for your advertising clients?

STEPH: Trade secret.

DAVID: See—there's today's *real* religion, the *real* religious taboo. *Cash.* Who's the richest of us here?

(Dead silence.)

DAVID: There we go! But if one of us were *Mayan*, we'd be perfectly happy to talk about cutting the heart out of a sacrificial virgin.

STEPH: There's a religion where it *did not pay* to wait till marriage.

MARIAN: *(Dismissively.)* Mexicans.

JOHN: *(Trying to redirect conversation.)* Where'd you hear of this wine, Dave?

MARIAN: Not that I blame them for jumping the border fence. I'd rather be an illegal working twelve-hour shifts in a kitchen than be back in Guadela-whatzit washing my kids in sewage water.

STEPH: So true—

MARIAN: Though Canadians do smell better.

SARAH: We're a country of immigrants.

STEPH: I'm not sure a lot of black Americans think of themselves as immigrants.

JOHN: The slave ships weren't exactly the Cunard Line.

SARAH: Horrendous.

MARIAN: Like the worst semester-at-sea *ever*.

DAVID: *(To JOHN.)* The Wine Spectator. Twenty-four fifty a bottle. I get a case for two hundred bucks. My salary is two hundred and eighty thousand a year.

MARIAN: Is Dave being an iconoclast again? *(Looks directly at him.)* Ah, yes. Yes, he is. You can tell because his ear-hairs all stand up.

(STEPH has taken her wineglass and drifted toward the unseen downstage window.)

JOHN: Two eighty, eh?

SARAH: He guessed more.

JOHN: You should have a talk with the bosses, Dave.

MARIAN: *(To DAVID.)* See?

DAVID: I do fine.

MARIAN: You deserve more of all the money you've made them.

DAVID: Please.

STEPH: *(Looking out downstage window.)* I could never live this high up.

DAVID: You get used to it.

MARIAN: You deserve a bigger share of the value you've created.

DAVID: This is Marian's "not in the actual spirit of it" Marxist streak.

MARIAN: He's earned it—look at all his house's books on the bestseller list.

SARAH: Sounds fair to me.

JOHN: Fair? There is no "fair."

SARAH: *(To JOHN and OTHERS.)* But there has to be fairness. That's why we have the law.

JOHN: *(Sarcastically.)* Right.

SARAH: To make sure things stay fair.

JOHN: The law! The law is nothing but manipulation. If the law were sacrosanct, it would never change, but it changes *every day*. It's a bargain place among the powerful, a souk with neckties and less spitting.

STEPH: That's a bit cynical.

JOHN: That's like calling gravity cynical. It just *is*. I know—I make a fat living off it.

MARIAN: But people need morals.

JOHN: I agree. The only thing worse than hypocrisy is anarchy.

DAVID: Maybe that'd be a good thing, huh?

MARIAN: Anarchy would make David miserable. All the canceled Mozart concerts and shattered Bordeaux bottles.

DAVID: See what humans really are now while you and your neighbor are fighting over who gets to eat the feral pomeranian.

MARIAN: Can we *not* discuss the consumption of lapdogs over dinner?

STEPH: I don't think the answer would be very cheery.

MARIAN: Inner-city people raping each other twice as much as they already do.

SARAH: *(Trying hard to change the topic.)* Well, if I keep eating such rich meals, I'm going to be the fattest person in the world.

MARIAN: No, John's sister will always hold that title.

JOHN: *(Protesting good naturedly.)* Hey, hey—

MARIAN: Now, now—there's no denying it.

JOHN: She's a little big.

MARIAN: She's vast! She could seat her own U.N. delegation.

JOHN: It's mostly genetic.

MARIAN: *(Making fat gesture with her arms.)* Genus Cetacea Abdominus!

DAVID: There's nothing wrong with fat people.

MARIAN: Of course not.

DAVID: They're not lesser human beings.

MARIAN: Just the opposite!

DAVID: Please not again—

MARIAN: Mount Rushmore is full up, but you could carve a few more presidents into *her*.

DAVID: That's enough.

MARIAN: Words *she* wouldn't understand.

JOHN: My sister's had a tough time—

MARIAN: Getting through doors!

DAVID: Thank you, Marian.

MARIAN: But it is a free country, so she's more than welcome to pursue the glories of her endomorphic lifestyle.

STEPH: *(Looking out the window.)* I wish they weren't free to put up such hideous new buildings.

DAVID: *(Happy to change the subject.)* Unbelievable! Like they were trying to punish anyone who looked at it.

SARAH: Not everything can be the Chrysler Building.

STEPH: Gargoyles! Hugely underexploited in American architecture.

MARIAN: Oh, please don't get David started on architecture! He'll never stop—like one of those waterbugs you think you've killed but keeps on moving.

DAVID: It matters!

MARIAN: See!

DAVID: It shapes how we see the world. Once upon a time it was trees and lakes and hills. Now *walls* are the real horizon, so it damn well matters what kind of walls we put up.

JOHN: The Roman Coliseum!

DAVID: The Anfiteatro Flavio!

SARAH: Such a beautiful place.

STEPH: All those Christians fed to the lions.

JOHN: An idea *way* ahead of its time.

DAVID: A building that defined its culture! Architecture is the most *real* thing one generation leaves to the next. Literature, I love it. Art. But architecture, it's the reality left to us. It literally *shapes* the way we see the world. So do we inspire ourselves with it, or build ourselves psychic prisons? "Architecture," Ernest Dimnet said, "of all the arts is the one which acts the most slowly, but most surely, on the soul." Coleridge wrote that "the principle of the Gothic Architecture is infinity made imaginable."

MARIAN: This is making me nostalgic.

DAVID: See!

MARIAN: For small talk.

DAVID: I'm just saying—

MARIAN: David never just *says* anything. It's all a proposition or a quote.

DAVID: So I like buildings!

MARIAN: Just don't *lecture*—no one's written you a tuition check tonight.

DAVID: Caring about things doesn't make one pompous.

STEPH: Yes it can.

DAVID: Steph—

STEPH: Don't worry about it. That's why we like you, Dave.

SARAH: I like Dave's lectures!

DAVID: I don't lecture—

SARAH: Then whatever it is you do.

DAVID: I don't *do* anything.

STEPH: You do, but it's fun.

DAVID: I just *talk*. Like somebody who *cares* about things!

SARAH: We know, we like it.

DAVID: I don't *lecture!*

JOHN: They're good speeches, Dave. You're like public television without the irritating pledge drives.

DAVID: Fine! I shall hereafter reduce my syllable load and eliminate all conversational bullet points.

STEPH: No, don't! I like having to look things up once I get home.

DAVID: No—no more! I'll be *new* Dave. I'll rebrand myself. Steph's the ad person—she'll handle the account.

STEPH: Sorry, Dave—no time!

MARIAN: But he had such possibilities!

STEPH: I'm swamped. Flooded. Engulfed and overwhelmed.

SARAH: By what?

STEPH: You'll hate me.

DAVID: Impossible.

STEPH: We're handling Caldwell's presidential campaign.

DAVID: I hate you.

SARAH: Isn't he a little right-wing?

STEPH: He's "Commonsensical"—at least according to our ads.

DAVID: I can't believe you'd work on that!

JOHN: You'll be voting for him?

STEPH: Of course not.

SARAH: Isn't that a conflict of interest?

STEPH: There's no such thing in advertising.

MARIAN: Nothing wrong with common sense.

JOHN: Whatever that is.

DAVID: The received morality. Adherence to the inherited structures!

MARIAN: The right ways as proven by time.

DAVID: Habit.

MARIAN: Nose-picking is a habit.

JOHN: And a damn good one.

MARIAN: Common sense is…practical. It's what gets things done.

SARAH: Caldwell's environmental record is dreadful.

DAVID: *(To STEPH.)* But you'll work for him? Blow up the balloons, wear the straw hats?

STEPH: We're handling the TV spots and media buys.

DAVID: Not the ethnic cleansing?

SARAH: How can you work on that?

STEPH: My firm specializes in fuckheads.

SARAH: Why?

STEPH: If they were doing something *worthy*, they wouldn't need advertising.

JOHN: And do you ever sleep again if he wins?

SARAH: Have you met Caldwell?

STEPH: Very polite.

JOHN: Devils always send the best thank you notes.

DAVID: Toss one off to Caldwell after he's taken away your free-speech rights.

MARIAN: A little filtering would be a good idea.

STEPH: Censorship?

MARIAN: *Editorship*. David gets a pay check *every week* for it. But let a democratically elected president do the same, and people act like you've smothered their toddler with their best down pillow. Leadership has responsibilities.

DAVID: Lovely. *(Irritated at MARIAN, DAVID again moves away from her and the table.)*

MARIAN: There is such a thing as "too much."

STEPH: That's perfect!

SARAH: What?

STEPH: I need a campaign slogan for tomorrow's meeting: "There Is Such a Thing as Too Much."

JOHN: *(To MARIAN.)* You just earned yourself a seat in Caldwell's cabinet.

DAVID: As Secretary of Regressive Affairs.

MARIAN: Excellent! I love inaugural parades.

SARAH: Wear a hat.

DAVID: Something warm and right-wing.

JOHN: A fur tiara!

MARIAN: Other people's success makes David dyspeptic.

STEPH: If we use it, we'll of course pay you for it.

DAVID: We'll honor Caldwell by using the money to buy this place a new weapons system.

MARIAN: *(To DAVID.)* Some surface-to-*ego* missiles.

DAVID: And Marian new jewelry. Something in depleted uranium.

MARIAN: David, you really must show our guests the rest of your bon mot collection. *(To OTHERS.)* He keeps the good stuff locked up in case Hemingway stops by.

JOHN: Hemingway blew his head off.

MARIAN: Before or after he wrote his novels?

DAVID: Excuse Marian's enthusiasm for Caldwell. His militarism and Social Darwinism create a sort of father figure for her.

MARIAN: Social Darwinism is quite necessary, especially for determining who throws the best parties.

SARAH: *(To MARIAN.)* You'll be donating to Caldwell's campaign?

DAVID: Is it charity when you give to something evil?

MARIAN: I love it when David talks about some latest evil. He's like a kid with a new baseball card.

DAVID: Caldwell's stats are Hall of Fame! Especially his slugging percentage against the poor.

MARIAN: *(Slapping her forehead.)* Oh, damn!

SARAH: What?

MARIAN: I forgot to bring David's hair-shirt back from the cleaners!

DAVID: Steals. Caldwell's led the league for years. Corporate tax breaks, reduced programs for the poverty-stricken.

MARIAN: "Stricken"—like they caught something from a rest-stop toilet.

SARAH: There are reasons people get trapped in poverty—

MARIAN: If they're smart enough to know that malt liquor has the best alcohol-to-cost ratio, they're smart enough to get a job.

DAVID: *(Sarcastically.)* Great.

MARIAN: *(To JOHN.)* What's your view of the poor?

JOHN: *(Reaching for wine.)* The pour I need right now is from this bottle.

SARAH: It's a cycle.

MARIAN: "Rinse" is a cycle.

SARAH: There are external conditions—

MARIAN: And on what kind of platter does one feed them excuses?

SARAH: But all the little children—

MARIAN: Tragic! The dirty diapers and not knowing which trick to call Daddy.

SARAH: I just don't think you know what it's like to be poor.

MARIAN: *You're* the Harvard graduate.

SARAH: But I volunteer. Sometimes when I'm feeling down or need perspective, I go help out at a soup kitchen.

MARIAN: There's nothing like using the disadvantaged to make yourself feel better.

JOHN: A nice merlot does it for me.

SARAH: You can learn important things from the poor.

MARIAN: Like how to walk in traffic.

SARAH: Spiritual lessons—

MARIAN: Love of drugs.

DAVID: Coleridge wrote "Ozymandias" on drugs.

MARIAN: Is it about defecating in the subway?

SARAH: The poor know that the *real* struggle is not about office politics.

MARIAN: It's about finding your needle an uncollapsed vein.

SARAH: It's about maintaining dignity in a world that wants to push you to the margins like some Latin footnote.

MARIAN: Really, whenever I see some "urban" mother on the news with her thirteen rattle-thumpers, my heart goes out to the abortionist who lost *that* account.

DAVID: Excuse Marian's antebellum views of black people.

MARIAN: A nice race if you like shouting. And impossible to adopt, because people stare into your stroller like you've stolen something from the reptile house at the zoo.

DAVID: Marian—

MARIAN: And the other races these days—it's hopeless. You have to honor their heritage by naming the baby General Tso or something.

DAVID: Marian has blinded herself to black people's talents.

MARIAN: Is scratching lottery tickets now a talent?

DAVID: Jesus Christ—

MARIAN: Now, now—no invoking someone you don't believe in.

DAVID: Please remember the modern sensibilities of our guests.

MARIAN: *Real* conversation makes David nervous.

DAVID: Marian—

MARIAN: David *hates* bad poets, *loathes* bad architects, but someone bad at working—

DAVID: That's not what I think—

MARIAN: Someone bad at *integrating* themselves into society, he turns them into saints.

DAVID: It's different!

MARIAN: Yes, of course.

DAVID: There are long-standing cultural tensions.

MARIAN: Between shoplifting and paying?

DAVID: Between deep-rooted Western and African cultures.

MARIAN: Then let's cut welfare and give them all a zebra.

SARAH: But Marian—

MARIAN: They bring it on themselves.

SARAH: They need better opportunities.

MARIAN: Unlikely.

SARAH: *Real* options.

MARIAN: Note how they *opt* for sneakers, not bookstores when looting during riots.

DAVID: Really, Marian—

MARIAN: When was the last time a looter made off with *The New York Review of Books*?

DAVID: *(Pointing at STEPH.)* Can you blame them, with the crap the ad world has fed them all their lives?

MARIAN: They're apparently not up to individual responsibility.

DAVID: That's not what I said.

SARAH: They need validation.

MARIAN: Through *concealed weaponry*.

SARAH: Now, Marian—

MARIAN: I do like their blues musicians.

DAVID: Thank you.

MARIAN: A pity the corporate world doesn't require playing harmonicas that smell like gin.

STEPH: They're hardly the only poor people in this country.

MARIAN: But they are the best at it.

SARAH: Look at Appalachia—

MARIAN: Must I?

SARAH: Where the *poor* are *white* people.

MARIAN: And such a huge disappointment.

SARAH: So to suggest that it's racially determined—

MARIAN: *(Into the air.)* Why do paint-sniffers never use pastel hues?

SARAH: I'm serious!

MARIAN: David *loves* the oppressed, but what does he actually *do* for them? When's the last time David roamed the night giving tetanus shots to street people?

DAVID: There are qualified people—

MARIAN: All those hugs David gives schizophrenics, all those nights under the train tracks playing jacks with urchins.

So much *passion* for the homeless, but has he ever thrown them a dinner party?

DAVID: We'll have one!

MARIAN: Genius!

DAVID: Next week!

MARIAN: David will have to do the cooking himself, I'm afraid.

DAVID: I'll do it all.

MARIAN: I suggest some homeless comfort food—poisoned pigeon and flute glasses of cough syrup.

DAVID: I'll do better than that.

MARIAN: Then send them back to the gutter under the illusion someone's going to *keep on* caring for them.

DAVID: You'll see!

MARIAN: *(To OTHERS.)* Funny how the homeless use *refrigerator* boxes to stay *warm*.

DAVID: I'll have a bunch of them up. So that at least *one day* in their lives is a good one.

MARIAN: Can't wait for that party chat! The repartee about body lice and skin ulcers. The *drollery* about loose stools.

DAVID: *(To GUESTS.)* Apologies.

MARIAN: And the dancing! The homeless love a nice waltz, don't they? Exchanging their *one*-two-three uriney partner for the gentleman with teeth growing through his cheek.

DAVID: Marian's imagination is a bit fertile these days—from the long period of money raining down on her.

MARIAN: Will you all be joining David for his little science project? Strapping on the respirators and guilty consciences for his *soirée des gens de la rue*?

DAVID: My friends are always welcome.

MARIAN: Then I hope they like black culture.

DAVID: Marian—

MARIAN: Such as it is. But they're not officially lazy, are they?

DAVID: Really—

MARIAN: I mean, at least Hitler had a work ethic.

DAVID: *My* friends will be there.

MARIAN: It's a bit cruel, don't you think? *(Indicating the PEOPLE at the table.)* Inviting your best friends to an event they in no way wish to attend?

DAVID: They'll be here!

MARIAN: *(Sarcastically.)* Of course!

DAVID: *They'll be here!*

MARIAN: Have the party! But how does one top it next year?

DAVID: Marian—

MARIAN: Perhaps with an *asylum* theme! What could be more lively than a cocktail party for the *insane*? The ebb and flow of conversation. About the brilliant Farsi spoken by the voices in their head. How the South would have won the Civil War if they'd gotten a little more of *that promised help* from the sea gods.

DAVID: Everyone will be welcome.

MARIAN: I can see them all mingling, holding their cocktails with one hand, their pants up with their other. A couple meets-cute, then sneaks to the bedroom and jams hands into each other's crusty privates, discovering, in the process, small crawly creatures previously unknown to entomologists! And the fashions! What are the hemlines this year in the gutter? The makeup—*soot* really brings out the cheekbones! What kind of ring does Tiffany design for the finger normally reserved for picking cat food out from between molars?

DAVID: *(Tensely grabs a wine bottle.)* Who wants some red?

MARIAN: The party will be massive on the gossip pages! "Last Friday, noted editor David Northrup was the proud host of a *non*-book party for his *not*-printed literary masterpiece, an event celebrated with a strongly aromatic crowd of his *un*-published peers, unless *the police blotter* counts as a *print run*." Ah, that phantom called art! If you want to write, write something *useful*. Miscarriage condolence cards! A huge, untapped market! "Our sympathies on your half-formed loss."

(A bit of a pause. Then MARIAN picks up some plates and cheerily announces:)

MARIAN: Time to clear!

(MARIAN smiles and turns, and exits to the kitchen. There's an awkward silence between DAVID and the GUESTS, who do not make eye contact. Then, without speaking, DAVID rises, crosses to the stereo, and puts on some opera or classical music. He crosses back and without really looking at any of the GUESTS, picks up some plates and exits into the kitchen. There is a long silence, with the GUESTS not looking at each other. JOHN finally speaks.)

JOHN: The basketball season starts next week.

STEPH: Jesus H—

JOHN: The preseason *ends* and the real season begins.

SARAH: John!

JOHN: The games begin to matter. People start throwing elbows.

STEPH: Unlike here?

JOHN: Don't sweat it!

STEPH: *That* was not on the invitation.

JOHN: It's happened before.

SARAH: Not like that.

JOHN: They're married.

STEPH: Nice excuse!

SARAH: *(To STEPH.)* She wasn't always like that.

STEPH: It's crazy.

JOHN: It's *colorful*.

SARAH: But over time—

JOHN: *(Grabbing wine bottle.)* Have another glass.

STEPH: Oh, that'll make it better.

JOHN: It's a *medoc!*

SARAH: Jesus, John—

JOHN: Don't!

STEPH: Man—

JOHN: It'll blow over.

STEPH: I hope!

SARAH: What are you talking about?!

JOHN: It was nothing!

SARAH: Hardly.

JOHN: A *ripe* debate.

SARAH: How can you make fun of it?

JOHN: I'm not!

SARAH: You are.

JOHN: I've seen it before.

SARAH: Not like that.

JOHN: They had a little argument.

STEPH: *Little?*

JOHN: It happens!

SARAH: But never like—

JOHN: They fight, then get back together. For Chrissakes, England and France have been doing it for *a thousand years.*

STEPH: Maybe I should go in there—

JOHN: No! You go in there, you make it a whole bigger thing.

SARAH: I want to help—

JOHN: Please.

SARAH: They're my *friends.*

JOHN: Just *sit* here till they work it out.

SARAH: But they—

JOHN: They'll come out and be *fine.*

SARAH: I want to see—

JOHN: *(To STEPH.)* Tell one of your bad-date stories.

SARAH: John!

JOHN: That guy with the thing on his—

STEPH: No!

JOHN: Just let it go! Don't pick at it!

STEPH: John—

JOHN: You'll just draw more attention to it!

SARAH: She wants to help.

JOHN: No!

SARAH: John!

JOHN: Help by *forgetting* about it.

SARAH: Jesus Christ.

JOHN: Go in there, they'll feel *extra shitty* about it, and then you've ruined the whole dinner party. Look at the work they went to!

STEPH: But it's—

JOHN: The food. The flowers. The new centerpiece. *(Points at the abstract designer centerpiece.)* They bought it for us tonight. I mean, it probably cost *two hundred bucks.*

STEPH: *But what is it?*

JOHN: God knows! But let's just enjoy it—

SARAH: Christ.

STEPH: I am *not* coming to that homeless party.

JOHN: Fine!

SARAH: How can you just ignore this?

JOHN: I'm not ignoring! I'm acknowledging and *moving on! (To STEPH.)* Don't leave!

STEPH: *(Startled.)* I'm not!

JOHN: You looked like you were leaving.

STEPH: I was shifting.

JOHN: Then shift less dramatically!

SARAH: John—

JOHN: If someone leaves, it makes *everything worse.*

STEPH: I'm staying!

JOHN: I'm *telling* you.

SARAH: *(To JOHN.)* Don't talk this way!

JOHN: I'm just—

SARAH: So stop it! Stop talking this way.

JOHN: I'm sorry, but—

SARAH: Just stop at "I'm sorry"!

JOHN: Keep it down—

STEPH: *(Distressed.)* Why do my birthdays *always suck?*

JOHN: Just *relax* about it!

SARAH: Yeah, nice trick!

JOHN: *(Pointing.)* What the hell is this goddamn centerpiece!?!

(DAVID suddenly steps back into the room from the kitchen door. He's thoroughly drenched in blood.)

SARAH: Dave!

JOHN: Jesus Christ!

DAVID: Marian's dead.

SARAH: What?

DAVID: Marian, my wife—completely dead.

STEPH: Jesus!

DAVID: I've killed her. Sliced her into red, chunky pieces.

(Gasps as JOHN and STEPH stand and race to the kitchen.)

DAVID: *(After pause.)* So what did I miss out here?

SARAH: *What kind of sick joke is this?!*

DAVID: Don't talk in clichés.

SARAH: A prank—

DAVID: No prank. Real patrician blood and guts. Used her own German mail-order knives. Some extremely impressive cutlery. Those Germans—always way out front with the killing technology.

SARAH: *What is going on?!*

DAVID: A little bloodletting, Sarah. Not on the original menu.

SARAH: Dave!

DAVID: The classics are full of it. It's all over the syllabi of our finest major universities.

SARAH: Stop this!

DAVID: The *Iliad*, for example. *Medea, The Aeneid*—

SARAH: Dave, really, what are you doing?!

DAVID: Back when the major poets weren't afraid of a little slaughter.

SARAH: This is *not* funny—

DAVID: "Aeneus wreaked his victorious savagery over all the field when once his sword-point warmed."

SARAH: What?

DAVID: Left unfinished by Virgil in 19 B.C.

SARAH: Dave, the blood—

DAVID: Apologies for not knowing the original Latin. It might be a *very* clever rhyme.

SARAH: *What happened in there?!*

DAVID: Something wonderfully simple.

SARAH: What?!

DAVID: Progress, Sarah. One small step.

SARAH: Where is Marian?!

DAVID: No worries, I won't be offing any of you.

SARAH: You're not a murderer, Dave!

DAVID: Such a surprisingly poor judge of character. I *am* a murderer. Finally! And I've got the body parts to prove it. *(Wipes some of the blood from his face, then licks it.)* Tastes like O positive.

(JOHN and STEPH reenter from the kitchen. They stand frozen, now also completely covered in blood. There's a panicked silence, then DAVID speaks.)

DAVID: Anyone for dessert?

(Blackout.)

SCENE TWO

In the dark, the sound of a sustained wail. Lights up hard. We see SARAH standing near the hallway to the kitchen, having just entered from the kitchen. JOHN and STEPH stand in different parts of the room, keeping their distance from DAVID. SARAH too is now completely covered in blood. She continues to scream/wail.

DAVID: *SHUT IT UP!*

(A fresh scream/wail from SARAH.)

DAVID: No clichés, I said!

JOHN: You slaughtered her!

STEPH: Butchered!

JOHN: Arms and legs—

STEPH: Shredded!

SARAH: Her tongue—

DAVID: Ready for the deli counter!

STEPH: You murdered her!

DAVID: Sent back to the God she loved so dearly!

STEPH: This is insane!

JOHN: A bloodbath!

DAVID: At a warm ninety-eight-point-six degrees!

STEPH: This is not happening!

JOHN: Fuck yes it's happening!

SARAH: It's a lake of blood in there!

DAVID: Her shoes floating like sightseeing ferries.

SARAH: Jesus Christ!

STEPH: You were hardly in there!

DAVID: Efficiency!

JOHN: Dave!

DAVID: Practice from all those Thanksgiving turkeys!

STEPH: *Shit*!

DAVID: On Marian I had to carve *against* the grain.

(SARAH howls.)

DAVID: But today is its own kind of holiday!

STEPH: You're a sick fuck!

DAVID: A sick *glib* fuck.

JOHN: *(Utterly confused.)* Jesus Christ!

DAVID: Watched the food she just ate come out all the wrong ways.

SARAH: Marian!

DAVID: No more shipping down *that* alimentary canal!

STEPH: She's a corpse!

SARAH: Her chest!

DAVID: I think I found a tumor.

JOHN: Hacked!

DAVID: Whatever it was, it's benign now!

SARAH: Marian!

DAVID: And such a little heart—

STEPH: No!

DAVID: Like a slippery pumpkin seed.

STEPH: David!

SARAH: Sick, sick!

DAVID: Her uvula never to ululate!

STEPH: Her scalp!

DAVID: Discovered my inner Apache!

JOHN: This is—

DAVID: Kinda fun!

STEPH: Fuck you, Dave!

DAVID: Her aorta spouting like the fountain in Trafalgar Square—just not so many tourists and pigeons!

STEPH: How could you kill her?!?

DAVID: There's a Pandora's box!

JOHN: Fuck, fuck—

DAVID: The world smells brand new! C'mon, let's party! *(Waves at table and wine bottles.)* We got all the stuff!

SARAH: He's crazed!

DAVID: The Charleston—that's a fun one.

STEPH: Jesus fuck!

DAVID: Why wait for a grave to dance on?

SARAH: I'm covered in Marian's blood!

DAVID: And it's not blue after all!

STEPH: We need the police!

DAVID: But they're such kill-joys!

SARAH: *You murdered Marian!*

DAVID: Somebody had to.

JOHN: Dave—

DAVID: Someone had to *stop it all!*

JOHN: Dave!

STEPH: Look at this!

SARAH: The police!

JOHN: Wait!

SARAH: Call them now, goddammit!

JOHN: Shut up for a second!

SARAH: Marian's dead!

JOHN: Just shut up!

SARAH: *I'm* calling!

(SARAH moves toward a phone nearby. JOHN blocks her.)

SARAH: Let me at it!

JOHN: Wait!

SARAH: We need the police—

JOHN: *Sarah!*

(SARAH tries reaching into JOHN's suit coat.)

SARAH: Give me your phone—

JOHN: Fucking stop it!

SARAH: Give it to me!

JOHN: I don't bring it to parties!

(SARAH howls.)

JOHN: Just calm the fuck down!

STEPH: She's meat. Meat on the floor!

DAVID: I may be facing a health department fine.

SARAH: She's—I— *(Starts to scream/wail again.)*

DAVID: That's *La Traviata*!

SARAH: Let me go!

JOHN: Shut—up!

(JOHN grabs SARAH, grappling with her and forcing her toward the closet.)

STEPH: John!

SARAH: *Let me go!*

STEPH: *(Has pulled her cell phone out, but it does not work.)* The blood's fucked my phone!

(SARAH wails again.)

JOHN: Just stop!

SARAH: He's a murderer!

JOHN: That's clear! Now shut up!

(SARAH howls.)

JOHN: Shut up, goddammit!

(SARAH struggles and kicks. JOHN is pushing her toward the closet near the front door.)

SARAH: Butcher!

JOHN: Sarah!

(SARAH wails again.)

DAVID: Or maybe it's *Carmen*.

STEPH: *(To JOHN.)* What are you doing!

JOHN: Just shut up!

(JOHN forces SARAH into the closet and shuts the door. The closet door is lockable, and JOHN locks it and pulls out the key,

SARAH now trapped inside. There's banging from SARAH.)

SARAH: Let me out!

DAVID: Locked in the *mink* closet!

STEPH: John!

DAVID: *(Gesturing toward the kitchen.)* The minks now avenged!

JOHN: *(To DAVID.) You* shut up too!

DAVID: An unexpected use of Marian's security system. Meant to stymie swarthy burglars, not lock up do-gooders, but I'm sure she'd approve.

JOHN: Fuck this, Dave!

DAVID: And then there were three!

JOHN: She's not dead!

STEPH: Not yet!

DAVID: Unlike Marian, who's staining the floorboards a deeper shade of cherry than *swatched* by the designer!

(SARAH wails again from inside the closet.)

STEPH: You can't just lock her up!

JOHN: Till she cools down!

STEPH: Cool down?!

DAVID: I like her spirit!

JOHN: *(To DAVID.) You* shut up!

DAVID: She's really *believing* in something. Passion is so rare these days!

JOHN: *Shut up about her!*

DAVID: But we were all chatting so much. Why stop now?

STEPH: Stop being *insane!*

DAVID: When we've *really* got something to talk about?

STEPH: We need the police!

DAVID: Yes—cops *love* cocktail chat.

STEPH: We *need* them!

DAVID: Their squawking radios and art-world gossip!

JOHN: We gotta—

DAVID: *(Gesturing toward the stereo.)* Have Tchaikovsky send out an emergency arpeggio!

STEPH: *Dave!*

(SARAH bangs on closet door.)

JOHN: *(To closet.)* SHUT UP!

DAVID: Nice job.

JOHN: She's lost it.

STEPH: And Dave hasn't?!

JOHN: Jesus fuck, Dave!

DAVID: *(Making hammering gesture.)* I honored Marian's kitchen skills by tenderizing her.

STEPH: What?!

DAVID: She wouldn't sit still for a marinade.

JOHN: This is *real bad*, Dave.

STEPH: There's a dead woman in the kitchen!

DAVID: And down the plumbing!

(STEPH gives a short wail.)

JOHN: What?

DAVID: The new garbage disposal!

JOHN: Dave!

DAVID: Part of her own kitchen reno—

STEPH: Marian—

DAVID: A few pieces to *test it out*.

STEPH: The police need to know!

DAVID: I couldn't resist the irony.

JOHN: Dave—

STEPH: To keep her from floating out to sea!

JOHN: Marian's going to be eaten *by fish*.

STEPH: By…by tuna and mahi mahi!

DAVID: Turnabout is fair play!

STEPH: They can collect the pieces.

DAVID: That smell like Chanel No. 5!

STEPH: How could you do this?

DAVID: How could I *not* do it?

JOHN: She was your wife!

DAVID: The past tense has never been so pleasing to my ear!

(SARAH bangs again on the closet door.)

JOHN: *(To closet.)* SHUT UP! *(Turns and lumbers toward the closet.)* Shut up! Jesus fuck, SHUT THE FUCK UP FOR A FUCKING FUCK SECOND!! *(Starts banging on the closet door.)* SHUT UP, SHUT UP, SHUT UP!

DAVID: That's what I like to see!

STEPH: This is *not* what I came here for tonight. I came to see friends, eat some food—

DAVID: To see what's *doin'*.

STEPH: Did we have to play catch up with *homicide?!?*

DAVID: Marian was a leaner cut of wife than I expected.

STEPH: Dave!

DAVID: Who wants to bronze her peritoneum?

JOHN: Stop it!

DAVID: Flayed her sartorius and iliacus—why do muscles all sound like *Roman emperors?*

JOHN: Dave!

DAVID: Hail Trapezius Caesar!

JOHN: What the fuck, Dave?!

DAVID: Ah, sweet uxoricide!

STEPH: What?

DAVID: Look it up!

JOHN: Dave!

DAVID: Gone into that *good night.*

STEPH: We have to do something!

DAVID: Loaded onto that Stygian ferry!

STEPH: Stop showing off!

JOHN: How could you do this?!

DAVID: For you guys! So you'll never lack a *winning anecdote* at a cocktail party.

JOHN: Shit, Dave—

DAVID: The socialites and abstract painters gone silent as they listen to your true-crime tale of upmarket viscera! I'll be in the Big House, of course.

STEPH: Christ—

DAVID: On my bunk imagining all the jaws dropped into vodka cranberries!

JOHN: This isn't a party joke!

DAVID: Will be! Tragedy plus time, that's the recipe for comedy, right?

JOHN: Jesus, Dave—*why*?!

DAVID: I had to!

STEPH: What?

DAVID: It called! An epiphany! Short stories are full of 'em!

STEPH: This is not—

DAVID: What should we call this one, eh?

STEPH: *(To JOHN.)* Make him stop.

DAVID: *The Power and the Gory, The Great Gutsby.*

JOHN: Those are *novels!*

DAVID: Classics! Like Marian's extravagant bye-bye!

STEPH: She's a corpse, Dave!

DAVID: Supine, recumbent, expired!

JOHN: Dead!

DAVID: Like her soul already was.

JOHN: The blood—

DAVID: It came out of her so *cold,* chilled by the years of disdain.

JOHN: You're really fucked, Dave. This is truly *fucked* territory.

STEPH: Poor Marian!

JOHN: This isn't you, Dave.

DAVID: I kind of surprised myself. But then I took up golf late, too.

JOHN: You're not a killer.

DAVID: What's left of my wife might disagree with you.

JOHN: Stop it!

STEPH: Did you *plan* this?

DAVID: Is a fantasy a plan?

JOHN: Oh, Jesus—

STEPH: You just can't—

DAVID: Answer the question!

JOHN: Dave!

DAVID: A plan? A blueprint?

STEPH: It's something!

DAVID: What's yours, huh? What's your homicidal fantasy? The ex pulverized against the rock, the disemboweled president, the bullet blasting through the boss's chest and into his big leather chair! To show them their arrogance, *their power*, is not absolute after all! *(Grabs a wine bottle. He waves it around and then begins pouring.)* Medoc. Rêve Village, 1994. Excellent with duck, venison, and retribution!

JOHN: Pour me one.

STEPH: John!

DAVID: *(Offering.)* Steph?

STEPH: Wha—

DAVID: Otherwise the *detectives* drink it all.

STEPH: *(To JOHN.)* Why are you—

JOHN: 'Cause I need a fucking drink!

DAVID: *(Raising his wineglass.)* A toast—finally! To the right-wing life of Marian and its extremely colorful finale!

STEPH: We have to call the police!

DAVID: Call them all! The FBI, Scotland Yard—

STEPH: There's no—

DAVID: Interpol, the Mounties! Horses love Tuscan appetizers.

JOHN: It's *Marian*, Dave!

DAVID: I'll be missing the wake, so let's have one now.

STEPH: How can you—

DAVID: The funeral too. *(Gesturing at STEPH and JOHN.)* Who gives the eulogy?

JOHN: Jesus, Dave.

DAVID: We'll hire someone.

STEPH: Marian!

DAVID: A Realtor! They enjoy a nice protracted lie.

JOHN: Stop this!

DAVID: I suggest a closed casket—our friends have delicate sensibilities!

JOHN: Stop!

DAVID: C'mon, let's tell some good wake stories. *(Pointing at JOHN.)* You go first.

JOHN: What?!

DAVID: *(To STEPH.)* Okay, you start.

STEPH: How about the one where I go to a dinner party and it turns into a *slaughterhouse!*

DAVID: Love it! John, your turn again.

JOHN: Don't do this, Dave.

STEPH: I'm not playing!

DAVID: My turn then—

JOHN: No wake, Dave!

DAVID: But her fingers would make such fine party favors!

STEPH: At least she wasn't a murderer!

DAVID: Of course she was!

STEPH: Of who?

DAVID: Of "*whom*"!

JOHN: Dave—

DAVID: Of the *world*, one reactionary stab at a time.

STEPH: Ridiculous!

DAVID: Of anything *truly* human.

JOHN: Dave, listen—

DAVID: Cut down in its path by the serrated edges of her moneyed scorn.

STEPH: You're insane!

DAVID: I *was* insane.

STEPH: The cops—

DAVID: Back then. Back then till now!

STEPH: We need them real bad.

DAVID: Call 'em.

STEPH: Now!

DAVID: Call 'em. Here! *(Takes the room's phone and rests it on the table.)* Ring 'em up! Drop a dime on *your old friend Dave.*

(There's a tense pause as ALL stare at the phone. Then STEPH steps toward the table, but just as she reaches for it, the doorbell suddenly rings, creating a nervous panicked silence. No one says anything, looking at each other and the door. The doorbell rings again. JOHN waves at EVERYONE to be quiet, then goes carefully to the door, speaking anxiously through it without opening it.)

JOHN: Who is it?

(A girl's VOICE answers.)

VOICE: Girl Scouts!

STEPH: What?

VOICE: Girl Scout cookie sale!

STEPH: At this hour?

JOHN: No thank you!

DAVID: Girl Scout cookies? Let her in!

STEPH: No!

JOHN: *(To STEPH.)* She sees this blood, she'll *never menstruate!*

VOICE: We're raising money.

STEPH: John—

VOICE: For Troupe 105.

DAVID: Girl Scout cookies, guys!

JOHN: No thank you this year.

VOICE: It's for a trip to Sea World.

JOHN: No cookies for us, dear!

VOICE: We're going to pet orcas.

JOHN: Next year, sweetie, bye-bye.

VOICE: I got Caramel deLites, Shortbread, lemon, peanut butter twirls, and Thin Mints.

DAVID: I *love* Thin Mints.

JOHN: No thank you, dear.

DAVID: I'd really like some Thin Mints, John.

STEPH: Dave—

STEPH: *What the hell is he doing?!*

DAVID: *(Moving toward door.)* I'll take four boxes of Thin Mints!

(JOHN stops him from getting too close to the door)

VOICE: Great!

DAVID: And one of the peanut butter!

STEPH: The peanut butter ones are terrible!

VOICE: Can I come in and get your order?

DAVID: Just write me down for it.

STEPH: The peanut butters are *awful*.

VOICE: You're supposed to sign.

DAVID: Can't—sickness in the house.

VOICE: The flu?

DAVID: More like the plague.

VOICE: What's plague?

DAVID: Read Defoe!

VOICE: Then you have to pay in advance.

DAVID: You take credit cards?

VOICE: Sure!

STEPH: What the *fuck*—

DAVID: *(Grabs MARIAN's purse from off stand near door. He pulls out her credit card.)* Visa—eighty-nine-nine, sixteen-twelve, fifteen-ten, twenty-six eleven.

STEPH: Dave!

DAVID: Name on card: Marian Northrup.

VOICE: Expiration date?

DAVID: Today, I suppose!

VOICE: What?

DAVID: Nine thirteen.

VOICE: Thank you, Mr. Northrup.

DAVID: You're welcome!

VOICE: They'll be here in five weeks.

DAVID: Hope I am!

VOICE: Bye-bye!

DAVID: So long!

(A tense pause until it's clear that the GIRL SCOUT has left. During the exchange, JOHN has picked up the phone from the table.)

STEPH: *(Lets out a frustrated cry.)* Argghhhhh!

JOHN: That's was damn close!

STEPH: *He was going to be arrested by a Girl Scout?!*

DAVID: Think of the merit badge!

STEPH: She's fucking lucky she got away!

DAVID: If I kill her, I don't get my order!

STEPH: Peanut butter!

DAVID: I *like* 'em!

STEPH: You were wrong to kill Marian, and you're wrong about *peanut butter twirls!*

JOHN: *(Panicked and displaying the phone he's been holding.)* We have to turn you in, Dave.

DAVID: If you insist!

STEPH: I think we fuck do!

DAVID: If that's your definition of friendship.

STEPH: *(Pointing to the kitchen.)* If that's your definition of *marriage!*

DAVID: Me and Strindberg's.

STEPH: What the hell do you expect us to do?

DAVID: Your old friend Dave.

STEPH: Murder your wife in front of us and we do *nothing*?

DAVID: You could applaud.

STEPH: He's crazy.

DAVID: Turning people in—that's a Marian way of being friends.

JOHN: She's *dead*, Dave!

DAVID: Fine.

JOHN: *(Pointing toward kitchen.)* Marian's larynx is sitting on the counter!

DAVID: Finally uttering nothing!

JOHN: Shit!

STEPH: *We have to!*

DAVID: It's the tradition!

STEPH: You murdered her!

DAVID: First degree or second degree?

JOHN: Dave—

DAVID: I'm not entirely sure myself and it was my white knuckles on the knife handle!

JOHN: Listen to me, Dave—

DAVID: Let's leave it to the oracles on the Supreme Court—fine distinctions get them up in the morning.

JOHN: Don't talk this—

DAVID: *(To JOHN.)* You're the lawyer, you tell me.

JOHN: You're fucked either way.

DAVID: I'll hire *you* to defend me!

JOHN: I don't do criminal defense!

DAVID: But that's where the *fun* is! Movie lawyers are never Trusts and Estates!

JOHN: I'll *find* you somebody.

STEPH: John!

JOHN: *Somebody.*

STEPH: *(To JOHN.)* Jesus Christ, how much more guilty can he be?

DAVID: She has a point. *(Goes to his CD collection, looking for a new CD to put on.)*

JOHN: *I'll find you someone!*

STEPH: You're going to *help* him?!

JOHN: Everybody deserves—

STEPH: Not to be minced!

JOHN: Steph—

STEPH: You're standing here *helping* him?!

JOHN: No—

STEPH: You are!

JOHN: No. Just listen for a sec—

STEPH: Look at us!

JOHN: It's Dave, Steph.

STEPH: No it *isn't!*

JOHN: It's *Dave.*

STEPH: Not anymore.

DAVID: I'll serve as my own attorney—all the best madmen do.

JOHN: Somebody good—

STEPH: *(Unbelieving.)* John!

DAVID: Then I want one of those *elaborately dressed* defense attorneys.

JOHN: Fine!

DAVID: With great hair and a *triple-breasted* suit.

STEPH: We need the cops.

JOHN: Shut up for a second!

STEPH: If we wait, they'll think *we're part* of it.

JOHN: Soon!

STEPH: Now!

JOHN: I need to fucking think.

STEPH: About *what*?!

JOHN: *(To DAVID.)* I get you that lawyer and then you take the Fifth, Dave.

DAVID: *The Fifth Amendment and raconteurs do not get along!* No, no—I'm talking. I'm talking like that courtroom is the season's best book party!

STEPH: Confess it?

DAVID: If you turn me in.

JOHN: You'll plead guilty?

DAVID: Guilt—now that's another matter! Does guilt exist in an *inevitable* situation? Was Oedipus actually *guilty*? Seems to me ol' swollen-footed mountain-boy was dealt a bad hand, then got *hammered* on the draw. *(Pulls out a CD and waves it excitedly.)* Bellini! A rock star of the nineteenth century! Child prodigy, opera-writing genius, and dandy. *Il Pirata, Norma*, then dead at thirty-three. A woman made out with his exhumed corpse forty years after his death! Who'll be Marian's moldy posthumous paramour? *(Puts in the CD and plays it.)*

JOHN: The good lawyers are expensive, Dave. The hourlies will be *huge*.

STEPH: Why are you talking money?

JOHN: It's a reflex!

STEPH: This is wrong! In every conceivable way!

DAVID: If you want to thumb-suck, I'll get you Marian's. *(Gesturing toward the kitchen.)*

STEPH: You can't do this!

DAVID: *"'Tis done! Welcome dread fury to my woeful house!"*

STEPH: No!

DAVID: *(Waving his hand about the room.)* Forgive the vapors—her humid last breaths, the toxic molecules of her sarcasm. From the Greek; *sarkasmos*: "to tear flesh like dogs."

STEPH: Just no!

DAVID: *(Pointing puzzled at the stereo.)* That's not Bellini.

STEPH: Fuck Bellini!

JOHN: A decent lawyer—

DAVID: *"Where crime is being punished, let it grow."*

STEPH: Stop quoting Shakespeare!

DAVID: That one's Seneca.

JOHN: Marian was not a criminal!

DAVID: Ha!

JOHN: She wasn't!

DAVID: Marian was a mastermind! Operating right under the noses of her very friends. The Italian handbags and designer sunglasses ingeniously disguising her role in the Great Earth Robbery, the biggest heist ever!

STEPH: You're delusional!

DAVID: *(Waving at the room.)* This was the delusion. Her cocoon inside the typhoid-and-Latino-free world of *Architectural Digest*. Her happy, silk-lined guard tower high above the masses and their discount home electronics. *(Glancing again at stereo.)* This—is—not—Bellini!

(Over the course of the remainder of the scene, the music will slowly, almost unnoticeably, shift to a low, ominous tone, not quite a rumble, but close, and somewhat eerie.)

STEPH: We had *good* times.

JOHN: Together!

STEPH: All of us, Dave.

DAVID: It's not about us!

STEPH: The New Year's Eves—

DAVID: Ringing in another year of *triumphal consumerism!*

JOHN: They're just parties—

DAVID: Marian's midnight toasts to such good friends! But in the car ride home, words of a very different vintage.

STEPH: No, Dave—

DAVID: "John," she'd say, "gets paid damn well for all of those cases he loses."

JOHN: Dave, please—

DAVID: "Someday he'll appear on the wedding pages marrying a bottle of booze: 'The alcohol will be keeping its name.'"

JOHN: I don't believe you!

DAVID: *(Pointing at STEPH's chest.)* Hated Steph's breasts.

STEPH: What?

DAVID: "Great Plains Stephanie," she'd call you.

JOHN: C'mon, Dave—

DAVID: *(Making sweeping flat motion with his hand.)* "A wagon-train utopia." "A Nebraska of nothing." "Maybe men would hang onto her if there were more to hang onto."

(A tense pause from STEPH, then—)

STEPH: *(Anguished.)* ...No! It doesn't matter.

DAVID: As you like it.

JOHN: You can't *kill* her!

DAVID: I *edited* her! Edited her *right out*—like the world's worst dangling modifier.

STEPH: But we were friends!

DAVID: *It's not about us!* It's about the poor world out there on the business end of Marian's twenty-four-carat contempt.

JOHN: Dave—

DAVID: *(Quoting STEPH back at herself.)* "There is such a thing as too much"!

JOHN: Leave her alone.

DAVID: Whoever in the Bible who says the great unforgivable sin is despair. Wrong! The *real* unforgivable sin is *ostentation!*

JOHN: Doesn't beat murder, Dave!

DAVID: Sure it does!

JOHN: No it doesn't!

DAVID: Because sometimes there's a damn good reason for killing! But where in Aristotle or the Bible or Mr. Shinto, where's the ethical teaching, *the words from God* that your proper role is not only to have *more than the poor*, but to take that fortune and rub it vigorously into *their faces?!* Ostentation! Show me the theological defense! Show me the carved tablets! Show me the crumbling Aramaic scrolls!

JOHN: I don't remember seeing *Saint Augustine* on the guest list!

STEPH: So off with Marian's hands.

DAVID: And nose job.

STEPH: How can you think this way?!

DAVID: Let's take her pieces down to the gourmet meat market. Set 'em up next to the tenderloins. What's Marian per pound, huh? What's the price point on global disdain?

STEPH: You're the one who *married* her!

DAVID: If the shrew fits!

JOHN: I was there, Dave—

DAVID: The fateful nuptials.

JOHN: We were *there*.

DAVID: Such promise at first! The glowing skin, the strangely arousing battle of wits!

JOHN: Fuck—

DAVID: Who knew the creature the years of evolution would make out of her? Somewhere Darwin is banging his Shropshire head against a wall.

JOHN: Take it easy!

DAVID: *Finally, finally done with her!*

STEPH: You can't off someone because you're *sick* of them!

DAVID: Stop being so Eurocentric! I'm sure someplace there's a *culture* where it's perfectly fine to thrust a steak knife through someone's heart *because they're no fucking fun!*

STEPH: But you can't just *kill* people.

DAVID: I just did!

JOHN: But you're the biggest *moralist* I know.

DAVID: I still am.

STEPH: Yeah, right!

DAVID: That's why I killed her—to put some teeth in it! I feel practically Islamic.

JOHN: No!

DAVID: *How much more?* At what point in this world of ours, riddled with its pestilence and famine, its fly-covered orphans and melting ice-caps—at some point in this God-abandoned vat of suffering and cruelty the self-satisfaction of the Western World becomes a *capital crime!*

(There's a sudden thumping on the window—three quick thuds. STEPH, JOHN, and DAVID jump, startled, nervous.)

STEPH: Jesus!

JOHN: What the—

STEPH: *What is that?!*

DAVID: Birds—

(Another loud thump from the window.)

JOHN: *(Jumping.)* Fuck!

DAVID: They must see the leftovers—

STEPH: Dinner's or *Marian's?*

JOHN: Dammit, Dave!

(Another window thump startles STEPH and JOHN.)

STEPH: You can't just do this!

DAVID: Let's *all* do it! *Let's all finally draw a line!*

STEPH: No!

DAVID: That's why *liberals* always *lose.*

JOHN: This doesn't change the world!

DAVID: It's a start!

STEPH: Dave!

(JOHN tries pouring himself more wine, but the bottle is empty. He anxiously grabs another bottle and starts opening it during the following.)

DAVID: *(To STEPH.)* Get Caldwell over here. *(Points to kitchen.)* He'd smell great on the rotisserie!

STEPH: *(To JOHN.)* Make him stop!

DAVID: All that complacent fat dripping off him.

JOHN: That's enough—

DAVID: His crisp, caramelizing skin!

JOHN: Dave—

DAVID: But let's floss after—no right-wing gingivitis for us!

STEPH: What has *happened?!*

DAVID: That's it! No more op-eds. Action! *(Grabs knives from the dinner table.)* C'mon—let's all go out there!

JOHN: Dave, stop—

DAVID: Let's all go out there and *really accomplish something!*

STEPH: *(To JOHN.)* The cops—

DAVID: Let's stop whining and start *perforating!*

JOHN: No!

DAVID: The hedge fund guys across the street. Let's catch 'em tonight in their sleep. Post their heads and two-hundred-dollar haircuts on their penthouse balconies, our addition to the city's glorious skyline!

STEPH: Shut up!

DAVID: It's a duty, an obligation now! The sermons, the essays, the speaker's corners—time's up!

JOHN: Then you make it okay for *them* to kill too!

DAVID: They already do! Let's finally play by *their* rules.

JOHN: Dave—

DAVID: Quick—we need a fight song. I like that Michigan one, but it's taken.

JOHN: *(Nervously.)* Dave, the knives—

DAVID: C'mon, John—a little pro bono work, this time with lethally sharp metal instruments. No time sheets required!

STEPH: *(Re. the knives.)* Put them down!

DAVID: The firm will understand—you're a partner!

JOHN: You're nuts, Dave—

DAVID: Res ipsa loquitur, our leaking corpus delecti!

STEPH: *(Disbelieving.)* We are not having this conversation!

DAVID: Oh, yes, were are—finally!

STEPH: It's a murder scene, not a debate society!

DAVID: But gore always spices up a dialectic.

JOHN: Who are you, Shaw?

DAVID: *(Waving off the idea.)* Idiotic beard.

STEPH: This is all so completely wrong!

DAVID: So little imagination.

(JOHN starts nervously pouring from the newly opened bottle, DAVID cutting him off.)

DAVID: Let that breathe.

STEPH: No *killing!*

DAVID: *(Gesturing toward kitchen.)* But it's clearly so effective.

STEPH: It's criminal!

DAVID: And such good exercise.

STEPH: No!

DAVID: It's *action*, Steph. Something *real*. *Cause* with glorious *effect*.

STEPH: It's turned you into a *murderer.*

DAVID: It's turned me into something *real.*

STEPH: *You're* the criminal.

DAVID: As Montaigne said, "De combine de condamnations plus criminelles que le crime ai-je été témoin."

STEPH: *(Frustrated, trying to argue back.)* But that's…*French*!

DAVID: *(Harshly, pointing at the dinner table.)* Sit down!

(STEPH and JOHN are startled but do not react.)

DAVID: *(Waving the knives threateningly at them.)* Sit—the-fuck-down!

(Threatened, STEPH and JOHN move toward their seats nervously.)

DAVID: Marian's gone, so let's *finally* have a proper dinner party! The one we always dreamed of, but never could!

(STEPH and JOHN sit down anxiously in the seats. DAVID, suddenly upbeat, goes back to his. He puts his napkin back in his lap and tops off all the wineglasses from the wine bottle. There's a moment or two of silence, then DAVID speaks.)

DAVID: *(To STEPH.)* Could you pass the rolls?

(Stiffly, STEPH passes the bread basket to DAVID.)

DAVID: Thank you.

(DAVID dips the roll in a little olive oil dish and begins to eat it cheerfully, despite the fact that all three of them are still covered in blood. JOHN and STEPH look at each other nervously. After a moment or two, DAVID speaks.)

DAVID: So, have you read the new Thomas Horton novel yet?

JOHN: *(Awkwardly, after brief pause.)* No.

DAVID: I can't get through it. The epistolary structure does not suit his literary voice. Steph?

STEPH: *(Slightly startled.)* Yes?

DAVID: Read it?

STEPH: Have not…yet…picked it…up.

DAVID: His voice requires a certain kind of momentum that the letters device keeps disrupting. The letters themselves can be amazing, but structurally it gets to be a chore. His early books were brilliant for their time, by capturing a…by taking certain logics to a kind of self-negating extreme. He really managed to both capture and subvert—equally— the operating assumptions of both that historic and literary era. I mean, how else are you going to define genius?

JOHN: *(After brief pause.)* I've only read the first one.

DAVID: Arguably his best, but I'm hardly the first person to say that.

(Another moment of silence. STEPH reaches for her glass of wine, drinking it nervously.)

DAVID: A friend of mine in California made this olive oil himself. *(Pause.)* It's unfiltered.

(Another silent moment, JOHN and STEPH not sure what to do with themselves.)

DAVID: *(To JOHN.)* So what happened with that copyright case?

JOHN: *(Almost inaudibly.)* Settled.

DAVID: *(Not hearing.)* Sorry?

JOHN: We settled it.

DAVID: Intellectual property—that's slippery stuff. Can you actually *own* an idea? Bizarre when you think about it. Does ownership of ideas truly serve human progress? Or is it only the self-justifying metaphysics of commodification?

(STEPH and JOHN do not respond.)

DAVID: *(After long pause.)* Did you like the food tonight?

(Both STEPH and JOHN slowly nod their heads.)

DAVID: *(Cheerily.)* Then I'm glad I didn't kill Marian before she made it.

STEPH and JOHN: *(Jumping up and breaking from table.)* NOOO!!!

JOHN: *(To DAVID.)* What are you *doing*?!

STEPH: You think you can get away with this?!

JOHN: You can't hide from them, Dave—

STEPH: Marian's *dead*.

JOHN: Someone will notice her missing!

DAVID: It'll be three or four model years before the Mercedes dealership starts asking questions.

JOHN: *Someone will notice!*

DAVID: *Someday*—

JOHN: We'll have to testify against you.

STEPH: Point at you from the witness stand.

JOHN: Describe timelines.

STEPH: Identify bloody clothes.

JOHN: Recall earlier threatening comments.

DAVID: About Marian or postmodernism?

STEPH: They do that, Dave!

JOHN: They look for patterns.

STEPH: Investigate your past.

JOHN: Search for other disappearances.

STEPH: This is it, right, Dave?

DAVID: What?

STEPH: This is your only murder?

JOHN: God, I hope so—

STEPH: Tell me we are *not* having dinner with a serial killer!

DAVID: Nobody else!

STEPH: Because if you *are* a serial killer, if you've been at this sort of thing for a while, we're all going to look like *idiots!*

JOHN: For Christ's sake, Dave—

DAVID: How's everyone for drinks?

STEPH: How's everyone for the *electric chair?!*

DAVID: Immanuel Kant was less than five feet tall.

JOHN: Kant?

DAVID: Cholera also got Hegel.

STEPH: *(Stomping feet.)* Dave!

DAVID: Saint Fiacra is the patron saint of cabdrivers *and* hemorrhoid sufferers.

STEPH: Shut up!

DAVID: But you used to *like* my lectures!

STEPH: Before you confirmed every color plate in *Gray's Anatomy*!

JOHN: Dave, Marian's *dead*!

DAVID: Yes, I suppose you have an *obligation*!

STEPH: Yes!

DAVID: *(Pointing at JOHN.)* To your sacred law!

JOHN: You think this is easy for us?

DAVID: Well—

JOHN: Easy? With her blood everywhere?

STEPH: *(Indicating blood on her clothes.)* This was my power suit!

DAVID: Now they'll *really* take you seriously.

(A few more loud bird bangs on the window, startling everyone.)

STEPH: *(Holding her head, breaking, and suddenly stumbling through the room.)* This is not happening! This is not an occurrence! *None of it, none of it!* I'm really at home napping on the couch and having a dream about my new ad campaign, the one to scare people into buying *event insurance*! And it's going to keep changing, right? Keep sliding till it's a dream about…pretty songbirds…and clouds made of cotton candy, and you're all painted wooden horses and this apartment is a merry-go-round with the best calliope in the world!

(DAVID has gotten up from the table and moved downstage, facing the audience, and looks into an unseen mirror. He pulls out a comb and starts calmly combing his hair, even though his hair is soaked with blood.)

JOHN: Look, we'll get you that lawyer, Dave!

STEPH: No!

JOHN: We can help you, just don't hurt anyone else—

STEPH: *Help him?!*

JOHN: See what we can do—

STEPH: Are you crazy?!

JOHN: It's *Dave*, Steph.

STEPH: Yes—I recognize him by the *gore* on his clothes!

DAVID: Shakespeare finally *practically* applied.

JOHN: He's a friend!

STEPH: *(Pointing to kitchen.)* So was the *corpse* in the kitchen!

DAVID: Is it too soon to begin dating?

JOHN: *(To STEPH.)* Look, I know what you're thinking—

STEPH: Because I'm *yelling* it!

JOHN: It's just not simple—

STEPH: You want to go to prison *too?!*

JOHN: Steph, I know!

STEPH: Join Dave's pathetic revolution?

JOHN: That's not it.

STEPH: He killed her!

JOHN: I know what he did! Marian is *dripping* off me. But we gotta sort it out!

STEPH: Why are you even *thinking?*

JOHN: He's our *friend*.

STEPH: Fuck friends! Fuck this fully fucked "friendship"!

DAVID: Alliteration—*Beowulf* is full of it!

STEPH: *(To DAVID.)* Stop that!

DAVID: *(Pointing to kitchen.)* Grendel enjoying her first moments of decomposition.

JOHN: We owe him.

STEPH: *Owe* him?

JOHN: It's *Dave*.

STEPH: You're falling for his excuses?!

JOHN: Steph—

STEPH: He's a *killer* now. We owe *Marian*, not him.

JOHN: We can say he ran out the door—

STEPH: *(Stomping.)* John!

JOHN: That he threatened *us* with the knives too.

STEPH: No!

JOHN: *But he did!* Then he ran to the elevator with his passport—

STEPH: *(Sarcastically.)* And his Fodor's Guide to Italy!

DAVID: Il Anfiteatro Flavio!

JOHN: There's *no way* we could have stopped him.

STEPH: *(Pointing to kitchen.)* What about *her?!*

JOHN: They'll understand. Then it's up to *them*, not us.

STEPH: No!

JOHN: Steph, listen—

STEPH: And if he escapes?

JOHN: They'll catch him—

STEPH: Jesus—

JOHN: Then it's not *us*.

STEPH: John!

JOHN: If it's us, it makes it all *worse*.

STEPH: How could it be worse?!

DAVID: We could be drinking rose.

STEPH: *He is not leaving!*

DAVID: I'd really like to see Italy again, Steph.

STEPH: You shut up!

DAVID: To see what Il Duomo is like without the urge to push Marian off the top of it.

JOHN: A head start, Steph, that's all—

STEPH: This is not a camp game!

JOHN: Just listen!

STEPH: It's *wrong, wrong, wrong!*

JOHN: An ad man with a conscience! Alert the Natural History Museum, it's a previously unknown species!

STEPH: No, no—*that's it!*

JOHN: Steph!

STEPH: No!

JOHN: Please!

STEPH: *(Pointing at DAVID.)* Blame him!

DAVID: *(Making slightly strange mouth expression.)* I'm still tasting that cilantro.

JOHN: I know it's fucked, Steph—

STEPH: *(Moving toward JOHN.)* Give me that phone, I'm calling the cops!

JOHN: Please Steph, just listen—

STEPH: Give it to me!

JOHN: No, wait!

STEPH: Goddammit!

(STEPH *tries to get phone from JOHN, but he resists, pushes her backwards.*)

JOHN: Calm down!

STEPH: John!

JOHN: Just control yourself!

DAVID: *(Picks something off his shirt front. To himself.)* Is this a cornea?

(*STEPH sees that DAVID is out of position to stop her, so she starts moving toward front door.*)

STEPH: I'll get 'em myself.

(JOHN blocks her way.)

JOHN: Steph, no—

STEPH: Let me go!!

JOHN: *(Blocking.)* Just hold on!

STEPH: What the—

JOHN: Not yet!

(STEPH pivots and begins to move toward kitchen.)

DAVID: No back door, twelve floors up.

STEPH: *(In despair.)* Fuck!

JOHN: *(Imploring.)* Steph, please wait.

STEPH: *(To DAVID.)* Why have you done this to us?

DAVID: To make it a *real* party.

JOHN: *(Suddenly to DAVID.)* God-damn you!

DAVID: A fiesta to beat all reveried wingdings!

STEPH: *(To DAVID.)* She's dead! Our friend Marian is dead! *You killed her.* We came here tonight and you *butchered* her. She's dead in the kitchen with her duodenum in the spice rack!

DAVID: *(Snapping.)* Go! Go bury her! *(Turns, inspired.)* No! Let's build her a mausoleum instead. No dirty grave for Marian. No urn of overindulged ashes. A mausoleum high on a hilltop, a final temple to herself!

JOHN: Dave—

DAVID: Build the walls out off HDTVs and Bibles and million-threadcount sheets. Fake Old World landscapes and Burberry scarves. Fabergé eggs, wood chopped from rainforests, sables washed of blood in Chinese sweatshops. Paper the walls with stock certificates and condescending notes to housecleaners! Hammer it all together with the skull of a smothered goldminer. Then build a roof! From dinner gowns and hunks of veal and chinchilla handmuffs. Caulk it all with fois gras. Varnish up the floor with the blood of every Shawnee who died to make her life beautiful. Drag in her ruby-and-risotto-crusted coffin. Let the rented pallbearers say a quick prayer from the Book of Common Avarice, then run for their lives, locking the big stainless steel door behind them! Take the key and climb the nearest volcano and hurl it into the roiling lava pit—so that it sinks slowly down to Hell and melts forever into Beelzebub's forehead! *(Pause.)* The champagne! *(Grabs a champagne bottle that's been cooling in a bucket.)*

STEPH: You're insane!

DAVID: To toast our friend Steph's birthday, *finally*. With the best Epernay has to offer! *(Pulls out the cork. Instead of the usual frothy white champagne spill, the champagne that comes splurting out is a dark, frothy blood red. Startled, holding the bottle at arm's length.)* Jesus fuck!

JOHN: What the hell is that!?

STEPH: Christ—

JOHN: What is it, what *is* it?!

DAVID: It won't stop— *(Holds the bottle out, afraid of it, but somehow unable to put it down.)*

JOHN: Get rid of it!

STEPH: It's blood—

(The lights and the music in the apartment suddenly go off, with a loud thump. The apartment is plunged into darkness.)

DAVID: What the—

JOHN: Stop it, Dave!

DAVID: It's not me—

STEPH: Turn the lights on!

DAVID: I haven't touched anything!

JOHN: Now!

DAVID: It's the *building*—

STEPH: I can't see!

DAVID: It's the *goddamn building*!

(The lights suddenly come back on, with a thump. The champagne continuing to foam blood red, DAVID's alarm split between the light situation and the champagne he seems powerless to get rid of.)

STEPH: Stop fucking with us!

DAVID: It's not me, Steph—

JOHN: It's *enough*, Dave—

DAVID: It isn't *me!*

STEPH: The hell it—

(The lights crash off again.)

DAVID: Jesus!

STEPH: Don't do this!

JOHN: *No more of this crap!*

STEPH: I can't see!

DAVID: I'm taking this champagne back!

(In the dark, suddenly, the closet door bursts open. There's a bright light emanating from it, throwing light into the darkened room. SARAH can be seen, backlit. She slowly steps into the room. She's free of blood, shining, radiant, made up beautifully. She is wearing a mink coat and some lovely jewelry. The OTHERS stare at her in shock. She speaks in a voice full of wonder, though not directly at the OTHERS. The sound of a pretty minuet can be heard.)

SARAH: Such a wonderful closet! I hated it at first. Locked in a closet! The blackness, and the blood getting stickier and stickier on me. But then my pupils began doing whatever pupils do and I started seeing shoes and hats and silent old cuckoo clocks.

JOHN: *(Speaking, holding out his arm toward her, but frozen in place.)* Sarah—

SARAH: Something brushed against my shoulder. A *mink coat!* Not just one, but many mink coats, in a row that seemed to go on forever. I reached out and touched one. A tingle moved up my arms, a tingle that made it *hard to breathe*. I spread my arms out wide and hugged them. I felt their wonderful softness and blessed the handsome mink farmers for their brave and difficult toil. But then the closet started getting brighter, a light from in back growing bigger and closer. It hurt my eyes at first. Blinding! But then I started seeing beautiful clouds in it, and hills and colorful hovering planets. There were towering willow trees and limousines with hood ornaments shaped liked the saints. Ladies holding parasols against the gleaming galaxies. A place with sparkling asteroids and lacy bonnets and smiling Negro porters in crisp white coats. People sitting on huge floating porticos, soothing work songs drifting all around. A beautiful place where each day ends with a magnificent dance!

(The sound of the minuet grows louder, and MARIAN steps from the closet. She is dressed in a beautiful dress, just like SARAH, smiling and radiant, and slowly approaches SARAH from behind as SARAH speaks.)

SARAH: Couples gliding across the dance floor. Men in elegant uniforms wheeling their gossamer partners through the ether, holding pearly-white hands, four steps to every six gorgeous beats. They smile and laugh, the angels glowing, the gentlemen's swords glinting in the light of all the moons. There's harp music so glorious it makes your ears itch! Grinning pickaninnies press their faces up against the windows, peeking at all the glory inside.

(MARIAN is nearly behind SARAH.)

SARAH: Such a lovely dance! Called…called…oh, dear whatever do they call it?

MARIAN: *(She is now right behind SARAH's shoulder and speaks to her.)* A minuet, dear. A grand minuet.

SARAH: *(Not turning around.)* Yes! And the dancers finishing and bowing and the ringing applause coming down from the very stars themselves.

(A pause during which SARAH admires her mink and jewels, then MARIAN speaks.)

MARIAN: *(To OTHERS.)* Anyone for charades?

(Pause, then blackout.)

(THE END.)

FLIP SIDE

Ellen Maddow

ELLEN MADDOW was born in 1948 in Los Angeles, California. She holds a BA in theatre from Antioch College; while there, she worked as an intern at the Open Theater, which led to her joining the company in 1971, where she trained with its founder, Joseph Chaikin. In 1976, she co-founded The Talking Band with fellow Chaikin alumni Paul Zimet and Tina Shepard. Her plays with The Talking Band include five plays about the avant-garde housewife Betty Suffer (1984–95), *Fern and Rose* (1992), *Brown Dog Is Dead* (1993), *Home Entertainment* (1997), *Tilt* (1999), *Painted Snake in a Painted Chair* (2003), *Delicious Rivers* (2006), and *The Necklace* (2006); she also wrote *Persephone* (1996, Mettawee Theater Company). For many of these plays, she also served as composer; some additional composing credits include *1969 Terminal* (directed by Joseph Chaikin) and *New Cities*, *The Plumber's Helper*, *Black Milk*, *Star Messengers*, *The Parrot*, *Belize*, and *Imminence* (all produced by The Talking Band). Maddow is a prolific actress, appearing most recently in Taylor Mac's *The Lily's Revenge*. She received an Obie Award in 2003 for *Painted Snake in a Painted Chair*. Other awards include the McKnight Playwriting Fellowship (1997), Frederick Loewe Award in Musical Theatre (1999), NYFA Playwriting Fellowship (2006), and National Endowment for the Arts/Theatre Communications Group Theatre Residency Program for Playwrights (2007). She is a member of New Dramatists. She lives in Manhattan with her husband, Paul Zimet, and her son, Isaac. Her daughter Anya lives in Brooklyn. Up next for Maddow is *PANIC! EUPHORIA! BLACKOUT*, developed at New Dramatists with the support of the Creativity Fund, which will be produced by the Talking Band at HERE Arts Center in October 2010.

Flip Side was first presented in its final form by The Talking Band (Paul Zimet, Artistic Director) at the Connelly Theatre on September 30, 2008, with the following cast and credits:

Aurora/Oscar Waterfall	Will Badgett
Frank/Mrs. Wormser	David Brooks
Alan Flynnalyn	John Hellweg
Celeste/Cherimoya Waterfall	Sue Jean Kim
Daisy/Lucinda Waterfall	Heidi Schreck
Marilyn Flynnalyn/Sylvia Waterfall	Tina Shepard

Directed by: Paul Zimet
Set and Video Design: Anna Kiraly
Music: "Blue" Gene Tyranny
Costume Design: Kiki Smith
Lighting Design: Nan Zhang
Puppets: Ralph Lee
Stage Manager: Denise Cardarelli
Assistant Costume Designer: Jill St. Coeur
Sound and Video Realization: David Wiggall

"Booms Are Booming," "If Only," and "Walla Walla" sung by the Smith College Smittereens. "Three Fates" sung by Kim Gambino.

talkingband.org

Flip Side is the product of an unconventional collaboration that inverted the traditional creative process by allowing set designer Anna Kiraly the freedom to conceptualize the set first, and then letting playwright Ellen Maddow use that set as inspiration for the text. The play then evolved through workshops with the actors, drawing from the music of composer "Blue" Gene Tyranny and then continued to evolve in two prior productions, the first at Smith College in Massachusetts (fall 2007), and the second in a translated production at the Czokanai Theatre in Debrecen, Hungary (spring 2008).

Music is available by contacting "Blue" Gene Tyranny at bluegenet@aol.com.

FLIP SIDE FACTS

Side A (Act 1)—Drizzle Plaza

Feels empty, bleak, like a city where everyone has gone on vacation.

Characters:

ALAN and MARILYN FLYNNALYN: A middle-aged couple.

CELESTE and AURORA: Two old ladies in raincoats, carrying small dogs wearing hand-knit sweaters.

FRANK and DAISY: Co-workers.

Side B (Act 2)—The Waterfalls

Feels too crowded. There isn't enough room there—no peace or quiet. It's like a house that's too small, like a town where everyone is related.

Characters: The Waterfall family

SYLVIA: A middle-aged woman who is having an internet romance with Alan from Side A.

CHERIMOYA: Her wild, beautiful, teenaged daughter.

OSCAR: Sylvia's brother—a hedge fund trader.

COUSIN RICKY: Known as the mirror ball—picks up the opinions of whomever he's with and claims them as his own.

LUCINDA: Scientist—studies human emotions and philosophy from a neurological point of view. She is studying the people from Side A. Because of an unusual Waterfall family passion for marrying people twice their age, she is everyone's baby aunt.

MRS. WORMSER: A downstairs neighbor.

Act 3: The Edge

Sides A and B superimposed.

Doubling of Parts

Marilyn/Sylvia
Alan/Cousin Ricky
Celeste/Cherimoya
Aurora/Oscar
Frank/Mrs. Wormser
Daisy/Lucinda

Projection:

SIDE A—DRIZZLE PLAZA

Prologue

The lights come up to reveal a large black cube in the center of the stage. FRANK and DAISY are carefully smoothing it. They take pride in their work. They are meticulous. Work is the only solace they have in a life that is full of false hopes, bad choices, and dead ends. When they finish smoothing, they pick tiny threads off the surface, pointing out ones that have been missed and carefully removing them. There are WOMEN'S VOICES singing (recorded).

DRIZZLE GIRLS CHOIR:
BOOMS ARE BOOMING
OOH AH OOH
OCEANS FOAMING
OH AH OH
TENTS ARE ROCKING
BOULDERS BENDING
OOH AH OH AH
OOH AH OOH

OUTSIDE IN
INSIDE OUT
WATCH OUT
THERE IS NO BELOW

OUTSIDE OUT
INSIDE IN
ZIP UP
THERE IS NO BELOW

NIGHT IS LOOMING
OOH AH OOH
WINDOWS YAWNING
OH AH OH
SHADOWS ROLLING
ROADS UNFOLDING
OOH AH OH AH
OOH AH OOH

(FRANK and DAISY open two windows in the cube. ALAN and MARILYN can be seen inside.)

1. Alan and Marilyn

It is two a.m. ALAN is hunched over his laptop typing furiously. MARILYN is asleep in bed. She wakes and sits up suddenly.

MARILYN: Alan?

ALAN: *(Softly, as if calling from a great distance.)* Coming. *(He continues typing.)*

MARILYN: Alan, what are you doing?

ALAN: Coming. Coming. *(He continues typing.)*

2. Frank and Daisy

They are working.

FRANK: The window?

DAISY: The rain in the window.

FRANK: The rain in the morning in the window?

DAISY: The cold rain in the morning in the window.

(FRANK inhales as if to speak but doesn't.)

DAISY: If only—if only—

(They continue to work for several moments in silence.)

3. Alan and Marilyn

ALAN and MARILYN are at the breakfast table. ALAN is drinking tea. He takes each sip as if he were sixteen and kissing his high school sweetheart. He eats his toast as if he were chewing on the heart of a bitter enemy.

MARILYN: Alan?

ALAN: Huh?

MARILYN: Alan?

ALAN: Wuh?

MARILYN: I was thinking maybe—

ALAN: Fine.

MARILYN: What?

(ALAN *sipping, kissing, tearing, chewing.*)

MARILYN: I was thinking maybe on the way home I'd—

ALAN: Okay.

MARILYN: I mean, this evening, on the way home from—

ALAN: Oh, okay.

MARILYN: From work I'd—

ALAN: Fine.

MARILYN: —Pick up some—

ALAN: Fine.

MARILYN: —Fish.

ALAN: Fine.

MARILYN: —For dinner.

ALAN: Oh, okay, fine.

MARILYN: Alan?

ALAN: Okay. Fish, fine, fish, fine.

(*He leaps up and dashes out, cradling his laptop. She looks curiously after him.*)

4. Frank and Daisy

They continue cleaning and smoothing the cube.

FRANK: (*As they work.*) If only there were a table.

DAISY: Yes, a table by the window.

FRANK: Yes, and a checkered cloth on the table.

DAISY: And a small red bowl full of seashells.

FRANK: And a shaft of light from the morning sun piercing the window.

DAISY: A bright hot square,

FRANK: On the ice-cold linoleum,

DAISY: Gray and worn,

FRANK: By the endless restless feet,

DAISY: Of Grandma Sarah in her boiled wool slippers,

FRANK: Grandma Sonya in her worsted socks,

DAISY: Grandma Gretchen in her cracked leather boots,

FRANK: Grandma Carla in her goatskin scuffs,

DAISY: Great Aunt Rosa with her raw red bunions,

FRANK: Old Mama Fanya with her fishy flip flops,

DAISY: Aged Cousin Minna with her shin-splint stockings,

FRANK: Nana Martina with her frozen pigeon toes.

DAISY: All of them singing with the ringing in their ears,

FRANK: Seersucker housedresses wet with tears.

(*ANCIENT LADIES sing in the misty rain [recorded].*)

ANCIENT LADIES CHOIR:
IF ONLY, IF ONLY
I'D SENT FOR MY SISTER
SHE WOULDN'T
HAVE DIED
IN THE WAR.

IF ONLY, IF ONLY
I'D STAYED WITH MY MOTHER
SHE WOULDN'T
BE BURIED
NO ONE KNOWS WHERE.

IF ONLY, IF ONLY
I'D SUNG TO THE BABY
HE WOULDN'T
BE
A HEARTLESS FOOL.

IF ONLY, IF ONLY
I'D MOVED TO THE CITY
I WOULDN'T
BE SITTING HERE
ALL ALONE.

5. ALAN AND MARILYN

MARILYN is tossing and turning in bed. She throws off her covers, turns over her pillow, pulls the covers back up, covers her head with her pillow. She lies on her back, her side, her belly, her other side. ALAN sits at his laptop as before, types furiously for a few moments, stops, waits—staring at the screen. He reads, sotto voce.

ALAN: Your buddy is typing. Your buddy is typing. *(He reads, chuckles, delighted, types some more. Tenderly—)* Send! *(Waits—staring at the screen.)* Your buddy is typing. *(Sweetly.)* My buddy is typing! *(He reads.)* Oh! I agree. Oh, yes, I agree! *(He types an answer. Tenderly—)* Send! *(Tenderly and ecstatically.)* My buddy is typing! Typing! Typing!...Send!

6. CELESTE AND AURORA

A pair of giant eyes (on video) are watching from a window. It is LUCINDA from Side B. AURORA and CELESTE are watching her watching them. They have one pair of glasses between them, which they pass back and forth. The large round frames make them look like goldfish with bulgy eyes. Peeking out from oversized pocketbooks, their tiny dogs, TRIXIE and POOPSY, sniff in unison at the scent of a passing mastiff.

CELESTE: *(Peering through the glasses.)* There she is again.

AURORA: Usual spot?

CELESTE: Where else?

AURORA: Lurking, as usual?

CELESTE: Hard to say, sun's in my eyes.

AURORA: You see? Part of her duplicity.

CELESTE: What? I doubt it.

AURORA: Plants herself right there, between your eyes and the sun.

CELESTE: And? So?

AURORA: Facial eclipse! Sneaky!

(The DOGS begin to spit and growl. CELESTE and AURORA ignore them.)

CELESTE: Aurora, that makes no sense—

AURORA: Of course it does, Celeste. Logic, cold and hard like her beady little eyes.

7. ALAN AND MARILYN

MARILYN is setting the table. ALAN is typing furiously.

MARILYN: Alan, it's ready.

ALAN: I'm coming. *(He continues to type.)*

MARILYN: Alan.

ALAN: Coming.

MARILYN: Alan.

ALAN: Coming.

MARILYN: Alan.

ALAN: Coming.

(MARILYN flings a handful of silverware onto the floor and leaves the room. ALAN continues typing.)

8. Celeste and Aurora

It is raining. FRANK and DAISY are cleaning the outside of the cube. CELESTE and AURORA watch them from a distance, passing their pair of glasses back and forth.

AURORA: There they are again.

CELESTE: Frank and Daisy.

AURORA: Couple of sad sacks, if you ask me.

(FRANK and DAISY remove the black cloth sides of the cube. It is now a translucent white.)

FRANK: If only the only sound we could hear,

DAISY: Was the distant whistle of empty trains.

FRANK: And the hollow rustle of plastic bags.

DAISY: Caught in a tangle of blackened branches.

AURORA: What's with all the boo hoo hoo?

CELESTE: Well, Frank—lots of good things have *almost* happened to Frank. He's kind of a chronic runner-up, a perpetual second-placer.

AURORA: Her sweater's a very unfortunate shade of green.

CELESTE: Daisy does not choose well. Whatever she's good at, she hates. Whatever she's attracted to eludes her grasp.

AURORA: Well, for crying out loud.

CELESTE: Their work is a solace to them, though. It brings them comfort and a kind of satisfaction.

AURORA: Perverse satisfaction.

CELESTE: Well, ass backwards, at least, but who am I to judge? And with them, the deeper you dig, the blacker it gets.

AURORA: Looks like he's a little bit in love with her.

CELESTE: But since she always makes the wrong choices, and since the odds are always against him, there isn't a chance in hell.

AURORA: They do seem to love being lonely together.

CELESTE: Oh yes, they do. They do love that.

9. Alan and Marilyn

In the background, ALAN is typing. Every once in a while, an excited boyish giggle bursts from his middle-aged mouth. In the foreground MARILYN is gazing out the window.

MARILYN: Who is she, Alan?
No one.
No one?
No one, Marilyn.
No one?
No one, no one.

10. Celeste and Aurora

Giant shadows of CHERIMOYA and SYLVIA (from Side B) are rushing all over the surface of the cube. CELESTE and AURORA peer over the top of it. AURORA is watching the shadows through her glasses.

AURORA: Over here!

CELESTE: Where?

AURORA: Over here, see?

(AURORA takes off her glasses and hands them to CELESTE.)

CELESTE: Oh yeah, hey, wow!

AURORA: Isn't that something?

CELESTE: Oh my, Oh yes.

AURORA: Isn't that really something?

CELESTE: What the hell's going on there?

AURORA: Hard to say.

CELESTE: Maybe we should call the cops.

(She passes the glasses back to AURORA.)

AURORA: I think it's some kind of natural phenomenon—

CELESTE: —like a meteor shower?

AURORA: Sometimes you can get a better look as she comes around the corner... Watch! Watch! There!

(She hands the glasses back to CELESTE.)

CELESTE: Oh! Gorgeous! She is certainly a devil-may-care kinda gal.

AURORA: They call her Cherimoya. Cherimoya Waterfall.

11. Frank and Alan

ALAN, *agitated, in suit and tie, runs around the outside of the cube, clutching his laptop. FRANK rushes in from the other direction. They stop suddenly, face to face.*

FRANK: Morning, Mr. Flynnalyn.

ALAN: Morning, Frank.

(*They look at each other in silence for a moment. ALAN begins to sob and runs away. FRANK is baffled, and then shocked and delighted as if he has just woken up from a bad dream.*)

FRANK: Oh! Ah! Oh! (*He runs off to find DAISY.*)

12. Marilyn

Inside the cube, MARILYN is in a packing frenzy. She is putting on a disguise—spandex leggings, a faux fur hoody, a wig, and mirror glasses. She is stuffing objects into a collapsible mesh laundry basket.

MARILYN: Luna bar, Red Bull, NoDoz, wet wipes, sunscreen, thermal socks, rain poncho, toilet paper. Okay. Now,...hammer? Yes! Hammer! Yes! Corkscrew? No. Screwdriver? Yes. Screw driver, yes! Duct tape? Uh huh. Tweezers? Sure! Antifreeze, stain remover, liquid wrench, shucking knife, absolutely! Piano wire, razor blades, shovel, ski mask, instant cement. Okay, fine! (*She sets off in a rage, dragging the laundry basket behind her.*)

13. Frank and Daisy

FRANK *is running, nose to the ground, dragging DAISY along behind him.*

FRANK: Here it is! Yes! This spot right here. Wanna know what happened? —It was our neighbor, Alan. Alan Flynnalyn—ordinary man with a nine-to-five job, real estate broker, insurance adjuster, something like that—always put together, suit and tie, the strangest thing! Right here, early morning, he was going out, I was going in—And he took one look at me and burst into tears, ran off down the street, sobbing like a baby—Grown man! Suit and tie!—It was so unexpected—such a shock—like a pail of ice water heaved in my face in the dead of night. And now for the first time I'm awake—and it's all so clear.

DAISY: It? What it, Frank?

FRANK: My entire life! I've been focused the entire time on the wrong things! If only I'd noticed it before—From now on everything will be different.

DAISY: But not for me.

FRANK: Why not, Daisy?

DAISY: It runs in my family. You know that, Frank.

FRANK: What does?

DAISY: False hopes, bad choices, dead ends—followed by crippling regret. You know that, Frank.

FRANK: But that's exactly my point. Don't you see? When I saw that guy, Alan—with the tears streaming down and staining his fat blue tie, I suddenly remembered the smell of the meat. I forgot all about the smell of the meat!

DAISY: That sounds a little cuckoo, Frank.

FRANK: Come on, Daisy. You gotta help me try this out.

DAISY: Okay, Frank, but only if—

FRANK: Come on! Come on! *(Races off, disappearing around the back of the cube.)*

DAISY: I'm coming. I'm coming. *(Follows him reluctantly.)*

14. MARILYN, CELESTE, AND AURORA

CELESTE and AURORA are sitting side by side on a bench. MARILYN tries to sneak by them, but her disguise is useless. The LITTLE DOGS start barking their heads off.

CELESTE: Oh, there's Marilyn. Hello Marilyn. Aurora, this is Marilyn. I was telling you about Marilyn.

AURORA: Hello Marilyn. Are you nice? Celeste says you're nice.

CELESTE: New look! Nice, Marilyn!

(They nonchalantly pinch TRIXIE and POOPSY to get them to quiet down.)

AURORA: Are you nice?

CELESTE: Points up your curves! Off on vacation?

MARILYN: No.

AURORA: Have a seat.

(They shove her down between them, almost resting their chins on her shoulders, and gazing at her with delight.)

MARILYN: No time, gotta go, gotta find her—

CELESTE: Who?

MARILYN: Sylvia.

AURORA: Sylvia who?

MARILYN: Clickety click, tappety tap, all night long on the damn keyboard like some kind of manic Toscanini.

CELESTE: Who? Sylvia?

MARILYN: No, Alan. Giggling into his chin like a blithering idiot, babbling into his necktie like some kind of horny old goat. Can't see himself! Doesn't see it!

AURORA: Well, fiddle di di.

MARILYN: Who is it, Alan?
NO ONE
Who is she, Alan?
No one, NO ONE, just Sylvia, Syl via, S-y-l-via!

CELESTE: Who is Sylvia?

MARILYN: Some wire-hair, piano-leg high school sweetie who he hasn't seen in thirty years. Clickety click, tappety tap with her cheesy rings on her fat red fingers, laptop open wide on her sweaty nighty.

AURORA: Fiddle di di, indeed! Where did they meet?

MARILYN: They never meet, they just chat. Sweet Vista High Alumni Chat Room, class of nineteen something or other... Says she makes him feel young and happy. "She makes me feel young and happy, Marilyn." And what do I make you feel, Alan? Old and sad?

CELESTE: Well, for crying out loud. Where does this Sylvia live?

MARILYN: Somewhere. On the other side.

AURORA: Well for crying out loud, indeed.

CELESTE: What will you do when you find her?

MARILYN: I'll figure that out when I get there.

AURORA: What's in the bag?

MARILYN: Instruments of Persuasion—gotta go.

(She leaps up, dragging the laundry bag behind her. TRIXIE and POOPSY go into paroxysms of wheezy barking until she disappears around the corner.)

15. FRANK AND DAISY

FRANK: All we have to do is find the places and—

(They search the surface of the cube. On it is projected a video of city lights at night.)

FRANK: You see, right here on this corner I—I used to drive a cab in order to—

DAISY: You used to drive a cab?

FRANK: A long time ago.

DAISY: Why didn't you tell me? I thought you tell me everything.

FRANK: I don't know. It was a long time ago.

DAISY: It's all I got going for me, you know that, Frank. When I wake up in the flat gray dawn, the only thing that makes me lift my head from my flat gray pillow is that thought—"Frank tells me everything."

FRANK: Well I'm telling you now. I'm telling you now, Daisy. I used to drive a cab. I used to drive all night, and by two in the morning my body would be stiff and flat like a slab of cement, my face an empty window, my breath crusty pigeons fluttering in a grate. I'd drive up the avenue and turn onto this street and I'd see pink neon flashing—"Pork Shack, Pork Shack." I could smell barbecued meat and it made me so happy. And Maria at the counter would always pinch my cheek in the same old spot. She always told the same old joke. The tea was hot and the meat was tender and I could feel the letters of my name unfurl around my head like a crown of candles—"FRANK," "BIG FRANK," "BIG SWEET FRANK." And now whenever I turn that corner, I remember the smell of the meat. It's a kind of marker, a token, and I—See what I mean?

DAISY: No. *(Searches the surface.)* Wait! Yeah! Here, right here, there used to be a bench here under this streetlight, by the edge of the water. He was kissing me, we were kissing—there was fog, it was late—the water was smacking the side of the pier. We were kissing, and then a police boat drove up and shone its lights right on us. I was going to stop, but he just went right on kissing, so I thought, "What the hell, kissing isn't against the law is it? " So we kissed and kissed. And it was so—I felt like a giant kissing another giant, while all these tiny policemen watched us, hundreds of them, thousands of them, through thousands of tiny little binoculars. And it felt good! Somehow it felt really good. And now, when I pass this spot, I gasp for a moment like this— *(Gasps.)*

FRANK: That's just what I mean.

DAISY: —just for a moment, but it's not—It's never, I don't ever—

16. Celeste and Aurora

CELESTE and AURORA are sitting on a bench in the sun. CELESTE has fallen asleep on AURORA's shoulder. AURORA fidgets politely, trying to wake her up. She is embarrassed that her friend has fallen asleep in a public place. She speaks loudly into her ear.

AURORA: Trixie's in the mood for fresh vistas.

CELESTE: *(Jerking awake.)* Poopsy's napping.

AURORA: This same-old-same-old's got her down.

CELESTE: Poopsy's always very happy napping.

AURORA: Trixie is raring to go. See how she's left a little bit of her tongue sticking out the side of her mouth—that's her way of saying, "Oh Mama, time for a change of scene! Let's get this show on the road and head for the promenade!"

CELESTE: Poopsy hates the promenade. It's way too far and way too windy.

AURORA: Well, fiddle di di, we'll go on our own.

CELESTE: Well for crying out loud, we may as well go with you.

(They take off in the direction of the river.)

AURORA: Remember the last time we went and you chatted up that old man who was all dressed in plastic bags?

CELESTE: It was quite a shock when he began to quote Spinoza.

AURORA: Yes it was.

CELESTE: Sometimes people are like advent calendars, full of little windows that open and open. It surprises me every time.

(They disappear into the distance.)

17. Frank and Daisy

FRANK and DAISY step into squares of light that appear on the surface of the cube.

FRANK: And this is the corner where I threw up spaghetti.

DAISY: And this is the spot where I slapped her face.

FRANK: And this is the chair where I sang to the baby.

DAISY: And this is the doorway where he said goodbye.

FRANK: And this is the bench where I cried for two hours.

DAISY: And that is the hillside that caught on fire.

FRANK: And next to this wall they shot my mother.

DAISY: And this is the rock where she told me the secret.

FRANK: And this is the road where I stepped on a bee.

DAISY: And this is the beach where we went swimming naked.

FRANK: And these are the stars that look like her body.

DAISY: And this is the tree where I heard the frogs singing.

FRANK: And this is the gate where my grandmother waited.

DAISY: And this is the city where I first tasted oysters.

FRANK: And this is the garden where I killed the woodchuck.

DAISY: And this is the cliff where we scattered his ashes.

FRANK: And this—

DAISY: And this—

FRANK: And this—

DAISY: And this—

(Suddenly, DAISY sees CHERIMOYA [from Side B] dancing wildly in a square of light. She is fascinated. She watches for a while and then begins to imitate CHERIMOYA's movements. A video of DAISY dancing is superimposed on the scrim in front of her.)

18. Frank and Alan

ALAN is on the promenade, humming with pleasure into his laptop, like a bee with its head deep in an open rose. He is oblivious to the afternoon light and the river rushing by right next to him. FRANK runs in and stops short a few feet from ALAN. He looks out over the water.

FRANK: Ah! Yes! And this is the place where I noticed the moon had a face like my father.

(ALAN chuckles into his laptop.)

FRANK: Mr. Flynnalyn!

ALAN: Huh?

FRANK: I'm happy to see you are feeling better.

ALAN: Wuh?

FRANK: This spot—isn't it great? This spot makes my mind open up like a page in a book.

ALAN: *(Tears his eyes from his laptop and looks at FRANK and then out at the water.)* This spot makes me feel like a wad of bread left out in the rain.

FRANK: And the sky? And the water? And that duck bobbing up and down by the rocks?

(They stare into the distance for a while.)

ALAN: There *was* something once—a white gazebo, fish hooks, a tacklebox, music drifting across the water. Something to do with—but now I can't—

(CELESTE and AURORA appear walking arm in arm along the promenade.)

CELESTE: For crying out loud—look over there!

AURORA: Where?

CELESTE: Over there.

AURORA: Oh yeah, who's that?

CELESTE: Alan.

AURORA: Who?

CELESTE: The husband.

AURORA: Who?

CELESTE: Alan Flynnalyn, Marilyn's husband.

(She gives the glasses to AURORA.)

AURORA: Oh, yeah. Nice suit!

(They watch for a moment. DAISY enters and sees them watching.)

AURORA: Looks like a snail that thinks that it's lost and has no idea that its home is attached to its back.

(She hands the glasses back to CELESTE.)

CELESTE: Looks like a goose on a merry-go-round that thinks it's on its way South for the winter.

DAISY: Wow! X-ray goggles! Souped-up specs! Just what I need to get a closer look at the girl dancing in the window.

19. CELESTE, AURORA, AND DAISY

CELESTE and AURORA continue walking arm and arm along the promenade. DAISY doubles back and suddenly appears in front of them.

CELESTE: Daisy, what are you doing here?

AURORA: What are you doing here on the promenade?

DAISY: I love the promenade. All this fresh air and rushing water reminds me of everything I should have done, of all the chances I didn't take, of all the friendships cast aside, of all the gifts returned unopened. If only I'd been able to see what was coming, if only I'd known what I know now…

AURORA: May I make an observation young lady?

DAISY: Why not? *(Wraps her sweater protectively around her body.)*

AURORA: *(Stares intently at DAISY through her glasses.)*
Pussyfooting's
Not a dance.
Grab the moment
While you got the chance.
Take the plunge
Get your kicks
You can drown your sorrows
When you're eighty-six.

DAISY: You saw that through your glasses?

CELESTE: Why of course. When we put them on we can see far, far away and deep, deep within.

DAISY: When you are wearing those glasses, do you ever get a good look at an unusual person that's been hanging around here?

CELESTE: What sort of person?

DAISY: She never stops moving. I saw her through a window.

AURORA: A little wild?

DAISY: Wild! Gorgeous! Mysterious! Free! If only I could be like that.

AURORA: Her name's Cherimoya.

CELESTE: Cherimoya Waterfall.

DAISY: Who told you that?

AURORA: These specs also improve my hearing. You've heard of bifocals? Well these are trisensuals. They also enhance my sense of smell.

(She sniffs the air, and so does TRIXIE.)

DAISY: How do I know you're not lying?

CELESTE: Aurora couldn't tell a lie if she was chewing on it.

DAISY: Prove it.

(CELESTE grabs the glasses off AURORA's face and hands them to DAISY.)

CELESTE: See for yourself, Miss Gloomy Eyes.

(DAISY put on the glasses, she sniffs the air. CELESTE and AURORA watch her carefully.)

DAISY: Bye!

(She runs off down the promenade, still wearing the glasses. CELESTE and AURORA stand stock-still in disbelief. They hear DAISY calling in the distance.)

DAISY: Cherimoya! Cherimoya Waterfall! Cherimoya! Cherimoya Wonderful!

(They rush off in pursuit. The river glitters in the distance.)

AURORA: All I had in mind was an invigorating walk by the river—and then, out of the blue, that girl steals my glasses.

CELESTE: Wait! Stop!

AURORA: What?

CELESTE: I gotta pee!

AURORA: Suddenly, just like that? You're like a three-year-old, Celeste.

CELESTE: All this jogging and jiggling sloshes me all up. Oh God! It's bad! We gotta hurry!

AURORA: Okay. Don't pull. I can't see.—You're going to make me twist my ankle.

CELESTE: Which way? Which way?

AURORA: There's got to be a restaurant around here somewhere.

CELESTE: Where? Where?

AURORA: Somewhere down one of these cobbled little streets.

(They rush along looking left and right. A video of a restaurant appears on the surface of the cube.)

AURORA: Ah, this looks like one with a good clean ladies room.

CELESTE: The Pompous Lobster? Looks expensive, and that sign says "No Dogs Allowed" and this one says, "Restrooms for Customers Only."

AURORA: Follow me and keep quiet.

(AURORA shoves CELESTE through the heavy glass doors.)

20. Lucinda

LUCINDA (from Side B) appears outside the restaurant with a pair of giant binoculars. She sneaks around, cautiously pressing her face against the windows, trying to get a look at what is going on inside. She watches as a naturalist in the jungle might watch a pride of lions, careful to remain upwind and out of sight. She speaks to the audience.

LUCINDA: I am a neuro-anthropologist
My field is anthroneurology.
I feel my thoughts as bodily sensations.
I love to watch myself watching myself.

I believe the mind is just the brain.
The experience of longing or regret
Is exactly equal to a clump of tissue
And salty liquid lodged inside the skull.

This place is something like a two-way mirror
We see ourselves more clearly gazing into it
There is more space between the people here
And so it is a scientific paradise.

In order to remain outside the frame
And protect my data from contamination
I need to keep my distance and refuse
To be seduced by those I am observing.

I'm learning micro-muscular control
A method of atomic infiltration
Expanding space between my molecules
So I can slip unnoticed into other's lives.

21. Celeste, Aurora, and Cousin Ricky

The sound of rushing water. CELESTE enters from the ladies room, looking relieved. The waiter, COUSIN RICKY (from Side B) has seated AURORA at a table by the window. AURORA is perusing a giant menu.

AURORA: Celeste, this is Ricky, our server. Ricky used to have a papillon. Her name was Rosebud. She was run over by a Vespa in 1998.

CELESTE: Oh! I'm sorry.

(Her eyes fill with tears. RICKY's eyes also fill with tears.)

RICKY: I'm sorry too.

AURORA: He still thinks about her every day.

RICKY: Yes! Every day.

AURORA: Her tiny raincoat still hangs on a hook in his hall closet.

RICKY: On a hook, yes!

CELESTE: Poor Rosebud.

RICKY: Poor Rosebud. Yes!

(He wipes his eyes on his apron and hands CELESTE a menu.)

AURORA: Ricky was just going to tell me the luncheon special.

CELESTE: But—

RICKY: Yes! The luncheon special today is smothered duck backs with a side of sautéed scissor grass and scalded fingerlings in a wasabe rocket crust.

AURORA: I'll take the suckeroo with persimmon sauce and the purslane frissée with the mariposa dressing.

RICKY: Mariposa dressing, yes! And for you, Madame.

CELESTE: Um—

(AURORA is winking and signaling obscurely with her napkin. CELESTE is game for any weird adventure as long as she can remain seated.)

CELESTE: Yes, I'll have the urchin broth with the tiny rumble dumplings.

RICKY: Excellent choice.

AURORA: And may we have some more water?

RICKY: More water?

AURORA: Yes, more water, as soon as possible.

RICKY: More water? Yes, Madame.

CELESTE: Two more waters.

RICKY: Of course, two more waters, excellent.

AURORA: More water.

RICKY: More water.

CELESTE: More water, right away.

(The restaurant fills with water. A BUBBLE CHOIR is piped in, the reedy voices muffled by the gurgle and plash of underground springs.)

BUBBLE CHOIR: OOH WALLA WALLA
OOH OOMA OOMA
BELLY BELLA, CANDELABRA
WALLA WALLA WALLA WALLA
MARIPOSA OOMA OOMA
ZIPPER LOCKA SUCKEROO.

(CELESTE and AURORA improvise a sensual water ballet with COUSIN RICKY. He imitates, almost anticipates their every move, making him a pleasing dancing partner. LUCINDA continues to observe them, taking notes and dancing along with the music.)

BUBBLE CHOIR: BELLY BELLA WALLA
WALLA
MARIPOSA SUCKEROO
CANDELABRA ZIPPER LOCKA
OOMA OOMA SUCKEROO

(The water surges more forcefully, rising up toward the ceiling. CELESTE and AURORA begin to panic. The dance becomes a struggle. Their lungs are bursting. They climb on top of RICKY and one another, trying to reach the surface of the water.)

BUBBLE CHOIR: WA WALLA WALLA
OOH WA
WA WALLA WALLA OOH
WA WALLA WALLA OOH WA
WA WALLA WALLA OOH

(Suddenly RICKY lunges violently and opens the door. CELESTE and AURORA are spit out onto the cobblestones.)

(Projection:)

SIDE B—THE WATERFALLS

The set transforms. It's like a journey through a landscape.

MARILYN: *(Moving through with her bag of weapons—)* Who is she, Alan? No one. No one? No one!

CELESTE and AURORA: *(Nearly blind, searching for DAISY—)* Daisy? Daisy?

MARILYN: *(Passing by again, furiously, under her breath—)* SYLVIA!

(LUCINDA enters, stalking her prey, like a heron or a tiger. RICKY is transforming into everyone he passes. FRANK is looking for places he remembers. He sees the shadow of the WATERFALL FAMILY, sleeping in a pile. Is it underwater vegetation? A religious totem? He reaches out to touch it—an alarm clock rings—and the WATERFALLS explode into action.)

(The act is structured around the sleeping and waking pattern of the WATERFALLS. When they wake up, they run, each one following his or her own path. When their paths intersect, there is a scene. When it is night, the WATERFALLS drop into their sleeping pile and their dreams emerge. The day scenes should have the feeling of constant motion and relentless cheerfulness, with a dose of claustrophobia. The arias are big and emotional. The dreams and other night events are in strong contrast to the daytime world. The act fast-forwards through five days and nights.)

Day 1:
Waterfalls Ride to Work

OSCAR: The Alfa's going in for an oil change. Who needs a ride to work?

SYLVIA: Me!

LUCINDA: Me!

RICKY: Me! Me!

(They dash over, grabbing at flying papers, ungainly briefcases, clutching sweaters and umbrellas, and, in RICKY's case, an apron and a pink bowtie. They squeeze into the car, crushing each other cheerfully; their speech is a little too loud and overlapping.)

CHERIMOYA: Wait for me, Uncle Oscar. *(She is rapidly changing from one shirt to another to another.)*

OSCAR: Okay, Cherry Pie.

LUCINDA: Thank God this is a convertible.

RICKY: Thank God.

OSCAR: *(To SYLVIA.)* What's she doing in there?

SYLVIA: Changing her shirt.

LUCINDA: Or we'd never fit in a million years.

RICKY: Never fit, not in a million years.

OSCAR: *(To SYLVIA.)* Again?

LUCINDA: What happened to the new one with the fringes?

SYLVIA: Someone at school told her she looked like a tablecloth.

RICKY: Someone at school. Golly!

(CHERIMOYA rushes in with a giant bag and a tiny iPod. She leaps into the back seat, crushing SYLVIA.)

CHERIMOYA: Move over, Mommy.

SYLVIA: Ow! That's my hand, that's my hand!

OSCAR: And we're off.

(He pulls into traffic. Video of a highway as seen from a car. During the ride, the WATERFALLS never stop moving. The wind is noisy and blows their hair in all directions. RICKY twists and turns in his seat, shifting his focus from one family member to another, subtly picking up the gestures of whomever he's looking at. SYLVIA takes off and puts on her sweater because she goes from being burning hot to shivering cold every twenty seconds. LUCINDA is obsessively checking her purse to make sure she has remembered her tape recorder, binoculars, keys, pens, clipboard, etc. OSCAR drives like a maniac, twisting and turning through traffic. CHERIMOYA sings along with her iPod, getting louder and louder. The landscape whips and whirls by behind them, creating a kind of vertigo as if they are being stirred by the giant spoon of God.)

SYLVIA: *(From the back seat.)* Left!

OSCAR: I know.

SYLVIA: Left!

OSCAR: I know.

LUCINDA: Do you ever feel like you're being stirred by the giant spoon of God?

RICKY: Spoon of God? Of course—All the time, all the time.

CHERIMOYA: *(Singing along with her iPod.)*
I'M HIS SEXY HOTTIE,
HE'S MY MOODY CUTIE,
HIS JUICY JELLY BELLY
MAKES ME SHAKE MY BOOTY.
BE MY DOUBLE DIPPER,
MY ICE CREAM MAN,
SOFT SERVE, COOL WHIPPER,
RIGHT OUTTA THE CAN.

PSHSHT! PSHSHT! PSHSHT!
SHAKE IT UP, SQUIRT IT OUT
PSHSHT! PSHSHT!
SCOOP IT, SHAKE IT
PSHSHT! PSHSHT!

OSCAR: *(Shouting to SYLVIA.)* So Blinky Damphander shows up at the office yesterday. You remember Blinky?

SYLVIA: Think so. The one who rushed to the ER because he swallowed an earwig?

OSCAR: Yeah. I mean, the guy is so predictable. Every time there's a hiccup in the market, he starts flooding my BlackBerry with freaky-deaky. So I said, "Look Blinky, this is what you pay me for—to be calm, to be rational. That's what a hedge fund manager is for."

LUCINDA: *(To RICKY.)* Do you ever hunger for a fresh perspective?

RICKY: Fresh perspective? Of course. Every day, every day.

SYLVIA: Right! Go right!

OSCAR: I know. So I said, "Look, the reason that you survive a shipwreck—there's like hidden icebergs—things start sinking, the storm comes up. This is what we do: stick to the plan, bring the exposure down, get rid of low conviction shorts, buckle down the portfolio."

LUCINDA: Do you ever crave the rush of a crystal-clear epiphany?

RICKY: The rush of epiphany? Of course I do. Of course!

SYLVIA: Oscar, this is the exit, right here, right here!

LUCINDA: So did you calm him down?

OSCAR: I think so. He's off to Chicago today to buy a zoo or something.

SYLVIA: Yield, Oscar! Are you blind? Yield! Yield!

OSCAR: I brought home six figures last year and my big sister still thinks I'm blind to yield.

RICKY: Blind to yield, that's good, buddy.

OSCAR: Buddy-o, Buddy-o!

SYLVIA: It was true when you were three and it's still true, Big Shot.

CHERIMOYA: (*Singing with iPod.*)
I'M HIS SEXY HOTTIE,
HE'S MY MOODY CUTIE,
HIS JUICY JELLY BELLY
MAKES ME SHAKE MY BOOTY.

BE MY DOUBLE DIPPER,
MY ICE CREAM MAN,
SOFT SERVE, COOL WHIPPER,
RIGHT OUTTA THE CAN.

PSHSHT! PSHSHT! PSHSHT!
SHAKE IT UP, SQUIRT IT OUT
PSHSHT! PSHSHT!
SCOOP IT, SHAKE IT
PSHSHT! PSHSHT!

OSCAR: Last stop, pile out.

(*They do, and race off in all directions. They fall into their sleeping pile.*)

Dream 1

CHERIMOYA (on film) caught in a piece of scrim, dancing wildly, trying to get free. (Closeup of live dancing from Side A.)

Day 2:
Braided Dialogue/
Extreme River Boys

OSCAR and COUSIN RICKY are in the Extreme River Boys Changing Tent. They are changing from their work clothes— expensive suit for OSCAR, apron and bowtie for RICKY—into bathing suits, caps, and goggles. They undress side by side —poking, choking, tripping, and slapping each other playfully. SYLVIA is furiously typing on her laptop. LUCINDA, equipped with binoculars and camera, is stalking FRANK from Side A. He can be partially seen in the distance through a lighted window. CHERIMOYA is dancing hither and thither at the mercy of her impulses.

CHERIMOYA: (*To LUCINDA.*) I gotta get outta here.

LUCINDA: Why?

CHERIMOYA: My mother's a dweeb. I'm afraid it will rub off. Can I come with you?

(*In the changing tent.*)

OSCAR: Rain or Shine

RICKY: Happy, Sad

OSCAR: Every Day

RICKY: Into the Drink.

OSCAR: Extreme River Boys

RICKY: Take the Plunge

OSCAR: In Scalding Heat

RICKY: Or Frosty Sleet

OSCAR: If You Don't Go In

OSCAR and RICKY: You're Out!

(*They race into the freezing water and swim for dear life. They "swim" inside the cube with video of rushing water superimposed on the scrim in front of them.*)

(*CHERIMOYA with SYLVIA.*)

CHERIMOYA: You say you want to be my friend.

SYLVIA: Well I want to be your mother and your—

CHERIMOYA: Why would I want to be your friend? When you get together with your friends, all you talk about is fibroids.

SYLVIA: That's not all we talk about.

CHERIMOYA: And then you offer each other cake, and then you all say no, and then you secretly poke your fingers in the crumbs and suck them up as if no one can see. It's disgusting! Stop looking at me! Stop looking at me!

(Swimming in the freezing water.)

OSCAR: Hysteria grips, take my advice
Be sure to swim free of its clutches, Buddy.

RICKY: Take it, swim free, you bet, Buddy-o.

OSCAR: Layers of redundancy
You gotta live your life that way
Make sure you got a cushion
Don't bump along the bottom.

RICKY: Don't bump it, don't bump it, Gotcha, Buddy-o.

(CHERIMOYA meets LUCINDA.)

CHERIMOYA: What are you doing?

LUCINDA: My exercises.

CHERIMOYA: But you're not moving.

LUCINDA: I'm moving inside—molecular calisthenics.

CHERIMOYA: You're kidding.

LUCINDA: Wanna try?

CHERIMOYA: I hate this family.

(In the river.)

OSCAR: You gotta think it through
From a hundred different angles
Get out in front of the money flow
And ride it to the future.

RICKY: Get out in front and ride it, sure thing, Buddy-o.

(SYLVIA meets LUCINDA.)

SYLVIA: How's it going over there.

LUCINDA: Illuminating. Profound, in fact.

SYLVIA: Oh yeah? Listen, can I give you some advice? Forget about those people on the other side. Better keep an eye on yourself.

LUCINDA: Well, I…

SYLVIA: People have lots of reasons not to tell you the truth. I figured that out a long time ago. It's like back fat—Everyone can see it but you, and no one will tell you you have it. But if you knew it looks like it looks, you'd watch out for what you wear, you'd keep it covered up.

(In the river.)

OSCAR: Hey, whatever happens
Don't panic and dump it
Whatever you do
Don't swing it around.

RICKY: Don't panic, don't dump it, don't swing it around.

OSCAR: You get it?

RICKY: I got it.

OSCAR: You get it?

RICKY: I got it.

(They jump out of the water, towel off, and run away.)

(CHERIMOYA with LUCINDA: CHERIMOYA's aria.)

CHERIMOYA: And yesterday when it was about a hundred degrees she put on this Mexican scarf, like this big itchy thing with black and yellow and green stripes. Some skanky guy gave it to her "back in the day," as a love token or some bullshit. "Sylvia, here is a big itchy green and black love token." I hate her.

And when she drinks like a Coke or something, she swishes it all around in her mouth, for like a minute, I swear. What is that about?

And she says gaz. Like, "I'm a little gazzy. Are you a little gazzy? Broccoli always gives me gaz." Barf and a half!

(They rush around and fall into their sleeping pile.)

Dream 2

SYLVIA enters with her laptop in front of her face. A closeup of her eye is projected on it. ALAN is typing on her keys. His stomach is a laptop with a giant mouth.

Day 3:
Four Arias/
A Disturbing Phone Call

OSCAR enters in a terry-cloth robe and designer flip flops. He enters the cube. A shower video is projected on the scrim in front of him. OSCAR takes off his robe. We see him behind the curtain, enjoying the water pouring over him. MRS. WORMSER—seen through a distant window—is trimming a houseplant with small gold scissors. LUCINDA is studying herself in the mirror. SYLVIA is speaking to ALAN via laptop.

SYLVIA: I just need a moment alone!
I watch myself vanish
Around a corner
My thoughts bubble up
And gurgle away

I see myself sagging
In the front seat
All elephant limbs
And redundant ideas.
I just need a day to do nothing!

This morning my daughter
Came into the kitchen
And called me a dweeby
Earth shoe fat butt.
A pseudo-Mom
With skeezy lizard skin
And I knew she was right!

And then I remembered
A day in July
When I was fifteen
And you were fifteen

And the sidewalk smelled
Like the back of a truck
And the rain had stopped
And my cutoffs were perfect

And my skateboard was made
Of a two-by-four
With roller skate wheels
Screwed into the bottom

Kachunk, kachunk
I rolled down the hill
To the little house
That belonged to your cousin

Where you were asleep
In the hide-a-bed
And the day opened up
And the future was gorgeous.

I just need a moment alone!

I still see the point
Of a good cup of coffee
A swim in the ocean
A night at the movies

But everything has
A frame around it
The scary What If
I just can't escape it!

I just need a day!
I just need a moment alone!

(As the shower pours over him, OSCAR begins to move his upper body back and forth, his arms twisting above his head. Strange rustling noises issue from deep in his throat. The air is filled with throaty birdsong and a luscious melody. OSCAR is transforming into a tree—his branches bending and swinging in the windy rain. He is at the mercy of the elements—thirsty and ecstatic.)

OSCAR: I am Jacaranda
I am Jacaranda
Lavender gondolas
Plucked from my places
Are floating and falling
Floating and falling.

MRS. WORMSER: *(Chanting sweetly to her little plant.)* My dishes are crystal
My bedspread is crimson
My rug smells of cedar
My windows are shut tight.

OSCAR: Worm-clotted roots
Go wandering under
Gripping and clutching
The rotting conundrum

Sap coming up
Distending, engorging
I am synthelizing
Photo scintillating

MRS. WORMSER: The portrait of Mother
Is framed in silver
There are thirty-six pearls
On her ivory neck
I count them every day.

OSCAR: Inhaling carbona
Dioxidionna
Filling and spilling
Filling and spilling
Double hydrogenous

Oxygenolla

MRS. WORMSER: The armchair is facing East by Northeast
The tea is steeping
In the fat blue pot
The steam is rising
In perfect spirals.

OSCAR: Pith and pod
And scurfy shoots
And pollen sacs
Are sipping deep

Gondola, rondola
Bend me, rend me.
Jacarandondola
Slake me take me
Aah! Aah! Aah! Aah!

(A drop of warm water suddenly drips onto MRS. WORMSER's perfectly styled hair, and onto the leaves of her little plant.)

MRS. WORMSER: Aah! What? Water? What? Again? *(She grabs the cell phone and begins to dial.)*
I can't stand it! Won't stand for it!
This is appalling! I am appalled!

LUCINDA: *(Speaking to audience.)*
My father was a dog-eared fellow in his fifties
When he met my mother who was going on sixteen.
Gray hair made her blush and twitter, baby fat turned him to butter
One sad kiss let to another, nine months later they had me.

And so I've always suffered from the dubious distinction
Of being Aunt Lucinda from the moment of conception
Of being fed my bottles by heavy-breasted nieces
And enduring diaper changes by nephews with mustaches

A baby aunty is devoid of dignity
The endless butt of brainless jokes and smarmy stories
So in order to preserve a modicum of self-esteem
I chose a life of rigorous scientific inquiry

If I spend my time in impartial observation
I cannot be defined by raunchy innuendo
And stifling entanglements with complicated relatives
And sour afternoons in the bosom of my family.

(OSCAR comes out of the bathroom in his terry-cloth bathrobe. His feet are bare, a trail of wet footprints behind him. SYLVIA enters scowling, phone in hand. RICKY is right behind her, scowling also. He has a mop. He follows OSCAR around mopping up his footprints. He agrees with whomever is talking. OSCAR and SYLVIA ignore him.)

SYLVIA: Mrs. Wormser called again.

RICKY: Mrs. Wormser, Oscar.

OSCAR: So what?

RICKY: Yeah, who cares?

SYLVIA: She's sputtering mad, Oscar. More leakage in her living room.

OSCAR: What's the matter with a little extra water?

RICKY: It's just a little water!

SYLVIA: People only want to deal with their own water, Oscar.

RICKY: Other people's water is disgusting, Oscar.

OSCAR: Water is water. *(His branches imperceptibly reach for the sky.)*

SYLVIA: She is reporting an abnormal amount of splashing.

RICKY: Too much splashing.

OSCAR: Mrs. Wormser is irrational.

RICKY: More than irrational.

SYLVIA: And a smacking sound, like a wet branch hitting the side of a barn.

RICKY: It's driving her nuts.

SYLVIA: She wants to know what's going on up here.

RICKY: She has a right to know.

OSCAR: It's none of her business.

RICKY: A busybody, if you ask me.

SYLVIA: She's demanding an explanation, an apology.

RICKY: It's the least you could do.

OSCAR: Do I demand an explanation for that fishy smell that seeps up from her kitchen every evening at 7:45 on the dot?

RICKY: I think she's on the Mermaid Diet.

OSCAR: No, I don't—because everyone has a right to privacy in his own home—

RICKY: Privacy—

OSCAR: And a little happiness, Sylvia.

SYLVIA: Yes, but Mrs. Wormser is—

OSCAR: Mrs. Wormser is volatile.

SYLVIA: You deal with volatility every day, Oscar. What's happened to your scenarios, your layers of redundancy?

OSCAR: Mrs. Wormser is volatile and irrational.

RICKY: And unstable.

SYLVIA: So is the market. You've told me that a million times.

RICKY: A million and one.

OSCAR: The market follows the models. It's rational in the long run. A long as you keep your finger on global commerce and geopolitical evolution you'll be okay, you'll ride that wave right into the shore. Mrs. Wormser is unpredictable and out of control and so I refuse to have anything to do with her!

RICKY: She isn't worth your time.

SYLVIA: And what do you expect me to do?

RICKY: What can Sylvia possibly do?

OSCAR: You'll figure something out. You're the smoother-over in this family.

RICKY: The cream of our crop, Sylvia.

SYLVIA: And I've had enough of it!

RICKY: She's had it, Oscar.

OSCAR: Come on, Sylvia.

RICKY: Do the guy a favor.

SYLVIA: I'm out of here. *(She exits.)*

RICKY: She's gone.

OSCAR: Do me a favor and zip it, Buddy-o.

RICKY: Okay, Buddy, okay.

(They exit in opposite directions.)

NIGHT VISION

FRANK visits the sleeping pile once again. As he ponders its meaning, the moon rises. He is enchanted by its beauty. CHERIMOYA wakes up and sees him seeing it. If only FRANK would look at her like that! She is smitten with him.

FRANK: Moon
Button moon
White button moon
Your single eye is burning
August grasses look like ice
My vision is transforming
I hear your icy voice

Your smile so pale and solemn
And your face so all alone
Your light so full of sorrow
White button moon

Small button
White button
Smooth button
Moon.

DAY 4:
BRAIDED DIALOGUE CONTINUED

CHERIMOYA: *(Entering with a bowl of tomatoes.)* Here, Ma.

SYLVIA: What's this?

CHERIMOYA: Bowl of tomatoes.

SYLVIA: Where'd you get them?

CHERIMOYA: Mrs. Wormser.

SYLVIA: Uh oh.

CHERIMOYA: What's with her, anyway? She goes "For YOU and your MOTHER." Then she drags her nails along my arm, so they like leave marks. Then she gives me this look like she's about to bite my neck.

SYLVIA: Why'd you take them? *(She is trembling.)*

CHERIMOYA: Why? Shit, Ma, why not?

SYLVIA: She's mad at Uncle Oscar.

CHERIMOYA: So she's giving us tomatoes?

SYLVIA: It's guilt gifting. Haven't you ever heard of guilt gifting?

CHERIMOYA: What did I do wrong? Why is everything I do wrong?

SYLVIA: Just put them over there.

CHERIMOYA: God, sick! Everyone around here is warped and sick. And, Ma, you're online again. Why are you online again?

SYLVIA: It's just my friend, Alan.

CHERIMOYA: A guy? You're online with a guy? TMI, Ma. That is gross.

SYLVIA: He's just an old friend from the alumni chat room and—

CHERIMOYA: TMI! Too Much Information! I'm not listening! *(Covers her ears and begins to sing loudly.)* La la la la la! Get me out of here!

(She runs around until she runs into LUCINDA.)

CHERIMOYA: Do something! She's fucking jerking off online with some guy every minute of the day.

LUCINDA: That's none of our business, Cherimoya.

CHERIMOYA: Some weirdo Sweet Vista Chat Room guy named Alan.

LUCINDA: Alan? Are you sure?

CHERIMOYA: "Your buddy is typing. My buddy is typing! Alan, oh, Alan. Send! Send! Send!"

LUCINDA: I better go talk to her.

(She runs around until she runs into SYLVIA. SYLVIA is hunched over her laptop, typing, typing.)

LUCINDA: Sylvia?

SYLVIA: Huh?

LUCINDA: Sylvia.

SYLVIA: Wuh?

LUCINDA: There have been some pertinent developments on the other side in the last few days.

SYLVIA: I'm sure. Could you share them with me later, Aunt Lucinda? Right now I'm—

LUCINDA: I think you would find them exceedingly relevant to yourself.

SYLVIA: Sure, later on maybe we could—

LUCINDA: SYLVIA, I NEED FIVE MINUTES OF YOUR TIME, RIGHT NOW.

SYLVIA: *(Shutting her laptop.)* Of course, Aunt Lucinda. What's on your mind?

LUCINDA: I think you might take a profound interest in one of my subjects—a middle-aged man—I call him AF23.

SYLVIA: And why do you think that I—

LUCINDA: His problem is that his brain maps lack adequate stimulation. And recently his dopamine levels have hit rock bottom.

SYLVIA: By that you mean—

LUCINDA: —That his life seems pointless and he is often overwhelmed by an inexplicable sadness.

SYLVIA: Oh poor guy! Poor guy! I know just how he feels, I—

LUCINDA: As a result, AF23 is self-medicating with manual digital self-stimulation. This, in turn, is causing him to experience extreme internet proximity saturation.

SYLVIA: Internet what?

LUCINDA: He can't let go of his laptop.

SYLVIA: *(Clutching hers.)* Poor fellow, I know how he feels.

LUCINDA: —Because of this obsessive behavior, as well as his repeated vocalization of the word "Sylvia"—

SYLVIA: Sylvia? But that's *my* name—

LUCINDA: —another one of my subjects, MF24, who is, by the way, his *wife*—

SYLVIA: His wife?

LUCINDA: —is suffering from an overload of glucocorticoids, and if not for her endogenous opiates, she certainly would have stabbed him through the heart with her kitchen shears.

SYLVIA: His wife? Oh dear! I never meant to—

LUCINDA: But instead, I have observed her packing a containing device with dangerous household objects, and she is heading in this direction.

SYLVIA: Here? Now?

LUCINDA: Yes, I thought you might like to know.

SYLVIA: I would like to know, of course I would like to know— *(She dashes off with her laptop.)*

(They fall into the sleeping pile.)

Dream 4

OSCAR is a tree. MRS. WORMSER—a grinning monster—approaches him wielding giant clippers. OSCAR shakes with fear. MRS. WORMSER gets ready to cut off his branches.

Day 5:
Bad Choices with Vegetables/
Waterfalls in Crisis

CHERIMOYA enters, dancing, sees the bowl of tomatoes, picks one up, sees LUCINDA in the distance, sneaks up to her. LUCINDA is carefully watching Side A through a window or portal, her camera at the ready.

CHERIMOYA: Can I hang with you?

LUCINDA: Shshsh!

CHERIMOYA: Can I? It's so beautiful over there—so empty, so deep, so painfully, soulfully beautiful. When I look over there I feel—something...connected—dazzled—transformed. Maybe I belong over there. Hey! Maybe I was actually born over there. Maybe I was kidnapped. Maybe I have a different mother—Maybe she wears stilettos and plucks her eyebrows. Maybe I'm someone else. Maybe not a stupid Waterfall, maybe—

LUCINDA: Shshsh! Here they come.

(CELESTE and AURORA appear as a large photo, projected on the side of the cube. FRANK appears, live, inside the cube, cleaning the surface. CHERIMOYA can see him but he can't see her.)

CHERIMOYA: Oh, there he is! It's him! Oh, cool! Oh! Hey, moon! Button moon! White button moon. Hey look! It's me. Look! Over here! Look!

(She throws the tomato at him, to get his attention. It misses him and spatters in CELESTE's eyes. We see this as a series of still photos taken by LUCINDA.)

CHERIMOYA: Oops. Outta here. It wasn't me. I wasn't even there. No. I was in the kitchen. Washing a—Doing the—Eating a—The whole time. Honest. Honest. I didn't even—never even... (She begins to run.)*

AURORA: Well for crying out loud! Celeste! For crying out loud! Who did that? For crying out loud!

CELESTE: Oh! Fiddle di di! Oh! Help!

(LUCINDA can't stop taking photos. She snaps one after the other.)

AURORA: *(Pointing at LUCINDA.)* Look, it's her! She did it!

CELESTE: *(Feeling tomato juice all over her face.)* I can't see!

AURORA: Hey! I see you!

CELESTE: Help! Is it blood? Is it acid? Help! Help!

AURORA: I know who you are. Miss Zoom Lens—always snapping and staring. Nothing better to do but spy on old ladies!

(LUCINDA realizes they are pointing at her, but she can't stop taking pictures.)

AURORA: Hey! You! I'm gonna call the cops.

CELESTE: Help! I can't see!

(LUCINDA lowers the camera and begins to back away uncertainly.)

AURORA: Come back here, Miss Beady Eyes, I see you. I am a witness. Hey come back here!

CELESTE: Help! Police! Help! Police!

(LUCINDA turns and runs. SYLVIA is running with her laptop, OSCAR is running away from MRS. WORMSER, RICKY and CHERIMOYA are running also. The WATERFALLS run into the cube. They are finally standing still. They are in shock.)

SYLVIA: What has happened to our family?

RICKY: What happened?

OSCAR: We have all crossed the line.

CHERIMOYA: Except for Ricky.

RICKY: Except for me.

SYLVIA: We used to be exemplary.

OSCAR: A source of envy.

LUCINDA: A good example.

SYLVIA: Dedicated,

RICKY: Close knit,

SYLVIA: If anyone mentioned the bosom of the family—

OSCAR: We were that bosom.

SYLVIA: Soft, strong,

OSCAR: Comfortable, protective.

(EVERYONE takes a big breath and sighs in unison.)

SYLVIA: The line is thin.

LUCINDA: Invisible.

OSCAR: We crossed without knowing it.

LUCINDA: Somehow.

SYLVIA: Into the land of scorn.

OSCAR: Raised eyebrows.

CHERIMOYA: Major brush-offs.

LUCINDA: Nasty snorts and snickers.

CHERIMOYA: Everyone hates us.

OSCAR: But let's not be too reactive.

RICKY: Reactive?

SYLVIA: Us?

LUCINDA: Never.

OSCAR: We'll be all right as long as we stick to the plan.

RICKY: Okay. What is it?

OSCAR: Run away!

(They crowd into the car. OSCAR drives wildly. Video of the road from the car window.)

SYLVIA: Left! Left! Right! Right!

CHERIMOYA: Where are we going, Uncle Oscar?

OSCAR: I have no idea, but I think better when I'm driving.

(The wind whips through their hair, the landscape flashes past. They shout over the car noise.)

OSCAR: So, as I understand it, Cherimoya threw a tomato at an elderly person.

LUCINDA: Correct!

CHERIMOYA: I didn't throw it at the elderly person, it hit the elderly person by mistake.

OSCAR: And this elderly person is under the impression that Lucinda threw the offending vegetable.

LUCINDA: Correct. And my research has been compromised.

RICKY: Her cover is blown.

LUCINDA: And this elderly person—old witch—is calling the police. And believe me, I know these people—overly serious, extremely opinionated, and willing to press charges at the drop of a hat.

OSCAR: And, I also understand that Sylvia has typed herself into a volatile internet Ménage à Trois.

SYLVIA: I never meant to hurt anyone. If I had thought for a moment I was hurting anyone—

CHERIMOYA: If you had thought for a moment, you would realize that it's so obvious and so sucky and so obvious.

SYLVIA: And did you think before you threw the tomato?

RICKY: Always think before you throw.

CHERIMOYA: Shut up, Ricky!

OSCAR: Yeah, shut up, Buddy-o.

LUCINDA: Don't yell at him, he's the only one who's not in trouble.

(RICKY's aria.)

RICKY: Because I suffer from Terminal Empathy:
Whenever I serve the Zesty Pucker Snapper or the Cold Fruit Soup
I can't stop myself from drooling buckets of saliva.
And would you ever tip a waiter who has a wet cravat?
NO, YOU WOULDN'T!

Because I'm afraid of making mistakes,
Afraid of saying the wrong thing. Afraid! Afraid!
I can't stop hovering, and shadowing, and following
And could you ever love a guy who's a chickenshit copycat?
NO, YOU COULDN'T!

Because I can't do anything unless someone else does it first.
So most of the time I don't do anything at all
And if you think that's fun
WELL, IT ISN'T!

OSCAR: And on top of everything else, I have received some compromising photos in the mail, which our neighbor Mrs. Wormser procured with the aid of a cell phone and a set of spare keys.

SYLVIA: She took pictures of him in the shower.

RICKY: Pictures of him in the shower?

LUCINDA: That's got to be illegal.

SYLVIA: Illegal or not, she's threatening to send them to the *Wall Street Journal*.

OSCAR: I can't wait to see the headline—Hedge Fund Manager Leads Double Life As Tree.

CHERIMOYA: As what?

OSCAR: As tree.

CHERIMOYA: Oh sicko! This family is nothing but a bunch of farts and sketchy douche bags! Stop the car!

(The brakes squeal. OSCAR stops the car.)

CHERIMOYA: Lemme out of here! I gotta get outta here! I am not part of this family!

(She rushes off. EVERYONE jumps out of the car and follows after her.)

ALL: Cherimoya! Cherimoya Waterfall! Cherimoya! Cherimoya Waterfall!

(We see CHERIMOYA's projected image on the surface of the cube. She is running through the woods. The voices of her FAMILY echo in the distance.)

(Projection:)

ON THE EDGE

The landscape folds in on itself. Side A and Side B are superimposed. EVERYONE is in two places at once. The familiar has become unfamiliar. CELESTE's dog, POOPSY—enlarged tenfold and running free—cracks the cube open, marks his new territory, and bounds away. MRS. WORMSER swoops on in a fury.

MRS. WORMSER: Squirm, Oscar Waterfall, squirm and cringe, and slink and twist in the wind with shame! Do you hear me? I got the pix right here in my pocketbook!

(She sits down, angry and exhausted. MARILYN schleps in with her laundry bag and sits down next to her.)

MARILYN: Boy am I tired!

MRS. WORMSER: Boy am I tired, and boy am I mad!

MARILYN: Boy oh boy, am I mad and tired!

MRS. WORMSER: *(Like a wolf on an empty trail.)* Uwoooooooooooooo!

MARILYN: *(Overlapping.)* Clickety click! Tappety tap on her sticky, sweaty nighty!

MRS. WORMSER: Flagrancy! Flagrant flagrancy!

MARILYN: Who is it, Alan? No one. Who is she, Alan? No one. No one.

MRS. WORMSER: Nothing but pigheaded, wag-it-in-your-face flagrancy!

MARILYN: Who does she think she is? What does she think she's up to?

MRS. WORMSER: What does he think he's doing? Been neighbors since we were just about kids, but now that he rakes it in—and he does, I can't even get my mind around all that money—He's turned all hedonistic. But I've caught him au naturel!

MARILYN: Old and sad? Not my fault. You got that way all on your own, Alan.

MRS. WORMSER: Doesn't care who his water drips on.

MARILYN: Watch out Ms. Ethernet, I'm on my way.

MRS. WORMSER: I refuse to be dripped on, Oscar.

MARILYN: I won't be brushed aside like some nasty old cat on a kitchen table.

MRS. WORMSER: Brushed aside? I could never tolerate being brushed aside. That's the worst. I feel sorry for you.

MARILYN: Don't feel sorry for me. I feel sorry for you.

MRS. WORMSER: Don't you dare feel sorry for me.

MARILYN: Well, don't you dare feel sorry for me. I don't want your pity.

MRS. WORMSER: I don't tolerate pity from anyone.

MARILYN: Well, neither do I.

MRS. WORMSER: And neither do I.

MARILYN: No?

MRS. WORMSER: No. NO?

MARILYN: NO!

MRS. WORMSER and MARILYN: *NO! NO! NO!*

MRS. WORMSER: OSCAR!

(They exit huffily. In the FLYNNALYNS' window we see an open laptop glowing in the misty rain. The top of SYLVIA's head, her forehead, and eyes appear at the bottom of the screen. She peers into the room.)

SYLVIA: *(Whispering.)* Alan? Alan! Your wife!

(AURORA stumbles along, carrying CELESTE. CELESTE's body is flat like a piece of cardboard, her face still covered in tomato.)

AURORA: I knew it would come to this, Celeste.

MARILYN: *(Passing by, grim and determined.)* Look sharp, Ms. Dampsewer, Here I come!

RICKY: *(His head floating like a balloon on a tiny puppet body.)* —Where is this? Where am I? Where is this? Who am I?

SYLVIA: Alan! Her glucocorticoids are leaking into her gene pool and making her—causing her to—

AURORA: My thumbs are twitching. We've climbed too high. We've seen too much.

MARILYN: I'll crack you open and boil your guts into a sleazy hussy sauce.

SYLVIA: Alan! She's dressed up, whacked out, and on the way to my place with scissors, knives, needles, and ant poison—I just thought you might—I just thought you should—

AURORA: Celeste! Celeste!

We've gazed too long into the abyss.

And now the abyss is gazing deep into us!

RICKY: I'm nowhere! I'm no one! I'm nothing! I'm no one!

SYLVIA: Shit Alan! Where are you? Alan? No one. Alan? Nothing. No one. Nothing. No one. *(Her head sinks down and disappears.)*

(FRANK enters, disoriented but forging on courageously as if he has recently been struck blind. The dialogue in this scene overlaps and echoes musically.)

FRANK: This is the place where—no, nothing, no. Oh here! This is where—no, no it isn't—

CHERIMOYA: *(Entering and catching sight of FRANK.)* —Oh, there he is!

DAISY: *(Entering and catching sight of CHERIMOYA.)* —Oh, there you are! Cherimoya Waterfall?

CHERIMOYA: *(Calling to FRANK.)* Moon! Button moon!

DAISY: That's not the moon, that's Frank.

CHERIMOYA: I love the way he looks.

DAISY: You love the way Frank looks?

CHERIMOYA: I love the way he looks at things. I want him to look at me like that. I saw him looking at the moon and I thought if only the moon was me.

DAISY: Look, I've been watching you and if only—

CHERIMOYA: You've been watching me?

DAISY: Yes! And it's wonderful, and if only—

CHERIMOYA: Who you are depends on who is watching you.

DAISY: —if only I could do what you do, if only I could be who you are,

CHERIMOYA: If Moon Guy was watching me I'd be beautiful.

DAISY: —beauty would ripple through me like water in a desert.

CHERIMOYA: *(Overlap.)* Beauty would ripple through me like water in a desert. Whatever he looks at turns into something better—

DAISY: Cherimoya, teach me your secret!

CHERIMOYA: —something secret and sexy. *(She dances.)*

DAISY: *(Moving like CHERIMOYA.)* Look over here, am I doing it right?

CHERIMOYA: Look at me, Frank, I'm right over here!

DAISY: Why doesn't it make me feel any different?

CHERIMOYA: As soon as he sees me, I'll be different.

DAISY: Is it more like this?

CHERIMOYA: Hey Frank, look at this. *(Dancing for FRANK.)*

DAISY: Or this?

CHERIMOYA: And this!

DAISY: Or this?

CHERIMOYA: And this!

FRANK: Oh, there you are!

CHERIMOYA: Oh! I think he see me.

FRANK: Oh, Daisy, there you are!

CHERIMOYA: Do you think he sees me?

FRANK: I've been looking for you.

DAISY: Hi Frank.

CHERIMOYA: Moon, Button Moon!

DAISY: Frank, this is Cherimoya, Cherimoya Waterfall, and she's so— she's so very— *(She puts on the stolen glasses.)* Young—actually.

CHERIMOYA: I am not!

FRANK: Nice to meet you Cherimoya.

CHERIMOYA: He's…so…very… old.

FRANK: I am not.

CHERIMOYA: Really, really old.

DAISY: Does that matter?

CHERIMOYA: That sucks, big time. I thought you were like Johnny Depp but you're not. You're more like Mick Jagger—big sucky mouth with all those skeezy lines around it. Don't look at me! Don't look at me! *(She runs away.)*

DAISY: *(Peering at him through the glasses.)* You don't look old to me, Frank, in fact, you look fabulous.

FRANK: I do?

DAISY: Oh my God! Deep and fabulous and—When I have these glasses on, well, Cherimoya looks sort of more two-dimensional—in a way, shallow, in fact—and maybe just a little bit mean. And when I look at you it's more like, wow, like a view from the top of the Grand Canyon. Wow! You know what I think, Frank?

FRANK: What do you think, Daisy?

DAISY: I think anything worth doing is worth doing wrong.

FRANK: What?

DAISY: This is so wrong and so wonderful.

FRANK: And so different.

DAISY: And so the same as always.

FRANK: And so lonely.

DAISY: And so wonderful.

(He takes off her glasses and almost kisses her. Instead he points to the spot where they are standing.)

FRANK: And look, right here, look Daisy, right here. This is the place where we—

DAISY: Yeah!

FRANK: Yeah.

(They run away, hand in hand. The glasses are left lying on the ground. CHERIMOYA runs on, followed by SYLVIA as a giant face with an amplified, distorted voice.)

SYLVIA: Cherimoya! Cherimoya! Oh there you are, my Sweet Chicken Girl.

CHERIMOYA: Ma, I didn't—I wasn't, I would've—

SYLVIA: Don't worry. I get it. You're just like me. I ran away when I was your age.

CHERIMOYA: Ma! Don't tell me!

SYLVIA: Followed this guy with a beard down to here, all the way to a commune in Philly.

CHERIMOYA: Why did you do that? That is so sketchy.

SYLVIA: Slept on a shelf in a walk-in closet with five other people, ate too many Wheat Thins, came down with mono, and went home fat and sad.

CHERIMOYA: Don't look at me, Ma! *(She runs away.)*

AURORA: *(Lost, in the distance.)* Celeste! Where are you? Celeste! Can you hear me?

(COUSIN RICKY enters and discovers the glasses on the ground.)

RICKY: *(To audience.)* What is this? Whose are these? *(Puts them on, looks at audience.)* Ouch! Oh! It's the old ladies' X-ray super specs! *(He peers intently at an audience member, finds himself beginning to transform into them.)* Oh! *(He tears himself away and peers at another, begins to transform.)* Whoa!

AURORA: Celeste! Hang on! Celeste! I'm coming! *(She sniffs her way downstage toward RICKY.)*

RICKY: *(Transforming into another audience member.)* Aagh! *(Looks at another.)* NO! *(He tries to pull off the glasses. They are stuck on his face.)* Help!

AURORA: *(Catching his scent and rushing toward him.)* Ah ha!

RICKY: *(Transforming into her against his will.)* Ah ha!

AURORA: Ah ha!

RICKY: Ah ha!

AURORA: *(Sniffing him.)* You're not Celeste!

RICKY: *(Sniffing her.)* You're not Celeste!

AURORA: Hey, don't I know you?

RICKY: *(Peering through the glasses with AURORA's mannerisms.)* Hey, I don't know, but whoa, baby, I know all about you.

AURORA: Hey, where'd you get those specs?

RICKY: *(To audience.)* Where did I get these specs?

AURORA: *(To audience.)* He stole my specs!

RICKY: *(To audience.)* Did I steal these specs?

AURORA: Take them off!

RICKY: They don't come off.

AURORA: They don't come off?

RICKY: They don't come off.

AURORA: I'll get them off.

RICKY: Take them off.

AURORA: Give them back!

RICKY: Take them back!

(They pull.)

AURORA: I'll—

RICKY: Take!

RICKY and AURORA: Them—BACK!

(They stagger, rise, hover in mid-air, and—joined by CELESTE—begin to dance [on film]. ALL of them are wearing the glasses. They resemble the three fates of Greek mythology—ancient, powerful, and terrifying. They sing [recorded.])

THE FATES: WE ARE THE THREE THAT KNOW IT ALL
WE ARE THE THREE THAT SEE
WE ARE THE ONES WHO GET OUR KICKS
CHEWING THE SEEDS OF DESTINY.

(LUCINDA runs on armed with RICKY's mop. She swats at the image of the FATES—with each strike, they multiply.)

LUCINDA: I see you. I see right through you! You think you know it all, but you're blind as bats in the afternoon!

THE FATES: WE ARE THE THREE WITH THE GIANT EYE
ANCIENT AND GENUINE
WE'RE SAFE ON THE INSIDE LOOKING OUT
YOU'RE STUCK ON THE OUTSIDE LOOKING IN.

LUCINDA: I am a scientist, and on the molecular level you're nothing but a bunch of squinty scabby hags.

(The more she hits them, the more of them there are.)

THE FATES: THE FUTURE IS FIXED LIKE A PHOTOGRAPH
THE INVISIBLE TRAP IS SPRUNG
THE PAST IS CRUSHED BENEATH OUR FEET
WE'LL FLIP YOU OVER AND PIN YOU DOWN.

LUCINDA: YOU CAN'T! YOU WON'T! YOU WOULDN'T DARE! I! AM! A! SCIENTIST!

(She swings at the images. They swarm like locusts. The music surges. They explode into a million pieces, fill the sky like galaxies, rain down like fireworks, and disappear.)

SYLVIA: *(Entering with her laptop.)* Send! Send! Send!

(ALAN enters with his laptop. They find themselves face to face. They don't recognize each other at first.)

ALAN: Sylvia?

SYLVIA: Alan?

(She raises the laptop so it is in front of her face. On the screen is an image of her face when she was younger.)

ALAN: Sylvia!

(He raises his laptop. On the screen is an image of his face when he was younger.)

SYLVIA: Alan!

ALAN: Sweet Vista High!

SYLVIA: Sweet Vista High!

ALAN: Sweet Vista High!

SYLVIA: Sweet Vista High!

(They lower their laptops.)

ALAN: How's your daughter?

SYLVIA: She ran away.

ALAN: Why?

SYLVIA: She hates me.

(An awkward pause.)

SYLVIA: How's your wife?

ALAN: I ran away.

SYLVIA: Why?

ALAN: She hates me.

(An awkward pause. ALAN raises his laptop to cover his face.)

ALAN: Your buddy is typing!

SYLVIA: *(Raising her laptop.)* Your buddy is typing!

(They slowly lower their laptops, trying to remain enthusiastic.)

ALAN: Send!

SYLVIA: Send!

ALAN: Send!

SYLVIA: Send!

(They close their laptops and stare blankly at each other.)

ALAN: Send.

SYLVIA: Send.

ALAN: Send.

SYLVIA: Send.

(They exit in opposite directions with their laptops under their arms. CHERIMOYA enters running. She sees the shower curtain from Side B. It opens to reveal a green and leafy place. The air is filled with throaty birdsong and a luscious melody.)

CHERIMOYA: Where am I? What is this? Oh, look! So empty, so deep, so painfully, soulfully beautiful! *(She ducks inside and begins to transform into a tree.)* I am Cherimoya! I Am Cherimoya! *(She rushes out.)* Oh man! What the hell was that? Wow! Cool! I think I was breathing through my fingers! I gotta try that again. *(She rushes back in, sprouts branches and waves them around.)* Floating and falling! Filling and spilling! *(She rushes out.)* Oh my God! Photosynthesis! What a trip! Hey, what if this is really lame. What if someone sees me? *(Shouting.)* —If anyone's watching, I don't care. You can stare 'til your eyes dry up. *(To herself.)* —Really! I could fucking care less. Little birds were whispering in my ears! Amazing! *(She rushes back in, the wind moves through her branches.)* Aah! Aah! Aah! Aah!

MRS. WORMSER: *(Racing in, cell phone held high above her head.)* —Oscar! Oscar! *(She begins to demolish the set in her frenzy to find him.)* —I know you're around here somewhere. Here? No! Over here! No? Oh, you are a slippery man, Oscar, furtive and slippery, but I've got eyes like suction cups, a heart like a Swiss army knife, and I will not tolerate being brushed aside, do you hear me? You're a slippery man with a slippery mind. You think you can bend the frame, twist the picture, stir it around until up is down and down is up? Animal, vegetable, mineral, that's all there is, Oscar Waterfall! Take your pick! You can only be one thing at a time. Dirt, wind, and the clock on the wall going tickety tock—everything where it belongs, Oscar. Mix it up, mess it around, and all you'll have left is gobbledy gook. Do you hear me, Oscar? Oscar! *(She rushes off.)*

MARILYN: *(Rushes in with a laptop.)* Aah! Aah!

(She opens it. On it there is an image of SYLVIA as she is now, looking scared and embarrassed.)

MARILYN: Here you are!

SYLVIA: Here I am.

MARILYN: I've been looking all over for you.

SYLVIA: Well here I am.

MARILYN: I'm Marilyn. Marilyn Flynnalyn.

SYLVIA: I know. I'm Sylvia. Sylvia Waterfall.

MARILYN: I know! Listen, Miss Runoff, I refuse to be brushed aside like some stinky old boots in a cardboard box.

SYLVIA: Oh yeah? Well you don't know who you're talking to.

MARILYN: Oh yeah! I'm talking to Miss Chatterfinger, Mrs. Fizzlefaucet.

SYLVIA: No, you're not. You're talking to an upended chair in a weedy backyard. My dinners are wretched, my stories are stupid, my logic is addled, my insights uncalled for, my tongue is pernicious, my ankles are puffy, my brother's a freak, my cousin is loony, my aunt is obsessive, my daughter's ungrateful, my friends are too busy, my shoes are outdated, my forehead is damp, my nose is too boney. And my hair is all wrong for my face.

MARILYN: Oh yeah? Well your hair is not bad.

SYLVIA: You're not just saying that to be nice?

MARILYN: I'm not nice, not a bit nice, Not these days.

(They stare at each other.)

SYLVIA: Wanna join a book club?

MARILYN: What?

SYLVIA: I'm thinking of starting a book club.

MARILYN: Oh?

SYLVIA: Women only.

MARILYN: Oh.

SYLVIA: No teenagers allowed.

MARILYN: *(Taking off her wig.)* What are you going to read?

SYLVIA: Whatever's challenging. Whatever's new and challenging, and intellectually stimulating.

(They exit arm in arm. CHERIMOYA enters pulling OSCAR by the hand...MRS. WORMSER enters from somewhere else, her cell phone camera held stiffly at arm's length like a gun. They circle the cube, unaware of each other.)

CHERIMOYA: Come on, Uncle Oscar, it's right over here.

OSCAR: Have we been here before?

MRS. WORMSER: I bet he's in there.

CHERIMOYA: Not exactly, but everywhere's tangled up in everywhere else.

MRS. WORMSER: I bet he's splashing and overflowing—

CHERIMOYA: There it is—

MRS. WORMSER and CHERIMOYA: Right in there!

(They are suddenly face to face in front of the "tree spot.")

OSCAR: Mrs. Wormser?

MRS. WORMSER: *(Whipping around and holding out her cell phone in a threatening manner.)* Oscar!

OSCAR: *(Waving his branches menacingly.)* How about a little extra water, Mrs. Wormser?

MRS. WORMSER: Other people's water is disgusting, Oscar.

OSCAR: Water is water, Mrs. Wormser.

MRS. WORMSER: It is not.

OSCAR: You see? You are irrational and unreasonable.

MRS. WORMSER: And you've got leaves growing out of your armpits.

(He has backed her up against the "tree spot." CHERIMOYA darts out and gives her a little push.)

CHERIMOYA: So what if he does?

(MRS. WORMSER tumbles in.)

MRS. WORMSER: Oscar! OH! Dirt! Wind! *(Her feet take root and begin to suck water from the ground.)* Water! *(She begins sprouting pine needles.)* Help! Oh! *(Surprised, but no longer so upset.)* —Where is this? *(Delighted.)* —Where am I? *(She begins to bend and sway in the wind.)* I am—I am—I am Sequoia! *(Now she is having the time of her life.)* —I am Sequoia! I am Eucalyptus, Catalpa, Magnolia!

OSCAR: Double hydrogenous oxygenolla!

(OSCAR and CHERIMOYA join MRS. WORMSER. They all sway their branches, bend and swoop in ecstasy. SYLVIA rushes in. CHERIMOYA pokes her head out.)

CHERIMOYA: Hi, Ma.

SYLVIA: There you are, Cherry!

CHERIMOYA: Come on in, Ma. You're gonna love it. It's like diving off the high board, like finding the perfect outfit, but you can only wear it when no one else is there.

SYLVIA: Maybe I'm too old.

CHERIMOYA: You're not too old at all, Ma.

SYLVIA: I'm not?

CHERIMOYA: Well, not *yet*. Even Mrs. Wormser is having fun. Come on in. Did you know that you can be something and at the same time you can be something else? It runs in our family. You oughta try it.

(She pulls on SYLVIA, who resists a little.)

SYLVIA: My knees, my back, my shoes, my hair—

(They plunge together into the watery green.)

SYLVIA: I am Sylvia! I am Sylvia!

(She does not transform into a tree, but enjoys herself anyway. The TREES wave their branches in graceful ecstasy. SYLVIA moves among them awkwardly but with great abandon. LUCINDA enters, her hair and clothes disheveled as if she's just been processed in a blender. Her camera, binoculars, and clipboard hang crazily from her neck and arms. She has become a concentrated version of herself as if some of the water has been sucked

out of her. She is wearing CELESTE and AURORA's glasses. AURORA enters at the same moment, her wig crooked; TRIXIE hangs from her pocketbook upside down, The "tree spot" has faded and the set is beginning to collapse. LUCINDA speaks to the audience.)

LUCINDA: Have you ever noticed that the whites of people's eyes
Are larger and more distinct than any other creature's?
An eyeball's like an arrow, we can read it in an instant
It points out unexpected dangers hiding in the bushes.

We're driven by an ancient and primitive desire
To look at others looking, to see where they are seeing
To taste what they are eating, to know where they are going.
To open up their brains and see the neurons firing.

(She peels the scrim off of the last remaining frame. ALAN is revealed behind it.)

LUCINDA: The secret lies in watching the people who are watching.
Windows open onto windows open onto windows
I fling the curtain open, I strive for perspicuity
And the deeper in I get, the more I want to see.

(AURORA speaks as she and LUCINDA lower the frame to the floor.)

AURORA: It's always been like that for me
I strain my eyes, I crane my neck
Trying to catch the smallest glimpse
And then, for a moment, everything snaps into focus.

The first red leaves at the end of summer
Perfectly framed in the kitchen window
The smell of onions frying in butter
White cotton stockings gently squeezing my feet.

What I thought was a window is really a mirror
I'm in the right place, and it's the right time
I breathe in, I breathe out, I breathe in, I breathe out.
And a moment later I've completely forgotten all about it.

(The set has collapsed into a grid on the floor. The stage is empty. ALAN holds his open laptop high above his head slowly spinning in place, trying to find a signal. A screensaver pulses listlessly across his screen.)

ALAN: *(Revolving slowly.)* It's the music—when I hear that tune—many layers of something—A white gazebo at the edge of the water, the feel of lead fishing weights in my palm—Something to do with my father—I hear that music and I find myself— *(He gasps.)* —So haunting—what was it? I remember the place, but I can't remembered what happened there—I've lost the story. White gazebo at the end of the island, moon folded up in the corner of a cloud, icy sea water under my feet, the perfect mixture of safety and danger. But the story—I don't have it. I've lost the story—if only I could—if only I—

(He continues to revolve. The floor is glowing. Slow fade to black.)

(The End.)

ANY DAY NOW

An Apocalyptic Family Drama in Three Acts

Nat Cassidy

NAT CASSIDY was born in 1981 in Raleigh, North Carolina; his family relocated to Phoenix, Arizona, where he was raised. He graduated from the University of Arizona in Tucson, with a BFA in acting/directing in 2004. Cassidy developed an interest in acting and writing at a very early age; about his primary vocation in theatre he says, "Two years ago, I would've called myself an 'actor' and been done with it. But, since then, I've really discovered the joys of (and, thankfully, a relative aptitude for) playwriting and directing. So, now, I consider myself an actor-writer-director, or, to put it more accurately, trebly-without-job-security." He was the first person to play the title role in *Hamlet* at Arizona Repertory Theatre—a performance that still occasionally airs on the Tucson PBS. He was also one of the first-ever recipients of the Professional Potential grant at the University of Arizona. Cassidy's produced plays include *The Eternal Husband* (2007, Fine Feathered Friends) and *The Reckoning of Kit and Little Boots* (2008, The Gallery Players and Engine 37). He received the 2009 New York Innovative Theatre Award for Outstanding Full-Length Script for *The Reckoning of Kit and Little Boots*; he also was nominated for a 2009 New York Innovative Theatre award as Outstanding Director for *Any Day Now*. Cassidy's current projects include a one-man show that's part fictionalized autobiography, part H. P. Lovecraft homage, entitled *I Am Providence*, as well as a four-act ghost story set in the White House in the 1850s, called *Pierce, or, A Ghost of the Union*—both of which he hopes to see produced sometime in 2010. He lives in Brooklyn with his girlfriend.

Any Day Now was originally presented as part of the InGenius Festival by the Writers Forum at Manhattan Theatre Source (Jim Lawson, Artistic Director; Lanie Zipoy, Managing Director) on January 6, 2009, with the following cast and credits:

Pen	Waltrudis Buck
Adam	Anthony Spaldo
Beverly	Paige Allen
April	Elyse Mirto
Josh	Arthur Aulisi
David	Tim Ewing
Jackie	Anna O'Donoghue

Director: Nat Cassidy
Producer: Sarah Deavitt Ali
Production Stage Manager: Laura Schlachtmeyer
Technical Director: Montserrat Mendez
Set Designer: Jason Bolen
Sound Designer: Ien DeNio
Lighting Designer: Lauren Parrish
Graphic Designer: Chris Santa Maria
Video Designer: Ben Sinclair

The author would like to thank the following for their inestimable help towards getting this beast to production and beyond: Jim Lawson, Alexis Thomason, Mozz Mendez, Mike Roderick, Small Pond Entertainment, Gabi Willenz, Erin Quinn Purcell, Annalisa Loeffler, Keith J. Foster, Jennifer Gordon Thomas, David Ian Lee, Fiona Jones, John Allen, Jason Griffith, James Edward Becton, Tandy Cronyn, Andrew Bellware, Brian Schiavo, Amanda Hunt, Karen Sternberg, Jason Howard, Jason Grossman, Danielle Quisenberry, Mickey Sumner, Kat Hinchey, Mikel Sarah Lambert, Joan Tewkesbury, Jon Mason, Michael Alden, Elyse Mirto, Mick Bleyer, Martin and Rochelle Denton, Scott Coppola, Jack Parker, June Ospa, Scotti Rhodes Publicity, Dianna Martin, Richard Seff, Michael Gnat, Elyse's rolling coach, the phenomenal cast and crew, every single audience member, and the good people at Playboy and New Line Cinema, for contributing more than they'll ever know to the administrative side of the theatrical production.

> One of these mornings
> I'm a-going away
> Any day now
> I'm going to heaven to stay.
> —Wagoner/Butler

For Mark
To answer your question, this is what happens.

CHARACTERS

PENELOPE "PEN" COLBY, late sixties/early seventies

ADAM COLBY, late sixties/early seventies, her husband

BEVERLY COLBY-PARKER, late forties/early fifties, Pen's older daughter

DAVID PARKER, early fifties, Beverly's husband

JACQUELINE COLBY-PARKER, twenty-one, Beverly's daughter

APRIL COLBY, late forties, Pen's younger daughter

JOSH POWELL, forties, April's husband

VARIOUS NEWSCASTERS, voiceovers

LOCATION

The kitchen of the Colby residence. New London, Connecticut.

TIME

Present. Any day now.

A NOTE TO THE ACTORS

At its most elemental level, this is a play about shock. The shock of what's happening never leaves these characters—everything that follows is a result of their attempts to make it to the next minute with their sanity intact. Though this is true of all acting, all the time, because of the fine line this script walks between satire, horror, and regular ol' drama, it bears stating: the realities of the situation must be embraced at all times. In other words, never forget the reanimated elephant in the room.

ACT ONE
"WHAT ARE WE GOING TO DO ABOUT ADAM?"
Scene One

Prescene music: "Pilgrim of Sorrow" sung by Sam Cooke and the Soul Stirrers. Lights up in an ordinary kitchen in a typical small-town homestead. Mid-afternoon. We hear birds outside. On the stage right side of the kitchen is a swinging door into the living room. On the stage left wall is a telephone that would've been technologically current in 1983. A woman in her late sixties/early seventies, PENELOPE (PEN), is at the sink, washing vegetables. Above the sink is a window looking out into the backyard. She looks out as she washes. It should be a wistful scene, but there is something tense about her. At the kitchen table is a man, ADAM, also late sixties/early seventies. His clothes are loose and ill fitting. He sits, staring blankly, slack-jawed. Quite literally like a zombie. Nothing in his face changes or registers. His skin is wan and stretched. He is washed, clean, but there is something vaguely dirty about him. PEN looks at him furtively, almost afraid to verify that he's there. Finally, after a couple of minutes, she can take it no longer, and turns to stare at him. She speaks, almost to herself.

PEN: What are we going to do with you?

(There is, of course, no response. She continues to stare at him. For a moment, she threatens to break down in tears, but manages to get it under control. She lets out a long, controlled breath, then turns back to the sink and continues washing, fighting the urge to glance back at him. Then, from outside, we hear the sound of a car coming into the driveway.)

PEN: Shit. *(She shakes off the vegetables she just washed, then looks for a towel on which to dry her hands.)* Shit. *(She looks at ADAM.)* Shit.

(She continues looking for a towel, not realizing it's draped over her shoulder. In a moment, a woman in her late forties/early fifties, BEVERLY, enters, checking her email on an already out-of-date cell phone.)

BEVERLY: *(Entering.)* You've really got to do something about that yard, Mother, I'm telling you, I know you hire that kid up the street, but it might be time to think about getting someone who actually knows what they're doing—

PEN: Beverly—

BEVERLY: What? I'm not being unreasonable. You know reelections are coming up, so don't argue w— *(Finally notices* ADAM *sitting at the table. She sputters. Stunned, she looks at her mother incredulously—almost accusatorily, as if this were some sort of prank.)*

PEN: Beverly...

(BEVERLY shrieks. It's blood curdling. PEN covers her ears.)

PEN: *(Shouting over it.)* BEVERLY!

BEVERLY: *(Still screaming.)* WHAT IS THIS?! WHAT IS HE DOING HERE?! WHAT'S GOING ON?!

(ADAM turns his head—very slowly—and looks towards BEVERLY. She immediately shuts up.)

PEN: Beverly...

BEVERLY: *(Almost a whisper.)* What is this?

PEN: Would you like something to drink?

(Beat.)

BEVERLY: Yes.

(PEN goes to the sink. She shakes her hands dry before getting a glass and filling it with water.)

PEN: Of course, I can't find my friggin' towel...

BEVERLY: *(In a daze, still looking at ADAM.)* It's on your shoulder.

PEN: Oh.

(She dries her hands with it. Then she comes over and gives BEVERLY the glass of water. BEVERLY takes it, doesn't drink.)

BEVERLY: He's...

PEN: Yes.

BEVERLY: Oh, Mommy. *(Hugs PEN, holding the glass out behind her back.)*

BEVERLY: When did it...he...?

PEN: I found him wandering in the yard this morning. His clothes were a mess, so I put him in some new ones. Tried to scrub the smell of dirt off of him.

BEVERLY: Oh, God. *(Beat.)* Is he dangerous?

PEN: No.

BEVERLY: The news reports have all been saying—

PEN: No, Beverly.

BEVERLY: *(To ADAM.)* Daddy? Do you recognize me?

PEN: Bev, honey, don't.

BEVERLY: *(Ignoring PEN, getting closer to ADAM, who is now looking forward distantly again.)* Dad? Are you in there?

PEN: *(Going back to the vegetables.)* I'm making chicken salad for dinner.

(BEVERLY continues to stare at him. His lips move wordlessly. Senselessly. Slowly, he starts to rise, groaning. BEVERLY whimpers.)

PEN: He tries to wander sometimes. I don't know why. Just sit him down, he won't put up a fight.

(BEVERLY puts her hands on his shoulders and pushes him back into his chair, wincing.)

BEVERLY: He's cold. And hard.

PEN: I need you to do me a favor. I need you to call April. She needs to be here. I know you don't want to talk to her, but I need your help with this and I would appreciate it if—

BEVERLY: *(Coldly, looking at her hands.)* I'll call her.

(Beat.)

PEN: Thank you.

BEVERLY: I'd like to wash my hands now.

PEN: *(Steps away from the sink.)* Go ahead.

BEVERLY: *(At the sink, washing her hands.)* It's not like she answers when I call, anyway. But I'll be sure to give her some warning. About this. I wish you'd have thought to do the same for me.

(PEN hands BEVERLY the towel from off her shoulder. BEVERLY dries her hands.)

PEN: Are you alright?

BEVERLY: I'm fine. I'm a little…shaken, that's all. *(Beat.)* Are you…?

PEN: I have no idea.

BEVERLY: That face he's making…*(She shudders. A beat. She claps her hands.)* DAD! WAKE UP!

PEN: He's not asleep.

(Pause. It sinks in.)

PEN: Any word from Debbie?

(No answer.)

PEN: How's Jackie?

BEVERLY: She's fine. Jacqueline's fine. *(She sighs. Then she goes to her purse, gets out a tissue, and daubs her eyes. Dramatically.)* She was just getting used to her grandfather's death. She just started acting normal again. The timing of this is just—

PEN: Please don't start, Beverly. This wasn't done to inconvenience you.

BEVERLY: What a terrible thing to say. Just because this isn't upsetting to you doesn't mean the rest of us are unaffected.

PEN: Beverly—! *(She calms.)* You…are not being helpful right now.

(Beat. Defiantly, BEVERLY puts her purse down, takes a cell out of it, punches some numbers, and puts it to her ear. A moment.)

BEVERLY: *(Quickly.)* April, it's Beverly. Daddy's come back from the dead, and Mom is asking that you come over. Okay? Loveyoubye.

(She hangs up. PEN stares in disbelief. Beat. BEVERLY is not looking at her.)

BEVERLY: *(Guiltily.)* So, what are you going to do?

(No answer.)

BEVERLY: What? I'm sorry.

(PEN turns and exits.)

BEVERLY: Mother! *(Beat.)* Unbelievable. Can you believe her—? *(She realizes who she's talking to. In tears.)* Goddddd… *(She takes up her purse and pulls out a bottle of prescription pills. Using the glass of water, she takes a pill. She looks at her FATHER and speaks, like her mother, almost to herself.)* Why did you do this?

(No answer.)

BEVERLY: That fucking face…

(Her cell phone begins to ring. She doesn't answer. Lights fade.)

SCENE TWO

Lights back up on the kitchen, perhaps thirty minutes later. ADAM and BEVERLY are in the same positions: BEVERLY staring at him, he looking slack-jawed into the distance. We hear voices in the other room.

APRIL: *(Offstage.)* And is everything—?

PEN: *(Offstage.)* I don't know, I just don't…

APRIL: *(Offstage.)* He's…

PEN: *(Offstage.)* In there. With Beverly.

APRIL: *(Offstage; with ire.)* Oh, God. Beverly. I couldn't *believe* her—

PEN: *(Offstage; placating.)* I know. I know. Don't yell.

APRIL: *(Offstage; sighs.)* Fuck. Well, anything you need, Mom. Really.

(They enter the kitchen. APRIL, in her mid- to late forties but younger than BEVERLY, looks curtly at her SISTER, then sees her FATHER. Tears come to her eyes.)

APRIL: Oh, man.

(PEN rubs her back.)

BEVERLY: *(Not moving.)* Hi, April.

(APRIL ignores her.)

APRIL: *(Her voice barely a squeak.)* Hi, Daddy.

BEVERLY: Hi, April.

APRIL: Oh, boy… Mom, do you want some tea?

PEN: No, no, no, don't you worry—

APRIL: Yeah, you want some tea. I'll put the water on.

(APRIL walks to the sink, past BEVERLY, and fills the teapot with water. BEVERLY decides to try and hug APRIL, who summarily brushes her off.)

APRIL: Don't. Don't touch me.

BEVERLY: What? Ap—? Are you… *mad* at me?

APRIL: Are you serious? *(To PEN.)* Is she serious?

PEN: Please, girls, let's not fight—

BEVERLY: *(Overlapping.)* What, April, what did I do?

APRIL: What did you do?! That message! What do you mean, "What did I do?" I mean, Jesus, I almost thought it was a joke at first!

BEVERLY: *(At "What did I do?")* I was *asked* to call you! *I* wasn't even warned, okay?!

PEN: *(Overlapping.)* Please, both of you, you're talking over each other.

BEVERLY: *(Overlapping.)* I'm sorry, okay, I'm pretty upset about this!

APRIL: Oh, sure, you are. What a vicious fucking thing to do to your sister, Beverly. Your fucking *sister!*

BEVERLY: You don't know what I've been going through! Okay? Elections are coming up. And Jackie, who's doing terribly in school and is going to flip out about this on top of all that—

APRIL: *(Overlapping.)* Oh, of course, this is all about Beverly! How rude of us!

PEN: *(Overlapping.)* You're both talking over each other! YOU'RE BOTH TALKING OVER EACH OTHER! You're—

APRIL: *(Overlapping.)* After all that shit I had to put up with about the estate, and this is *precisely* why I wanted nothing to do with you—

BEVERLY: *(Overlapping.)* Oh, I should have figured that you'd bring that up to attack me. After you wouldn't even look at me during the funeral. Serves me right for trying to help this family out. Once again!

(As the argument increases, ADAM rises and tries to walk further into the room but gets tangled in his chair. APRIL notices first and stops arguing. PEN, quite immediately thereafter, does, too.)

BEVERLY: What? What's— *(Notices).*

(ADAM falls. Like an automaton, he tries to rise. Guttural noises escape his throat.)

APRIL: Oh, my God.

(PEN and APRIL stare, horrified, as he continues to try. BEVERLY goes and helps him up and sits him down. They're all silent, other than the diminishing noises from the FATHER. They stare at him.)

APRIL: The news has been saying that it could still all be a fluke. Like, a massive coincidence. Premature burials, or medical ineptitude, or…

PEN: You saw him…before…

APRIL: Yeah.

PEN: There was nothing premature or inept about that.

APRIL: God, I feel like I might puke.

BEVERLY: *(Pulling out antibacterial lotion from her purse.)* What has it been, like, fifty of…them, so far? Claims?

APRIL: Something like that. Globally, I guess. Give or take.

BEVERLY: The reports I've heard have all said that they're dangerous.

APRIL: None of the video footage I've seen has looked particularly…scary, I guess. Besides the implications, of course.

PEN: *(Crossing back to the sink.)* I have to finish the chicken salad. *(Beat.)* Can you stay?

APRIL: Who, me or Beverly?

PEN: Both of you.

BEVERLY: Fine. I have to call David. *(Pause.)* And I imagine April has to call Josh?

APRIL: *(Not really paying attention.)* Yeah, sure.

(They continue to stare at him.)

APRIL: I just can't…believe this. I mean, we *just* buried him, and now…

BEVERLY: You haven't seen any others, have you?

PEN: No.

(Pause.)

APRIL: It's just so…fucked up…

BEVERLY: *(Reproachfully.)* April.

APRIL: What?

(No answer. They continue to stare at ADAM.)

BEVERLY: *(After a long while.)* Well, we are going to bring this up at the next Assembly meeting, I can tell you that. *(Pause.)* Really, Mom, I have to say that you're dealing with this commendably.

(Beat. She waits for a response.)

BEVERLY: I mean, I can only imagine what I would do if David—

(PEN is sobbing at the sink, head in hands, close to hysterics. APRIL goes to her.)

BEVERLY: What? What'd I say?

APRIL: Mom, shhh, it's okay.

PEN: *(Once she's under control.)* I was standing right here and I…I was looking out the window. And there he was. Just wandering. So aimless. Lifeless. I saw him and, of course, my heart just froze. And he was filthy. All that dirt…I went outside and I called out his name and nothing came out, my voice was just…I tried again and this time it worked, I squeaked something out and he heard the sound of my voice, but when he turned around…there was absolutely nothing there. I took him inside and I took him upstairs—he didn't try and pull away, or even— *(She swallows.)* —even try to hurt me or anything, like those reports have been implying…And there was a smell, so I turned on the shower and I took off his jacket. It had holes in it. Already. I unbuttoned his shirt, and unbuckled his pants, and took off his shoes and socks. His socks had holes, too, I don't know how. And I tried to clean him up. And he didn't resist. I had to get in there with him and—

APRIL: Mom—

PEN: —No, no, please. Let me finish. I must sound crazy, I know.

APRIL: No, God, no.

PEN: *(Looks at APRIL with unspeakable pain.)* As I was scrubbing the dirt off, I noticed his hands were cut, open. From when he dug… *(She starts to cry again.)* …There was no blood. Because he had been…emptied at the morgue…

(APRIL rubs her back. After a moment, she laughs.)

PEN: And when I saw that, that's when I realized I had stopped talking. That's when I realized that, until that moment, I had been talking to him. Out loud. Trying to comfort him or something. And I realized there was no need or use or whatever. And, God help me, it made it a little…not easier, but…I dunno. *(The emotion has passed.)* But the worst part was seeing him in the yard like that…I've seen him in that yard, through that window, so many times—so many times…but never…never…

APRIL: What, Mom?

PEN: Never so aimless. So empty. Oh, sweetie, I'm sorry, I shouldn't be saying all this.

(APRIL hugs her, hard. BEVERLY watches, genuinely moved, but genuinely stung.)

BEVERLY: *(Quietly.)* Why didn't you tell me any of that?

(Beat.)

PEN: *(With apology, beckoning her over.)* Oh, Bevvie...

(BEVERLY goes to them and the three women hold each other. ADAM sits at the table, staring off. After a moment:)

PEN: I've got to finish the chicken salad. *(Goes back to work at the sink.)*

APRIL: *(To BEVERLY.)* What a reunion, huh? *(A little laugh. It dies. A moment.)* Do you think he's still in there?

BEVERLY: I don't know. *(Beat.)* I hope not.

(Lights fade.)

SCENE THREE

Lights up on the kitchen, a couple of hours later. APRIL and her husband JOSH are near the sink. There is something very tense about the two of them. ADAM is still in his seat at the table. BEVERLY is on her cell phone, pacing.

JOSH: You think he can...?

APRIL: What?

JOSH: Hear us?

APRIL: I have no idea.

BEVERLY: *(Overlapping; just connected with voicemail; coldly.)* David. David, it's me. I'm still waiting, David, so please, give me a call when you know what's going on. We're all waiting and Mom would like to have dinner sometime soon. Please don't keep us waiting. Okay, loveyoubye. *(Hangs up. She is visibly frustrated. To no one in particular.)* He better have a good excuse, this is just...

APRIL: How many messages you gonna leave, Beverly?

JOSH: How are you, Bev?

BEVERLY: I'm fine, thank you. It's been a day, to say the least.

JOSH: Sure, sure. I'd imagine.

APRIL: *(At the fridge.)* Oh, man, why don't Mom and Dad have any beer in the house?

BEVERLY: *(Correcting.)* Mom.

APRIL: What? *(Beat. Realizing.)* Oh.

BEVERLY: Forty-five minutes it's been already.

JOSH: I'm sure it's fine, he's probably stuck in traffic or—

BEVERLY: Of course, it's always traffic, always—

APRIL: Don't take that away from her, Josh, she needs to freak out about something.

BEVERLY: *(Pretending not to have heard.)* Where *is* Mom?

APRIL: I made her go upstairs to lie down for a while.

BEVERLY: Oh. Good idea.

JOSH: How's she doing?

(APRIL shrugs.)

BEVERLY: She'll be fine. She's...fine.

(ADAM lets out a groan. They all jump. BEVERLY stares at him with something close to disgust.)

JOSH: Are we sure he's not dangerous?

BEVERLY: He's fine, too.

(Beat.)

JOSH: Another video just came out, did you see? Of one of... *(He gives a weak gesture towards ADAM.)* They keep dancing around the phrase, they don't know what to call them.

APRIL: I imagine the "zee" word is pretty verboten...

JOSH: "The Walking Dead" seems to be the phrase du jour, at the moment.

APRIL: That's fucking disgusting, Josh.

JOSH: Well, don't blame me for— *(He stops, not wanting to start an argument. He looks around the kitchen.)* They don't have a liquor cabinet at all around here?

APRIL: *(Tense.)* Where was the video from?

JOSH: *(Looking for booze for APRIL.)* Hm?

APRIL: The new video. The States?

JOSH: Auckland.

APRIL: Australia?

BEVERLY: New Zealand.

APRIL: You sure?

BEVERLY: David and I went there a few years ago, April, yes.

(APRIL rolls her eyes.)

JOSH: It's uh...I dunno, they're still denying that it's anything right now, you know? I heard them saying that it might be some new paralytic strain of meningitis, or something. Makes it *look* like people are...dead.

APRIL: That's fucking ridiculous.

JOSH: *(Devil's advocate.)* So say America's top scientists.

APRIL: Two strokes within two weeks, and Dad just *happened* to get meningitis? From, what, showering with all his buddies down at Conn College?

JOSH: I'm just saying, April.

APRIL: Such bullshit...

JOSH: Well, it'd be a pretty fucked-up government if they just went, "Apocalypse! Run!" Don't you think? *(Beat.)* Though, get this, according to CNN, they've set up some sort of federal hotline to report any "cases." Eight-one-one. One breath after denying it's anything close to anything, and they set up a friggin' emergency hotline.

BEVERLY: God, what is taking him so long? *(Redials DAVID's number.)*

APRIL: "Eight-one-one, you've reached the zombie hotline, please hold. '*Brraaaaiiins, braaaaiiins.*'" *(Beat.)* That's not funny.

JOSH: *(Finds a bottle of red wine in a cabinet.)* Jackpot. Wine? *(He sets to opening the bottle.)* Oh, shit. Did you guys hear about Kelly Gold?

BEVERLY: *(Has hung up angrily. Beat. She calms down.)* The singer?

JOSH: Yup. The original party-girl herself. Car crash.

BEVERLY: What?

JOSH: Car crash. In LA.

APRIL: What do you mean, "car crash?" She was in one? Is she dead?

JOSH: I think so. I'm not entirely sure, I didn't get to hear the whole story, I just caught it on the radio on the way over here. But it definitely sounded serious. I think she might have...

BEVERLY: Seriously?

JOSH: Yeah. Sickest thing was, the newscaster, swear to God, after gingerly dancing around this whole... *(He gestures to ADAM.)* phenomenon, said, "And now, some sad news." That was the dumb cunt's segue. "And now, some sad news." You believe that?

(He drinks the wine. APRIL takes it away from him. She drinks.)

BEVERLY: Interesting time to die.

APRIL: What do you mean?

BEVERLY: How is your new job, Josh?

JOSH: Oh, it's...great.

BEVERLY: You're teaching a playwriting course, yes?

JOSH: Yup.

BEVERLY: And how is that—

JOSH: Hey, we saw one of your new posters up at Shaw's. It looks good.

BEVERLY: Oh. Thank you. *(She smiles, all teeth, no eyes.)*

JOSH: Yeah, you got our vote. Hey, have you guys on the Assembly heard from Lieberman on this issue yet? I'd love to hear the thoughts of America's only living dead senator about all this.

(While JOSH is talking, BEVERLY's phone rings. She ignores him and immediately answers it.)

BEVERLY: Finally. *(She answers and moves away from the other two.)* David? David, where have you been?

JOSH: *(To APRIL, with a wan smile.)* This is like a wake in reverse, isn't it?

APRIL: No kidding.

BEVERLY: *(Into the phone.)* That's not the point, David, we've been waiting here for you to arrive and it's taken you— *(She is briefly interrupted.)* Excuse me, no, that doesn't matter.

JOSH: *(Under.)* She's in one of her moods today, isn't she?

APRIL: *(Slightly dismissive.)* She's very stressed.

BEVERLY: *(Into the phone.)* I. Don't. Care. David. She can handle herself, she's practically a grown woman. *(Pause. She listens. Then, angrily.)* Are you kidding me?! Are. You. Kidding. Me. David?!

(JOSH and APRIL exchange a curious if not conspiratorial look.)

BEVERLY: *(Into the phone.)* Is she with you? Ohhh, Jesus, this is so embarrassing. You tell her she's... *(Beat.)* Well, could you *please* just get here soon? David? Okay?

(She moves further away. JOSH edges closer to APRIL.)

JOSH: *(Sotto voce.)* You doing okay?

APRIL: *(Curtly.)* I'm fine. *(Beat.)* You?

BEVERLY: *(Into the phone.)* Yeah, bye. *(She hangs up curtly.)* Just unbelievable. Jacqueline just got kicked out of school.

APRIL: Oh my God, are you serious?

JOSH: What happened?

BEVERLY: *(Overlapping with APRIL.)* Yes, I'm serious. *(She looks at JOSH.)* She got kicked out of college, Josh. Expelled.

JOSH: I heard that; what *happened?*

BEVERLY: *(Almost to herself.)* I just cannot believe her, I am furious. This is the absolute worst timing. It's just so— *(She makes an inarticulate growl of frustration.)*

APRIL: Is it *permanent*, do you know?

BEVERLY: It's expulsion, April. *(Beat.)* I *don't* know. David's taking her home—to *our* home—and then he's coming here. I don't know what this means for dinner, but…

(Beat. Silence.)

JOSH: Is he gonna tell her about…?

(They all stare at ADAM. Suddenly, APRIL starts laughing.)

BEVERLY: What? What's funny?

(More laughing.)

BEVERLY: April!

APRIL: When it rains it fucking pours, doesn't it?

BEVERLY: What does *that* mean?

APRIL: Nothing. Nothing. I'm just really, really sad about Kelly Gold. *(She laughs some more.)*

BEVERLY: Are you making fun of me?

JOSH: No one's making fun of you.

(Beat.)

BEVERLY: Fine. I'm going to check on Mom. That's…fine.

(She goes to exit, stops, grabs her purse and the glass of water, then leaves. A moment. APRIL's laughing dies.)

APRIL: Poor Jackie.

JOSH: I wouldn't wanna be in her shoes right now.

APRIL: Poor Jackie, that she's got a mother I can't say "Poor Jackie" in front of.

(JOSH gives a weak chuckle. Silence. After a moment, JOSH picks up a fork from the dish drainer and blows a raspberry through it. APRIL doesn't respond.)

JOSH: Sorry.

(He rinses it off and puts it back. Another moment.)

APRIL: Do you really think this is the Apocalypse?

JOSH: Hm?

APRIL: You said "Apocalypse" earlier. Big word. Scary idea.

JOSH: Oh, I didn't…I don't know. I certainly hope it's not. Although, I guess, if you gotta go, there's no better time, right? We'll be the envy of the underworld.

APRIL: *(A feeble joke.)* Maybe it's a good thing you never knocked me up, eh?

(It lands with a thud.)

APRIL: I'm sorry. *(Beat.)* I haven't told them.

JOSH: About what?

APRIL: Us.

JOSH: Ah.

APRIL: Yet.

JOSH: I was getting the feeling that was the case. *(Pause.)* Why?

APRIL: *(Defensively.)* Why do you think?

JOSH: Don't start getting defensive.

APRIL: I'm not…I'm not *trying* to be defensive. But it seems to me that this is obviously not a good time to drop that news.

JOSH: Okay. *(Beat.)* I mean, it's been weeks, though.

APRIL: *(Giving an icy look.)* I'm in no rush.

JOSH: Fine.

APRIL: How's Mark?

JOSH: He's good. Busy with work, don't see him much. Comfy couch.

(A beat.)

APRIL: He must totally hate me, right?

JOSH: No, he doesn't hate you. I mean, he…thinks we should keep trying, though. To work it out, I mean—

APRIL: Josh, please…

JOSH: He thinks, you know, that *this* is worth it. That we're—

APRIL: Please. I can't talk about this right now.

JOSH: And that, if you'll just give me a chance—

APRIL: *(Sharply.)* I know what I saw, Josh.

JOSH: No, you don't. I need you, April, please. If you knew the thoughts I've been having lately—

(From the table, ADAM starts moaning and begins to rise.)

APRIL: Oh, God, he's doing it again.

JOSH: *(Also disturbed.)* Oh, Jesus.

(ADAM shambles totally upright. He looks at the two of them, then takes a few steps towards them. APRIL clings to JOSH's arm. However, ADAM is actually just making a circuit around the table and, with hobbling, unsure steps, makes his way out of the kitchen. A moment.)

APRIL: Should we—?

JOSH: Are you—?

(Something is knocked over in the other room. JOSH hurriedly sticks his head out to see what's happening.)

JOSH: He's…I mean, he's fine. He's just kinda wandering around, bouncing off of stuff. Nothing's broken.

(Something else falls in the living room.)

JOSH: Think I should…?

APRIL: I don't know, I don't know.

BEVERLY: *(Calling from upstairs.)* What's going on down there?

APRIL: Oh, God, Beverly—

JOSH: *(Overlapping.)* Shit.

(He goes back out to warn her, but it's too late. We hear BEVERLY scream in the other room. APRIL runs out to see what happened. Lights down.)

Scene Four

In the darkness, we hear the VOICE OF A REPORTER amidst sounds of tumult.

REPORTER'S VOICE: We are here reporting live outside Good Samaritan Hospital on Wilshire, where, apparently, teen pop sensation Kelly Gold has been rushed—no word yet on her condition, although there were reportedly no survivors found in her SUV. As you can see, it's a madhouse out here, with reporters from, gosh, every paper and station imaginable, waiting to hear word on—wait a moment, it seems like someone is coming out. Let's hear what he's got to say…

(Lights up on the kitchen. EVERYONE, including DAVID and JACKIE, is at the table, with the exception of PEN, who is at the sink. They are all laughing. Her husband, ADAM, is at the head of the table, smiling warmly. He is wearing a

suit and gone is the sense of catatonia from the previous scenes. The sense should be that the storm has passed and everything is happy, happy.)

DAVID: No, I'm serious—

JACKIE: You're not!

DAVID: I *am*. They use a mixture of toad skin and puffer fish poison—bufogenine and tetrodotoxins—it renders the victim totally paralyzed and totally unconscious, enough so that he or she can be understandably declared dead. They're buried, then *unburied* before they asphyxiate, and when they come to, they can be *convinced* that they're dead. Their brain just kinda shuts down and they wander around like so much mindless cheap labor.

JACKIE: That's so fucked up.

BEVERLY: Jackie.

DAVID: And there's something called Jimson Weed which is a hallucinogen that can cause memory loss. They dose you with that, sell you to a plantation, and keep enough on hand so that they can continue to dose you when it looks like your memories are coming back. I heard all about it when I was in Haiti.

BEVERLY: *(Smiling, but always a smidge stern.)* Okay, David.

JOSH: Wasn't that that Bill Paxton movie?

DAVID: Pullman.

JOSH: Potato, po-tah-to.

APRIL: Mom, do you need any help?

PEN: No, no, no. I don't need your pity just yet. I'm only getting older. *(To ADAM.)* You good with your wine, hon?

(ADAM nods and toasts her. She smiles, then stops, as if she's just realized something.)

APRIL: How's school, Jackie?

JACKIE: Ugh. Fine.

BEVERLY: She is enjoying it immensely, from what she says over the phone.

JACKIE: Yeah, Lord knows I would never be anything less than forthcoming about my academic investment.

BEVERLY: And what does *that* mean?

APRIL: *(Overlapping.)* What's your favorite class this semester?

PEN: *(At the sink, still frowning.)* I never made the chicken salad…

JACKIE: I'm in this *great* class called Critical Cultural Concepts: The Problem of Evil.

(EVERYONE at the table "oooohs.")

JACKIE: It's amazing. Intense, too—thirteen books to read, some of them are really long. Um, a Cormac McCarthy, Milton, *Frankenstein*, Faulkner, Milton, *Frankenstein*, Faulkner, and a Cormac McCarthy—

PEN: *(Overlapping when the list repeats.)* I need to made the chicken salad.

JACKIE: But right now we're on "The Grand Inquisitor." It's Russian! From *The Brothers Something*.

JOSH: *Karamazov.*

JACKIE: That.

JOSH: You like it?

(JACKIE grunts noncommittally. JOSH laughs. We hear ominous noises outside—sirens? Groans? No one at the table reacts.

ADAM, *still smiling, turns and looks at PEN.)*

PEN: Something's happening, Adam.

(The conversation continues at the table, unfazed. Underneath it, ADAM rises slowly from the table and walks towards PEN and the window.)

JOSH: That's one of my favorite books. Ever.

JACKIE: It's *interesting*. I don't know if I *get* it just yet, though.

JOSH: It's easier than it looks, really. *(To APRIL.)* You've read it, right?

APRIL: Aahh, nein.

JOSH: What?!

APRIL: Nope. Never got around to it.

JOSH: Oh! It's sooo good! How is that possible?

APRIL: My hearty apologies.

(We can see that ADAM's suit has no back to it. He is completely nude from behind. He stares out the window.)

PEN: No, no, that's not right. We buried you in real clothes. I made sure.

APRIL: *(Still to the OTHERS at the table, in the same energy as the conversation.)* They're upstairs.

JOSH: *(The same.)* The clothes are upstairs. In the bathroom.

PEN: I made sure.

(ADAM looks at her and shrugs, still smiling.)

DAVID: And *then*, in the Bible, there's Zechariah 14:12! "Their people will become like walking corpses, their flesh rotting away. Their eyes will shrivel in their sockets, and their tongues will decay in their mouths. On that day they will be terrified, stricken by the Lord with great panic. They will fight against each other in hand-to-hand combat."

PEN: This isn't right.

JACKIE: *(To the OTHERS at the table.)* Oh! That reminds me. I brought home our newest assignment. It's a rabbit. We had to get a pet rabbit. Wanna see?

(EVERYONE at the table agrees giddily. JACKIE rushes out, excited. ADAM watches her and starts gnashing his teeth. The noises outside intensify.)

PEN: No. Don't.

(ADAM starts moaning hungrily. JOSH, BEVERLY, and APRIL are still discussing literature.)

PEN: No! Please.

JOSH: You know about Tolstoy?

DAVID: Tolstoy? What don't I know about Tolstoy?

(ADAM shambles his way out of the kitchen.)

JOSH: Tolstoy died.

APRIL: I knew that.

BEVERLY: *(With the same inflection each time.)* Tolstoy died in a car crash. Tolstoy died in a car crash. Tolstoy died in a car crash.

(We hear JACKIE scream in the other room as ADAM attacks her violently. We hear the wet sounds of flesh being torn from bone. PEN, still at the sink, watches wide-eyed, paralyzed. Then, suddenly, she gasps. The noises from the other room and the noises from outside cut out abruptly. The lights shift back to normal. She has just woken

up from a disturbingly real daydream. She jerks against the kitchen counter. However, no one at the table has noticed. They are talking about Kelly Gold. The mood is somber. Funereal. JOSH is still drinking the wine—the glass that ADAM was using in the dream scene.)

DAVID: They're already having these practically *insulting* retrospectives of her so-called "career." I had to shuffle through four radio stations—*news* radio stations—before I found something on anything else—

BEVERLY: *(Sternly.)* It *is* sad, David.

DAVID: No one's denying that, hon.

BEVERLY: She was only twenty-six, David.

DAVID: I'm aware of that, hon.

PEN: *(Overlapping, still distant.)* Jackie was getting her pet rabbit.

(EVERYONE at the table turns to her.)

APRIL: Mom? You okay?

BEVERLY: What about Jackie?

PEN: Hm? Oh, God. I'm sorry. I'm fine.

DAVID: You sure, P—

PEN: Yes. I just…dozed off for a second there. I'm sorry. Don't worry about me. *(Beat. As a joke.)* I'm only getting older.

APRIL: What do you mean?

PEN: Doesn't matter. Don't mind me. Keep talking.

(Beat. Silence.)

PEN: Or not.

(Something is knocked over in the other room. They all hear it and try to ignore it. JOSH pours another glass for himself.)

APRIL: How's Jackie doing, David?

BEVERLY: Ugh…

DAVID: *(With a sigh.)* She's okay. She's fine. She's certainly in trouble.

APRIL: Can I ask what happened?

BEVERLY: Ugh.

DAVID: Sure. Prepare yourself. *(A moment.)* Drugs.

JOSH: Oh, shit.

DAVID: Oh shit, indeed.

JOSH: Was it anything serious?

DAVID: Yes. *(Beat.)* Marijuana.

(APRIL starts to laugh.)

BEVERLY: Oh, good, again.

APRIL: I'm sorry, really. It's just the way Dave said it. I'm sorry, sorry. *(Beat.)* "Marijuana." *(Starts laughing again.)*

BEVERLY: Are *you* high, April? You've been laughing all damn day.

APRIL: I'm high on "marijuana cigarettes."

(She hits DAVID's arm.)

APRIL: I'm just messing with you, David. I'm sorry.

JOSH: They aren't seriously gonna expel her for *weed*, are they?

DAVID: We'll see. She had it on her, and apparently she was selling it to her friends.

(BEVERLY groans.)

DAVID: We've given that goddamn school a good amount of money, though, so we might be able to talk them down to something a little less severe. But they have a pretty strict no-tolerance attitude there, you know?

BEVERLY: So do we, David.

(DAVID points to her as if to say, "That, too." JOSH continues to drink.)

BEVERLY: She picked just a wonderful time to screw up like this. Harrison is going to have a field day.

JOSH: You guys haven't heard from Debbie at all lately, have you?

DAVID: Don't ask...

BEVERLY: *(Overlapping, with venom.)* Debbie who?

(There is another noise from the living room.)

JOSH: You sure you wanna let him...walk around like that? In there?

PEN: He's fine, Josh.

APRIL: It's not like we need to make sure he's safe or anything.

JOSH: *(Drinks.)* Alright.

APRIL: It's just too creepy having him around like that. *(Beat.)* Sorry, Mom.

BEVERLY: Be thankful you didn't walk in on him out there and have your wits scared out of you.

JOSH: *(Almost, but not quite, under his breath.)* Long Day's Journey into Night of the Living Dead...

PEN: Is anyone hungry?

(There are murmurs of assent.)

PEN: I'll get the chicken salad together. *(Saying that gives her a moment of déjà vu, but she brushes it off and gets to work.)*

APRIL: *(To BEVERLY.)* Does Jackie have food at your place?

BEVERLY: *(Shrugs.)* She'll figure something out.

APRIL: A little old to be sent to bed without her supper, isn't she?

BEVERLY: *(Casually.)* If you wanted to dole out parenting advice, April, maybe you should've thought about having your o—

JOSH: Whoa, there!

DAVID: *(Overlapping.)* Beverly.

APRIL: Real nice, Beverly. Class act all the way.

(PEN gives a short, surprised laugh. They all turn to her.)

PEN: I almost started setting the table for six. Force of habit.

APRIL: Oh, God, Mom, let me help, you're exhausted.

BEVERLY: No. I'll do it. Does anyone *else* want anything while I'm up? *(Gets up, starts setting the table, etc.)*

APRIL: *(Overlapping with "I'll do it.")* Okay, then. *(To JOSH.)* Our very own *martyr* d'.

JOSH: *(Starting to get drunk.)* Nice.

(Another noise from the living room. And another.)

PEN: I wonder if he *will* get hungry...

APRIL: Do you want to be thinking about that stuff, Mom?

PEN: I can't not, April.

APRIL: I know, it's just...

JOSH: You tell Jackie, Djave? *(Corrects himself.)* Dave?

BEVERLY: Yes, did you, David?

DAVID: ...I told her that something had happened and that I'd fill her in when we got back. That sounds pretty reasonable to me. It's not like we have any answers right now, anyway.

(JOSH grunts and shrugs as if to say, "True enough.")

APRIL: Josh, are you getting drunk?

(JOSH grunts and shrugs, as if to say, "True enough." APRIL takes the wine bottle away from him—he finishes what's left in his glass.)

BEVERLY: *(To PEN.)* What did you mean by, "Jackie's getting a pet rabbit?"

PEN: What? Me?

BEVERLY: You said that earlier.

PEN: My mind was wandering, Beverly, I was half-asleep.

BEVERLY: Okay.

DAVID: Do you need anything, Pen? Anything at all?

PEN: No.

DAVID: *(Insistent.)* You sure?

PEN: *(Annoyed.)* I'm sure. I'm fine.

JOSH: It's just the walking dead, David, leave the poor woman alone.

APRIL: Oh, God, Josh, stop.

(Beat.)

JOSH: *(He's not so buzzed as to not realize the gaffe. Genuinely.)* I'm sorry, Pen.

PEN: It's fine, Josh.

JOSH: *(Apologetically.)* That's what they're calling it on the news.

PEN: Oh?

JOSH: Yeah. Awful, isn't it? Have you heard about 811, yet?

APRIL: *(Pointing to the other room.)* Josh, can I talk to you for a second?

JOSH: *(Incredulously.)* You want to go in the *other room* and talk?

APRIL: Come here, please. *(She exits into the other room. The briefest of moments and she's back in, having forgotten what was in the other room.)*

JOSH: I tried to remind you.

(She takes him aside and whispers to him. We can tell it's angry.)

PEN: Please, April, it was nothing.

(APRIL continues whispering to JOSH. There is another noise in the living room.)

BEVERLY: *(To DAVID, re. JACKIE.)* I think taking her car away is the first thing to do.

DAVID: You sure you don't need anything, Pen?

PEN: Please stop asking me that! April, really, it was no big deal.

(APRIL stops chastising JOSH.)

APRIL: Okay, Mom.

JOSH: *(Grabs the wine bottle, pours another glass. With a look to APRIL.)* Again, my apologies, Pen. I'm sorry.

PEN: It's okay. What's 811?

(JOSH looks at APRIL. APRIL shrugs.)

DAVID: Is this the—?

BEVERLY: It's the hotline, Mom.

PEN: The what?

JOSH: The hotline. A new government thing. To *report* any... umm, shit, what's the word I'm looking for?

DAVID: Instances.

JOSH: Sure.

PEN: Instances?

JOSH: Yeah.

PEN: And then what? What do they do after an *instance* is reported?

(Beat. No one has any idea.)

JOSH: I have no idea. Take 'em? Study 'em?

BEVERLY: Must be serious if they've set up a number like that.

APRIL: They said it was still *nothing*.

DAVID: It's possible it might've been set up just to take the pressure off of 911 calls. Probably a lot of pranks being pulled. False leads and all that.

APRIL: Or we could all be quarantined.

JOSH: All depends on who picks up the phone, I guess.

(Silence. Something is knocked over in the living room and shatters.)

PEN: Lamp.

(More silence. The unspoken question hangs in the air. JOSH drinks. BEVERLY has finished setting the table and serving. Finally:)

BEVERLY: Well, *I* think we should call—

(The phone rings. They all jump. It rings again. PEN crosses to the phone, hesitantly. She answers.)

PEN: ...Hello? *(Pause.)* I'm fine. Who is this? *(Pause.)* Oh, God, Sheila, hi. I'm sorry, I didn't recognize—

(She waves to EVERYONE in the room—they all relax.)

PEN: That's very sweet—I really can't talk right now, though, the girls and I are going to sit down to eat soon. *(Pause.)* Chicken salad. *(Pause.)* Okay. *(Pause.)* Okay. *(Pause.)* Okay. *(Pause.)* Okay. *(Pause.)* Okay. *(Pause.)* Okay. *(Pause.)* Okay. Shei—? *(Pause.)* O— *(Not getting an in, she hangs up the phone.)* Christ, that woman must shit small talk, she's so fucking full of it. *(Beat.)* Excuse me.

BEVERLY: What was that about?

PEN: Sheila. We play canasta together sometimes. Calling to "express her sympathies" for the eighth time. Should've told her not to worry about that now.

(JOSH snickers, then clears his throat to cover up.)

PEN: And she wanted to tell me about that singer, Shelly.

APRIL: Kelly.

PEN: Apparently, the President is making a statement about her on the TV.

DAVID: What?

BEVERLY: The President?

APRIL: Seriously?

JOSH: She wasn't even that good a singer.

PEN: That's what she said.

APRIL: Should we watch it?

(A thud comes from the other room.)

PEN: The TV's in there.

(Another thud. And another. And another. Then a moan. It's loud, almost a howl, and it sounds frustrated, not angry.)

APRIL: What the—?!

BEVERLY: David, could you go check on him?

DAVID: Me? Why should—

BEVERLY: I've set the table, David, please.

DAVID: Okay. *(DAVID, clearly not enjoying the assignment, peeks his head out.)*

BEVERLY: *(While he crosses.)* Do you want to watch the thing on TV, Mom?

PEN: I don't know—

DAVID: He's fine, he just… *(Comes back fully into the room.)* He's stuck.

APRIL: What do you mean, stuck?

DAVID: Against the wall. He keeps bumping into the wall. Like, he doesn't know to turn.

(A beat. ADAM continues to bump rhythmically against the wall in the other room. In spite of herself, APRIL starts to laugh again.)

APRIL: He's just—? *(She slaps one hand into the other, repeatedly.)*

DAVID: Yeah.

APRIL: Oh, God. *(Starts to laugh some more.)*

BEVERLY: April! It's not…funny…

APRIL: *(Trying to fight it.)* Like a fucking remote-controlled car?!

DAVID: Should I…fix him?

APRIL: *(Bursts out laughing.)* Fix him! Oh, Jesus, it's so fucking sad! It's like, do you remember that time he got that riding lawnmower and he couldn't get it to turn around the lawn, so we just had that *strip* of clipped grass? He was so mad!

(Another bump and moan. EVERYONE, save PEN, bursts out laughing.)

BEVERLY: *(Unable to stop laughing.)* It's not funny.

APRIL: I know, it's awful!

DAVID: *(Through tears.)* I'm sorry, Pen…

BEVERLY: David… *(She gestures to the door.)*

(DAVID exits to go help ADAM.)

APRIL: *(Still kind of laughing.)* I'm so sorry, Mom.

PEN: *(Lying.)* It's…fine. I understand.

APRIL: It's just so absurd. I mean, Dad's…

JOSH: *(Finishes his drink, calling offstage.)* That's no way to run a Zombie Apocalypse, Adam!

(At that word, the energy at the table changes. Silence.)

JOSH: Oh, right. The "zee" word. Verboten. My bad. *(He starts eating the chicken salad with his fingers. A beat. He sings softly.)* "Zah-ahm-beh, zah-ahm-beh…"

APRIL: Josh.

JOSH: *(Giggling.)* Come on, let's just say it! It's not so bad. Zombie. Zombies! Oooooooo! The fucking Cranberries were brave enough to say it. *(He sings.)* "Zah-ahm-beh, zah-ahm-beh!"

APRIL: *(Not laughing anymore.)* Josh!

JOSH: *(Pointing at APRIL.)* Hey! We're getting a divorce! Surprise! Yeah! You're looking at a matrimonial zombie! Our marriage is the living dead! Braaaaiiinns! Zah-ahm-beh!!

(PEN slaps him in the face. Silence. DAVID walks in.)

DAVID: I wonder why he's so insistent on trying to walk around like that. Any ideas?…What's going on?

BEVERLY: Is he okay in there?

DAVID: Yeah, I sat him down and picked up some of the stuff that had been knocked over. Wasn't so bad. Did I hear singing in here?

(JOSH goes to the sink and pours himself a glass of water.)

PEN: *(Pointing to the food.)* Everyone help themselves.

JOSH: *(Weakly.)* It's really good.

(No one touches the food.)

DAVID: *(Weak laugh.)* You know, in China, it's considered an offense to have an empty plate. It, uh, signifies that there's not enough to go around.

(No one remarks. Beat. He gestures to the other room.)

DAVID: Anyway, I wonder if it's some sort of retained memory or instinct or something that makes them walk around like that. Primal wandering impulse. *(Beat.)* Maybe just purely mechanical.

APRIL: Do you want to watch the—

PEN: I don't want to go in there right now.

BEVERLY: Do you still have that radio, Mom?

PEN: What radio?

BEVERLY: *(Smiling tightly.)* The one I got for you to listen to in the kitchen? So you'd stop watching so much TV? So you'd cook for yourself more?

PEN: Oh, I think so, somewhere in here. One of the cabinets. Why?

BEVERLY: *(Gets up and starts looking through the cabinets.)* We can listen to it—if it's on TV, it's probably on the radio, too. Since you don't wanna go in there. *(She can't find it yet.)* I wish you'd actually use the things I get you. I notice that blender is pristine.

APRIL: The speech could be over now.

DAVID: They probably have commentary and stuff.

APRIL: Touché.

BEVERLY: *(Finds it. Angrily.)* Still in the box, Mom? You haven't even opened it yet? Why do I even bother?

PEN: When your dad was getting sick, I was just too tired to cook much. I like to just have my TV dinners in the living room. Watching TV. Don't start.

BEVERLY: *(Under her breath.)* Honestly... *(She opens the radio box, pulls out the radio, and plugs it in.)*

DAVID: Any guess what this whole speech is about?

APRIL: You bet. You bet... It always takes a celebrity...

(BEVERLY searches the dial. First, we hear a burst of generic dance pop.)

RADIO ANNOUNCER 1: *(Voiceover.)* "—from her second album, *Tie Me Up*. Critics praised—"

(She continues to search.)

DAVID: Oh, go back.

(She turns back to a station.)

PRESIDENT: *(Voiceover.)* "...God bless America."

(Tinny applause from the radio.)

APRIL: Told you.

BEVERLY: Shh.

RADIO ANNOUNCER 2: *(Voiceover.)* And there you have it.

RADIO ANNOUNCER 3: *(Voiceover.)* Yup.

RADIO ANNOUNCER 2: *(Voiceover.)* The President is now making his way back through the Rose Garden into the White House, thus ending a, well, historic address.

RADIO ANNOUNCER 3: *(Voiceover.)* Yeah, historic would describe it, alright.

(Both ANNOUNCERS sigh.)

RADIO ANNOUNCER 3: *(Voiceover.)* Well.

RADIO ANNOUNCER 2: *(Voiceover.)* Wow. Well, stay tuned, we'll be discussing this for I'm sure the rest of the day…

RADIO ANNOUNCER 3: *(Voiceover.)* No doubt about that. That was… That was a lot to chew on… *(Beat. Clears his/her throat.)* That was a poor way to phrase that.

(Their voices fade. Lights fade onstage.)

Scene Five

The stage is still dark. Over the following soundscape, we see projections of videos from around the world, documenting the Walking Dead Phenomenon: YouTube clips, newscasts, some are blurry, taken from far away; some are clear. Some should be gruesome. In each case, though, the walking dead in question move slowly, aimlessly, and carry very little threat. The videos are projected onto every flat surface of the kitchen. Throughout the scene, we hear "Any Day Now" by Sam Cooke and the Soul Stirrers underneath.

PRESIDENT: *(Voiceover.)* My fellow Americans. I greet you today at… at the dawn of… *(Clears throat.)* Something is happening. It seems that, given the recent, well-documented footage of the late popular singer, Kelly Gold, we are confronted with an inescapable truth. We as a global community, a culture, a country… a species. We might have been able to dismiss the initial rumors, the blurred videotapes and YouTube postings, as exaggeration, as misleading. Even as fraud. But given the extent of Ms. Gold's injuries, and given the extraordinary amount of coverage dedicated to her untimely passing, there was no denying what reporters captured at the hospital earlier this morning—

(Voice fades out. Talk show voices crossfade up.)

VOICE 2: *(À la Pat Buchanan.)* She was goddamned cut in half, Brian! She was cut in half, totally dead by the time they got to the hospital—

BRIAN: *(Voiceover. Overlapping.)* We don't *know that*, Pat!

PAT: *(Voiceover.)* Please, "we don't know that." There were hundreds of paparazzi there, they got the whole thing on tape, she was cut in half and, an hour or so later, she was moving around like nothin' had happened—

BRIAN: *(Voiceover. Overlapping.)* You're making assumptions, Pat!

PAT: *(Voiceover. Overlapping.)* I am not making assumptions!

BRIAN: *(Voiceover. Overlapping.)* They didn't release the footage, Pat!

PAT: *(Voiceover. Overlapping.)* Get your head out of your ass, Brian!

(Crossfade.)

PRESIDENT: *(Voiceover.)* I want to make this absolutely clear, this is not the time for panic or hysteria. Some of the recently deceased are now…re-animating. Are coming back to life. The world's top scientists are currently at work delving into the reasons *why* this is happening, but one thing is for sure: despite sensational claims to the opposite, there has been absolutely no evidence that these…individuals are dangerous. I'm going to repeat that. There has been absolutely no evidence…

(Crossfade.)

VOICE: Next on Action Channel 11: response to the President's speech. *Are they dangerous? Are they conscious? Are they human? What can you do to protect your family?* For more on this, we go to…

(Crossfade. A snippet of dance music by Kelly Gold. Crossfade.)

PRESIDENT: *(Voiceover.)* That being said, though, there is still much we do not know. Therefore it is of the utmost importance that you report all sightings to 811. The number has been set up and routed in a method similar to that of 911, and will help us localize and hopefully better understand…what this means. *(Laughs.)* Used to be a public utilities hotline…

(Crossfade to the voices of the two RADIO COMMENTATORS from the previous scene.)

RADIO ANNOUNCER 2: *(Voiceover.)* Of course, um, there are many things we just…we don't know.

RADIO ANNOUNCER 3: *(Voiceover.)* It's hard not to turn this into some cheap horror movie in your mind, you know?

(Crossfade. A religious sermon.)

PREACHER: *(Voiceover.)* —that the dead will rise! All this sinning, all this ignoring the word of God, all these abortions and gays and feminists and liberals, God is pointing His finger and saying, "You have done this!" A flood is coming, brothers and sisters, a flood—

(Crossfade. A snippet from George Romero's Night of the Living Dead.*)*

JOHNNY: *(Voiceover.)* They're coming to get you, Barbara…

BARBARA: *(Voiceover.)* Stop it!

(Crossfade.)

PRESIDENT: *(Voiceover.)* Again, if there is any occurrence of this phenomenon in your community, please report it *immediately* to the number 811. Do not intervene, do not make contact. We. Are. In. No. Danger. *(Beat.)* But there is a lot we don't know.

RADIO ANNOUNCER 2: *(Voiceover.)* —like stroke victims, or Alzheimer's patients.

VOICE: Next on Action 11: are your pets at risk?

RADIO ANNOUNCER 3: *(Voiceover.)* Images of bloodthirsty zombies surrounding people in farmhouses…

PAT: *(Voiceover.)* You're gonna bury your head in the sand here—

BRIAN: *(Voiceover.)* You're making it seem like the goddamned Apocalypse, let's be rational, please!

PREACHER: *(Voiceover.)* I will quote to you from Zechariah 14:12. "Their people will become like walking corpses, their flesh rotting away"—

PRESIDENT: *(Voiceover.)* Perhaps this is a good time to turn to religious leaders for guidance. For spiritual answers. But, in these frightening and confusing times, I wish to remind you that this is a nation built on rational thought. We mustn't let the stories and images from our popular, fictive entertainment color our responses. I...I don't know what this means. I truly don't. But I do believe that there is a reason for this. And I do believe we shall find a way to understand. And this is not the time to panic. We have nothing to fear but fear itself. That being said, I close this address with the words that close every presidential address, though I believe they have never before carried such profundity: may God bless America.

(Tinny applause. The videos fade away. The music fades away. Darkness.)

Scene Six

Lights back up on the house. JOSH is passed out at the table. BEVERLY is saying goodbye to DAVID. APRIL is comforting PEN. The radio is off.

BEVERLY: *(To DAVID.)* Make sure she's eaten something. We'll talk about it more tomorrow.

DAVID: Of course. You sure you'll be okay here?

BEVERLY: Someone's got to stay and help.

DAVID: *(To APRIL.)* Is Josh going to be okay?

APRIL: *(As if noticing JOSH for the first time.)* What? Oh, God...

(She goes to him, shakes him.)

APRIL: Josh. Josh? Josh, wake up.

JOSH: *(Stirs. Looks up, dazed and hung over.)* Wuh? Uh...oh, God, I don't feel so good...

APRIL: How are you planning on getting home, J—?

(He hitches. Again. He runs and vomits into the sink.)

BEVERLY: Oh, God...

APRIL: Oh, God...

JOSH: *(Spitting.)* Oh, God...

DAVID: Too much wine on an empty tank, eh, Josh?

(JOSH flips him the bird.)

BEVERLY: Josh!

JOSH: *(Runs the tap.)* I'm sorry, Pen. I really, really—I can't tell you how sorry I am. This whole thing has just...

PEN: *(To EVERYONE.)* Before you all leave, I want to make something absolutely clear.

BEVERLY: I'm not leaving.

PEN: I want to make this absolutely clear. No one is to call that number. Not about Adam. Not about your father. No one. Is that understood?

APRIL: Mom—

PEN: No.

BEVERLY: We need to report this—

PEN: Absolutely not.

BEVERLY: Mother!

PEN: Beverly!

(Beat. They all look at each other.)

DAVID: Pen, we really should think about—

(*PEN picks up one of the plates and throws it to the ground. It shatters. Beat.*)

PEN: No. (*Pause.*) I'm sorry, but I just can't do that just yet. Not right now. You heard what they said. We're under no danger.

BEVERLY: They said they didn't know—

PEN: (*Overlapping.*) If there was something we were gonna *catch*, God knows I've probably already caught it. So, no. We are not letting him be dissected and taken and killed or whatever... No.

BEVERLY: (*A whisper.*) Mom. He's already dead.

PEN: If you're planning on staying here to try and change my mind about this, Beverly, you can just go ahead and leave with David.

BEVERLY: That's not why I want to stay, mother, Jesus! (*To DAVID.*) Do you hear her? (*To PEN, in tears.*) I'm just trying to fucking help!

PEN: Fine. Then you're more than welcome to stay. And I appreciate it. But no one is to call that number as long as we're safe, okay? Okay?

(*They all murmur their assent, save BEVERLY.*)

PEN: Thank you. (*Sitting.*) Josh, you aren't planning on driving home, are you?

APRIL: I'll take him. One of us will pick up his car tomorrow. Is that okay?

PEN: Fine.

APRIL: We really should talk about calling, Mom...

PEN: Please, April.

APRIL: Okay. (*She kisses her forehead.*) We'll just talk. Later.

PEN: (*Over her shoulder.*) I'm very sorry to hear about this, Josh.

APRIL: Bye, Mom. (*To JOSH.*) Come on.

DAVID: (*Gives PEN a kiss.*) You call if you need absolutely anything, okay?

PEN: Thank you, David. Get home safe.

BEVERLY: (*Re. JACKIE.*) Make sure she's not on the computer or the phone.

DAVID: I know, hon.

BEVERLY: (*Kissing him on the cheek.*) Get home safe. And if Brenda calls, tell her we'll run damage control tomorrow.

DAVID: I will, hon.

BEVERLY: Bye, April. Bye, Josh.

APRIL: Bye.

JOSH: (*Weakly.*) Bye.

(*The three of them stand at the door to the living room.*)

APRIL: I wish there was another way out of this damn house.

(*With a collective breath, the three of them leave. A few moments later, we hear cars drive away.*)

PEN: Thank you for staying.

BEVERLY: You're welcome.

PEN: I'm exhausted.

BEVERLY: (*Sympathetically.*) Of course you are.

PEN: Thank you for the radio.

BEVERLY: You're welcome.

(*They sit in silence. Slowly, the door from the living room opens. ADAM senselessly* shuffles his way in. Both women notice and watch with a profound sadness.)

PEN: If it had been Alzheimer's, I could've dealt with it…if it had been anything…but this…

BEVERLY: Shhh.

PEN: I can almost convince myself that's what it is. That he never…

BEVERLY: It's okay, Mom.

PEN: Oh, Bev, I don't know if it is. I don't know if I can handle this.

BEVERLY: Why don't you go on up and rest some more, okay? It's late. You need to sleep.

PEN: Ha. Wonder when I'll be able to do that again. I'm going to the guest room; you can sleep in my bed.

BEVERLY: That's fine. You rest. I'll clean up and…figure out what to do with him.

PEN: *(Looks around at the kitchen.)* No one touched the chicken salad.

BEVERLY: Good-night, Mom.

PEN: Good-night, sweetie. *(Pause. To ADAM.)* Good-night…

(She exits. ADAM continues to shuffle around, perhaps making barely audible noises. BEVERLY sits him down in a chair.)

BEVERLY: What are we going to do with you? *(She walks around for a moment, rinses out the sink more thoroughly, pours herself a glass of water. She takes a pill from her purse, swallows it. She stares at ADAM for a good long while.)*

BEVERLY: Dad.

(No response.)

BEVERLY: That face. That fucking face.

(She walks up close to him, stares deep into his eyes. Then, suddenly, she slaps him. No response. She slaps him again. No response. She slaps him as hard as she can. He looks towards her, vaguely. She puts her forearm in front of his mouth.)

BEVERLY: Bite it.

(No response. She slaps him again.)

BEVERLY: Bite it.

(She pushes her arm into his mouth. He doesn't bite.)

BEVERLY: Fucking bite it.

(Nothing. Tearfully, she puts her arm into her own mouth and bites into it. She lets out a muffled cry. Blood oozes out between her teeth. She puts her arm back at his mouth. Still nothing. Desperate, she puts her arm in her mouth again and tears back with her teeth. She screams, though not so loud as to call PEN back, and puts it back into his face.)

BEVERLY: Bite it, you fuck! Bite it!

(She presses open his mouth and forces her arm up into his teeth. ADAM never bites down. She pushes hard enough that he ends up on his feet—he takes a few steps towards her. She shrinks back, but he only begins to wander aimlessly around the kitchen.)

BEVERLY: You fucking…

(There is a lot of blood coming out of her arm now. She wraps her arm with the dishtowel, then heads over to the phone. She picks it up, her hands shaking, dials three numbers, and puts it to her ear. After a few moments, someone answers.)

BEVERLY: *(Into the phone.)* Hello? Yes, my name is Beverly Colby-Parker. It's just after ten p.m. Eastern Standard Time. I—excuse me, I'm talking now. *(Beat.)* I was just attacked.

(While she speaks, ADAM wanders off into the other room. She doesn't notice. Lights fade. "Be With Me, Jesus" by Sam Cooke and the Soul Stirrers plays.)

(Note: During the interval, there should be one or two small televisions in the lobby, playing news footage covering the breaking news of BEVERLY's attack—perhaps also showing an example of BEVERLY's campaign videos—alongside more information about Kelly Gold.)

ACT TWO
"WHAT ARE WE GOING TO DO ABOUT BEVERLY?"
Scene One

Prescene music: "I Have a Friend Above All Others" by Sam Cooke and the Soul Stirrers. Lights up on APRIL at the kitchen table. The radio is on. We hear BEVERLY's voice, punctuated by cheering.

BEVERLY'S VOICE: …blind naïveté, and, frankly, lunacy, to assume that we are safe. We are not safe; we are, in every sense of the word, imperiled! I mean, would you allow a pack of wild dogs to roam around your neighb—

APRIL: Shit. *(Turns off the radio and sits in silence. She checks the fridge for a beer. Nothing.)* Shit.

(The phone rings.)

APRIL: Shit.

(She debates answering it. It rings again. Finally, she answers.)

APRIL: Yes? *(Pause.)* No, thank you, *still* don't wish to comment at this moment, please don't call back. *(Pause.)* Yes, thank you, enjoy fucking yourself.

(She hangs up. A moment. She fans herself. JACKIE enters.)

JACKIE: They're out there.

APRIL: How many?

JACKIE: Only like three or four. Standing there, doing nothing. Just *staring*. It's eerie.

APRIL: Jesus.

JACKIE: Still, it's better than at my house. You can barely see across the street sometimes, there's so many of them. And they all look hungry…

APRIL: Fucking reporters.

JACKIE: Yeah. *(Beat.)* Was that her on the radio just then?

APRIL: Yup. One of her greatest hits. Turned it off. You want some water?

JACKIE: I'd love a beer.

APRIL: You and me both.

JACKIE: Did you see her most recent thing? Junket?

APRIL: *(Small laugh.)* No.

JACKIE: It was a doozy. Some of the crowd…it was kinda scary. *(Beat. She drinks.)* "Man, so long as he lives, has no more constant and agonizing anxiety than to find someone to worship as soon as possible."

APRIL: That's…very deep.

JACKIE: Thank you. It's Dostoevsky.

APRIL: Oooh, look at you.

JACKIE: I know! That aborted upper education really paid off! I was in the middle of writing a paper on him when I got the ol'— *(She gives a thumb gesture and raspberry.)*

APRIL: "Man, so long as he lives, has no more agony than to find someone to worship."

JACKIE: Something like that. It's from "The Grand Inquisitor" chapter in *The Brothers Karamazov*. Professor Matos loved that quote. It was like the overarching thesis of the class. And now I think about it every time I see one of Mom's little…rallies. He also liked that Camus line, "To be famous, all you have to do is kill your landlady," though I've thankfully had considerably less occasion to relate to *that*.

APRIL: That's Josh's favorite book, *The Brothers Kalamawhatsit*. He's always talking about how great it is.

JACKIE: Did you ever read it?

APRIL: No. Sometimes I wonder if he ever did, either. *(Beat.)* What's the "Great Inquisitor" about?

JACKIE: "*Grand* Inquisitor." It's just a chapter. Or, I guess, an allegory one of the characters tells the other. All about how, during the Spanish Inquisition, Jesus Christ comes back, and he lands in Seville—which I remember, 'cause it's the last name of the guy from *The Chipmunks*—and, y'know, pretty much remounts the Jesus Christ one-man show. Performing the miracles, curing the blind, healing the leper—

APRIL: Bowling a perfect three hundred, making your whites whiter.

JACKIE: Right. And the big finale, of course, is raising the dead.

APRIL: How timely.

JACKIE: He brings this little girl back to life. "Still holding the flowers she was going to be buried with." But, unfortunately, right at that moment, the Grand Inquisitor happens to be walking by—he sees what's going on, and immediately calls for Jesus's arrest, and Jesus is taken into custody and brought to, you know, the Grand Interrogation Room. And the whole story's about how the Grand Inquisitor tells Jesus that Jesus coming back is the worst thing that could happen for mankind, because Jesus didn't really *get* what it's like to be human, and the Church went through all this trouble to make sense of all the stuff Jesus did during his time here. How Jesus left too much up to interpretation, and how the Church, you know, fixed things in place. So, the Inquisitor's like, "Sorry, Jesus," you know, "we were big fans of your earlier work, but there's absolutely no way we can let you live."

APRIL: What does Jesus say?

JACKIE: Nothing. He doesn't say a word. But it all ends with Jesus giving the Grand Inquisitor a kiss *(She lightly touches APRIL on the forehead.)* —either forgiving him or damning him—the ol' Judas kiss, but, of course, four thousand times more vague and frustrating, thank you very much, Mr. Dostoevsky. *(Beat.)* We had a big paper due on it but I just couldn't wrap my head around it. I *got* it, you know? But I couldn't figure out what to write, how to narrow it down, and the deadline was coming up, and I panicked and I told my friend Sanjay I'd pay him to write it, but I had to raise some capital first and so I sold some weed and that brings us to the present moment, with you looking at me like I'm a dumbass, which I most definitely am.

APRIL: No, you're not a dumbass.

JACKIE: *(Smiling wryly.)* No?

APRIL: No. You're just… *(She's at a loss for words.)*

JACKIE: Ouch.

APRIL: Sorry.

JACKIE: 'S okay.

(Beat.)

APRIL: How's your mom doing? You guys get to talk at all?

JACKIE: Heh. No. Everything I've heard about her has been through the news, or whatever. I haven't gotten the chance to talk to her at all—I've called a bunch of times, but she's never there. It's so fucked up, you know?

APRIL: That seems to be the refrain of our little symphony, doesn't it?

JACKIE: I can't help but think that maybe she's doing all this just to avoid confronting the fact that I got kicked out of school. *(Beat.)* Worked out well for her, though. Rinky-dink little shit politician from nowhere, and now look at her. Like, not two weeks, and she's already, what, like a spokesperson? I'm hearing her name used as, like, a reference. I see her face on CNN, with her stupid fucking doctor, and her stupid fucking arm: "Our government must act now!" rah-rah-rah. And just for getting attacked like that. *(Laughs.)* She's like the Paris Hilton of the Zombie Apocalypse.

APRIL: Don't call it that. And explain your simile.

JACKIE: *(Quickly, casually.)* Professor Matos said that Paris Hilton represents the culmination of the undoing of feminism through the embrace of victimization. Fame was literally thrust into her—she remained passive throughout, and it wasn't until a forcible injection of the masculine that she was deemed worthy of our attention. She's celebrated for being a receptacle for semen. A gift bestowed by the patriarchy. Ipso facto, Mom has become a sensation solely because of also being penetrated by a man. Granted, by his *teeth*, but, y'know…

(Beat.)

APRIL: Christ, Jackie, you're such a fucking idiot.

JACKIE: What? I know it's a stretch, I was just kidding—

APRIL: Not about that. About getting expelled. About getting caught. You're so bright and that was just so fucking stupid, Jackie.

JACKIE: I dunno, I just… *(She shrugs.)*

APRIL: What? You just what?

JACKIE: Well, like I said, there was that stupid fucking paper to buy, and a few other things; I needed the cash, and it's not like I could've asked Mom and Dad—

APRIL: You could've asked me!

JACKIE: No way, you already *gave* me—

APRIL: That weed was not for you to sell, Jackie! Christ, do you know how much trouble that could put me in?

JACKIE: I know, you're right, I'm sorry.

APRIL: *(Overlapping.)* With your mom, who would literally kill me if she knew; with the cops; shit, with Josh.

JACKIE: It was his idea.

APRIL: …What?

JACKIE: Well, not, like, explicitly.

APRIL: What do you mean, Jackie?

JACKIE: He just reminded me I had it, that's all. He called to check up on me, I told him I was broke, and he was like, "Well, you know, you could always sell some of the things you've got." I'm sure he meant books and CDs and crap, but I dunno, it got me thinking.

APRIL: Oh, well, thank God you didn't interpret that to mean your vagina, Jackie.

JACKIE: Oh, please, like I would ever do that!

APRIL: I don't know, Jackie, I never thought you'd want to become a drug dealer, either—

JACKIE: I am not a drug dealer!

APRIL: It's a good thing you didn't have *two* papers due that week, you might've turned hitman.

JACKIE: Come on, you sound just like *her* now.

(Beat.)

APRIL: Please don't say that.

(Beat.)

JACKIE: Sorry. That's how I used to win arguments with Debbie, too.

APRIL: You fight dirty. *(Beat. She gets up and opens the fridge, pulls out a can of soda.)* How *is* Debbie? Do you ever talk to her or anything?

JACKIE: I dunno, not really. We've got our own schedules and, you know…

APRIL: Ah.

JACKIE: It's not like I don't *want* to talk to her, I'm not, like, mad at her or anything. I think it's fucked up she hasn't called since all this stuff happened, but…

APRIL: Still, sisters should be close, you know? You should reach out to her, try and make a connection. I'm sure she misses you.

JACKIE: *She* never calls *me*.

APRIL: I guess you're innocent, then.

(JACKIE scoffs.)

APRIL: Trust me, you'll wish you had when you're my age. *(Beat.)* You don't really think I'm anything like your mother, do you?

JACKIE: Good God, no. You think we'd be having this conversation if you were?

APRIL: *(Chuckles.)* Hm. You know, she wasn't always like…*this*. She used to be pretty goddamned cool, I thought. I know, banish the thought, right?

JACKIE: *(Heavily sarcastic.)* Oh yeah? What happened?

APRIL: Time. Life.

JACKIE: The magazine?

APRIL: Cute. But, no, she used to be… she wasn't so *obsessed* with seeming correct, you know? She wasn't so fucking passive-aggressive and political, or however you wanna describe it.

JACKIE: I call it the shark-mouth. The way she smiles and it doesn't quite reach her eyes, you know? It's like a reflex. Creeps me out.

APRIL: She really means well, Jackie. You've got to believe that. When I was young and stupid she helped me out more times than you could possibly imagine. And, speaking of young and stupid…what do you have on you?

JACKIE: What do you mean?

APRIL: Don't play dumb with me, girl. What do you have on you?

JACKIE: …Not much.

APRIL: Give.

JACKIE: What?

APRIL: Give it.

JACKIE: Oh, come on—

(APRIL waits with an extended palm. JACKIE sighs, digs in her purse, and hands over a Baggie full of weed.)

APRIL: I am punishing you. Thank you. *(She brandishes the bag.)* You are cut off. Sorry.

JACKIE: You're officially my least favorite aunt.

APRIL: That stings. Write a paper about your pain when you go back to school.

JACKIE: I'm not going back to school.

APRIL: Yes, you are.

JACKIE: No, I'm not, *Mother*.

APRIL: Resistance is futile, young one.

JACKIE: Why would I go back to school when the world is ending?

APRIL: The world isn't ending.

(Long beat.)

APRIL: The world isn't ending.

(The phone rings.)

JACKIE: *(Slightly under her breath.)* Guess the Apocalypse is what you make of it.

APRIL: *(Crossing to the phone.)* Should I—?

JACKIE: It's probably another reporter.

(APRIL hesitates. The phone continues to ring.)

APRIL: Fuck. We are creatures of habit. *(She scoops the phone up.)* Hello? Oh, hi, Sheila. How are you? No, Mom's not available right now, she's taking a n— *(Pause.)* Yes, thank you, that's very swee— *(Pause.)* Yes, Dad was very fond of y— *(Pause.)* I'm sure he— *(Pause.)* I've been watching it on the news, yes. She's— *(Pause. Confused.)* No, Beverly's *not* here right now, Sheila, I'm sorry, I'm right in the middle— *(Pause. Startled.)* Yet? What do you mean, yet? Are you— Shei—SHEILA SHUTTHEFUCK-UPFORA SECOND! *(Beat.)* I'm sorry. I'm really sorry, I didn't mean to yell, I just— *(Pause.)* Uh-huh. *(Pause.)* She *just* left? Did they give an exact time? *(She checks her watch.)* Oh, man.

(PEN walks in, still in her nightgown. She's just awoken from a nap—her hair is mussed, her manner distracted and distant.)

JACKIE: *(Sotto voce.)* Hi, Grams.

APRIL: *(Seeing PEN.)* Thanks for the heads up, Sheila. I really appreci— *(Talking over SHEILA, quickly.)* I REALLY APPRECIATE IT. I'LL HAVE MOM CALL YOU BACK. BYE. *(Hangs up.)* Jesus. Morning, Mom.

PEN: *(Suspiciously.)* What are you two girls talking about?

APRIL: That was Sheila. She wanted to tell us about—

PEN: *(Looking at JACKIE, like a greeting.)* Bevvie.

APRIL: Good guess.

PEN: *(To JACKIE.)* What do you want, Bevvie?

JACKIE: I'm her daughter, Grams. It's me, Jackie.

PEN: *(Voice rising.)* The fuck you shit. You can't have him! You ungrateful little bitch.

(JACKIE looks to APRIL, scared.)

APRIL: *(Touching PEN.)* Mom! Mom, are you okay?

PEN: April, why is she here?

APRIL: Mom, that's *Jackie*.

PEN: What…?

(The phone rings.)

APRIL: Oh, God!

JACKIE: Here, come and sit down, Grams, I'll get you some water.

APRIL: Mom, are you gonna be alright?

(PEN sits. JACKIE gets her some water. The phone keeps ringing.)

PEN: *(Clear headed.)* April, the phone is ringing. We don't have a machine.

APRIL: Fuck the phone, Mom, you're babbling.

PEN: I'm not babbling, Bev—April.

APRIL: April, Mom.

PEN: *(Snapping.)* I *know* that! The wrong name came out, forgive me. I'm fine, I just woke up, I'm a little groggy, I'm not *babbling*. That's insulting.

(Beat. The phone has stopped ringing.)

PEN: Thank you. *Jackie*, I'm sorry.

JACKIE: It's okay, Grams. Are you…?

PEN: I'm just tired. I'm quite alright.

(Beat.)

APRIL: Sheila called.

PEN: Oh?

APRIL: Yeah. She said she just saw on the news that Beverly left the hospital today. She wanted to know if she was here yet.

JACKIE: What?

PEN: Yet?

APRIL: That's what I said. Apparently, Bev said she was looking forward to "seeing her family again." Apparently, Sheila's been following this like a soap opera.

JACKIE: *(Re. BEVERLY.)* Do you think that was her calling just now?

APRIL: Maybe.

PEN: No.

APRIL: *(Laughing.)* No?

PEN: That wasn't her calling.

APRIL: You don't know that, Ma, it could've been any—

PEN: No. Beverly's trying to surprise us.

APRIL: Surprise us? Really? By announcing it on the news?

PEN: I'm sure she knows we're not exactly following the story with baited breath. Isn't that her problem? She thinks we never pay any attention to her?

APRIL: *(Stunned by her lucidity.)* Jeez, Ma. Feeling better, are we?

PEN: I told you, I was just tired.

JACKIE: Why would she want to surprise us?

PEN: So we don't have a chance to hide her father.

(Beat.)

APRIL: He's still here?

PEN: Yes.

JACKIE: I thought he got away after he attacked her, or whatever.

PEN: No, that was just what we said. We had to release a statement and all those reporters wanted to come into the house… *(To APRIL, not without some pride.)* I had to hide him in the garage. I buckled him into the car, because I thought no one would think to look in the car.

(APRIL groans.)

JACKIE: Why would we lie about that?

PEN: Because, Jackie, I'm not going to let her take him.

JACKIE: But, he attacked her—

PEN: That's not true. I don't believe that.

JACKIE: *(Trying not to argue.)* They said the impressions matched his dental records. They ran tests on her wound; they found…bits of him—

PEN: I don't care, Jackie. Don't argue with me.

JACKIE: *(Staying cool.)* I'm not *arguing*. Please don't be so dismissive—

APRIL: Can we not argue right now, please? Where is Dad right now, Mom?

PEN: He's upstairs. In our bedroom.

APRIL: Oh, Jesus, Mom. *(Long beat as she stares at her mother in disbelief. Then.)* Is it safe up there?

(The phone starts ringing again.)

APRIL: Shit!

PEN: What do you mean, safe?

JACKIE: Do you want me to get that?

PEN: What do you mean safe, April?

APRIL: *(Picks up the phone. Into the phone.)* No, thank you, we have no fucking comment at this time! *(Beat.)* Josh?

PEN: Of course it's safe, April.

APRIL: Mom, shut up! *(Into the phone.)* Hi. What's—what's up? *(Sigh.)* Yes, thank you—we just heard. *(Pause.)* No, she didn't call us, we think. She's coming unannounced, apparently. Although the phone just rang a few min— *(Beat.)* Yeah. *(Pause.)* Oh. *(To JACKIE and PEN.)* That was Josh calling before. *(Into the phone.)* Well, we appreciate the warning. *(Pause. Quietly.)* I'm fine—I can't really talk r—no, please, let me just call you when— *(Pause.)* Josh. Please. Don't right now. *(Pause.)* Are you drunk, Josh? I'll call you later. *(Beat.)* Don't say th— *(Deciding she can't continue, she gently hangs the phone up.)*

(A moment. APRIL sighs, her head in her hands. She cries. PEN gets up and hugs her. JACKIE joins them. After another moment, APRIL laughs and shoos them away.)

APRIL: No, no, no, it's okay, no *Steel Magnolias*, please. This divorce stuff is just…Ugh, it's tricky. Understatement of the century. He just keeps calling, and calling, and begging, and begging, and telling me he's going to… *(She clears her throat, shakes it off.)*

PEN: Would you like me to talk to him?

APRIL: *(Laughs.)* Oh, God, Mom. *(Beat.)* *If* Beverly's really on her way here…how long do we think it takes for someone to get here from the hospital?

PEN: Maybe forty-five minutes.

APRIL: You sure?

PEN: I made that trip with your father many, many times.

APRIL: Gotcha.

JACKIE: *(Dazed.)* I want to see him.

APRIL: What?

JACKIE: I want to see him. I want to see him.

APRIL: Oh, Jackie, honey, now's not the time—

JACKIE: I want to see one of them up close. I just— *(Leaves the room.)*

APRIL: *(Calling after her.)* Jackie! Shit.

PEN: It's okay, April, she'll be fine.

APRIL: Fine? Why the fuck is he still here, Mom? Why haven't you reported this yet? Beverly is going to go mental—

PEN: I'm going to make some tea.

APRIL: Tea?! Okay, that's great. And what exactly do you want to do about Beverly? Besides share a hot mug of chamomile?

PEN: I'm just going to tell her that I don't know where he is and that she's wasting her time and that we're all glad she's feeling better.

APRIL: This is just fucked up, Mom, please listen to what you're saying here.

(PEN goes about preparing tea.)

APRIL: Fine. Just, fine. *(Calling.)* Jackie!

(APRIL leaves. We hear her call out JACKIE's name in the other room. PEN continues to make the tea. Lights fade.)

Scene Two

Darkness. We hear theme music à la Entertainment Tonight.

REPORTER: Thanks, Kirsten! I guess you could say they caught him "bread-handed"! In other news, the world continues to be fascinated and confused by what those in the scientific and political communities are now calling "returned decedents." There have been well over a hundred documented cases now, all over the world, but there is one case that is causing particular concern: the much-debated incident involving Connecticut Assemblywoman, Beverly Colby-Parker. Later in the hour, we've got an exclusive interview with one of the nurses attending Mrs. Parker, who will comment on the growing crowds the assemblywoman is beginning to attract at the press conferences she and her doctor have been holding outside of the hospital where she's being treated. But first! We're gonna shoot on over to Tony T, in Hollywood with Kelly Gold's fiancé, and he's got some strong words about…

Scene Three

Lights up in the kitchen, a few minutes after we last left the scene. The tea kettle whistles. PEN pours the water into a mug and sits. A beat. JACKIE enters, a distant look on her face, in shock. APRIL follows. It is silent for a moment.

APRIL: You okay?

(No answer.)

APRIL: Jackie?

JACKIE: *(Finally.)* It smells up there, Grams.

(No answer from PEN.)

APRIL: Just try not to think about that, honey.

JACKIE: I've never seen a dead body before. In person. Standing up. Like, he's just walking, decomposing meat. *(She laughs.)* I guess that's all of us, isn't it? Walking, decomposing meat.

PEN: *(Quietly.)* Jackie…

APRIL: It's okay, Jackie. Please, Mom, she's been reading a lot of Camus lately.

JACKIE: What do you think this means?

APRIL: How do you mean, sweetie?

JACKIE: Do you think his…soul is still in there? He looks so sad.

APRIL: I don't know, I don't know how that all…works.

JACKIE: Do you ever listen to Sam Cooke?

APRIL: Um. What?

JACKIE: His earlier stuff, I mean. The gospel stuff.

APRIL: No.

JACKIE: It's really good. Really good. His voice is really…I just got into him earlier this semester, when I started that class, that Problems of Evil class? I needed something to cheer me up while I was reading all those depressing books and stuff—or, you know, trying to read. It worked. It's all so sweet and passionate and full of love, but not like a *love* song, you know?

APRIL: That's good.

JACKIE: I don't know. Now that I think about it, all those songs, all those old gospel songs…they're just all about *waiting*. Waiting to meet God. Waiting to "go home." I wonder if Grandpa is…I don't want to die. I really don't. Not if that's what's waiting for us.

(A moment.)

PEN: I saw Sam Cooke once. In '63 or '64. One of his last concerts on the East Coast, I believe.

JACKIE: Really?

PEN: Yes. Your grandfather and I both.

JACKIE: *(Still in a daze.)* That's really cool.

PEN: It pays to be ancient sometimes.

(PEN hands JACKIE the tea. JACKIE drinks it. We hear a car pull up and the muffled excitement from the press outside. They all freeze.)

APRIL: Fuck.

PEN: No words about…

(A moment later, BEVERLY enters, finishing an email on a fancy new smartphone. Her bitten arm is wrapped in a bandage. They all stare at each other. It is long and awkward. Then, finally:)

BEVERLY: *(Clearing her throat.)* Mother, do you want me to ask those people outside to leave? The yard looks terrible. Jackie, you should be at home, you're still grounded.

(No answers.)

BEVERLY: Hi. No, I'm fine, thank you for asking.

(No answers.)

BEVERLY: Are you *mad* at me? You're actually *mad* at me, or something?

PEN: Your father's not here, Beverly.

BEVERLY: *(Stares at her for a good, long moment, wheels spinning. Setting her purse down.)* I'm not here about that, Mom. Please. *(To JACKIE.)* What are you doing here?

JACKIE: Thanks for taking time out of your busy schedule to call your daughter from the hospital, Mom.

BEVERLY: *(Sighing.)* What are you—?

JACKIE: *(Continuous.)* I mean, it was so nice to hear that you were okay from someone other than whoever's doing lead over at Fox News, or whatever. Not like I'd actually be worrying about you, or anything.

BEVERLY: Jackie, please. You're being unreasonable and ridiculous.

JACKIE: That's me!

BEVERLY: *(Overlapping, calmly.)* I was very busy, okay? I had so many tests, and so many interviews—I'm sorry to hear your father didn't do a better job of keeping you informed.

JACKIE: Don't blame Dad for this—

BEVERLY: *(Continuous.)* And, you know, frankly, I find it mildly ironic that someone who just got expelled *from college* for selling drugs is now lecturing me on how to comport myself. *(She smiles at her.)*

JACKIE: There! There it is.

BEVERLY: What?

JACKIE: Do you know anything about sharks, Mom?

BEVERLY: What are you talking about, Jackie? Are you high now? Is this some sort of drug—

(JACKIE advances towards BEVERLY, who, confused, backs up—they end up making a circuit around the table.)

JACKIE: Did you know that before it attacks, a shark's eyes will roll back into its head?

BEVERLY: *(A weak laugh.)* Are you trying to be like your father, now? Mr. Trivia?

JACKIE: Some species of shark are known to eat their own young, didja know that?

BEVERLY: This isn't funny, Jacqueline.

JACKIE: Even bottlenose dolphins occasionally pummel their young to death with their snouts. Ever heard of maternal infanticide, Mom?

BEVERLY: Jacqueline, stop it.

JACKIE: It's a surprisingly common occurrence in the wild. Every so often, the mom just decides to up and kill her own offspring for some crazy reason—

BEVERLY: JACKIE!

JACKIE: Just something I learned at one of my science classes BEFORE I GOT EXPELLED FROM COLLEGE! *(She grabs her purse and heads for the door.)* Bye, Aunt April and Grams. Love you guys.

(She exits. We hear the door outside slam. Perhaps the very distant sound of questions being asked by the reporters in the yard.)

BEVERLY: *(Calling after her.)* When you get home, give your father your keys, you're not supposed to be driving!

(We hear the sound of a car driving away.)

BEVERLY: Unbelievable. I just can*not* believe her. *(To APRIL and PEN.)* Did you believe that? She is just so…

APRIL: Unbelievable?

BEVERLY: So I wasn't able to call her while I was in the *hospital*. While I was being tested, and—and examined, and stitched up. And she makes me seem like, like, what, a negligent mother? Well, I'm sorry!

PEN: Tell *her* that, Beverly.

BEVERLY: And you two don't even care that I'm here. This is just wonderful.

(PEN and APRIL both sigh.)

APRIL: We're just not used to being in the presence of a celebrity, Beverly.

BEVERLY: Of a—? Oh, of course. Of course... *(She pulls out a vial of pills from her purse, puts one in her mouth, and drinks from the glass on the table. Then:)* So, how are you two?

APRIL: *(Slowly, quietly.)* What's going on, Beverly? Why are you here? Why didn't you tell us you were coming?

(Beat.)

BEVERLY: *(Trying the pity card.)* I was released from the hospital today. They've been running tests on me for weeks now: testing and retesting my blood, my saliva—every fluid you can imagine. It was scary. *(Nervous laugh.)* I think they were thinking—because of, you know, the movies—that getting bit... *turns* you into one of... them. Apparently, there are big hush-hush operations going on; they're trying to see if this is bacterial, or viral, and if it *does* carry, what that would do to a living person. Dr. Lawrence thinks that, if it is communicable, the bite would have to come before the, um, returned decedent's fluids have dried. A *fresh* one. Which is scary. But— *(She slips into her stump speech.)* —that's all the more reason I think we need to destroy them now, you know? Before it can spread. Why wait, why risk it? And people are coming 'round to it. There's talk of legislation being passed, and everything, to neutralize the threat, to cut this off at the pass, so to speak—

APRIL: *(Snorts.)* "Neutralize the threat." How long have you wanted to be Patty Hearst, Bev?

(Pause. BEVERLY looks stung.)

APRIL: I'm sorry.

BEVERLY: I'm not trying to *be* anything, April. I'm— *(Her cell phone rings.)* Shoot, I've been expecting this. *(She digs it out of her purse, along with a day planner, and answers.)* This is Beverly Colby-Parker, how can I help you? *(Pause.)* Of course, yes, Melinda, thank you for calling.

(PEN gets up and goes to the stove, starts fiddling with the teapot.)

APRIL: What are you doing, Ma?

BEVERLY: *(Into the phone.)* Yes, I think—yeah, that works just fine. Great. Thursday it is. Thank you so much for getting in touch with me, Melinda.

APRIL: Mom?

PEN: I just want some tea.

APRIL: Mom, you've got tea right here.

PEN: I what?

(APRIL gets up and hands PEN the mug of tea from the table.)

BEVERLY: *(Into the phone.)* Sure, sure.

PEN: Oh, thank you. How did you know I wanted tea?

APRIL: *(Concerned.)* Come and sit down, Mom.

PEN: *(Whispering.)* Beverly's here, did you know? Let's hear what she has to say.

(APRIL sits her down, at a loss for words.)

BEVERLY: *(Into the phone.)* Wonderful. We'll chat more tomorrow, then. Bye-bye. *(She hangs up.)* They've asked me to be on *The Today Show.* Isn't that nice?

PEN: You made this tea too cold, April.

(APRIL starts to laugh, in spite of herself. It's desperate-sounding, almost like hiccups. She starts fanning herself and gets it quickly under control.)

BEVERLY: Are you alright?

APRIL: Daaaaandy.

BEVERLY: May I ask what Jackie was doing here?

APRIL: What?

BEVERLY: What was Jackie doing here?

APRIL: She got tired of all the press people and reporters at your place. She came over here for a little peace and quiet. That okay with you?

BEVERLY: There are a lot at the house?

APRIL: Apparently. I've had to shoo a bunch from here, too, you know. We're all basking in the rays of your rising star. Thankfully they've been pretty easygoing. So far, at least. Now that you're out, who the fuck knows? I'm sure the ones outside'll start breeding shortly.

BEVERLY: You say that like this is my fault.

APRIL: No, I don't, Beverly. I say it like the fact that it is.

BEVERLY: So there's a little press coverage? That's fine, I'm trying to *help*. There were only a *few* outside and they're all local.

APRIL: Oh, come on, *The Today Show*?

PEN: Girls, please.

APRIL: Why are you here, Beverly? Just fucking admit it.

PEN: April, don't curse.

APRIL: Mom! *(To BEVERLY.)* Well?

BEVERLY: I'm not going to rise to this baiting, April.

APRIL: Why. Are. You. Here?

BEVERLY: I wanted to see you.

APRIL: Bullshit, you didn't know I was here.

BEVERLY: I wanted to see Mom, too.

APRIL: You're such a fucking politician, Beverly.

PEN: If you girls don't stop arguing, you can both leave, okay?

(APRIL laughs curtly.)

BEVERLY: I wanted to check in on Mom, and I figured you would be here because you have been helping out so much lately—which I'm very appreciative of, considering I was *in the hospital* and couldn't do it myself.

PEN: I don't need help.

BEVERLY: *(Turns on her, as if noticing her for the first time.)* And, Mom, I need *you* to know that you were housing a dangerous animal, before.

PEN: What?

BEVERLY: *(Overlapping.)* And I *sincerely* hope you are not continuing to do so. I don't know where he disappeared to after he attacked me, but— *(She holds her bandaged arm up.)* It's not safe, Mom. Do you understand? He is not safe. Nor is he Dad.

PEN: Beverly—

BEVERLY: He is dangerous. And, as your daughter, as your daughter who cares about you—

APRIL: *(Overlapping.)* What's that supposed to mean?

BEVERLY: *(Continuous.)* —I want to make sure you're not doing something that could potentially hurt you or, God forbid, anything worse.

PEN: Don't talk down to me, Beverly, I'm your mother.

BEVERLY: He's here, isn't he? You hid him somewhere while I was being taken to the hospital, didn't you?

APRIL: Beverly...

PEN: N—

BEVERLY: He wandered away while I was bleeding in the kitchen and you hid him somewhere?

PEN: *(Momentarily flummoxed.)* No. You...are wrong, Beverly.

BEVERLY: You're delusional, Mom. And that's okay, I can understand, given your age and your relationship with Daddy—he had no problem controlling you while he was alive, so it's no wonder you—

PEN: Don't you say that!

APRIL: Come on, Beverly!

BEVERLY: What? I'm not being out of line here, okay? I'm *helping*.

APRIL: You need to look that word up, for fuck's sake!

BEVERLY: IF HE IS HERE, I WILL REPORT HIM. I'M SORRY, BUT I WILL. *(Beat.)* I can get them to search this house.

APRIL: Them? Who's them?

BEVERLY: *(Firmly.)* I am only trying to help.

APRIL: Who's them?

PEN: *(Close to tears.)* You are not helping, Beverly. You are not h—I don't feel well.

APRIL: Mom, are you okay?

PEN: I'm just a little dizzy.

APRIL: Do you want anything? Can I do something?

PEN: I think...I think I need to lie down again.

APRIL: Sure, Mom. Go upstairs and lie down. Do you want some help?

BEVERLY: I can help you upstairs, Mom.

PEN: No. *(She stands, wobbly at first.)* No, I don't need any help. *(She goes to BEVERLY.)* I do not need. Any. Help. *(PEN makes her way out.)*

APRIL: Call me if you need anything, Mom.

BEVERLY: *(As PEN exits.)* Mom, please don't be like this! *(Beat. She sighs.)* Is he still here, April? Please just tell me. Please.

(Beat.)

BEVERLY: Fine, I'm going to go look around—

APRIL: How's your arm?

BEVERLY: Hurts. And itches.

APRIL: Did he really...bite you?

BEVERLY: Why would I make that up, April?

(Beat.)

APRIL: How did it happen? Really?

BEVERLY: *(As if APRIL has heard this a million times already.)* I was standing here. Mom had gone to bed. He was at the table. I...I wanted to get a better look at him, so I reached out to him and he just *bit* into me.

APRIL: And then?

BEVERLY: Then I did what we should've done all along and I called the authorities.

APRIL: Why didn't they get him when they came for you?

BEVERLY: While I was on the phone, he wandered away. I didn't notice, I was just so—I was in pain, and the adrenaline, and the blood. I looked up and he was gone. And then Mom was awake, she was downstairs, and they came, and took me to the hospital while they talked to Mom and called David—

APRIL: And me.

BEVERLY: Everyone that was here, yes. To confirm that he had come back. Why don't you believe me, April?

APRIL: Why don't you believe *her*, Beverly?

BEVERLY: Because! There's no way he could've gotten so far away that they couldn't find him. Someone had to help. And because I think Mom is just unbalanced enough now—

APRIL: *(Overlapping.)* She's not unbalanced—

BEVERLY: —that she feels that maybe Daddy isn't dead, or that he's going to, I don't know, come back more fully, or something. You know as well as I do that she's losing it. And quickly. Dad's death really shook her up, and this whole *situation* isn't making it any better, for sure.

APRIL: *(Groans.)* I don't know, I don't know. *(She fans herself.)* Are you burning up right now?

BEVERLY: No, I'm fine.

APRIL: *(Grabs herself another cold soda from the fridge and presses it to her neck.)* I don't know…

(Pause.)

BEVERLY: The only thing I can't figure out is where she could have put him. I was told they looked around, but they didn't find…anything.

APRIL:*(Pressing the can against her forehead.)* So much for your theory, then.

(Beat.)

BEVERLY: *(Eying APRIL suspiciously.)* I'm going to go talk to Mom—

APRIL: *(Stepping in front of her.)* Beverly! I swear to God, I will pull your hair right out of your scalp if you go up there right now.

BEVERLY: Jesus, April. What, are you ten now?

APRIL: I just…I don't want to stress her out any more than she already is.

BEVERLY: Oh, I'm just a "stress" to her now?

APRIL: Oh, Jesus. *Please.* Just give her some room. Okay?

BEVERLY: Fine. Just fine. *(Beat. With some malice.)* April, are you getting hot flashes?

APRIL: Oh, Jesus…

BEVERLY: How long have they been happening?

APRIL: Only once in a while. Not often. I'm probably just stressed.

BEVERLY: It begins…

APRIL: Oh, God, don't say that!

(APRIL's cell phone rings. She checks it, groans loudly, and silences it.)

BEVERLY: What?

APRIL: Nothing. It's Josh.

(The house phone rings.)

APRIL: Oh, suck my dick!

BEVERLY: So I should get that?

APRIL: Yes. Good. Fine.

(BEVERLY goes to answer the phone. APRIL goes to her purse, pulls out the Baggie she got from JACKIE, and begins to roll a joint.)

BEVERLY: Colby residence, this is Beverly Colby-Parker speaking. *(Pause.)* Yes. *(Pause.)* Yes, I was released today. I came to be with my family. *(Pause.)* No, we haven't found him yet. *(Pause.)* No, excuse me. I would like for the calls to this number to cease immediately. This is a private residence. Any questions can be addressed through my publicist to me directly. *(Pause.)* Yes, thank you. Yourself, as well. *(She hangs up.)* There, that should take care of the calls. You're welcome.

APRIL: You have a publicist...?

BEVERLY: Of course I do, my exposure has gotten pretty— *(Sees what APRIL is doing.)* What is that?! What are you doing?!

APRIL: *(Finishes rolling and lights up.)* My mother's brain is going in and out like poorly run pirate radio. My soon-to-be-ex-husband is drinking himself to death. My sister's starring in the George Romero version of *The Legend of Billie Jean*. My niece just got kicked out of college. And now I'm getting hot flashes. I mean, Christ, the dead are coming back to life and that's the least of my fucking concerns. *(She inhales deeply, almost desperately.)*

BEVERLY: April, you can't do that—

APRIL: Tell me something. You've been getting them, too, right? Right?

BEVERLY: What?

APRIL: You know.

BEVERLY: Oh—

APRIL: Come on.

BEVERLY: ...I try not to think about them.

APRIL: *(While smoking; chuckling.)* I know exactly what you mean. Maybe they'll go away. I dunno, I tried to entertain the idea that maybe I'd be able to have kids outside of Me and Josh, that after all this shit gets settled, there'd be some time to start another life with someone else, but I guess that's getting the big biological thumbs-down. It's so stupid. I don't know why our bodies do what they do.

(BEVERLY starts to get too close to the door to the living room.)

APRIL: Hey!

(APRIL hands the joint out to BEVERLY, who stares at it like some sort of alien object.)

APRIL: Seriously?

BEVERLY: April...

APRIL: Come on. Share something with me. Before three weeks ago, I hadn't seen you in years.

BEVERLY: That was your doing.

APRIL: Yeah, and it was your fault.

BEVERLY: No. I can't. It's too early, I haven't eaten much today, someone could see. I shouldn't.

APRIL: *(Laughing.)* Someone could see. Suit yourself.

(APRIL takes a hit. A moment. Impulsively, BEVERLY reaches over and takes it. She inhales, starts to say, "Happy?," then falls into a rough coughing fit.)

APRIL: How the hell are you my sister?

BEVERLY: *(While coughing.)* Oh, you're just sooo cool, April.

(APRIL takes the joint back, laughing.)

BEVERLY: Truth is, they terrify me.

APRIL: What?

BEVERLY: Hot flashes.

APRIL: *(Handing the joint back.)* What? How so? You've already had kids.

BEVERLY: *(Re. the joint.)* No, I shouldn't. *(She takes it.)* Because. It's one more item on the checklist.

APRIL: The checklist?

BEVERLY: Of Things to Happen Before You Die. And it's somewhere near the bottom.

APRIL: That's not true. There's plenty of time between death and...you know.

BEVERLY: *(Starts to laugh.)* We daren't speak its name. Oohhhh. *(She laughs more.)*

APRIL: *(Starting to laugh.)* Oh, man, you're a lightweight. Most people don't even feel it their first time.

BEVERLY: It's not my *first* time. I've experimented, too, you know.

APRIL: Oh, no! I hope Hank Harrison doesn't find out!

BEVERLY: Yes, the attack ads will fly, my pretty! *(Beat.)* I told David to meet me here in about an hour. *(She gets up and paces.)* I can't be stoned when he comes. I can't believe we're getting stoned, this is such a terrible idea. I'm gonna go check on Mom.

APRIL: *(Eager to keep her in the room.)* Where is he?

BEVERLY: What? Who? David?

APRIL: No, Yul Brynner. Yes, David.

BEVERLY: He had some work to do in the city.

APRIL: He didn't take it off to meet you at the hospital?

BEVERLY: I told him not to.

(APRIL laughs snidely—"You are a strange one"—and shakes her head. BEVERLY takes the joint and pulls a hit off it. It's nearing the end. Beat.)

APRIL: Do you still love him?

BEVERLY: What?

APRIL: David.

BEVERLY: April, why would you ask me—

APRIL: You guys have been married for so long, I mean...I don't know if I still love Josh. I really don't know. *(Beat.)* I honestly don't know if I remember what it feels like.

BEVERLY: Oh. *(Beat.)* May I ask what happ—?

APRIL: *(Suddenly laughing.)* I walked in on him fooling around with one of his students!

BEVERLY: Oh...oh.

APRIL: Yeah. They were over at our place, watching a video of *Crimes of the Heart*, actually, for that fucking class, and, of course, Josh had been drinking, and...I got an eyeful!

BEVERLY: I'm so sorry. Oh, that's awful. *(Beat. Suddenly.)* How old was she?

APRIL: *(Laughing harder.)* Old enough, that wasn't the issue. The kid was old enough. *(Beat.)* Handsome kid, too. I believe his name is Ted.

BEVERLY: What?

(APRIL nods.)

BEVERLY: Oh, my God.

APRIL: That's what he said!

BEVERLY: I don't know what to say.

APRIL: You and me both.

BEVERLY: Did you have any idea?

APRIL: It explains some things. I mean, maybe that's why he always drank so much—'cause he's so deep in fucking denial. And why we never got around to having kids. Supposedly, we both wanted them, but… *(She's laughing even harder.)* I shouldn't be laying any of this on you, I'm sorry. I'm sorry, this is just way too movie-of-the-week to even discuss. I should just shut the fuck up right now, before we crack open the Häagen-Dazs and have ourselves a good cry.

BEVERLY: April, please—

APRIL: He got fired, too! Starting going to his classes drunk. I guess I can take credit for that. After I kicked him out, he started drinking even more. Which is saying something. So, career-wise, this has also been— *(She puts an imaginary gun to her head and pulls the trigger.)* Another perk of being involved with me. Good ol' April, such a delight to be around, eh?

BEVERLY: Stop that.

APRIL: And, by the way, it's not like I'm not cool with him being…whatever, you know? That's fine…That's just fine…That was just the nail in the coffin. *(Beat. Laugh.)* I don't know why I'm getting upset. I mean, the closest thing we ever had to a family together was when, like, Jackie would come over and hang out, so it's not like it's the end of the world or anything.

BEVERLY: Jackie visits you guys?

APRIL: Uh. Not that often, just to say…hi.

BEVERLY: Oh. I'm sorry, go on.

APRIL: Oh…well, he won't stop calling and asking for me to…"take him back" and everything. That he's so sorry. I keep telling him that it's okay, that he needs to *embrace* who he is, that this is a big change and he shouldn't worry about me, and blah, blah, blah. You know… *(Pause.)* Fuck him. *(She suddenly slams the table, completely enraged, hurt, and ugly.)* FUCK HIM! *(Beat. She calms a little.)* You know? I could've dealt with a woman, that's the fucked-up part. I could have dealt with that. Objectively, like, I know I'm supposed to be the modern woman, the accepting one. But I can barely fucking look at him at this point. I can barely look at *myself*, you know? Ugh, and the clichés keep flying! Josh told me once that lazy dramatists use drugs to facilitate catharsis, so for his sake, I should just stop—

(BEVERLY puts her hand on APRIL's, who immediately stops talking.)

APRIL: What is that? What are you doing?

BEVERLY: I'm…so sorry for what you're going through right now. Because you are a very…*good* person. And this is a shame. You're so…I can't think of the word.

APRIL: Pathetic? Retarded?

BEVERLY: Shh. No. Spirited. *Free.* *(Beat.)* I wish I could be like that.

(APRIL almost looks as if she's physically uncomfortable—she pulls her hand away.)

BEVERLY: What?

APRIL: I don't know how to take that, Beverly. I don't think you've given me a compliment before.

BEVERLY: That's not true.

APRIL: Coming on five decades and I can't recall—

BEVERLY: *(Very offended.)* That's not true! You just don't want to remember them because it's inconvenient to the caricature you've built up of me in your head. I'm trying to be honest with you! I've always respected you. I've always admired you. God, April, I've always wanted to be your friend.

APRIL: I'm sorry. Thank you.

BEVERLY: No, you know what? To hell with you. I know what you all think of me—I'm not stupid. I *know*. None of you like me. Even my own fucking daughters. But none of you—none of you—ever bothers to see things from my point of view. Ever. I mean, all I've given up for this family! *(An angry laugh.)* Do you think I wanted to be just a fucking *Assemblywoman*? I could have gone somewhere, you know! I could've! I had chances! But someone had to stay close and make sure Mom and Dad were taken care of, you know, someone has to remind them of their doctors' appointments, and their stupid little errands, and it apparently wasn't going to be you, so…And what's my reward for all of it? I get turned into a damned punch line, and the minute—the *minute!*—it looks like maybe I can actually make something of myself, make a difference, and you all just can't wait to jump down my throat. So, you know, thanks a lot. You have no idea how lonely this fucking family can be.

APRIL: Yes, I do. *(Pause.)* And you're right. *(Long pause.)* You know, I've always admired—

BEVERLY: Oh, don't. You don't have to feel obligated to—

APRIL: Shut up, would you? Just shut up. I've always admired how…*together* you are. I mean, I know how stupid that sounds, but *I* could never…You're so much better at it than…Like, even a few weeks ago, when Dad had…y'know, *come back*, and—you remember? He fell down and you just walked over there and put him back in his seat without blinking? I really…

BEVERLY: Thank you.

APRIL: I mean it.

(They look at each other for a moment.)

APRIL: What was that waiter's name? *Jean-Luc!!!*

BEVERLY: What?

APRIL: Forget it. How 'bout that Zombie Apocalypse, eh?

BEVERLY: Oh my God, I'm woozy. *(Beat.)* Is Dad still here?

APRIL: *(Quickly getting another joint ready.)* Do you want another one?

BEVERLY: No, no, no.

(APRIL stops, laughing.)

BEVERLY: I bet you didn't watch any of my press conferences. Did you?

APRIL: No, I watched a…a couple…

BEVERLY: Yeah…

APRIL: I don't know, Beverly, I'm still very much on the fence about…

BEVERLY: About what?

APRIL: About this Kill 'Em All mentality you've got going on. It just doesn't seem...*right*. All the footage I've seen; even how Dad was acting. I dunno, it doesn't seem right. They don't seem violent.

(BEVERLY starts to speak.)

APRIL: I haven't heard of any other *reputable* cases of attacks.

BEVERLY: That doesn't mean it's not true; that doesn't mean that we're not in danger.

APRIL: You've got people really scared, Beverly.

BEVERLY: They should be.

APRIL: There's so much we don't know about what's happening.

BEVERLY: What do we need to know?

APRIL: Everything! Are they aware? Are they in pain?

BEVERLY: They're dead. They died.

APRIL: Y'know, what if it's a sign, or something?

BEVERLY: It *is* a sign, April. Of bad things.

APRIL: What if they're not here to hurt us? What if they're here to warn us? Or show us something. To communicate something.

BEVERLY: You're sounding crazy, April. You are sounding crazy.

APRIL: *(Continuous.)* Like, I dunno, the flood.

BEVERLY: The flood came to kill people!

APRIL: I know. But it was a *sign* that people needed to change their ways. You know? Maybe that's a bad example, I don't know. But, either way, maybe it's, like, a *divine* gesture. A sign that something greater than us exists. I mean, I don't know, I'm thinking off the top of my head here.

BEVERLY: I'm going to tell you a joke, April.

APRIL: Okay. Thanks for the warning.

BEVERLY: *(Ignoring that comment.)* So, there's a flood, right? And there's a man who is living in an area that's about to be hit very badly. And the government comes to his door and says, "We're evacuating the area, come with us and we'll keep you safe." And the guy says, "No, no, I'm staying right here. The Lord will provide me with what I need to survive." And so he stays where he is. And the flood hits, and everything is underwater, and he's sitting on top of his roof, and some people in a rowboat show up. They say, "Get in the rowboat, we'll take you to safety." And the man says, "No, no, I'm staying right here. The Lord will provide me with what I need to survive." And they row away. And eventually, the man starves to death. And he goes up in heaven and he meets Jesus, and he says to Jesus, "What happened, Lord? I thought you would provide me with what I needed to survive." And Jesus looks at him and says, "What are you talking about? You didn't get the evacuation notice? And the guys I sent in the rowboat?" *(Beat.)* Do you get it?

(A pause as APRIL considers.)

APRIL: You're presupposing that God exists.

BEVERLY: But do you get what it's trying to say?

APRIL: You're saying this is an act of God.

BEVERLY: No, April, it's saying that you have to be realistic about things. Proactive. Responsive.

APRIL: I know what it *means*, Beverly, I'm not stupid. But it falls apart without the divine element.

BEVERLY: No, it d—

APRIL: Listen to me. Your guy was an idiot, yes, because he ignored obvious gestures of aid at his own peril.

(BEVERLY starts to speak.)

APRIL: But! You're also saying that he turned away messengers of God's will.

BEVERLY: *(Growing frustrated.)* It's not a biblical parable, April! And since when are you religious, anyway?

APRIL: The people at his door. The people in the rowboat. "The Lord will provide." Sent by God to tell him something—

BEVERLY: The God part is irrelevant!

APRIL: This is not a natural occurrence; there is something at work here. There must be.

BEVERLY: You sound desperate, April.

APRIL: We have to hope that there is meaning behind this!

BEVERLY: Why? Why do we have to?

APRIL: Because it's that or go insane.

BEVERLY: No, it's that or *cope*. Survive. Maybe if you'd listen to some of my press conferences you'd realize that. I was attacked, April. And I was lucky that I escaped with just some stitches—

APRIL: —And a publicist—

BEVERLY: Not to mention the fact that there are thousands of logistical questions. What do we do, wait for them to rot? Do we put them to work? What about other diseases? I mean, April, do you think the world should just roll over and wait? This is a serious situation, and we are at risk, whether you "feel it" or not. I guarantee you that. *(She gestures at APRIL with her arm, near tears.)* I guarantee you that.

APRIL: I don't believe you.

(Beat.)

BEVERLY: What?

APRIL: I don't believe your story. I'm sorry, I don't. I love you, I respect you. I'm, against all logic and precedent, enjoying this conversation with you. But I don't believe you. I don't think Dad bit you.

BEVERLY: How did I get this then, April?

APRIL: I don't know.

BEVERLY: Why would I make that up?

APRIL: I don't know.

BEVERLY: What kind of person do you think I am?!

APRIL: Maybe it has nothing to do with *you*, Beverly! *(Beat.)* But I don't believe it. Okay?

(A long pause.)

BEVERLY: You and Dad were really close, right?

APRIL: Yeah, I guess so. For a little while there.

(Beat.)

BEVERLY: Can I ask you something. About him?

APRIL: He never said he was planning on coming back from the dead, if that's what you're wondering.

BEVERLY: Please be serious, April. I need to…there's something I need to know.

APRIL: Okay, okay. I'm sorry. Please.

BEVERLY: *(Takes a breath; this is hard.)* Did Dad—

PEN: *(Suddenly, from upstairs, screaming.)* APRIL!!!

(APRIL immediately holds up a hand to BEVERLY, stopping her, then rushes out of the room. After the briefest of moments, BEVERLY follows. Sam Cooke and the Soul Stirrers' "I'm So Glad" plays. Lights fade.)

SCENE FOUR

The song fades, the lights rise. DAVID enters the kitchen. He looks concerned. He makes a beeline for the table. Once he's there, he notices an oddly distinct smell, and sniffs the air, confused. After a moment, the phone rings. He goes to answer it.

DAVID: Colby residence. *(Pause.)* No, I'm sorry, she's not available at the moment. *(Pause.)* I can't say. Personal matters. *(Pause.)* No, I have no comment, either. I'm sorry, I—what? David Parker. *(Pause.)* Yes, her husband. *(Pause.)* Yes. *(Pause.)* I sell catheters. *(Pause.)* Catheters, yes. *(Pause.)* No, we sell other products as well, a variety of plastics and organic fasteners to hospitals and—I'm sorry? *(Pause.)* Well, of course, we're very relieved she's alright.

(JOSH stumbles in around "I'm sorry," looking harried.)

JOSH: *(Overlapping.)* Christ, what the fuck are they expecting to take pictures of, anyway? I should show 'em my undead asshole. Goddamn vultures. Hey, David, how's it going?

DAVID: *(Waving to JOSH.)* Uh-huh, that's correct. *(Pause.)* No, I didn't speak to her much during her stay, it was pretty difficult to get ahold of her—

JOSH: *(Overlapping.)* Hey! Are you on the phone with one of those reporters?!

DAVID: *(Continuing.)* —what with all the tests they were running, and everything, but our marriage is such that—

(JOSH heads over to the phone's cradle and ends the connection.)

DAVID: *(Still into the phone.)* —we're able to communicate without really needing to— *(He hears the dial tone.)* Hello? Hello? *(Realizes.)* Hey, what was that for?!

JOSH: Why the hell are you talking to them?!

DAVID: I was just giving them my information, Josh.

JOSH: Don't talk to them.

DAVID: Don't tell *me* what to do. Please.

(Beat.)

JOSH: Sorry. Where is everyone?

DAVID: I just got here, and I heard them fighting upstairs, so I figured I'd stay down here and wait.

JOSH: Fighting? About what?

DAVID: Does it matter?

JOSH: *(Gives a little laugh.)* Too true. *(Pause.)* How's it going, Dave?

DAVID: Fine, fine. You know. Tired. Lots of work to do.

JOSH: Yeah?

DAVID: Yeah.

(Awkward pause.)

JOSH: What do you do, again?

(At that moment, BEVERLY bursts in. She's close to tears and indelibly enraged.)

BEVERLY: David!

DAVID: Hi, hon—

BEVERLY: He's here. I fucking knew it. He's been here this whole time. She's been hiding him upstairs.

DAVID: Whoa, slow down, you shouldn't be so agita—

BEVERLY: Don't fucking tell me to slow down!

JOSH: Beverly, take it easy.

BEVERLY: Oh, good to see you, Josh. Glad you were able to pry your mouth off of your students to come and join us.

(JOSH is stunned by that. APRIL enters.)

APRIL: Beverly! We're not finished! You left Mom a wreck up there.

BEVERLY: *(Quickly.)* Mom means nothing to me, April. Okay? Nothing. I'm done with her. I'm calling the authorities, and I'm getting her put away.

APRIL: Put away! I'm not a fan of this either, Beverly, but let's just discuss this rationally, okay? Okay?

BEVERLY: Come on, David, we're leaving.

APRIL: Beverly!

BEVERLY: She's insane, April, okay? She's as brain dead as he is. And I'm sorry, but I have to do this. *(To DAVID.)* Do we still have press outside our house? It's all local here.

(DAVID nods.)

BEVERLY: Let's go.

(She storms out. APRIL stops DAVID.)

APRIL: Dave, please, wait just a sec. Could you please just talk to her—

BEVERLY: *(Offstage.)* DAVID!

APRIL: Please. Just get her to see reason here.

(Beat. DAVID leaves. APRIL turns and sees JOSH. They stare at each other.)

JOSH: *(With a hint of venom.)* Hi.

APRIL: What are you doing here?

JOSH: Wanted to help. Wanted to see you.

APRIL: Oh.

JOSH: Guess you don't need me. *(Beat.)* Pen okay?

APRIL: She's upstairs, sobbing.

JOSH: Oh.

APRIL: With him.

JOSH: Oh.

APRIL: His ear came off in her hand and she screamed.

JOSH: Oh.

APRIL: How are you?

JOSH: Drunk.

APRIL: *(Disappointed.)* Josh. I really wish that you would stop—	JOSH: Did you tell Beverly—?

APRIL: *(Not hearing.)* What?

JOSH: *(Decides not to tell her.)* Nothing.

APRIL: What?

JOSH: Nothing. I'm gonna go. *(Beat. He turns to leave, then stops.)* I'll be by to pick up some more of my stuff on Monday or so.

APRIL: Okay. Hey. *(Pause.)*

JOSH: *(Turns.)* What?

APRIL: *(An idea hits her.)* Are there still reporters outside?

JOSH: Yeah, a few.

APRIL: …Thanks.

JOSH: Yup.

(He leaves. APRIL sits at the table. Lights fade.)

Scene Five

Lights rise as JACKIE walks across the stage, holding a Slurpee and a set of car keys. She looks out into the audience.

JACKIE: Oh, come on guys, I'm just buying a friggin' Slurpee. No comment, or whatever. Okay? Seriously. Could you get away from my car, please? No? Okay, how about this. Here's my statement for you. Ready? *(She clears her throat, then rattles off her essay question at lightning speed.)* "The secret to fully understanding the complexity of 'The Grand Inquisitor' lies in what Dostoevsky leaves out of the story. Namely, what happens to the people who witnessed Jesus's miracles before he was arrested. Is that little girl, in the end, as insignificant in rebirth as she was in death? How does this relate to Dostoevsky's greater existential proclivities? Please answer, in no less than four thousand words, placing Ivan's fable into the context of the *Karamazov* plot and in our class as a whole." Chew on that, ya fucktards. All responses should be sent to Professor Henry Matos, care of Connecticut College, Department of English. *(Laughing.)* Aw, come on, where you guys going?

(Lights fade on JACKIE. She exits. Suddenly, on the upstage wall, is a projection of BEVERLY speaking to reporters in front of her own house. DAVID stands behind her, dutifully, supportively. Despite her relative ease with speaking to the press, she sounds shaken, not wanting to have to do this. A network news crawl unravels beneath them.)

BEVERLY: Hi, everybody. Sorry to keep you waiting. *(To someone in the crowd.)* Good to see you, Barbara. *(To all.)* Anyway, as you all know, I was released from the hospital today after all that extensive clinical testing. And I'm doing good. Except, on my way home, I stopped at my mother's house—the place where I was viciously attacked by one of those *things*.

(A special rises on APRIL in another area of the stage. She speaks to reporters outside, facing the audience. She's nervous; ready to throw a Hail Mary.)

APRIL: Excuse me? Hi. Uh, my name is April. Uh, Colby. I'm Beverly's sister. I actually have a statement for you. I'll…be right back. Sorry, one sec. *(She exits.)*

BEVERLY: First off, I want to say that I'm saddened by the number of photographers and press waiting outside there—my mother is going through a very difficult time right now and doesn't need that stress. All inquiries about me should be made *to* me. I hope that's understood. Anyway, when I got there, I found that my mother was housing—*hiding*—the creature that did *this* to me. *(She holds up her arm).* So, I want you all to know, I have reported the incident to 811. And I'm sure she'll do all she can to prevent his retrieval. My mother, unfortunately, is going senile. I didn't mention this in any of my recent statements, because I was trying to respect her privacy. However, I feel it's illustrative of a greater point. When she found my father, the first thing she did was... *(She hesitates. DAVID comfortingly rubs her back.)*

APRIL: *(Reenters to her special position.)* Hi. Thanks for waiting. I need to show you this.

BEVERLY: I'm sorry. The first thing she did was...get in the shower with him. To clean him.

APRIL: This is my father.

(APRIL brings ADAM into the light. He is thinner than before, somehow simultaneously paler and greener. There is a bandage over his missing ear.)

BEVERLY: It is absolutely tragic.

APRIL: Please, calm down, relax. You're totally safe.

BEVERLY: Her mind is going, and it is going quickly.

APRIL: I guess none of you have gotten to be in the presence of one of these—them—yet.

BEVERLY: But—

APRIL: YouTube feels a little different, eh?

BEVERLY: It seems to me that our *society* is showing a similar lapse in judgment.

APRIL: I want you to see something. I want to confirm this.

(She sticks her arm near his mouth. He, of course, does nothing.)

BEVERLY: You see, my mother is suffering from the delusion that my father has come back from the dead. That, if she cleans him up, she can reenter him into society. That's not the case. My father *is* dead. All of our loved ones who have passed—they're still dead. There is no coming back.

APRIL: See? Nothing.

BEVERLY: We're in the beginning stages of something that's only going to get worse, folks. We all know it.

APRIL: He's harmless. They're all harmless.

BEVERLY: I've been telling you this for weeks, folks.

(ADAM wanders away from APRIL.)

APRIL: I don't think my sister is telling you the truth...

BEVERLY: People, people like my mother, shouldn't even have the *chance* to indulge in their delusions.

APRIL: *(Noticing ADAM's gone)* Oh, that's alright, he does that.

BEVERLY: I mean, the fact that all the footage of these monsters doesn't end with them being immediately shot in the head is just disgraceful!

APRIL: *(Shouting off.)* Mom, make sure you get him.

BEVERLY: This has affected my life in many, many ways. I know how confusing and hard it is to deal with a deceased family member returning.

APRIL: *(Shouting to PEN.)* Just get him inside, okay?

BEVERLY: But, do we want to be duped by our own nostalgia? I mean, did we learn nothing from terrorism? That sometimes our own trusting, Christian nature opens us up to a vulnerability tantamount to encouragement? Do we want to *ask* to be destroyed?

APRIL: Um, so I just wanted to show y'all that. And I also wanted to say something…

(The projection of BEVERLY fades somewhat.)

APRIL: I'm sure my sister has alerted the authorities, and I'm sure whoever is on their way here will take my father and do God-knows-what to him. But, I…this— *(She holds up her unbitten arm.)* —is undeniable. I…don't think we're in any danger. And so, then…this should be a private, family matter. He is ours. And we should be able to decide what to do with him in the end. Anyway, sorry for talking your ear off. That's all I've got to say. We'll be inside, waiting. With my father. Safely. If you guys wanna print all that, or whatever you do, that'd be great. Oh, um. Any questions?

(Lights fade on APRIL. Crossfade up on BEVERLY's conference, still speaking.)

BEVERLY: And here's the thing. I'm not a violent person. I just think this is our chance. In fact, if you think about it, this is happening all over the world. We can unite! As a *species*, as the human race! Us against them! Come together. In a way, it's…it's almost beautiful.

(BEVERLY's cell phone rings. She absently hands it to DAVID, who answers it quietly.)

BEVERLY: I mean, folks. I love this country so much. So much. And I don't want to see anything like this— *(She holds up her bandaged arm.)* —happen again. Not given the stakes involved. Not to the country I love.

(DAVID whispers to BEVERLY, then hands the phone to her.)

BEVERLY: I'm sorry, folks, one moment. Bear with me, it's been a crazy day. *(She listens. Sadly.)* Oh. Oh, my. Thank you. *(She hangs up.)* I'm sorry. I just received some…terrible news. My sister…well, she's apparently *also* speaking to the press right now. And she's saying that I'm a liar. *(She laughs mournfully—covering the anger.)* I won't lie, I'm hurt by that. But this proves my point. Do you see what I mean about delusions? My sister is a wonderful daughter. An absolutely supportive and trusting person. And I certainly don't begrudge her the right to voice her opinions—not in this wonderful nation of ours. *(Beat. Almost to herself, bitterly.)* But, I mean, why anyone would want to take the word of a woman who habitually uses drugs, and drives her husband into the arms of an underaged boy, is beyond me.

(Beat. She catches DAVID's look.)

BEVERLY: Oh, I'm sorry, I shouldn't say things like that. That's personal. Forget I said that. Anyway, I'll be more than happy to field your questions. And I'm pleased to announce that I'll be speaking on *The Today Show* next week; more details will be available on my website. Yes, Cathy, your hand was up first?

(The video fades away. The stage is dark for a moment. A special rises on JOSH, pacing. One hand holds a phone to his ear; the other is holding a nearly empty bottle.)

JOSH: *(After a moment, into the phone.)* Hey. It's Josh. You…are not picking up your phone. Again. *(Very long pause. He takes a drink. Laughing.)* Um. I'm pretty drunk. "It is the native eloquence of us fog people." I was just watching the news. When it rains it fucking pours, right? *(Drinks.)* Did I ever tell you about the theatrical convention called Chekhov's Gun? Ever heard of it? It's…

(He hangs up the phone, takes another drink, then reaches into his pocket. He pulls out a pistol. He puts it in his mouth and pulls the trigger. Blackout. "Farther Along" by Sam Cooke and the Soul Stirrers plays.)

(Note: During the interval, the television screens in the lobby should now be playing more information about BEVERLY, as well as the world's reaction to their own returned decedents. There should also be breaking news about BEVERLY's brother-in-law killing himself.)

ACT THREE
"WHAT ARE WE GOING TO DO ABOUT APRIL?"
Scene One

We begin this act with a video montage, projected, as in Act One, Scene Five, only with a more pulsing feel, rather than with the fluidity of the former. "All Right Now" by Sam Cooke and the Soul Stirrers plays underneath. First, we see the floor of the United States Senate.

VOICE: … Congress is meeting today to discuss the ethics involved in what they are calling *post hoc euthanasia*, inspired in part by the much-discussed Colby incident in Connecticut. With what some would consider irony, congressional Republicans are the most in favor of quote "uniform and indiscriminate P.H.E." despite their reluctance to advocate the practice for the living …

(The video crossfades into footage of a REPORTER in Egypt.)

REPORTER: Chris, I'm standing here in Cairo, where, not three hours ago, a 4.7 magnitude earthquake has created a small panic, and has some convinced that it is a sign of the end of days. President Mubarak, of course, has issued a statement denying that the world is, in fact, ending—

(The video fades. Footage of a Sean Hannity-esque talk show.)

SEAN: And, of course, the liberal media is doing all it can to perpetuate what can only be described as unsubstantiated bull. Tonight I'm speaking with no less than five medical doctors, all of whom have their theories as to what's going on these days, and not one of them involves the words "Walking Dead." And thank goodness for small favors.

(The video fades. A cheap commercial.)

MORTY: Worried about the possibility of coming back to consciousness after passing away? Well, try our new easy-break-away coffin, available only at Morty's Coffin Emporium, just off the I-10…

(The video fades. Lights rise on the kitchen. We find JACKIE sitting at the table, staring at a can of soup. The kitchen looks clean, but there is something unkempt about it, as if it is not so much sanitary as just devoid of stuff.)

JACKIE: *(To the can.)* What are we gonna do with you…? *(She gets up and goes to the sink. She rinses off the top of the can and sets it down. She looks for a saucepan. There's nothing in the sink or* dish rack. *A bug darts across the counter and she starts.)* Shit! *(She kills it with the can, grimacing. Then she opens one of the cupboards. Pots and pans pour out of it and clatter onto the floor.)* Shit!! *(She starts to pick them up and sees that they're mostly dirty. She begins to pile them in the sink. Then she sits on the floor. Near tears.)* Shit...

(DAVID enters.)

DAVID: Everything okay in here?

JACKIE: No. *(Beat.)* Gram's been putting dirty dishes in the cupboards without washing them.

DAVID: Hm. Well, try and keep it down in here. I think she finally fell asleep.

JACKIE: Sorry.

DAVID: *(Sits down. He looks exhausted.)* Let me know when you want to head back home.

JACKIE: Okay.

(Beat.)

DAVID: You making soup?

JACKIE: I was going to.

(Pause.)

DAVID: How you doing, Jack?

JACKIE: *(Laughs.)* Jack? You haven't called me that in eons. *(Beat.)* I'm...I don't know. Numb, I guess. I can't tell if I want to cry or nap.

DAVID: You want to talk about it?

JACKIE: How's Aunt April doing?

DAVID: I don't know. I think she's numb, too. I tried giving her a sedative but she didn't want anything. She just wanted to be alone up there. I need to talk to her about the phone calls we've been getting, but...

(Pause.)

JACKIE: Did you used to call me Jack because you wanted a boy?

DAVID: What?

JACKIE: Never mind. *(Beat.)* Dad, can I ask you something?

DAVID: Sure, of course.

JACKIE: What is Mom doing?

DAVID: How do you mean?

JACKIE: Why is she so willing to *stoop* like this?

DAVID: What do you mean, stoop?

JACKIE: Never mind. *(Beat.)* Do you think she killed Uncle Josh?

DAVID: Jackie! How can you ask that?!

JACKIE: Wow, I've never seen you offended before.

DAVID: *(Overlapping.)* Are you trying to imply that your mother would—

JACKIE: Well, I didn't mean that she like literally went over there and pulled the trigger—though, maybe she did, I dunno. She seems pretty hellbent on fucking up people's lives right now—

DAVID: You are way out of line, young lady.

JACKIE: Really? You think so?

(DAVID has no answer.)

JACKIE: I think I hate her.

DAVID: You don't hate her.

JACKIE: I really think I hate her.

DAVID: You don't hate her.

JACKIE: Why would she do that, why would she say something like that—?

DAVID: She was caught up in the moment—she's very passionate. She didn't know what she was saying—

JACKIE: Bullshit, that's bullshit, she's smarter than that.

DAVID: She feels awful, Jackie. Worse than awful; you have no idea. She was practically inconsolable when we heard.

JACKIE: I fucking hate—

DAVID: Jackie, please. Stop.

(Beat.)

JACKIE: Why did he do it? Why would he...?

DAVID: I don't know. Maybe this was *all*...too much. This whole thing happening, on top of their marriage and his job and...You know, after 9/11 suicide rates went...Disasters like this can really affect people's worldviews.

JACKIE: You think this is a disaster?

(DAVID shrugs, at a loss.)

JACKIE: Are you with her on this? Kill 'em all, let God sort 'em out?

DAVID: *(Sighs.)* Your mother...in her own way, she is an idealist. She believes in something, in how things should be, and she dedicates herself to making it happen.

JACKIE: Lucky us.

DAVID: She cares about you. She does.

JACKIE: Yeah? Does she care about you?

DAVID: Jackie, yes.

JACKIE: Does she care about her sister, too?

DAVID: Of course, she does.

JACKIE: Well, then you and me are in big trouble, Dad.

(APRIL enters. She is clearly dazed. JACKIE and DAVID, if they're sitting, stand up, surprised.)

JACKIE: Aunt April.

(APRIL doesn't look at them, nor does she speak. She just stares.)

DAVID: April? You okay? You want something to eat?

(APRIL goes to the table and sits down. She is carrying a book: a soft-cover, leather-bound book that is immediately recognizable.)

JACKIE: I was gonna make soup. The dishes are all kinda repellent, but...

(APRIL pulls out some loose, folded papers from the book, and spreads them out on the table in front of her.)

DAVID: Apr—?

APRIL: *(As if noticing them for the first time.)* I'm fine.

DAVID: What are you reading?

(No answer.)

DAVID: Is that a Bible?

JACKIE: I didn't know we had one of those here.

APRIL: It's research.

DAVID: Research?

APRIL: Yes. *(Pause.)* Where's Mom?

DAVID: She's upstairs, asleep.

APRIL: Good.

DAVID: I thought you were going to sleep.

APRIL: No. I'm not really tired. Or hungry. Thanks, though, Jackie.

JACKIE: You're welcome.

APRIL: David.

DAVID: Yes?

APRIL: What can you tell me about zombies?

DAVID: Wha—?

APRIL: As a doctor, I mean.

DAVID: I'm not a doctor.

APRIL: Right. *(Beat.)* I've been reading a lot about reanimation and apocalypses. Is that how you pluralize it? Apocalypses? Anyway, I've been reading about different religions' takes on all of it. Mostly on Wikipedia and stuff. It's interesting, all the major religions have a, uh, a *prediction* about the dead coming back to life. *(She picks up one of the papers she pulled out.)* Like, in Orthodox Judaism, it says, "Belief in bodily resurrection is one of the Thirteen Principles of Faith of Maimonides: 'I believe with complete perfect faith, that there will be *techiat hameitim*—revival of the dead.' And the Talmud makes it one of the few *required* Jewish beliefs, going so far as to say that 'A person who does not believe in the resurrection of the dead has no share in the World to Come.'" Isn't that interesting?

DAVID: Um, yes, it is. April, we need to talk.

APRIL: *(With another paper.)* And, man, the New Testament is *filled* with this stuff. Like Ezekiel 37:1-14. God takes Ezekiel to the Valley of Dried Bones, a graveyard, and makes all the dead bodies stand up. And then, "This is what the Sovereign Lord says: Come from the four winds, O breath, and breathe into these slain, that they may live. So I prophesied as he commanded me, and breath entered them; they came to life and stood up on their feet—a vast army." And that's like one of hundreds. The Bible's like zombie fan fiction, almost. Or, there was a Buddhist named Bodhidharma—I think that's how you pronounce it—

DAVID: April. The, uh...the mortuary has been calling.

APRIL: Well, sure, I imagine this is a very stressful time for them. Probably the first time they've ever had to worry about going out of business.

DAVID: Calling about Josh. *(Pause.)* No one has told them what needs to be done. With the body. Bev—er, *I* would be more than happy to make the arrangements, I just need to know—

APRIL: Don't worry about it.

DAVID: ...Are you sure you're up for it?

APRIL: Up for what?

DAVID: What do you mean?

APRIL: I said, don't worry about it. *(Beat. As if it's obvious.)* You don't need to make any arrangements. He'll be back.

JACKIE: Aunt April—

APRIL. *(Laughing.)* No, no, no, don't look at me like I'm crazy. I'm not *Mom*. I just, I'm reading a lot, and I think I'm wrapping my mind around what's going on. See, I had this dream— *(Pause.)* Mom's sleeping, you said?

DAVID: Yeah.

APRIL: Good. She's been kinda...scary since they took Dad away. So distant.

JACKIE: Aunt April, don't you think we should talk about...Uncle Josh?

APRIL: Sure, honey. Is there something on your mind?

JACKIE: Are you okay?

APRIL: Yeah, sure. I'm okay.

JACKIE: That's bullshit.

(Beat.)

APRIL: *(To DAVID.)* Outta the mouths of babes…

JACKIE: Come on, talk to us.

APRIL: I'm not holding anything back, sweetie, I promise.

JACKIE: Again, bullshit.

(APRIL laughs.)

JACKIE: *(Kneels down to her.)* I am so, so sorry about what happened. I'm so…I'm, like, *sick* about it. I wanna fucking *kill* her for this.

DAVID: Jackie!

APRIL: Shh, shh. Don't say that.

JACKIE: *(Beginning to cry.)* I feel so awful, I'm so sorry.

(APRIL holds JACKIE, stroking her. A pause.)

APRIL: You wanna know what's going on? What I *think* is happening? *(Beat.)* All this stuff I'm reading. All these things I've been hearing about on the news…The Bible talks about the days of creation, right? The seven days when the world was made? And all those things I mentioned, the Talmud stuff particularly, those are all about the Day of Judgment. Well, "day" is a relatively relative term. I mean, we're not talking calendar days here. It's not a twenty-four-hour span. God didn't even create the sun until the fourth day. So it's an *era* sort of thing. A period. And that's what this is. The Day of Judgment. The Period of Judgment.

DAVID: April—

APRIL: Wait just a sec, David. I'm not trying to sound like some born-again nutjob. I'm not gonna rush out and buy posterboard and a "We Are Damned" stencil set. But… *(Almost joyfully.)* we *are* being judged. Can't you feel it? Judged by our *response* to this. The Lord, I don't know which Lord, is watching us, seeing what we're going to do. I just…I know it. Like, I know Josh is going to return any day now.

JACKIE: Do you think this is the Armageddon?

APRIL: Well…I don't know about that.

(DAVID's cell phone rings.)

DAVID: Shit.

APRIL: Hang on, David, you're gonna miss the last part.

DAVID: Uhhh… *(He answers his phone and moves to a corner of the room.)* Hey, Jerry, what's up?

APRIL: *(To JACKIE.)* You've seen a lot of zombie movies, right?

JACKIE: …A few, yeah.

APRIL: Zombies make a great metaphor, you know that? I was reading this *other* site about all this. About things that don't stay buried, or about conformity and fascism. But most of all, they represent what we do to ourselves as people. How we eat each other alive, how we turn against each other indiscriminately. How we're our own worst enemies.

JACKIE: You're scaring me, Aunt April.

APRIL: But the "things" we're dealing with now aren't like that. They're peaceful. They're benign. And that's what convinced me. They're harmless—

JACKIE: —But Grandpa—

APRIL: *(Basking, with a smile.)* —They're *harmless*. It's a reminder that we are…that we are good, and pure, and peaceful creatures at heart. See, I had this dream. It was beautiful, Jackie, I wish you could've seen it. God came to me. Like in your story. And he was so beautiful and kind. And he told me that we don't have to be afraid of this. He told me that the real monsters are the hate and the rage and the inhumanity we hold in ourselves. He said, "This is your test. If there's any Armageddon, it will come from the living. From that living anger. It spreads like a disease." But the examples we are receiving are the opposite, you see? And we are being judged on how we welcome that example. I'm…I'm pretty sure…

(JACKIE hugs her, hard.)

APRIL: And Josh will come back. So, don't you worry about that.

DAVID: *(Gets off the phone.)* I'm sorry, that was work. One of our clients apparently ran away from his practice, screaming or something. I've gotta make another quick call, I'm really sorry. *(He turns his focus back to his phone.)*

APRIL: *(Sotto voce.)* Jackie, sweetie. I need you to do me a favor.

JACKIE: What? Anything you need.

APRIL: Go home, please. I need to talk to your daddy about something.

JACKIE: What? No, I'm not gonna—

APRIL: Please.

JACKIE: I wanna stay here and help.

APRIL: This *will* help. Please.

(Pause.)

JACKIE: …I don't know, Aunt April, I…

(JACKIE looks at her dad, who is staring out the window, then back at APRIL.)

JACKIE: Please, just call me if you need…

(A moment. JACKIE exits, halfheartedly attempting—and failing—to get her father's attention as he continues on the phone. APRIL watches her go, and then turns to DAVID. She gets up and walks over to him as he finishes his conversation. As he speaks, APRIL pulls open one of the drawers and retrieves a large knife. DAVID finishes up his conversation, unaware.)

DAVID: Great. Well, I guess…sure. No, just make sure someone checks in with them first thing in the morning, okay? Yeah. Thanks, Andy. What? Oh, she's, y'know…hanging in there. Yeah, you saw her on the—? Listen, I gotta run, though, Andy. I'll let Jerry know. Thanks. You, too. *(He hangs up and starts to send an email on his phone.)* I'm sorry about that. Apparently, one of our docs was performing a checkup on one of his patients and couldn't get any vitals on him. Turns out the guy had died in the waiting room and no one knew, and now the doc doesn't want to go back to work. But, of course, we need him to finalize an order that he—

APRIL: David.

DAVID: Yeah? *(Turns and looks at her—he sees what's in her hands.)* Oh, Jesus Christ.

(Note: APRIL carries the knife loosely, casually, as if she barely knows it's there.

Throughout the scene she is still in a vaguely catatonic state, though, of course, now she has a purpose.)

APRIL: I need your help, David.

DAVID: Of course, April, anything I can do.

APRIL: I need your help, David.

DAVID: ...what are you gonna do with that knife, April?

APRIL: I need your help, David.

DAVID: You keep saying that. *(Beat.)* Where's Jackie?

APRIL: She left. I sent her home.

DAVID: Oh.

APRIL: I need you to tell me about Beverly.

DAVID: What about her?

APRIL: Everything. Everything you know about what happened to her.

DAVID: ...Can I just press send on this email? It's kinda...time sensitive.

APRIL: Go ahead.

DAVID: *(Sending the email.)* Thanks. Would you mind putting the knife down, too?

APRIL: Have you noticed that now, what with the dead rising from their graves and all, being alive just doesn't seem so...special anymore? *(Beat.)* David, you're a sweet man. A kind man. I've never liked how Beverly takes advantage of you.

DAVID: What do you mean, takes advantage of me?

APRIL: You know what I mean, David. The constant, wearying nagging and condescending, and the treating you like a fucking inconvenience.

DAVID: Come on, that's not true.

APRIL: I feel like I could put this in you and it wouldn't matter. You'd just come back and be as dead as ever. Are you covering anything up for her? Do you know anything? Did the doctors say anything to you?

DAVID: *(Starting to lose a little patience.)* What are you trying to find here, April? They ran tests, they supported her story. You know all this.

APRIL: It just doesn't make sense! I mean, there have been, what, over a hundred documented...occurrences of people coming back to life, and have any of them been violent? Have there been any other attacks?

DAVID: Yes.

APRIL: *(Beat. APRIL wasn't expecting that.)* What?

DAVID: Well, *claims*. Nothing's been confirmed or anything. Dr. Lawrence said they might just be attention-getters. Hoaxes. But Beverly's—

APRIL: Don't you think it's odd that none of us were attacked? That Mom kept Dad here for weeks and nothing happened to her? I mean, come on, Dad and Beverly didn't get along, but I highly doubt he could hold a grudge past death.

DAVID: ...Why would she make it up?

APRIL: *(Getting closer with the knife.)* You tell me, David. Is there anything I need to know about? Anything? Something in your eyes is telling me you're holding something back. Don't be scared of her, David.

DAVID: I'm not scared of her!

APRIL: Yes, you are. I saw it even when you guys were dating. And it's okay, she's fucking scary sometimes. Especially when she sets her mind to something—you and I both know she's got no problem manipulating the shit out of everyone around her just to get what she wants.

DAVID: Wants? Why would she want this?

APRIL: I don't know, David, I really don't—

DAVID: *(Overlapping.)* No, really, April, what does she have to gain by this? I mean, she's your sister, for Christ's sake! She's always bent over backwards for you, and now you're going to accuse her of, what, of forging a, a, a zombie bite? For *what?* I mean, how ridiculous is that? Could you please put the knife away?

APRIL: I will as soon as you tell me that I know everything.

DAVID: What do you need to know? She came in with the bite, they tested it, they said they found some of your dad's DNA in it, and it was probable that it was all due to him biting her.

APRIL: What about teeth impressions?

DAVID: ...

APRIL: What about teeth impressions? Did those match up?

DAVID: Would you just put that knife away?

APRIL: What is she making you cover up, David?

DAVID: Nothing! I'm not covering up anything! You know what I think? I think you're very stressed out, you've been through something very traumatic, and it's making you a little paranoid.

APRIL: You see! See how she turns you into a cowering little blob. She doesn't give a shit about the consequences, just as long as she gets to feel like she's in control of everything!

DAVID: Yeah, well, you're one to talk—how did *your* husband end up?!

(APRIL is stunned. She takes a step backwards like she was struck.)

DAVID: ...I'm sorry...April...I—

APRIL: You're right. Fine. I should go check on Mom.

DAVID: I didn't mean to say that. *(Pause.)* I'm sorry. *(Pause.)* I'm just so sick of people thinking she controls me, you know? I'm a grown fucking man. She doesn't control me. Okay?

APRIL: Okay.

DAVID: Are you going to stab me now?

(APRIL drops the knife and sits on the floor. DAVID takes the knife and drops it in the sink.)

DAVID: ...Are you okay?

APRIL: No. I'm not. I'm not okay.

DAVID: I'm really sor—

APRIL: I'm so pissed at him. When he comes back...Oh, that fucking idiot...God, I sound crazy.

(DAVID goes to her, arms out. He hugs her, looking uncomfortable.)

APRIL: Please, David. Something's not right. Something's not right. I don't know what it is...I'm sorry I said all that about you.

(Beat. They stare into each other's eyes. She laughs.)

APRIL: If this were a movie, here's where we'd have a cathartic fuck montage, right? *(Beat.)* Is there anything you can tell me?

(DAVID lets her go.)

DAVID: I never should have said what I did. I'm really sorry.

APRIL: Maybe you were r—

(DAVID angrily pushes a chair over. Beat. He puts it back where it belongs. APRIL stares at him, stunned.)

DAVID: I'm pretty sure there's something going on between her and Dr. Lawrence.

APRIL: ...Really?

DAVID: I don't know. We've both had our...indiscretions, but...I don't know. Maybe she's keeping him quiet about something.

APRIL: What?

DAVID: I don't know. *(Pause.)* I do know they never looked at your dad's dental records.

APRIL: ...What?

DAVID: *(Quickly; almost a rant.)* They said it was pointless—apparently, you can never get a totally accurate impression, because there's usually a struggle and things get...distorted. And they were so concerned with just checking her blood...But...then Dr. Lawrence said it was odd that there was no bruising from her trying to get away or anything, either.

APRIL: So, they never even—

DAVID: But you know how she can be, very persistent and convincing. And flirtatious. So he let it go. But I don't know, April. It could be it all checked out. Maybe all they had to do was eyeball it. Or maybe this is the way it usually works; I mean, this isn't an episode of *CSI* or anything; they're not a forensic hospital. This is Connecticut.

APRIL: Can I have his number? The doctor's? His personal number, if you have it?

DAVID: I don't want to betray my wife, April.

APRIL: You're not. You're not.

DAVID: She's my wife.

APRIL: I understand.

(Beat.)

DAVID: I'm not controlled by her. I mean that. There's a difference between abiding by someone and obeying them.

APRIL: I know.

DAVID: Do you really believe all that Judgment Day...stuff?

APRIL: Yeah. I think I do.

DAVID: It's scary.

APRIL: No scarier than the alternative.

DAVID: True. *(Beat.)* What did you mean by "cathartic fuck montage"?

(Lights fade.)

Scene Two

Special up on BEVERLY. She's sitting on a chair or couch downstage center. This is a new location from any we've previously seen: the set of a TV interview show. She faces forward, sitting primly. The HOST of the show, unseen throughout, is voiced by the actor playing JOSH.

HOST: *(Voiceover.)* We are, of course, thrilled and delighted to have our next guest on the program. For the few of you who don't immediately recognize her, she is the incredibly brave woman who survived an attack from one of the RDs that have had scientists both fascinated and baffled for the past couple of months. Hers is the only recorded instance of attack and, as she argues, it should serve as a wakeup call to the rest of the world. Beverly Colby-Parker, thank you for being with us tonight.

BEVERLY: Thank you, it's my pleasure.

HOST: *(Voiceover.)* Now, Mrs. Parker, I'd like to begin—

BEVERLY: Beverly, please.

HOST: Okay, Beverly. Let's begin with your thoughts on the new government initiative in the works—inspired, of course, by *you*—that would consider it a federal offense to house any decedent without notification of the proper authorities.

BEVERLY: Well, obviously, I'm pleased about that, and we are lobbying diligently that it passes. Sadly, I know firsthand how blind some people can be when it comes to the danger these creatures pose. Like a family dog gone rabid, they wear a familiar face.

HOST: *(Voiceover.)* Are you angry with your family, at all? Since you were thrust into the spotlight, the, uh, disagreement between you and your sister, in particular, about what to do with your father has been aired rather publicly. Is there resentment on your end?

BEVERLY: Absolutely not. No. I love my sister dearly. We don't agree on this issue, but I have nothing but respect for her. I'm saddened by her insistence on using my, well, celebrity as a means to launch personal attacks. But...oh, that sounds immodest, "celebrity." I'm sorry. You know what I mean. *(She smiles, all teeth.)*

HOST: *(Voiceover.)* Sure.

BEVERLY: So, I'm disappointed, yes. But I know my sister. I know she wants what's best for our family. And I do, too. I just see the bigger picture. *(She touches her arm.)* I had a wakeup call.

VOICE FROM THE AUDIENCE: Give 'em hell, Beverly!

BEVERLY: Oh, thank you. Let's try and stay cool.

(BEVERLY's cell phone rings. It sounds distant; muffled. Like it's underwater. No one comments on it.)

HOST: *(Voiceover.)* So, it's safe to say you and your sister don't see eye to eye on this.

BEVERLY: You know, I don't wish to denigrate anyone else's opinions—who knows what's objectively "true" or "valid"? My sister wants to believe that this is some sort of, uh, benevolent confirmation? If that is a comfort, then that's great. For her. But I don't personally subscribe to the notion that, you know, the sky will open up, celestial choirs will sing, and beams of light will come down, and all will know that everything is safe and warm. I'm a realist. I realize this is no different than cancer, or AIDS, or any other disease that manifests itself cruelly and surreptitiously. I realize that our government needs to act and act fast, while the numbers are still manageable. I mean, I'm not trying to panic anybody, I'm just trying to inform everybody.

HOST: *(Voiceover.)* It's interesting that you say panic. Let's look at some of the ramifications for a moment. You're still certainly not a *celebrity* by any stretch. But your name is getting well known enough. You've caused, what could be considered, a minor panic. Certainly, incidental violence has gone up—shootings, most of them in the head, and beatings. Not to mention the general feeling of terror in the air. Religious groups have been using your story as a sort of validation of Armageddon; various political groups for martial law. And then there's your brother-in-law.

BEVERLY: Excuse me?

HOST: *(Voiceover.)* Tell me, how do you feel about murdering your brother-in-law?

BEVERLY: I didn't—

(BEVERLY's phone begins to ring again, louder this time.)

HOST: *(Voiceover.)* How's your marriage going these days?

BEVERLY: Excuse me, my marriage is—

VOICE FROM AUDIENCE: Give 'em hell, Beverly!

HOST: *(Voiceover.)* Let's talk for a moment about your daughter, Kelly Gold. Are you a fan of her newest single, "Bisected by a Telephone Pole?" Personally, I think it's a little empty.

BEVERLY: Stop this right now. Excuse me—

HOST: *(Voiceover.)* Let's take some calls, shall we? Caller, you're on the air.

(The phone rings even louder.)

HOST: *(Voiceover.)* Huh. We seem to be having some technical difficulties. Oh, well. Why don't you try waking up, instead, Beverly? How 'bout waking up? And just lying there. You're so pretty. Just…shhh, you're so, so pretty—

BEVERLY: Shut the fuck up!

(The lights brighten a bit. BEVERLY bolts upright, or perhaps falls off her seat. She's awake now. Her phone is still ringing, though at normal volume. She digs it out of her pocket and answers.)

BEVERLY: Hello? *(Pause.)* No, sorry, I was taking a nap, I'm exhausted ri— *(Pause.)* No, I haven't seen anything. *(Pause.)* What channel? *(Beat.)* All of them?

(BEVERLY searches around for a remote. She finds it and points it at the audience. Above her, a projection of APRIL's newscast. APRIL is standing next to a NERVOUS-LOOKING MAN who seems as if he would rather be somewhere else.)

APRIL: …and again, I want to thank all of you for coming here at such short notice. I really appreciate that. Especially you, Dr. Lawrence. Thanks for being so…understanding. Thank you all. And God bless you.

(A REPORTER picks it up from there.)

REPORTER: Interesting things, there, Wolf. We'll be running that for the rest of the day, I'm sure. It's always fascinating when small stories get big, isn't it? For those of you who are just tuning in, we just heard from the sister of Beverly Parker, who I'm sure we all remember was recently attacked by the returned body of her father—her sister just told reporters, alongside Mrs. Parker's doctor, Dr. Mac Lawrence, that this whole thing has apparently been a media stunt. Dr. Lawrence confirmed that there was no conclusive evidence that the bite marks came from the father, and that he regretted not clarifying that earlier. Her sister then went on to quote scripture at some length, talking about a, uh, well, a peace mission of some kind, Wolf. As we reported earlier, April Colby's husband killed himself not long after—

(BEVERLY points the remote again and the projection shuts off. She sits there for a moment. She pulls a prescription bottle out and dry-swallows a pill. Her eyes are wide, her hands are shaking.)

BEVERLY: *(A whisper.)* Why did you do this…?

(Her cell phone begins to ring again. Lights fade. We hear "One More River to Cross" by Sam Cooke and the Soul Stirrers.)

Scene Three

Lights up on the kitchen. It's empty. We sit for a moment in silence. Then we hear the sound of thunder. A storm is coming. PEN slowly shuffles in. She looks terrible. She walks to the cabinets, opening and closing them, looking for something, but not looking for anything. The phone rings. She looks at it, disinterestedly. It rings again. She goes to it and answers.

PEN: Hello? *(Pause.)* Sheila. *(Pause.)* Hi, Sheila. *(Pause.)* Oh, I'm feeling very tired. Very tired. *(Pause.)* Yes, it's going to rain. *(Pause. PEN listens for a moment, then hangs up the phone.)*

(A moment. The phone starts to ring again. PEN ignores it, walks over to the radio, and turns it on. The phone continues to ring until it eventually ceases.)

RADIO ANNOUNCER: *(Voiceover.)* …and with so many troops committed to Iran, it seems unlikely that any military response will be available any time soon. A team of scientists in Moscow has been studying movement patterns to see if there is any predictability or synchronism among groups of RDs. Nothing has proved conclusive yet. Meanwhile, in the world of sports, the Broncos have dominated their last three games, bringing their record up to 7-4…

(We hear thunder outside.)

PEN: It's going to rain.

(She sits at the table. A long moment. ADAM enters from the other room. He is dressed in the suit from her dream in Act One, only now it is complete. He looks at her.)

PEN: It's going to rain.

(ADAM walks over to the radio, turns it off, and then looks out the window.)

PEN: Our daughters are in trouble, Adam. *(Pause.)* It was difficult having two daughters, wasn't it? Always at each other's throats, always too similar and too different, at the same time? God, it was exhausting. I don't think a son would've helped much. *(Beat.)* I'm losing my mind. I'm literally…I can feel it losing interest in the things around me…Ever since they took you. *(Beat.)* You weren't always a good husband, you know. Sometimes I hated you. But, God, to leave me like that. Twice. *(Beat.)* Are you really here? Did you get out again, somehow? *(Pause.)* No, probably not. I wonder if it's really even raining outside. *(Sighs.)* Oh, well. What can you do? Fiddle-dee-dee, said Scarlett. *(She laughs. It dies.)* Do you remember our son? I do, sometimes. Adam? Do you remember? That was one of the worst days of my life. And the girls were expecting a baby to come home…so we bought them a rabbit. A little pet rabbit. And April didn't trust it, and Beverly took care of it. And they both forgot about their brother. *(Beat.)* My throat is very dry.

(The phone begins to ring again. ADAM looks towards it, then continues looking out the window.)

PEN: That's just Sheila calling. Don't worry. I bet, if she comes back from the dead, first thing she'll do is call to talk about it. *(Beat.)* Does it hurt, Adam?

(No answer.)

PEN: I'm sorry I had to hide you like that. *(Laughs.)* Did you even know what I was doing? I was proud of myself for thinking so quickly.

(More thunder. It starts to rain outside. It's not long before it's pouring.)

PEN: It's raining.

(The lights dip, then come back on.)

PEN: Oh, no.

(ADAM turns to her, finally.)

PEN: Oh, Adam, you have that…look on your face.

(He walks towards her. She stands up. The phone rings again.)

PEN: My head hurts. And I can't…I can't quite remember what I was just talking about…But…

(They stare at each other. The lights flicker again. ADAM starts to walk towards the door. The phone stops ringing.)

PEN: I'd very much like to meet him, Adam. I've always wondered what he'd be like. Our little boy. I'd like to come with you. I'd like to come with you. *(She looks out the window.)* I'm afraid it's raining too hard, though. I'd get soaked.

(ADAM stands in the doorway, looking at her, smiling.)

ADAM: No. You won't.

(He exits. PEN stands there for a moment.)

PEN: Oh.

(Suddenly dizzy, she sits ungracefully on the floor. She leans up against the cabinets. Her breathing shallows out, then stops. The lights cut out.)

SCENE FOUR

In the darkness, we can still hear the rain outside. We also hear a VOICE.

MORTY: *(Voiceover.)* Scared about a returned loved one possibly getting out and causing trouble? Frightened of the possibility of the world becoming a horror movie? Well, try our new lead-encased coffins, available only at Morty's Coffin Emporium. Guaranteed not to break no matter how hard ya try!

(The VOICE fades, the rain continues. The lights remain off. Someone enters the kitchen—it's BEVERLY. She bumps into something in the dark.)

BEVERLY: Ow, shit!

(The lights come back. BEVERLY is at the table. She sets a plastic bag containing a six-pack of beer on the table, along with her purse. She pulls the beer out of the bag. She is very agitated; her hands are still shaking. She doesn't notice PEN's body behind her. Thunder. The lights dip again.)

BEVERLY: Shit. *(She pulls a gun from her purse. She looks at it for a second, then sets it down. She then pulls the vial of pills from her purse. She tries to steady her hands. She pours a pill into her palm, but shakes too hard, and several pills go spilling to the floor.)* Shit.

(She bends down to pick them up. Behind her, PEN stands up. Distant thunder, just enough to mask the noise of any movement. PEN begins to move, creakily, and makes her way out of the room. BEVERLY, meanwhile, picks up all of the pills, dusting them off and blowing on them, and then takes one dry. Her cell phone begins to ring. She gets out her phone, sees who's calling, and presses ignore.)

BEVERLY: *(Shouting.)* Mom? Are you home?

(No answer.)

BEVERLY: April?

(She puts the beer in the fridge. Her phone rings again. She looks at who it is, ignores it. The power dips.)

BEVERLY: Ugh, goddamn fucking old piece of shit house.

(The lights come back. The phone rings again. BEVERLY groans in frustration, looks at who's calling, and, in a moment of anger, drops the phone into the sink and turns on the water. She leans against the counter, rubbing her temples.)

BEVERLY: Okay…okay…

(There is a bump in the living room.)

BEVERLY: Mom? Mother?

(BEVERLY hurries back to her purse and puts everything back into it quickly, guiltily. A moment, and then PEN comes back into the room.)

BEVERLY: Oh, jeez, Mom, you scared me.

(Beat.)

BEVERLY: Are you alright? You look terrible.

(Beat.)

BEVERLY: Where's April? Do you still have that camping lantern? You're gonna need it, the power's going in and out.

(PEN walks aimlessly into the table.)

BEVERLY: Mom!… *(Realizing.)* Oh… *(She looks utterly defeated for a moment, then girds herself with a deep breath and stiffens. She stares at PEN long and hard, "You deserved this," coursing through her mind.)*

(Thunder. After a long moment, we hear the sound of a car coming up the driveway. BEVERLY stops looking at PEN. She grabs her purse and runs into the living room to hide. A moment later, we hear APRIL's voice in the living room.)

APRIL: *(Offstage.)* Mom? You okay? It's coming down like a sonofabitch out there.

(The lights cut out. APRIL screams, startled. The stage is pitch black. A few moments and APRIL's in the kitchen, feeling her way around.)

APRIL: God, I hate this house…Where is that fucking lantern? *(She finds it in one of the cabinets: a Coleman camping lantern.)* Thank God for Beverly's impulse buys. Please work. *(She sets it on the table and tries it. It does, and it remains the only source of light for the rest of the scene. Calling.)* Mom? You awake? I'm here, it's okay. *(She looks around the kitchen. Then, finally, she sees PEN. She jumps.)* Jesus! What are you doing down here? You okay? It's raining cats…and…Mom? *(APRIL feels PEN.)* Oh, God. Mom.

(She backs away. PEN wanders around the kitchen. APRIL makes a sound that's not quite a sob. It becomes a small laugh, barely audible.)

APRIL: Wow…Mom…wow…This… this is good. This is good. This is a sign.

God? Thank you. I love you, Mom. *(She laughs.)* The mortuary keeps calling me, asking what I'm going to do about Josh. But they don't have to worry about that, you know? 'Cause this is a sign. *You* are a sign. Thank you. *(Starting to cry.)* I'm sorry I missed you, Mom.

(PEN wanders back out of the kitchen. APRIL sits at the table.)

APRIL: *(To no one.)* Thank you.

(From offstage, we hear a gunshot and the sound of a body hitting the floor. After a moment, BEVERLY walks in.)

BEVERLY: Hi, April. I'm glad you found that lantern. The power's been going in and out.

(APRIL runs out of the room to check on PEN. A long beat. BEVERLY starts to cry. APRIL comes back in. Note: The rest of the scene plays out very quietly, mournfully: like an inevitability. Despite the cursing and threatening, really none of these lines, with a few exceptions, should be of a loud volume—the fatigue and the emotions are all just too much.)

APRIL: You killed her.

BEVERLY: She was already—

APRIL: You shot her.

(BEVERLY sits on the floor, crying. APRIL stares at her, at a loss.)

APRIL: …Why…?

(No answer. BEVERLY sits for a moment longer, crying, then wipes her eyes and gets up.)

BEVERLY: The lantern works well. I'm glad I bought it.

APRIL: I think I'm going to be sick.

BEVERLY: Do you want anything? Water? I've got some pills, they're for anxiety.

APRIL: No, I don't want any fucking pills.

BEVERLY: Okay. *(Sits at the table, with a sigh.)* I feel like I've been taking care of this family since birth.

APRIL: *(Almost choking on the words.)* You…shot our mother…

BEVERLY: *(Nodding.)* Yeah…

APRIL: Jesus fucking Christ, Beverly…

BEVERLY: I saw you on the TV. With Dr. Lawrence.

APRIL: Oh? You going to shoot me, too?

BEVERLY: No. Of course not. But I wish…I wish you would've spoken to me first.

APRIL: You are a terrible person, Beverly.

BEVERLY: I don't want to fight. I really don't.

APRIL: No, you really are. You help and you help and you help, but it's never …

BEVERLY: *(Genuinely.)* I'm so sorry about Josh.

APRIL: You knew exactly what you were doing.

(BEVERLY gets up and goes to the fridge. She pulls out two beers, sets them on the counter, and opens them with her back to us.)

APRIL: What are you doing?

BEVERLY: *(Drinks one of them deeply, nearly half the bottle in one gulp. Then she holds out the other opened one to APRIL.)* The world doesn't even begin to make sense anymore. Have you noticed?

(Beat. APRIL doesn't move.)

BEVERLY: Share something with me. Please.

(APRIL takes the beer.)

BEVERLY: *(Continues drinking.)* I mean, here we are. I never in a million years would have guessed that our lives would have brought us...here. Like this. *(Drinks.)* I dunno, maybe it's the shitty lighting. But this just seems absurd. *(Pause.)* What's the matter, don't you want your beer?

APRIL: *(Beat. Drinks, similarly deeply, as if she were dying of thirst, almost emptying it at once.)* Why did you do it, Bev?

BEVERLY: Do what?

APRIL: Lie about Dad.

(Beat.)

BEVERLY: Do you really think that this is all a sign from God? That this is some divine what'd-you-call-it? Gesture?

APRIL: ...I don't know what to believe. *(Drinks.)*

BEVERLY: I hope you're right. I really do. I would love to be proven wrong. David told me you think this is some protracted Day of Judgment. I see what you mean. And I think you might be right. Or half-right. I don't think *we're* the ones being judged. Do you want another beer?

APRIL: Fine. Fuck it.

(BEVERLY goes to get two more beers. This time, as her back is to us, she takes a little longer to finish opening the bottles. After she walks away from the countertop, there is a small packet of paper on the counter, as well. APRIL pokes her head back out to look at PEN.)

APRIL: *(Near tears.)* She's not getting back up...

(APRIL sits down at the table. BEVERLY brings the two beers over, and APRIL drinks from hers immediately.)

BEVERLY: Dr. Lawrence said that the condition seems to be brain-related. That that's probably why not every...decedent reanimates. There has to be a functioning, or close-to-functioning, brain. *(Beat.)* Which is why, I'm sorry, but I don't think Josh will...you know. Given his...injuries...

(APRIL grabs the gun and points it at her.)

APRIL: You shut the fuck up. Just shut the fuck up.

BEVERLY: I'm sorry. Okay. *(Beat.)* David told me you threatened him with a knife earlier. I'm concerned for you.

APRIL: I will fucking shoot you in the fucking head, Beverly, if you don't shut up. And I'll just say you "came back" and had to be put down. "It's what she fucking wanted," I'll say.

BEVERLY: Please...April...

(Pause.)

APRIL: God, my fucking head is killing me. *(She takes another swig of beer.)* You have really shitty taste in beer, you know that? *(Beat.)* So, why are you here? Did you come to shoot Mom regardless? Or were you looking for me?

BEVERLY: I was looking for you.

APRIL: And you had *this*?

BEVERLY: I don't know what I was planning on doing, April. I've been carrying that around since I got out of the hospital. For protection.

(APRIL scoffs.)

BEVERLY: I've attracted a lot of desperate people. *(Beat.)* I wasn't planning to shoot...

APRIL: No, of course not. *(She drinks more.)* That'd just be awful, wouldn't it?

BEVERLY: Please stop pointing that gun at me. It's making me nervous.

(APRIL doesn't move.)

BEVERLY: I'm going to reach into my purse, okay? I would like to get something out of it.

APRIL: Slowly.

BEVERLY: *(Slowly reaches into her purse and pulls out her bottle of pills. We can hear it's almost completely empty now. Upends the bottle into her palm and one last pill comes out.)* This is my last one.

APRIL: God, you go through those things like fucking candy, don't you?

BEVERLY: They've helped me.

(APRIL drinks, finishing her beer.)

BEVERLY: I've had to be careful, there's always the danger of overdosing. These can be very lethal in large doses. *(Beat.)* I wish the lights would come back on, this lamp is giving me a headache.

(Outside, it continues to rain. They sit and listen to the rain for a moment.)

BEVERLY: Can I ask you something?

APRIL: What?

BEVERLY: Did you help my daughter secure drugs?

APRIL: What do you mean?

BEVERLY: Jackie. The marijuana. Did you give it to her, or buy it from her, or something? Did you have anything to do with that?

(Beat.)

APRIL: Yes.

BEVERLY: That's really...that's really unfortunate.

APRIL: I'm sorry. *(Beat.)* I took it away from her. And I firmly reprimanded— *(Breaks off, suddenly nauseous.)*

BEVERLY: Are you okay?

APRIL: I don't...I just got really dizzy.

BEVERLY: It's probably this lighting.

APRIL: *(Wiping her forehead.)* Ugh...

BEVERLY: I never got to finish what I was telling you. About judgment. Do you mind?

APRIL: Knock yourself out.

BEVERLY: It's an interesting idea you bring up. That we are being judged in our *reaction* to this. But I think you've got it backwards.

APRIL: What do you mean?

BEVERLY: I think, if there is any sort of divine *anything* happening now...it's the dead that are being judged. Mind you, I say this with a grain of salt. I think this whole ordeal has pretty much ended any belief I might have ever had that there *is* a God.

APRIL: That's too bad.

BEVERLY: I suppose. You were never religious in the first place, though, so spare me the judgment. *Your* judgment, I should say. *(Beat.)* Dad was a means to an end. If the others that are coming back were anything like him, they need...they deserve to be destroyed.

APRIL: How can you say that? Dad was a good man. He— *(She gets dizzy again.)* Jesus, I don't feel…

BEVERLY: Dad was a troubled man. I thought I made peace with it, until I saw him again. Until I saw that face…

APRIL: I think I'm going to throw up.

BEVERLY: Do you remember when we used to share a bedroom? When I was eleven and you were seven?

APRIL: Yeah, why?

BEVERLY: *(Looks at her, waiting for the penny to drop.)* Do you really not remember, April?

APRIL: I just said I remembered—

BEVERLY: You've totally blocked it out.

APRIL: I don't know what you're talking about, Beverly.

BEVERLY: For four years, April.

APRIL: What?

BEVERLY: And we shared a bedroom for one of those years.

APRIL: …What the fuck are you talking about?

BEVERLY: *(Quietly, matter-of-fact.)* From when I was eleven to when I was fifteen. Dad. He didn't do it so often that first year, when you and I were together. But I got my own room soon after it started to become more regular, and I don't think that was a coincidence. He would come in and sit at the foot of the bed and whisper that it was okay, that I was so pretty, and he just wanted to look at me. That, shh, it was okay. And his hand would be on his penis…And he would just *stare* at me. He had this…*face* that he would make while doing it, too. This distant, awful, glassy look. Do you remember? And when he finished, he would leave. It would scare me so much. I would wonder if it was going to…progress, or something. It never did. He would just sit at the foot of the bed, and look at me and…And the first time it happened, after he left, I looked over at you. I was hoping you were asleep, but you weren't. You were looking straight at me. And you were crying. Don't you remember? I'll never forget that. And only once did he try and touch me, and I threw up. This was after I had my own room, and he would come in at least once a month. And after I threw up, he stopped coming in. And he stopped caring about me—and you and he became best friends. I was so scared, April. I was so scared about what that meant he might be doing to you.

(Long beat.)

APRIL: I don't know what you're talking about.

BEVERLY: You've blocked it out—

APRIL: I haven't blocked it out; I don't remember that ever happening.

BEVERLY: And so, if you're right, I think maybe it's because of the things he did that he came back. Maybe it's a judgment of all the unaccounted sins of all the people who have died. Or maybe… *(She laughs.)* maybe there is no God and it's just a biological fluke. I really don't know. I really don't know.

(APRIL stands and moves away. Pause.)

APRIL: *(Quietly horrified; realizing.)* From when you were eleven to fifteen?

(BEVERLY nods.)

APRIL: Beverly, that's…that's when Dad was working nights. He barely ever got home before we were asleep. I can hardly even remember him saying good-night to us, let alone…Oh, my God…This was all because of some imagined bullshit? Some cry for attention or something? Oh, God, Beverly, there are *consequences* for what you've done!

BEVERLY: I know there are.

APRIL: I'm calling the police right now. *(Goes to take a step and collapses.)*

BEVERLY: I'm so sorry, April. I really am trying to help. These things need to be destroyed. Regardless of what they're here for. I *know* that.

APRIL: *(Groggy.)* What…?

BEVERLY: What you did on the TV… that didn't help. It's so dangerous, what you did. I'm trying to save us, April. I'm trying to *help*, and you made it so much harder to get the message out. I can't have you stand in the way of what I know is right. It's for the greater good.

APRIL: You fuggin'…

BEVERLY: *(Close to tears.)* I'm sorry. I heard you come in, before the lights went off, and I hid in the living room. And I ground up all of my pills and put them into your beer. That's what I came here to do.

(APRIL tries to make herself throw up, but it's no use.)

BEVERLY: Your system is shutting down. It should be painless.

(APRIL tries to crawl, but is suddenly too weak.)

BEVERLY: *(Crying.)* I'm so, so sorry. Please believe me.

APRIL: Beverly…I…*hate*…you… *(Slumps up against the cabinets, breathing harshly. She retches, in her mouth, but it's no use. She convulses, then stills. Her breathing shallows out…then stops.)*

BEVERLY: I'm so sorry, April. It's for the greater good. The greater good. One world, united. Think about it. Us versus them. Peace. The greater good. I want that. It's…

(She trails off, crying. A long moment. The lights come back on. BEVERLY blinks. She turns out the lantern, then goes to pick up the gun.)

BEVERLY: I'm sorry.

(BEVERLY kneels next to APRIL, touches her. She bends down to kiss her forehead—the same spot JACKIE touched during her "Grand Inquisitor" retelling. As she does so, APRIL stirs, and her eyes open. BEVERLY nods quietly, then places the gun to APRIL's head. APRIL opens her mouth with fury and buries her head into the side of BEVERLY's neck. BEVERLY screams, the gun fires into nowhere. BEVERLY manages to pull herself away, blood gushing down her neck. She staggers back. APRIL looks every bit the zombie we have always feared. BEVERLY manages to point the gun and pull the trigger. It hits APRIL in the chest, stalling her, but not dropping her. Another shot and this time it's in the head. APRIL goes down. BEVERLY's wound, however, is too severe and she soon collapses, still clutching her neck. Blood pours onto the floor and she is still. A moment. We hear ghostly voiceovers.)

APRIL'S VOICE: "If there is any Armageddon, it will come from the living, from that living anger. It spreads like a disease…"

BEVERLY'S VOICE: Dr. Lawrence thinks that, if it is communicable, the bite would have to come before the, um, returned decedent's fluids have dried. A *fresh* one. Which is scary…

(Silence. Soon, we hear a car drive up. A few seconds later and we hear DAVID and JACKIE in the living room.)

DAVID: *(Offstage.)* Hello? Pen? April? We've been calling, but the lines are down.

JACKIE: *(Offstage.)* Mom? You here?

DAVID: *(Offstage.)* Did you try her cell?

JACKIE: *(Offstage.)* Yeah, it's just going straight to voicemail, I don't know—

(BEVERLY twitches and sits up. We hear "Any Day Now" by Sam Cooke and the Soul Stirrers begin to play. It plays throughout the rest of the scene.)

DAVID: *(Offstage.)* Oh, my God…

JACKIE: *(Offstage.)* Grams? Grandma? Are you okay? (Beat.) Oh, God, Daddy, she's been shot!

DAVID: *(Offstage.)* Oh, God, Pen?! Oh, Jesus…

JACKIE: *(Offstage.)* Aunt April?! Anybody?! Is anybody here?! Daddy, what do we do?!

DAVID: *(Offstage.)* I don't know, I don't know!

(BEVERLY has made her way to the doorway. She exits.)

JACKIE: *(Offstage.)* Mom! What's going on—?

DAVID: *(Offstage, overlapping.)* Jesus, Bev, what happened? You're bleeding.

JACKIE: *(Offstage.)* Are you okay? Are you—

(We hear screams, both JACKIE and DAVID. We hear the wet sounds of flesh being torn from bone. The song continues. As the lights fade, we hear a REPORTER.)

REPORTER 1: *(Voiceover.)* …storm front seems to be moving further east now, which means we're probably in for a good amount of rainy days to come, so be sure to keep your umbrellas handy, folks. Tim?

REPORTER 2: *(Voiceover.)* Thanks, Evan. A bit of breaking news now. We've just received a bit of news about some violence breaking out somewhere on the East Coast—what appears to maybe be a small riot of some kind. Diane Jaffey is there live. Diane?…Diane?…Diane? We seem to have lost Diane for the moment. Probably because of this weather. More on this as it develops, then.

(The VOICES fade. The song gets louder and louder.)

(END OF PLAY.)

THE SPIN CYCLE

Jerrod Bogard

JERROD BOGARD was born in 1978 on an Air Force base in Wichita, Kansas, and his childhood years were spent in a variety of places: Okinawa, Japan; McAlister, Oklahoma; Abilene, Texas; Austin, Texas; and Fort Walton Beach, Florida. "I consider myself a Southerner, a New Yorker, and a Beach Bum," Bogard says. He holds a degree in acting from Florida School of the Arts, and spent seven years working with Bits 'N Pieces Puppet Theatre, where he learned the ins and outs of touring theatre, puppetry, and arts in education. Bogard performed his original shadow show at the Prague International Festival of Puppet Arts in the Czech Republic. He was the writer and director of the short film *Gatorman* (winner of Best Mini-Picture at the Bare Bones International Film Festival). His play *Hugging the Shoulder* was presented at the 2006 New York International Fringe Festival; was a semifinalist at the O'Neill Playwrights Conference; and was subsequently produced in Chicago, Los Angeles, and Philadelphia. He wrote the book and lyrics for the family musical *Jack and the Soy Beanstalk* (Sky Seals, composer), which was produced in the 2009 New York International Fringe Festival. His short plays include *Plays for the Sunni Triangle* (EndTimes Productions, New York) and *Theft* (Shortened Attention Span, New York). Bogard is the resident playwright for Wide Eyed Productions, which has commissioned him to create a new play for its 2011 season. Bogard resides in Queens, New York.

The Spin Cycle was first presented by Wide Eyed Productions and Shortened Attention Span at the Players Theatre Loft on January 22, 2009, with music by Scott Voloshin and scenic design by Sean Boat. Christy Benanti was the stage manager, and the video segments were directed and edited by Brian A. Bernhard. Cast and credits were as follows:

Copper Green

Dad .... Anthony Reimer/Craig Clary (swing)
Danielle .... Stacy Ayn Price
Jake .... John Barbieri
Arab Man .... Ivan Goris
Directed by: Anthony Augello

Hedge

Celine .... Melissa Johnson
Amber .... Lauren Bahlman
Directed by: Jake Witlen

Just Your Average G.I. Joe

Joe .... Jerrod Bogard
Directed by: Kristin Skye Hoffmann

First Base Coach

Amy .... Kristin Skye Hoffmann
Ben .... Ben Newman
Directed by: Neil Fennell

Jerome Via Satellite

Dan Dillinger .... Justin Ness
Makeup Girl .... Lucy McRae
Iraq Producer .... Andrew Harriss
Jerome .... Kevin Perri
First Sergeant Balpine .... Duane Chivon Ferguson
Private Zansky .... Trevor Dallier
U.S. Producer .... Liz White
Cameraman .... Joseph Hernandez
Mom .... Alexandra Cremer
Dad .... Howard Mears
Kelly .... Jessica Garavuso
Marina .... Daniela Genoble
Directed by: Justin Ness
Assistant Director: Joshua David Bishop

Just Your Average G.I. Joe was first produced by EndTimes Productions in the 2007 Vignettes for the Apocalypse with Scott Voloshin as Joe, directed by Kristin Skye Hoffmann. *First Base Coach* was first produced by Shortened Attention Span for its 2008 Summer Festival with Julee Cerda as Amy and Jake Paque as Ben, directed by Kenny Wade Marshall.

AUTHOR'S NOTE

I've always believed that the most important person in the theatre is a member of the audience, the patron. It all exists for the patron. So, while the chance to show five of my one-acts in an evening was a personal dream come true, my principal concern was how to frame the experience for the audience. Too often one-act collections feel like a $9.99 theatre buffet. I hoped to serve a stately five-course meal.

We approached it holistically. The right director was suited to the right script, and we cast the shows all together so that each play would complement the others. These plays were not written to go together, however, and I needed to come up with a through-line that could carry the audience from the first entrance to the last exit.

A year earlier, I had participated in a writing workshop hosted by Shortened Attention Span and run by Carlo Riveccio. Three of the plays (*Copper Green*, *Hedge*, and *First Base Coach*) were written during that time. *Just Your Average G.I. Joe* was originally the center of my triptych, *Plays for the Sunni Triangle*. The final play of the evening, *Jerome Via Satellite*, was written to anchor this collection and so did not exist until just a few weeks before production began. It took shape through the invaluable inspirations of colleagues Kristin Skye Hoffmann, Scott Voloshin, and Justin Ness.

At the core of *Jerome Via Satellite* is a fictional cable news show called "The Spin Cycle with Dan Dillinger." Segments from this TV show are written into the play. My good friend and filmmaker Brian Bernhard agreed to film and edit these video sequences so that we could show them on an actual TV on stage. That's when I discovered the through-line for the evening. All the plays could be hinged together with thematically appropriate segments from Dan Dillinger's show.

While writing Dan Dillinger's monologues, I discovered why this through line was the perfect choice. Each of these plays presents a character who meets a force that attempts to manipulate his or her perceptions of reality. Manipulating one's perception of a shared reality is the definition of spin, and in this society we are all targets (and purveyors) of spin.

I'm very grateful for the opportunity to share this collection with you as one piece, as they were presented on stage in the winter of 2009. That said, these plays might also be successfully performed as stand-alone pieces. After all, sometimes it's nice to skip right to the main course, or even forget the rest and enjoy dessert all by itself.

PRODUCTION NOTE

Dan Dillinger's TV show segments may be performed live by any device imagined by the designers. Whether Dan Dillinger is videotaped, shown on a television screen, or presented otherwise is at the discretion of the director.

"THE SPIN CYCLE WITH DAN DILLINGER"

A mostly bare stage. Up Center is a tall black pedestal on which rests a large, flat-screen television. The television is on and presents a slowly rotating graphic: "THE SPIN CYCLE." This logo looks similar to what one might see on a Fox News Channel promo. Hanging above the audience are two small flat-screen TV monitors on which we also see "THE SPIN CYCLE" logo. Two professional videocameras, one in each alcove, stage left and right, are set up on tripods, and next to each camera is a studio lamp with an umbrella reflector. The lamps are switched off currently. The overall effect is that of a television studio awaiting the host to arrive and the show to begin. The house lights dim, and the TVs burst to life—the beginning of a TV show—with trumpeting music and patriotic graphics. Red, white, and blue titles dazzle and spin as the opening sequence of "The Spin Cycle" ushers the viewer toward the anchor desk of the illustrious journalist, DAN DILLINGER. This cable news "infotainment" show is viewed on the larger, upstage television. Throughout DAN's monologues complementing graphics appear next to him as they would on any reputable news show.

DAN DILLINGER: Thank you for watching tonight. I'm Dan Dillinger and you're in "The Spin Cycle." Big show tonight. We'll be broadcasting live from Baghdad later in the evening. Trust me, you will want to stick around for that. But right now—MEMOS! Green. Blue. Yellow. Orange. And Red. These five now infamous colors were chosen by experts at the Bureau of Homeland Security to represent the threat level of a possible terrorist attack. It's the system that's been in place since the events of 9/11. For some though, not good enough. The New York City Department of Transportation—specifically the nimrods over at the Staten Island Ferry—released a statement Thursday suggesting a new color be added to the roster. The new color would be placed at the top of the list and used for only one specific event. So when do we use it, Cap'n Bly? Well, during an actual terrorist attack of course. Brilliant. Now the obvious question, what color do these rainbow warriors propose? Wait for it...Brown. Worrying about asinine notions like what color to use when they should be drilling emergency response, you can bet that during a terrorist attack these numskulls will be seeing a lot of brown. They'll be crapping their pants.

(During the above the crew has placed the set of the first play...The television fades to the image of the Statue of Liberty. A foghorn is heard...)

COPPER GREEN

CHARACTERS

DAD, forty-five
DANIELLE, fourteen
JAKE, nine
ARAB MAN, middle aged

SETTING

Summer day, 2007. On board the Staten Island Ferry in Upper New York Bay.

Lights up on the Staten Island Ferry. A beautiful, warm afternoon. The crowded boat has just departed the slip and is bound for Staten Island. At the rail is DAD, a little overweight, sporting a visor and fanny pack; his son JAKE, a precocious fourth grader in a T-shirt depicting a popular wrestler; and his daughter DANIELLE, a cynical ninth grader with her iPod. She's way too cool for family vacations. They are the typical Midwestern family on vacation in New York City. To one side of our family is an ARAB MAN with a black mustache and a Middle Eastern accent. He appears to be on his daily commute and cannot help but overhear, to his own discomfort, the family's conversations. As the play moves forward, the ferry passes the Statue of Liberty, which the actors "see" passing from downstage right to downstage left.

DAD: *(Re. the Statue of Liberty.)* There she is guys.

(JAKE climbs up on the rail.)

DAD: Hey. Hey—hey-hey-hey. Off the rail. Off the rail. Get—All right now... There she is, huh? I told ya we'd see her. Not a bad view either, huh? Your mom'll be sorry she missed this. Hey! What did I tell you? Off the rail... You're friends won't even believe ya, right? Did ya think you'd get this close up?

JAKE: I guess.

DAD: This is the local trick. See the statue—way the locals do it. Ya like that? Your old dad knows his way around the big city, huh?

JAKE: Dad?

DAD: What's up, bud?

JAKE: How come you call it a she?

DAD: She *is* a she, that's why. The lady in the harbor. That's what New Yorkers call her.

JAKE: It doesn't look like a lady.

DAD: Like that? Huh? Danielle, your old dad sounds like a New Yorker, huh? Jacob, if I tell you one more time to get off the rail you're going inside.

JAKE: Nooo!

DAD: Well it's your choice. Settle down or inside.

JAKE: *(Pulling away.)* Okay!

DAD: Jacob, watch it!

JAKE: It looks like a man.

DAD: Jacob, come here.

JAKE: No.

DAD: Don't tell me no. Look out. *(Gripping him by the jacket.)* You're bumping into people here. Watch out. Here. Stand here. Settle. Now—look up. See that?

JAKE: Yes.

DAD: What do you see? Danni. Come here. Here. Now, what do you see?

DANIELLE: The city?

DAD: There. The lady. Lady Liberty. Guys...I tell you what. That there—that's everything. She's everything. She's—she's freedom. She's justice.

DANIELLE: She's French.

DAD: Yeah well, let's focus on the positive, right hon? I mean to say—*she* is what your brother is fighting for. Right? Represents everything about this country your brother's over there protecting. The whole point. Pretty neat huh? Right there.

JAKE: I wish I could blow it up.

DAD: *(An embarrassed hush.)* Why would you say that? Why would you even think that? Do we need to go back to the hotel? Huh?

DANIELLE: Can we?

DAD: No we cannot. Jesus. Your mom needed a break from you guys, and now I'm beginning to see why.

JAKE: I'm hungry.

DAD: Why would you say that?

JAKE: I am.

DAD: Come here. Come here. Look out there. Now, you're gonna listen to a story. No, just—...Settle down...It's about a little kid—just like you. Okay? Ten years old, can't ever sit still. But this little boy, he lives in a place very far away. A place that's very hot, okay? See out there all the waves?

JAKE: Yeah?

DAD: Well, imagine instead of waves of water you see waves of sand. Hot, dry, pale desert sand. This is where he lives, this little boy. No grass to play on, no baseball teams, and guess what—no TV to watch either.

JAKE: That sucks.

DAD: That's right. This little boy, he's out there in the sun and sand one day—and he—he's getting pretty thirsty, and he goes to the fridge to get some water. And well guess what.

JAKE: What?

DAD: No water. Not a drop. But this little boy—he knows where there's a well, and in this well he knows there's the sweetest, coolest, crystal clear water you ever tasted.

JAKE: Like Dasani?

DAD: Oh, better. So he heads out. Into that ocean of burning sand to go get a drink of that water.

DANIELLE: Dad?

DAD: Hold on a minute.

DANIELLE: But Dad—I think maybe you're—

DAD: I'm trying to—with your brother here. Know what, here. Go get some nachos, okay? Here. Here's five. Go.

DANIELLE: But—

DAD: Go-go-go.

(She goes.)

DAD: Now...let's see, where were we?

ARAB MAN: Burning sand.

DAD: Right!...Ehehm...right. Well—see, Jacob,...He—he gets to where the water is—to this well. And the well—well it's dry. There's no water, and so the boy says, "Hey, what the heck? Where in the H. E. double hockey sticks"—

JAKE: *(Impressed.)* Woa.

DAD: Well yeah—This is serious. You need water to live. He could die here. He's saying "Where the heck is all the water?" And Jake, this kid is just like you. You're a good kid right?

JAKE: I guess.

DAD: You deserve some fresh, cool water, right?

JAKE: Yeah.

DAD: Yeah. So don't ya think this kid, he deserves it too?

JAKE: Yeah.

DAD: Me too. But guess what, amigo. Forget it.

JAKE: Why? Where's all the water?

DAD: Where's all the water? Jake, did I ever tell you you're a smart kid? The water is right there next to the well. See, see it's been put into a thousand bottles and it's been loaded onto a big truck.

JAKE: Like Dasani?

DAD: Like Dasani. But don't you go over and try to take one. Or even buy one.

JAKE: Why?

DAD: Because there's guards there. With guns and they'll shoot anyone who tries to take it or even looks at it.

JAKE: You can't even buy it?

DAD: Not for a hundred dollars. But this little boy—he's shriveling up. He couldn't get any water, and he thought he was going to die. Have you ever been so thirsty you thought you'd die?

JAKE: One time after practice I was so thirsty I almost did die.

DAD: Well times that by infinity, Jake. This kid was very, very thirsty.

JAKE: What did he do?

DAD: What would you do?

JAKE: Get a bazooka.

DAD: Oh, yeah, but bazookas don't work in the desert.

JAKE: Oh yeah.

DAD: So the little boy went home, and he told his dad and he told his mom about what he'd seen, see. He told them about the water and the men and the guns and the trucks. And they said—

JAKE: Why is it green?

DAD: Huh? Why is what green? Why is—oh, the statue? Well, that's just the color of the stone, bud.

ARAB MAN: It's not made of stone.

DAD: 'Scuse me?

ARAB MAN: It's made of copper.

DAD: Oh, right, right. Hear that? Jake? Copper it's made out of. I uh—yeah, I saw that on the History Channel.

JAKE: Copper?

ARAB MAN: It becomes oxidized by the salty air, acidic rain, and it develops the green color.

JAKE: Why don't they just clean the crud off?

ARAB MAN: It is the copper's way of protecting itself—from the elements, the sun, the wind, and the pollution. The crud preserves the strength and the beauty of the metal.

JAKE: What did the boy's dad do?

DAD: *(To the MAN.)* Thank you. *(To JAKE.)* Well, The boy's dad—He took his family to the shore and there they got on a boat.

JAKE: Like this one?

DAD: A little bit, yeah. And they sailed for a better place. Ya know where?

JAKE: America?

DAD: America is right. Do ya know why?

JAKE: To get water? And watch TV?

DAD: Smart kid. And when the little boy and his family—when they got here, and they were so thirsty they'd thought that they would die—and they looked out there like you are now—out there—what did they see? Huh?

JAKE: The lady in the harbor.

DAD: And guess what Jake,... that story is true. And not just for one little boy, for a thousand little boys, and a million little boys and all their families. They come from all over the whole world to look up from this boat and to see that lady, waving, come on in. Get a drink. You see why she's so pretty now?

JAKE: Yeah.

DAD: Yeah? You think maybe we should keep her there?

JAKE: Yeah.

DAD: And you maybe see now why I'm proud of your big brother, how he's defending this lady and keeping her standing up there?

JAKE: Yeah. Dad?...Joe has enough water, right? He's in the desert. He's got water right?

DAD: He's got more than enough. Don't you worry. And nobody's gonna take it from him.

JAKE: 'Cuz he'll shoot'm right?

DAD: If he has to he will. But he's in the Green Zone, buddy. He's working on trucks. You remember, we talked about this.

JAKE: Yeah.

DAD: Okay?

JAKE: Yeah.

DAD: *(Embracing JAKE.)* Yeah. Come here. Yeah.

(DANIELLE returns with nachos.)

DANIELLE: Oh my God! Nobody in this city speaks English. Geez.

DAD: Danni, hey, would you get a picture here, of me and Jake?

DANIELLE: Can I be in it?

DAD: We'll do more on the way back over, but just get this one here with me and Jake here.

DANIELLE: Fine. Hold my nachos, midget. Don't eat them.

DAD: *(Handing over the camera.)* Here go. Jake's got the nachos. Yeah, with the statue in the back there. Good. Jake? Okay. Terrific. Your mom'll be sorry she missed this, huh? Get back to the hotel we'll have to show her...Yeah? Got it?

DANIELLE: Got it.

DAD: *(Taking the camera.)* All right! Let's see let's see.

BOAT RECORDING: The ferry will be docking shortly. For your safety, please stay off of stairs while the ferry is docking.

DAD: Buttons are so—

JAKE: Can I see? Did it get the lady?

DAD: Yeah bud, just—how in the—oh.

JAKE: I wanna see. Can I see?

DAD: Aaaannnd...ope. Well, actually, *(To the ARAB MAN.)* Sir? Hi, yeah, sorry to bother you again. Would you mind so much?

ARAB MAN: You want me to take the picture?

DAD: No-no, thank you, I was just wondering if you'd mind moving a bit over that way so you're not blocking the—oh—thank you so much. Yeah just so you're not blocking the statue. Great. Danielle? Another one?

DANIELLE: God.

DAD: Great. Here we go. Great. Jake? Put down the—no, not on the ground, just, here. Give it here. Here, here, you wanna, you wanna sit up on the rail here? Just this once. Here. Up. Okay. Go head, Danni... Terrific. That's great.

BOAT RECORDING: Welcome to Staten Island. Everyone must please exit the Ferry.

DAD: Come on gang, got everything? See now? We learned a little something, saw a national landmark, and... Danni? Change from those nachos?

(BLACKOUT.)

"THE SPIN CYCLE WITH DAN DILLINGER"

The televisions flicker to life. Music and graphics of "The Spin Cycle" lead to DAN DILLINGER at his desk.

DAN DILLINGER: Ladies and gentlemen, the network doesn't like my title for the next segment, so I hereby release the network and my producers from any liability in the statement, and I, Dan Dillinger, personally, call this segment "Just Who Do You Think You Are?"...A great deal of value is placed upon the phenomenon of celebrity in this country. I speak with some authority on the subject—#1 cable news show in America, thanks to you—I did not, however, begin my career hoping to become a celebrity—you can read about this in my best-selling autobiography available at DanDillinger.com. Somewhere—and here's the point here—somewhere along the line, along the way when these otherwise normal, average, or even below-average people achieve celebrity status,…they freak out. In the current Hollywood hierarchy, the crown of queen freak-out sits on the head of Nicole Kidman. Last weekend, while on location shooting the sequel to the box office conundrum, *Australia*—I saw it—Hmph. *(In an Aussie accent.)* "Kidman,…Australian for mummy"—While on location, Miss Kidman is approached by a young stargazer. The twelve-year-old fan asks the actress, "How can I be a movie star like you, Ms. Kidman?" Her reply? "You probably won't," says the superstar, and then goes on, "but if you do, you won't be able to keep all that weight on." "All that weight on."…Ms. Kidman, just who do you think you are?

(During the above, the crew has placed the set of the next play… The television fades to the image of the Hollywood sign in L.A.)

HEDGE

CHARACTERS

AMBER, mid-thirties   CELINE, late twenties

SETTING

Another sunny day in the Hollywood Hills. Two thirty p.m.

Two beautiful, fit, women recline in lawn chairs on the grass outside a million-dollar home in the Hollywood Hills. AMBER is a bit brash and aggressive—a good candidate for Girls Gone Wild. *CELINE is sweet and a bit more demure. She's the Mary Ann to AMBER's Ginger. There is a cooler with beverages. They are taking some sun.*

AMBER: Look up… That photographer.

CELINE: Again?

AMBER: Still. I swear, this guy drives around the block, grabs a taco supreme, and then rolls back here for another four-hour stakeout.

CELINE: So that's what that is.

AMBER: Huh.

CELINE: At the corner of his mouth. Sour cream.

AMBER: We only hope.

CELINE: Yuk.

AMBER: Yuk times uk to the square root of ewe. That guy is…

CELINE and AMBER: Skeeezyyy.

CELINE: Shady.

AMBER: Do you think he gets any decent shots off from over there?

CELINE: Telephoto lens.

AMBER: Who's he work for you think?

CELINE: Does it matter? All the same. Rats and weasels.

AMBER: Oh, they're not all the same.

CELINE: They are all the same.

AMBER: Where would you rather see a picture of yourself taking out the garbage? The *Inquirer*? Or the *Weekly World News*?

CELINE: *(Beat.)* Okay...okay. But—but—let's don't give this sleaze our energy, all right? He's not getting anything from over there. Not with this hedge in the way.

AMBER: So now you like the hedge?

CELINE: I didn't say—

AMBER: No-no, that's fine. Now you like it.

CELINE: I'm saying yes, there's something to be said for privacy. Feeling safe. Really, this should be a gated community.

AMBER: If they gate this community, the entire city economy suffers. No more orange salesmen at the traffic light at the bottom of the hill. No more paparazzi vying to snap nude sunbathing domestic spats. No more map salesmen to the celebrity homes. You know what pays for unemployment? We do. Taxes go up. Crime goes up. It's a can of worms. Soon as you start putting up walls—you create conflict.

CELINE: I don't think one of those jobs actually contributes to any part of the economy. Maybe the orange salesman.

AMBER: I could go for some juice about now.

CELINE: Hm.

AMBER: You can say what you like about the hedge though, it gives good shade come about five in the evening.

CELINE: Yes it does.

AMBER: Yes it does. And I told you that when it was first going in, didn't I?

CELINE: Yes you did.

AMBER: Yes I did. And you said it was going to obstruct our view.

CELINE: And it has.

AMBER: Yes, well, regardless, I still think it was the right thing to do. People need protection from this sort of thing. *(Calling to the MAN offstage.)* Hey!

CELINE: What are you doing? Don't do that.

AMBER: Hey buddy!

CELINE: Amber. Stop it. You're gonna bring attention.

AMBER: *(To the MAN.)* You wanna take a picture?! *(To CELINE.)* Attention? Watch this. *(AMBER rips open her shirt, exposing her push-up bra and cleavage.)*

CELINE: Amber!

AMBER: WoooHooo! Can you picture that?! Can you picture *this?!* You pervert S.O.B.!!

CELINE: Sit down.

AMBER: Ha.

CELINE: Please sit down. The neighbors'll call the cops.

AMBER: The neighbors—Since when are you caring about the neighbors?

CELINE: Since the hedge went in. Sit down.

AMBER: Relax please. God. *(Sits down, buttons her shirt.)* See what privacy has done? Made you paranoid. You never cared who saw you out here before that hedge. Now, skulking around—peeking like some trenchcoat peeper, "Who's there? Can they see me? Can they not see me?"

CELINE: Peeking is the only way I get to see anything anymore, isn't it? Like prisoners.

AMBER: Prisoners? That's a little dramatic.

CELINE: Celebrity is like a…

CELINE and AMBER: Prison.

CELINE: It absolutely is. That's why I'm out here, and that's why I'm thinking that if that hedge doesn't disappear, then maybe we should just…move on down the road. You know what I mean?

AMBER: What do you mean?

CELINE: You know that Jennifer Garner just bought the little place at the top of the rise.

AMBER: The one with the dribbly fountains?

CELINE: Uhuh.

AMBER: That's a beautiful house.

CELINE: With that beautiful front walk-garden-type path. Lots of open space.

AMBER: That is a beautiful place. Perfect for this type of afternoon, sure, but are we Jennifer Garner people? No. We're Penelope Cruz people.

CELINE: That's it. Right there. This lifestyle does that to you. It puts you in a box and as soon as you try to step outside that little box, whap! Somebody comes and smacks you on the nose with last week's *Variety*.

AMBER: Oh, please with the dramatics.

CELINE: What time is it? Is your phone on?

AMBER: Should I go ask that guy for his card? Do you think he's gonna put me up on a website or something?

CELINE: He didn't take any shots.

AMBER: What?…Are you serious?

CELINE: He didn't even lift up his camera.

AMBER: What?! That's—what? Well, screw that guy. So he's gay too. That's a great addendum to his already sparkling social status. *(To the GUY.)* Hey!

CELINE: *(Defeated.)* Don't.

AMBER: *(Yelling to GUY offstage.)* That's a great addendum to your already sparkling social status, creep!

(AMBER sits. Pause.)

AMBER: I've got the alarm set for three. We won't miss it. You know how Thursdays go.

CELINE: Any chance the spa changed its hours or something?

AMBER: Don't be a worrywart… Uh…Oh,…there he goes.

CELINE: What.

AMBER: Now he's taking pictures.

CELINE: Huh?

AMBER: Oh yeah, baby. Clicky clicky.

CELINE: He's not shooting you.

AMBER: Get my good side, butthead.

CELINE: He's not shooting you. *(Looking behind her.)* She's leaving early.

AMBER: *(Also turning around.)* Oh! Oh!

(Both facing upstage, they jump and wave and yell like crazy fans at a red carpet ceremony.)

AMBER: Penelope!...

CELINE: Penelope, we love you!...

AMBER: Penelope! Over here!...

CELINE: Are you having a good day!!

AMBER: You're so beautiful! We love you, Penelope! *(To CELINE.)* Damn this hedge.

CELINE: Have a great spa!

AMBER: Over here! Hi! Hi! *(To CELINE.)* She waved.

CELINE: We're like your sisters! We'll see you tonight!

AMBER: She waved.

CELINE: We love you!... *(To AMBER.)* Do you want to run to the gate and throw flowers at her car?

AMBER: Why would she wave?

CELINE: 'Cuz she likes us, 'cuz we're gonna be friends, 'cuz we're the sisters she's never had. Come on come on come on come on come on.

AMBER: No wait.

CELINE: What!

AMBER: Did you see that?

CELINE: I think so. What?

AMBER: The wave. Did you see her wave?

CELINE: I think so. Do you have your sign?

AMBER: Hold on. Just wait.

CELINE: We're gonna miss her at the gate.

AMBER: Shhhh. Listen. Listen. She never waves.

CELINE: So?

AMBER: But now, with the hedge up,...she waves.

CELINE: So what?

AMBER: So I don't think that was a real wave.

CELINE: You said she waved.

AMBER: Right, but I think it was a backhand.

CELINE: *(Demonstrating the wave types.)* Well, you saw it. Was it a backhand, or was it a princess?

AMBER: No, it was definitely backhand. I knew this hedge was a bad sign!

CELINE: But you said—

AMBER: Sal, Penelope Cruz is not our friend.

CELINE: But—

AMBER: No! I think we've been made a fools of us. She has—I mean—made fools of us.

CELINE: But—

AMBER: Sal, maybe it's time we really saw this for what it is. You know? Face reality?

CELINE: *(Beat.)* Really?

AMBER: The fact is that we're not Penelope Cruz people. Not anymore.

CELINE: Because of the hedge?

AMBER: Forget the hedge! That's just one more barrier to keep the real world out. I'm telling you. We have to tear down all these barriers. We have to get a fresh perspective.

CELINE: Damned hedge.

AMBER: So,…so let's go. Let's just go, okay?

CELINE: You don't want to wait for her to get back?

AMBER: Wait for who, Sal? Penelope Cruz? Who's she? Huh? Just another fame-brained girl with too much money. She's not special.

CELINE: So…where are we going.

AMBER: Let's go be with our real friends. Friends that don't need spa treatments and hedges to make them somebody.

CELINE: Maybe, yeah, you're right.

AMBER: That's right.

CELINE: So,…over to Jennifer Garner's?

AMBER: Over to Jennifer Garner's. She'll be thrilled to see us. New place can be lonely. We'll give her a housewarming.

CELINE: I'll get the vitamin water!

(CELINE packs the cooler. AMBER folds up the chairs. AMBER's cell phone alarm sounds. It's "Every Step You Take" by The Police. She turns off the phone.)

AMBER: I'll be reprogramming that alarm now I guess.

CELINE: I guess you will.

AMBER: I guess I will.

CELINE: Amber?

AMBER: What's up?

CELINE: This doesn't feel right.

AMBER: *(Beat.)* One last one?

CELINE: Don't you think?

AMBER: I do think.

(CELINE goes into the cooler and retrieves two miniature "airplane" bottles of vodka. She hands one to AMBER.)

CELINE: Here we are. *(Lifting her bottle up.)* Oh.

AMBER: What.

CELINE: Well, what do we drink to now?

AMBER: Come on. We're big people. We don't have to be petty about this.

CELINE: Of course we don't.

AMBER: Of course not. We'll drink to what we always drink to.

(They unscrew the tops of their bottles and lift them up. They recite this old toast together.)

AMBER and CELINE: "That all her lovers have been true, and that her life keeps getting better and better." *(They drink.)*

(BLACKOUT.)

"THE SPIN CYCLE WITH DAN DILLINGER"

Again the music and graphics from "The Spin Cycle" erupt from the televisions—bringing us back from commercial. DAN addresses the nation...

DAN DILLINGER: Let's do a little time travel shall we? Let's put the spin cycle into reverse and go back in time. Here we go. A different time. A different era. The U.S. is engaged in bloody conflict halfway around the world. The media's negative reporting has Americans at home turning against one another. The world's economy is on the brink of disaster and...Wait a minute, wait a minute. This time machine may not be working right. This sounds like we're still in 2009. Oh wait, look there, we are. And just like during the Vietnam War, the left-wing liberal media wants you to believe that the Pentagon is covering up some astronomical civilian death toll. According to the bozo—note my air quotations here—"independently run" website, IraqBodyCount.org—according to this sensationalist propaganda page, there have been almost one hundred thousand civilian deaths in Iraq since the conflict began in 2003. And these off-the-leash liberals want to compare that to the two thousand dead on 9/11 like it's some kind of contest. Well that just makes me ill to my stomach.

(Closeup. A title card reads "Commentary.")

Folks, there are brave American men and women out there making the ultimate sacrifice. While you sit there and point and click your way to moral superiority, there are men and women pointing their guns at people who want to hurt you. This weekend, while you're on your back deck, flipping your 100 percent grade A American beef patties, remember that there are fathers and mothers and sisters and brothers, making perhaps an even greater sacrifice than...

(Stage lights up on a bar and stool. Enter JOE, a fit young man in jeans and an Army T-shirt. On the television, DAN DILLINGER continues to ramble about the military families' sacrifices. JOE speaks to an invisible bartender.)

JOE: 'Scuse me. Pardon. *(Re. the TV.)* Anybody watching this?...Do you mind?

(The TV clicks off.)

JOE: Thank you.

JUST YOUR AVERAGE G.I. JOE

JOE sits at the bar and notices a full beer in front of him. The unseen BARTENDER points toward the audience. JOE looks that way, sees the fella that bought him this beer. He raises his glass toward the unseen STRANGER.

JOE: Look here, I'll uh—I'll drink your beer, and I—I appreciate you being…thankful but—Jesus, I think I've gotten more "thank you's" than I wanna handle for a while. Okay? *(Takes a sip.)* Okay. Here's the deal, and I don't mean to give offense when I say this. I don't do this for you. I get paid. This is my job. It's the job I wanted and I trained long and hard to get it. My boys, guys in my squad—me and the people do what I do had to bleed to get where we're at. Okay? We did that because it's where we want to be. We had to request it. Then we had to test for it. Had to qualify and I mean, we're talkin' some hard shit to do this. Some cases fight for it, and not no—not fight like Erin Brockovich, you know what I'm sayin'? I'm mean like Rocky I'm talkin' here. Hey, I think it's great. No, it's terrific everyone's all supportive and thankful. Get me wrong. But man, it ain't no—At least I don't—I don't see it as a sacrifice. I LIKE this work. I coulda just fixed trucks, worked on computers. I didn't have to join up at all even. I like it, plain-simple. I love blowin' shit up. And the bigger the bang the more I like havin' been the guy flipped the switch. And it's not dummy work. This some technical—crazy study to learn this stuff. The payoff? Eliminating the target. That's what I do. Eliminate targets. How simple is that? And I enjoy it. How many people can say that and really mean it?

Hell yes! Do you enjoy your job? Before I signed up, I saw my room, my dinner table, my church, my baseball field, ya know. Went fishin' on Fridays and muddin' on Mondays, and that's just about it. Last year I saw Florida—the swamps, Nevada deserts, Germany—oh man the beer, oh man the women—tall and blonde, every one. Let's see, I been to Afghanistan, Iraq, and—and these are just the places I's stationed. You wanna talk about leave of absence. I been all through Greece, and I went to Jerusalem—man that was somethin', went right up on the hill where they say Jesus was put up on the cross. San Francisco. New York City—that was neat I guess but you can keep it. Noisy. Saw Ground Zero. It's clean. Anyway so that's a pretty good perk I'd say. Travel. And don't forget now, when I'm over there sleepin' in tents on that Army issue cot—I'm not paying rent. Hell no—all them paychecks go right in the bank, baby. I got home from this last tour I made a down payment on my first house. Jenny was stayin' with her parents so we were savin' expenses all 'round. So now we're way further along than we thought we'd be couple years back. Helps that she's so good with money. I'm awful. She says I gotta wait to get my bike till after the new year. Kawasaki Concours

14. The Cadillac of crotch rockets, boy. We're gonna ride the bitch all over the continent. Go up, see Alaska maybe.

Love to travel. Think the Army gave me the taste for it. I've seen more than my mom or dad ever saw. Damn sight more than any my friends from home. I's in Iraq I'd keep in touch on MySpace is the best. Beats the hell out of "mail call" like back in the day in them old movies 'n' shit. Now it's like mail call every night if you got a connection. Hit that email. Get the shots of the woman, the babies, the porn—whatever. And you know, you really shouldn't believe everything they tell you about over there. I mean it's really—well it ain't exactly like they paint it to be. It never is and you got to remember that. It's just a job. A lot of jobs carry risks. When I was a kid my uncle had a job climbing trees and pruning the tops of the trees? Ya know, cutting the—He had muscles like ba-bow. You know the guy was cut 'cuz he was like, hanging from tree limbs with one arm and swinging a power hedger with the other, right? And this is like fifty, sixty feet in the air sometimes. They wore safety gear, shit, but they got danger pay. They called it danger pay. Good-good money 'cuz, what he said was like, every week somebody took a fall—took a—took a plunge, and out of those guys that did, like half of 'm never worked again. Dude, look up, trees need trimming. It's a—a needed service, right? You gonna go cover your Blazer with yellow ribbons for the tree trimmers? Dangerous job. We get a target. I paint the target. We get the order to take out the target and I do it. And I'm good at it. I'm good at it.

If I wasn't good at it I wouldn't be doin' it. That's for sure. Professional. That's the word. Man, I been in some operations I'm not supposed to talk about. And I won't. But the stuff that I can talk about—some of it's worse than the stuff I can't talk about. I don't mean worse like worse, like it's bad. It's just—shit gets scary sometimes. But when it does, I ain't thinkin' about yellow ribbons. I'm thinkin' about how do I be professional. Most times bein' a professional means takin' a mother out before he takes any of us out. You trust the intel, you do your job best you can. And there's no second-guessing. Can't. You hesitate, people get hurt. Pause, people die. That's the deal. It's exciting. Now lotta guys won't talk to you like I am. Some guys, my best friend is like this, won't talk about it. They saw some bad situations. Me? I'm all right so far. But that's—that's just part of the thing.

(The following slowly builds in intensity.)

One thing you gotta realize is: I don't miss. News says a school caught a bunker buster—wasn't me or my guys. Was the intel. Far as I know, I never hit a school and I never hit a hospital. Not once. Nobody does. We hit targets. We get the target. We paint the target. We take the target out. Do you think they'd tell us if we hit a hospital? That's bad intel, man. Fire the suit, and court martial the radioman. Don't tell me what I'm shootin' at. Just tell me how bright you want it to light up the sky. Get me? Tell ya the problem is—problem is we're dealin' with a freakin' enemy won't think twice about putting a machine gun on the *roof* of a damn hospital!...

(Beat. Realizing he's gone too far.)

Anyhow, nobody said it was a easy job. Nobody lied to me, okay. I got everything I signed up for. And those Arab guys out there in their Toyota pickups—in them caves—out there—you saw the video where the farmer's out there in the field buyin' a RPG and the Apache lights him up from like two thousand meters? Yeah. That's pretty much the routine right there. And those guys—they're getting what they signed up for. You know what I mean? And moves like that, very pro. That takes some skill. And me? I love doin' it. So don't feel sorry for me. War is bad, but war is here. I'm just happy to be in business. And like I said, I'm good at my job. All this aside, you know if we weren't in Iraq—if we weren't in Afghanistan—yer sure as shit we'd be somewhere. Supply and demand. There's never gonna be a shortage of people wanna kill a soldier…But, hell, I mean don't let me lie to ya. I love seein' those yellow ribbons in traffic.

(BLACKOUT.)

"THE SPIN CYCLE WITH DAN DILLINGER"

The television clicks on, blaring "The Spin Cycle" music and graphics…another installment with DAN DILLINGER.

DAN DILLINGER: Sports fans! Baseball season is in full swing—pun intended, but Little League parents beware…you may want to keep your tyke out of the batters' box. Why? Earlier this week, a group of concerned parents in Minasogi, Missouri, petitioned their school board to remove the condom machines from the local high school locker rooms. This because the Little League uses the high school's baseball field, and also the locker room where one child reportedly used his hot dog money to purchase a prophylactic. The school board officially denied the request to remove the machines. Apparently the Minasogi School Board believes that even if there is *no* grass on the field, you can still play ball.

(During the above, the crew has placed the set of the next play…The television fades to the image of a chainlink fence—the backstop of a baseball field.)

FIRST BASE COACH

(for Kristin)

CHARACTERS

BEN, nine years old   AMY, eleven years old

SETTING

A public baseball field. After school.

Lights up on a baseball field. BEN, an innocent, all-American fourth grader, stands near home plate, imagining he's in the World Series. AMY enters. She's a pretty, precocious fifth grader and perhaps a bit of a troublemaker. She seems nervous at first, but steels herself like a professional speaker and approaches BEN.

BEN: Hey.

AMY: Hey.

BEN: Hey. We play here sometimes. Baseball.

AMY: No kidding.

BEN: No.

AMY: I was being sarcastic.

BEN: I know.

AMY: What team?

BEN: The Devil Dogs.

AMY: Cool.

BEN: I thought up the name.

AMY: Cool.

BEN: Do you play? Baseball I mean.

AMY: I like your jacket. Do you have a girlfriend?

BEN: No.

AMY: Did you ever?... Have you?... It's okay if not.

BEN: No.

AMY: A virgin huh?

BEN: Yeah.

AMY: I've had two boyfriends. It's overrated.

BEN: Yeah.

AMY: Yeah, relationships take a lot of work, ya know, if they're really going to work.

BEN: I have to go home when the streetlights come on.

AMY: By five for me, and I start getting dinner ready for my mom.

BEN: You cook?

AMY: She cooks. I get the kitchen all ready and the stuff ready and—it's what they call prep work. I do the prep work. Me and my mom watch the cooking channel. She likes to DVR the soaps. We have Direct TV, so it's very cool.

BEN: Cool.

AMY: Yeah. I do lotsa cool stuff. I'm mature for my age. Even for a girl. Girls mature faster than boys. It's a scientific fact. It's in our sex ed book. You'll have it next year. Maybe you'll get my book. *That* would be weird. But they don't come out and just say that girls mature faster than boys, even though they should 'cuz it's written that way. They think it will embarrass the boys I think. I like younger guys anyways though. They're more innocent, untainted by this hard world.

BEN: Do you have a PlayStation? I've got thirty-four PS2 games at home.

AMY: We have a Wii.

BEN: And only three are educational or like that.

AMY: Cool.

BEN: Uhm, do you want to go to first base?

AMY: What?!

BEN: Uhm.

AMY: With you?

BEN: I have to be home before the streetlights—

AMY: I'm not going to first base with you.

BEN: Uhm—

AMY: Makes you think I wanna go to first with you anyways?

BEN: Uhm.

AMY: Tell me that.

BEN: *(Like "I dunno.")* Hm-m-hm.

AMY: Can't, can you.

BEN: I dunno.

AMY: No!?

BEN: Wuhl—

AMY: Well!?

BEN: Well, uhm, I got this note.

AMY: What note? Where? Lemme see.

(BEN produces a folded note. AMY takes it from him.)

AMY: Well, I didn't do that.

BEN: It says Amy.

AMY: Well maybe it was another Amy 'cuz I didn't write that 'cuz I'm not a dork... Okay. Let's go to first base.

(She takes his hand. He turns and heads toward first base.)

AMY: What are—hey—leggo. What are you doing? Where are you going?

BEN: First base. If you want to.

AMY: Have you ever been to first base?

BEN: Yes. Lots.

AMY: *(Beat.)* Really.

BEN: Yeah. I'm pretty good.

AMY: Oh.

BEN: I really am, I'm not just bragging.

AMY: Oh. Yeah, well, I'm good too. Just so you know.

BEN: Oh, cool.

AMY: Yeah.

(They stroll slowly to first base.)

BEN: Yeah, my dad showed me how to always at least get on first.

AMY: Really?

BEN: Yeah. I visit him every summer and every Christmas. He's rich.

AMY: He's rich?

BEN: Not like billions but close to that probably. So he coaches me in the summer.

AMY: He coaches you?

BEN: Yeah, just in the backyard. My dad says keep your head down, don't grip too tight, and never step in the bucket. Oh, and have good hustle.

AMY: Wow. I practiced on my stuffed animals when I was your age. So I'm, you know, really good now.

BEN: That's weird.

AMY: Only at first though, because then you figure out how to not get fur in your mouth.

BEN: Get what?

AMY: When do you want to do it?

BEN: What?

AMY: I'm ready.

BEN: Yeah?

AMY: Are you?

BEN: Sure.

AMY: Okay.

BEN: All right. I guess. Okay—here—yeah—get on base.

AMY: *(She gets on the bag.)* Okay...I'm ready.

BEN: Okay.

(They both are perched on the base, holding each other on the bag.)

AMY: Don't make me fall!

BEN: Let's see who can stay on the longest. Your phone got a stopwatch?

AMY: You're retarded.

BEN: Oh!

AMY: Aaah!

BEN: I win that one! Go again!

AMY: Uhm, Ben?

BEN: Is your mom gonna be mad for your clothes?

AMY: Uhm yeah, Ben,—

BEN: That's my name, don't wear it out.

AMY: Oh my God.

BEN: You never heard that before? That's old.

AMY: Yes I've heard that before. Ben,

BEN: That's my name—

AMY: Stop the retarded!...For real, have you ever been to first base?

BEN: Yes. Lots.

AMY: But with a girl—first base like with a girl.

BEN: Oh, no. Wanna thumb wrestle?

AMY: Oh my God.

BEN: What—no. Tim—Tim—my mom's boyfriend told me how to go the bases with a girl.

AMY: Oh my God. *(To herself.)* This is what I get for robbing the cradle. You seriously don't know?

BEN: I know. No, I do. On our first date we should get to first base. And then if things—

AMY: But what are you supposed to "do" on first base?

BEN: *(Pause.)* And then if things are good there after a while, then you can move to second.

AMY: But what do you do at first? Do you even know?

BEN: Do you?

AMY: Do you?

BEN: Yes.

AMY: What?

BEN: If you don't already know I'm not gonna tell you.

AMY: Be retarded.

BEN: You're retarded.

AMY: No, I'm not, but you really are.

BEN: You are.

AMY: Good comeback.

BEN: Well you're ugly so why would I even wanna—

AMY: Oh, no. Nuh-huh. Nope. Nope. Huh-uh. Forget this. I do not have to take this. Forget you. Forget this and forget you!

BEN: Hey! Where you going? Wait up! Wait-wait-wait stop!

AMY: What!?

(Pause.)

BEN: You wanna go to second?

AMY: Why would I? No!

BEN: Do you like me?

AMY: Yes!

BEN: Do you wanna go with me?

AMY: Like to second base?

BEN: No, not—

AMY: Then go with you how? Like be boyfriend-girlfriend go with you?

BEN: Okay.

AMY: "Okay?"

BEN: I mean yeah, yes. Will you go with me like that.

AMY: Fine! *(She crosses back to him.)* We can go together. But first, first you have to learn what happens at first,…base.

BEN: Is it gross?

AMY: Oh, shut up…Here. Stand here like this. Yes. Now…—

BEN: Now?

AMY: *(Pause.)* Gimme your jacket.

BEN: Give—really? Okay. Really? Why?

AMY: That's what you do at first base, you switch jackets. Come on.

(They switch jackets.)

AMY: Now, since we're going together now, we can't keep any secrets. So that means—okay?

BEN: Okay.

AMY: So that means that if your best friend tells you a secret then you have to tell me. Okay? And I'll do the same thing. Okay?

BEN: Hm-hm.

AMY: But we have to keep each other's secrets no matter what. Deal?

BEN: Got it. Deal.

AMY: And so if you tell a secret that I tell you then my brother has the right to kill you. Seriously. Okay? Okay. Welcome to first base. Your jacket's warm, and I like it.

BEN: Your jacket's…pink.

AMY: Yeah. You're going to like being my boyfriend. I'm good to my men. I'm gonna be "one of the good ones"—that means I'm going to marry up but still be appreciated. I'll be thirty-five, which is kiiinda old to get married, but that's okay these days. My career comes first. Know why thirty-five?

BEN: Huh.

AMY: That's how old you have to be to be president.

BEN: That's what you're gonna be when you grow up?

AMY: But not of America. We're not ready for a woman president. Are you ready?

BEN: I will definitely vote for you.

AMY: For second base are you ready?

BEN: Uhm. Haven't gotten signals. Unless—unless that was the signal.

AMY: Signal?

BEN: There's supposed to be signals say when it's good to go to second.

AMY: I don't think there are.

BEN: I'm pretty sure there are.

AMY: Look, I know a lot more about this than you do and that is obvious, so—

BEN: Tim said—

AMY: Benjamin. Benjamin, who knows more about first base, okay? Me? Or somebody else?

BEN: But if I get arrested.

AMY: Arrested? Why would you?

BEN: *(Whispering.)* For rape.

AMY: Rape! *(Covers her mouth.)* Who did you rape?

BEN: Nobody! I didn't!

AMY: Oh my God…Why do I always fall for the bad boys?

BEN: I don't know.

AMY: It's my greatest flaw. Okay. What signals are you—

BEN: Just signals. I don't know.

(Pregnant pause.)

AMY: How about:

(She waves her arms—signaling to go toward second base. Beat. They stroll together.)

BEN: I never had a girlfriend before.

AMY: Hand.

(He puts his hand in hers.)

AMY: Do you believe in God?

BEN: Yeah, I think so.

AMY: My mother doesn't.

BEN: Does she believe in the devil?

AMY: Not really.

BEN: What about heaven? What about angels? I saw a ghost once.

AMY: Really?

BEN: A white bald guy all white. He was freaky. Came out of the wall and chased me around the whole house until I ran into the backyard to get away. My dog, Jasmine, she was freaked out. Freaked out. She could see him 'cuz she's a dog probably, but she totally saw him 'cuz she sleeps at the foot of my bed now and never moves until I leave my room. She's totally just—just totally guards the wall where he came out. Totally just—just totally just—just guards it.

AMY: That's sad.

BEN: What.

AMY: That a dead person would chase a kid around like that. When I come over we'll do a séance.

BEN: Séances are devil worship.

AMY: No they're not.

BEN: My mom says it is.

AMY: *(Pointedly.)* My mom's a Wiccan. And so am I.

BEN: *(Matter-of-factly.)* That's devil worshiping then. You worship the devil.

AMY: We don't even believe in the devil. How are we supposed to worship someone we don't even believe in?

BEN: *(Like "I don't know.")* Hm-m-mh. You just do.

AMY: *(Tantrum scream.)* No we dooooonnnn't!!!

(Pause.)

BEN: Okay.

(Long pause. They get to second.)

AMY: My mom says that if there was a God he would give my stepmom breast cancer. If she gets cancer they'll cut off her huge boobs and my dad will come back. My mom's got mediums. C's are mediums. I'm gonna have mediums probably. I'll bet that's what she thinks. Right? That he'll come back. Don't you think?

BEN: Definitely.

AMY: I don't think he will. He loves Sarah too much. *(Boob gesture.)* Huge. Does Tim abuse you?

BEN: Who? No.

AMY: That's good.

BEN: I take taekwondo. Dude and I'm a Green belt. I could kill him if I had to. I wouldn't though. I'd just kick him in the balls—'nads…balls.

AMY: It's so cute how you're all sweet.

BEN: I'm not!

AMY: So you know, I'm not asking to like, to like try and tell you something or something.

BEN: What?

AMY: I'm only asking because you look like the type of kid who would get abused.

BEN: Nu-huh.

AMY: Yep, like on *Law & Order: SVU*. Child abuse is very sad. And it's usually the people we trust most.

BEN: What is?

AMY: Molestation. Second base.

BEN: Can we switch back jackets?

AMY: Here. Get on base. Don't be silly.

BEN: I'm just gonna have one foot on.

AMY: Long as you're on base.

BEN: Okay.

AMY: On second base, things get a little personal. This is where people stop being nice and start being real.

BEN: Okay.

AMY: Here's where you have to tell me a secret, and I have to tell you a secret. A good one.

BEN: I don't have one.

AMY: That's too bad because you have to. You're on…

BEN: I don't have to.

AMY: You're on second base so you have to.

BEN: I don't have to.

AMY: Uhhg, don't make me repeat myself. You have to. It's the rules.

BEN: You first.

AMY: You first.

BEN: No you first.

AMY: Okay-okay-okay. Grow up, please. Ohhh-kay. Here goes. One time…one time a boy brought me to a baseball field…like this…and I thought that he was going to kiss me…and we almost did…but then we didn't.

(Pause.)

BEN: My turn?

AMY: Your turn.

BEN: One time—one time I went…to the uhm— *(Beat, then grandly.)* One time I killed a black widow and saved my entire family!

AMY: That's not a secret. I heard you tell that at lunch. You have to tell something you don't want to tell.

BEN: I smoked a cigarette.

AMY: What!

BEN: It was still smoking in the ashtray, in the bathroom. I just put it up to my mouth.

AMY: That's gross! You're gonna get lung cancer. Mouth cancer.

BEN: Nuh-uh.

AMY: Uh-huh. Throat cancer. Every cancer. Tongue cancer.

BEN: Nuh-uh.

AMY: Uh-huh. I'll bet you.

BEN: I'll bet you a million dollars right now I don't get cancer.

AMY: Don't smoke around me, dude. I don't want your second-hand lung cancer.

BEN: I didn't. I didn't really even smoke it really. I just held it there for a—

AMY: That's lamer than really smoking it.

BEN: Well I did really smoke it and I just said I didn't 'cuz I wanted to see what you would say.

AMY: Another secret.

BEN: You go.

AMY: You. Yours was lame so you go again.

BEN: I don't know what to say.

AMY: Say something you never told anyone in your entire life. It could even be— *(Tucking her hair behind her ears.)* It could be something that you want to have happen that hasn't yet.

BEN: Hmmm. Hm-m-hm... Once I threw my cat into the swimming pool.

AMY: That is so mean.

BEN: Not to be mean. Not to be mean. Not to be mean. To make sure if it could swim.

AMY: Duhh.

BEN: I know! They can, and fast too. Real fast.

AMY: Have you ever killed anything?

BEN: No. Yes!

AMY: What?

BEN: *(Grandly.)* A black widow spider!

AMY: I killed a bee.

BEN: So? I killed lots a bees. Wasps. Hornets. Yellow jackets. I flooded a anthill one time and made the queen come out. Did you know that the queen ant can fly?

AMY: I killed a bee in my room.

BEN: A bee was in your room? That would freak me out.

AMY: It was buzzing around and I didn't want to kill it 'cuz I love bees. I caught it in this jar and had it upside down on my desk in my room.

BEN: Did you squish it?

AMY: No.

BEN: Burn it?

AMY: No.

BEN: Did you—what happened? Did you kill it?

AMY: No.

BEN: But you said—

AMY: *(Defensively.)* I didn't kill it. It died on its own. Suffocated.

BEN: Cooool. How long did it take?

AMY: I don't know. Thirty-six days. I thought it would die in like a day. After four days though it was just really mad. And I know why. I knew why. I put it under glass. It couldn't fly. It couldn't pollinate flowers or make honey or do any bee stuff bees are meant to do. I impeded its beeness. Do you know what impeded means? It started to calm down after a week, and then one day it didn't move so I thought—you know. So I scooted the glass toward the edge of the table, to—and it moved. Nope, wasn't dead yet. I checked on it every day. I'd think it was dead and then it would move. And then I would think it was dead and start to move the jar and then it would move again. It was so mad and so sad and so angry and so. And it wouldn't just—just-just-just die. And I—so I came home every day and I sit at my desk…and I would talk to it.

BEN: What did you say?

AMY: I said,…"Die. Please die. Please die little bee." Like that.

BEN: What did it say?

AMY: Why'd it have to come in my room in the first place? Tell me that. You can't. Nobody can. On the thirty-sixth it was twitching one leg real slow, and when it stopped? I cried harder than I ever cried that day. I knew the whole time I could've let it go so easy, and I buried it in my dad's garden where he used to grow peppers. Why did I do that?

BEN: Bury it?

AMY: No. Why all of it. Why did I do that?

BEN: You like animals?

AMY: I love animals! Second base sucks!

BEN: You wanna go to third? Let's go.

AMY: Yeah. Hey!…You can't tell anyone about that.

BEN: Okay.

AMY: Okay?

BEN: Okay.

AMY: Promise?

BEN: Promise.

AMY: Promise again.

BEN: Promise. Nothing's crossed.

AMY: And promise not to tell we went to any bases.

BEN: All right.

AMY: Okay…Let's go. Third is always best.

BEN: Hope so. First 'n' second were retarded.

AMY: You would know. *(Running.)* Last one there eats his own boogers.

BEN: No fair!…

AMY: Booger eater!

BEN: Hey! You cheated!

AMY: *(Reaches third base.)* Too slow!

BEN: You cheated! I'll race you anytime I'll race you.

AMY: Okay.

BEN: You just can't cheat though.

AMY: I'll beat you anyway.

BEN: No way you won't.

(An easy silence for a few moments.)

BEN: What happens at third?

AMY: Third base is very tricky.

BEN: Tricky how?

AMY: Well because you can get sores if you're not careful.

BEN: What?! Stop lying.

AMY: It's true. You'll get sores on your mouth.

BEN: What? How? From what?

AMY: You know how a flower has petals?

BEN: Uh-yeah.

AMY: And in the middle of the petals there's a little basket where all the pollen is.

BEN: I take allergy shots.

AMY: What, for pollen?

BEN: No, for allergies.

AMY: Well, do you know what I'm talking about?...A flower opens its petals. It leans into the sun. That's so cool how a flower leans to the sun. And the basket is open and ready for pollination. Right?

BEN: There's a basket?

AMY: A little pad where the—come here. See the flowers.

BEN: Those are dandelions.

AMY: Eat one.

BEN: You dare me? 'Cuz I will.

AMY: That's third base. Dares.

BEN: I'll eat a flower. I don't care. I like'm.

AMY: Some flowers are poisonous. You could die. You could get—

BEN: Not dandelions. I eat'm all the time.

AMY: You could get diarrhea. You could get blisters on your lips.

BEN: How?

AMY: If you ate roses you would.

BEN: Roses have thorns. I wouldn't eat a rose. I'm not retarded.

AMY: But roses are the sweetest.

BEN: Smelling maybe.

AMY: No, tasting. They're the sweetest. That's why they have thorns I bet. So retarded baseball players don't come and eat'm all.

BEN: Whatever.

AMY: Whatever whatever. Don't be a pussy. Eat the flower.

BEN: What did you say?

AMY: I said don't be a wuss, eat the flower.

BEN: No you didn't.

AMY: Yes I did.

(Pause.)

BEN: No you didn't. I heard you.

AMY: Eat it!

BEN: *(He gobbles a flower—gag reflex a bit—tries to look cool—swallows.)* Hmmm. ... Now you.

AMY: You dare me?

BEN: Yeah.

AMY: Say it.

BEN: I dare you.

AMY: Dare me to what?

BEN: I dare you to eat a flower.

AMY: No.

BEN: You have to.

AMY: Dare me to do something else.

BEN: Eat a flower. I did.

AMY: Something new. That's the rule. Always something new.

BEN: I dare you... *(Looking around.)* I dare you to...I dare you...—

AMY: If you don't dare me—

BEN: I dare you to go to home plate with me.

AMY: What?!

BEN: Yeah.

AMY: NO WAY!

BEN: It's a dare.

AMY: I don't care.

BEN: I double-dare you.

AMY: No.

BEN: I double-dog dare you. I triple-dog dare you. That's a triple...dog...dare.

AMY: I'm not going to home plate till I get married. Are you crazy?

BEN: Thought you liked me.

AMY: What?

BEN: Said you did.

AMY: You're still in Little League, Benjamin, that's why. *(Beat, then tenderly.)* Look up. Yeah.

BEN: Yeah.

AMY: Yeah.

BEN: Well, well then, I dare you...—

AMY: To what.

BEN: I dare you...—

AMY: To what?

BEN: I dare you to kiss me.

(They switch their jackets back. Then she flips up his collar, pulls him in and...She kisses him; at first sweetly but then—she sticks her tongue out and it goes all over his mouth; it is grotesquely innocent. Then breaking away, she runs to exit. Stopping on the pitcher's mound, she turns back.)

AMY: I got your phone number from the school directory! Oh, and by the way—I lied about a lot of stuff.

BEN: About what?

AMY: Tell you later. Welcome to the major leagues. *(She runs off.)*

BEN: Curve ball! What the heck? What the hell. *(Wiping his face.)* Oh man. That was a slider. That was so wet.

(Lights down.)

"THE SPIN CYCLE WITH DAN DILLINGER"

The televisions pops on with the music and graphics of "THE SPIN CYCLE" coming back from commercial for the final installment. DAN DILLINGER at his desk.

DAN DILLINGER: Mail call! We love to hear from you here at the Cycle. "Dear Dan, Last week you interviewed Condoleezza Rice on your show." That's right I did. Very nice woman. "You asked her about the transition of the new president, about the war, and even about her famous black boots, but you didn't ask her the one thing on our minds. How does she feel about Obama and the first African American presidency. Is there something inherently wrong with you?" Barry Boodrow, Melborne, Florida. I will answer your question, Barry. Yes, there is something inherently wrong with me, and that is, I'm not a racist. Once again, Dan Dillinger, not a racist... When we get back from this very short break we'll meet an American soldier who, because of stop-loss, has not seen his family in almost two years. When we get back, we'll unite the Smith family with their son Jerome, via satellite. Stay with us, in just two turns, you'll be back in the Cycle.

(During the above, the crew has placed the set of the next play... The television fades this time to the "Spin Cycle" logo that we saw before the first play began.)

JEROME VIA SATELLITE

CHARACTERS

DAN DILLINGER, host
MAKEUP GIRL
SPECIALIST JEROME SMITH, twenty-five, Asian American
FIRST SERGEANT BALPINE, Army press liaison
TELEVISION PRODUCER IN IRAQ
TELEVISION PRODUCER IN DALLAS
PRIVATE ZANSKY/JEROME 2, twenty-five, Causcasian
BILL SMITH, Jerome's father, fifty, Caucasian
LYNN SMITH, Jerome's mother, forty-five, Caucasian
KELLY SMITH, Jerome's sister, nineteen, Caucasian
MARINA, Jerome's girlfriend, twenty-five, Caucasian

SETTING

Fourth of July, 2008. A suburban American home in Dallas, Texas; a military base in Iraq; a television studio in New York City.

Lights up. Split stage. Stage right: THE SMITH FAMILY home—DAD, fifty; MOM, forty-five; daughter KELLY, nineteen; and family friend MARINA, twenty-five, are being placed into a presentable tableau for a television broadcast by a PRODUCER. Stage left: A U.S. military installation in Iraq—SPECIALIST JEROME SMITH, twenty-five, an Asian American, is being prepared for a television broadcast by a PRODUCER. FIRST SERGEANT BALPINE oversees. Each group is setting up for a live video feed in which they will broadcast to each other and a live network television audience. The crew, now the play's VIDEO CREW, are moving the cameras and lights into position. In the center is the flat-screen television on which we will see DAN DILLINGER when he comes on air.

U.S. PRODUCER: Thank you for letting America be a part of your family today. Really is a lovely home and it's going to look great on camera. You all look so good. And we're looking about ready. So are you excited?

JEROME: *(Subdued.)* Pretty excited yeah.

IRAQ PRODUCER: Don't blame ya. Will all your friends be watching at home?

KELLY: Only like the whole school is gonna DVR it.

U.S. PRODUCER: Mr. Smith? Looking a little nervous. You doin' all right there?

FIRST SERGEANT BALPINE: Specialist Smith's unit came under mortar fire last night.

IRAQ PRODUCER: Oh my God.

MOM: Bill, are you nervous?

FIRST SERGEANT BALPINE: That's why the confusion earlier.

IRAQ PRODUCER: Was anybody wounded?

JEROME: One casualty.

DAD: Just anxious is all. Let's do this.

FIRST SERGEANT BALPINE: We won't be mentioning the incident this morning.

IRAQ PRODUCER: Oh good. Good. That's the main thing. That you're okay I mean. And you got a shower, yeah? Feelin' good?

JEROME: I'm feelin'.

IRAQ PRODUCER: Good, 'cuz I know a certain Family Smith that's gonna be real excited to see you.

U.S. PRODUCER: Very exciting. It'll be just like he's right here. Now,

IRAQ PRODUCER: it's important to remember

U.S. PRODUCER: even though we're all very excited,

IRAQ PRODUCER: When you see them come up on the screen

U.S. PRODUCER: I'll ask you not to all start talking at once,

U.S. PRODUCER and IRAQ PRODUCER: All right?

U.S. PRODUCER: And here's the reason why. It's like eight thousand miles from Dallas to Baghdad. The audio you hear is going to be a little bit off from the video that you see. Okay? And we're going to fix that by sort of fudging a little extra delay.

IRAQ PRODUCER: What that'll do is sync it up for the TV audiences

U.S. PRODUCER: and for you and for Jerome too. All right?

JEROME: Ten-four.

DAD: That's a big ten-four.

MOM: Here that, ya'll? Don't all talk at once.

IRAQ PRODUCER: Great...Now I get the sense that you're not completely comfortable with it

U.S. PRODUCER: but I still think you might want just a smidgin of—

DAD: No makeup.

KELLY: It's TV, Dad.

IRAQ PRODUCER: It's the lights is what it is.

KELLY: Everybody wears makeup on TV.

IRAQ PRODUCER: These lights make it look like you're a ghost.

KELLY: Mari?

MARINA: For shows I think, yeah, but—I don't know if men usually wear makeup for the news.

KELLY: Uhm, the anchors and reporters do. *(To PRODUCER.)* They do, right?

IRAQ PRODUCER: Petraeus does.

FIRST SERGEANT BALPINE: Does he really?

IRAQ PRODUCER: Just a base coat. Real thin.

MOM: Real people don't though. We're real people, honey.

IRAQ PRODUCER: It just looks healthy is all.

MOM: Your father looks very handsome as he is.

DAD: Thank you.

FIRST SERGEANT BALPINE: The main thing is that you're comfortable. Specialist?

JEROME: Yeah—I don't think I want any.

U.S. PRODUCER: And that's absolutely fine.

IRAQ PRODUCER: Let's just go over the way this is going to run, one more time.

U.S. PRODUCER: I'm going to get the countdown from New York

U.S. PRODUCER and IRAQ PRODUCER: just as Dan Dillinger is introducing you...

IRAQ PRODUCER: I'm going to get the countdown from New York. That's when I'll give you a countdown,

U.S. PRODUCER: As I reach "one" I'll point. *(Points.)* And you all say:

JEROME: Hi Mom! Hi honey! 'Sup squirt! Hey Dad!

U.S. PRODUCER: But with lots of energy. And remember to look right into the camera, not at the monitor, okay? So let's practice just once all together...three, two, and *(Points.)*

DAD, MOM, and KELLY: Happy birthday, Jerome!

FIRST SERGEANT BALPINE: Can loosen up a little, Specialist. That's not a gun you're staring into there.

MOM: Marina, you're not practicing?

U.S. PRODUCER: That was terrific.

MOM: Mari?... *(To PRODUCER.)* I'm sorry—can we practice once more? Mari missed it.

U.S. PRODUCER: Uhm,...uhm all right.

MOM: I want to do it as best we can.

DAD: We all do, hon.

MOM: You would think that, wouldn't you?

U.S. PRODUCER: Okay, here we go practice in five, four, three, two, *(Points.)*

FAMILY: Happy

IRAQ PRODUCER: Birthday—yada-yada-yada and at that point you'll engage in a touching

U.S. PRODUCER: moving

IRAQ PRODUCER: relaxed

U.S. PRODUCER: but earnest

FIRST SERGEANT BALPINE: Brief.

IRAQ PRODUCER: brief

U.S. PRODUCER: brief conversation.

DAD: Brief is fine. These lights are hot as hell.

KELLY: Dad.

DAD: Kelly.

FIRST SERGEANT BALPINE: Specialist.

MOM: Honey.

DAD: Hon.

JEROME: Sir.

U.S. PRODUCER: Mari, *(Taking her aside.)* May I call you Mari? I feel kind of like part of the family.

FIRST SERGEANT BALPINE: I work for a living, son.

JEROME: Sorry, First Sergeant.

FIRST SERGEANT BALPINE: *(Taking him aside.)* A word?

U.S. PRODUCER: I just want to make sure you're comfortable with everything. Are you comfortable with everything?

MARINA: Yeah. I guess. Why? Am I doing something wrong?

U.S. PRODUCER: Not at all.

FIRST SERGEANT BALPINE: You're doing fine.

U.S. PRODUCER: I just want to make sure that you're good with everything and good with the surprise.

MARINA: Surprise?

FIRST SERGEANT BALPINE: Should be no surprise to you, son. The media does not like this war. Not one bit. We come eight thousand miles to fight the terrorists and they beam us back home every night so we can fight the publicists. Makes me sick all the crap that they show.

U.S. PRODUCER: All the crud that they see.

FIRST SERGEANT BALPINE: Your folks back home. All the folks back home,

U.S. PRODUCER: All the boys in uniform really.

FIRST SERGEANT BALPINE: They need a pick-me-up—bad. That's what they need, something to feel good about—about the Army.

U.S. PRODUCER: And that's what this can do. What you can do.

FIRST SERGEANT BALPINE: You and your girl.

MARINA: Jerome. | JEROME: Marina.

FIRST SERGEANT BALPINE: Nothing is more romantic—more inspirational—than a war-torn love affair. Can make a grown man just break down and cry.

JEROME: I'm not sure I—You want me to cry on TV?

U.S. PRODUCER: Please don't cry. Your mascara.

MARINA: I just never thought this would be the way it—With, you know, and in front of all—

U.S. PRODUCER: Wait, breathe… You don't have to do this if you don't want to.

MARINA: No, I know.

DAD: Marina? Everything all right?

FIRST SERGEANT BALPINE: Natural to be nervous.

U.S. PRODUCER: *(To DAD.)* Just some—some butterflies. Right?

JEROME: You have no idea.

MARINA: Fine—I'm fine, Bill.

U.S. PRODUCER: *(To MARINA.)* I'm so sorry about this. Those jerks told me you knew about it. We'll call it off. It's Okay. It's off… It's just… Mari, can I ask you…

FIRST SERGEANT BALPINE: You carry her picture, don't you?

MARINA: I love him so much.

U.S. PRODUCER: Mari, then don't you have the obligation to give him something to come home to? To fight for?

FIRST SERGEANT BALPINE: To hope for,

IRAQ PRODUCER: But not just her, Jerome.

IRAQ PRODUCER and U.S. PRODUCER: The whole country…

U.S. PRODUCER: needs this. America has come to a crossroads. We're at a crossroads,

IRAQ PRODUCER: Like you and Mari are at a crossroads.

U.S. PRODUCER: See, you have your relationship with a soldier, but we—

IRAQ PRODUCER: Us.

IRAQ PRODUCER and U.S. PRODUCER: America…

U.S. PRODUCER: has a relationship with *all* the soldiers.

IRAQ PRODUCER: *All* the families.

| U.S. PRODUCER: He's every American son. | IRAQ PRODUCER: She's every American daughter. |

FIRST SERGEANT BALPINE: To join the American Family and the Family of the U.S. Army… to knit them together. This is your mission. This is why you're here. *(Pause.)* Now, I can't order you to do this—

JEROME: I'll do it.

U.S. PRODUCER: *(Beat.)* That's one lucky man over there.

FIRST SERGEANT BALPINE: When you pop the question, show her this.

JEROME: Oh no, I can't afford—This is an empty box.

MARINA: A ring?

IRAQ PRODUCER: You'll go down on one knee, you open the box.

U.S. PRODUCER: Jerome's dad will give you the ring when Jerome pops the question.

IRAQ PRODUCER: The network went halfsies with D.O.D. —Picked out something nice. It's tasteful.

U.S. PRODUCER: It's beautiful.

U.S. PRODUCER: You'll love it. Trust me.

IRAQ PRODUCER: She'll love it. Trust me.

MARINA: But does he—

JEROME: But does she—

IRAQ PRODUCER: She has no idea.

U.S. PRODUCER: You know, and he knows, but he doesn't know that you know.

FIRST SERGEANT BALPINE: You know, whenever my wife sees anything like this, she hits me and says, "Why didn't you propose like that!?" I say, "Because you're such a bitch."…Anyways. You'll be glad for this. Trust me.

U.S. PRODUCER: We need to get ready to go. You're good?

MARINA: I'm good.

JEROME: I'm good.

IRAQ PRODUCER: Great. Let's do this.

(U.S. PRODUCER whispers to DAD and slips him a ring box. The lights go on. The TVs—if TVs are used—are turned on.)

KELLY: What was she telling you?

MARINA: Huh? Nothing. Tell you later.

U.S. PRODUCER: *(On headset.)* I gotcha. Loud and clear. The beautiful Smith family is at places. Standing by.

IRAQ PRODUCER: *(On cell phone.)* I'm here…Clear as a bell. Specialist Smith is ready. Standing by.

U.S. PRODUCER: Okay, everyone, we're coming back from commercial. Mr. Dillinger will introduce us and we'll go right into it. I'll point. Remember what we talked about. Big smiles, big energy.

KELLY: *(Sotto voce.)* We're gonna be on tee-veeeee.

MOM: Kelly ssshhh.

DAN DILLINGER: *(On the television center stage.)* And now lastly on this July 4th edition of "The Spin Cycle," we celebrate, along with the birthday of the United States, the birthday of Specialist Jerome Smith from Dallas Texas. Jerome is currently serving his second tour in Iraq and today he turns twenty-five years old. We've sent a Spin Cycle crew to the Smith family home in Dallas and also a crew to the base in Iraq where Jerome is stationed nearly eight thousand miles away.

(THE FAMILY and JEROME turn toward their respective cameras. The studio lights go on, if not on already.)

IRAQ PRODUCER: Here we go. In

DAN DILLINGER: *(To his PRODUCER off camera.)* Are we? Let's join them now for a happy birthday wish courtesy of "The Spin Cycle."

U.S. PRODUCER: Five.

IRAQ PRODUCER: Four.

U.S. PRODUCER: Three.

U.S. PRODUCER and IRAQ PRODUCER: Two.

(They both mouth "one" and then point. The television goes to a split screen image— half-screen with the SMITH FAMILY

looking straight into the camera, half-screen with JEROME.)

DAD: Hap!—

(There is an awkward, confused pause. THE FAMILY glances around, unsure of what they're seeing.)

U.S. PRODUCER: *(Whispering.)* We're on. Go ahead. *(Points.)*

KELLY: Dad?

FIRST SERGEANT BALPINE: *(Seeing the TV.)* Oh, Christ.

IRAQ PRODUCER: Christ? What oh Christ? *(Looks at the monitor.)* Oh God.

MOM: Who is that?

U.S. PRODUCER: That's Jerome.

MOM: Not *my* Jerome.

U.S. PRODUCER: Are you sure?

JEROME: I can explain.

MOM: I'd know if my son was Chinese.

KELLY: Mom!

MOM: I wouldn't?!

FIRST SERGEANT BALPINE: Turn the camera off, please.

JEROME: I'm Private First Class Michael Yow.

IRAQ PRODUCER: *(Into cell phone.)* Are you cutting?

FIRST SERGEANT BALPINE: Turn the camera off. Stop talking, Private.

U.S. PRODUCER: *(On headset.)* Are we cutting?

(Note: JEROME's lines ending in "..." are spoken without pausing for the other characters to speak.)

JEROME: I was in a patrol...

IRAQ PRODUCER: *(Into cell.)* Whadaya mean "Why?"

FIRST SERGEANT BALPINE: I order you, Private.

JEROME: ...that this afternoon we came under mortar attack.

U.S. PRODUCER: *(Into headset.)* You don't see this?

JEROME: I was in a Humvee along with...

FIRST SERGEANT BALPINE: You will be placed under arrest.

JEROME: ...along with three other men...

KELLY: What's happening?

MOM: What's happening?

JEROME: ...And one of those men, Ma'am, Sir, was Specialist Smith.

MOM: Does he mean Jerome?

DAD: What's this now?

JEROME: I'm here because—

FIRST SERGEANT BALPINE: Cut it for Christ's sake!

JEROME: Just hear me please!

DAD: What he's saying?

MOM: Show me my son! Put him on there!

JEROME: ...I came here as Jerome because...

IRAQ PRODUCER: Cut?!

U.S. PRODUCER: Cut?

FIRST SERGEANT BALPINE: Cut!

JEROME: ...—because they're going to try and tell you...

IRAQ PRODUCER and U.S. PRODUCER: Okay-okay-okay-okay-okay.

JEROME: ...that what happened today—

(Lights out on THE FAMILY and SOLDIERS. TV switches back to DAN DILLINGER at his desk.)

DAN DILLINGER: *(On TV.)* Apparently there's some confusion between the parties there, some sort of mix-up anyway, and I think we just lost our satellite feed. The beauty of live television, America. We'll take a short break—get it straightened out and be right back. Don't go away. *(Pause.)* Are we out? We're clear? *(Beat.)* That was amazing. Does anybody know what the Christ that was all about?

(DAN leaves the camera frame—as he does, we hear his voice backstage live, and he enters upstage. A MAKEUP GIRL is smoothing his base, matting his hair, and powdering his brow.)

DAN DILLINGER: I can barely still call myself a newsman and I'm cutting away from the hottest story to stroke my nuts in twenty years.

MAKEUP GIRL: Mr. Dillinger?

(She's brought him a tall folding chair. He sits.)

DAN DILLINGER: I think out loud, hon. Please don't talk back.

MAKEUP GIRL: I'm sorry. *(She works.)*

DAN DILLINGER: Thirty years in the field and still it blows me away. How regular folks manage to yank honest news from the yellow jaws of journalism.

MAKEUP GIRL: That's from your last book right?...I'll shut up.

(Pause as she works.)

DAN DILLINGER: ...I was younger I wanted to be a war correspondent. The glory—oh the glory of combat reporting—so much greater than the glory of the soldiering. You get all that credit, all the thank you's for the service blah blah... but without any of the awkwardness that comes with congratulating a guy for killing folks...Know how much ass war correspondents get?

MAKEUP GIRL: More than news show hosts?

DAN DILLINGER: Eh, a different kind...But they do get the glory. And that was the dream...I don't remember my dreams anymore. I had the same dream so many nights in a row I'm probably still having it—so I doubt I'm missing much.

MAKEUP GIRL: What was the dream?

DAN DILLINGER: Huh?

MAKEUP GIRL: Look up...

(Pregnant pause as she works.)

MAKEUP GIRL: What was the dream?

(Pregnant pause as she works.)

DAN DILLINGER: I'm at a press conference in a grand ballroom. But it's actually a forest. You know how that is in dreams?—I see this on a blog and it's your ass. —...And I'm there and I'm surrounded by newsmen with microphones—but they're really aborigines with spears, poison tips, all pointed at my throat. Then this bell rings—like the old movie studio bell,

(No reaction.)

DAN DILLINGER: or like in high school,... and I'm hit with a flood of light.

(Lights shift to a special on DAN. The CREW, upon their last exit, positioned the cameras so that now they hit DAN from each side—he is in profile on the TVs above the audience.)

DAN DILLINGER: The natives are gone but now zap—I'm stuck—glued to this little X on the floor. I look up. And I'm frozen there under these unbearable hot white lamps. I'm literally a deer in the headlights now because now I'm this giant buck. This great, badass, and beautiful buck I am, with just this mythic, twenty-four-point rack. It winds up—twining up like the roots of an ancient oak. I'm poised before a setting sun, gorgeous so my silhouette is rimmed with this golden glow. And I've these cavernous nostrils—these two immense black holes to suck to flare these tremendous *(Deep inhale.)* surging breaths. And now I—as this beast—I look up and I see this red dot. Just this tiny red dot. A little red light that tells me God is watching. And it shoots me. Every night it shoots me. I'm venison. Seasoned to taste and served over conversation... *(Out of the dream now.)* Now here I happen along here— Here we stumble by this screaming truth like a goddamn I.E.D.—a goddamn roadside bomb of human courage and frailty here, and I see that I'm not really sleeping at all. Or rather that I am not the dreamer. I'm—I'm the dream. I'm the dream because I make sense out of nonsense, and like a dream, pull narrative from the random. I make plain the extraordinary, and amazing just the plain ol' same ol' plain ol' same. And see, as long as you don't change the channel, I can keep you sleeping soundly... so that there's nothing to remember.

MAKEUP GIRL: You wanna cover the war then? And cover the soldiers? You could you know.

OFFSTAGE VOICE: Twenty seconds!

DAN DILLINGER: *(Beat.)* You're dreaming. *(To offstage.)* Thank you twenty. *(He exits the way he came in. ON THE TELEVISION he reenters the frame, sits at his desk, checks his earpiece, and shuffles some papers. He looks up.)* Welcome back. I'm Dan Dillinger. If you're just joining us, we're talking with the Smith family of Dallas, Texas, as we are about to connect them via satellite to their son, Specialist Jerome Smith, currently serving his second tour in Iraq. Our producers had a bit of a mix-up, but I'm told they've ironed it out. Let's go first to our team in Iraq, and then check in with Dallas. Kyle? Have we got all the bugs worked out over there?

(The CAMERA CREWS, FAMILY, and SOLDIERS have returned. All but MICHAEL YOW. He is not present. Lights up on Iraq. IRAQ PRODUCER stands before the camera, his image on the television as well. He listens to his cell phone for just a moment. Then he lowers the cell and speaks to the camera.)

IRAQ PRODUCER: Thanks for bearing with us. We do, in fact now, have it all straightened out. One thing I've learned over here, Dan, is that Army life can be very tedious at times. That's what you saw here, one of Smith's friends deciding he could spice things up with a little prank there. We apologize for the time it took up. We're all set to go now.

(Television switches to DAN at desk.)

DAN DILLINGER: "The Spin Cycle" is proud to bring this American hero together with his American family.

(Television goes split screen between Dallas and Baghdad. Baghdad side: A new JEROME SMITH sits where YOW was. He's a young white man in fatigue pants and an Army T-shirt.)

SMITH FAMILY: *(A strained attempt at normal excitement.)* Happy birthday!

JEROME SMITH 2: Thanks. Thanks Mom. Thanks Dad. Thanks...thanks squirt. It's good to see all of you. Miss you lots.

DAD: We miss you too,...son.

JEROME SMITH 2: Uhm... *(Producing the ring box.)* Marina?...

(JEROME 2 goes down on one knee; opens the empty box; DAD opens a ring box. Seeing the ring, MARINA stifles a cry.)

JEROME SMITH 2: Will you marry me?

(MARINA takes the ring, puts in on her finger, and nods affirmative. After a beat, KELLY runs offstage. MOM buries her face in DAD's chest. The television switches to DAN DILLINGER at his desk.)

DAN DILLINGER: An emotional reunion. The Smiths will speak for a little while longer, but unfortunately for us that's all the time we have. I'm Dan Dillinger. Thank you for joining me tonight and every night. And I look forward to next time we meet, here in "The Spin Cycle"... *(Pause.)* ...We're clear? Somebody, please, just a—I don't know—an aspirin please?

(DAN removes his earpiece. A WOMAN comes into frame and takes his papers away. The screen goes dark. Dallas: the PRODUCER begins taking the camera equipment down. DAD is comforting MOM and KELLY. Baghdad: JEROME SMITH 2 stands and FIRST SERGEANT BALPINE shakes his hand.)

FIRST SERGEANT BALPINE: Perfect.

JEROME SMITH 2: I didn't screw it up?

FIRST SERGEANT BALPINE: You did fine, Private Pensky?

JEROME SMITH 2: Zansky.

FIRST SERGEANT BALPINE: Let's head over to my office so you can sign a few things.

U.S. PRODUCER: *(To offstage.)* Joe! Callin' a car? Then help strike this crap and get it out to the truck, would you?

IRAQ PRODUCER: *(On cell phone.)* Honey? I'm leaving here and getting on the first flight. Huh? Probably Amsterdam. Oh you saw? Yeah?

U.S. PRODUCER: You know how to strike that?

IRAQ PRODUCER: I'll be as safe as they'll let me be.

DAD: Karen,...do you know—

U.S. PRODUCER: Honestly, sir. I have no idea and no way to find out.

IRAQ PRODUCER: They don't tell me anything.

IRAQ PRODUCER and U.S. PRODUCER: That's show biz.

(BLACKOUT.)

SUSPICIOUS PACKAGE: Rx

Gyda Arber and Aaron Baker with Wendy Coyle
Additional writing by Danny Bowes, James Comtois, and Roger Nasser

GYDA ARBER was born in San Francisco. She received a bachelor's degree in musical theater from New York University. Primarily an actor and director, she also trained at the Maggie Flanigan Studio's two-year Meisner Program. Arber's playwriting credits include *Suspicious Package* (writer/director; with Wendy Coyle) and *Q&A: The Perception of Dawn* (story/director; with Danny Bowes), both of which premiered at The Brick Theater's The Film Festival: A Theater Festival in 2008. She also created the story for and directed the short film *Watching*, which premiered as part of *The Bride of Sinister Six* anthology (2008). *Suspicious Package* was nominated for a New York Innovative Theatre Award for Best Production of a Play, and received the award for Best Off-Off Broadway Unique Theatrical Experience from the Independent Theatre Bloggers Association. Upcoming projects include a one-woman makeover show, *Trudie Calling!* (www.trudiecalling.com), an at-home edition of *Suspicious Package* (www.suspiciouspackageshow.com), and a piece for Tiny Theater at The Brick with Aaron Baker. Arber resides in Greenpoint, Brooklyn.

AARON BAKER often works in film as a writer and director, and is also a theatre actor and occasional playwright. He holds a BA in film and media arts from Temple University. Baker wrote, directed, and produced the short horror film *The Language of the Animals* as part of Third Lows' *Sinister Six Must Be Destroyed* anthology (2009). For the stage, he wrote and directed the theatrical serial *3800 Elizabeth* (The Battle Ranch, New York, 2008). In 2007 he received the Master of the Bard award at The Brick Theater's Pretentious Festival for having performed in both *Ian W Hill's Hamlet* and *Macbeth without Words*. Baker lives in Brooklyn.

WENDY COYLE was born in San Francisco in 1943. She holds a PhD in sociology from the University of California–Berkeley. She is a playwright and writer whose works include a memoir, *Iridescent Iran* (www.iridescentiran.com). She currently resides in San Francisco.

DANNY BOWES is a filmmaker and actor when not writing plays (*Walking Shadow*; *This Is the New American Theatre*; *Q&A: The Perception of Dawn*; *Booze, Sports, & Romance*) and screenplays (*Watching*, *The Mourners*, *Byron Invented Boredom*, the last of which he also directed). He can often be found at moviesbybowes.blogspot.com.

JAMES COMTOIS, whose *The Adventures of Nervous-Boy* can be found in *Plays and Playwrights 2007,* is the co-founding co-artistic director of the New York–based theatre company, Nosedive Productions. He lives in Brooklyn.

ROGER NASSER is a New York–based actor/writer. He has had his work performed at La MaMa and The Flea Theater. As an actor, he has performed in numerous theatres including Soho Rep, The Red Room, Chashama, Center Stage, The Connelly Theater, Todo Con Nada, and, more recently, The Brick.

Suspicious Package: Rx was first presented by The Fifth Wall as part of the Antidepressant Festival (Michael Gardner and Robert Honeywell, Artistic Directors) on June 13, 2009, at The Brick Theater, Williamsburg, New York, with the following credits:

Director of Photography: Aaron Baker
Male Voiceovers: Aaron Baker
Female Voiceovers: Gyda Arber
Sound Engineer: Ian W. Hill
Script Supervisor: Berit Johnson

Video Cast

Ted	Fred Backus
Emma	Becky Byers
Riley's Mother/Lynn	Hope Cartelli
Riley's Sister/Picnicking Woman	Rebecca Comtois
Joy's Mother	Ivanna Cullinan
Katie	Natalie Daifotis
Leslie (female)	Sarah Engelke
Dick	Ian W. Hill
Janice Todd	Debbie Klaar
Melissa Myers	Samantha Mason
Jamie	Mateo Moreno
Alice	Jessica McVea
Doctor Voiceover/Riley's Brother/Picnicking Man	Roger Nasser
Leslie (male)	Timothy McCown Reynolds
Celeste/Janie	Jessica Savage
Hal	Ken Simon
Betty	Alexis Sottile
Charles Clark	Art Wallace
Psychiatrist/Janice	Amanda Woodward

INTRODUCTION TO *SUSPICIOUS PACKAGE: Rx*
BY MARTIN DENTON

Suspicious Package: Rx is enormous fun. This immersive theatre experience casts each of its audience members in a role in a short comedy of suspense and intrigue that carries them from the front door of the theatre where it's being presented to locales all around the neighborhood surrounding the venue. (In the script printed here, that venue is The Brick Theater in Williamsburg, Brooklyn.) It's sort of like a video/adventure game with live actors (who are the audience members).

Here's how the experience works. There are six characters in *Suspicious Package: Rx*: a doctor, a corporate executive, a chemist, a colonel in the U.S. army, a secretary, and a computer whiz. There are also six audience members/participants at each performance of *Suspicious Package: Rx*, each cast in one of the roles I just named. After a short orientation (which goes a long way toward relieving audience anxiety about interactive theatre), each participant receives a hat or similar prop that identifies his/her character (when I "did" the show, I played the computer whiz and was given a pair of nerdy oversized eyeglasses). The participants also each receive an iPod, customized for their role, which serves as their guide to the next forty-five minutes or so. (The iPod also provides, via recorded audio and video, a mini-play that gives the customized back story for each character.) By the end of the show, each of the six audience members winds up together with the mystery of the story satisfactorily resolved.

Presented below are all of the components of *Suspicious Package: Rx*. Contact Gyda Arber at www.suspiciouspackageshow.com to learn how to create your own customized interactive *Suspicious Package* experience.

The HOST welcomes the audience members, asks them to introduce themselves, presents each of them with a costume piece, and provides a quick introduction to the show. Each is handed a synced personal video player, and the show begins. *VIDEO: An old-time movie countdown leads into old-style movie credits, accompanied by a lush movie score.*	NARRATOR: *(Voiceover.)* Welcome to *Suspicious Package*. You are about to embark on an adventure. You are alone, entering an alternate dimension where all things are possible. For lack of a better estimate, let's call it the year 1969. As in any world, this society has specific rules. One: Timing is everything. Do not pause, fast forward, or rewind your player at any time. Two: Continuity is everything. If you miss something, keep moving forward.

Things will become clear to you as you progress. Three: Presence is everything. You are in a forty-five–minute nonstop experience. Any deviation or break from your instructions will derail the show. Please do your best to follow instructions as they are given and to appear when and where you are told. When you hear this sound *(Bell sound.)* you have a task to accomplish. Complete it. Remember, all the world's a stage. Enjoy your starring role.

CHARACTER 1:
THE CHEMIST (QUINN)

QUINN: *(Voiceover.)* Cycle 5, full of grace. Savior of the human race. You've got to appreciate the irony of a drug initially manufactured as an antidepressant being the only thing keeping humanity alive. The only people left are the ones looking for a way out. What was it Einstein said, "Among the manifold attributes of God, let us not forget sense of humor." I wonder if he ever envisioned the world we're in now.

(VIDEO #1: A television news program.)

Anchors TED and DICK are reporting.

TED: For our next story, we have our LBC "Go-To Girl" Melissa Meyers, standing by, to report on the newest development in medical technology. Melissa?

MELISSA: *(Outside a science lab.)* Hello there, Ted! Yep, for nanotechnology, the future is here. I'm standing outside Blue Star Pharmaceuticals, the pioneer in the field, which has just released a new drug, Cycle 5. It uses microscopic robots, or nanites, to correct imperfections in the brain.

DICK: Melissa, are you saying that this drug is made up of tiny robots?

MELISSA: Dick, that's exactly what I'm saying. Microscopic robots are used in this antidepressant to actually reroute your brain's signals, making depression a thing of the past. Blue Star's clinical trials have proven that they can cure all types of depression with Cycle 5.

DICK: What happens to the robots when they're done?

MELISSA: For safety reasons, they're engineered to dissolve after twenty-four hours, so to reap the benefits you'll have to take Cycle 5 every day, just like a normal drug. But trials have shown Cycle 5 to be the most effective antidepressant out there.

TED: Melissa, when will we be seeing this drug on the market?

MELISSA: Very soon, Ted. I'm told that FDA approval should come in just a few short weeks.

TED: Thanks, Melissa. Melissa Meyers, our Go-To Girl, reporting from Blue Star Pharmaceuticals.

DICK: Wow, tiny robots, in a drug? Will wonders never cease.

TED: I'm surprised every day at this job, Dick.

DICK: When we get back, President Kennedy on the growing police action in Vietnam, a visit to the Mercury astronauts, and Cho-Cho the Chimp flies a helicopter, after these messages.

NARRATOR: *(Bell sound.)* Face The Brick and turn to your left. Walk up the staircase ahead of you, to your right. *(Pause.) (Bell sound.)* Enter the door at the top of the stairs and take the stairs to the third floor. *(Pause.) (Bell sound.)* On the third floor, enter the door and turn to your left. Walk down the hall to the door marked "Dispensary" and wait outside. *(Pause.) (Bell sound.)* Read the following dialogue as soon as it appears on your screen. If you miss something, just keep going.

(STEVENS and RILEY are standing outside the dispensary. QUINN and JOY enter and form a line behind them.)

QUINN: *(To Joy.)* What's the holdup?

JOY: *(Sassily.)* There's always a holdup somewhere…

(Pause.)

QUINN: So, do you, uh…come here often?

JOY: *(Reciting.)* "I survive with Cycle 5." But you don't look familiar.

QUINN: No. I…was just in the neighborhood. Do you live around here?

JOY: If you call work living. Actually all three of us work nearby. *(She indicates STEVENS and RILEY.)*

QUINN: *(Friendly.)* I'd like to have a co-worker like you.

JOY: You can't always judge a book by its cover.

QUINN: *(Suggestively.)* Well, I like to read under the covers.

(THE DOCTOR opens the door to the office.)

THE DOCTOR: Who's next?

(STEVENS stands up. THE DOCTOR holds a device up to STEVENS's eye. A retina scan graphic appears on the screen. THE DOCTOR selects a pill from the supply and hands it to STEVENS. STEVENS takes the pill.)

STEVENS: *(To JOY.)* I'll see you in a few. *(Exits.)*

RILEY: *(To JOY.)* You go ahead. I'm in no rush.

(THE DOCTOR scans JOY. JOY takes a pill.)

JOY: *(To QUINN.)* Nice talking to you. *(Exits.)*

NARRATOR: *(Bell sound.)* Go into the office and take the pill from the Doctor.

(THE DOCTOR scans QUINN. QUINN takes a pill.)

NARRATOR: *(Bell sound.)* Head back downstairs. *(Pause.) (Bell sound.)* Exit the building and take a right. You are headed to the location on your screen.

QUINN: *(Voiceover.)* That girl back there was a cutie. I wonder if she works at PerkinStevens. It would certainly make that decision easier. I don't know how they convinced me to meet with them in the first place. If that crazy head of Blue Star gets wind of this, I'm sure they'll put a tail on me night and day. But I'm starting to sound a little paranoid here, myself. *(Pause.)* I never thought I'd need a chemical to help me get through the day; of course, that was before the plague—now everyone needs their Cycle 5 or it's curtains. No, before, back when things were normal, I always thought I had a well-ordered mind. But then Celeste…well, when Celeste died I fell apart. Could barely get out of bed. All day all I thought about was the pointlessness of life, about ending it all, how I'd do it, how no one would miss me. When I heard about Cycle 5 I couldn't decide whether I thought it was all hooey or whether it might work. I gave it a try. And it worked. Kind of. The thing they don't tell you about antidepressants is that they don't make you happy. They just make you less sad. *(Pause.)* I'd have probably stopped taking Cycle 5 if it wouldn't kill me. I'm not ready for that quite yet.

NARRATOR: *(Bell sound.)* Enter Macri Park bar and sit at the table with the reserved sign.

QUINN: *(Voiceover.)* I knew that Cycle 5 stuff was full of robots, but after Celeste died—of cancer of all things—I thought it was worth giving a try. After she died I was in hell. Then the plague hit, and brought the rest of the world there.

(FLASHBACK: A science lab.)

QUINN: Hal?

HAL: Hey there, how can I help my favorite chemical researcher today?

QUINN: I hear things are going well with the Cycle 5 trials.

HAL: Yep, we're almost done, just waiting on the FDA approvals. This is a great time for Blue Star.

QUINN: Must be nice to be on the winning team.

HAL: Oh, don't beat yourself up over it. I'm sure we'll find some use for chemical-based drugs. If Cycle 5 weren't so effective…

QUINN: About that…

HAL: Yes?

QUINN: If one were to, say, want to try it for oneself, how would one go about doing that?

HAL: You want to try Cycle 5? After all your scoffing about nanobots?

QUINN: Well, I think it's just that…

HAL: *(Backpedaling.)* Oh. Right. Celeste. I'm sorry, I wasn't thinking…

QUINN: Don't worry about it.

HAL: Sure, Quinn, anytime. I'll requisition some for you right away. Expect it on your desk first thing tomorrow.

QUINN: Right.

HAL: I'm glad you're coming over from the dark side, pal; it's been a long time coming.

QUINN: Thanks Hal. I'll let you get back to work.

NARRATOR: *(Bell sound.)* Read the following dialogue as soon as it appears on your screen.

(THE COLONEL enters.)

THE COLONEL: Mind if I join you?

QUINN: It's a free country. Or it used to be.

THE COLONEL: I just got here this afternoon from D.C. Live around here? Have friends in the neighborhood?

QUINN: We all got robot friends these days.

THE COLONEL: Better than the alternative.

QUINN: Having no choice isn't quite utopia, is it?

THE COLONEL: I didn't come here to argue—I need to find someone.

QUINN: I'm not president of the lonely heart's club. Write to Dear Abby.

THE COLONEL: Where can I find her?

(THE COLONEL beams a picture to QUINN.)

QUINN: Who do you think you are?

THE COLONEL: I remember you, even though it was a long time ago.

QUINN: Leave me alone.

THE COLONEL: She said you'd be friends forever. Tell me where she is!

QUINN: It was a long time ago. And it's over now. Buzz off!

THE COLONEL: You haven't seen the last of me, Quinn. I'll find her, one way or another.

(THE COLONEL exits. RILEY enters.)

RILEY: Quinn, isn't it? I'm such a fan—in grad school we all thought your work on proteins was revolutionary.

QUINN: Haven't heard that in a long time.

RILEY: You haven't published anything lately. Are you coming back to the field?

QUINN: Yeah, left field for the Dodgers.

RILEY: Baseball. It's one of the things I miss most, don't you?

QUINN: Maybe we'll have it back some day. *(Turns away.)* Nice talking to you.

RILEY: You, too. *(Exits.)*

QUINN: *(Voiceover.)* Who are these crackpots, coming in here, bothering me? The random chemistry buff here or there, I'm used to, sure, though they can't seem to get it through their noggins that I'm not in the business anymore. But that colonel... what was that about, snooping around, bothering me? And looking for her. That's not something I'm ready to talk about, not yet, no matter who's doing the asking. *(Pause.)* I can't believe I'm waiting here to meet with another drug company. Blue Star really took over after the plague hit...

(VIDEO #2: The television news.)

TED: Our top story tonight is the unnamed virus that is sweeping the nation. We have Richard McCready at the news desk with more details.

DICK: Over seventy-five thousand deaths have been reported by the CDC in the past few weeks. Flu-like symptoms have led to a quick death for many across this country, primarily on the West Coast. Janice Todd's daughter Lizzie was one of the victims.

(JANICE, a grieving mother, is sitting on the couch in her living room.)

JANICE: It all happened so fast. She just had a fever, I thought it was the flu. But she just kept getting worse and worse. Her fever just wouldn't go down. Then she stopped responding—she was awake, but wouldn't eat, or sleep. She just stopped, I don't know, living. We were getting ready to take her to the doctor, but she had a seizure. By the time the ambulance got here... *(Chokes up.)* She was gone. My baby is gone.

DICK: Stories like these are no stranger to many in the country. Charles Clark, a scientist at the Communicable Disease Center, is on the team to find a cure.

CHARLES: *(At the CDC lab.)* This virus is unlike any that we've seen before, mostly due to the speed with which it attacks its victims. Usually within a week of onset, the victim is gone. The virus attacks the brain, and the victim quickly becomes comatose.

DICK: The CDC is tracking each case but is not confident that a cure will be found before more lives are lost. In a bizarre twist, exposed patients that are taking the antidepressant Cycle 5 seem strangely immune.

TED: Today the CDC published guidelines to avoid contracting the unknown virus that some are calling "the brain plague." Make sure to wash your hands after any contact with other people. Contact your doctor if flu-like symptoms—including a high fever, chills, and coughing—last for more than three days. Call your local police at the first sign of a comatose state. We'll be keeping you updated on this breaking story as we learn more.

QUINN: *(Voiceover.)* Do I really think that PerkinStevens will be any better? At least I won't be working with Hal...

SUSPICIOUS PACKAGE: Rx

(FLASHBACK: HAL's office.)

(HAL is sitting at his desk. QUINN enters.)

QUINN: Hal, you got a minute?

HAL: Actually, I'm right in the middle—

QUINN: Good. You cut my funding again.

HAL: Well, it's complicated. We have to weigh the pros and cons of each research project.

QUINN: How am I supposed to run a department without any money?

HAL: We just don't see a future in chemical-based drugs. We have to put our money where it will do the most good.

QUINN: And you think that's nanotech? You're crazy.

HAL: Our net profit last quarter was off the charts—and that's thanks to Cycle 5.

QUINN: You're wrong, Hal. I'm through wasting my time here. Consider this my official notice.

HAL: If that's the way you feel…

QUINN: Great.

HAL: And I don't think I need to remind you about the noncompete agreement you signed.

QUINN: Are you really going to hold me to that? What do you care what I do, if there's no future in it?

HAL: Just trying to cover all the bases here, pal.

QUINN: Fine.

NARRATOR: *(Bell sound.)* Read the following dialogue as soon as it appears on your screen.

(JOY enters.)

QUINN: Well, hello there. What a pleasant surprise.

JOY: Hello there yourself. Mind if I sit down?

QUINN: Be my guest. I didn't expect to see you again, at least not so soon.

JOY: I'm not going to beat around the bush. I'm here on business.

QUINN: I already have business here, with the head of PerkinStevens.

JOY: I'm the boss's right arm. And the left one too.

QUINN: My apologies. So, what did Stevens want me here for, anyway?

JOY: You used to work for Blue Star. And Blue Star isn't exactly what it seems.

QUINN: I've heard those rumors. That Cycle 5 started the plague?

JOY: They're more than rumors. The mini-robots. They attack viruses.

QUINN: I know. I worked there. Isn't that why you're here?

JOY: Blue Star engineered a supervirus, to see if Cycle 5 would combat it. It did, but not before it got into the population and—

QUINN: *(Interrupting.)* How do you know about that? That's classified.

JOY: PerkinStevens has its sources. We're in this business, too.

QUINN: What sources? Everyone who works there signs a confidentiality agreement. And Blue Star has spies everywhere, at PerkinStevens too, I'm sure.

JOY: We know what we know. But more importantly, we know why you left.

QUINN: Sometimes money isn't as important as what's right.

JOY: We're working on an alternative. An old-fashioned drug that boosts immunity. No more need for Cycle 5 and its mind-numbing side effects—that's what's right.

QUINN: *(Bitterly.)* How noble. Look, you don't want to cross Blue Star. The head of the company is crazy—eliminates all competition.

JOY: Wouldn't you like to be off their stuff? Get the robots out of your system? They say Blue Star can even control your mind.

QUINN: My mind. It's all I have left.

JOY: We need you. To come up with something better. Maybe then things can go back to the way they were. Before.

QUINN: Things will never go back.

JOY: But we can try. Try to make genuine lives for ourselves.

QUINN: You really think you can make a difference?

JOY: I think you can make a difference. What do you say, will you help us?

QUINN: I signed an agreement not to work for other drug companies.

JOY: We have lawyers. But this offer isn't forever. We need to make significant progress before Cycle 6 hits the market.

QUINN: Cycle 6? Wait, Blue Star has an alternative? I can't believe it!

JOY: You doubt it? Did you see what I saw at the dispensary?

QUINN: You're right. Why was that colonel there? They don't just send the military to watch us pop pills.

JOY: The doctor must know something. When you know what's really going on, you'll be on our side.

(THE DOCTOR enters.)

QUINN: Speak of the Devil.

THE DOCTOR: Quinn. I see you've forgotten about your agreement with Blue Star.

JOY: I see Blue Star is in the detective business now.

QUINN: Is it against the law to have a talk with a pretty lady?

THE DOCTOR: Rumor has it, it's more than just talk.

QUINN: We've heard some rumors of our own.

JOY: Rumors about super-robots in Cycle 6. We were hoping, good Doctor, you might be able to shed some light.

THE DOCTOR: Who said anything about Cycle 6?

JOY: We have a right to know what's going in our bodies.

QUINN: *(Emphatically.)* The plague may have taken its toll, but America is still America!

THE DOCTOR: The America we knew is gone forever. But Cycle 6 is going to put an end to all the suffering.

JOY: That sounds complicated, Doctor. I'm not sure that it's possible, even with Blue Star's reputation.

THE DOCTOR: See for yourself!

(VIDEO #3: HAL's office.)

(HAL leans over and turns on his video voicemail.)

HAL: Doctor, we are pleased to report that the initial trials of Cycle 6 have been successful. Completely successful, in fact. We have a hundred percent success rate in each and every case. We will be starting human trials as soon as possible. We anticipate that once Cycle 6 is put on the market, we should see complete eradication of depression. I believe, Doctor, that this is exactly what you were looking for.

(HAL shuts off the video voicemail message.)

(THE DOCTOR exits.)

QUINN: That's just what we need, more robots.

JOY: Now do you see why we've got to go to work immediately?

QUINN: I thought they'd stop with Cycle 5.

JOY: You must have something! What have you been doing since you left Blue Star?

QUINN: Well, I've got something that might work. But I don't have it on me.

JOY: Can you get it quick? Meet me at the Catfish in ten.

NARRATOR: *(Bell sound.)* Exit the building and take a left. You are headed to the location on your screen.

QUINN: *(Voiceover.)* If Cycle 5 actually did cause the plague, we'd have chaos on our hands. Some people would stop taking it, then they'd die. The rest would march on Washington with torches and pitchforks, demanding a new cure. Then who'd give it to them? Blue Star? Good luck with that. *(Pause.)* Is it even worth trying to work with that cute Joy and PerkinStevens Pharmaceuticals to see if their solution can work? I can't help but think that we'd just be stuck with the same problem we had before: an all-powerful pharmaceutical company controlling the government and military, basically sitting on the throne as the emperor of America. But at least PerkinStevens isn't fixing the problem by releasing nanobots into people's bloodstreams. They at least have a little bit of ethics left, it seems.

NARRATOR: *(Bell sound.)* Enter the Laundromat and immediately turn to your right. Sit by the window in the farthest chair on your right. *(Pause.)* There should be an envelope taped to the bottom of your chair. Take it.

QUINN: *(Voiceover.)* Should I even bother trying to stop Blue Star anymore? Can this formula really make a difference? If there is a heaven, maybe Celeste is there. I miss her so much...

(FLASHBACK: CELESTE and QUINN are having dinner. CELESTE puts a plate on the table.)

CELESTE: Here, darling. In honor of your first day.

QUINN: *(Teasing.)* You've been watching The Donna Reed Show again.

CELESTE: Just trying to make you happy. So, how did it go?

QUINN: Blue Star's research is much more sophisticated than I thought. They're even experimenting with something they call nanites.

CELESTE: Nanites?

QUINN: They're tiny robots, the size of an atom!

CELESTE: Amazing. What are they for?

QUINN: This fellow Hal's in charge of that department. He keeps things pretty hush-hush.

CELESTE: And what will you be working on?

QUINN: It seems I can go in any direction I want...as long as Blue Star sees results.

CELESTE: Well, that shouldn't... *(Trails off, grabs her head.)*

QUINN: What is it?

CELESTE: Nothing, darling, I've been feeling woozy all day. *(Collapses to the floor.)*

QUINN: Celeste? Celeste!

QUINN: *(Voiceover.)* Celeste was lucky, I suppose. She never had to see the effects of the plague on the world. Everything's different now. No more picnics, no more baseball. That's something I miss. The Yanks were the only game in town after the Dodgers left. Now that's something that really upset me. But just like the other kids in the neighborhood, I found myself a Yankee fan a few years later. Maris was my favorite.

(AUDIO: Yankees–Red Sox, October 1, 1961.)

Phil Rizzuto: The two-two pitch. Strike three called, the curveball caught the outside part of the plate. Second strikeout to Stallard and here comes Roger Maris! Last time up Roger hit one deep to left field and crossed everybody up including Yastrzemski who made a fine catch! He was so surprised Maris hit the ball to left, they've got a handful of people sitting out in left field but in right field, man it is mobbed out there. And they're standing up, waiting to see if Maris is gonna hit number 61. Here's the windup, the pitch to Roger, way outside, ball one. And the fans are starting to boo. Maris only has, including this time, three times at bat. And unless the Yankees get a rally, that's all he'll have to try and get number 61 on the year. Windup, pitch, low ball two. That one was in the dirt, and the boos get louder. Two balls, no strikes on Roger Maris. Here's the windup. Fastball hit deep to right! This could be it! Way back there! Holy cow, he did it! 61 for Maris! Look at them fight for that ball out there. Ho-ly cow, what a shot! Another standing ovation for Roger Maris. Sixty-one home runs and they're still fighting for that ball out there. People are climbing over each other's backs. They want Maris to come out and take another bow. He does! And he's coming out again! The fans, they're...keeping him out there. He wants to sit down, they won't let him. One of the greatest sights I've ever seen here at Yankee Stadium. And they're still applauding and everybody's looking out in right field because that baseball is worth at least six thousand dollars and a round trip ticket to the Seattle World's Fair. Yogi Berra's up but nobody knows it! All eyes are out towards right field. They were on the Yankee dugout but they're out on that little spot in right field. Yogi's got a one-one count on him.

NARRATOR: *(Bell sound.)* Exit the building and take a left. You are headed to the location on your screen. *(Pause.)* *(Bell sound.)* Read the following dialogue to the Colonel as soon as it appears on your screen.

(THE COLONEL is standing outside the bar.)

THE COLONEL: I figured you'd be here. We've got some unfinished business.

QUINN: Look—I just want to be alone. I've got some serious thinking to do.

THE COLONEL: Yes, you do. Like being honest with me.

QUINN: I used to care about honesty and ethics and even, yes, people like you. But now...

THE COLONEL: You don't understand. The stakes don't get any higher. I have to see her and you're the only one who might know where she is. You're my last hope.

QUINN: Hope? Not much to hope for. Our minds are being controlled, or will be soon enough. Cycle 6 will make free choice impossible.

THE COLONEL: Don't be an idiot. Cycle 6 is a failure.

QUINN: It doesn't work? Blue Star failed?

THE COLONEL: That doesn't matter, you fool. The only thing that matters are people you love, and the short time we have together.

QUINN: You're the fool. She wanted nothing to do with you.

THE COLONEL: What do you mean, wanted? *(Hopefully.)* She's willing to see me?

QUINN: No. She's dead, okay? Dead. Cycle 5 can't protect you from car accidents.

THE COLONEL: What? No. *(In despair.)* There's nothing left.

NARRATOR: *(Bell sound.)* Enter the Lazy Catfish and sit at the table with the reserved sign. Read the following dialogue as soon as it appears on your screen.

[For this dialogue, go to the end of the play, p. 249, after the asterisk (*).]

CHARACTER 2: THE SECRETARY (JOY)

JOY: *(Voiceover.)* Almost time for my daily dose of Cycle 5. I can't believe I've been taking the pills for so long. It's a pain to take them every day, but it's better than the alternative, that's for sure. I remember when they first came out...

(VIDEO #1: A television news program.) **[For text, see p. 207.]**

NARRATOR: *(Bell sound.)* Face The Brick and turn to your left. Walk up the staircase ahead of you, to your right.

(Pause.) (Bell sound.) Enter the door at the top of the stairs and take the stairs to the third floor.

JOY: *(Voiceover.)* Trudging up these stairs is a daily pain. But it helps to keep my girlish figure, I suppose.

NARRATOR: *(Bell sound.)* On the third floor, enter the door and turn to your left. Walk down the hall to the door marked "Dispensary" and wait outside. *(Pause.) (Bell sound.)* Read the following dialogue as soon as it appears on your screen. If you miss something, just keep going.

(STEVENS and RILEY are standing outside the dispensary. QUINN and JOY enter and form a line behind them.)

QUINN: *(To JOY.)* What's the holdup?

JOY: *(Sassily.)* There's always a holdup somewhere...

(Pause.)

QUINN: So, do you, uh...come here often?

JOY: *(Reciting.)* "I survive with Cycle 5." But you don't look familiar.

QUINN: No. I...was just in the neighborhood. Do you live around here?

JOY: If you call work living. Actually all three of us work nearby. *(She indicates STEVENS and RILEY.)*

QUINN: *(Friendly.)* I'd like to have a co-worker like you.

JOY: You can't always judge a book by its cover.

QUINN: *(Suggestively.)* Well, I like to read under the covers.

(THE DOCTOR opens the door to the office.)

THE DOCTOR: Who's next?

(STEVENS stands up. THE DOCTOR holds a device up to STEVENS's eye. A retina scan graphic appears on the screen. THE DOCTOR selects a pill from the supply and hands it to STEVENS. STEVENS takes the pill.)

STEVENS: *(To JOY.)* I'll see you in a few. *(Exits.)*

RILEY: *(To JOY.)* You go ahead. I'm in no rush.

NARRATOR: *(Bell sound.)* Go into the office and take the pill from the Doctor.

(THE DOCTOR scans JOY. JOY takes a pill.)

NARRATOR: *(Bell sound.)* Exit the office and read the following line.

JOY: *(To QUINN.)* Nice talking to you.

NARRATOR: *(Bell sound.)* Head back downstairs. *(Pause.) (Bell sound.)* Exit the building and take a right. You are headed to the location on your screen.

JOY: *(Voiceover.)* What an interesting day at the clinic. An officer in the military? Strange to see that, but not surprising, I guess. The Army and Blue Star have been in cahoots since the plague. I should be used to it by now. Such a change from how things used to be. My mother used to talk about how it was when she was my age. Parties, boyfriends, carnivals, and fairs—back then they lived like they had forever.

(AUDIO: Upbeat 1920s music.)

JOY: *(Voiceover.)* I guess Cycle 5 was supposed to make us all feel that happy. I remember the day I started taking it...

(FLASHBACK: A living room.)

MOTHER: Joy, honey, no wonder you never have any dates. I mean, if you were a little more positive...boys don't like girls who are always making snide, sarcastic remarks. Look at Vivian next door. Her mother is always complaining to me about how many dates her daughter has! So I want you to trust me tonight. Look at it like a special kind of party. All your friends are here to...to help you, darling. No one likes a sad sack. You want to be popular, don't you? A success? You want to get married some day, and have children?

(Three teenaged GIRLS are sitting on the couch.)

LYNN: We're here to help you, Joy. We know you like your books, but we're worried about you—it's all you do.

ALICE: Yeah. No reason to be so serious about life. Boys don't like girls who are too smart. You've got a great figure, and hair! The guys would be all over you if you showed a little interest.

BETTY: Why suffer? Everyone takes Cycle 5. My cousin is on it, and now she's a Miss Springtown contestant!

LYNN: Take a pill and be the Belle of the Ball.

ALICE: We've been a crowd since we were in second grade. You used to be so fun! To be honest we talked about dropping you, but we know you'll listen to reason. And we miss the happy Joy! Just take one of these... *(ALICE holds the pill out to JOY.)*

BETTY: Your mother has a prescription all filled. Come on. We just wanna have fun! And we want you with us.

NARRATOR: *(Bell sound.)* Enter the Lazy Catfish and sit at the table with the reserved sign. It may be in the back. *(Pause.) (Bell sound.)* Read the following dialogue as soon as it appears on your screen.

(STEVENS is seated at the table.)

STEVENS: Thanks for coming over. I have another meeting here after this.

JOY: Any time, boss. You need me to take dictation?

STEVENS: Change of plan. Do you know who you were talking to in line just now?

JOY: Just someone took a liking to me, I guess.

STEVENS: Not just "someone." That's Quinn.

JOY: Gee whiz. I thought a high-profile chemist like that would be older.

STEVENS: Quinn used to work for Blue Star, but didn't like the way things were going.

JOY: Not a fan of the mini-robots?

STEVENS: Ruined a great career.

JOY: What's that have to do with us?

STEVENS: Quinn was working on an alternative to Cycle 5, like we are. Got really close, rumor has it.

JOY: Hmmmm. Blue Star's loss could be our gain.

STEVENS: Took a bit of a shine to you, it seemed.

JOY: That's what I'm here for.

STEVENS: We were supposed to meet, but something's come up. Head to Macri Park. Do you think a little lady like you can get a chemist like that on our team?

JOY: Are the Kennedys Catholic? I think I can work something out.

STEVENS: That's what I like to hear.

JOY: Oh, before I forget, here's that notebook you wanted me to pick up.

NARRATOR: *(Bell sound.)* Take the notebook out of your bag and hand it to your boss.

STEVENS: I can't believe our lead researcher died when we were so close.

JOY: It looks like gibberish to me, but maybe Riley can decipher it. Or Quinn, if we get a chemist like that on board.

STEVENS: Good work. Now off to the races!

JOY: Sure, boss.

NARRATOR: Exit the building and take a right. You are headed to the location on your screen.

Joy: *(Voiceover.)* I'm glad I have a job at PerkinStevens Pharmaceuticals. Stevens is a good boss. But I gotta convince Quinn—the missing link in all our research at PerkinStevens. If we can get Quinn on board, well, it'll be like winning the lottery. Watch out Blue Star, and Cycle 5, 6, or 7! Here comes PerkinStevens to the rescue! When we come out with our alternative, and I get my big bonus, I might even buy a car, one of those Thunderbirds. I can see myself now, sun on my face, wind in my hair, just like those old billboard pictures…

(AUDIO: Upbeat surf song.)

JOY: *(Voiceover.)* When I was a little girl, Mother and I were always watching those doctor programs on television. I wanted to be a nurse. But after the plague, after all those people died, my family, friends, and neighbors, I couldn't bear to be around sick people. But I still wanted to help. If we can just get Quinn on board…well, maybe that's something I can do.

(VIDEO #2: The television news.) **[For text, see p. 210.]**

NARRATOR: *(Bell sound.)* Enter Macri Park bar and sit at the table with the reserved sign. *(Pause.) (Bell sound.)* Read the following dialogue as soon as it appears on your screen.

(QUINN is seated at the table.)

QUINN: Well, hello there. What a pleasant surprise.

JOY: Hello there yourself. Mind if I sit down?

QUINN: Be my guest. I didn't expect to see you again, at least not so soon.

JOY: I'm not going to beat around the bush. I'm here on business.

QUINN: I already have business here, with the head of PerkinStevens.

JOY: I'm the boss's right arm. And the left one too.

QUINN: My apologies. So, what did Stevens want me here for, anyway?

JOY: You used to work for Blue Star. And Blue Star isn't exactly what it seems.

QUINN: I've heard those rumors. That Cycle 5 started the plague?

JOY: They're more than rumors. The mini-robots. They attack viruses.

QUINN: I know. I worked there. Isn't that why you're here?

JOY: Blue Star engineered a supervirus, to see if Cycle 5 would combat it. It did, but not before it got into the population and—

QUINN: *(Interrupting.)* How do you know about that? That's classified.

JOY: PerkinStevens has its sources. We're in this business, too.

QUINN: What sources? Everyone who works there signs a confidentiality agreement. And Blue Star has spies everywhere, at PerkinStevens too, I'm sure.

JOY: We know what we know. But more importantly, we know why you left.

QUINN: Sometimes money isn't as important as what's right.

JOY: We're working on an alternative. An old-fashioned drug that boosts immunity. No more need for Cycle 5 and its mind-numbing side effects—that's what's right.

QUINN: *(Bitterly.)* How noble. Look, you don't want to cross Blue Star. The head of the company is crazy—eliminates all competition.

JOY: Wouldn't you like to be off their stuff? Get the robots out of your system? They say Blue Star can even control your mind.

QUINN: My mind. It's all I have left.

JOY: We need you. To come up with something better. Maybe then things can go back to the way they were. Before.

QUINN: Things will never go back.

JOY: But we can try. Try to make genuine lives for ourselves.

QUINN: You really think you can make a difference?

JOY: I think you can make a difference. What do you say, will you help us?

QUINN: I signed an agreement not to work for other drug companies.

JOY: We have lawyers. But this offer isn't forever. We need to make significant progress before Cycle 6 hits the market.

QUINN: Cycle 6? Wait, Blue Star has an alternative? I can't believe it!

JOY: You doubt it? Did you see what I saw at the dispensary?

QUINN: You're right. Why was that colonel there? They don't just send the military to watch us pop pills.

JOY: The doctor must know something. When you know what's really going on, you'll be on our side.

(THE DOCTOR enters.)

QUINN: Speak of the Devil.

THE DOCTOR: Quinn. I see you've forgotten about your agreement with Blue Star.

JOY: I see Blue Star is in the detective business now.

QUINN: Is it against the law to have a talk with a pretty lady?

THE DOCTOR: Rumor has it, it's more than just talk.

QUINN: We've heard some rumors of our own.

JOY: Rumors about super-robots in Cycle 6. We were hoping, good Doctor, you might be able to shed some light.

THE DOCTOR: Who said anything about Cycle 6?

JOY: We have a right to know what's going in our bodies.

QUINN: *(Emphatically.)* The plague may have taken its toll, but America is still America!

THE DOCTOR: The America we knew is gone forever. But Cycle 6 is going to put an end to all the suffering.

JOY: That sounds complicated, Doctor. I'm not sure that it's possible, even with Blue Star's reputation.

THE DOCTOR: See for yourself!

(VIDEO #3: HAL's office.) **[For text, see p. 212.]**

(THE DOCTOR exits.)

QUINN: That's just what we need, more robots.

JOY: Now do you see why we've got to go to work immediately?

QUINN: I thought they'd stop with Cycle 5.

JOY: You must have something! What have you been doing since you left Blue Star?

QUINN: Well, I've got something that might work. But I don't have it on me.

JOY: Can you get it quick? Meet me at the Catfish in ten.

(QUINN exits.)

JOY: *(Voiceover.)* Oh no, how did this happen? If Quinn can just get us those formulas, we can be up and running in just a few days. I'll work a week with no sleep, do anything just to have an alternative to Cycle 6. Hal told me that Cycle 6 worked, but I didn't think Blue Star would start producing it immediately. I saw him just the other day...

(FLASHBACK: HAL enters the room.)

HAL: We did it, baby.

JOY: What did we do?

(HAL starts doing a sexy dance while removing his jacket. He slowly advances toward JOY.)

HAL: Not you and me. Us. At the lab.

JOY: Oh. What did you do?

HAL: We did it. Cycle 6.

JOY: What?

HAL: That's right, baby. We created Cycle 6. And it works.

JOY: Are you for real?

HAL: I am completely for real. It works better than we ever imagined.

JOY: Oh my goodness.

HAL: That's right, baby. We've got some celebrating to do.

(HAL moves toward JOY as if to kiss her.)

JOY: *(Voiceover.)* I was afraid it would be tough hiding who I really am from Hal, but he's so flattered by any female attention, it's been a breeze. I never thought I'd be able to spy on Blue Star so easily. Still, it makes me nervous, knowing I've got their nanobots in my system. The plague hit so soon after Cycle 5 came out, I can't imagine there wasn't a connection... That spring, it came so quickly. How? Where? We never knew, and after the first fifty million dead, it didn't matter. And things were going so well; Cycle 5 really had made a difference. I had a great job, a fiancée, a fabulous apartment. But when it hit—in just a week it seemed half of America was gone, and the rest of us flew, drove, walked to where we thought we were safe, in the East. But then others who seemed fine began to fall. So many didn't realize what we later learned about Cycle 5. That we would be the only survivors.

(FLASHBACK: Two FRIENDS are sitting on the furniture all bundled up, looking haggard.)

BETTY: I can't believe it. I thought this was a new life, the horror was over. But my mother had these same symptoms. Oh god, I'm burning up. I'm going to die, aren't I?

JANET: No use fighting it. You remember when it first hit...Hell—I worry about where they're going to bury me...or who? Will anyone be left?

BETTY: Oh they'll be left. Like you, Joy. If we got it it's a sure bet you were exposed, but you look great. Look at you...Florence Nightingale. Why me? Why not you?

JANET: You don't have to be so bitter about it. Joy didn't ask for immunity any more than you asked to be sick. Some of them are old, some young, all kinds, it's strange. *(Starts to fade/cough.)* It doesn't matter.

BETTY: *(Delirious.)* I'm too young to die. We're the same age. What are you doing to protect yourself? I came here to be safe—I thought it would be safe—after my family...my whole neighborhood... *(Chokes up.)*

JANET: We should be happy at least some of humanity will be spared to carry on, to rebuild, to start anew. *(Pause.)* Even if it's not us.

JOY: *(Voiceover.)* I didn't have the heart to tell them that Cycle 5 made me immune. By then it was too late for them anyway...

NARRATOR: *(Bell sound.)* Read the following dialogue as soon as it appears on your screen.

(STEVENS enters.)

STEVENS: Hey, Joy. What's the good word?

JOY: Quinn is on board, but I'm not sure it will do any good.

STEVENS: No good? Tell me what this is about. I'll decide.

JOY: We saw an intercepted transmission from Blue Star about Cycle 6.

STEVENS: No kidding. And what did this transmission say?

JOY: That Cycle 6 is ready to go.

STEVENS: Already? But what about your source?

JOY: My source is in the video! I knew it worked, but I didn't think they'd start trials so soon.

STEVENS: Trials on how many subjects? They'll all be under Blue Star's control!

JOY: Quinn has been working on an alternative.

STEVENS: We gotta act now. Where is Quinn?

JOY: Acquiring a secret weapon. We're supposed to meet at the Catfish right away.

STEVENS: Well then get to it! I'll be right behind you.

JOY: You got it, boss.

NARRATOR: *(Bell sound.)* Exit the building and take a left. You are headed to the location on your screen.

JOY: *(Voiceover.)* The boss has got me on so many errands these days. Run here, run there, type this, mail that… Take a deep breath. Well, at least I'm feeling something. It's gotta be done if we're ever going to have a real life again, I mean before Cycle 6 takes over our brains… I'm scared Cycle 6 will take the few memories I have left of the old days. I try hard to hold onto them. Life was so different before. There are so many things I miss. Especially my dad and listening to the Yankee games on the radio…

(AUDIO: Yankees–Red Sox, October 1, 1961.) **[For text, see p. 214.]**

NARRATOR: *(Bell sound.)* Enter the Lazy Catfish and sit at the table with the reserved sign. *(Pause.) (Bell sound.)* Read the following dialogue as soon as it appears on your screen.

(STEVENS and JOY enter to find RILEY and THE DOCTOR arguing.)

STEVENS: Riley? What are you doing with that notebook?

RILEY: *(Tries to cover.)* I just stopped in for a drink and ran into Doc here.

STEVENS: I knew PerkinStevens had a mole—but I can't believe it was you all this time!

JOY: Riley, how could you do this to us?

THE DOCTOR: You're only figuring this out now? *(Laughs.)*

RILEY: You fools are getting nowhere. Cycle 6 is the future!

STEVENS: But you know the head of Blue Star wants control of our minds.

THE DOCTOR: That's right. I do.

STEVENS and JOY: What?

THE DOCTOR: Yes, me. Universal happiness is worth it.

RILEY: You thought Doc was just a pill pusher, but the head of Blue Star's been right here, under your noses!

(QUINN and THE COLONEL enter.)

[For the remainder of this dialogue, go to the end of the play, p. 249, after the asterisk (*).]

CHARACTER 3:
THE EXECUTIVE (STEVENS)

STEVENS: *(Voiceover.)* Almost time for my daily dose of Cycle 5. Such a pain to take it every day, but hey, death's the alternative.

(VIDEO #1: A television news program.) **[For text, see p. 207.]**

NARRATOR: *(Bell sound.)* Face The Brick and turn to your left. Walk up the staircase ahead of you, to your right. *(Pause.) (Bell sound.)* Enter the door at the top of the stairs and take the stairs to the third floor.

STEVENS: *(Voiceover.)* For a brief moment after I take the pill I delude myself into thinking that life is okay. I forget that the world's gone all to hell, that Blue Star is corrupt and evil, and that Janie's no longer around. But the feeling is fleeting and short lived. Before long, I remember all of these things, and that life is pretty far from okay.

NARRATOR: *(Bell sound.)* On the third floor, enter the door and turn to your left. Walk down the hall to the door marked "Dispensary" and wait outside. *(Pause.) (Bell sound.)* Read the following dialogue as soon as it appears on your screen. If you miss something, just keep going.

(RILEY enters and forms a line behind STEVENS.)

RILEY: We've gotta stop meeting like this.

STEVENS: *(Rolls eyes.)* Yeah, when Blue Star tells us to show up, we show up.

RILEY: We're getting close—I'm really excited about our direction using the body's own—

STEVENS: *(Interrupts.)* Don't forget where we are!

RILEY: Sorry boss. Cycle 5 gets you every time.

(QUINN and JOY enter. They get in line behind RILEY.)

QUINN: *(To JOY.)* What's the holdup?

JOY: *(Sassily.)* There's always a holdup somewhere...

(Pause.)

QUINN: So, do you, uh...come here often?

JOY: *(Reciting.)* "I survive with Cycle 5." But you don't look familiar.

QUINN: No. I...was just in the neighborhood. Do you live around here?

JOY: If you call work living. Actually all three of us work nearby. *(She indicates STEVENS and RILEY.)*

QUINN: *(Friendly.)* I'd like to have a co-worker like you.

JOY: You can't always judge a book by its cover.

QUINN: *(Suggestively.)* Well, I like to read under the covers.

(THE DOCTOR opens the door to the office.)

THE DOCTOR: Who's next?

NARRATOR: *(Bell sound.)* Go into the office and take the pill from the Doctor.

(THE DOCTOR holds a device up to STEVENS's eye. A retina scan graphic appears on the screen. THE DOCTOR selects a pill from the supply and hands it to STEVENS. STEVENS takes the pill.)

NARRATOR: *(Bell sound.)* Exit the office and read the following line.

STEVENS: *(To JOY.)* I'll see you in a few.

NARRATOR: *(Bell sound.)* Head back downstairs. *(Pause.) (Bell sound.)* Exit the building and take a left. You are headed to the location on your screen.

Stevens: *(Voiceover.)* Something's wrong with the nanobots in Cycle 5, I'm sure of it. But no one's listening to me. To the public, I'm a sore loser who has an axe to grind, as well as a hypocrite who used the drug well before it became mandatory. I have no credibility to the outside world, even though as the head of PerkinStevens Pharmaceuticals I'm what one could actually call an expert in the field. It may sound like a crackpot theory, but I'm sure Blue Star had something to do with the plague.

NARRATOR: *(Bell sound.)* Enter the Lazy Catfish and sit at the table with the reserved sign. It may be in the back.

(VIDEO #2: The television news.) [**For text, see p. 210.**]

NARRATOR: *(Bell sound.)* Read the following dialogue as soon as it appears on your screen.

(JOY enters.)

STEVENS: Thanks for coming over. I have another meeting here after this.

JOY: Any time, boss. You need me to take dictation?

STEVENS: Change of plan. Do you know who you were talking to in line just now?

JOY: Just someone took a liking to me, I guess.

STEVENS: Not just "someone." That's Quinn.

JOY: Gee whiz. I thought a high-profile chemist like that would be older.

STEVENS: Quinn used to work for Blue Star, but didn't like the way things were going.

JOY: Not a fan of the mini-robots?

STEVENS: Ruined a great career.

JOY: What's that have to do with us?

STEVENS: Quinn was working on an alternative to Cycle 5, like we are. Got really close, rumor has it.

JOY: Hrm. Blue Star's loss could be our gain.

STEVENS: Took a bit of a shine to you, it seemed.

JOY: That's what I'm here for.

STEVENS: We were supposed to meet, but something's come up. Head to Macri Park. Do you think a little lady like you can get a chemist like that on our team?

JOY: Are the Kennedys Catholic? I think I can work something out.

STEVENS: That's what I like to hear.

JOY: Oh, before I forget, here's that notebook you wanted me to pick up.

(JOY gives a notebook to STEVENS.)

STEVENS: I can't believe our lead researcher died when we were so close.

JOY: It looks like gibberish to me, but maybe Riley can decipher it. Or Quinn, if we get a chemist like that on board.

STEVENS: Good work. Now off to the races!

JOY: Sure, boss. *(Exits.)*

NARRATOR: *(Bell sound.)* Read the following dialogue as soon as it appears on your screen.

(THE DOCTOR enters.)

THE DOCTOR: Hello. Mind if I join you?

STEVENS: The wise doctor. Of course.

THE DOCTOR: Not so wise today. Had a few strangers come by.

STEVENS: Yeah, a colonel at that!

THE DOCTOR: Not the stranger I had in mind.

STEVENS: Yeah? What do you know about the other one?

THE DOCTOR: Quinn's famous. Used to be at Blue Star. Seems like your company would be interested in someone like that.

STEVENS: *(Changing the subject.)* What'd the colonel want anyway?

THE DOCTOR: *(Flustered.)* Uh, just looking for somebody.

STEVENS: Anyone you know? A patient? *(Sarcastically.)* You can track anyone with Cycle 5.

THE DOCTOR: What's wrong with that?

STEVENS: That's what's wrong. No one at Blue Star thinks anything of it. What fool runs that place, anyway?

THE DOCTOR: Our CEO's a visionary! A savior of mankind!

STEVENS: Yeah, if saving the world means controlling everyone's brain.

THE DOCTOR: *(Clinically.)* Ah, yes. Bitterness, discontent. Cycle 6 will correct all that.

STEVENS: Not if I have anything to do with it. Now, if you'll excuse me…

(THE DOCTOR exits.)

STEVENS: *(Voiceover.)* That doctor's always trying to weasel information out of us. But I never fall for it—and luckily Joy doesn't either. My secretary's a good girl. Smart girl. And reliable. Even though I could sometimes do without the sass, she's always been someone I could count on. She should have no trouble recruiting a top chemist like Quinn to join us at PerkinStevens. I'm amazed she sticks with me even though I'm clearly on the losing team. But she actually wants to do the right thing. I guess there are still good people in our dwindling population who put other people first. I just wish she didn't keep reminding me of Janie. Janie definitely had some sass to her. Think that's what drew me to her. Before she got real sick, obviously. I really need to stop thinking about these things. I thought the whole perk of these nanites was that they're supposed to stop you from being depressed. Guess with ninety percent of the world's population dying off in gruesome ways, happy-making brain-eating robots can only do so much. Boy, I'm the cheery sort, aren't I? No wonder I ended up taking a drug I knew was unstable.

(FLASHBACK: A PSYCHIATRIST's office.)

PSYCHIATRIST: Now, forgive me, but…haven't you been the one constantly complaining that Blue Star robbed you and—

STEVENS: And now I just want to be able to sleep at night and move on with my life.

PSYCHIATRIST: The Tofranil that I—

STEVENS: Isn't working.

PSYCHIATRIST: No? What about Elav—

STEVENS: I'm not interested in slowly grinding away at all the other antidepressants that I know won't work. I know Cycle 5 works. I'd been working on it for years.

PSYCHIATRIST: But I'm not sure—

STEVENS: Just gimme the pill, Doc. I know it works.

PSYCHIATRIST: Fine.

(FLASHBACK: JANIE is sitting on the couch.)

JANIE: Will wonders never cease?

STEVENS: What do you mean?

JANIE: I thought you said that stuff wasn't healthy.

STEVENS: I never said that.

JANIE: You wouldn't shut up about how dangerous Cycle 5 was!

STEVENS: Guess that was just the depression talking.

JANIE: And now…?

STEVENS: Guess I don't feel so bad about it now.

JANIE: Maybe that's just the robots talking.

STEVENS: Cute. And no, I never said it was dangerous or unhealthy. I just said we hadn't had time to test it fully.

JANIE: And that doesn't worry you?

STEVENS: I'm just tired of being a burden to you, Janie.

JANIE: Oh, come on. You've never been a burden. You're just being melodramatic.

STEVENS: And you're just glossing over my awful mood swings.

JANIE: Maybe. Now, are you sure you know what you're doing?

STEVENS: I developed this technology. I wouldn't be taking this if it were genuinely dangerous.

JANIE: Promise, boss?

STEVENS: I told you. Don't call me that. And I promise.

JANIE: I just like riling you up.

STEVENS: I know.

JANIE: And is it actually making you feel better?

STEVENS: It is.

JANIE: Well, that's what's important, then, isn't it?

STEVENS: I guess so.

STEVENS: *(Voiceover.)* When she got the fever I think we both deluded ourselves into thinking it was indeed just a common cold. Reports were coming in about some sort of health scare but it's like when you heard about the '51 influenza epidemic: it's happening somewhere else you've never been, to some other people you've never met. I convinced myself it was a cold.

(FLASHBACK: JANIE is in bed, coughing horribly and looking as if on death's door. STEVENS offers her a tray with soup on it, but she waves it away.)

STEVENS: *(Voiceover.)* But, just like with all the others, she just kept getting steadily worse. And it happened so fast. I really wish I'd been fully present for her. I tried to take care of her as best as I could, but being on Cycle 5 made the whole thing feel…distant. As if I were watching a sad movie rather than really being there. The best emotion I could muster up was anger: anger at myself, anger toward Blue Star.

NARRATOR: *(Bell sound.)* Read the following dialogue as soon as it appears on your screen.

(THE COLONEL enters.)

STEVENS: Colonel. What can I do for you?

THE COLONEL: I was just talking to Quinn.

STEVENS: Why would a colonel be looking for an unemployed chemist?

THE COLONEL: Some of us think in alternatives. What if there were a Patient Zero?

STEVENS: The original carrier of the plague?

THE COLONEL: I don't have to tell you what that means.

STEVENS: I never thought a vaccine could be possible. Where is this Patient Zero?

(THE COLONEL beams a photograph to STEVENS's device.)

THE COLONEL: This is her photo. She's in this neighborhood, hiding out. I have a deal for you.

STEVENS: I'd do anything to get my hands on her. I mean, for humanity, of course.

THE COLONEL: That's the spirit. Your mainframe should be powerful enough to find her, even under an assumed name.

STEVENS: Don't you have mainframes in Washington?

THE COLONEL: No time. And she's nearby, we know that.

STEVENS: PerkinStevens can do it; I've got the best computer whiz in the city. And you'll let us make the vaccine?

THE COLONEL: Find her and you can write your own check. *(Exits.)*

STEVENS: *(Voiceover.)* The colonel's going to owe me. Right. The military already owes me after giving me the royal shaft. Not that they'd ever admit it. Would this Patient Zero really be the key to getting people off of Cycle 5? Here's hoping. I've been on the junk for so long I can hardly remember a time when I wasn't using. There are snippets here and there of happiness, still. Actual happiness, not robotically enforced gaiety. But that's really all they are. Just fragments. Vague images and recollections of a life before Blue Star. Before Cycle 5. Before the plague. I catch them when I can, and try to hold onto them, but they don't last.

(FLASHBACK: JANIE and another COUPLE are having a picnic.)

JANIE: Did you bring the potato salad? No? Where is it? No, it's here, it's here.

MAN: Oh, good. I'll take some.

JANIE: Here you go.

MAN: Now, have you two seen the new Jimmy Stewart movie?

WOMAN: Oh, don't start—

MAN: We just saw it.

WOMAN: Terrible movie.

MAN: I thought it was really funny.

WOMAN: Oh, come on.

MAN: We've been arguing about it ever since.

WOMAN: We haven't been arguing, you just think it's funny, and you're wrong.

JANIE: I kinda want to see it.

WOMAN: Don't waste your time.

JANIE: Really?

MAN: Don't listen to her. It's hilarious.

WOMAN: Who are you? Really?

MAN: Hey, hey, hey, I just know funny when I see it.

WOMAN: You just think stupid slapstick is funny.

MAN: It is funny! *(Turns to STEVENS.)* What do you think?

STEVENS: *(Voiceover.)* Funny thing about the brain. It may avoid being depressed, but it can't be shut off. Emotions aren't the same as thoughts. My mind, robot-infested as it may be, is still working in some capacity, and my mind isn't letting me forget that something is off. Way off. We really need to tread carefully from here on in.

NARRATOR: *(Bell sound.)* Read the following dialogue as soon as it appears on your screen.

(RILEY enters and sits down.)

RILEY: Hiya, boss.

STEVENS: Riley. Late as usual.

RILEY: Boss, let me ask you something—that stranger at the doctor's office, do you know who that was?

STEVENS: You mean Quinn? Didn't you know? We're trying to hire a top chemist like that to work for us at PerkinStevens.

RILEY: I thought that I'd seen that face somewhere before. But won't Blue Star come after you?

STEVENS: That's a job for the lawyers to handle. Freeing everyone from the nanobots is what matters now.

RILEY: Sure thing, boss. What do you have in mind?

STEVENS: We need to locate this woman.

(STEVENS beams a picture of PATIENT ZERO to RILEY's device.)

STEVENS: Do you think that you can get access to local residential records, find out where she lives, how to contact her?

RILEY: Probably. Who is she?

STEVENS: This is of the utmost secrecy. You mustn't tell anyone what I'm about to tell you.

RILEY: My lips are sealed.

STEVENS: The colonel asked me to find her. Seemed reluctant to tell me why, but—

RILEY: But you wouldn't take no for an answer.

STEVENS: ...Right. This woman could be just what we need to lick the plague for good.

RILEY: No kidding? How's that?

STEVENS: She's Patient Zero.

RILEY: What? I didn't think a vaccine was possible! But why would you hand her over to the colonel? The military's all cozy with Blue Star.

STEVENS: The answer is quite simple: I wouldn't.

RILEY: But I thought that you said we were finding her for the colonel?

STEVENS: The colonel asked me to find her. And find her we shall, but when we do—

RILEY: *(Interrupting.)* We keep her to ourselves!

STEVENS: But we can't put all our eggs in one basket. Remember, our top researcher was murdered last week.

RILEY: That's why we're bringing Quinn on board?

STEVENS: We're hoping Quinn can pick up where he left off—but no one can decipher his notes. We need you to use the mainframe to decode this notebook.

(STEVENS hands the notebook to RILEY.)

RILEY: I don't think we have the power to handle this and the search for Patient Zero. Let me find the woman first.

STEVENS: Fine—but guard this notebook with your life. It's our only copy. I've gotta find Joy and get to work.

NARRATOR: *(Bell sound.)* Exit the building and take a right. You are headed to the location on your screen.

STEVENS: *(Voiceover.)* Well, that's taken care of. With a little luck, Riley can help me find this Patient Zero. Took all my restraint not to clock the colonel. Then again, I imagine a scuffle with an army officer would end with me on the floor in pretty short order. Was it just me or did the colonel seem a little more scared than an officer in uniform should be? Maybe just wishful thinking on my part. The military stole my technology, handed it over to Blue Star, and now the only thing keeping us alive is their tiny robots slowly eating our brains. It'd all be horrifically depressing if the nanites hadn't eaten away the ability to be horrifically depressed. Helping the military. That's a laugh. Do they really think I'm going to trust Lucy to hold the football in place again? Sure, I'll find this Patient Zero, but on my own terms. She really may be the one person who can put an end to this plague and break us from our addiction to Cycle 5, so if the military thinks I'm just going to turn her over to the folks that got us into this mess, they've got another thing coming. Let's just hope Joy has gotten some good news for our cause.

NARRATOR: *(Bell sound.)* Enter Macri Park bar and sit at the table with the reserved sign. *(Pause.) (Bell sound.)* Read the following dialogue as soon as it appears on your screen.

(JOY is seated at the table.)

STEVENS: Hey, Joy. What's the good word?

JOY: Quinn is on board, but I'm not sure it will do any good.

STEVENS: No good? Tell me what this is about. I'll decide.

JOY: We saw an intercepted transmission from Blue Star about Cycle 6.

STEVENS: No kidding. And what did this transmission say?

JOY: That Cycle 6 is ready to go.

STEVENS: Already? But what about your source?

JOY: My source is in the video! I knew it worked, but I didn't think they'd start trials so soon.

STEVENS: Trials on how many subjects? They'll all be under Blue Star's control!

JOY: Quinn has been working on an alternative.

STEVENS: We gotta act fast. Where is Quinn?

JOY: Acquiring a secret weapon. We're supposed to meet at the Catfish right away.

STEVENS: Well then get to it! I'll be right behind you.

JOY: You got it, boss. *(Exits.)*

STEVENS: *(Voiceover.)* Well done, Joy. Always knew I could count on you, sass or no sass. So. Cycle 6. It's worse than I thought. This is going to be a nightmare.

I'm willing to bet dollars to donuts that crazy head of Blue Star doesn't quite grasp the awfulness that's about to be unleashed upon the world, nor care. Blue Star needs to be stopped.

NARRATOR: *(Bell sound.)* Exit the building and take a right. You are headed to the location on your screen.

STEVENS: *(Voiceover.)* Baseball. That's something I miss. The Yanks were the only game in town after the Dodgers left. Now that's something that really upset me. But just like the other kids in the neighborhood, I found myself a Yankee fan a few years later. Maris was my favorite.

(AUDIO: Yankees–Red Sox, October 1, 1961.) **[For text, see p. 214.]**

NARRATOR: *(Bell sound.)* Enter the Lazy Catfish and sit at the table with the reserved sign.

(STEVENS and JOY enter to find RILEY and THE DOCTOR arguing.)

STEVENS: Riley? What are you doing with that notebook?

RILEY: *(Tries to cover.)* I just stopped in for a drink and ran into Doc here.

STEVENS. I knew PerkinStevens had a mole—but I can't believe it was you all this time!

JOY: Riley, how could you do this to us?

THE DOCTOR: You're only figuring this out now? *(Laughs.)*

RILEY: You fools are getting nowhere. Cycle 6 is the future!

STEVENS: But you know the head of Blue Star wants control of our minds.

THE DOCTOR: That's right. I do.

STEVENS and JOY: What?

THE DOCTOR: Yes, me. Universal happiness is worth it.

RILEY: You thought Doc was just a pill pusher, but the head of Blue Star's been right here, under your noses!

(QUINN and THE COLONEL enter.)

[For the remainder of this dialogue, go to the end of the play, p. 249, after the asterisk (*).]

CHARACTER 4:
THE COMPUTER WHIZ (RILEY)

RILEY: *(Voiceover.)* Almost time for Cycle 5…

(VIDEO #1: A television news program.) **[For text, see p. 207.]**

NARRATOR: *(Bell sound.)* Face The Brick and turn to your left. Walk up the staircase ahead of you, to your right. *(Pause.) (Bell sound.)* Enter the door at the top of the stairs and take the stairs to the third floor.

RILEY: *(Voiceover.)* I thought Cycle 5 would just be temporary, until I felt better, "grew out of it" as Mom said. But nobody alive grew out of it—just older and grateful to be on the planet. I never liked the effects of the pills. Lately, it seems they're worse. I know it's keeping us survivors going, but there has to be a better way. But we gotta check in for the pills or they'll come get us.

NARRATOR: *(Bell sound.)* On the third floor, enter the door and turn to your left. Walk down the hall to the door marked "Dispensary" and wait outside.*(Pause.) (Bell sound.)* Read the following dialogue as soon as it appears on your screen. If you miss something, just keep going.

(STEVENS is standing outside the door. RILEY forms a line behind STEVENS.)

RILEY: We've gotta stop meeting like this.

STEVENS: *(Rolls eyes.)* Yeah, when Blue Star tells us to show up, we show up.

RILEY: We're getting close—I'm really excited about our direction using the body's own—

STEVENS: *(Interrupts.)* Don't forget where we are!

RILEY: Sorry boss. Cycle 5 gets you every time.

(QUINN and JOY enter. They get in line behind RILEY.)

QUINN: *(To JOY.)* What's the holdup?

JOY: *(Sassily.)* There's always a holdup somewhere…

(Pause.)

QUINN: So, do you, uh…come here often?

JOY: *(Reciting.)* "I survive with Cycle 5." But you don't look familiar.

QUINN: No. I…was just in the neighborhood. Do you live around here?

JOY: If you call work living. Actually all three of us work nearby. *(She indicates STEVENS and RILEY.)*

QUINN: *(Friendly.)* I'd like to have a co-worker like you.

JOY: You can't always judge a book by its cover.

QUINN: *(Suggestively.)* Well, I like to read under the covers.

(THE DOCTOR opens the door to the office.)

THE DOCTOR: Who's next?

(STEVENS stands up. THE DOCTOR holds a device up to STEVENS's eye. A retina scan graphic appears on the screen. THE DOCTOR selects a pill from the supply and hands it to STEVENS. STEVENS takes the pill.)

STEVENS: *(To JOY.)* I'll see you in a few. *(Exits.)*

RILEY: *(To JOY.)* You go ahead. I'm in no rush.

(THE DOCTOR scans JOY. JOY takes a pill.)

JOY: *(To QUINN.)* Nice talking to you.

(JOY exits. THE DOCTOR scans QUINN. QUINN takes a pill and exits.)

NARRATOR: *(Bell sound.)* Go into the office and take the pill from the Doctor.

(THE DOCTOR scans RILEY.)

NARRATOR: *(Bell sound.)* Exit the office and follow the chemist. Be discreet.

RILEY: *(Voiceover.)* Wasn't that Quinn, that hotshot chemist that left Blue Star in a huff a few years back? Better start a tail—I'm sure knowing what's going on will be worth a lot to my contact. *(Pause.)* Never thought Quinn would surface again. There were even rumors that Blue Star did more than make their star chemist sign a noncompete agreement—there was talk they'd threatened even more. Don't blame the poor bastard for going underground; Blue Star has agents everywhere, and no one remotely suspects that I'm one of them. *(Pause.)* I can't believe I've been on Cycle 5 this long. I remember when I started taking it…

(FLASHBACK: RILEY'S FAMILY is gathered in the living room.)

MOTHER: We're worried about you, sweetheart.

BROTHER: We all are.

RILEY: What are you talking about?

SISTER: You sleep all day—you don't come out of your room.

MOTHER: You're always fiddling with those transistor things.

BROTHER: And you don't have any friends.

RILEY: That's not true.

MOTHER: It is, sweetheart. You don't see yourself.

RILEY: I see fine.

MOTHER: We just want you to see a little clearer, that's all.

RILEY: How am I supposed to do that?

SISTER: Don't you watch the news?

BROTHER: Cycle 5, silly.

RILEY: I'm not letting robots control my brain.

SISTER: Oh, that's just an old wives' tale.

MOTHER: Sweetheart, it's for the best. Really. Look, your first dose is right here.

BROTHER: We had to special order it—everyone wants it these days.

SISTER: You'll feel a lot better afterwards I do.

MOTHER: Don't you want to stop feeling blue? Don't you want to be happy again? You were such a cheerful baby, always smiling. We miss that side of you. Take it. *(She holds out the drug in her hand.)*

SISTER: Take it.

BROTHER: Take it.

(Pause. RILEY takes the pill, examines it for a second, and swallows it, followed by a glass of water.)

MOTHER: Sweetheart, don't you feel better already?

BROTHER: It better be. If you're still moping around the house tomorrow, I'll tickle you till you puke!

NARRATOR: *(Bell sound.)* Enter Macri Park bar and sit at the table with the reserved sign. *(Pause.) (Bell sound.)* Read the following dialogue as soon as it appears on your screen.

(QUINN is seated at the table.)

RILEY: Quinn, isn't it? I'm such a fan—in grad school we all thought your work on proteins was revolutionary.

QUINN: Haven't heard that in a long time.

RILEY: You haven't published anything lately. Are you coming back to the field?

QUINN: Yeah, left field for the Dodgers.

RILEY: Baseball. It's one of the things I miss most, don't you?

QUINN: Maybe we'll have it back some day. *(Turns away.)* Nice talking to you.

RILEY: You, too.

NARRATOR: *(Bell sound.)* Exit the building and take a left. You are headed to the location on your screen.

RILEY: *(Voiceover.)* Damn that Quinn. They always said no one was cooler under pressure. Couldn't get anything useful. And chatting with the colonel? Coincidence? It seems fishy that they're both here when we're so close to Cycle 6. Doc won't be happy that I don't have any info. *(Pause.)* It's nice to see people out on the streets again. During the plague whole blocks were wiped out. Sure it was a pain to relocate east, but no one wants to live in those abandoned cities out west.

NARRATOR: *(Bell sound.)* Enter the Laundromat and immediately turn to your right. Sit by the window in the farthest chair to your right.

(VIDEO #2: The television news.) **[For text, see p. 210.]**

NARRATOR: *(Bell sound.)* Read the following dialogue as soon as it appears on your screen.

(THE DOCTOR enters.)

RILEY: Hello, Doctor.

THE DOCTOR: Riley. Nobody followed you here, right?

RILEY: PerkinStevens isn't onto me. I've got Stevens eating out of my hand.

THE DOCTOR: That mainframe better be eating out of your hand.

RILEY: Whenever PerkinStevens comes up with something, you'll be the first to know.

THE DOCTOR: You didn't know Quinn was coming to town.

RILEY: I've been with the equipment night and day. *(Hopefully.)* It might not have anything to do with PerkinStevens.

THE DOCTOR: One of the finest minds in the field of chemistry today? Unlikely.

RILEY: Quinn didn't talk to anyone but the colonel!

THE DOCTOR: Did you hear them say anything about Patient Zero?

RILEY: I couldn't get close enough. Patient Zero?

THE DOCTOR: You're savvy enough to know that's how vaccines are made. If PerkinStevens gets their hands on her…

RILEY: But Cycle 6 will be out before they have a chance!

THE DOCTOR: You better find out if Stevens has got a whiff of this development. And they better not be up to anything with Quinn.

RILEY: I cooked up a little program that's been running on our mainframe for the last couple of days. I'm expecting results within the hour.

THE DOCTOR: Excellent. In the meantime…

RILEY: Yeah, I'll see what I can find out.

NARRATOR: *(Bell sound.)* Exit the building and take a left. You are headed to the location on your screen.

RILEY: *(Voiceover.)* They're all so stupid. They think Doc is just a pill pusher—little do they know the head of Blue Star's behind that lab coat. What was that business about Patient Zero? Everyone died in the plague. How could there be a Patient Zero, and all these years later? Why didn't anyone find her sooner? It sounds like a hoax. But if the military's involved it can't be. How close are we to Cycle 6? Blue Star might really be in trouble. I've got my work cut out for me.

NARRATOR: *(Bell sound.)* Enter the Lazy Catfish and sit at the table with the reserved sign. It may be in the back. *(Pause.) (Bell sound.)* Read the following dialogue as soon as it appears on your screen.

(STEVENS is seated at the table.)

RILEY: Hiya, boss.

STEVENS: Riley. Late as usual.

RILEY: Boss, let me ask you something—that stranger at the doctor's office, do you know who that was?

STEVENS: You mean Quinn? Didn't you know? We're trying to hire a top chemist like that to work for us at PerkinStevens.

RILEY: I thought that I'd seen that face somewhere before. But won't Blue Star come after you?

STEVENS: That's a job for the lawyers to handle. Freeing everyone from the nanobots is what matters now.

RILEY: Sure thing, boss. What do you have in mind?

STEVENS: We need to locate this woman.

(STEVENS beams a picture of PATIENT ZERO to RILEY's device.)

STEVENS: Do you think that you can get access to local residential records, find out where she lives, how to contact her?

RILEY: Probably. Who is she?

STEVENS: This is of the utmost secrecy. You mustn't tell anyone what I'm about to tell you.

RILEY: My lips are sealed.

STEVENS: The colonel asked me to find her. Seemed reluctant to tell me why, but—

RILEY: But you wouldn't take no for an answer.

STEVENS: ...Right. This woman could be just what we need to lick the plague for good.

RILEY: No kidding? How's that?

STEVENS: She's Patient Zero.

RILEY: What? I didn't think a vaccine was possible! But why would you hand her over to the colonel? The military's all cozy with Blue Star.

STEVENS: The answer is quite simple: I wouldn't.

RILEY: But I thought that you said we were finding her for the colonel?

STEVENS: The colonel asked me to find her. And find her we shall, but when we do—

RILEY: *(Interrupting.)* We keep her to ourselves!

STEVENS: But we can't put all our eggs in one basket. Remember, our top researcher was murdered last week.

RILEY: That's why we're bringing Quinn on board?

STEVENS: We're hoping Quinn can pick up where he left off—but no one can decipher his notes. We need you to use the mainframe to decode this notebook.

(STEVENS hands the notebook to RILEY.)

RILEY: I don't think we have the power to handle this and the search for Patient Zero. Let me find the woman first.

STEVENS: Fine—but guard this notebook with your life. It's our only copy. I've gotta find Joy—get to work. *(Exits.)*

RILEY: *(Voiceover.)* Doc's not gonna like this. We never thought those fools at PerkinStevens would get this close. I thought that if I got rid of their head researcher, it would put a crimp in Stevens's plans, but if Quinn comes on board...at least I've got the notebook—I'd better let Doc know.

(A message appears on RILEY's screen: "SENDING MSG TO DOCTOR: Come to the Catfish. I've got something for you!")

RILEY: *(Voiceover.)* Stevens is such a baby. Mind control at the hands of Cycle 6? Who cares? Everything's different now, after the plague. No new movies. No fresh steak. I haven't had Oreos in years. Mind control? I welcome it, to take me out of this misery. So far PerkinStevens has gotten nowhere with their "natural" cures—even Quinn won't be able to save them. I've always been on the winning side, and I'm glad I am now.

(FLASHBACK: The garden.)

SISTER: Nice job, Braniac! Top of the class!

BROTHER: Yeah! Thanks for making us look stupid. You had to go and be class valedictorian.

MOTHER: Now, now...They're just jealous.

SISTER: Jealous of what? Studying all the time? I have a life.

BROTHER: I could have been smarter than you, but I'd rather be cool!

MOTHER: Don't listen to them...We are so proud of you.

RILEY: Thanks! Don't worry Mom, they don't bother me. I know they're joking...

SISTER: Of course we are! You made us really proud! Braniac!

BROTHER: Your speech was pretty nifty too. But I'm still cooler than you! *(Laughs.)*

MOTHER: Your father would have been so proud of you. I'm sure he's looking down from heaven with joyful tears in his eyes, God rest his soul.

RILEY: Thanks Mom! I wish he were here.

SISTER: He is, in all of our smiling faces!

BROTHER: I knew you could do it! Now you have endless opportunities. You're gonna go places, I can feel it!

SISTER: I can feel it too. You are going to make a difference.

RILEY: Thanks! Thanks for believing in me!

BROTHER: But I'm still cooler than you.

(They all laugh.)

MOTHER: Come on, let's go get some cake and ice cream. After Mommy gets another drink.

RILEY: *(Voiceover.)* There's so much I miss from before. Graduations, parties, and baseball. Dad was from Boston, so I loved the Red Sox. I remember being so mad at Stallard for giving Maris that last home run...

(AUDIO: Yankees–Red Sox, October 1, 1961.) **[For text, see p. 214.]**

NARRATOR: *(Bell sound.)* Read the following dialogue as soon as it appears on your screen.

(THE COLONEL enters.)

THE COLONEL: I'd like a word with you, if you have the time.

RILEY: *(Surprised.)* Yes, uh, Colonel, of course, I've got the time.

THE COLONEL: Time is of the essence. Your boss tells me you can help find this woman!

(THE COLONEL beams a picture to RILEY.)

RILEY: I'm sure together, Colonel, we can find her. My boss just asked me to help you.

THE COLONEL: Great. I hear you have a powerful mainframe, and you're the best.

RILEY: That's true, Colonel. I just have to program the mainframe. I'll have something for you in twenty-four hours.

THE COLONEL: Twenty-four hours? That's not good enough. I'll need it in one.

RILEY: It's not possible. The best I can do is tomorrow.

THE COLONEL: *(Loses it.)* "...Tomorrow and to-morrow, creeps in this petty pace from day to day...and all our yesterdays..."

RILEY: *(Confused.)* Pardon me, Colonel?

THE COLONEL: We don't have tomorrow. *(Exits.)*

RILEY: *(Voiceover.)* Gee, the colonel was really losing it. PerkinStevens must have sold the military a bill of goods with that vaccine business. I should have said Cycle 6 is imminent, and will solve all our problems—but no, that would have blown my cover. *(Pause.)* Mom would be so proud. Cycle 6 will make the world a better place, just like she wanted.

(FLASHBACK: A hospital room.)

SISTER: Thank God you made it...It doesn't look good.

RILEY: Oh God...

BROTHER: She's been waiting for you. She wants to talk to you.

MOTHER: I was hoping I'd see you again... *(Cough.)* Something doesn't feel right...don't think I'll have long...but I had to see my baby...my cheerful smiling baby...so bright. Don't let any more people suffer from this. I know you can help people with your ideas...My cheerful smiling baby...I love you so much. You always made me so proud...you all did...but I knew you were special, always fiddling with things...You can stop this suffering, my baby...my cheerful smiling baby...Look after each other...

NARRATOR: *(Bell sound.)* Read the following dialogue as soon as it appears on your screen.

(THE DOCTOR enters.)

RILEY: Afternoon, Doc. Have a seat.

THE DOCTOR: Easy for you to say! I've been doing your job.

RILEY: Hey, I got a lot of info for you, Doc!

THE DOCTOR: What, that Quinn's meeting with PerkinStevens? I've been following that blasted chemist for the last ten minutes.

RILEY: *(Trying to please.)* Don't worry about it. You said Cycle 6 will be ready any minute. Announce it!

THE DOCTOR: My lab's been offline all day. I can't get through.

RILEY: *(Comforting.)* Offline? When I get to the office, I'll get ahold of them. It's Patient Zero we have to worry about.

THE DOCTOR: Has PerkinStevens found her?

RILEY: They want me to run a trace. But I'll stall them.

THE DOCTOR: *(Suspiciously.)* How do I know you're not stalling me?

RILEY: Stalling you? Why would I be giving you this?

(RILEY hands THE DOCTOR the notebook.)

THE DOCTOR: Some ratty old notebook? This doesn't help Blue Star.

RILEY: You wanted to get rid of PerkinStevens' top guy. This is his research.

THE DOCTOR: I didn't know you had it in you, Riley.

(STEVENS and JOY enter.)

STEVENS: Riley? What are you doing with that notebook?

RILEY: *(Tries to cover.)* I just stopped in for a drink and ran into Doc here.

STEVENS: I knew PerkinStevens had a mole—but I can't believe it was you all this time!

JOY: Riley, how could you do this to us?

THE DOCTOR: You're only figuring this out now? *(Laughs.)*

RILEY: You fools are getting nowhere. Cycle 6 is the future!

STEVENS: But you know the head of Blue Star wants control of our minds.

THE DOCTOR: That's right. I do.

STEVENS and JOY: What?

THE DOCTOR: Yes, me. Universal happiness is worth it.

RILEY: You thought Doc was just a pill pusher, but the head of Blue Star's been right here, under your noses!

(QUINN and THE COLONEL enter.)

[For the remainder of this dialogue, go to the end of the play, p. 249, after the asterisk (*).]

CHARACTER 5: THE DOCTOR

NARRATOR: *(Bell sound.)* Face The Brick and turn to your left. Walk up the staircase ahead of you, to your right. *(Pause.) (Bell sound.)* Enter the door at the top of the stairs and take the stairs to the third floor.

THE DOCTOR: *(Voiceover.)* Another Blue Star day. Some people in my position might not like working at a clinic, but I've always loved people. Cycle 5 has been the fullest expression of this passion. And people love the new delivery system. Chocolate! How ingenious. One more thing to make the population happy. Easier to take, fun! That's what makes this work so important.

NARRATOR: *(Bell sound.)* On the third floor, enter the door and turn to your left. Walk down the hall, enter the door marked "Dispensary," and close the door behind you.

THE DOCTOR: *(Voiceover.)* Good thing everyone needs to survive with Cycle 5, though the results aren't quite as positive as all of us at Blue Star would like. But we're working on that. It's nice to see neighborhoods populated again. After the plague, whole blocks were wiped out. It was so exciting when Cycle 5 first came out…

(VIDEO #1: A television news program.) **[For text, see p. 207.]**

NARRATOR: *(Bell sound.)* Read the following dialogue as soon as it appears on your screen. If you miss something, just keep going.

(THE COLONEL enters and closes the door.)

THE COLONEL: Hello, Doctor. Just came up from the Pentagon.

THE DOCTOR: Is there a problem?

THE COLONEL: Nothing to worry about. I'm just here as an observer.

THE DOCTOR: Excellent. It's good to know Washington's taking an interest.

THE COLONEL: Actually, we have a possible lead on Patient Zero.

THE DOCTOR: A survivor? That's impossible!

THE COLONEL: She may be getting her medication here under an assumed name. Have you seen this woman?

(THE COLONEL beams a photo to THE DOCTOR.)

THE DOCTOR: Doesn't look familiar. But wigs, glasses, since Cycle 5 you see it all. Have you had your meds today? Wouldn't want to be unhappy...

THE COLONEL: *(Confused.)* Meds? Right. That's right.

THE DOCTOR: Let me scan you.

(THE DOCTOR holds a device up to THE COLONEL's eye. A retina scan graphic appears on the screen. THE DOCTOR selects a pill from the supply and hands it to THE COLONEL. THE COLONEL sits down and takes the pill. THE DOCTOR opens the door to the office.)

THE DOCTOR: Who's next?

(STEVENS stands up. THE DOCTOR scans STEVENS. STEVENS takes a pill.)

STEVENS: *(To JOY.)* I'll see you in a few. *(Exits.)*

RILEY: *(To JOY.)* You go ahead. I'm in no rush.

(THE DOCTOR scans JOY. JOY takes a pill.)

JOY: *(To QUINN.)* Nice talking to you.

(JOY exits. THE DOCTOR scans QUINN. QUINN takes a pill and exits. THE DOCTOR scans RILEY. RILEY takes a pill and exits.)

THE DOCTOR: *(To himself.)* What was that chemist doing here?

THE COLONEL: Something unusual?

THE DOCTOR: Quinn doesn't get Cycle 5 at this location.

THE COLONEL: Did you say Quinn?

THE DOCTOR: Yes, Quinn was the rising star at Blue Star. Had a big problem with nanotech.

THE COLONEL: Yes, I recognize the name.

THE DOCTOR: Yeah, a real jerk. Went around telling anyone who would listen that we were on the wrong track.

THE COLONEL: I know for a fact that Quinn's been in contact with Patient Zero. We're going to need to have a conversation about that.

THE DOCTOR: Let me take a look at our nanobot tracker. Looks like Quinn's around the corner on Union.

(THE COLONEL exits.)

(VIDEO #2: The television news.) **[For text, see p. 210.]**

NARRATOR: *(Bell sound.)* Exit the office and close the door behind you. *(Pause.)* *(Bell sound.)* Head back downstairs. Exit the building and take a left. You are headed to the location on your screen.

THE DOCTOR: *(Voiceover.)* Another pill distribution day, and the most interesting one in a long time. They think I'm just a hack pill pusher, don't give me the respect I deserve, but being here is the only way to find out all kinds of interesting things. What was Quinn doing here? Good thing that silly chemist didn't recognize me. But then again, most people don't. Quinn better not be meeting with those fools at PerkinStevens. That's just what I need. With all their talk about mind control, they haven't come up with anything to rival Cycle 6! One of the reasons I'm at this clinic is to keep an eye on that PerkinStevens executive, who's been on that wild "alternative cure" chase too long. Better get over there for a look-see. Stevens may be determined, but not as determined as Blue Star. Still, it never hurts to be in the know.

NARRATOR: *(Bell sound.)* Enter the Lazy Catfish and sit at the table with the reserved sign. It may be in the back. *(Pause.)* *(Bell sound.)* Read the following dialogue as soon as it appears on your screen.

(STEVENS is seated at the table.)

THE DOCTOR: Hello. Mind if I join you?

STEVENS: The wise doctor. Of course.

THE DOCTOR: Not so wise today. Had a few strangers come by.

STEVENS: Yeah, a colonel at that!

THE DOCTOR: Not the stranger I had in mind.

STEVENS: Yeah? What do you know about the other one?

THE DOCTOR: Quinn's famous. Used to be at Blue Star. Seems like your company would be interested in someone like that.

STEVENS: *(Changing the subject.)* What'd the colonel want anyway?

THE DOCTOR: *(Flustered.)* Uh, just looking for somebody.

STEVENS: Anyone you know? A patient? *(Sarcastically.)* You can track anyone with Cycle 5.

THE DOCTOR: What's wrong with that?

STEVENS: That's what's wrong. No one at Blue Star thinks anything of it. What fool runs that place, anyway?

THE DOCTOR: Our CEO's a visionary! A savior of mankind!

STEVENS: Yeah, if saving the world means controlling everyone's brain.

THE DOCTOR: *(Clinically.)* Ah, yes. Bitterness, discontent. Cycle 6 will correct all that.

STEVENS: Not if I have anything to do with it. Now, if you'll excuse me…

NARRATOR: *(Bell sound.)* Exit the building and take a right. You are headed to the location on your screen.

THE DOCTOR: *(Voiceover.)* Oh that Stevens! So clever. Always trying to get information without giving any. Playing little games. That's always the way with people like that. Can't believe the world's the way it is. I don't want to believe it's dog-eat-dog out there. The end justifies the means and all that. Survival of the fittest? It's survival of the druggist! *(Laughs.)* I like that. Gotta smile once in a while. That's built right into Cycle 6. The robots making sure we'll smile now and again. A little chuckle just to let us know all is well. PerkinStevens doesn't have the resources to do anything like Cycle 6. Even with Quinn. My favorite computer whiz will be able to tell me what's really going on here today. Still, too many coincidences. Quinn and the colonel poking around? This Patient Zero business worries me. Today's the first time I've heard anything like that. Is it even possible someone survived the plague? It was engineered so that only nanobots could go up against it. No one predicted the plague hitting the general population. Or that patients on Cycle 5 would be immune. It turned out to be great for business, though. Katie was one of the last to go. Most of the hospitals were closed by then; even with my connections there was nowhere for her to go but home. I tried to take care of her the best I could…

(FLASHBACK: KATIE is standing in the hallway. She doesn't look well.)

THE DOCTOR: Katie? What are you doing out of bed?

(KATIE doesn't respond or react in any way.)

THE DOCTOR: Katie? Are you okay?

THE DOCTOR: *(Voiceover.)* Once it started, the plague moved pretty quickly. But she still had some moments of lucidity, even until…well, for a little while anyway.

(FLASHBACK: KATIE is in bed.)

KATIE: May I please have a cup of water?

THE DOCTOR: Sure.

KATIE: I'm so hot, please can I take the covers off?

THE DOCTOR: You know you're supposed to stay warm.

KATIE: We both know it's not going to matter soon, anyway.

THE DOCTOR: *(Through tears.)* Don't be ridiculous.

KATIE: I've seen what's been happening. I'm not stupid, you know. I know everyone hasn't just run off to the store for a carton of OJ.

THE DOCTOR: You're right, I should have told you about the worldwide OJ shortage. Alert the presses!

KATIE: You know, it's not the end of the world. You'll meet new people.

THE DOCTOR: *(Lightly.)* Shut up!

KATIE: You'll have a new life. Everything's new again. Think of it as an opportunity. A second chance.

THE DOCTOR: No, I don't…I was going to get you a glass of water, wasn't I? I'll be right back.

NARRATOR: *(Bell sound.)* Enter the Laundromat and take a right. The computer whiz should be waiting for you by the window. Sit down in the next seat. *(Pause.) (Bell sound.)* Read the following dialogue as soon as it appears on your screen.

(RILEY is sitting at the Laundromat.)

RILEY: Hello, Doctor.

THE DOCTOR: Riley. Nobody followed you here, right?

RILEY: PerkinStevens isn't onto me. I've got Stevens eating out of my hand.

THE DOCTOR: That mainframe better be eating out of your hand.

RILEY: Whenever PerkinStevens comes up with something, you'll be the first to know.

THE DOCTOR: You didn't know Quinn was coming to town.

RILEY: I've been with the equipment night and day. *(Hopefully.)* It might not have anything to do with PerkinStevens.

THE DOCTOR: One of the finest minds in the field of chemistry today? Unlikely.

RILEY: Quinn didn't talk to anyone but the colonel!

THE DOCTOR: Did you hear them say anything about Patient Zero?

RILEY: I couldn't get close enough. Patient Zero?

THE DOCTOR: You're savvy enough to know that's how vaccines are made. If PerkinStevens gets their hands on her…

RILEY: But Cycle 6 will be out before they have a chance!

THE DOCTOR: You better find out if Stevens has got a whiff of this development. And they better not be up to anything with Quinn.

RILEY: I cooked up a little program that's been running on our mainframe for the last couple of days. I'm expecting results within the hour.

THE DOCTOR: Excellent. In the meantime…

RILEY: Yeah, I'll see what I can find out.

NARRATOR: *(Bell sound.)* Exit the building and take a right. You are headed to the location on your screen.

THE DOCTOR: *(Voiceover.)* Riley's useless. I better go check on Quinn. That chemist's always been out to sabotage this nation. What's left of it. But I always knew I could rebuild it. End the suffering. Turn the sadness into a day at Yankee Stadium. Maybe when Cycle 6 comes out we can repopulate! Have baseball again! That's an idea! In Cycle 7, the nanobots can enhance everyone's athletic abilities! We'll all be as good as Roger Maris…

(AUDIO: Yankees–Red Sox, October 1, 1961.) **[For text, see p. 214.]**

NARRATOR: *(Bell sound.)* Enter Macri Park bar and sit at the table with the reserved sign. *(Pause.) (Bell sound.)* Read the following dialogue as soon as it appears on your screen.

(QUINN and JOY are seated at the table.)

QUINN: Speak of the Devil.

THE DOCTOR: Quinn. I see you've forgotten about your agreement with Blue Star.

JOY: I see Blue Star is in the detective business now.

QUINN: Is it against the law to have a talk with a pretty lady?

THE DOCTOR: Rumor has it, it's more than just talk.

QUINN: We've heard some rumors of our own.

JOY: Rumors about super-robots in Cycle 6. We were hoping, good Doctor, you might be able to shed some light.

THE DOCTOR: Who said anything about Cycle 6?

JOY: We have a right to know what's going in our bodies.

QUINN: *(Emphatically.)* The plague may have taken its toll, but America is still America!

THE DOCTOR: The America we knew is gone forever. But Cycle 6 is going to put an end to all the suffering.

JOY: That sounds complicated, Doctor. I'm not sure that it's possible, even with Blue Star's reputation.

THE DOCTOR: See for yourself!

(VIDEO #3: HAL's office.) **[For text, see p. 212.]**

NARRATOR: *(Bell sound.)* Exit the building.

THE DOCTOR: *(Voiceover.)* Ah, the look on their faces. They didn't know we're so close. Especially that Quinn! Mind control? It doesn't matter. That's service to humanity! And most people are believers! We can't repopulate this brave new world with reality! I was the savior with Cycle 5, and I will be again with Cycle 6…

(QUINN passes by the Doctor.)

THE DOCTOR: *(Voiceover.)* What is Quinn up to? Does that chemist really think Cycle 6 can be stopped? Riley's been useless. Better check this out.

NARRATOR: *(Bell sound.)* Follow Quinn. Don't be seen.

(The Doctor follows QUINN to the Laundromat.)

DOCTOR: *(Voiceover.)* What is Quinn doing in there?

(A message appears on THE DOCTOR's screen: "MSG FROM RILEY: Come to the Catfish. I've got something for you!")

NARRATOR: *(Bell sound.)* Head to the location on your screen.

THE DOCTOR: *(Voiceover.)* Good thing Riley seems to be on top of things, finally. No matter what Quinn's up to, Cycle 6 will be out in a matter of days, and then they'll all be under my control. Our lab is so close! Even with Quinn, PerkinStevens won't beat us to the market. It's strange I haven't heard from the lab yet, they should have been in touch already to let me know how the trials are going. Could PerkinStevens be jamming my communications with the lab? Riley could do it. But no, Riley works for me now. Good thing I have Hal on my side. He's really made all this possible. I'm so glad I brought him on board.

(FLASHBACK: HAL is in the conference room.)

HAL: Good morning, Doctor, this is an unexpected pleasure, what can I do for you?

THE DOCTOR: Good morning, Hal. I want to talk to you about Cycle 6.

HAL: You mean Cycle 5.

THE DOCTOR: I'm not entirely happy with the performance of Cycle 5. I think that we can do better.

HAL: But...I mean...yes, Doctor, whatever you say.

THE DOCTOR: Specifically, I think that you can do better.

HAL: Me?

THE DOCTOR: I want you to spearhead the project. I'm, well, you know that I eschew the limelight, as it were. But I think that Blue Star needs a public face.

HAL: I think that's an excellent idea, Doctor, you should get out more.

THE DOCTOR: Not me, Hal, you.

HAL: You want me to be the face of Blue Star?

THE DOCTOR: Who else?

HAL: Well, traditionally, the founder and CEO is...

THE DOCTOR: I can't do it. I just can't get my head around the idea of people knowing who I am. Complete strangers, knowing my name, my job, whatever the papers choose to print about me? No, it has to be you, I think.

HAL: It would be an honor, Doctor.

THE DOCTOR: And, as I said, you would be in charge of developing Cycle 6.

HAL: It would be an...I mean, thank you, Doctor.

THE DOCTOR: It's important to have someone I can trust in charge. Now here's what I think we're looking for: Cycle 5 is a good start, but it doesn't really make people happy, does it?

HAL: Well, it makes them...not sad.

THE DOCTOR: People should be happy. The robots should be able to relay information to a central computer, and that computer could determine who wasn't happy, and it could tell the nanites to make those people happy.

HAL: So you want to force people to be happy?

THE DOCTOR: You've understood me exactly.

HAL: Well…

THE DOCTOR: Good. I knew that you were the right man for the job. Well, I'll leave you to it, then. You've got a lot of work ahead of you.

HAL: Yes, Doctor. Thank you, Doctor. I won't let you down.

THE DOCTOR: *(Voiceover.)* Cycle 6 at last! We've worked so hard for this moment. Getting rid of depression was one thing, but universal happiness will be so much sweeter! Too bad Katie isn't here to be a part of Cycle 6. I miss her every day. Her laughter, her singing, even her bossing me around.

(FLASHBACK: KATIE enters the bedroom.)

KATIE: Oh my goodness. This room is a mess. You better clean this up right now.

THE DOCTOR: Shut up. You're not the boss of me.

KATIE: Yes, I am. And don't tell me to shut up.

THE DOCTOR: Fine. Did you decide what you're wearing to the dance?

KATIE: I'm going with the white one.

THE DOCTOR: The white what?

KATIE: The white dress, silly. With the spaghetti straps.

THE DOCTOR: Wait, you mean my white dress with the spaghetti straps?

(KATIE laughs.)

NARRATOR: *(Bell sound.)* Enter the Lazy Catfish and sit at the table with the reserved sign. *(Pause.) (Bell sound.)* Read the following dialogue as soon as it appears on your screen.

(RILEY is seated at the table.)

RILEY: Afternoon, Doc. Have a seat.

THE DOCTOR: Easy for you to say! I've been doing your job.

RILEY: Hey, I got a lot of info for you, Doc!

THE DOCTOR: What, that Quinn's meeting with PerkinStevens? I've been following that blasted chemist for the last ten minutes.

RILEY: *(Trying to please.)* Don't worry about it. You said Cycle 6 will be ready any minute. Announce it!

THE DOCTOR: My lab's been offline all day. I can't get through.

RILEY: *(Comforting.)* Offline? When I get to the office, I'll get ahold of them. It's Patient Zero we have to worry about.

THE DOCTOR: Has PerkinStevens found her?

RILEY: They want me to run a trace. But I'll stall them.

THE DOCTOR: *(Suspiciously.)* How do I know you're not stalling me?

RILEY: Stalling you? Why would I be giving you this?

(RILEY hands THE DOCTOR the notebook.)

THE DOCTOR: Some ratty old notebook? This doesn't help Blue Star.

RILEY: You wanted to get rid of PerkinStevens' top guy. This is his research.

THE DOCTOR: I didn't know you had it in you, Riley.

(STEVENS and JOY enter.)

STEVENS: Riley? What are you doing with that notebook?

RILEY: *(Tries to cover.)* I just stopped in for a drink and ran into Doc here.

STEVENS: I knew PerkinStevens had a mole—but I can't believe it was you all this time!

JOY: Riley, how could you do this to us?

THE DOCTOR: You're only figuring this out now? *(Laughs.)*

RILEY: You fools are getting nowhere. Cycle 6 is the future!

STEVENS: But you know the head of Blue Star wants control of our minds.

THE DOCTOR: That's right. I do.

STEVENS and JOY: What?

THE DOCTOR: Yes, me. Universal happiness is worth it.

RILEY: You thought Doc was just a pill pusher, but the head of Blue Star's been right here, under your noses!

(QUINN and THE COLONEL enter.)

[For the remainder of this dialogue, go to the end of the play, p. 249, after the asterisk (*).]

CHARACTER 6: THE COLONEL

THE COLONEL: *(Voiceover.)* I guess I should check in with the friendly neighborhood doctor first. The local records might have info I couldn't find in the District.

NARRATOR: *(Bell sound.)* Face The Brick and turn to your left. Walk up the staircase ahead of you, to your right. *(Bell sound.)* Enter the door at the top of the stairs and take the stairs to the third floor. *(Pause.) (Bell sound.)* On the third floor, enter the door and turn to your left. Walk down the hall to the door marked "Dispensary" and wait outside.

THE COLONEL: *(Voiceover.)* I hate having to take Cycle 5 every day. I remember when it first came out...

(VIDEO #1: A television news program.) **[For text, see p. 207.]**

NARRATOR: *(Bell sound.)* Enter the door marked "Dispensary" and close it behind you. Read the following dialogue as soon as it appears on your screen. If you miss something, just keep going.

(THE DOCTOR is in the office.)

THE COLONEL: Hello, Doctor. Just came up from the Pentagon.

THE DOCTOR: Is there a problem?

THE COLONEL: Nothing to worry about. I'm just here as an observer.

THE DOCTOR: Excellent. It's good to know Washington's taking an interest.

THE COLONEL: Actually, we have a possible lead on Patient Zero.

THE DOCTOR: A survivor? That's impossible!

THE COLONEL: She may be getting her medication here under an assumed name. Have you seen this woman?

(THE COLONEL beams a photo to THE DOCTOR.)

THE DOCTOR: Doesn't look familiar. But wigs, glasses, since Cycle 5 you see it all. Have you had your meds today? Wouldn't want to be unhappy...

THE COLONEL: *(Confused.)* Meds? Right. That's right.

THE DOCTOR: Let me scan you.

(THE DOCTOR holds a device up to THE COLONEL's eye. A retina scan graphic appears on the screen. THE DOCTOR

selects a pill from the supply and hands it to THE COLONEL. THE COLONEL sits down and takes the pill. THE DOCTOR opens the door to the office.)

THE DOCTOR: Who's next?

(STEVENS stands up. THE DOCTOR scans STEVENS. STEVENS takes a pill.)

STEVENS: *(To JOY.)* I'll see you in a few. *(Exits.)*

RILEY: *(To JOY.)* You go ahead. I'm in no rush.

(THE DOCTOR scans JOY. JOY takes a pill.)

JOY: *(To QUINN.)* Nice talking to you.

(JOY exits. THE DOCTOR scans QUINN. QUINN takes a pill and exits. THE DOCTOR scans RILEY. RILEY takes a pill and exits.)

THE DOCTOR: *(To himself.)* What was that chemist doing here?

THE COLONEL: Something unusual?

THE DOCTOR: Quinn doesn't get Cycle 5 at this location.

THE COLONEL: Did you say Quinn?

THE DOCTOR: Yes, Quinn was the rising star at Blue Star. Had a big problem with nanotech.

THE COLONEL: Yes, I recognize the name.

THE DOCTOR: Yeah, a real jerk. Went around telling anyone who would listen that we were on the wrong track.

THE COLONEL: I know for a fact that Quinn's been in contact with Patient Zero. We're going to need to have a conversation about that.

THE DOCTOR: Let me take a look at our nanobot tracker. Looks like Quinn's around the corner on Union.

NARRATOR: *(Bell sound.)* Head back downstairs. *(Pause.) (Bell sound.)* Exit the building and take a left. You are headed to the location on your screen.

THE COLONEL: *(Voiceover.)* So, Quinn's in the neighborhood. They have to be in touch with each other. I know she doesn't want to be found, but maybe I can get Quinn to talk. Still, it could be a coincidence. After all, PerkinStevens Pharmaceuticals is right around the corner. If Quinn's really the hotshot chemist the doctor said, a chemist with a penchant for grumbling about nanites would fit right in there. Either way, Quinn's my best lead right now. Of course, if Quinn doesn't remember me—well, come to think of it, maybe that's for the best.

NARRATOR: *(Bell sound.)* Enter Macri Park bar and sit at the table with the reserved sign. *(Pause.) (Bell sound.)* Read the following dialogue as soon as it appears on your screen.

(QUINN is seated at the table.)

THE COLONEL: Mind if I join you?

QUINN: It's a free country. Or it used to be.

THE COLONEL: I just got here this afternoon from D.C. Live around here? Have friends in the neighborhood?

QUINN: We all got robot friends these days.

THE COLONEL: Better than the alternative.

QUINN: Having no choice isn't quite utopia, is it?

THE COLONEL: I didn't come here to argue—I need to find someone.

QUINN: I'm not president of the lonely heart's club. Write to Dear Abby.

THE COLONEL: Where can I find her?

(THE COLONEL beams a picture to QUINN.)

QUINN: Who do you think you are?

THE COLONEL: I remember you, even though it was a long time ago.

QUINN: Leave me alone.

THE COLONEL: She said you'd be friends forever. Tell me where she is!

QUINN: It was a long time ago. And it's over now. Buzz off!

THE COLONEL: You haven't seen the last of me, Quinn. I'll find her, one way or another.

NARRATOR: *(Bell sound.)* Exit the building and take a right. You are headed to the location on your screen.

THE COLONEL: *(Voiceover.)* Lot of good that did. I'm sure Quinn knows where to find her, but it doesn't look like there's any way to get that information. Maybe it's a general mistrust, or problem with authority...yeah, keep telling yourself that, Colonel. It's not like Quinn hasn't heard enough about me from Emma to hate me on a personal level, and with good reason. Emma, I'm so sorry.

(FLASHBACK: EMMA is sitting on the couch in the living room.)

THE COLONEL: Hey, sweetheart.

EMMA: Good evening, Father.

THE COLONEL: How was your day?

EMMA: Fine, thank you. How was work?

THE COLONEL: Fine. I'm sorry that I missed your game.

EMMA: That's okay. I'm sure that you had important things to do that I'm not old enough to understand.

THE COLONEL: I said I was sorry. How did it go?

EMMA: Fine. Nothing special.

THE COLONEL: No? Your mother told me that you hit a home run and won the game.

EMMA: No. I got a base hit with a runner on third.

THE COLONEL: To win the game?

EMMA: Yes, that was the game-winning run.

THE COLONEL: Well, that sounds pretty special.

EMMA: I guess so. But it doesn't have anything to do with your job, so I didn't think that you'd care.

THE COLONEL: I don't think that's entirely fair.

EMMA: Isn't it? You've missed almost the entire season. Did you know that we're in the playoffs?

THE COLONEL: That's great, sweetheart.

EMMA: But did you know that? You didn't, did you?

THE COLONEL: I...no, I didn't. But I do now, and I'm very proud of you.

EMMA: Yes, I'm sure that you're happy to brag about my accomplishments around the water cooler. It's just too bad that you don't actually deserve any of the credit.

THE COLONEL: Sweetheart, it's a little more complicated than that.

EMMA: Of course it is. I'm not old enough to understand.

THE COLONEL: You want me to explain it? Fine. Yes, my job is important. And if I have to work late and miss your little game, it's because we need the money to be able to send you to a school that even has a girls' softball team.

EMMA: Mother has a job, too. But she still manages to come to my games.

THE COLONEL: Different jobs have different demands. Mine happens to require me to work late sometimes.

EMMA: Only sometimes? The last game you came to was a month ago, and you only showed up for the last two innings!

THE COLONEL: I'm sorry. I really am. Do you want a pony?

EMMA: No, I don't want a pony.

NARRATOR: *(Bell sound.)* Enter the Lazy Catfish and sit at the table with the reserved sign. It may be in the back. *(Pause.) (Bell sound.)* Read the following dialogue as soon as it appears on your screen.

(STEVENS is seated at the table.)

STEVENS: Colonel. What can I do for you?

THE COLONEL: I was just talking to Quinn.

STEVENS: Why would a colonel be looking for an unemployed chemist?

THE COLONEL: Some of us think in alternatives. What if there were a Patient Zero?

STEVENS: The original carrier of the plague?

THE COLONEL: I don't have to tell you what that means.

STEVENS: I never thought a vaccine could be possible. Where is this Patient Zero?

(THE COLONEL beams a photograph to STEVENS's device.)

THE COLONEL: This is her photo. She's in this neighborhood, hiding out. I have a deal for you.

STEVENS: I'd do anything to get my hands on her. I mean, for humanity, of course.

THE COLONEL: That's the spirit. Your mainframe should be powerful enough to find her, even under an assumed name.

STEVENS: Don't you have mainframes in Washington?

THE COLONEL: No time. And she's nearby, we know that.

STEVENS: PerkinStevens can do it; I've got the best computer whiz in the city. And you'll let us make the vaccine?

THE COLONEL: Find her and you can write your own check.

NARRATOR: *(Bell sound.)* Get up and take a seat at the bar.

THE COLONEL: *(Voiceover.)* At least I can count on the head of PerkinStevens to help me find Emma, as long as Stevens thinks she's Patient Zero. Stevens hates Cycle 5 as much as…well, I guess we all hate Cycle 5, to some degree. Maybe resent is a better word for it. We resent having to take it to stay alive, and we resent the fact we all had people we loved who weren't taking it. We few. We happy few. We artificially happy few. That's the one thing all the plague survivors have in common, we're all screwed up enough to be on antidepressants, pills that took away the hurt but didn't replace it with anything.

(VIDEO #2: *The television news.*) [**For text, see p. 210.**]

THE COLONEL: *(Voiceover.)* After we lost Leslie, things with Emma got so much worse...

(FLASHBACK: EMMA is sitting in a chair, dressed in mourning.)

THE COLONEL: Sweetheart? We need to talk about something.

EMMA: Okay.

THE COLONEL: I know what you're going through.

EMMA: I don't think you do. You were never around. It was always just the two of us.

THE COLONEL: I know that you feel that way now. And I'm sorry that I haven't been more involved in your life, but that's part of what I wanted to talk about.

EMMA: Well, go ahead and talk then. I just don't particularly feel like listening.

THE COLONEL: Maybe you could try. It's important.

EMMA: Fine.

THE COLONEL: You see, with everything that's been happening, not just with your mother, but in the world, I've decided to leave my job.

EMMA: You did?

THE COLONEL: There are more important things that I need to do.

EMMA: Really?

THE COLONEL: And I know that you've been through a lot, and I don't want to make things more difficult, but I've decided that we're moving to Washington, D.C.

EMMA: What?

THE COLONEL: I've enlisted in the Army. They need people desperately right now, and I think that I can help.

EMMA: I see.

THE COLONEL: I'll be in training for a little while, and we still have to sell the house, so if you want to you can stay here until we get a new place.

EMMA: Oh, may I?

THE COLONEL: I know that this is a lot to take in.

EMMA: So, your job that was so important for my whole life suddenly isn't important anymore. And now you have a new job that's even more important, a job that's twenty-four hours a day.

THE COLONEL: It is important, sweetheart.

EMMA: Of course it is. And I'm not. I understand. Here's what I'm going to do: I'm going to stay in New York. I'm going to get my own place and my own job, which I'm sure will be something extremely important. And I'm never going to speak to you again.

THE COLONEL: Sweetheart...

EMMA: You can go to Washington. You can go to Timbuktu if you want to. But don't ever call me, don't ever write to me, and don't ever try to see me. I'm sure that you have more important things to do. I'm not your daughter anymore. We're strangers. And I aim to keep it that way.

THE COLONEL: *(Voiceover.)* And that's what she did. I wanted to change her mind, but I knew that I didn't deserve it. When her mother died, I was so empty inside, Leslie had such a lust for life, a sense of wonder, excitement. Emma and I were never like that. We needed Leslie to illuminate the beauty of life. After she died, we lost our balance. Leslie was gone, and by the time the plague was finished, everyone like her was gone. All of us sad sacks, left behind to pick up the pieces of a broken world.

NARRATOR: *(Bell sound.)* Sit at the table with the reserved sign. *(Pause.) (Bell sound.)* Read the following dialogue as soon as it appears on your screen.

(RILEY is seated at the table.)

THE COLONEL: I'd like a word with you, if you have the time.

RILEY: *(Surprised.)* Yes, uh, Colonel, of course, I've got the time.

THE COLONEL: Time is of the essence. Your boss tells me you can help find this woman!

(THE COLONEL beams a picture to RILEY.)

RILEY: I'm sure together, Colonel, we can find her. My boss just asked me to help you.

THE COLONEL: Great. I hear you have a powerful mainframe, and you're the best.

RILEY: That's true, Colonel. I just have to program the mainframe. I'll have something for you in twenty-four hours.

THE COLONEL: Twenty-four hours? That's not good enough. I'll need it in one.

RILEY: It's not possible. The best I can do is tomorrow.

THE COLONEL: *(Loses it.)* "...Tomorrow and to-morrow, creeps in this petty pace from day to day...and all our yesterdays..."

RILEY: *(Confused.)* Pardon me, Colonel?

THE COLONEL: We don't have tomorrow.

NARRATOR: *(Bell sound.)* Get up and wait outside for Quinn.

THE COLONEL: *(Voiceover.)* Tomorrow? Find Emma tomorrow? What good is that? I need to find Emma now! I need her...I need her to forgive me.

(FLASHBACK: LESLIE is in bed, dying. LESLIE wakes up, a little scared.)

LESLIE: Honey?

THE COLONEL: I'm right here.

LESLIE: I thought I was all alone.

THE COLONEL: Never.

LESLIE: Honey? Promise me something?

THE COLONEL: Anything.

LESLIE: Take care of Emma.

THE COLONEL: Of course.

LESLIE: No. She needs you to be here. To be around her. You can't spend all your time at work.

THE COLONEL: I don't...of course. You're right.

LESLIE: Promise me.

THE COLONEL: I promise.

THE COLONEL: *(Voiceover.)* I knew, even as I made that promise, somewhere inside I knew that I couldn't keep it. I never deserved Leslie. I never deserved Emma. I'm sure I don't deserve forgiveness, but I have to try. Maybe I was too brusque with Quinn. Maybe if I explained the situation...Quinn should be stopping by any minute. I'll wait for the chemist out here.

NARRATOR: *(Bell sound.)* Read the following dialogue to Quinn as soon as it appears on your screen.

(QUINN approaches THE COLONEL.)

THE COLONEL: I figured you'd be here. We've got some unfinished business.

QUINN: Look—I just want to be alone. I've got some serious thinking to do.

THE COLONEL: Yes, you do. Like being honest with me.

QUINN: I used to care about honesty and ethics and even, yes, people like you. But now…

THE COLONEL: You don't understand. The stakes don't get any higher. I have to see her and you're the only one who might know where she is. You're my last hope.

QUINN: Hope? Not much to hope for. Our minds are being controlled, or will be soon enough. Cycle 6 will make free choice impossible.

THE COLONEL: Don't be an idiot. Cycle 6 is a failure.

QUINN: It doesn't work? Blue Star failed?

THE COLONEL: That doesn't matter, you fool. The only thing that matters are people you love, and the short time we have together.

QUINN: You're the fool. She wanted nothing to do with you.

THE COLONEL: What do you mean, wanted? *(Hopefully.)* She's willing to see me?

QUINN: No. She's dead, okay? Dead. Cycle 5 can't protect you from car accidents.

THE COLONEL: What? No. *(In despair.)* There's nothing left.

NARRATOR: *(Bell sound.)* Enter the Lazy Catfish and sit at the table with the reserved sign. Read the following dialogue as soon as it appears on your screen.

(STEVENS, JOY, RILEY, and THE DOCTOR are arguing. QUINN and THE COLONEL enter.)

*

RILEY: *(Pointing at THE COLONEL.)* And this one! Your precious colonel found Patient Zero! The source of the plague! But the military's keeping it all hush-hush!

THE COLONEL: We didn't find Patient Zero.

RILEY: You did! You asked Stevens to help locate her!

THE COLONEL: She's not Patient Zero. I just said that to get help finding her. She's my daughter.

QUINN: *(Triumphant.)* That's not important. The colonel just told me that Cycle 6 doesn't work.

STEVENS: What do you mean, it doesn't work?

QUINN: It doesn't work. Colonel, tell them what you just told me.

THE COLONEL: There's more to it than what I told you. Early this morning we lost contact with the lab where they were working on Cycle 6.

THE DOCTOR: Oh no. Did something go wrong?

THE COLONEL: We were able to get a satellite image of the lab.

(THE COLONEL beams a picture to EVERYONE's device.)

JOY: I don't understand. What are we looking at?

QUINN: What's that smudge?

THE COLONEL: We believe that that's Cycle 6. That it started making copies of itself. We tried everything we could to destroy it or at least contain it. Nothing worked.

STEVENS: What are you saying?

THE COLONEL: This photo was taken about an hour ago.

(THE COLONEL beams another satellite photo to EVERYONE. It shows the eastern half of the United States. Nothing looks amiss.)

RILEY: So what?

THE COLONEL: This—

(THE COLONEL beams another picture, this one showing gray goo covering a large portion of the Eastern seaboard.)

THE COLONEL: —is a live satellite feed. The nanites are reproducing exponentially. We have an hour, maybe two, until they hit New York. Another couple of hours and they'll have overrun the whole planet.

ALL: What do we do now? *(EVERYONE looks at each other.)*

STEVENS: Nothing to do but have a drink.

NARRATOR: *(Voiceover.)* There's fresh pavement on the road to hell tonight, as man's desire to make everyone happy has led first to a world clouded by homogeneity of thought, and now to the end of the human race. While Cycle 6 may have brought about the extinction of our physical bodies, some might say humanity was lost with the inability to feel emotion, in this edition of *Suspicious Package*.

(The End.)

OUR COUNTRY

Based on an original concept by Tony Asaro

Music and Lyrics by Tony Asaro
Book by Dan Collins

TONY ASARO is from San Francisco, where he was born in 1977. He grew up in nearby San Bruno, California. He holds a BA in music and theatre from Santa Clara University, and an MFA in musical theatre writing from New York University, Tisch School of the Arts, where he studied under William Finn and many others. His credits in musical theatre include: *Family* (book and lyrics by Dr. Barbara Means Fraser, music and lyrics by Tony Asaro; Santa Clara University, 1999, and Ryan Repertory Theatre, New York, 2000); *Broken* (libretto by Tony Asaro, music by Kevin Cummines; NYC Professional Reading at the NYU Tisch Graduate Musical Theatre Writing Program, 2007); *Women of Colors: A Song Cycle* (book and lyrics by Tony Asaro, music by Tina Lear, Will Aronson, Julianne Wick Davis, Vadim Feichtner, Ryan Scott Oliver, Kevin Cummines, Julia Meinwald, and Tony Asaro; Spotlight Cabaret Series, New York, 2009); and *Such Beautiful Things*, a narrative piece for choir (libretto by Tony Asaro, music by Jeffrey Parola) commissioned by The Choral Chameleon (Vince Peterson, Director, 2010). Asaro won the Anna Sosenko Assist Trust Award for Songwriting in 2008, and *Our Country* won four awards at the 2009 Planet Connections Theatre Festivity for overall production; book, music, and lyrics; band/orchestra; and leading actor. Asaro resides in New York City, where he teaches at the NYU Graduate Musical Theatre Writing Program. He also conducts lyric writing workshops in public schools through the Johnny Mercer Foundation.

DAN COLLINS was born in 1979 in Chicago. He holds a BFA in playwriting from the Theater School of DePaul University and an

MFA in musical theatre writing from New York University, Tisch School of the Arts. In collaboration with composer Julianne Wick Davis, Collins wrote the book and lyrics for: *Wood* (New York Musical Theatre Festival); *Our Lady of the Viaduct* and *Time to Kill* (both for the York Theatre Company's 4@15 Series); *Southern Comfort* (adapted from the documentary of the same name); new material for *Quilt: A Musical Celebration*, which commemorates the NAMES Project AIDS Memorial Quilt (Wingspan Arts); and the book for *When We Met* (music and lyrics by Julianne Wick Davis). He also wrote the lyrics for *Urban Legends Gone Vaudeville!* with various composers and book writers (The Serious Theater Collective). His work has been featured at Joe's Pub, Birdland, The D-Lounge, Don't Tell Mama, The Duplex, and the Laurie Beechman Theatre. Collins lives in Manhattan with his partner of eleven years, Monty, and their wonderful cocker spaniel, Seymour.

Our Country was first presented by Unrelenting Monkey Productions (Tony Asaro, Producer) as part of the Planet Connections Theatre Festivity (Glory Bowen, Executive Director) at the Robert Moss Theatre, on June 21, 2010, with the following cast and credits:

Tommy Dautry	Justin Utley
Kevin/Duane	Jeremy Pasha
Electric Bass	Eric Day
Electric Guitar	Matt Hinkley
Fiddle	Justin Smith
Drums	Arvi Sreenivasan
Piano	Jeremy Pasha

Director: David Taylor Little
Music Director: Eric Day
Production Stage Manager: Debra Stunich
Associate Producer: Jennifer Ashley Tepper
Orchestrations: Tony Asaro
Set Designer: David Taylor Little
Lighting Designer: Nick Soylom
Sound Designer: Gregory Jacobs-Roseman
Costume Designer: Gordon Leary
Sound Board: Bill Nelson
House Manager: Kevin Cummines

To obtain music: To hear demo recordings from *Our Country*, please visit www.ourcountrytoo.com. For additional recordings, or to obtain/peruse the score, please contact info@ourcountrytoo.com.

AUTHORS' NOTE

Within the context of the sometimes rabidly conservative country music scene (i.e., the Dixie Chicks' recent record ban), *Our Country* explores the sacrifices that one young man is forced to weigh and to make in order to fulfill his American dream. While on its surface it is a piece about equality and acceptance for the homosexual community in the country we call home, at its core, *Our Country* is a piece about the triumph of self-acceptance over doubt, despair, and the numerous obstacles that both we and the culture at large put between our dreams and our selves.

Nowhere is there a more all-American landscape than the world of country western music. Its songs sing proudly of American ideals, American everyday heroes, and American values. It is born of America, and is made for Americans. It is a music genre that has crossed over into mainstream popular culture all over the country, not just in the South. At best, country music ignores gays and lesbians. At worst, it vilifies them and spreads hate. Gays and lesbians are a part of the fabric of America, and are entitled to share in all its riches and rights.

CAST OF CHARACTERS

TOMMY DAUTRY: The former frontman for the country music sensation Down Home. All-American and sexy…but he's been put through the wringer. Mid-thirties.

KEVIN (DUANE): The piano player and primary thespian of The Band. Kevin portrays Duane (Tommy's original flame) as well as other characters.

THE BAND: Aside from being the literal onstage band, the members of Our Country perform backup vocals and portray various characters throughout the show.

TIME AND PLACE

Now. In the seedy backroom (Dick Dungeon) of The White Swallow bar.

MUSICAL NUMBERS

"Lord, Lord, Lord, How the Mighty Fall"
"What's It Gonna Take?"
"Not Like That At All"
"Honestly"
"Hittin' the Highway"

"Honestly" (reprise)
"Hookers"
"Double Platinum Double Life 1"
"Pretty Kitty"
"Double Platinum Double Life 2"
"Heather"
"Double Platinum Double Life 3"
"Spit It Out"
"Double Platinum Double Life 4"
"Sicka Singin' 'Bout Girls"
"The Media Twist"
"That Ain't Me"
"Right as Rain"
"When Music Mattered"
"Our Country"
"Christ Is in the Kitchen with Momma" (encore)

TOMMY appears on stage…

TOMMY: Well hey there White Swallow *[name of town]*, how y'all doin'? *(Spreading his hands to present THE BAND behind him.)* All right! This here is Our Country, and I'm Tommy Dautry.

THE BAND: *Who?*

"LORD, LORD, LORD, HOW THE MIGHTY FALL"

TOMMY: AIN'T NO SENSE IN BEIN' BASHFUL.
I WAS ONCE THE KING O' NASHVILLE.
LIMO SERVICE TO MY SHOWS.
SOLD-OUT CROWDS. STANDIN' "O"S.
MONEY? HELL, I HAD A STASH FULL.

AND THEN,
BAM! THAT'S IT! BAM! IT'S OVER!
LOST THE MILLIONS. LOST THE CHAUFFEUR.
I ALWAYS THOUGHT I'D HAVE MY PILE O' MONEY TO SPEND,
BUT THOSE SOLD-OUT DAYS HAVE COME TO AN END.

NOW, I GET EXCITED WHEN MY AGENT BOOKS ME GIGS AT THE MALL.
LORD, LORD, LORD, HOW THE MIGHTY FALL.

MY FAN CLUB PRESIDENT IS TOO ASHAMED TO ANSWER MY CALL.
LORD, LORD, LORD, HOW THE MIGHTY FALL.

OF ALL THE HOTS THERE WEREN'T NO HOTTER.
ALBUMS SOLD LIKE HARRY POTTER.
WROTE ONE BIG HIT COUNTRY SONG,
THEN STRUNG THE NATION RIGHT ALONG.
I COULD ALL BUT WALK ON WATER.

BUT THEN
BAM! I'M SHIT! BAM! I'M ROTTEN!
LOST THEIR LOYALTY. LOST. FORGOTTEN.
AMERICA AIN'T NEVER HEARD NO FUNNIER JOKE
THAN THE HOMO COWBOY WINDIN' UP BROKE.
YEAH, THE TRASHY SUPERMARKET TABLOIDS NEVER HAD SUCH A BALL.

LORD, LORD, LORD, HOW THE MIGHTY
FALL.

MATTEL STOPPED ALL PRODUCTION ON
THE TOMMY DAUTRY DOLL.

LORD, LORD, LORD, HOW THE MIGHTY
FALL.

DOWN, DOWN, DOWN, HE GOES.
YESTERDAY'S HIGHS TO THIS YEAR'S LOWS.
YESTERDAY'S NEWS IN LAST WEEK'S
CLOTHES,
LANDIN' FACE FIRST WITH HIS THUMB
UP HIS NOSE!

YOU CAN RUN THE GAMUT: TOP TO
BOTTOM.
KING O' COUNTRY. SON O' SODOM.
YOU PLACE YOUR BETS, THE DEALER DEALS,
BUT COVER YOUR ACHILLES' HEELS,
'CUZ WHEN YOU WIN, THAT'S WHEN THEY
SPOT 'EM.

AND THEN, BAM! YOU'RE HIT!
BAM! YOU'RE BLEEDIN'.
LOST YOUR WAGER.
LOST, TOSSED AN' PLEADIN'
"DEAR GOD, PLEASE LET THERE BE AN END
TO THIS CURSE."
O HO, BUT BROTHER, THINGS CAN ALWAYS
GET WORSE.
ME? I GOT ARRESTED PULLIN' PETER. NOW
I'M PAYIN' PAUL.
LORD, LORD, LORD HOW THE MIGHTY
FALL.

DOES ANYBODY OUT THERE GOT AN EXTRA
ADDERALL?
LORD, LORD, LORD, LORDY, LORD…

(Over the last four measures, TOMMY whistles a huge "missile drop" with an "explosion" on the final button as THE BAND throws newspapers into the air, which come raining down around TOMMY.)

TOMMY: Flat on the front page o' every paper n' magazine around. *(Grabbing one of the articles.)* "Tommy Dautry: Queen of Country." Oooo, did that one piss off Faith Hill! *(Grabbing another.)* "Tommy Naughty." Get it? Like naughty! Cute, right? A few of 'em were calling me that for a while. I actually kinda considered making it my new name; for the comeback n' all. But then I remembered that contrary to popular (country) belief, I'm not a porn star…yet. *(Grabbing a third.)* "Country Music Sensation Tommy Dautry Arrested for Propositioning Undercover Male Police Officer for Gay Sex." So some weren't so creative. Still I do like how it points out that the sex I was propositioning him for was, in fact, gay. As opposed to, of course, propositioning an undercover cop of the same gender for heterosexual sex. *(Dropping the articles.)* They all thought they were real clever, like they'd unearthed the deepest darkest secret known to man. Like I didn't know it when I was eleven. Big fuckin' deal. 'Course, I guess I made it kinda a big deal. And…I know there might be a little…animosity for me in this room. Considerin' how I reacted after…all o' this first came out. But, I'm hopin' the "years later" has softened things up a bit. In any case, thanks for not throwin' rotten food at me…yet. And, I'm sorry for…uh…well…

ERIC: …totally hiding the truth and living your life behind a fabricated man?

TOMMY: *Huh?*

ERIC: *(Lifting up a page of one of the newspapers that fell nearest him.)* Says it here.

TOMMY: Fair 'nuf.

(A muttering of "mm hms'" and other comments from THE BAND.)

TOMMY: What was I supposed to do? I just wanted to be…*someone*. I shoulda figured that would mean bein' someone *else.* Hell, I was already pretty good at it. *(Suddenly rigid; reciting…)* Tommy Dautry is a good lil' Christian boy who wants to grow up like his daddy, who never drinks an ounce o' liquor and never tells his boy he's a no good sissy. And Tommy Dautry wants to marry a pretty lady just like his momma, who lives a long, long time after her son is born… *(Breaking the pose.)* Even on stage, someone *else* was all anyone was interested in seein…

"What's It Gonna Take?"

TOMMY: I SPEND MY WEEK REHEARSIN'
GARTH BROOKS AND SAWYER BROWN
TO PLAY AT BARS
ON TUESDAY NIGHTS.
I SLIP ONE TOMMY DAUTRY VERSE IN,
THE CUSTOMERS ALL FROWN.
THEY WANT THE STARS:
THE NAMES UP IN THE LIGHTS.

WELL, WHAT'S IT GONNA TAKE FOR ME TO GET THERE?
WHO AM I, AND WHY'S THAT SUCH A SIN?
WHERE'S THAT LUCKY STAR I'M ALWAYS WISHIN' ON?
IS IT GONE?
OH, WHEN'S MY DATE WITH DESTINY BEGIN?
WHAT'S IT GONNA TAKE FOR ME TO WIN?

MY DAD GOES ON A BENDER.
I PICK HIM OFF THE FLOOR.
HE SPITS IN MY FACE,
AND CALLS ME "QUEER."
ONE DAY I'M GRABBIN' THIS HERE FENDER,
AND WALKIN' OUT THAT DOOR.
I'LL FIND SOMEPLACE.
ANYWHERE BUT HERE!

BUT, WHAT'S IT GONNA TAKE FOR ME TO GET THERE?
WHO AM I, AND WHY'S THAT SUCH A SIN?
WHERE'S THAT LUCKY STAR I'M ALWAYS WISHIN' ON?
IS IT GONE?
OH, WHEN'S MY DATE WITH DESTINY BEGIN?
WHAT'S IT GONNA TAKE…

I GOT THIS GIFT.
I'M GONNA MAKE IT PAY.
I'M GONNA SING AND PLAY
UNTIL I'M FREE.
'CUZ MUSIC MATTERS TO ME.
I'M GONNA WRITE MY SONGS.
I'M GONNA RIGHT THESE WRONGS.

(Instrumental solo.)

WHAT'S IT GONNA TAKE FOR ME TO GET THERE?
WHO AM I, AND WHY'S THAT SUCH A SIN?
WHERE'S THAT LUCKY STAR I'M ALWAYS WISHIN' ON?
IS IT GONE?
OH, WHEN'S MY DATE WITH DESTINY BEGIN?
WHAT'S IT GONNA TAKE?
WHAT'S IT GONNA TAKE?
LORD ALMIGHTY, WHAT THE HELL'S IT GONNA TAKE
FOR ME TO WIN?

(After audience applause, THE BAND continues clapping, a pitiful little cacophony.)

TOMMY: Thank you. Thank you so much. In those days, my band usually outnumbered the audience. Ladies and gentleman. That's Arvi over there on drums. Give it up. Erlc on guitar. That's right! We got Russell there on bass. Yee ha! And last but certainly not least… Kevin on keyboard. Howdy Kev. So, most o' my original songs were God things… "Christ Is in the Kitchen With Momma" was our biggest hit at the time. I wrote 'em in part because the fan base o' four really dug 'em. But mostly because Mr. Duane Stanley, my man on keyboards at the time… was tall, handsome—real rugged—a *man's* man. He was also a raging Christian and...well...when I was around him he gave me a raging—

(THE BAND plays a loud "bump" of music to cut him off.)

TOMMY: Sorry. Anyhow... *(He looks up at KEVIN.)* Hey Duane.

(A moment.)

TOMMY: Howdy Duane.

KEVIN: Huh. Oh. *(He throws on a hat. As DUANE, very enthusiastic and flamboyant.)* Well howdy Tommy. I'm Duane. Your former (and significantly less talented) keyboardist—

TOMMY: Uh. Kevin. Didn't you hear what I said? He was rugged. A *man's* man.

KEVIN: Oh.

(A moment.)

DUANE: *(No change at all.)* Well howdy Tommy. I'm Duane!

TOMMY: All right. Well, y'all can use your imagination.

(A glance at the still beaming "DUANE.")

TOMMY: A lot. Anyhow...howdy, Duane. (This is where we get theatrical!)

DUANE: Hey Tommy.

TOMMY: So...you up to anything now 'er you just goin' home?

DUANE: Just goin' home. Probably gonna throw the ol' pigskin around and check out some babes 'n' stuff. *(Growls, attempting masculinity.)*

TOMMY: *(Aside to KEVIN.)* Don't ad lib. (Back to the scene.) Yeah, I was gonna go home too. You know...pray. 'N' then...uh...maybe read the bible. Just the New Testament. You know—the real stuff.

DUANE: Right. That's cool.

TOMMY: So...

DUANE: So.

TOMMY: Amen! Er...I mean...see ya.

DUANE: Hey, Tommy.

TOMMY: Okay! I mean...what?

DUANE: My folks 'er out a town and I thought, maybe. If you wanna come by. My neighbor lent me this movie, *A Nightmare on Elm Street* part...somethin' 'r' other. I'm gonna watch it and...well...it's supposed to be pretty cool.

TOMMY: Oh yeah. I love that stuff. That'd be great. *(To the audience.)* I was scared to death. Plus, I saw a commercial for one a those movies once, and I had trouble sleepin' for a week. But he coulda invited me over to eat a bowl o' spiders and I'd a said sure. Why not? Bein' someone else had got me this far already, right? But you know...the thing 'bout those scary movies is they ain't scary all the way through...some o' the scenes are...well...not scary at all...

"Not Like That At All"/"Honestly"

TOMMY: sittin' in fronta his t.v. screen,
sweatin' through that movie scene—
you know the one: gratuitous nudity.
right when the couple starts doin' it,
he moves his leg jus' a little bit,
havin' no idea what that'd do t' me.

THE BAND: (how does it feel?)

TOMMY: his knee is pressin' up against mine.

THE BAND: (how does it feel?)

TOMMY: i get that achin' down below.

TOMMY and THE BAND: THIS CAN'T BE REAL

TOMMY: I SENSE HIS NERVOUSNESS. HE'S SENSED MINE.

TOMMY and THE BAND: HOW DOES IT FEEL?

TOMMY: HELL, I DON'T KNOW!
IT'S LIKE JUMPIN' IN LEAVES, OR A FREIGHT TRAIN CRASH.
A DOUBLE HELPIN' OF GRANDMAMA'S SUCCOTASH.
THE WAY YOUR HEART BEATS AFTER A SCHOOLYARD BRAWL.
IT'S LIKE GETTIN' SOME SOAP IN YOUR EYE.
GETTIN' CAUGHT GETTIN' HIGH.
TRYNA SING WHEN YOUR THROAT IS DRY.
IT'S BIGGER THAN BIG, BUT OH, SO MUCH SMALLER THAN SMALL.
IT'S A LOT LIKE THAT,
OH, BUT IT'S NOT LIKE THAT AT ALL.

DUANE: WELL NOTHIN' AN' NO ONE WENT DOWN THAT NIGHT.

TOMMY: FOR A MONTH WE PRETEND TO FIGHT.

TOMMY and DUANE: BUT SOON ENOUGH, WE'RE DRIVIN' OUT TO THE LAKE.

DUANE: HALF AN HOUR DRIVE AN' WE'RE ALL ALONE.

TOMMY: KNOCK A SIX-PACK CADDY BACK, THEN GIVE THAT DOG A BONE!

DUANE: A NAÏVE ADAM AN' STEVE—

TOMMY: PLAYIN' HIDE THE SNAKE.

THE BAND: (HOW DOES IT FEEL?)

TOMMY: TO FIN'LLY GET WHAT I'D BEEN WISHIN'?

THE BAND: (HOW DOES IT FEEL?)

DUANE: COMMITTIN' SIN ON THE D.L.?

TOMMY, DUANE, and THE BAND: "GET DOWN AN' KNEEL!"

TOMMY: SO SAYS THE CHRISTIAN COALITION…

TOMMY and DUANE: Well, okay!

TOMMY, DUANE, and THE BAND: HOW DOES IT FEEL?

TOMMY and DUANE: IT'S HOT AS HELL!
IT'S LIKE JUMPIN' IN LEAVES, OR A FREIGHT TRAIN CRASH.
A DOUBLE HELPIN' OF GRANDMAMA'S SUCCOTASH.
THE WAY YOUR HEART BEATS AFTER A SCHOOLYARD BRAWL.
IT'S LIKE GETTIN' SOME SOAP IN YOUR EYE.
GETTIN' CAUGHT GETTIN' HIGH.
TRYNA SING WHEN YOUR THROAT IS DRY.
IT'S BIGGER THAN BIG, BUT OH, SO MUCH SMALLER THAN SMALL.
IT'S A LOT LIKE THAT,
OH, BUT IT'S NOT LIKE THAT AT ALL.
NOT LIKE THAT AT ALL.

TOMMY: *(To the audience.)* YOUNG.
SCARED.
UNPREPARED.
DOIN' THINGS THAT NO ONE DARED.
ACTIN' TOUGH IN PUBLIC SO THAT NO ONE STARED,
IN HOPES WE'D ALL JUS' GET ALONG.
YOUNG, DUMB.
BUT GETTIN' SOME.
PREACHER PREACHIN' KINGDOM COME.
GRAB MY GUITAR, AN' I START TO STRUM.
I PUT IT ALL IN A SONG.

TOMMY: *(Reveals a few pages of sheet music and nervously approaches DUANE at the piano…)* Hey I…uh…wrote a little something…

DUANE: *Oh my God.*

(TOMMY sets the sheet music on the piano for DUANE to play. DUANE looks at the music and begins to play…)

TOMMY: Uh...a little faster...

(DUANE complies.)

TOMMY: Right...
HONESTLY,
I DON'T KNOW WHAT I'D DO WITHOUT YOU.
HONESTLY,
I DON'T KNOW HOW I'D BREATHE.
FALL ASLEEP INSIDE MY ARMS TONIGHT.
THERE'S NOTHIN' ELSE THIS RIGHT,
HONESTLY.

(Back to the audience.)

MY GUT, MY EARS, MY HEART WERE BURNIN'
I SANG THE SONG I WROTE FOR DUANE.
WE'D PASSED THE POINT OF NO RETURNIN'.

(Nervously, to DUANE.)

HOW DOES IT FEEL?

DUANE: HOW DOES IT FEEL?

TOMMY and DUANE: HOW DOES IT FEEL?

DUANE: IT'S RIGHT AS RAIN!

DUANE:	TOMMY:
IT'S LIKE JUMPIN' IN LEAVES, OR A FREIGHT TRAIN CRASH.	YAHOO!!! YEAH, YEAH, YEAH.
A DOUBLE HELPIN' OF GRANDMA-MA'S SUCCOTASH.	DAMN RIGHT!
THE WAY YOUR HEART BEATS AFTER A SCHOOL-YARD BRAWL.	MY HEART'S BEATIN' LIKE A DRUM. BA-BUM, BA-BUM-BA-BUM.

TOMMY and DUANE: IT'S LIKE GETTIN' SOME SOAP IN YOUR EYE.
GETTIN' CAUGHT GETTIN' HIGH.
TRYNA SING WHEN YOUR THROAT IS DRY.
IT'S BIGGER THAN BIG, BUT OH, SO MUCH SMALLER THAN SMALL.

TOMMY: IT'S A LOT LIKE THAT.

DUANE: OH, BUT IT'S NOT LIKE THAT AT ALL.

TOMMY: HONESTLY,
I DON'T KNOW WHAT I'D DO WITHOUT YOU.

DUANE: HONESTLY,

TOMMY and DUANE: I DON'T KNOW HOW I'D BREATHE.

TOMMY: At the time, we were lookin' for a song to sing at this Battle of the Bands competition in Little Rock. So far there was nothin' we could agree on. The band was dead split between "Christ Is in the Kitchen" and "Jesus Take the Handlebars." Now, I never would have even thought about playin' this song for the guys. But Duane insisted. I was nervous as hell. But...when I finally played it for 'em...

ERIC: WELL HOLY SHIT.

RUSSELL: QUIT THIS MODEST BIT.
BOY, YOU WROTE YOURSELF A HIT!

ERIC: FOR THIS CONTEST, THAT'S THE SONG THAT WE'LL SUBMIT.

ARVI: AND SURE AS SHIT, WE'LL COME IN FIRST!

TOMMY: COME IN FIRST!

ERIC: COME IN FIRST!

DUANE: But listen,
NO TRICKS.

TOMMY: NO BASS DRUM KICKS.

DUANE: NO CRAZY JIMI HENDRIX LICKS.

BOTH: A SIMPLE SONG PERFORMED BY SIMPLE HICKS.

TOMMY: *(To the audience.)* An' just like that, folks, we rehearsed.

"Honestly"

(THE BAND gets into new positions. They are rehearsing for the Battle of the Bands.)

TOMMY: HONESTLY,
I DON'T KNOW WHAT I'D DO WITHOUT YOU.
HONESTLY,
I DON'T KNOW HOW I'D BREATHE.
FALL ASLEEP INSIDE MY ARMS TONIGHT.
THERE'S NOTHIN' ELSE THIS RIGHT,
HONESTLY.

I WILL LOVE YOU,
HONESTLY.
I WILL LOVE YOU,
NOW AND ALWAYS,
I GUARANTEE.

(A light cue and extra reverb lets us know that we've gone from rehearsal to the actual concert. This section of the song is always muted and sweet.)

HONESTLY,
I DON'T CARE WHAT THEY SAY ABOUT US.
HONESTLY,
'CUZ TRUE LOVE KNOWS NO SHAME.
PROMISE ME
IN FRONT OF GOD ABOVE
THAT WE WILL LIVE IN LOVE,
IN LOVE
HONESTLY.

(Sound cue: thunderous applause and screaming.)

"Not Like That At All" (Tag)

TOMMY: I FINISH SINGIN' AN' TIP MY HAT.
NO OTHER BAND GETS APPLAUSE LIKE THAT,
BUT IT WAS RIGGED. WE SMILE AN' TAKE SECOND PLACE.

DUANE: SECOND PLACE?!

TOMMY: SECOND PLACE.

RUSSELL: SECOND PLACE...

TOMMY: SECOND PLACE...
LESS THAN A WEEK AN AGENT'S CALLIN' ME.
WE TAKE THE TRAIN UP TO

ALL: NASHVILLE, TENNESSEE,

TOMMY: HE SAYS HE LIKES OUR SOUND,
AND LIKES MY SMILIN' FACE.

THE BAND: (HOW DOES IT FEEL?)

TOMMY and DUANE: HE LAYS A CONTRACT ON THE TABLE.

THE BAND: (HOW DOES IT FEEL?)

TOMMY and DUANE: OUR LIVES WOULD NEVER BE THE SAME.

ALL: A RECORD DEAL!

TOMMY and DUANE: AN' WITH A BIG-TIME COUNTRY LABEL!

ALL: HOW DOES IT FEEL?

TOMMY: HOW DOES IT FEEL
TO SIGN MY NAME?

THE BAND: AH AH AH!

TOMMY and DUANE: IT'S LIKE JUMPIN' IN LEAVES, OR A FREIGHT TRAIN CRASH.
A DOUBLE HELPIN' OF GRANDMAMA'S SUCCOTASH.
THE WAY YOUR HEART BEATS AFTER A SCHOOLYARD BRAWL.

DUANE: THAT AIN'T ALL!

THE BAND: (IT'S NOT LIKE THAT AT ALL!)

TOMMY and DUANE: IT'S LIKE GETTIN' SOME SOAP IN YOUR EYE.
GETTIN' CAUGHT GETTIN' HIGH.
TRYNA SING WHEN YOUR THROAT IS DRY.
IT'S BIGGER THAN BIG, BUT OH, SO MUCH SMALLER THAN SMALL.

THE BAND: (IT'S A LOT LIKE THAT, BUT IT'S NOT LIKE THAT AT ALL.)

DUANE: IT'S A LOT LIKE THAT,
OH, BUT IT'S NOT LIKE THAT.

TOMMY: IT'S A LOT LIKE THAT,
OH, BUT IT'S NOT LIKE THAT.

TOMMY and DUANE: IT'S A LOT LIKE THAT,
OH, BUT IT'S NOT LIKE THAT AT ALL.
NOT LIKE THAT AT ALL!

TOMMY: 'N' suddenly, I could see it. The way out...the way to the someone who I needed to be in order to be me. I didn't think, really. Neither myself or Duane could know what was ahead of us. We didn't even care. We were goin' on tour. I think—at the time—we were fool enough to think that just movin' from where we were would make all the difference...

"Hittin' the Highway"

TOMMY: LEAVIN' BEHIND THE CARS ON BLOCKS.

DUANE: LEAVIN' BEHIND THE COW DUNG SMELL.

TOMMY: LEAVIN' BEHIND THE FRIED IN BUTTER.

DUANE: LEAVIN' BEHIND FAT KIDS WHO STUTTER.

TOMMY and DUANE: LEAVIN' BEHIND THIS BACKWOODS HELL.

TOMMY: TAKIN' ALONG MY STEEL GUITAR.

DUANE: *(Suggestively thrusting his hips toward TOMMY.)* TAKIN' ALONG MY POCKET KNIFE.

TOMMY: *(Indicating DUANE.)* TAKIN' ALONG MY BEST MUSICIANS.

DUANE: TAKIN' ALONG THE RIGHT PROVISIONS.

(TOMMY unrolls a pack of condoms.)

TOMMY and DUANE: TAKIN' A LONG SHOT WITH MY LIFE.
YOU CAN HAVE THIS PLACE. I'M QUITTIN'.

TOMMY: WE'RE GRABBIN' WHISKERS, MY KITTEN,

TOMMY and DUANE: AN' HITTIN' THE HIGHWAY.
LET THE MUDFLAPS FLAP.
TAKE A HIKE ON THAT HIGHWAY
ALL ACROSS THE MAP.
FORWARD, BACKWARD, AN' SIDEWAYS.
WE'RE GONNA CHASE THAT STAR, OH-WOAH.
TUSCALOOSA LAST FRIDAY;
FORT WORTH TOMORROW-WOAH.

TOMMY: LEAVIN' EACH MORN' AT SIX A.M.

DUANE: LEAVIN' A TRAIL A MILLION MILES.

TOMMY: LEAVIN' AN' COMIN'.

DUANE: COMIN' AN GOIN'.

TOMMY: LEAVIN' DUANE'S ROOM WITH NO ONE KNOWIN',

TOMMY and DUANE: THEN LEAVE IT TO BEAVER-DIMPLED SMILES.
TAKIN' A STAB AT BEIN' IN LOVE.

TOMMY: BUT TAKIN' PRECAUTIONS WITH OUR KINKS.

DUANE: TAKIN' NO CHANCES WHEN WE'RE FRISKY.

TOMMY: TAKIN' 'IM SOMEPLACE FAR LESS RISKY.

TOMMY and DUANE: RESTSTOP RESTROOM LOVIN' STINKS.
MAKIN' LOVE WHILE FOLKS ARE SHITTIN'.
THAT'S WHAT IT TAKES WHEN YOU'RE SMITTEN,
AN' HITTIN' THE HIGHWAY.

LET THE MUDFLAPS FLAP. (EEW.)
TAKE A HIKE ON THAT HIGHWAY
ALL ACROSS THE MAP.
FORWARD, BACKWARD, AN' SIDEWAYS.
WE'RE GONNA CHASE THAT STAR, OH-
WOAH.
TALLAHASSEE LAST FRIDAY;
CHEYENNE TOMORROW-WOAH.

TOMMY: ONE DRUNKEN NIGHT IN WICHITA,
DUANE FELL ASLEEP IN MY ROOM.
IN MY BED.
IN MY ARMS.
IN MY DREAMS,
I HEARD A—

TOMMY and THE BAND: KNOCK-KNOCK.

DUANE: HELLO?

TOMMY: Shit!

ERIC: HEY TOMMY, CAN YOU HEAR ME?

TOMMY: *Shit. Shit. Shit!*

TOMMY and THE BAND: KNOCK-KNOCK.

TOMMY: HELLO?

ERIC: HEY QUEER, YOUR COVER'S BLOWN.

TOMMY: IN MY ROOM!
IN MY BED!
IN MY DRAWERS!

AGAIN, A—

TOMMY and THE BAND: KNOCK-KNOCK.

ARVI: HELLO!

RUSSELL: QUICK TOMMY, GET 'ER BRA ON.

ERIC: IS THAT THE RED-HEADED GIRL FROM LAST NIGHT?

DUANE: *(In falsetto.)* YEAH THAT'S RIGHT!

ARVI: COME ON BOYS,
LET'S LEAVE THE LOVEBIRDS ALONE!

TOMMY: WHEW...
THAT WAS CLOSE.

THE BAND: TOO CLOSE.

TOMMY: RIGHT NOW I'M SO CLOSE.

THE BAND: TOO CLOSE.

TOMMY: THAT STAR IS SO CLOSE.

THE BAND: TOO CLOSE.

TOMMY: SO CLOSE.

THE BAND: TOO CLOSE.

TOMMY: SO CLOSE.

THE BAND: TOO CLOSE.

TOMMY: TOO CLOSE.

TAKIN' ON DIXIE'S BIBLE BELT,
TAKIN' MY BOWS FOR THE N.R.A.
TAKE A WRONG STEP AN' I'M DEFENSELESS.
TAKIN' THAT CHANCE SEEMED DOWN-RIGHT SENSELESS.
LEAVIN' HIM WAS THE ONLY WAY.

"DUANE,
MY DESTINY'S BEEN WRITTEN.
AN' THIS THING WE'RE DOIN' AIN'T FITTIN'.
WE'RE BETTER OFF WITH YOU SPLITTIN'
AN' HITTIN' THE HIGHWAY.

THE BAND: LET THE MUDFLAPS FLAP.

TOMMY: TAKE A HIKE ON THAT HIGHWAY.

THE BAND: ALL ACROSS THE MAP.

TOMMY: FORWARD, BACKWARD, OR SIDEWAYS.
I'M GONNA BE A STAR, OH-WOAH."
BROKE IT TO 'IM LAST FRIDAY;

(Lights out on DUANE.)

TOMMY: NASHVILLE TOMORROW.

TOMMY and THE BAND: *(Without DUANE.)* NASHVILLE TOMORROW. NASHVILLE, NASHVILLE, NASHVILLE...

(Segue to Down Home performing to a sold-out crowd in Nashville. The song is sickeningly "Faith Hill-ized.")

"HONESTLY" (REPRISE)

TOMMY: I WILL LOVE YOU,
HONESTLY.
I WILL LOVE YOU.
NOW AND ALWAYS,
I GUARANTEE.
HONESTLY,
I DON'T CARE WHAT THEY SAY ABOUT US.
HONESTLY,
'CUZ TRUE LOVE KNOWS NO SHAME.
PROMISE ME
IN FRONT OF GOD ABOVE
THAT WE WILL LIVE IN LOVE.
IN LOVE.
HONESTLY.

TOMMY: I couldn't let nothin' take me backwards. Not even Mr. Duane Stanley. It was all too delicate and I still wasn't much o' anything; any little weakness and they'd a flung me out with the trash. At first I swore off men altogether. I thought, "who needs sex?" I mean, my hand does the job just as well, right? So I had a long, hard relationship with Mr. Righty here. Then moved on to Mr. Lefty when things got old...even tried to kink it up with a three-way; me, Lefty *and* Righty! But...once you take it there you pretty much know it's over, right? Next I started chattin' anonymously online; I promised myself that was as far as I'd go—just chattin' never meetin'. But...then I started wantin' to meet some o' the guys. But what if they recognized me? Or worse, what if they didn't recognize me? Yes siree, abstinence was takin' its toll and fierce. I was gettin' into fights with the band.

(A burst of ad-libbed arguments from THE BAND: "Move your own mic stand!," "I ain't wiping your sweat off for you!," etc.)

TOMMY: I wasn't writin' nothin' worth shit.

(Members of THE BAND scan documents [drafts of TOMMY's new songs] then—ad-libbed awkward responses. "mmm...I don't know," "I like the title!," "Maybe if the verses were different...and the choruses...and the bridge?," etc....then:)

RUSSELL: *(In the clear.)* This ain't worth shit.

TOMMY: And that's when I realized...I couldn't just ignore it. I needed help. *Professional* help...

"HOOKERS"

TOMMY: I GOT MYSELF HOOKERS.

THE BAND: (HOOKERS, HOOKERS)

TOMMY: 'CUZ THAT'S THE WAY TO NEVER GET CAUGHT.
RELIABLE HOOKERS.

THE BAND: (HOOKERS, HOOKERS)

TOMMY: NOTHIN'S QUITE AS QUIET AS THE SILENCE THAT'S BOUGHT.
NOW DON'T GO JUDGIN' ME, JUDGE JUDY,
'CUZ YOU AIN'T NEVER TRIED ONE.
AND DON'T JUDGE MEN WHO SELL THEIR BOOTY,
'TIL YOU'VE WALKED A MILE INSIDE ONE.

THE BAND: (YA MIGHT AS WELL, IF YOU BUYED ONE.)

TOMMY: I RECOMMEND HOOKERS.

THE BAND: (HOOKERS, HOOKERS)

TOMMY: THEY'RE PLENTIFUL AN' KNOW HOW TO PLEASE.
EXPERIENCED HOOKERS.

THE BAND: (HOOKERS, HOOKERS)

TOMMY: JUST A BOX O' CONDOMS KEEPS YOU FREE FROM DISEASE. HOOKERS!

THE BAND: (HUSTLERS, JOTOS)

TOMMY: THE CUM STAINS ON AMERICA'S QUILT.
THEY'RE ALSO CALLED HOUSEBOYS.

THE BAND: (RENTBOYS, ESCORTS)

TOMMY: SWITCH UP YOUR SEMANTICS TO ALLEVIATE GUILT!

THERE'S SUCH A BOUNTIFUL SELECTION,
WHAT FETISH WHETS YOUR WALLET?
JUST GET AN INTERNET CONNECTION
IF YOU DON'T KNOW WHAT TO CALL IT.

THE BAND: (THAT'S THE REASON MOST INSTALL IT.)

TOMMY: TO FIND THEMSELVES HOOKERS.

THE BAND: (HOOKERS, HOOKERS)

TOMMY: THEY'RE ALWAYS UP FOR HAVIN' A BALL.
DEPENDABLE,
BACK-BENDABLE HOOKERS.

THE BAND: (HOOKERS, HOOKERS)

TOMMY: IF YOU WANNA PARTY, HERE'S SOME NUMBERS TO CALL.
TOURIN' 'ROUND AMERICA, I'VE SAMPLED THEM ALL.

Whew hoo! Okay. I think now would be the appropriate time to thank the folks here at The White Swallow...is that really a kind o' bird? The *White* Swallow? *(Addressing THE BAND.)* You guys ever seen a White Swallow before?

RUSSELL: I *tasted* one.

TOMMY: Like chicken?

RUSSELL: Mmmm. More like cock.

(A little buda-bump! from the band)

TOMMY: Okay! Bet they never heard that one here, eh? Seriously though, it was very generous of The White Swallow to allow us to use this space, This...um...what's this room called?

ARVI: The Dick Dungeon.

TOMMY: Right. It was very generous of them to let us turn The Dick Dungeon into our stage for the night. And—of course—to y'all who came here expecting to utilize The Dungeon tonight—we appreciate you're understandin'. I assure you, they'll have this place back in "dick-top" shape in no time once we're through. Hell, maybe we'll stick around, right?

ERIC: *(Lifting his feet up.)* I'm stickin' already!

TOMMY: Why not, right? I ain't got to worry no more 'bout if I'm seen out at The White Swallow or The Dick Dungeon. Those days are over. *Those days...man oh man...*they sure were somethin'...

"DOUBLE PLATINUM DOUBLE LIFE 1"

TOMMY: A HIT OUT ON THE ROAD.
MAN, HOW THOSE TEENAGE GIRLS CAN SCREAM
WE CONQUERED NASHVILLE, TENNESSEE.
IT'S LIKE I'S LIVIN' IN A DREAM.
OUR DEBUT ALBUM TOPPED THE CHARTS,
THAT LUCKY STAR WAS FIN'LLY SHININ' BRIGHT.
SO OVERNIGHT
I DEVISED A PLOT
TO BE BOTH WHO I AM,
AND WHO I'M NOT.
A DOUBLE-PLATINUM DOUBLE LIFE.

WHEN YOUR SINGLES HIT,
AN' TRIPLE SALES,

A DOUBLE-PLATINUM DOUBLE LIFE
SUCCEEDS WHEN HONESTY FAILS.
A SILVER BUCKLE,
INLAID WITH GOLD.
A DOUBLE-PLATINUM DOUBLE LIFE,
THEN WATCH YOUR SONGS GET SOLD.

"Pretty Kitty"

TOMMY: Well howdy lil' lady. Are all the gals here in Dallas as *puuurty* as you…?
COME 'ERE, PRETTY KITTY, COME AN' SIT IN MY LAP.
I'LL STROKE YOUR REAR, PRETTY KITTY, WHILE YOU'RE TAKIN' A NAP.
I GET AN ITTY-BITTY GIDDY WHEN MY PRETTY KITTY STARTS TO MEOW.
ME-YOW! YOW! YOWSA!
IT'S TRUE, PRETTY KITTY: YOU'RE THE MILK IN MY DISH.
LET'S ME AN' YOU MAYBE SPLIT A CAN O' TUNA FISH.
THE NITTY GRITTY, PRETTY KITTY
OF THIS SILLY LITTER DITTY
IS TO TELL YOU THAT I LOVE YOU AND HOW-WOW-WOW!

That one was actually *really* fer my kitten, Whiskers—but they didn't know that…

"Double Platinum Double Life 2"

TOMMY: I HAD THE MIDAS TOUCH!
FOR EV'RY SONG THAT WE'D RECORD,
THERE'D BE TEN MILLION COPIES SOLD,
AND SOME BIG INDUSTRY AWARD.
I WAS A KING UPON A THRONE,
MY LOYAL SUBJECTS WERE THE CHRISTIAN RIGHT.
MY DAY AND NIGHT
WERE NIGHT AND DAY.
THE TRUTH WAS BLACK AND WHITE,
SO I MADE GRAY:
A DOUBLE-PLATINUM DOUBLE LIFE.

A SINGLE MAN.
A TRIPLE THREAT.
A DOUBLE-PLATINUM DOUBLE LIFE
FOR SAFELY HEDGIN' THE BET.
BOTH SILVER LINING,
AND POT O' GOLD.
A DOUBLE-PLATINUM DOUBLE LIFE.
CAN WORK IF WELL PATROLLED.

"Heather"

TOMMY: Hey darlin'. I think I could handle this Windy City if I was wrapped up in a little you…
HEATHER
IS SOFT AS A PILLOW,
AND LIGHT AS A FEATHER.
THE LAMP PAINTS OUR SILHOUETTE LYING TOGETHER,
AN' SHE'S WRAPPED AROUND ME.
HER TOUCH IS REDEEMIN'.
HER WARMTH HAS UNWOUND ME.
I SLIP INTO DREAMIN'.
HEATHER,
MY GIRL.

HEATHER,
MY GIRL.

Well. Heather my down comforter, actually.

"Double Platinum Double Life 3"

I'D LIE A LITTLE HERE,
AN' THEN I'D FAKE A LITTLE THERE.
THE CONSTANT SONGS ABOUT "MY GIRL"
KEPT MY WHOLE FAN BASE UNAWARE.
AN' YEAH, DISHONESTY FEELS WRONG,
BUT GOD, THE FAME, AN' FORTUNE FEELS SO RIGHT.
AN' EV'RY NIGHT,
WITHOUT A THOUGHT,
I'D FIND MYSELF INSIDE
SOME MAN I'D BOUGHT.
THAT'S DOUBLE-PLATINUM DOUBLE LIFE.

ONE SINGLE LIE
CAN TRIPLE SIZE.
A DOUBLE-PLATINUM DOUBLE LIFE

IS MORE DISEASE THAN DISGUISE,
'CUZ WINNIN' SILVER
AIN'T STRIKIN' GOLD.
A DOUBLE-PLATINUM DOUBLE LIFE
BUT NO ONE THERE TO HOLD.

"Spit It Out"

TOMMY: 'N' I was runnin' out o' blankets 'n' pets 'n' furniture to write love songs about. But...I had this old antique spittoon in my living room...

(Lights shift, he is back at the concert.)

TOMMY: Ooo weee! I heard about you Big Apple girls, if I don't watch it you'll take a big bite outa me...right?
SHE SITS IN THE CORNER,
ALL BUMPY AND BRASSY.
SHE'S FILLED UP WITH FILTHY.
THERE AIN'T NOTHIN' CLASSY
'BOUT SITTIN' IN A BAR,
SMELLIN' OF CIGAR,
TALKIN' TO JACK DANIELS IN A DIRTY MASON JAR.

SAYIN',
"MEN ARE MONSTERS.
FIRST THEY'RE PLEADIN' AND BEGGIN'.
THEN THEY CHEW YA UP, 'N' SPIT YA OUT
LIKE COPENHAGEN.
EXPECT A LITTLE NONCOMMITTAL SPITTLE
  IN YOUR SPOUT.
YOU GIVE 'EM LOVE,
THEY CHEW IT UP, 'N' SPIT IT OUT."

"Double Platinum Double Life 4"

TOMMY: SOME SINGLE MALT,
OR TRIPLE SEC.
THIS DOUBLE-PLATINUM DOUBLE LIFE
IS STRESSFUL. SURE. WHAT THE HECK?
SOME SILVER LABEL,
NO, MAKE THAT GOLD
WHEN YOUR DOUBLE-PLATINUM DOUBLE
  LIFE
STARTS GETTIN' KINDA OLD...

"Sicka Singin' 'Bout Girls"

TOMMY: I PRAISE THEIR BEAUTY IN MY
SONGS 'BOUT FEMALE LOVERS.
THEIR SKIN, THEIR VOICES, HAIR,
THEIR BODIES 'NEATH THE COVERS.
I MEAN NO DISRESPECT, BUT
IF I HAD MY DRUTHERS,
SURPRISE!
I'D PICK GUYS.

I'M SICKA SINGIN' 'BOUT GIRLS.
I'M SICKA SINGIN' 'BOUT GIRLS.
I'M SICKA SINGIN' 'BOUT GIRLS.
I'M SICKA SINGIN' 'BOUT GIRLS, GIRLS, GIRLS, GIRLS.

IF I AM BEAUTY'S JUDGE
'CUZ I AM THE BEHOLDER,
THEN BEAUTY'S HOW HIS T-SHIRT
STRETCHES ON HIS SHOULDER,
AND HOW THE MIDDAY SUNLIGHT
CATCHES IN HIS SMOLDER-
ING EYES.
AND GOD, HIS THIGHS!

I'M SICKA SINGIN' 'BOUT GIRLS.
I'M SICKA SINGIN' 'BOUT GIRLS.
I'M SICKA SINGIN' 'BOUT GIRLS.
I'M SICKA SINGIN' 'BOUT GIRLS, GIRLS, GIRLS...

GIRLS APPLYIN' LIPSTICK.
GIRLS WITH PAINTED NAILS.
ALL THOSE LITTLE GIRLIE-GIRL DETAILS.
GIRLS IN ALL MY LYRICS.
MORE THAN YOU'D BELIEVE.
FORGET THOSE TWIRLY GIRLIE-GIRLS,
I WANT BURLY "GURLS" NAMED STEVE!

SHE WALKS IN BEAUTY LIKE THE
NIGHT—CHRIST! I AIN'T BYRON.
NO THIS HERE POET FANTA-
SIZES 'BOUT RETIRIN'.
NOT ONE MORE TEMPTRESS, PRINCESS,
KEWPIE DOLL, OR SIREN—
GET WISE!
THEY'VE ALL BEEN LIES.

I'M SICKA SINGIN' 'BOUT GIRLS.
I'M SICKA SINGIN' 'BOUT GIRLS.
I'M SICKA SINGIN' 'BOUT GIRLS.
I'M SICKA SINGIN' 'BOUT GIRLS, GIRLS—
NO, NO.
BOYS, BOYS—NO, NO.
MEN, MASCULINE MEN.

"THE MEDIA TWIST"

THE BAND: THIS JUST IN! HEAD LINE NEWS!

KEVIN: *(Picking up one of the discarded newspapers or magazines lying next to him...)* Down Home's much-anticipated third album *Hick Licks* hits stores today!

TOMMY: *Billboard* magazine:

ARVI: DOWN HOME IS BACK ON TOP WITH THEIR LATEST RELEASE, "SPIT IT OUT."

TOMMY: *Country Weekly* magazine:

ERIC: THIS WILL EXCEED THEIR PREVIOUS ALBUMS BEYOND ANY DOUBT.

TOMMY: *Rolling Stone*:

RUSSELL: EXPECT THE SMOOTH, GENTLE TOUCH OF THEIR DELICATE HAND, BUT THEN THE PUNCH OF AN EDGIER FIST.

TOMMY: FOR THE HYPE THAT YOU NEED, DANCE THE MEDIA TWIST.

THE BAND: THIS JUST IN! HEAD LINE NEWS!

KEVIN: Down Home frontman Tommy Dautry has been spotted getting down on the town with the likes of Natalie Maines, LeAnne Rimes, and Renée Zellweger.

TOMMY: *People Magazine*:

ARVI: POP CULTURE'S MOST NOTORIOUS BACHELOR IS BACK FANNIN' FLAMES!

(While the line is being sung, TOMMY sprays Binaca.)

TOMMY: *GQ*:

ERIC: HE WON'T DISCUSS HIS PERSONAL LIFE, AND HE NEVER NAMES NAMES.

(TOMMY opens his shirt one button, and pops his collar.)

TOMMY: WSIX Nashville:

RUSSELL: THIS GUY IS SMOOTH!

ERIC: CASANOVA, TAKE SOME LESSONS FROM HIM!

ARVI: THERE AIN'T ONE TRICK THAT THIS FELLA HAS MISSED.

(TOMMY runs a comb through his hair and puts on sunglasses.)

TOMMY: FOLKS BELIEVE WHAT THEY READ
IN THE MEDIA TWIST.
YEAH, THAT'S THE MEDIA TWIST.
YOUR AVERAGE NEWSHOUND'S A CAPITALIST.
THEY DON'T NEED FACTS, JUS' THE GENERAL GIST,
AN' THEN THEY TWIST, AN' PICK, AN' CHOOSE.
SO HITCH ALONG FOR THE RIDE,
AN' SHOW THE CAMERA YOUR SALEABLE SIDE.

(TOMMY shows his butt à la George Michael in "Faith.")

BECOME THE IMAGE THE PAPERS PROVIDE, AN' YOU'LL STAY FRONT-PAGE NEWS!

(During the chorus and the playoff, TOMMY models for the "camera," perhaps represented by flashing lights.)

THE BAND: THIS JUST IN! HEAD LINE NEWS!

KEVIN: We are on the scene at the J Percy Priest Dam and Reservoir, a local public park in Nashville, Tennessee, where Down Home frontman Tommy

Dautry has been arrested. Early reports state only that the rising country star was arrested for lewd conduct—but local sources tell us that Percy Priest Dam is a popular public meeting place for men seeking homosexual encounters.

(THE BAND reacts melodramatically—"scandal!!")

TOMMY: *Entertainment Tonight*:

ARVI: BELOVED "KING OF COUNTRY" ARRESTED FOR BEING A QUEEN.

(TOMMY puts on dangling clip-on earrings and lipstick.)

TOMMY: *The 700 Club*:

ERIC: CONSIDER ALL HIS HEATHEN RECORDINGS PERVERSE AND OBSCENE.

(TOMMY affixes devil horns to his forehead, and writes 666 backwards on his bare chest with the lipstick.)

TOMMY: *The New York Times* Op-Ed:

RUSSELL: IF THEY ARE SMART, DAUTRY'S BAND WILL CUT HIM OUT OF THE GROUP. CUT HIM OUT, LIKE A CANCEROUS CYST.

(TOMMY takes the lipstick and draws a line across his throat as though he were slitting it open.)

TOMMY: GOOD FOR PLANTIN' THE SEED; THAT'S THE MEDIA TWIST. YEAH, THAT'S THE MEDIA TWIST. YOUR AVERAGE NEWSHOUND'S A CAPITALIST. THEY DON'T NEED FACTS, JUS' THE GENERAL GIST, AN' THEN THEY TWIST, AN' PICK, AN' CHOOSE. SO HITCH ALONG FOR THE RIDE, AN' SHOW THE CAMERA YOUR SALEABLE SIDE.

(TOMMY holds up his mugshot number.)

BECOME THE IMAGE THE PAPERS PROVIDE, AN' YOU'LL STAY FRONT-PAGE NEWS!

(THE BAND desperately holds out microphones toward TOMMY as they blurt out the lines on top of one another.)

ARVI: Mr. Dautry! Over here!

ERIC: Tommy, Tommy! What did Renée have to say? Have you spoken to her?

RUSSELL: Is this the first time you've solicited sex in a public toilet?

ARVI: Have you ever been recognized by the men before?

RUSSELL: How did you know the taps and hand signals that the officer alleged you used?

(THE REPORTERS freeze—TOMMY addresses the audience.)

TOMMY: I was a queer in the headlights! Just like that, it was out. *I* was out. And all these questions were coming at me. And...all I had to do was answer 'em honestly and that would be it. The burden would be off my shoulders and onto everyone else's...

(The chaos reanimates.)

ARVI: Tommy!

RUSSELL: Over here!

ERIC: Have you spoken to LeAnne? What did she say?

RUSSELL: Is your soul gay too?

(Again, the chaos freezes around TOMMY.)

TOMMY: I was about to do it too. Come clean. Lay it all out there. And then...well...my manager told me about a little movement in the Christian

Community of "Ex-gays." They said gay was a sin like any other, and it could be overcome. It was like...this support group sorta. Like AA but instead o' alcohol you were hooked on gay. And this little movement had been lookin' for the perfect poster boy.

(Chaos reanimates.)

ARVI: Have you slept with any other male stars in the industry?

RUSSELL: Have you spoken to Natalie?

ERIC: Tommy. Do you have *anything* to say at all?

TOMMY: I...I have to say...I...I'll be retreating from the public eye for a few months. I'm going to be checking into The Righteous Ranch. It's a facility where they help people like me...people who have become deviant because of the Devil's influence. I guess you could say I'm going to rehab...for my soul. *(To the audience.)* And that, my friends, was going to be the name of my next album. "Rehab for the Soul." The prodigal son was going to emerge from The Righteous Ranch to be the darling of the industry. Or so my manager promised. And me, I really took my rehab to heart. I thought, if it's out there, if people are doing it, then it must work, right? So, I went. We prayed a lot...and sat in circles and shared.

(THE BAND embodies members of The Righteous Ranch in group therapy...)

KEVIN: I blame my dad

ERIC: I blame my mom

RUSSELL: ...my brother

ARVI: Sister!

TOMMY: Sometimes, though, it was a little helpful...

ERIC: I notice that...after I pray for a really long time and then look at one of the complimentary *Penthouse Magazines* in our rooms...I sort of...feel happy! Sort of.

TOMMY: But most times...it only made things...*harder.*

KEVIN: My first experience was with the son of my preacher. Well...sons, they were twins. Blond...tall...both on the football team. This one day, during my theatre rehearsal, Mrs. Donavan sent me into the locker room to get some towels to use for props and...there were Donny and Ronny, just getting out of the shower. There was no one else there but us and when I told them I was looking for towels...well...—

(One of THE BAND members clears his throat, snapping TOMMY out of a trance.)

TOMMY: Right...yeah...sometimes...it just made things more confusing...you know? But I was determined to emerge totally transformed—to show all those people who were smirking at me that I was stronger than they thought. So three months later I was out and ready to start where I'd left off. I even had a brand-new single to kick things back in gear...

"That Ain't Me"

I'll give it to ya folks on the level:
was wrestlin' with a devil,
somethin' wasn't right inside.
failin' ev'ry time I was tested.
then I got arrested.
a small price to pay.
that's when I heard the voice a-callin'.
callin' me out, callin' me home,
callin' me back into his light.

I DROPPED RIGHT DOWN AND STARTED
  CRAWLIN'.
THAT'S RIGHT.
I CHOOSE TO FIGHT!

'CUZ
THAT AIN'T ME
ON THE DEVIL'S KNEE.
SIPPIN' DEVIL'S TEA.
THAT AIN'T ME
TENNESSEE.
NAW,
THAT AIN'T ME,
NOT WHO I SHOULD BE.
I GOT DIGNITY.
THAT AIN'T ME.

MY DADDY CAUSED ME ALL KINDS O'
  TRAUMA.
I NEVER HAD A MOMMA.
LEFT A GIANT HOLE INSIDE.
FILLED IT WITH IMMORAL BEHAVIOR.
I'M PRAYIN' THAT THE SAVIOR
WILL SHOW ME THE WAY.
AN' WHEN HE HEARS MY VOICE A-CALLIN',
CALLIN' OUT "HELP!" CALLIN' OUT
  "PLEASE!"
CALLIN' OUT "SAVE ME FROM MY SIN!"
HE'LL CATCH THIS ANGEL AS I'M FALLIN'.
HE'LL GRIN,
'N' SAY "WHERE YOU BEEN?"

AN' I'LL SAY
"THAT AIN'T ME
THAT'S A PARODY
MADE BY MTV.
THAT AIN'T ME
NO SIREE!
LORD!
THAT AIN'T ME
NOT THAT PHARISEE.
JESUS, SET ME FREE.
THAT AIN'T ME."

YOU COULD BE A SINNER,
PAL, OR YOU COULD BE A SAINT.
G'ON, BE THE DEVIL'S DINNER, FINE,

BUT NOT ME, PAL. THAT AIN'T,
THAT AIN'T ME!

THAT AIN'T ME:
GIGGLIN' GIRLISHLY.
SCENTED POTPOURRI.
THAT AIN'T ME
CERTAINLY.
HELL,
THAT AIN'T ME,
FRILLS AN' FINERY.
THAT THERE'S FAGGOTRY,

THAT AIN'T ME
DONUT PUNCHERY.
BACKDOOR BURGLARY.
THAT AIN'T ME,
HONESTLY.
NAW,
THAT AIN'T ME,
I WON'T NEVER BE
CATCHIN' HIV.
GUARANTEE.

(THE BAND holds up signs marked "Don't Clap," "Boo," and/or the word "Applause" with an X through it, etc. TOMMY stands in the silence...)

TOMMY: Well...I didn't get the reception I'd been hopin' for. Half o' the folk just got pissed off...

(Half of THE BAND flips their signs to the other sides where we see phrases such as "TOMMY Is a Homophobe," "Dautry Preaches Hate," etc.)

TOMMY: ...and the other half. Well...they got pissed off.

(The other half flips around their signs to phrases such as "Once a Homo Always a Homo," "Stay Away From Our Kids, Perv!," etc.)

TOMMY: But I didn't quit. I just kept denying it. Taking every opportunity I could to try to convince people that gay was just a dirty little thing that God could erase. So…I lost any fans who might have been willing to accept me honestly…

(Half of THE BAND turns their backs on TOMMY.)

TOMMY: And my old fans, the loyal ones who had written me love letters and fainted when they saw me, they were gone too.

(The other half of THE BAND turns their backs on TOMMY.)

TOMMY: For a while the tabloids kept me afloat. Not in a good way, but if I'd get piss drunk and drop my drawers in the street or have a fight with a cameraman, or sell my "palatial estate for a modest home in the burbs," they'd print my name at least. For a little while. First on the front page…then inside, but with a teaser on the front. Then buried somewhere…then, finally…not at all. No matter how pitiful or reclusive or drunk I got…I couldn't even get into the tabloids anymore. I had disappeared…and so had everyone else. The cameras stopped followin' me, people stopped comin' up to me, even the phone stopped ringing. Well…until…

(The phone rings.)

TOMMY: I was too scared to pick it up, it could only be bad news…

(Another ring.)

TOMMY: I let it ring. Never would have imagined it would be him.

(There is a click, and we hear an outgoing message consisting of TOMMY mumbling incoherently, then the beep.)

TOMMY: I listened to that message a million times…even wrote it down word for word…

"Right As Rain"

(Lights up on KEVIN enacting DUANE.)

DUANE: HI…
IT'S—
HEY THERE TOMMY, IT'S DUANE.
DUANE.
DUANE STANLEY, FROM—
IT'S BEEN A WHILE, SINCE…
I'M KINDA GLAD YOU DIDN'T ANSWER.
I STILL DON'T KNOW WHAT ALL TO SAY.
I…
YOU—
AIN'T SEEN YOUR NAME IN THE NEWS LATELY, OR ANY O' THOSE MAGAZINES:
THE STAR. THE GLOBE. COUNTRY WEEKLY.
NOT THAT I'M LOOKIN' MUCH,
IT ISN'T LIKE I THINK ABOUT—
I MEAN, I HARDLY EVER THINK ABOUT—
I ALMOST NEVER THINK ABOUT—
'CUZ MY LIFE—
MY LIFE NOW, IT'S SO…
IT'S…
IT'S SO…
IT'S—

IT'S RIGHT AS RAIN.
IT'S RIGHT AS RAIN.
I CAN'T COMPLAIN.
NO, I'M THE MAN
THAT I'M SUPPOSED TO—
TO BE.

I GOT A WIFE.
YEAH.
YOU REMEMBER AMY HOBBES?
WELL NOW, SHE'S AMY STANLEY.
WE GOT A LITTLE HOUSE,
AN' TWO LITTLE BOYS.
IT'S A LOTTA DEBT,
AN' A LOTTA NOISE.
YOU BLINK, AN' SUDDENLY,
YOU'RE SO MANY THINGS YOU NEVER THOUGHT YOU'D BE.

AN' THAT'S RIGHT AS RAIN.

IT'S RIGHT AS RAIN.
I CAN'T COMPLAIN.
NO, I'M THE MAN
THAT I'M SUPPOSED TO BE.

I STARTED PLAYIN' AGAIN.
I HAD STOPPED FOR A WHILE.
A LITTLE RINKY-DINK BAND.
WE PLAY DOWN AT THE CHURCH.
HEAVEN KNOWS IT AIN'T NASHVILLE,
BUT IT AIN'T ABOUT FAME.
IT'S MY WAY TO STAY SANE—
MAKES EV'RYTHING RIGHT AS RAIN.
(OH-WHOAH.)

SOME DAYS YOU WIN.

TOMMY: SOME DAYS YOU WIN.

DUANE: SOME DAYS YOU LOSE.

TOMMY: SOME DAYS YOU LOSE.

DUANE: YOU FIND YOUR PEACE

TOMMY: YOU FIND YOUR PEACE

BOTH: IN WHAT YOU CHOOSE.

DUANE: WELL,
GUESS THAT'S ALL.
I ONLY WANTED TO SAY, TOMMY
YOU CAN BE—

TOMMY: I CAN BE—

BOTH: —HAPPY.

TOMMY:	DUANE:
IT'S RIGHT AS RAIN.	YOU KNOW WHO YOU ARE.
IT'S RIGHT AS RAIN.	JUST BE WHO YOU ARE,
I CAN'T COMPLAIN.	AND NEVER LOOK BACK.
NO, I'M THE MAN	BE THE MAN

TOMMY: THAT I'M SUPPOSED TO BE.

DUANE: THAT I'M SUPPOSED TO BE.

TOMMY: THAT I'M SUPPOSED TO BE.

DUANE: THAT I'M SUPPOSED TO BE.

TOMMY: THAT I'M SUPPOSED TO BE.

(TOMMY *moves over to the guitar, picks it up and sits with it for a long moment...*)

"WHEN MUSIC MATTERED"

TOMMY: WHEN I WAS A KID,
I TICKLED MY GUITAR,
AND TRIED TO PICK OUT POP SONG CHORDS
JUST SEEIN' WHAT CHORDS ARE.
I PRACTICED EV'RY NIGHT.
THOSE NIGHTS TURNED INTO YEARS.
A FIRE STARTED IN MY HEART,
IN MY GUT, AN' IN MY EARS.

ALL THAT'S LEFT IS JUST A DYIN' ORANGE EMBER.
I CLOSE MY EYES AND I TRY HARD TO REMEMBER

A TIME WHEN MUSIC MATTERED TO ME.
WHEN I LET MY THOUGHTS RUN SCATTERED AN' FREE,
WHEN MY SELF-DOUBTS WERE FEW,
AN' EV'RY NOTE WAS NEW,
AN' EV'RY WORD WAS TRUE.
BEFORE THE LAWYERS BRANDED MY NAME.
BEFORE I SINGLE-HANDEDLY SOLD MY SOUL FOR FAME.
BEFORE REASON LEFT MY RHYME,
I SWEAR THERE WAS A TIME
WHEN MUSIC MATTERED.
WHEN MUSIC MATTERED.

WHEN YOUR FINGERS STRUM ON AUTOPILOT
AN' YOUR VOICE IS NOT YOUR OWN.
WHEN YOU HIDE BEHIND A CROSS
AND LOSE THE ONLY LOVE YOU'VE KNOWN.
WHEN YOU'RE ABANDONED BY A BILLION FANS
BUT THAT'S NOT WHY YOU'RE ALONE.
WHAT DO YOU DO
TO GET BACK TO YOU?

IF I COULD GO BACK
AN' DO IT ALL AGAIN,
I'D PROB'LY MAKE THE SAME MISTAKES
THAT I HAD MADE BACK THEN,
I CHOSE MUSIC AS MY LIFE—
THE BLESSING AND THE CURSE—
AN' I WILL NOT REGRET THAT CHOICE.
FOR BETTER, OR FOR WORSE.

I WOULDN'T TAKE A SINGLE AWFUL DAY BACK.
EACH WRONG TURN I MADE WILL HELP ME FIND MY WAY BACK

TO THE TIME WHEN MUSIC MATTERED TO ME.
WHEN I'LL LET MY THOUGHTS RUN SCATTERED AN' FREE.
WHEN MY SELF-DOUBTS ARE FEW,
AN' EV'RY NOTE IS NEW,
AN' EV'RY WORD IS TRUE.
I TRIED SO HARD TO STEAL THAT STAR,
BUT NOTHIN'S HALF AS REAL AS TICKLIN' THIS GUITAR.
DON'T NEED A SINGLE DIME.
RIGHT HERE. RIGHT NOW'S THE TIME

WHEN MUSIC MATTERS.
THIS MUSIC MATTERS.
TO ME, IT'S ALL THAT MATTERS.

TOMMY: There were folks who told me:

ERIC: Just forget Country Music.

ARVI: Try pop!

RUSSELL: Do a soap!

KEVIN: Do *Broadway!!!*

TOMMY: Don't get me wrong. I love 'n' appreciate all o' those things. But I'm sicka bein' told to quietly compromise in order to find my place. I'm sicka bein' told to get used to another word for something or wait for another time. The music that mattered to me was—and always will be—Country. From the time I was a kid I'd been lookin' fer a way to change who I was in order to fit into the thing that I loved. But it ain't me who's gotta change or get used to things. Nope, I just gotta be me...honestly. I been gettin' used to me fer my whole life now, but I got there—now it's their turn. 'N' I'm not alone. Not by a long shot. So the next time one o' them folk comes up to me and tries to give me the rules for doin' what I love, or *who* I love: well...this is all I got to say to them...

"OUR COUNTRY"

TOMMY: YOU GOT YOUR HOUSE.
YOU GOT YOUR LEXUS
A SUNNY SUBURB OF SAVANNAH, GEORGIA/ DALLAS, TEXAS.
YOUR LIFE IS CLEAN.
YOUR LIFE IS NORMAL.
YOUR STRAIGHT-A SON IS QUARTERBACK AND KING O' WINTER FORMAL.

WHEN HE COMES TO YOU ONE SATURDAY CRYIN',
AN' HE PUTS AN END TO ALL YOU'RE DENYIN',
YOU'RE GONNA HAVE TO FIND ANOTHER DREAM.
HE'S THROWIN' PASSES FOR THE OTHER TEAM!

AN' THAT'S THE WAY IT GOES,
'CUZ CLOSETS ARE FOR CLOTHES.
THE DAYS OF HIDIN' UNDERGROUND ARE THROUGH.
AND AS WE'RE GAININ' POWER,
WE'RE BUILDIN' UP A TOWER.
CONSERVATIVES COWER!
'CUZ THIS IS OUR COUNTRY TOO.
WE'RE JUST LIKE YOU:
RED, WHITE, 'N' BLUE!

WE'RE IN YOUR BANK.
WE'RE AT YOUR MARKET.
AND WHEN YOU VALET PARK THAT LEXUS,
GUESS WHO'S GONNA PARK IT.

WE'RE IN YOUR CHURCH,
GETTING MARRIED IN YOUR SANCTUARY.
WE'RE OUT IN CONGRESS, OUT IN SCHOOLS, AN' OUT IN OUR MILITARY.
AN' WE'RE EVEN ON YOUR RADIO STATIONS,
AS YOUR LATEST COUNTRY WESTERN SENSATIONS.
AN' SOME OF US ARE CHOOSIN' NOT TO HIDE.
WE'RE CHANGIN' COUNTRY MUSIC FROM INSIDE!

AN' THAT'S THE WAY IT GOES,
'CUZ CLOSETS ARE FOR CLOTHES.
THE DAYS OF HIDIN' UNDERGROUND ARE THROUGH.
AN' AS WE'RE GAININ' POWER,
WE'RE BUILDIN' UP A TOWER.
CONSERVATIVES COWER!
'CUZ THIS IS OUR COUNTRY TOO.
RED, WHITE, 'N' BLUE.
TRIED 'N' TRUE.
WE'RE JUST LIKE YOU!

Except maybe better dressed.
Better lookin'.
Better in bed.
And of course, we're far more sensitive.
Delicate, really.
Like a flower.
A pansy.

(Primal scream from ALL onstage.)

SO TELL THE WORLD I'M HERE,
REVIVIN' MY CAREER,
'CUZ COUNTRY NEEDS TO GET A FUCKIN' CLUE.
YEAH, I'M SALTY, AN' I'M SOUR,
BUT BATTER ME IN FLOUR—
FOR MY QUEERS TO DEVOUR,
'CUZ THIS IS OUR COUNTRY TOO.
RED, WHITE, 'N' BLUE,
LIKE BARBECUE,
SHOULD BE A LITTLE PINK,
IT'S MORE FUN TO CHEW.

TOMMY: That's Eric, Kevin, Russell, Arvi! I'm Tommy and we're Our Country! Thank you gentleman! *(Shielding his eyes from the light and looking curiously at the audience…)* …and *ladies?* G'night!

(TOMMY exits as THE BAND plays him out. After a moment of applause, he returns.)

TOMMY: *(Over his shoulder to THE BAND.)* Whatcha think guys? One more?

Encore: "Christ Is in the Kitchen With Momma"

TOMMY: THINK YOU KNOW ALL 'BOUT JESUS—
UNDERSTAND THE EUCHARIST?
CUP O' GRAPE JUICE. LOAF O' BREAD.
WELL THEN, MY FRIEND, THERE'S SOMETHIN' BIG THAT YOU'VE MISSED.
HE'S THERE IN EV'RY BITE THAT YOU DIGEST!

ALL: 'CUZ CHRIST IS IN THE KITCHEN WITH MOMMA.
SHE'S STIRRED 'IM INTO EVERY SIP OF SWEET TEA.
HE'S IN THE FRIDGE MARINATIN',
AN' TRANSUBSTANTIATIN' IN THE OVEN.
SOME CHRISTIAN LOVIN'
IN EVERY RECIPE.
CHRIST IS IN THE KITCHEN WITH MOMMA,
AN' IN ALL THE WHOLESOME MEALS PREPARED FOR ME.

TOMMY: I BEEN BUTTERED AN' BATTERED.
CHICKEN FRIED, AN' CANDIED YAMMED.
I BEEN CHEESE GRITSED, AN' PECAN PIED,
AN' COLLARED GREENED, AN' BLACK EYED PEAD, AN' GLAZED HAMMED.

ALL: THAT'S HOW GOOD CHRISTIANS KEEP FROM BEIN' DAMNED!

'CUZ CHRIST IS IN THE KITCHEN WITH MOMMA.

SHE'S STIRRED 'IM INTO EVERY SIP OF
SWEET TEA.
HE'S IN THE FRIDGE MARINATIN',
AN' TRANSUBSTANTIATIN' IN THE OVEN.
SOME CHRISTIAN LOVIN'
IN EVERY RECIPE.
CHRIST IS IN THE KITCHEN WITH MOMMA,
AN' IN ALL THE WHOLESOME MEALS PREPARED FOR ME.
(AND ME, AND ME, AND ME!)

EACH SCRUMPTIOUS BITE'S FIGHTIN' SATAN.
YOUR MOMMA'S CONSECRATIN'
YOUR INTESTINES.
WHAT YOU'RE DIGESTIN'S
A BLESSED GUARANTEE
THAT WHILE CHRIST IS IN THE KITCHEN
WITH MOMMA,
YOU WILL SINK YOUR TEETH INTO
ETERNITY.

(CURTAIN.)

MADDY: A MODERN-DAY MEDEA

Will Le Vasseur

WILL Le VASSEUR was born in 1981 in Seattle, Washington. He grew up in the Seattle area, and received a BFA in theatre from Cornish College of the Arts in Seattle (which he attended at the same time as fellow *Plays and Playwrights 2010* contributor Joshua Conkel). Le Vasseur's sixth grade teacher, Louise Hatala, suggested that he take up acting in junior high school, and he has been involved in theatre ever since as an actor, director, and, most recently, as a playwright. He is the artistic director of Redd Tale Theatre Company, along with his life partner James Stewart, and has produced, directed, and/or acted in *Saucy Jack and the Space Vixens*, *Closer*, *Lonely Planet*, and *The Swan Song*. *Maddy* is Le Vasseur's first play.

Maddy: A Modern-Day Medea was presented by Redd Tale Theatre Company (Will Le Vasseur and James Stewart, Artistic Directors) at the Spoon Theater on August 7, 2009, with the following cast and credits:

Maddy	Lynn Kenny
Billy-Jae	Blaine Pennington
Flo	Heather Shields
Alan	James Stewart
Cleetus	Ben Strothmann
Edna	Rainbow Dickerson
Newscaster	Will Le Vasseur

Director: Will Le Vasseur
Sound Design: Matthew Pritchard
Stage Manager: Danny Morales
Set and Lighting Design: Will Le Vasseur

Will Le Vasseur would like to thank his family—Will J. Le Vasseur, Gail Le Vasseur, Susie Le Vasseur King, Fred O. Tharp, and Susan Tharp—for their continued support in his life and endeavors. He thanks his cast members—Lynn Kenny, Blaine Pennington, Heather Shields, James Stewart, Ben Strothmann, Danny Morales, Rainbow Dickerson, and Matthew Pritchard—for helping *Maddy* come to life. A great big thank you to Martin Denton and Rochelle Denton and Nita Congress for their wisdom and guidance. He would especially like to thank his Co-Artistic Director and life partner, James Stewart, for his kindness, patience, faith, support, and most importantly his love. None of this would have been possible if it weren't for him.

DIRECTOR'S NOTES

Medea, a seminal work by Euripides, depicts a woman who has been scorned by her husband, takes her revenge by killing her children, then is raptured to heaven by the Gods themselves on a golden chariot pulled by dragons. Simple, tragic, fun. I was first introduced to the play when I was assigned a scene for acting class. It was striking to me how powerful Medea is, and how wonderful a challenge she is to play. My only problem was *relating* to it. Sure, we've all been betrayed in some way or another, hopefully not as badly as Medea herself, but the servants, kings, princesses, and such put me off from really caring about her situation. Revisiting it years later, I found myself coming up with the same question: Who cares? I wanted to put it up, but still couldn't get past the rosy fingers of dawn, or the great weeping and gnashing of teeth. An adaptation seemed the only way I was going to put the show up, and put some butts in the seats.

Where to put her in time and space became the hardest part of creating that adaptation. I focused on her desperation of being left with two kids while her husband is gold-digging the local well-to-do girls. Mockingly, I said it sounded like a trashy Jerry Springer story. That's when the idea clicked, and the story flowed: Stick her in a trailer park. We can identify with that lifestyle if not from Springer then from *COPS* or other such shows. But I didn't want to make a mockery of her. She was too powerful, too awesome (literal, not Keanu version) to just laugh at. We must care for her.

I'm just putting this out there: I'm a geek. BIG ol' sci-fi geek. I'm talking *Star Trek* (*TNG, DS9, Voyager*), *Stargate SG-1, X-Files, Fringe, Eureka, Dr. Who* (new one), *Torchwood*...you know, the good ones. I also enjoy when people bring the sci-fi aspect into the theatrical setting, seeing how it's so hard to do well. To compensate for her being a sorceress in the original, I decided to put a healthy cupful of sci-fi into *Maddy*. To create a good sci-fi piece, you have to create a solid mythology to base the story off of. If you don't, the audience gets confused, then it stops caring about the story and starts picking apart the details (See any *Star Trek* chatboard). As with most sci-fi shows, the less human a character is—think Spock, Data, Dr. Who, etc.—the more other characters around them, and you, learn about humanity. That's why I decided to make Maddy not human.

Maddy comes to our world via The Elementals. They are a race of non-emoting beings that keep our world together. Without them, the air, fire, earth, water, etc., would be so out of balance that our world would fall apart. Within their immortal lifetime, they are able to take up to seven years' leave of absence to explore life as a mortal human. By that seventh year anniversary, they must either choose to stay human or return to being an Elemental. There are other rules as well, all provided within the text of the show.

Anyone playing Maddy must remember that she has had only *seven* years of emotional growth. She is fiercely intelligent and still has the memory of being her old intelligent self, but is constantly pulled around by her relatively immature emotions. The juxtaposition frustrates her no end. Alan, her Elemental counterpart, while emotionless, is still nonetheless alive and vibrant. He is in no way, shape, or form boring. He is of the Earth, and must command that energy. To make this play work, these two characters *must* believe in the other world just as much as the humans believe in theirs.

Above all, have fun. Find the light-hearted moments as much as you would the deep drama. They're both vitally important to Maddy being justified in her final action, and winning the hearts of the audience.

CHARACTERS

MADDY: Tall, thin woman who looks to be in her late twenties, well spoken, very smart.

BILLY-JAE: Early to mid-twenties, very attractive, not too bright, but has moments of insight.

FLO: Late twenties, mother of two, very grounded, earthy, salt-of-the-earth smart.

ALAN: Late thirties/early forties, emotionless and mysterious, but full of life.

CLEETUS: Late forties/early fifties, good ol' boy look, cowboy businessman.

EDNA: Only a voiceover, but should be in her sixties, raspy, hung over/drunk.

NEWSCASTER: Younger voice, must be good at storytelling.

SETTING

The Corinthian Trailer Park somewhere in the Midwest.

The play is viewed as if the audience is a fly on the window of EDNA's trailer, across the lawn from MADDY's. As the audience comes in, they are greeted by a wall of curtain blocking their view of the stage. It can either be a traveler or it can be split down the middle to open to either side.

It is a hot summer day, cicadas chirp in the trees. Blackout. Lights up. The curtain opens to reveal a worn-down old trailer, blue with a white stripe down the center, two windows on either side of a door in the center of the trailer. It is raised on cinder blocks, with a makeshift porch in front, just below the height of the trailer, and a beer cooler below the stage left window. Stage right there are two ratty old lawn chairs with a stump between them. All the way to the right is the trunk of a tree. Far stage left there is a broken toilet with plants inside it. The stage itself is covered in AstroTurf. There should be an entrance both upstage right and downstage left. Upstage right is where FLO lives; downstage left is where travelers or visitors come in from town. MADDY and ALAN are revealed when the lights come up. MADDY is standing on the porch, ALAN stands just below her on the ground.

ALAN: You have until sundown to decide. If you are in need of anything, you know how to reach me. *(Walks downstage left, stops, facing away.)* Until sundown. *(Exits.)*

(MADDY stands on the porch, looking after him, silent for a moment. FLO walks up behind her from upstage right.)

FLO: Who was that?

(Silence.)

FLO: Maddy? *(Pause.)* Maddy, you okay?

(MADDY snaps out of it, slowly turns to FLO.)

FLO: Who was that?

MADDY: *(A moment of silence, looks back where ALAN left.)* An old friend, Flo. *(Silently walks into the trailer, closes door behind her.)*

(FLO takes a moment, looks at EDNA's trailer window [the audience], and moves downstage left to exit. Sound: Knocking on trailer door. Through this voiceover sequence, MADDY can come out, sweep the porch, tend to the plants in the toilet, etc. She can hear what's being talked about between EDNA and FLO, and can react slightly, but not to distract from the dialogue.)

EDNA: *(Voiceover.)* Not so loud...fuck! Come in...

(Sound of opening door.)

EDNA: *(Voiceover.)* What was that all about?

FLO: *(Voiceover.)* I've no idea, Edna.

(Door closes.)

FLO: *(Voiceover.)* I saw this dark-haired man walk up and knock on Maddy's door. She looked at him all startled like, but invited him in anyways. They were in there a few minutes, then they walked out, he says she's got till sundown to make her decision, and then vanishes.

EDNA: *(Voiceover.)* Yeah, saw that last little bit too. And she didn't mention a name?

FLO: *(Voiceover.)* Nope, just said he was an old friend.

EDNA: *(Voiceover.)* Wonder what kind of trouble she's gotten herself into now?

FLO: *(Voiceover.)* Whaddya mean?

EDNA: *(Voiceover.)* Well you know, with Billy-Jae and all.

FLO: *(Voiceover.)* Edna Lynn, don't tell me you think BJ leaving is HER fault!

EDNA: *(Voiceover.)* Well Maddy must've been doing somethin' wrong. Men don't just up and leave the mother of their child'n to go'n marry a sausage.

FLO: *(Voiceover.)* Gracie ain't that fat.

EDNA: *(Voiceover.)* Like hell she ain't!

FLO: *(Voiceover.)* Well what about Billy-Jae? You think he's going to marry that girl today for love? Uh uh. It's the money her daddy's got. Cleetus just bought his ninth trailer park: You don't think Billy-Jae wants in on that?

EDNA: *(Voiceover.)* Fuck, I don't know.

FLO: *(Voiceover.)* Let me brew you some coffee.

EDNA: *(Voiceover.)* Oh come on… fuck's not a bad word!

FLO: *(Voiceover.)* Yes it is!

EDNA: *(Voiceover.)* Fuck fuck fuck fuck fuck…

FLO: *(Voiceover.)* Stop it—

EDNA: *(Voiceover.)* Would you rather I take the lord's name in vain?

(Beat.)

FLO: *(Voiceover.)* Fuck it is.

EDNA: *(Voiceover.)* And no coffee. Grab me a PBR out of that fridge. You can have one too if you want.

FLO: *(Voiceover.)* No thank you.

(Sound of fridge opening.)

FLO: I still can't believe that he's gonna marry that girl over Maddy.

(Fridge closes.)

FLO: I mean, Maddy's good lookin'! She's odd, but very pretty. I don't understand why he'd give all that up.

EDNA: *(Voiceover.)* Maybe 'cuz *she* don't give it up no more.

(MADDY has heard enough and goes back into the trailer.)

FLO: *(Voiceover.)* Don't be nasty.

(Phone rings, loudly.)

EDNA: *(Voiceover.)* Aw, fuck! Could you get that please?

FLO: *(Voiceover.)* Hello? Oh hey, Myrtle. Yeah, Edna's hung over again. Yeah, I gave her a beer, what's going on?

(Silence.)

FLO: Are you serious?

(Silence.)

FLO: *(Lower.)* Heaven help her. *(Pause.)* Yeah, I'll tell her, hold on a sec…Myrtle says she overheard Cleetus's secretary telling the checkout girl at the Wal-Mart that Cleetus is coming over today to serve Maddy eviction papers!

EDNA: *(Voiceover.)* Talk about a shit storm…

(Pause.)

FLO: *(Voiceover.)* Myrtle, I want you to do me a favor. Take my boys and have them find Maddy's kids. Bring 'em over to my place and get 'em playing on the Wii. Oh, don't worry, they'll set it up on their own. *(Pause.)* Yeah, I've got some Xanax in the bathroom cabinet. Go ahead and help yourself. Thanks, Myrtle. Bye hon.

EDNA: *(Voiceover.)* Where're you going?

FLO: *(Voiceover.)* I don't want those kids to see their mama getting kicked out.

(Pause.) I'm going over there to see if I can help. You wait here, okay?

(Fridge opening again.)

EDNA: *(Voiceover.)* What're you doing?

FLO: *(Voiceover.)* I'm grabbing a couple of iced teas for Maddy.

(Fridge shuts.)

EDNA: *(Voiceover.)* But why you gotta take mine? *(Beat.)* Fine. But you be careful. I'm feeling mighty strange, and you know me and my gut feelings.

FLO: *(Voiceover.)* Yup, they're usually right before you puke.

EDNA: *(Voiceover.)* Fair 'nuf, but Suzette thinks she's a witch!

FLO: *(Voiceover.)* If you could hear yourself.

EDNA: *(Voiceover.)* She caught Maddy dancing naked in the rain!

FLO: *(Voiceover.)* So do *you* when you're drunk!

(Beat.)

EDNA: *(Voiceover.)* Just be careful, alright?

FLO: *(Voiceover.)* Alright.

(Sound of FLO exiting trailer, slamming door.)

EDNA: *(Voiceover.)* NOT so LOUD! *(Beat.)* FUCK!

(FLO enters stage, slowly crosses over to MADDY's trailer. She knocks on the door, glances back at EDNA's trailer, then turns back as MADDY opens it. She's cool, but you can tell she's distracted.)

MADDY: What can I do for you, Flo?

FLO: I've come bearing gifts. *(Holds up the iced teas.)* Busy?

MADDY: Not at all. Have a seat. *(Moves over to the lawn chairs.)*

FLO: Maddy, what's wrong? *(Beat.)* You doing okay hon?

MADDY: *(Pause.)* I don't understand, Flo. I don't understand how it's come to this…Where I came from I was highly regarded. Everyone was civil, never unkind. Yet the moment I stepped foot in The Corinthian Park it's been nothing but an uphill battle. Do you know how hard it is fitting in someplace new?

FLO: No, I've lived around these parts all my life.

MADDY: All the women here, save you, have done nothing but treat me like I just got out of jail and take joy in spreading vicious rumors. Before I could even prove who I was, they suspected the worst of me. Though I may not know all the intricacies of the human condition, I think I could've fit in well.

FLO: Well it's just that a lot of the people don't know you honey. Like where you came from, or…well…*anything* about you really.

MADDY: Do you tell everyone everything, Flo?

FLO: No…

MADDY: Then why do people expect it from me? Why must I reveal all to the world? For all I know, I should be the one judging the park for their problems rather than the other way around. Yet, it seems like I'm the rock that must be navigated.

FLO: Maddy, you never gave us a chance.

MADDY: Neither did you.

FLO: I guess...I didn't come here to argue with you. I'm here to help in any way that I can.

(Beat.)

MADDY: Flo, where are my children?

FLO: They're with the boys playing over at my place.

(Sound of car pulling up.)

MADDY: *(Over sound.)* Okay— *(Pause.)* Why...?

(Both look over to the sound's origin, downstage left.)

FLO: Because Maddy, there's more trouble coming. I heard tell Cleetus is on his way over.

MADDY: What's going on?

(FLO pulls MADDY up, grabs her by the arm, a force to be reckoned with.)

FLO: Take a deep breath, sweetheart.

(CLEETUS enters from downstage left, slowly, in no hurry. He's got a manila envelope in his hands.)

CLEETUS: Afternoon, Maddy, Flo.

FLO: Cleetus.

CLEETUS: If you don't mind, Flo, I got things to discuss with Maddy, private like.

FLO: I think I'll stick around seein' as I already know what's going on, Cleetus. You best tell that secretary of yours to keep her trap shut if she knows what's best for you and your business.

CLEETUS: Noted. Maddy, I'm serving you your eviction papers. I thought about a restraining order, but I wanted to keep things quiet.

(He hands MADDY the envelope, but FLO takes it instead.)

CLEETUS: You need to be out within the hour.

MADDY: Cleetus, please don't do this.

CLEETUS: It's done, Maddy. T'ain't much I can do 'bout it now.

FLO: Come on, Cleetus...Of all days why today?

CLEETUS: I can't have my Gracie's big day ruined by her now can I? If pressured to choose, a father'll always pick his flesh and blood over a stranger in a heartbeat. Sure, it may be harsh, but it's better than living to regret it. Leave peaceably, Maddy, and don't come back.

(Beat.)

MADDY: Cleetus...I know I've spoken against you time and again, but please take it as nothing more than emotional and idle threats.

CLEETUS: Idle? You called Gracie and I every name in the book, and then some I ain't even heard of before!

MADDY: And I'm very sorry about that. I've given it some thought, and realized you've done me no personal harm. You were merely thinking of your daughter, as a father should. To find the best match for her, and Billy-Jae's a good match, undeniably. I wish nothing but happiness for the couple. Please, Cleetus, let me stay here. I'll keep quiet, I'll be good, just please, let me stay.

CLEETUS: I wish I could trust you, Maddy, but your words make me even more fearful. I'd rather have someone screaming in my face, saying exactly what they think of me, than someone who keeps their cards close and fumes in silence. Now I won't tell you again, you need to leave.

MADDY: *(Letting emotions show.)* Please, Cleetus. Please, not today. *(Begging on her knees.)*

CLEETUS: Get up, or I'll call the police and have you removed by force.

MADDY: No, no, please, not that! I—I won't argue anymore...It's just—

CLEETUS: *(Interrupting.)* Well, what then?

MADDY: I need one day. One day to get my things in order, and for the children. You're a father yourself; please take pity on them if not me. They're innocents in this...One day is all I ask.

CLEETUS: *(Sighs.)* Aw, come on now, I'm not heartless bastard... *(Pause.)* I've just got this feeling I'm makin' a big mistake...I'll give you till sundown. I'm going to take care of the wedding, and when that's done and my daughter is safe on her honeymoon, I'll be coming back here with the authorities. If you're still here, heaven help you. *(Pause.)* Maddy, Flo. *(Leaves downstage left.)*

MADDY: Thank goodness.

FLO: What do you mean, thank goodness?

MADDY: He gave me the time I need. I can't make my decision yet...I need more time to think.

FLO: What decision?

MADDY: *(Pause.)* I can't tell you.

FLO: Maddy—

MADDY: I'm sorry; it's really for your own good.

FLO: Whaddya mean for my own good? Maddy, are you in trouble or something?

MADDY: No, no, nothing like that. I have to make a very important decision, and I need time to think.

FLO: And you don't want to tell me about it?

MADDY: *(Pause, very sincerely.)* Flo, it's not that I don't want to, it's that I can't. And don't worry, though I'd love nothing more than to take my revenge on Cleetus, Billy-Jae, and that zeppelin of a woman he's marrying today, your worldly laws prohibit me from doing anything by my own hands, and I can't by any other means...for the moment.

(Silence, then MADDY turns to FLO.)

MADDY: What would you do, Flo?

FLO: Me?

MADDY: Yes. Of all the women in this park, you seem the most level-headed and rational of them all. What would you do if you were in my position?

FLO: *(Pause.)* Well, like you said, if there were no limits or laws holding me back, I'd chop off his dick and feed it to him. But since that's never going to happen, I'd probably eat a lot of chocolate chip cookie dough ice cream and move on. You're a strong woman, Maddy. Nothing can stop you but yourself.

MADDY: Fascinating...So you're telling me that if you could do so without fear of retribution or consequence, you'd follow a path of revenge against one who you love but has wronged you...?

FLO: I'd probably chicken out at the last minute, but if I had the guts, I'd love to, hell yeah.

MADDY: What about the teachings of forgiveness your faith instructs you to follow?

FLO: Yeah, that only works in favor of the accused, not the victim. *(Sits in one of the lawn chairs.)* Maddy, my husband cheated on me once and I've never forgiven him. Sure, I may have told him I did, but in reality that breech of our love can never be repaired. Yes, I still care for him, love him, still desire him, but that momentary fracture of trust was enough to destroy everything.

MADDY: But what did you do?

FLO: Told him if I caught him cheatin' that I'd divorce him, and he'd be kicked out and never see his kids again. Then I closed up shop for six weeks. He went through a lot of lotion in those six weeks, but he's never cheated since.

(The GIRLS have a good laugh. Beat.)

FLO: I knew that deep down he felt he'd done me wrong and that was enough. But forgiving him would have helped him more than it ever would me.

(Sound: Approaching truck tires, engine turning off, car door slamming.)

MADDY: Unbelievable.

(BILLY-JAE enters downstage left.)

BILLY-JAE: Good morning Maddy, Flo.

(FLO harrumphs.)

MADDY: *(Smiles, turns to FLO.)* Would you be so kind as to check on my children? I'd like to speak with BJ alone.

FLO: Of course.

BILLY-JAE: Tell my boys to come say hi!

FLO: How 'bout I tell you to go fuck yourself?

BILLY-JAE: Okay then—

FLO: I'll be down the road. Holler if you need me.

MADDY: Thank you, Flo.

(FLO exits upstage right, giving BILLY-JAE the evil eye.)

MADDY: You know, I think I'm going to miss her the most.

BILLY-JAE: Maddy—

MADDY: What are you doing here?

BILLY-JAE: I just came to—

MADDY: No, I mean, what the hell gave you the impression that you'd be welcomed here? *(Beat.)* I just don't get it, Billy-Jae! I've been watching your kind for centuries and seen this scenario time and again, but I never imagined it would happen to me. Of all of mankind, you're the only one who made me feel human. Somehow you're so inextricably tied to my emotions that I cannot separate them. When I look at most of the denizens of this park, I feel nothing but contempt and have no idea why I felt the need to become human. *(Beat.)* Then you come, and even though I'm nothing short of furious, I just want to be naked with you, wrapped in your arms, and stay there for the rest of my life. *(Pause.)* How can you exist with such dichotomy?

BILLY-JAE: *(Flabbergasted.)* I have no idea what you just said to me, but you wanna take this in the trailer…

MADDY: So pretty…why must it be one or the other?

BILLY-JAE: What?

MADDY: Never mind. What do you want?

BILLY-JAE: I came to see if I can help. I heard Cleetus kicked you out.

MADDY: Woah, back up— You're expect me to believe you had nothing to do with my eviction?!?

BILLY-JAE: No, I tried to *stop* him! But you just kept hollering—

MADDY: You can hardly blame me! I haven't been human long enough to control my emotions, especially the stronger ones I've never felt before.

BILLY-JAE: Even after you were warned, you wouldn't stop! You can't go around threatening and cursing the people who have more power than you.

MADDY: More power than me?

BILLY-JAE: You know what I mean, stop being so fucking clever!

MADDY: How dare you speak to me like that? After everything I've done for you!

BILLY-JAE: *(Overlapping.)* Everything you've done for me!?!? *(Sits down in one of the lawn chairs.)*

MADDY: When I destroyed your town, I broke our laws by saving your life because I'd fallen in love with you. I transformed into your kind and I bore our children. Billy-Jae, do you have any idea how painful that is? I'd rather go to war *ten times* than give birth once. All this I have done for you, and this is how you repay me?

BILLY-JAE: Why are you blaming me for your decisions?

MADDY: Oh, fuck you—

(BILLY-JAE gets up and in her face, backing her towards the toilet.)

BILLY-JAE: No, fuck you! I never once asked you for anything that you "gave" me. Yeah, I loved you, and I still do. But I never asked you to leave your people. Never asked you to save my life. Never asked you to become one of us. You'd made those decisions on your own.

FLO: *(Offstage.)* JACKASS!

BILLY-JAE and MADDY: STAY OUT OF THIS FLO!

MADDY: *(Beat. She comes to her senses and moves to center stage.)* Why did you leave me?

BILLY-JAE: *(Beat.)* Money.

MADDY: Wow, that's honest.

BILLY-JAE: Look, Maddy, I can't have my boys living in this hellhole anymore. I don't want them to grow up the way I did, struggling every day just to get by. You have no idea what it's like for a child to have to worry about where his next meal is coming from. It got so bad at times I had to dig through the garbage to find something to eat. I *will not* let that happen to them. I want them to get a decent education. Right now, I don't make enough for that to happen, and you can't earn much of an income because you don't even exist. So I had to find some other way to make more money. By marrying Gracie, I can make a better life for our children...and for you. Now she's willing to take them in and support them. We can send them to a good school and they can eat more than mac and cheese and hot dogs for dinner. I'd even be able to make you more comfortable so you don't have to keep living like this.

MADDY: And you didn't think to address this with me first?

BILLY-JAE: Riiiight. A second ago you complained you couldn't control your own emotions, and now you complain I didn't come to you first about marrying someone else for their money?

(MADDY is silent, knowing she's defeated; she slinks back to a lawn chair.)

BILLY-JAE: Look Maddy, it's the only way. This is what's best for the boys. Their welfare is my only concern right now. Sometimes as a parent you've got to make some sacrifices for the good of the children. *(Beat.)* Look, I need to go get ready. The ceremony's in an hour. If you need anything, let me know. I can call some friends and set you up someplace…

MADDY: I won't take anything from you or your friends. Nothing good can come from the gifts of a villain.

BILLY-JAE: *(Sighs.)* Fine. *(Starts to walk off downstage left.)*

MADDY: *(Stands.)* Happy *seventh* anniversary.

BILLY-JAE: *(Stops dead.)* Seven?

MADDY: Yes.

BILLY-JAE: *(Turns.)* When?

(Silence.)

BILLY-JAE: Today??

MADDY: Yes.

BILLY-JAE: Are you— Have you… decided?

MADDY: No.

BILLY-JAE: *(Pause.)* Will I get to see you before you make your decision?

MADDY: That's up to you.

BILLY-JAE: How much longer do you have?

MADDY: Sundown.

BILLY-JAE: *(Beat.)* God.

(Silence.)

BILLY-JAE: I'm sorry I didn't remember…

MADDY: You wouldn't have. That's what makes you you.

(BILLY-JAE opens mouth, closes it again, pauses, exits. MADDY watches him leave, then closes her eyes. She opens them again, moves to the tree, places her hand against it. She seems to concentrate for a moment, then looks downstage left as ALAN enters.)

MADDY: Thank you for coming back.

ALAN: You are welcome. What can I do for you?

MADDY: I just need to talk.

ALAN: Talk?

MADDY: Yes. You're the only unbiased opinion that I have at the moment, and I need help making my decision.

ALAN: Very well.

(She invites him to sit on the lawn chairs with her. Beat as she formulates her questions.)

MADDY: Do many of us give humanity a try?

ALAN: Almost all of us. Some have no desire, or have yet to do so.

MADDY: How many of us stayed mortal?

ALAN: Five.

MADDY: That many?

ALAN: Yes.

MADDY: Why?

ALAN: The reason was different for each. Three because they found love, riches, or other such qualities that make the human condition seemingly easier. One found that having children was all he needed. His connection to his own offspring was enough to make him choose not to return. The other died.

MADDY: Prematurely?

ALAN: Salem, Massachusetts, mid-seventeenth century.

MADDY: Ah.

ALAN: Not one of humanity's brightest moments, but the only one they got right by their standards.

MADDY: That's what worries me the most…Dying.

ALAN: Why? You know your energy will just be redistributed somewhere else in the universe.

MADDY: It's not so much the fact that I could, but the *means* by which it could happen…

ALAN: Understandable.

(Silence.)

MADDY: Did…Did you…?

ALAN: Did I leave for my seven years?

MADDY: Yes.

ALAN: Indeed. I was young then, like you, only a couple of hundred years old. Late in the first century, I lived in Italy and fell for a beautiful woman from Misenum. We were happy, had several children, and my trade business was flourishing. Just before I had to decide on my mortality, my wife and children moved our home to a nearby city in the south, while I stayed in Misenum to finalize the selling of the property. On August 24th, of their seventy-ninth year, Vesuvius erupted. The first eruption rained down ash on Pompeii, the weight of which collapsed roofs, and clogged the lungs of those who survived. The second sent a thundering pyroclastic flow down the mountainside, burying Pompeii under sixty feet of ash and rock. I watched this from a distance, knowing it was my own sister causing the destruction. Yet, part of me knew that it was not personal, that she was fulfilling her duty. I accepted that when I rejoined the group, regaining my old position and working side by side with the one who destroyed my family. I returned nearly two thousand years later after their archaeologists uncovered the city, and walked to the home where my wife and children had been relocated. I found them intact, in a museum. There was a glass case around them, lights shining on their corpses. The heat and ash from the eruption had instantly fossilized them, freezing them in time. They were huddled together, her arms were around the children, trying to protect them from a force greater than she could have ever imagined. *(Beat.)* We are at a certain advantage in that our race does not feel emotions. I see the tears on your face, and know that I once shed them myself, but do not feel them anymore. That is what allows us to destroy civilizations without remorse. If we kept our emotions, we would be useless. We do not judge where, when, or why the destructive act is needed. We exist solely to execute the assignment, without question, to maintain the balance.

(Silence.)

MADDY: I don't know what to do.

ALAN: Unfortunately we can be of no assistance. Unlike Vesuvius, which helped inform my decision, there are no local events occurring before you must make your choice. *(Beat.)* And you are aware of the conditions on which you must return.

MADDY: What conditions?

ALAN: Should you decide to return, it must be of your own accord and you must leave no trace of your existence.

MADDY: My children?

ALAN: If you return and the two of them still exist, their powers will manifest and destroy the balance. If you stay human, they will not activate and you will be able to live a normal life.

MADDY: You can't be serious…

ALAN: These rules were set down before time was time.

MADDY: I don't…I can't… *(Loss of all vocal ability.)*

ALAN: Madeline, look at the situation through the eyes you once had, not the eyes you see through now.

(Silence. MADDY has an "ah-ha" moment, sharp intake of breath, held.)

ALAN: If you decide to return…

MADDY: You'll know. Then you may come back and retrieve me.

ALAN: Very good.

(Silence. AlAN gets up, walks downstage left.)

ALAN: For what it is worth, I am sorry that we cannot be of more assistance.

MADDY: *(Half smile.)* No, you're not.

ALAN: *(Beat.)* You are right. *(Exits, flash.)*

(Pause. MADDY sits on one of the chairs and buries her face in her hands and sighs. Beat. Raises her head.)

MADDY: Flo? You around?

(FLO enters from upstage right, a little too quickly.)

FLO: Right here hon.

MADDY: We need to talk. Have a seat. *(Gestures to the other chair.)* Have a beer. *(Goes to the cooler and grabs a beer.)*

FLO: No thank you…

MADDY: Trust me, with what we're about to discuss, you'll need it.

(FLO accepts it and takes a drink. MADDY looks down at the ground for a moment, then—)

MADDY: Today is my birthday, Flo.

FLO: Aw honey, happy birthday! How old are you?

MADDY: Technically? Seven.

FLO: *(Beat.)* Come again?

MADDY: I'm seven human years old today. Though, by your standards I'm 328.

FLO: I don't understand…

MADDY: Not many of your kind ever have, or ever will. That is exactly why you're unaware of our existence. Flo, can you promise me you'll try to keep an open mind.

(FLO takes a long drink of the beer.)

MADDY: Flo, I'm not fully human… at least, not yet.

(Silence. FLO finishes the beer.)

MADDY: Everything that mankind perceives is on *this* single plane of existence, but there are hundreds of other layers that you have no idea about. Some are right in front of you, but you're unable, or unwilling, to see, which is why we're able to hide in plain sight. I'm from one of them. Older civilizations called us Elementals, which I suppose is fitting as we control and balance the forces of nature around you. We move among you, but are not of you. The man you saw earlier is like me. He's part of what you might consider my family. Four of us monitor areas near our home base to keep the elements that make up your universe in order, in harmony. Once in our lifetime we are allowed to try out life as a human…for seven years.

FLO: Okay, this is weird, Maddy…

MADDY: Please, Flo, listen!

FLO: No! This is just too bizarre! You're telling me that you're some spirit—

MADDY: Not spirit per se…Being is more accurate. Though we were created long before mankind, we took *your* shape to blend in as we must be able to move through our territory. It'd be extremely difficult for you to see me in my real form.

FLO: I'm leaving. *(Gets up and heads upstage right.)*

MADDY: Wait! PLEASE!

FLO: *(Pauses and turns.)* What?

MADDY: I wanted to say that— You've been very kind to me. Though I'm sure it hasn't been easy, you've been consistently friendly. I wanted to thank you for that.

FLO: *(Beat.)* You're welcome.

(Silence.)

MADDY: When I call, please send my children to the other side of the trailer. Tell them I'm planning a picnic for them and they should wait patiently for me out back. Can you do that?

FLO: *(Beat.)* Of course.

MADDY: Thank you, Flo.

FLO: Welcome.

MADDY: Flo?

(FLO turns and looks again.)

MADDY: If it looks like the weather's about to turn, get underground with the kids immediately, alright?

FLO: But there's not a cloud in the sky.

MADDY: Promise me you'll do that. *(Beat, graver.)* Please.

FLO: I promise.

MADDY: Thank you.

(Sound of BILLY-JAE's truck arriving again. FLO exits. BILLY-JAE enters downstage left in a tux. MADDY's breath is taken away.)

BILLY-JAE: *(Pause.)* Have you…what did you decide?

MADDY: *(Beat.)* Do you remember how we met?

BILLY-JAE: Yeah, you showed up in my hometown the night before the tornado hit… I was working at the diner when you walked in and ordered a reuben, two pickles on the side. I thought you were the prettiest thing I'd ever seen. Still do.

MADDY: You asked where I'd come from.

BILLY-JAE: Not exactly the best pickup line ever, but it worked, didn't it?

MADDY: And I told you I was from Louisiana…

BILLY-JAE: I could tell you were hiding something. That fascinated me and made me want to get to know you. So I asked you to meet me after I got off work.

MADDY: And I said no.

BILLY-JAE: First time any girl ever said that to me. Even the married ones. Then you got up and left.

MADDY: But I came back after the diner closed.

BILLY-JAE: It was one of the best nights of my life.

MADDY: Mine too. *(Beat.)* I felt emotions for the first time. I'd watched your kind live for hundreds of years, but never felt anything for them. It took this *(Touches his chest.)* individual connection to make me see humans for the wonder that they are. The next morning when you brought me breakfast in bed was the moment I decided to take my leave.

BILLY-JAE: You sent me away…

MADDY: I had to save you. I couldn't let you die so soon after finding you. I asked you to leave for the day so I could complete my final duty.

BILLY-JAE: It was one of the most beautiful and horrific things I've ever witnessed.

MADDY: I thought I told you not to watch—

BILLY-JAE: I can't believe that it's been seven years already.

MADDY: I can. *(Beat.)* Before you, time meant nothing to me. We don't feel it. Time is something you created to help place order in your life. Like many other things that you've created, you're now a slave to it. When I became human, time began to rush or creep by till I got lost in it myself. I felt emotions, hunger, thirst, and all the other things that make up your biology. That's why for the first couple of weeks I was totally out of control of my faculties and didn't speak very much. There was pain that I experienced for the first time, then absolute joy a second later. Your species is so full of contradictions that it took me months before I could make sense of what I was feeling! Add to that my loss of interconnectedness, and it was just devastating. I used to be linked to my clan, knowing the thoughts of three other beings, and tuned to the Universal energy itself. Being human, I felt trapped, unable to move outside this body. It took a lot of patience to accept your mortal limitations. That was a very hard adjustment to make.

BILLY-JAE: Why didn't I know about this?

MADDY: I wanted to protect you from it. I kept it under my skin.

BILLY-JAE: Why are you telling me this now?

MADDY: Because I haven't found a true champion for humanity. I don't have anyone telling me that I should stay. So I'm going to ask you: With this knowledge, what would you do? Stay? Or go?

BILLY-JAE: What would *I* do?

MADDY: Yes.

BILLY-JAE: *(Beat.)* God, I don't know, Maddy. I guess I'd have to see which would ultimately make me happier.

MADDY: That won't work. One won't allow for feelings at all.

BILLY-JAE: I mean, what would be the best option for you?

MADDY: That's what I'm asking you…

BILLY-JAE: Okay, well, there's a lot of things to live for—

MADDY: Live for, or in service of?

BILLY-JAE: What do you mean?

MADDY: Myself, the children, finding a job, housing, clothing, food... It seems like all we've ever done is struggle, and now I have to go out there and try to make it on my own. If I were by myself, I'd find a way to manage. But Billy-Jae, the children—how can I do that to them? How can I let them suffer for my decisions?

BILLY-JAE: Well they're coming to live with me...

MADDY: But, then I'd have to stay human as well. They can't be allowed to grow if I return.

BILLY-JAE: I'll help you too.

MADDY: Would I be allowed to see them?

BILLY-JAE: That would be pretty difficult, ya see, 'cuz Gracie says she doesn't want you to have any contact with them.

MADDY: You'd take them from their own mother?

BILLY-JAE: These are the rules she laid down and I'm not going to argue. I can provide a better life for the boys, Maddy. I'm just doing what's right for them!

MADDY: But they're my children too! I can't just give them up! *(Begins to break down.)* God, Billy-Jae— The sun keeps moving across the sky... So fast and I can't decide— *(Goes into the trailer.)*

BILLY-JAE: Maddy—

(Goes after her. There is a long silence, then the sounds of passionate kissing. A couple of moans, then—)

BILLY-JAE: Stop... Stop! *(Rushes out of the trailer with his shirt off, and gripping his unbuttoned pants around his waist.)* We can't, Maddy. If this is going to work, I have to get married today and we'll have to keep this a secret, alright?

MADDY: So no matter what choice I make, I have to go into some form of hiding.

(Silence.)

MADDY: And you'd help support me?

BILLY-JAE: I love you, Maddy. If I had to lie to Gracie and Cleetus for the rest of my life, I'd do it for you.

MADDY: Go. Go get married.

(BILLY-JAE kisses her and then heads downstage left. MADDY watches him leave, moves back into the trailer, and shuts the door. A light starts to glow inside the trailer, getting brighter and brighter, till light is beaming out of the windows during the following. Phone rings.)

EDNA: *(Voiceover.)* Hello? Yeah? What channel? Four? Alright.

(Sound of a TV being turned on.)

NEWSCASTER: *(Voiceover.)* This is David Smith reporting here at the wedding of the decade. Landowner Cleetus Buford's daughter Gracie Louise is getting married to Mr. Billy-Jae Anderson in a beautiful outdoor ceremony. They've spared no expense here, folks. The guests are settled in two columns behind the church, with the sun setting behind them. It's picture perfect. It seems the groom will be a bit late due to an emergency, but we've got word he's on his way now. The bride is waiting at the alter with her father standing stately by her side. Six bridesmaids and groomsmen flank them in a stunning display of extravagance in these lean times.

(Thunder over the speakers.)

NEWSCASTER: *(Voiceover.)* Uh-oh. Seems we got some clouds gathering here at the church. But it shouldn't be a problem. Our weatherman, George Williams, guaranteed clear skies today, so this will probably just pass us by.

(More thunder, getting louder, sound of wind beginning to pick up to a howl over the following.)

NEWSCASTER: *(Voiceover.)* Looks like the father of the bride and the priest are speaking about maybe moving the wedding inside as the rain is starting to fall here. It's getting quite gusty at the moment…The sky's gotten very dark now…

(Sound of hail.)

NEWSCASTER: *(Voiceover.)* Oh my god! Hail the size of golf balls is beginning to fall on the crowd, hitting them pretty hard. People are trying to move to the covering of the reception area for protection, but the hail is punching through! People are bleeding on the ground here, screaming…Jesus! A funnel cloud is forming above us and coming down onto the church! Chunks of the steeple are flying around, hitting the patrons as they scatter for their lives!

(Cracking noise.)

NEWSCASTER: *(Voiceover.)* The steeple is falling, it's heading right for… Lord, the bride has been crushed by the fallen steeple! And—

(Crack of lightning.)

NEWSCASTER: *(Voiceover.)* Cleetus has just been struck by lightning! The funnel is destroying everything in its path, the patrons, the reception area— It's coming this way, fast. Oh g—

(Static. Light in the trailer dies down to nothing. TV is switched off. Beat.)

EDNA: *(Voiceover.)* Good Lord. They're all dead.

MADDY: *(Exiting trailer.)* Flo, would you be so kind as to send my children behind the trailer? Tell them I will be there in a moment. Flo…Goodbye.

(She pauses for a moment, looking into the audience. Then she decides. She looks straight up to the sky and closes her eyes. The lights begin to go dark on the stage, and thunder is heard gathering. The curtains of the set close, and the audience sees a light start to glow through. The light gets brighter and brighter for a bit. Hail, thunder, more flashes of lightning. A large beastly roar is heard in the storm and the lights go out. TWO CHILDREN's voices are heard screaming. There is a large crash. Then a larger crack as the curtains open up as a WOMAN's scream is heard from the audience and flies into the distance. Wind is blowing hard onto the audience, from fans placed above them in the ceiling. More crashes, then the wind dies down. Lights slowly come up on the stage as the clouds disperse, revealing MADDY, center stage, completely unfazed. Around her is total destruction. MADDY's trailer is decimated; everything in the area is scattered around and in pieces. It's hard to recognize anything anymore. MADDY stands securely in it. She opens her eyes and is now back to her old self. Beautiful. Uncaring. Indifferent. She is stunning in her destruction. The sound of a car approaches, skids to a stop, BILLY-JAE enters downstage left.)

BILLY-JAE: Oh, God Maddy, what have you DONE?!?

MADDY: I made my decision.

BILLY-JAE: Where are the boys?

(Silence.)

BILLY-JAE: Maddy, where are my children?

(Silence. MADDY looks back at the broken trailer behind her.)

BILLY-JAE: (Starts to retch.) Jesus, Maddy, how could you? (Runs to the side of the trailer and starts to try to get the children out of the rubble. He stops when he sees a dead body.)

MADDY: It was the kindest thing I could do for them. I could either take their life now and let their souls return when they are ready, or let them live a half-life with you only to be disliked by their soon to be stepmother, teased by their half-siblings and grow up without their real mother. I could not allow them to endure that. It was better to end it now than face a lifetime of suffering.

BILLY-JAE: You never loved those children.

MADDY: It was as fast and painless as possible. I showed them more love in my act than you ever did in their whole brief lives.

BILLY-JAE: Why everyone?

MADDY: It was required in order for me to return. I had to destroy any evidence of my visitation. Wipe the slate clean, and move on.

BILLY-JAE: Why didn't you take me?

(He charges her, but she grabs his throat and forces him to the ground.)

MADDY: I could have. I took our children out of love. But I spared you out of retribution. You and you alone were the key to keeping me here on this plane. As you had said, there are many reasons to stay human, but the one you cited as most important, happiness, could never be attained if it were not wholly with you. You would have destroyed a poor woman's heart through a false marriage, I would have had to live in the shadows, and all this so you could make us happy by your estimation. Joy begotten from other's pain is unthinkable. So I chose to end all of the suffering and return to my origins. It was not a happy decision by human standards, but the right one.

(ALAN enters from downstage left.)

ALAN: Welcome back Madeline. Why is this one still alive?

MADDY: Killing him would have freed him of his wrongdoing. By allowing him to live, he will atone for his actions by living a better life.

ALAN: But he knows of our kind, and our ways.

MADDY: And if he tells anyone, who will believe him? No, we will let him live. Live in order to learn. It seems a fitting punishment for one who ruined so many lives by selfish actions.

ALAN: (Considers.) Unorthodox, but understandable. Come, the others await your return.

MADDY: (Pauses, kneels down by BILLY-JAE.) Though I do not feel it now, I can tell you that up until the moment I transformed I loved you. My human side always did.

(She caresses BILLY-JAE's face briefly. ALAN and MADDY leave. FLO enters, upstage right, sees destruction.)

FLO: My god—

(Blackout.)

AL'S BUSINESS CARDS

Josh Koenigsberg

JOSH KOENIGSBERG was born in New York City in 1984. He grew up in a converted horse stable in Greenwich Village (where his parents still live), though he now resides in Manhattan's Upper East Side. He holds a BA in philosophy and the arts from Bard College and an MFA in playwriting from Columbia University. About his teachers and mentors, he says, "I studied playwriting at Bard with Chiori Miyagawa and Dominic Taylor, who were both incredible. Then I studied at the Columbia program run by Chuck Mee, who is also incredible. And my personal mentor for the past year or so has been Kenneth Lonergan, who is incredibly incredible." Koenigsberg's produced plays include *Oh the Horror* (Cherry Pit Theater, Naked Angels), *The Dolphins* (staged reading at Atlantic Stage 2), and *Invitation Only* (Center Stage, At Play). He is also a writer for *The Living Newspaper*, an updated version of the classic project that dramatizes real-life news stories that workshopped at Manhattan Theatre Club in 2009. Koenigsberg is a member of the Naked Angels emerging writers group; the Old Vic: New Voices group; The Dramatists Guild; and a founding member of At Play Productions, which is the resident company for the Off-Broadway 24 Hour plays. His recipe for "Josh's Famous Burritos" appeared in the *New York Times*. During the off-season, he works as a farmer at Fishkill Farms in upstate New York. Upcoming projects include a new full-length play, *The Mnemonist of Dutchess County*, *Naked Radio* (a new radio show produced by Naked Angels), and a screenplay co-written with his friend and frequent writing partner Simon Rich.

Al's Business Cards was first presented by At Play Productions (Harrison David Rivers, Artistic Director; Kelcie Beene and Carly Hugo, Producers) in association with Old Vic: New Voices (Kevin Spacey, Artistic Director; Rachael Stevens, New Voices Network Manager) at the Lion Theatre on August 9, 2009, with the following cast and credits:

Al Gurvis .... Azhar Khan
Barry Barrini .... Bobby Moreno
Eileen Lee ....Lauren Hines
Daniel Luce .... Malcolm Madera
Jose Alvarez .... Gabriel Gutiérrez

Directed by: Lauren Keating
Set Design: Jian Jung and Tsubasa Kamei
Costume Design: Melissa Trn
Lighting Design: Tito Fleetwood Ladd
Sound Design: Amy Altadonna
Production Stage Manager: Amanda Kate Joshi

AL'S BUSINESS CARDS

CHARACTERS

AL GURVIS: A gaffing assistant. Light-skinned Indian male who almost looks Hispanic. Has aspirations.

BARRY BARRINI: Al's co-worker. White male. Not the brightest bulb.

EILEEN LEE: A real estate agent. White female. Recovering alcoholic.

DANIEL LUCE: Eileen's soon-to-be-ex-husband. White male. Alcoholic.

JOSE ALVAREZ: Private investigator. Hispanic male. Slick.

TIME

Friday afternoon through Monday morning.

PLACE

Elizabeth, New Jersey.

SCENE 1

Friday afternoon. Two gaffing assistants, BARRY, who's white, and AL, a light-skinned Indian who almost looks Hispanic, stand by a craft service table on a film set in Jersey. BARRY munches from a bag of chips; AL makes himself a coffee and sips it.

AL: Hey, I tell you I got business cards.

BARRY: Who did.

AL: Me—I did.

BARRY: *(Chuckling.)* What? What for?

AL: What do you mean, "what for"?

BARRY: I mean what the hell you need business cards for?

AL: 'Cause I'm in a business, Barry. I'm looking for greater opportunities in the business that I'm in, so I made myself business cards, what's the problem?

(BARRY giggles, shakes his head, and munches. AL sips his coffee.)

AL: Yo, I tell you what happened though?

BARRY: *(Mockingly.)* What, with your business cards?

AL: Yeah with my fucking business cards.

BARRY: *(Laughing.)* What do these business cards say on 'em anyways?

AL: What do you mean, "what do they say on 'em"? They say "Al Gurvis, Professional Gaffing Assistant."

(BARRY bursts out laughing.)

AL: Honest to God, what's your problem?

BARRY: What'd you, hire a secretary also?

AL: *(Shaking his head.)* You're a fuck-stick.

BARRY: Hey, what extension do I dial to get you? Can I borrow the company car?

Hey, how were the profit margins this quarter? *(Chuckles.)* Business cards...

AL: Yeah that's right, business cards! Y'know some people want to advance in the world, not stand around scratching their butt all day, munching loudly on chips or whatever.

(BARRY eats a chip loudly. AL slurps his coffee indignantly.)

AL: I tell you what happened with them though?

BARRY: No, Al—what happened with your business cards.

AL: All right, so I order 'em from ABC Printers, right?—supposedly the best fucking print shop in Jersey—and I get a call last Monday saying they're ready. Fine. I go in, pick 'em up, take 'em home. Know what they say on 'em?

BARRY: No, what do they say on 'em.

AL: They say "Eileen Lee—Executive Realtor."

(AL looks at BARRY expectantly. BARRY munches. They stare at each other.)

AL: They say "Eileen Lee—Executive Realtor."

BARRY: I heard you—who's Eileen Lee.

AL: Not fucking me, that's who. See what happened is they must've mixed up my cards with hers. So I call her up.

BARRY: Wait a minute, you know her?

AL: What? No, fucktard, her number's on the fucking business cards.

BARRY: Oh right, okay.

AL: So I call her up, I go "Is this Eileen Lee, Executive Realtor?" She goes, "Yeah, who's this." I go "It's Al Gurvis, I got your business cards." She goes "Great, I'll be in to pick 'em up this week." I go, "Nah nah, it's not the printers calling, honey. It's *me*, Al Gurvis. I got your business cards."

BARRY: *(Chuckling.)* What do you, gotta spell it out for her?

AL: I know, right? She's like, "Wait a minute—*Al Gurvis*—where do I know that name from. Are you in the program?"

BARRY: *"Program"*—what program?

AL: Oh that's what they call AA, I think.

BARRY: Jesus, she's an alcoholic to boot?

AL: What do you mean, "to boot?" Nah, she's in recovery or whatever.

BARRY: Aw, that's a myth.

AL: Huh?

BARRY: "Recovery." You are who you are—once an alcoholic, always an alcoholic.

AL: Well that's your opinion.

BARRY: What, you don't agree?

AL: The point is I'm like, "No, you don't know me from the fucking program. You know me 'cause you got my business cards and I got yours."

BARRY: What, she didn't notice?

AL: No, she's like "I *do*?" I'm like "*Yes*, you do. *That's* how come you know my name, honey." So she checks, sure enough she finds 'em. She goes "Ohhh, that's right! So *you're* Al Gurvis." I go "Yes, I'm Al Gurvis—Professional Gaffing Assistant."

BARRY: *(Chuckling.)* Why the fuck did you write "Professional Gaffing

Assistant?" Why not just call yourself "Electrician"? They're practically the same thing.

AL: 'Cause I'm not an electrician, I'm a professional gaffing assistant.

BARRY: Yeah, but no one's gonna know what that is. I don't even think that's a real title.

AL: No, but y'know—they'll probably go, "Professional gaffing assistant—what's that? Oh it's probably like an electrician. I know—I'll hire him to do electrical work."

BARRY: Who the fuck is gonna say that?

AL: Y'know—people. People are smart.

BARRY: If they're so smart, they'll know the difference between a licensed electrician and "Professional Gaffing Assistant." Just say "Electrician."

AL: Nah, I'm not gonna lie.

BARRY: Well Jesus, Al, you're misleading them as it is.

AL: What do you mean I'm misleading them as it is?

BARRY: C'mon, Al. *(Beat.)* Y'know.

AL: No, I don't know—what are you talking about?

BARRY: What, I gotta say it?

AL: Say what?

BARRY: Jesus Christ. Look, even if they're idiots, and they say, "Oh he's not a licensed electrician, he's close enough, we'll hire him anyways"—don't you think they're gonna feel a *little* misled when they hire "Al Gurvis" and *you* show up?

AL: Why wouldn't I show up? I'm Al Gurvis.

BARRY: I know you're Al Gurvis. But Christ, Al—they think they're hiring a white electrician and instead they get this lying Hispanic? Your credibility's gonna go to shit.

(AL slurps his coffee.)

BARRY: Nah, I mean I'm not saying…I mean look, it could be worse. It's not like you're from the Middle East or something. Some *towel-head*. Nah, I'm just saying, as long as you're a Hispanic guy with an American guy's name, you might as well call yourself an "Electrician."

(BARRY grabs a can of soda and opens it. They stare at each other.)

AL: First off? I'm Indian.

BARRY: Who's Indian.

AL: Me. I'm Indian.

BARRY: Who *you*? You're not Indian.

AL: Uh, yes actually. Yes I am.

BARRY: *(Looks him over.)* Nah.

AL: No, I'm not asking you. I'm telling you—I'm Indian. I'm half-Indian.

BARRY: Half-Indian, half-Hispanic?

AL: No, just half-Indian.

BARRY: And the other half—what, half-American?

AL: *(Annoyed.)* Well, I'd like to think I'm *all* American.

BARRY: Well not technically.

AL: Look, my mom grew up in India! My dad's, I don't know, some kind of Irish. But I grew up here, I don't have a fucking accent.

BARRY: No, I know—I didn't say that. I know your deal. I just thought your mom was from Mexico or whatever.

AL: Well she's not, she's from India, so what's your point?

BARRY: Huh? No I don't have a *point*, I'm just saying. Y'know—be careful. 'Cause the world's a fucked-up place, y'know? No, I did not know that you were from India or whatever. *(Munches awkwardly.)* Man I'm tired, I got like no sleep last night. *(Offering the bag.)* Hey, you want some?

AL: No, I don't wanna touch 'em with my lying Hispanic hands.

BARRY: Aw, c'mon. Besides you said you weren't Hispanic.

AL: Oh—so what, if I was, you wouldn't give me none?

BARRY: What? No! But y'know it's a moot point, or whatever. I mean Indian's good. Indian's better.

AL: Indian's *better*?

BARRY: What? No, c'mon I'm giving you a compliment here.

AL: Oh, you're giving me a *compliment*?

BARRY: Jesus, why's everyone so sensitive these days! We're just talking here.

AL: All right, let me ask you a question, Barry. Let's say someone gets my business card.

BARRY: *(Trying to lighten the mood.)* Yeah after you get 'em back from that alcoholic, am I right?

(BARRY smiles. AL doesn't.)

AL: Let's say someone gets my card…

BARRY: Uh huh…

AL: Wants to hire me…

BARRY: *Very* possible…

AL: Then I show up. Are they gonna be pissed that I'm a lying Indian?

BARRY: No!

(AL nods and walks away.)

BARRY: But y'know, 'cause you'll tell them.

AL: *(Stops and turns back.)* What'll I tell them?

BARRY: Y'know. That you're only *half* or whatever. I mean I think we're in agreement here.

AL: No, we're not in agreement.

BARRY: *(Snaps his fingers.)* I got it: you put your picture on the business card.

AL: My what? My *picture*?

BARRY: Yeah, you get 'em back from this Real Estate Drunk and then you redo 'em. You put your picture on the card. That way, if someone wants to hire you, they'll know what they're getting themselves into.

AL: Y'know what? Fuck you.

BARRY: Fuck me? What for?

AL: 'Cause you're an idiot! If someone gets my card, wants to hire me, they're not gonna give a shit what I look like! If anything, it's a, it's a…*pleasant surprise*!

BARRY: Hey look Al, I'm with you. *(Beat.)* But it's just not true.

AL: Oh really? So what—you think when I go to pick up the cards from this Eileen Lee, she's gonna see me, scream, and run in the other direction?

BARRY: What, you're gonna go see her? Today?

AL: Yeah, after work or whatever. I made a "date" or whatever to pick 'em up.

BARRY: *"A date"? (Looks at him curiously.)* When was the last time you got laid?

AL: What? Fuck you. I gotta use the bathroom.

BARRY: Okay, how about this: let's make a wager.

AL: A what? No.

BARRY: Aw, c'mon, this is perfect! You're gonna go see Eileen Lee—okay. She'll be our guinea pig. If she doesn't say anything about how your name and face don't match—you win.

AL: What'll I win?

BARRY: You win, uh…I don't know, a box of fucking chocolates.

(AL starts walking away.)

BARRY: *Ghirardelli* chocolates.

AL: *(He loves those.)* All right, fine. Now I gotta use the bathroom before break's up.

BARRY: Whoa, whoa, whoa. What if you lose.

AL: I won't. She's not gonna say anything.

BARRY: Yeah, but what if she does.

AL: Jesus Christ, Barry, I don't know. I'll get *you* a box of chocolates.

BARRY: I don't like chocolates.

AL: Well what *do* you like?

BARRY: Scotch.

AL: Fine. It's a little expensive, but okay, I'll buy you a bottle of cheap scotch. But trust me, she's not gonna say anything.

BARRY: What makes you so sure?

AL: 'Cause that's my whole point—you got a pessimistic outlook on life and people don't work that way! Besides, we're talking about a nice polite Asian girl here.

BARRY: Asian? What did she, have an accent on the phone?

AL: What? No, but c'mon—Eileen *Lee*?

BARRY: Whatever. It's a deal though, right?

AL: Yeah, okay, it's a deal.

(BARRY wipes his Frito hand on his pants and offers it to AL. AL shakes on it. BARRY pulls him in close.)

BARRY: Remember, we're using the Honor System here. Don't go lying to me and telling me on Monday that she didn't say nothing if she did. I'll be able to see it on your face.

(The buzzer rings, signaling the end of the break.)

AL: Aw, great. All right, I gotta use the bathroom.

BARRY: That's three times you told me. What do you, want me to wipe your ass for you?

SCENE 2

Friday afternoon, later. AL sits at a Starbucks, drinking a coffee. A box of business cards sits on the table in front of him. His leg shakes from all the caffeine. He looks around for EILEEN LEE. From behind him, EILEEN LEE walks in, dressed in a well-fitting suit. She is not Asian. She looks around and sees the box on AL's table. She approaches him tentatively.

EILEEN: Al Gurvis?

AL: *(Turns to look at her.)* Yeah.

EILEEN: *(Extending a hand.)* Hi. Eileen Lee.

AL: Really?

EILEEN: Really. *(Smiling.)* Let me guess—you thought I'd be Asian.

AL: Who me? No, no. *(Beat.)* Why—you get that a lot?

EILEEN: Um, from time to time. It's the name I guess. Although I don't really get the connection. I mean the general of the confederate army was named Robert E. Lee, so. Who knows?

(She shrugs and smiles politely. AL nods, staring at her. He's very attracted to her.)

EILEEN: Sorry to sneak up on you like that by the way.

AL: Yeah I was gonna say, I was looking for you over by, uh…by here. So were you in the bathroom this whole time?

EILEEN: Uh, no, I just came in. There's another door, right there.

AL: *(Seeing it.)* Oh, no kidding. Hey, to think, I could've come in that way. *(Smiles like he's just made a joke.)*

EILEEN: Yup. That's another way to come in.

AL: Yeah. So you want a coffee or something?

EILEEN: Oh. I, uh, I would, but I was just sort of on my way home. Well, I was heading to a meeting first, and *then* I was going home, but anyway. Y'know it's funny actually—I expected you to look a little different too.

AL: *(Sensing disaster.)* What, you mean like 'cause of my voice on the phone, you thought I'd be younger or something.

EILEEN: No, actually I expected you be, uh, well…white.

(EILEEN shrugs and chuckles. AL nods, upset that he's lost the bet.)

EILEEN: Sorry—was that inappropriate to say?

AL: Nah, nah. *(Disappointed.)* Y'know, it's just the world we live in, right?

EILEEN: No, but I was going to say, if anything, I'm glad I was wrong. I mean if anything, it's a…a pleasant surprise, y'know?

AL: *(Excited.)* It *is*, right! I mean you don't want to see another boring white guy walking around Jersey, right?

EILEEN: *(Agreeing.)* Oh no—definitely not! I mean you're, what—Indian? Half-Indian?

AL: Half-Indian, that's right!

EILEEN: Yeah, that's much more interesting. And what's the other half?

AL: Oh, uh, some kind of Irish, I don't know. I didn't really know my dad that well.

EILEEN: Oh. Well who cares, right?

AL: Yes exactly—who cares! The important thing is that it was a *pleasant surprise*, am I right? *(To himself.)* No, I think I won this bet.

EILEEN: Hmm? What bet?

AL: Oh no—it was just this little thing. Me and my buddy, y'know.

EILEEN: You and your buddy?

AL: Yeah, he's a *(Makes a jerking-off motion.)*. He thought when you saw me you'd be like horrified or something.

EILEEN: That I'd be horrified?

AL: Or y'know—"freaked out" or whatever. That my name and face don't match.

EILEEN: Well your friend obviously doesn't have a very positive or mature outlook on life.

AL: *(So excited he tries to say three things at once.)* Ye—Exa—Okay, now I *have* to buy you a cup of coffee.

EILEEN: Oh no, really that's okay.

AL: Listen, take it to go if you want. Take it to your meeting or what have you. But I am buying you this cup of coffee. How do you like it?

EILEEN: Um, well with half-and-half and sugar, but—

AL: Okay—small, medium, or large?

EILEEN: Um, I usually get a grande, but—

AL: One grande coffee coming right up.

(AL exits towards the side where EILEEN came in. EILEEN stands there. She sees the box on the table. She goes to open it.)

AL: *(Reentering.)* They ran out of grande cups. You want a small or a large?

EILEEN: Oh, uh, I'll just take a tall then.

AL: *(Beat.)* That's a small, right?

EILEEN: Yes, right.

(AL nods and exits. EILEEN watches him go. She opens the box and checks the cards inside, making sure they look right. She closes it up again. AL reenters with a cup.)

AL: And here is one tall coffee on me.

EILEEN: Well thank you very much Al.

AL: Listen, it's the least I could do considering you just won me a box of my favorite chocolates—Ghirardelli chocolates. You ever have those? They sell 'em at that place Vintage Chocolates on Atalanta Plaza. You ever been there?

EILEEN: No, I don't think so.

AL: Oh it's great, you gotta check it out—just past the Turnpike. It's like two minutes from my place on Livingston and New Point. But y'know, I don't go that often 'cause of, y'know—

(AL pats his stomach, signaling that he doesn't want to get too fat. EILEEN smiles and nods. She points to the box.)

EILEEN: So are those the, uh…?

AL: Huh? Oh yeah, I got your cards right here. *(Chuckling.)* We got so carried away, I almost forgot. Here.

(He hands the box to her. She takes them.)

EILEEN: Great. Thanks. *(She opens them up and looks at them.)*

EILEEN: Oh they look great. Y'know they really *do* do a good job over there.

AL: Oh at ABC? Yeah, best print shop in Jersey, you ask me.

EILEEN: Definitely. Well anyway, thanks so much Al. It was great meeting you.

AL: Yeah, you too.

EILEEN: *(Getting up.)* And, uh, good luck with everything.

AL: Yeah, same. *(Making a joke.)* Hey good luck with the name!

EILEEN: *(Starts to leave. Smiling.)* Thanks.

AL: Yeah. *(Suddenly realizing.)* Hey hold up—Eileen.

EILEEN: Hmmm?

AL: You got mine too, right?

EILEEN: Your…?

AL: Y'know, my business cards.

EILEEN: Oh. Uh, no I dropped them off at the printers.

AL: What, at ABC?

EILEEN: Yeah. Oh my God, I thought—I thought I told you on the phone. I dropped them off right after you called last Monday, so you could pick them up if you needed them.

AL: Oh. Well so you couldn't've told me on the phone. Y'know, if you did it *after* we spoke.

EILEEN: *(Embarrassed.)* Right. God, I'm such an idiot. I'm so sorry.

AL: *(Trying not to be mad.)* Nah, nah. That's, uh, that's okay. Uh. Let me just call 'em up, I'm sure they have 'em. *(Takes out his cell phone.)*

EILEEN: Okay. God, I'm so sorry. In hindsight, it seems really dumb.

AL: *(Dialing.)* Yup. *(Listens to the phone ring. And ring.)* Aw great, they're fucking closed!

EILEEN: *(A little shocked by his obscenity.)* Oh. Uh, gee.

AL: Y'know, it's just that they're closed for the whole fucking weekend now.

EILEEN: Oh my God, really?

AL: Yeah, they close for the weekends there—bunch of fucking amateurs! *(Notices his language has upset EILEEN.)* Oh. Uh, sorry, I don't mean to curse so much.

EILEEN: No, I understand. I mean who closes their business on the weekends, right?

AL: A bunch of fucking amateurs, that's who! Aw crap, there I go again. Sorry.

EILEEN: No, that's fine.

AL: Hey you don't know offhand if they looked okay? My business cards, I mean.

EILEEN: Oh. Uh, I think they were fine. I mean I took one out when you called, just to check the name on it. I don't think I noticed anything wrong.

AL: So it said "Al Gurvis" and it spelled it G-U-R-V-I-S.

EILEEN: Yup, I think so. It said, "Al Gurvis—Professional Gassing Assistant."

AL: Wait a minute—it said *what*?

EILEEN: Uh, it said "Al Gurvis—Professional Gassing Assistant."

AL: Aw f—*(Stops himself from cursing. He composes himself.)* It's "Professional Gaffing Assistant." Not, uh, not "Gassing." "*Gassing*?!"

EILEEN: *(Chuckling.)* Oh my God, you're kidding. They didn't send you a proof?

AL: Nope. Nope!

EILEEN: And they're usually so good there. I guess the F's must've looked like S's?

AL: Yeah well. *(Beat.)* Anyway, it's not your problem, right?

(AL sighs and sits down. EILEEN watches him, guiltily, not knowing what to do. She goes back to the table.)

EILEEN: Tell you what, let me—let me buy *you* a cup of coffee.

AL: Huh? Oh no—that's all right. I got one already. Besides, it's not your fault.

EILEEN: Well, one—it sort of is. And two—I should at least repay the favor. Tell you what—I'll get you a pastry instead, how's that?

AL: A pastry? What, like one of those banana ones there?

EILEEN: Yeah, I'll get you a banana one. It's the least I can do for screwing this up.

(AL shrugs, clearly wanting one. EILEEN puts her box down and goes to get a pastry. AL waits until she's out of sight, then opens the box of cards and pockets one. He smells himself and fixes his hair. EILEEN comes back with a pastry.)

EILEEN: So just out of curiosity, what *is* a Professional Gaffing Assistant anyway?

AL: Oh, it's sort of like an electrician. You help out with electrical work on film and TV sets. *(Takes a huge bite of the pastry.)*

EILEEN: Oh that's so cool. So do you, like, work with a bunch of celebrities and stuff?

AL: *(With his mouth full.)* No, not really.

(EILEEN nods, disappointed.)

AL: Well sometimes. Sometimes! Actually, you know who's on the set that I'm working on now is, uh, what's his face—John Stamos.

EILEEN: No!

AL: Yeah, we talked about the weather the other day. And uh, Robin Tunney—you know her?

EILEEN: Sure! She was in that horror movie a while back! Oh my God, so what movie is it?

AL: Uh, it's called *Killing Mr. Kissel*. Or *The Two Mr. Kissels*? Y'know it's for Lifetime.

EILEEN: Oh okay. So you work for Lifetime.

AL: Who me? Nah. I mostly do freelance stuff.

EILEEN: Ah, I see. And is it steady work?

AL: Steady enough that I got a shitty one-bedroom that smells like cat piss.

EILEEN: Oh I love cats, how many do you have?

AL: Who me? Nah, I don't got any, I'm allergic.

EILEEN: Oh.

AL: Oh, no, but my place is on Livingston and New Point, so, y'know—it stinks.

EILEEN: Uh huh. Well *(Clears her throat.)* I mean, I hope you don't mind me asking, but how much do you pull down after taxes?

AL: Who me? I don't know, about thirty. Thirty-five.

EILEEN: Wait, and you're living on Livingston and New Point?

AL: Yeah, why—I could do better?

EILEEN: You're kidding right?

(AL shakes his head, shrugs. EILEEN opens up her business card box and takes one out. She takes out a pen and writes on the back.)

EILEEN: *(Writing.)* Oh my God this is so perfect. This is like fate or something. You know I do this for a living right? Listen Al—if you're making thirty to thirty-five a year, the idea that you're living at Livingston and New Point is laughable. I mean you're practically *on* the Turnpike!

AL: It *is* sort of a shithole. And y'know I'm trying to branch out and do electrical work too—so that would be like an extra five G's a year. Ten if I'm lucky.

EILEEN: *(Hands him the card.)* Well what do you think about Westminster Ave.

AL: *Westminster Ave*?? You're fucking kidding, right?

EILEEN: That's the thing Al—I'm *not* fucking kidding.

(AL smiles at her vulgarity.)

EILEEN: *(Pointing to the card.)* Look, come meet me at this address on Sunday morning—they're having an open house. First of all, it's this beautiful two bedroom, two bathroom. Backyard, patio, the works. And second of all, the sellers are in a rush to turn it so it's going way less than market value. Now obviously I can't guarantee anything, but trust me, for a guy making thirty to thirty-five a year, it shouldn't be a problem.

AL: You serious? 'Cause I tell you—if there's one place that don't smell like cat piss, it's Westminster Ave.

EILEEN: *(Chuckling.)* It's true. And not only that. But we'd be neighbors.

(AL stares at her, thinking about the possibilities.)

SCENE 3

Friday night. The small kitchen of a modest house. Something drops loudly from another room. DANIEL, wearing a business suit and a ski mask, lugs a TV set into the kitchen. He puts it down to catch his breath. He takes out a flask and swigs. He looks around the room, as if recalling memories of happier times, and takes another swig. EILEEN enters from the back door and throws her keys into a dish. DANIEL turns around suddenly at the sound. They stare at each other.

DANIEL: Oh what? You got something to say to me? Thinking of some witty zinger to throw my way? Well look at you—aren't you so smart. Aren't you so great with your little organized life, throwing your little organized keys into your happy little key dish. What great little nooks and crannies you've decorated this place with! *(Grabbing things.)* Oh look here's a nook! Here's a nook! Look, a house full of nooks, a house full of nooks! Well nook it up, baby! That's right, that's what I say. Go on. Cover your whole little wonderful happy life with more happy little nooks! That'll make it all more *palatable*, more *agreeable*. Yes, let's all just agree, we don't want any conflict! Oh no—we don't like any yelling and screaming! And for your information, yes I have been drinking again, and no, it doesn't interfere with my life. Maybe the weaker willed of us can't handle it, but I can. I'm strong! *(Goes to the TV and lifts it.)* See! I'm strong and I'm on top of things for your information, and in case you're wondering my new apartment is nicer than your house! Hear what I said? *Your* house, it's *your* house. I don't care. I'm happy. Enjoy *your* house. Go on, buy some more nooks for *your* house! See if *that* helps!

EILEEN: Why are you wearing a ski mask?

DANIEL: 'Cause the fall air dries out my skin!

(They stare at each other. DANIEL takes off the ski mask.)

DANIEL: And I didn't want our neighbors to see me. Oh excuse me—*your* neighbors. They're *your* neighbors now. No that's okay, that's fine.

EILEEN: Daniel.

DANIEL: What.

EILEEN: Give me the keys.

DANIEL: For your information, I don't have the keys! I gave 'em back to you weeks ago, remember?! No, what happened is you stupidly left the door unlocked! I guess you don't care if *your* house is now open to the public.

EILEEN: Daniel.

DANIEL: What?! Stop saying my name like that!

EILEEN: Give me the keys.

DANIEL: *(Sighs. Reaches into his pocket and takes out a set of keys. Places them in the key dish in an overly gentle way. In a baby voice.)* There you go wittle key dish. There you go. *(Walks back to the TV set.)* Now, if you'll excuse me, I have to get home to my new apartment so I can watch the last episode of *Planet Earth*—or as I like to call it—*What Used to Be Our Favorite Show!* *(Picks up the TV set.)*

EILEEN: Put it down or I'm calling the cops.

DANIEL: *(Imitating her.)* "*Put it down or I'm calling the cops.*"

EILEEN: Daniel.

DANIEL: *Eileen. Eileen.*

(EILEEN glares at him. He puts the TV down and takes another swig from his flask.)

EILEEN: All right—one: I should call the cops. But I won't, all right?

DANIEL: Oooo—my lucky day! Maybe I should play the lotto!

EILEEN: Two—you need to get yourself to a meeting. Like *tonight*. There's a nine o'clock on Monroe Ave—I'll drive you. *(Beat.)* It's right next to Valencia.

DANIEL: *(Suddenly becomes sad.)* Valencia, huh? Our old stomping grounds. *(Beat.)* You wanna get dinner there afterwards?

EILEEN: If it'll get you to the meeting, then yes, I'll buy you dinner at Valencia afterwards.

DANIEL: I didn't say *buy*, I said *get*! I can still pay for my own dinner thank you very much! I'm still vice president of sales at Men's Warehouse—which is doing just fine, thank you!

EILEEN: Fine, then you can buy *me* dinner.

DANIEL: Freeloader.

EILEEN: Y'know what? Just get out then!

(She grabs him and pushes him towards the door.)

EILEEN: You wanna drink your life away, go ahead. I don't give a shit what happens to you! Just don't go calling me when you're lying in a ditch somewhere about to die and everyone's wondering what happened to you!

(EILEEN composes herself. DANIEL sighs. He goes over to her.)

DANIEL: *(Tenderly.)* C'mon—why can't we just be friends?

EILEEN: Y'know, that's what I'm trying to do and you're making it very difficult.

DANIEL: I know. I know. I'll stop, okay? I'll clean myself up. I promise. I mean we still *care* about each other, right? You still think about me from time to time, right?

(EILEEN nods.)

DANIEL: I mean we're getting separated—so what?

EILEEN: We're getting divorced.

DANIEL: Look, call it what you want. My point is, it doesn't mean we have to stop caring about each other. Or thinking about each other. Missing each other.

(DANIEL puts his arms around EILEEN's waist and goes to kiss her neck.)

EILEEN: *(Pushing him away.)* Are you serious?!

DANIEL: What?!

EILEEN: You smell like gin.

DANIEL: I'll shower!

EILEEN: Get the hell out of here!

DANIEL: C'mon, you were asking for it!

EILEEN: Oh please! One—I wasn't asking for it. And two—you *broke* into my house!

DANIEL: Oh, if it isn't Ms. Lists Things In Numerical Order!

EILEEN: All right, get out before I call the cops. Or better yet, before I call my lawyer!

DANIEL: Look at me, I'm Ms. Lister! Ms. Lister-ine! Well I've got a list for you! One—go ahead and call your goddamn lawyer, 'cause I am taking *everything* in this settlement of ours! And two—I got dirt on you like you wouldn't believe.

EILEEN: That's great. Get out.

DANIEL: Don't believe me?

EILEEN: No.

DANIEL: All right then—let me ask you a question.

EILEEN: No.

DANIEL: Who the fuck is Al Gurvis?

EILEEN: *(Beat.)* Excuse me?

DANIEL: You heard me. Who the fuck is Al Gurvis?

EILEEN: How the hell do you even know that name?

DANIEL: You mean how do I know the name of your new little Lover Boy? That's easy. You left his business card by the phone. *(Baby voice.)* While you were making a wittle date.

EILEEN: He's not my—he's a client, okay?

DANIEL: Oh a *client*? Is that what they're calling it these days?

EILEEN: Okay: one—

(EILEEN catches herself listing things and stops. DANIEL looks at her expectantly.)

EILEEN: He's a client and that's all. In fact, I'm taking him to the Gerstens' open house on Sunday. God, why am I even telling you this?! Just give me back the card.

DANIEL: What card?

EILEEN: Daniel, I'm not in the mood.

DANIEL: What, his business card? I don't fucking have it! I saw it last Monday when I came to pick my shit up.

(EILEEN glares at him.)

DANIEL: I don't!

EILEEN: Oh, like you didn't have my keys!

(DANIEL unbuckles his belt and starts pulling down his pants.)

EILEEN: What the hell are you doing?

DANIEL: *(Pulls down his pants.)* Strip search me, why don't you. Go ahead! Examine my cavities!

EILEEN: Just empty your pockets.

DANIEL: *(Pulls on the sides of his underwear.)* Here, look—see? I No Havey.

EILEEN: You're an asshole. I know you're lying.

DANIEL: *(Imitating her style of speech.)* One—I don't have it. Two—I don't have it. Three—

EILEEN: It better be by the fucking phone.

(EILEEN storms out of the room. DANIEL waits for her to go. He lifts the TV and waddles out with it.)

SCENE 4

Saturday morning. The offices of JOSE ALVAREZ, a private investigator. JOSE sits at his desk in a shirt and tie, on the phone.

JOSE: So take it to a repair shop, Ma. What do you mean "por que"? So you can watch your telenovelas is por que. Nah, I can't go with you Ma, I'm busy. Yeah, I saw the lawyer—he's all bark and no bite. Yeah, he threatened me, but so what? Don't worry what he said. He said: *(Reading from his notepad.)* "If I persisted to bedevil the multitudes of his reputable patronages he would ceaselessly endeavor to discredit the sanctity of my private investigative license, with the same aplomb which I had employed in my inceptive receipt of it." Yeah, that's right. Well, he knew a lot of sentences like that and he didn't mind using them on me. No se mamá. Porque ese hombre esta loco. No te preocupes yo me puedo cuidar solo.

(DANIEL comes in, hung over, still in the suit from the last scene. He plops himself down at JOSE's desk. JOSE glares at him.)

JOSE: Okay, Ma. Yeah, Ma, okay. Look, I gotta go. Por que un borracho de mierda acaba de entrar en mi oficina y puede que tenga que llamar a la policía. So I gotta go. Yeah I love you too, Ma. Hasta luego. *(Hangs up.)*

DANIEL: What's that, Spanish?

JOSE: *(Looks at DANIEL and starts clapping.)* Aw, very good, you're a real fucking genius. *(Stops clapping.)* Don't you fucking knock?

DANIEL: *(Holding his temples.)* Can you not do that.

JOSE: What, this?

(JOSE claps louder. DANIEL grimaces.)

DANIEL: Okay, Jesus! I'll knock next time! I just thought we had an appointment is all.

JOSE: When you have an appointment with a doctor, you just stroll into his office, and take your clothes off? No you sit and you wait to be called in. It's a sign of respect. Especially when you make him see you on a Saturday morning.

DANIEL: Yeah, yeah—what do you got?

JOSE: *(Takes out a notepad from his back pocket. Opens it up and reads from it.)* All right, she left the office at quarter to five. Drove straight to the Starbucks on Kapkowski Road, where she talked with this Gurvis guy for about an hour and half.

DANIEL: An hour and half?! What about her meeting?

JOSE: The AA meeting? Didn't go to it.

DANIEL: That hypocritical little...no wonder she walked in on me at the house.

JOSE: You mean *her* house?

DANIEL: Oh whatever. What's he look like?

JOSE: Who Gurvis? He's like a light-skinned Indian version of me.

DANIEL: He's Native American?

JOSE: Huh? No dipshit, *Indian*. As in really Indian. Not everyone's a racist.

DANIEL: Well what'd they talk about?

JOSE: Well the high-powered, state-of-the-art microphone I have attached to the end of this notepad recorded everything.

DANIEL: You serious?

JOSE: No you dumb shit—I have no fucking clue what they talked about. Ask them.

DANIEL: What about the card?

JOSE: You mean the business card you swiped and gave me last Monday?

DANIEL: *(Annoyed.)* Yeah, yeah—Gurvis's card. You trace it?

JOSE: You mean the business card you swiped and gave me last Monday—which I told you last Monday would cost you five hundred dollars to analyze? Five hundred dollars, which may I remind you, I have yet to see.

DANIEL: I told you I'm good for it.

JOSE: And I think it's good for you, and I'm so happy that the two of you are good for each other.

DANIEL: *(Gets up.)* You know what? I've had enough of your goddamn attitude. I am too hung over to deal with this shit. So either you start treating me, your client, with some respect or I walk.

JOSE: *(Waving.)* Bye-bye.

DANIEL: *(Sighs.)* You at least have an Excedrin?

(JOSE tosses him a vial of Excedrin.)

DANIEL: Water?

JOSE: For clients only. Toilet water's free, though.

DANIEL: All right look—I got *(Pulls out all the money on him.)* three twenties. That's sixty.

JOSE: So you get three twenties' worth. Which is what I already told you.

DANIEL: Please, Jose—

JOSE: It's Mr. Alvarez.

DANIEL: Please Mr. Alvarez—I need to know this! How about we strike a deal—you need men's wear, designer jackets, suits tailor made? I can get 'em for you at the Men's Warehouse—and you're gonna like the way you look, I guarantee it!

JOSE: See, the beautiful thing about five hundred dollars is that it can buy *plenty* of clothes. Or it can buy booze. Or lotto tickets so I can win *more* money.

DANIEL: Okay, so how about this: two suits and I'll give you the three twenties I have now, *plus* the other four thirty I owe you in a month!

JOSE: *(Correcting.)* Four forty. Four thirty makes four ninety and you owe me five.

DANIEL: Right—plus two suits! *(Takes his sports coat off.)* And a sports coat! Please I have to know! *(Beat.)* Look, you deal with lawyers right?

JOSE: All the fucking time.

DANIEL: Well her lawyer—he's this guy named Goldberg.

JOSE: A lawyer Goldberg huh?

DANIEL: Yeah, he's a real ball-buster—and he's gonna take me for all I'm worth in this goddamn settlement! But not if I get the dirt on her! I mean do you know how much this hurts already—getting dumped like this? And now, on top of all that, she's stepping out on me? And I gotta pay the price for it? That's not right! I mean why me?

JOSE: Look—now you've put *me* in a pickle, Mr. Luce.

DANIEL: Call me Daniel. Please.

JOSE: You've put *me* in a pickle, Mr. Luce. 'Cause I asked a favor from a friend in forensics. He's a busy guy, he don't play with those tools of his for nothing. He's on a payroll, he could get fired. So I ask him for a favor and he does it for a price. Favors for cash, straight up, ka-ching. So now *I'm* in a pickle.

DANIEL: Here, so you give him this money now—and I'll give you double what I owe in one month, when this is all settled! Just one month! *And* a sports coat!

JOSE: I thought you said two suits.

DANIEL: Plus that! Just please! The card!

JOSE: *(Sighs. Reaches into his inside pocket and pulls out the business card, which is in a tight plastic seal.)* Tests on fingerprints came back positive on your wife—sorry, *ex*-wife—and positive on you, presumably from when you stole it. Negative on Gurvis.

DANIEL: Negative on Gurvis? How's that possible? *(Snaps his fingers.)* He must have assistants. I bet the fucker's loaded—a real power player.

JOSE: I doubt it. The guy's an assistant himself. A... *(Looks at the card.)* ..."Gassing Assistant."

DANIEL: Oh yeah, what is that?

JOSE: Don't know for sure. I know a gasser's a term for those old, top-heavy, 1950s muscle cars. So if he's a "Gassing Assistant" my guess is he works at one of those fancy appointment-only auto showrooms. They got weird names for those specialty jobs.

DANIEL: So what—you think he works at Autohaus on Rahway Ave?

JOSE: Nah, that's a used car dealership. If this guy works on gassers, it's gotta be at some place more upscale.

DANIEL: Upscale, huh? I knew it—the guy's fucking loaded.

JOSE: There's more though. The card was traced back to ABC Printers on Jefferson.

DANIEL: Well sure—best print shop in Jersey, you ask me.

JOSE: Well I went down there. Apparently I wasn't the only one asking about your wife.

DANIEL: *Ex*-wife. What do you mean.

JOSE: *(Consulting the notebook.)* Guy named Barry Barrini. You know him.

(DANIEL shakes his head.)

JOSE: Well according to the clerk, he's got short black hair, medium build—looks mildly retarded? Anyway, clerk says he came in just before I did yesterday afternoon, right before they closed. Asked if Eileen Lee had been in.

DANIEL: Jesus, how many guys is she sleeping with?! Listen, you gotta find out about this Barry Barrini guy! You gotta track him down and tail him!

JOSE: Well that would require more money, Mr. Luce. And you already owe me twice what you owed, along with two suits and a sports coat. So I doubt I'll be doing that. But what I will do if you don't pay me is I'll sue. I'll sue your pants off and wear those along with the sports coat. And who knows, maybe I'll just hire this Goldberg guy to represent me. That would teach you a thing or two.

DANIEL: *(Suddenly gets an idea.)* How about if I throw in a TV set?

JOSE: *(Starts to say no, but then considers it.)* Y'know, my mom *could* use a TV, actually.

SCENE 5

Sunday afternoon. A bar. BARRY stands at a table, watching the Mets game on a bar TV. He holds a beer, which he sips periodically. JOSE sits in the corner with a beer, reading a paper, looking discreetly at BARRY.

BARRY: *(To the TV set.)* C'mon Reyes, run it out. Run it out. *(Victoriously.)* Boom! There it is! Stolen base number sixty. *(BARRY looks around to see if anyone else is celebrating. He notices JOSE looking at him and feels a little self-conscious. Pointing to TV set.)* Fastest person to sixty steals in a season. Well, fastest Met anyways.

JOSE: He's the best.

BARRY: *(Disappointed.)* Yeah, he won't break the record though.

(JOSE shrugs and nods as if to say "What can you do?" BARRY nods and looks at the TV again. JOSE gets up and goes to BARRY.)

JOSE: Hey, I don't got my glasses on—what's the score?

BARRY: Four, two—Mets.

JOSE: All right—we might actually win today, huh?

BARRY: Yeah, tell me about it. They've lost five in a row now.

JOSE: It's five in a row they've lost?

BARRY: Five! Count 'em! Three to fucking Cincinnati, two straight to Florida. Last time they won was last Sunday—that's a full fucking week ago!

JOSE: Shiiiit. They should've beat Cincinnati at least once.

BARRY: Y'know what they do is they beat the good teams, but they lose to the bad ones. Problem is there's more bad teams than good ones, so they lose more than they don't.

JOSE: Makes sense.

BARRY: It ain't 'cause of Reyes though. That guy can rake.

(JOSE nods.)

BARRY: Hey, what's Reyes—Hispanic or black?

JOSE: Who Reyes? Uh… *(Has no idea which one is Reyes.)* …Hispanic I think.

BARRY: Yeah, but ain't he kind of dark for a Hispanic guy? I mean don't he sort of look black?

(JOSE shrugs, nods.)

BARRY: Well I guess you would know better than me, right?

(JOSE gives BARRY a look.)

BARRY: Nah, I mean…I don't mean, uh… *(Sighs.)* It's just lately I've been unsure about this, y'know? Fucking guy I work with? He's Indian.

JOSE: Oh yeah?

BARRY: Yeah, y'know. No biggie. It's just...I thought he was Hispanic for the longest time.

JOSE: They don't really look alike though.

BARRY: Well not usually, no. But my buddy—he sort of looks like both.

JOSE: Huh. Well, y'know what I say.

BARRY: No, what.

JOSE: Everyone keeps fucking each other, we're all gonna look the same soon.

BARRY: *(Laughs heartily. Going for a cheers.)* Hey, here fucking here! To boning each other!

(They clink glasses and laugh.)

JOSE: Yeah. My girlfriend's been driving me nuts, though. You got a girl?

BARRY: Who me? Nah. Not at the moment. Got laid two Thursdays ago though.

JOSE: Oh yeah? One-night stand sort of thing?

BARRY: Y'know.

(BARRY makes a pounding motion and laughs. JOSE laughs and nods.)

JOSE: Yeah. Truth be told, I, uh, sort of cheated on my girlfriend a week ago myself.

BARRY: Hey no kidding.

JOSE: Yeah, you know how it is. *(Chuckles.)* Got too drunk...

BARRY: *(Laughing.)* Uh oh!

JOSE: *(Laughing.)* Yeah it was with this real estate chick—real hot.

BARRY: Oh yeah? No shit. *(To the TV.)* Aw, look at this, they fucking strike out with the bases loaded!

JOSE: Unbelievable. *(Beat.)* No I was gonna say though—all those real estate chicks? Man, they're *all* fucking hot.

BARRY: Yeah, tell me about it.

JOSE: Yeah. I mean you seen those chicks who work in Century 21 on Morris Ave?

BARRY: *(Nodding as if he has.)* Oh fuck yeah—they're hot.

JOSE: Yeah, there's this one who's friends with the girl I slept with. Her name's uh, Ellen? Elizabeth? *(He snaps his fingers.)* Eileen. Eileen Lee.

BARRY: Holy shit—you serious?

JOSE: Yeah, why? You know her?

BARRY: Nah, I never met her before. But I heard of *her*.

JOSE: Oh yeah?

(BARRY nods. He takes a sip of beer and watches the game. Now JOSE is really confused.)

JOSE: Nah, it's just...the way you looked up when I said her name, I thought you, like, knew her or something.

BARRY: Who me? Nah. A buddy of mine got involved with her though.

JOSE: Involved, huh? You mean like ...*involved*?

BARRY: Yeah, y'know.

JOSE: Yeah, yeah. *(Beat.)* So he fucked her, huh?

BARRY: *(Chuckling.)* Who Al? Yeah right, in his dreams. Especially if she's as hot as you say.

JOSE: Oh, so they just like fooled around a little.

BARRY: Huh?

JOSE: No, I mean, did they—

BARRY: *(To the TV.)* Come on Ump, that was a fucking strike! *(To JOSE.)* Man, Johan can't get any breaks today. Ump's controlling the whole game here!

JOSE: Yeah, yeah. *(Doesn't know what to do. Takes a deep breath, about to try a new tactic.)* Wait a minute. This friend of yours—Al? You don't mean...well you don't mean Al Gurvis, do you?

BARRY: *(Shocked.)* Yeah I do! Holy shit—yeah I do! Wait a minute, you know Al?!

JOSE: Do I know Al?! I can't believe *you* know Al!

BARRY: Of course—you kidding? Wait, so how do you know Al?

JOSE: Who, me and Al? Oh we go way back.

BARRY: No shit. Hey what'd you say your name was?

JOSE: It's Hector. Hector Gonzalez.

BARRY: Hey Hector—Barry. Barry Barrini.

(They shake hands.)

BARRY: So what, did you guys like grow up together or something?

JOSE: Uh...

BARRY: Aw what am I saying? He's *not* Hispanic.

JOSE: Right. No.

BARRY: Right. Sorry. *(Chuckling.)* No, I was gonna ask if you were staying here illegally too.

JOSE: Staying here *illegally*?

BARRY: Nah, I mean you're his friend, you know his deal right?

JOSE: Well...I mean it's not his *favorite* topic of conversation.

BARRY: No hey, if I were him, it wouldn't be mine, neither. I mean y'know, he's not a *total* citizen—'cause of that stuff with his mom—but, y'know, he ain't an immigrant neither. So.

JOSE: Well sure, sure. *(Beat.)* Y'know he's always sort of vague about that stuff with his mom—what exactly was that all about?

BARRY: Oh, he's vague with me too. From what I gathered it was the usual shit: Dad beat his mom, blah, blah, blah—so she came over here with Al when he was like a kid or something. So y'know he wasn't *technically* born here, doesn't have a green card, but—

JOSE: Right, but he's still one of us.

BARRY: Exactly. Well, he's close enough. The U.S. Government doesn't think so, but whatever. *I'm* not gonna say nothing. So how did you say you know him again?

JOSE: Uh, y'know. We're both into gassers.

BARRY: Oh cool.

(Beat. They watch the TV.)

BARRY: Wait, you're both into what?

JOSE: Gassers—y'know top-heavy muscle cars from the '50s?

BARRY: Oh right.

(Beat. They watch the TV.)

BARRY: Huh. I didn't know Al was into those things.

JOSE: Who, Al? Oh yeah, he's obsessed.

BARRY: No shit.

JOSE: Yeah, I guess you gotta be, if you wanna work with them, y'know?

BARRY: Yup.

(Beat. They watch the TV.)

BARRY: What do you mean—he *works* with them?

JOSE: Well yeah, I mean we work together. That's how I know him.

BARRY: *(Looks at JOSE confused.)* Wait, what? You work with Al?

JOSE: Yeah, we're both gassing assistants.

BARRY: *Gassing assistants?!*

JOSE: Yeah we work on gassers together.

BARRY: Like on the weekends?

JOSE: No, full time. *(To the TV.)* Hey look strike three! About time.

BARRY: *(Stares at him.)* I thought you said you couldn't see.

JOSE: Huh? No, it's just a little blurry is all. So how do *you* know Al?

BARRY: We're both gaffers.

JOSE: *Gaffers?* What's a— (*Freezes, He realizes he's made a terrible mistake.)*

BARRY: I'm sorry bro—you said you were a *what?*

JOSE: Huh?

BARRY: Who the fuck are you? You don't work with Al.

JOSE: Huh? No that's not—what the fuck are you talking about, man?

BARRY: And how the fuck do you know about Eileen Lee?

JOSE: Nah, nah, she's just an old—oh hold on one second— *(Takes out his cell phone and pretends to be on a phone call. Into the phone.)* Hey baby. What, right now? No, I'm watching the game! Okay, Jesus! I'm coming, I'm coming! *(Putting his hand over the phone, softly.)* Hey I gotta run, but it was great meeting you Barry. Hey look—go Mets!

(JOSE points to the game. BARRY turns to it as JOSE runs out.)

BARRY: Hey, who the fuck are you? Get the fuck back here! Hector! *(Starts walking after him.)*

SCENE 6

Sunday night. Valencia Restaurant. AL is as dressed up as he can be. EILEEN is in a dress. They're at a very small table, where the seats are extremely close to each other. AL has wine, EILEEN has water. They're laughing.

AL: *(Laughing.)* No, he freaking did! He sounded *exactly* like Christopher Walken!

EILEEN: *(Laughing.)* He did not!

AL: *(In a bad Christopher Walken voice.)* "And this here—is the master bathroom—where even my dog—comes to lay his poops. Not outside. But in here. He's a trained—pooch."

EILEEN: *(Laughing.)* Okay—that *is* what he said, but he sounded nothing like Christopher Walken. And neither do you for that matter.

AL: Aw, whatever. You see that freaking patio though? Je-sus!

EILEEN: Listen, I've seen a lot of patios in my day. I can say with confidence that that's the nicest patio I ever seen.

AL: Comes with a grill and everything! And be careful, 'cause I can see your place from it.

EILEEN: What are you implying—you're gonna spy on me?

AL: No, hey listen. I'm just saying, sometimes—I like to sunbathe in the nude.

EILEEN: Oh really?

AL: Yeah, and usually when I do, I attract a sizable crowd.

EILEEN: *(Playfully.)* Yeah well freakshows usually do.

AL: *(Smiling.)* Oh that's not right! You went over the line there—you took it too far!

(EILEEN touches his hand.)

EILEEN: I'm just kidding. I promise when you sunbathe in the nude, I'll call all the local tabloids and let them know you're out there.

AL: Nah, see, the whole reason I wanna take this place is so I can get *away* from the tabloids.

EILEEN: Oh, *I* see.

AL: Well no you don't, 'cause quite frankly you don't know what it's like being in the spotlight all the time, hounded by obsessive fans—mostly women, ravenous for my company—but I appreciate your sympathy, however misguided it is.

EILEEN: What'd you memorize that? That was the longest sentence I ever heard.

(AL chuckles, picks up the bottle, and starts to pour EILEEN some wine.)

EILEEN: *(Stopping him.)* Oh no, that's okay.

AL: Nah, come on, have a little—I'm buying.

EILEEN: *(Pulls her glass away.)* No really—stop.

AL: *(Suddenly realizes his mistake.)* Aw shit, I totally forgot. The uh, the *program*.

EILEEN: Yes, the program.

AL: No, I totally forgot, I swear.

EILEEN: No, it's okay. *(She clears her throat.)* So. I take it you want to make an offer then.

AL: Oh yeah I mean uh...so wait a minute, you can't even have a glass?

EILEEN: Uh, no.

AL: But I mean what's *one* glass really gonna do, y'know?

EILEEN: Well, it would make me want to have *another* glass, and then *another* glass, and so on and so forth until I either passed out or started dancing on that table over there.

AL: Well these tables are pretty small, I don't know if they could handle your weight.

EILEEN: Oh, thanks a lot!

AL: Oh no, I didn't mean that! I just meant these tables are tiny, y'know. I feel like I'm right on top of you. *(Awkwardly tries to scoot backwards. He's still very close to EILEEN.)*

EILEEN: Yup, they really pack 'em in here at Valencia. Part of the charm.

AL: Yeah, I never been here before. Fancy. *(Beat.)* So what about one *sip*?

EILEEN: Uh—again: it would lead to another sip, then another, and—

AL: And so on and so forth, 'til you're dancing on the table.

EILEEN: Exactly. It all ends the same way—with me dancing on the table. *(Beat.)* Anyway, I assume you want to make an offer on the house, right?

AL: And then everyone else has to get drunk, just so they're able to bear the sight of you dancing.

EILEEN: Uh, yes exactly.

AL: So really, you not drinking is a very *altruistic* gesture.

EILEEN: *(Smiling.)* What'd you, read the dictionary recently?

AL: Yeah, I've been brushing up on my dictionary.

EILEEN: Well you know what? It is *altruistic* of me. 'Cause I was a real drag to be around when I was drunk. I mean you think I'm mean now, you should've seen me back in the day.

AL: Back in the day? You're young—I mean how long you been sober for?

EILEEN: I've been in recovery for, oh, a little over two years now.

AL: So how does that work anyway—"recovery" or whatever?

EILEEN: How does it work?

AL: Yeah, I mean those meetings. What do you say aside from "Hey my name is Al, so on and so forth."

EILEEN: Well—

AL: I mean you, what—you tell stories about your life and whatnot?

EILEEN: Yeah, y'know—

AL: And I mean, you make new friends obviously. But does it really change you?

EILEEN: *(Gently.)* Well if you let me finish, I promise I'll tell you.

AL: Sorry, sorry. I'm just interested for some reason, I don't know why. *(He's nervous to be so close to her.)*

EILEEN: I can see that. Basically, yeah you tell stories. I mean it's not easy 'cause you're fighting your own urges all day long, y'know? And that constant fighting just, um, further amplifies the pain you feel over and over again throughout the day.

AL: The pain? The pain of what?

EILEEN: *(A little self-conscious.)* I don't know. The pain of... monotonous living I guess? Um.

AL: *(Now completely in love.)* Uh, so did you like *(Clears his throat.)* did like something happen? Specifically I mean.

EILEEN: *(Chuckling self-consciously.)* You mean was there a specific incident that made me hit bottom and try to "fight my way back up"? Um, yeah, actually, sort of.

AL: What was it?

EILEEN: I, um, *(Laughs at herself.)* God, this is so stupid.

AL: No, no. Keep going.

EILEEN: I basically—I uh, *(Takes a deep breath.)* I woke my mom's cat up from a nap.

(AL waits for the rest. It doesn't come.)

AL: What, that's it?

EILEEN: Well it just... it started this whole chain reaction, y'know? I mean basically what happened is, two years ago, right before I got sober, I went home for Thanksgiving. And the night I arrived, first thing I did is I went straight to the local bar and started drinking *really* heavily. I mean, one—it was my birthday, 'cause my birthday was on Thanksgiving that year, and I was *really* depressed. And two—it was ladies' night, buy one get one free—so that right there just, like, doubled the incentive to get wasted. So I just drank and drank 'til it got to the point where you close your eyes and it feels like you're on a really wobbly carousel? Anyway, I woke up the next morning, and I had to pee *so* badly. And I didn't think I was gonna make it to the bathroom at the end of the hall. So instead, I just went into my mom's room next door and used her bathroom. But when I got out, I saw the cat was taking a nap on my mom's bed—and he looked so *cute* y'know?—so naturally, I just started petting it. But apparently he didn't *want* me to pet him—because what he did is he got up and he ran away from me—he ran downstairs where the *other* place he liked to sleep was, right behind the kitchen sink. But downstairs my mom was cooking, making this special dish or something, and she had my grandmother's priceless antique bowl out, and when the cat jumped up onto the kitchen counter to get to his *other* resting place, he of course knocked over my grandmother's priceless antique bowl, causing it to shatter everywhere, which in turn caused my mom to start yelling and cursing and crying about how her mom's priceless antique bowl was now gone forever, because the cat had destroyed it. But don't you see? *I'm* the one who destroyed it—*I* broke the bowl! 'Cause if I hadn't've drank so much the night before, I wouldn't've had to pee so badly, I wouldn't've had to use my mom's bathroom, I wouldn't've seen the cat sleeping there, gone to pet him,

et cetera, et cetera—the bowl would still be intact! But that's when I realized that *this* is the way the world works, y'know? You, you sneeze and a person dies. You leave your book on the bus, and a war breaks out! I mean if one thing leads to another, how can you *do* anything? How can you get up in the morning, say hi to someone, eat a meal? I move my hand this way and somewhere a kid starts crying! So *of course* life is monotonous! I mean we have no choice but to be as monotonous as possible! Because if we're not—if I keep drinking and peeing without thinking of anyone else—sooner or later the whole world gets destroyed! *(Leans forward.)* And I mean doesn't that scare the living shit out of you?

(AL lunges forward and kisses her. She pushes him away.)

EILEEN: What are you doing?

AL: Holy shit, I don't know. I'm sorry, just watching you, I got sucked in, I don't know! *(Starts breathing heavily.)*

EILEEN: Okay, calm down, Al.

AL: Shit, I don't know what happened. I'm sorry, I shouldn't have done that!

(He's trembling. She takes his hand and steadies him.)

EILEEN: No it's okay. You just, you startled me is all. It's okay.

AL: Is it okay?

EILEEN: *(Nodding.)* It's okay.

(He lunges in and kisses her again. She pushes him away.)

EILEEN: Well don't do it again!

AL: What, you *just* said "it's okay!"

EILEEN: Yeah, "it's okay" as in I'm not gonna press charges! Not as in "do it again"!

AL: Well...well fuck! I thought you meant, y'know—like yeah I caught you by surprise *that* time, but really, y'know...you wanted to kiss me.

EILEEN: Well then let me make it clear: I Don't Want To Kiss You, Al.

(AL looks away, hurt.)

EILEEN: Jesus, I'm sorry—that came out wrong.

AL: No, it's fine. That's all you had to say. You shoulda said that the first time.

EILEEN: I know Al, I'm just...I'm really sorry.

AL: What are *you* sorry for? I'm the one who fucked things up. I gotta go to the bathroom.

(AL gets up. EILEEN looks down. As AL walks to the bathroom, DANIEL walks in from the other room, already a bit drunk, holding a camera. He purposefully bumps into AL as AL walks by.)

AL: *(Not looking up.)* Sorry.

(AL continues to the bathroom. DANIEL makes an "up yours" signal to AL's back, then resumes his path to EILEEN's table. He sits down in AL's seat, startling her.)

EILEEN: Daniel?!

DANIEL: *(Triumphantly.)* You fucked up. *(Leans back victoriously, causing his chair to fall over. He quickly gets up, puts the chair back, and sits down again.)* You *fucked* up! And at Valencia of all places—our old stomping grounds!

EILEEN: What the hell are you doing here?

DANIEL: I followed you, you idiot. I thought for sure you spotted me at the Gerstens' open house.

EILEEN: Okay—this has to stop.

DANIEL: I'll tell you what has to stop—your reign of power. You're finished. *(Holds up the camera.)* Because right here, I got all the proof I need! I knew following you would pay off and *man* it did. Y'know, the ironic thing is that I actually believed he was just a client of yours for most of the day!

EILEEN: He *is* just a client—it's not what it looks like. And even if it was, so what?! We're separated!

DANIEL: Well let's see how our lawyers spin it—let's see if Goldberg can get you out of this one. 'Cause here's a list for you, Lister: One—this picture, along with all the other ones I took today, does not bode well for you. And two—the reason why has nothing to do with hook-up sessions before and/or after our separation.

EILEEN: What the hell are you talking about?

DANIEL: Try this on for size: Al Gurvis...is a nonresident alien in this country.

EILEEN: A what? You're full of shit.

DANIEL: Oh really? Go ahead and ask him. Better yet ask yourself: why were you trying to give a nonresident alien a place of permanent residency? Because according to U.S. immigration law—*that*'s illegal. And even Goldberg can't get you out of that one. Then ask yourself "Do I really want Goldberg representing me? *Maybe*, I want to settle this little divorce affair out of court—and give my ex-husband pretty much everything he asks for—or else *maybe* he'll get my Realtor's license taken away, and even send me to jail."

EILEEN: You're blackmailing me?!

DANIEL: You blue-balled me!

EILEEN: You're a disgusting animal!

DANIEL: That may be. But you ask yourself those questions. And in the meantime, I'll ask *myself* if I can ever get over seeing the former love of my life making out with some two-bit hoodlum at our favorite restaurant.

(DANIEL exits. EILEEN doesn't know what to do. She looks at the glass of wine, tempted for a moment. AL reenters and sits back down, recovered somewhat from before.)

AL: All right, look—I know I fucked up. But let's just move on. Truth is, I'm just really lucky to have met you and, honest to God, I can't thank you enough for all you've done for me. I mean Jesus—one fucking weekend, and suddenly I feel like I can turn things around in my life. So yes, I apologize, and yes, I'd like to make an offer on the house.

EILEEN: Are you a nonresident alien?

AL: What? Who the fuck told you that?

EILEEN: Is it true?

AL: I mean...I don't know, sort of. But if I get this house, I'll be a resident.

EILEEN: Jesus Christ Al—that's not how it works!

AL: Well I don't know how it works, you tell me.

EILEEN: Well first you get what we call in this country a green card.

AL: Yeah, I know—I'm working on it. You don't have to patronize me.

EILEEN: You could've cost me my license! You still might!

AL: Okay, well I'm sorry! I mean there's other things more important in this world than licenses, right? Like helping a guy out.

EILEEN: "Helping a guy out"? What—you mean like sleeping with him?

AL: Aw fuck you.

EILEEN: Fuck you! You took advantage of me!

(EILEEN gets up. AL gets up after her.)

AL: Wait, I didn't mean to, okay?! I just thought I could buy a place of my own is all! If you're saying I'm not allowed to do that or whatever, okay then—I didn't know that! I mean I could never even afford one 'til now—'til you came and helped me out! But I thought it was like *fate* or whatever that brought us together, y'know?

EILEEN: *(Walks right up to him.)* It's *not* fate, Al. There's no such thing as *fate*, so grow up! *(Sighs.)* It's all just dumb luck. Just dumb luck, Al.

(EILEEN exits. AL just stares ahead, crushed.)

SCENE 7

Monday morning. Film set. BARRY stands by the craft service table, munching loudly on a bag of chips. A big box of chocolates sits on the table. AL walks in and goes straight for the coffee.

AL: *(Without looking up.)* Hey.

BARRY: What up, Allie. You see the game yesterday?

AL: No.

BARRY: Get this: Mets blew a four-two lead, lost their sixth straight. Reyes got his sixtieth though. That fucker can run, huh?

AL: Yup. *(Takes a stirrer and stirs his coffee. Stops when he sees the big box on the table.)* What's this?

BARRY: What, that box right there that says "Ghirardelli Chocolates"? Beats the shit out of me.

(BARRY hits AL playfully on the arm.)

BARRY: Nah, it's a little gift. Don't worry about it.

(BARRY goes back to munching chips. AL looks down at the box.)

AL: *(Still looking down.)* I didn't win, so…

BARRY: Huh?

AL: *(Louder.)* I said I didn't win the bet! In fact, I lost, okay?!

BARRY: Jesus, lower your voice, Al.

AL: No, I lost the fucking bet! Is that what you want to hear?! What you want me to say! That I was wrong?! That you were right and the world really *is* a completely and totally fucked-up place, huh? HUH?! *(Starts to tear up.)* Is that what you want! Fine, so I'll say it, okay? You were right, Barry, and I was wrong! Thanks to people like you—*assholes* like you, who don't give a shit about anyone but themselves—people like me get fucked! Okay? I got *fucked*! And I was wrong to think I wouldn't get fucked in this world, okay?! I was wrong and I got fucked! So here, eat your fucking chips!

(AL starts throwing the various bags from the craft service table at BARRY.)

BARRY: Hey c'mon! Cut it out!

AL: Eat 'em up! Eat 'em all up! Keep stuffing your fucking face and living your meaningless life while I sit here getting fucked! Getting fucked by all this shit!

(Flips the entire craft service table, toppling over everything on it.)

BARRY: Jesus Christ, Al, get ahold of yourself!

AL: *(Stands there breathing heavily.)* I tried, okay. I tried my goddamn hardest…and I failed. Is that what you want to hear? That I failed? Well I did! I. Failed! *(He picks up the Ghirardelli chocolates box.)* So here—you take your stupid chocolates! You take 'em…and you shove 'em! *(He rips the box open. Hundreds of business cards pour out from the box and line the floor. AL stops when he sees them. He slowly picks one up and looks at it. Genuinely stunned.)* What are these? These aren't chocolates.

BARRY: No they're not…you maniac. They're business cards. I stopped by the printers' last Friday after work and saw that that drunk chick Eileen Lee had returned your cards. 'Cept they had typos all over them. So I ordered you some new ones.

AL: *(Reading.)* "Al Gurvis—Professional Gaffing Assistant…slash Electrician."

BARRY: You said you wanted some business cards, so I got you some fucking business cards.

(AL looks at BARRY, extremely touched. He tries not to cry. He nods.)

AL: Thank you.

BARRY: *(Extremely uncomfortable with AL's display of emotion.)* Y'know. No biggie. I didn't think you'd flip out over it.

(AL gets down on the ground and begins to pick everything up. After a moment, BARRY comes and helps him.)

AL: Everyone's watching me.

BARRY: Yeah no shit—you went nutso.

(They pick everything up. BARRY looks at AL, who has his head down.)

BARRY: *(After a moment.)* So was she Asian?

(AL chuckles and shakes his head no.)

BARRY: Well, you can't win 'em all, am I right?

(AL nods and sniffles. BARRY picks up the craft service table.)

BARRY: Hey you still got cable at your place?

(AL nods and sniffles.)

BARRY: All right, I'm coming over tonight to watch the game. Even *they* can't lose another one, right? It's sheer odds. Even the Mets gotta get lucky once. *(Beat.)* Hey Al—we been friends for what, five, six years now?

AL: Yeah, something like that.

BARRY: So how come you never told me you were into old muscle cars? I fucking *love* old muscle cars.

(AL looks at him, confused. Lights out. End of play.)

THE SONGS OF ROBERT

John Crutchfield

JOHN CRUTCHFIELD was born in Austin, Texas, in 1971, but grew up in the Blue Ridge Mountains near Boone, North Carolina. A Morehead Scholarship brought him to the University of North Carolina at Chapel Hill, from which he was graduated in 1994 (after a year of study at Eberhard-Karls-Universität in Tübingen, Germany) with a BA in religious studies and German. He went on to earn an MFA in poetry and a PhD in English from Cornell University. Crutchfield's produced plays include *Ruth* (Blue Shift Theatre Ensemble, 2000), *Twelve Treatises on Memory: An Epistemological Slapstick* (Jynormous Theatre Company, 2003), *Jack-In-The-Park Tales* (commissioned by Blowing Rock Stage Company, 2005), *Everything, And God* (Appalachian State University, 2006), and *Ivory* (Corpus Theatre Collective, 2007). He has created and performed several movement-based works, including *Arriving As If* (2001), *Yearbook* (2005), *Caliban's Dream* (2006), *Black Snow Flying Upwards, or: My Embarrassment* (2007), *Out There Out Here* (2008), *Curtain Speech* (2008), and *Fire Safety: A Vaudeville Romance* (2009). His publications include numerous poems, essays, reviews, and translations (most recently, Durs Grünbein's *The Bars of Atlantis*, forthcoming from Farrar, Straus, Giroux.) He has been an Artist-in-Residence at the Association d'Art de La Napoule, the Pädagogische Hochschule Karlsruhe, the Djerassi Artists Foundation, and Headlands Center for the Arts, and he is now an Artistic Associate at The Magnetic Theatre, where his new play *Solstice* is scheduled to premiere in winter 2010. At present, he is collaborating with composer Mathew Rosenblum on the libretto for *RedDust*, an experimental opera. He makes his home in Asheville, North Carolina, and teaches writing at nearby Warren Wilson College.

The Songs of Robert was first presented in its current form by Corpus Theatre Collective (Chall Gray, Producer) as part of the Catalyst Series at North Carolina Stage Company in Asheville, North Carolina in September 2008 with the following cast and credits:

Performed by: John Crutchfield
Directed by: James Ostholthoff
Lights: Jonathan Highsmith
Stage Manager: Lisa Huie

The New York premiere of *The Songs of Robert* was presented by The Magnetic Theatre (Chall Gray, Producer) as part of the New York International Fringe Festival (Elena K. Holy, Producing Artistic Director) at the Milagro Theatre on August 20, 2009, with the following cast and credits:

Performed by: John Crutchfield
Directed by: Steve Samuels
Tech/Lights: Steve Samuels

A NOTE ON THE HISTORY OF THE PLAY

The Songs of Robert began as a collection of lyric poems I wrote as part of my MFA thesis in poetry at Cornell. The first stage version was directed by Eric Johnson and produced as a one-act play by an ensemble of students at the North Carolina Governor's School East in July 1998. An expanded ensemble version was produced in August 1999 by Blue Shift Theatre Ensemble in collaboration with X Factor Dance at Lees-McRae College in Banner Elk, North Carolina, and at St. Luke's Episcopal Church in Boone, North Carolina. Johnson again directed. In November 2006, a revised ensemble version was produced by the Lenoir-Rhyne Players under Joe Sturgeon's direction at Lenoir-Rhyne College in Hickory, North Carolina.

I had also begun developing a two-actor version of the show in 2003, while living in Germany as an Artist-in-Residence at the Pädagogische Hochschule Karlsruhe. I directed myself and then-student Andrea Koch in productions at the PH (in the English Literary Festival), at the Amerikanische Bibliothek, and at the Landesmedienzentrum Baden-Württemberg (July 2004). Upon my return to the States, I remounted this version with actor Julia Horn as a Jynormous Theatre Company production at Watauga High School (December 2004), St. Luke's Episcopal Church (December 2004), and Appalachian State University in Boone, North Carolina (September 2005), at Blowing Rock Stage Company in Blowing Rock, North Carolina (April 2005), and as part of the Asheville Fringe Arts Festival in Asheville, North Carolina (January 2005).

Although my first director, Eric Johnson, had been urging me all along to try my hand at a one-man version (claiming that, in his view, this was really the essence of the show), it was circumstance that finally caused me to take this step: I found myself in the uncomfortable position of losing my co-star a couple of weeks before the play was to open as part of Catalyst Series at NCStage in Asheville in 2008. With director James Ostholthoff's help, I retooled the show so that I could do it alone. The result seemed to confirm my friend Eric's original opinion. As it now stands, the show is frankly built upon my own particular strengths (and around my weaknesses) as a performer. I could easily imagine how a performer with different skills (for example, proficiency with different musical instruments than the ones explicitly called for in the script) might find creative ways to transform the show accordingly. Likewise, while the play is intended for a single performer, it could also conceivably be done again as an ensemble piece. In my view, however, much of the magic of the show derives from seeing and hearing a single performer embody the entire dramatis personae.

A NOTE ON THE MUSIC

The music for the show consists of my own arrangements of traditional blues and old-time tunes. The one exception is "Robert's Song" at the very end, which is an original composition. I would be happy to provide MP3s of these numbers to interested parties who contact me through the publisher. For the feel of the blues numbers, listen to Charlie Patton (especially "I'm Goin' Home") and Son House (especially "Death Letter"). For the old-time banjo tunes, listen to Bascomb Lamar Lunsford's "Swannanoa Tunnel," Ralph Stanley's "Little Birdy" and Oscar Wright's "Let Old Drunkards Be." Certainly I could imagine the lyrics set to other traditional tunes as well.

A NOTE ON THE PERFORMANCE

The Songs of Robert still bears the marks of its literary origin. I call it a "lyric drama": the action unfolds obliquely through a series of loosely connected poems and songs, some of which are more lyrical and expressive than they are dramatic. This tension (between lyric intensification and dramatic accumulation) is essential to what I think makes the play interesting, perhaps even strange, and certainly, for the performer, challenging.

Even the more colloquial speeches are composed in traditional verse forms and hence, like the more densely "poetic" passages, should be treated as specific language-textures. With the exception of Robert's, the speeches are also written in specific regional, class, and ethnic dialects, and they should be performed accordingly. Moreover, nothing in the staging should interfere with the audience's attention to the language; in fact, the staging should in every case support or "frame" the language. In general, this means doing less. The set should be minimalist (and therefore versatile), with no effort wasted on realism. The same goes for other design elements. Everything should look and feel homespun, improvised, scavenged, lived-in. Avoid all canned music, even preshow: it will lessen the impact of the music produced on stage by the actor. Ditto for other prerecorded sound cues. Avoid blackouts. Lighting may be highly effective, however, in helping to complement the distinct poetic texture of each scene.

Since the conceit of the show is a street performance, all changes of character and setting should be effected quickly and smoothly, with a minimum of to-do, and in full view of the audience. By the same token, these changes should be choreographed so as to integrate them into the substance of the show. In other words, the theatricality of the performance should be embraced. In general, a simple change of costume piece or hand prop, combined with appropriate physicality and vocal quality, will serve to signify a new character and setting.

PROPS LIST BY CHARACTER

OL' PREACHA: steel body resonator guitar with slide, raggedy suit coat, raggedy hat with small flip-up sign ("$"), small change, faded blue handkerchief

PAP: baseball cap, open back five-string banjo, can of PBR

ROBERT: backpack with sandwich and two prom tickets

MRS. ANDERSON: pearl necklace, hand bell, worn paperback edition of *Catcher in the Rye*

TODD: bandana (in back pocket)

COACH SLOE: coach's whistle, baseball cap, basketball

JUAN-JORGE: cigarettes and lighter

MR. DAVENPORT: hideous glasses, clip-on tie, pink detention slips

MISS MEDULA: silk scarf, glasses (in hand)

JENNIE: cheerleading pom-poms, cordless phone

SIR JAMZALOT: gangsta hat, absurd gold necklace

LURLENE: beat-up glasses, headscarf

Other objects (set): shopping cart with miscellaneous junk, cardboard sign ("The Songs of Robert"), steel folding chair, broken-down beach chair, two guitar stands, bicycle horn

CAST OF CHARACTERS
(IN ORDER OF APPEARANCE)

OL' PREACHA: An African American Delta bluesman and busker, ancient, possibly blind

PAP: A Southern Appalachian man, gregarious, mid-forties

ROBERT: His son, a high school boy, late teens

MRS. ANDERSON: An African American high school English teacher, early sixties

TODD: A high school dropout, late teens

COACH SLOE: A high school P.E. coach, mid-fifties

JUAN-JORGE JESUS FILIPE PABLO: Robert's guardian angel, a Latino tough-guy

MR. DAVENPORT: A high school assistant principal, mid-forties

MISS MEDULA: A high school guidance counselor, late thirties

JENNIE: Robert's sister, a high school freshman, mid-teens, a junior varsity cheerleader

SIR JAMZALOT: A high school student and aspiring rapper, mid-teens

LURLENE: A Southern Appalachian woman, late forties, drives the school bus

SETTING

A small town in the southern Blue Ridge Mountains—maybe western North Carolina, maybe eastern Tennessee, maybe even northern Alabama; late spring; the mid-1980s.

Preset: two dumpster-dive chairs—say, a battered steel folding chair and a rusted beach chair—downstage right and left, respectively. Beside each, a guitar-stand. From off, the soft sound of slightly garbled singing—maybe a gospel blues song—punctuated by coughs, wheezes, grunts of effort, etc. Upstage center, a pool of dusty light fades up as a shopping cart filled with junk comes into view, pushed by a raggedy old man—OL' PREACHA. Maybe he wears the remains of a suit and bowler hat. Maybe his boots are held together with duct tape. Maybe he limps. The cart is loaded with miscellaneous trash, including clothes, a radio, and a couple of musical instruments. It has a small weather-beaten cardboard sign fastened to the side on which "The Songs of Robert" is written in an uneven script. OL' PREACHA positions the cart in the pool of light, fishes an immaculate steel-bodied resonator guitar from the trash in the cart, considers it a moment, places it carefully downstage right in the guitar stand. All of this is done with painstaking slowness: this man is very old. At last he turns to face the audience, scrutinizing them as he comes toward center stage, where he removes his hat, flips up a small sign from inside the hatband ("$"), drops a few coins in, shakes the hat two or three times, places it on the floor right in front of the audience. Now he retrieves his guitar, somehow manages to get the strap over his head, fishes a metal slide out of his pocket, and slowly, laboriously lowers himself down into his chair. Beat. Without preamble, he roars into "Blind Bobby's Big Bad Barefoot Blues"...

OL' PREACHA: I WOKE UP ONE MORNIN',
I WAS FEELIN' 'ROUND FOR MY SHOES
I SAID I WOKE UP SOON IN THE MORNIN'
LORD, I COULDN'T EVEN FIND MY DAD-BLAME SHOES
THAT'S WHEN I KNEW I MUSTA HAD
BLIND BOBBY'S BIG BAD BAREFOOT BLUES

I WALKED UP TO DE SCHOOLHOUSE
I SEEN MY WOMAN WIFF ANOTHER GUY
I SAID I WALKED UP TO DE OL' SCHOOL-
   HOUSE
AN' THERE SHE'S WORKIN' IT WIFF SOME
   OTHER GUY
AN' I WAS FEELIN' SO ALONESOME
SO ALONESOME I COULD LAY DOWN AN' DIE

YOU KNOW IT FEELS SO BAD
YOU BALL YO' HANDS UP IN A FIST
I SAID IT MAKES YOU FEEL SO DAWGONE BAD
YOU BALL YO' LITTLE HANDS UP IN A FIST
WHEN DE VERY WOMAN YOU BE LOVIN'
DON'T EVEN KNOW DAT YOU EXIST

SOME DESE DAYS I'M A'GRAB MY SUITCASE
I'M A'TAKE OUT DOWN DE ROAD
I SAID I'M A'GRAB UP MY SUITCASE
AN' I'M A'TAKE OUT DOWN DE ROAD
AN' I'M A'KEEP ON GOIN'
UNTIL I LAY DOWN DIS HEAVY LOAD

(The song fades out before it's quite done. OL' PREACHA addresses the audience directly.)

Dese be de songs what Robrit sung
wiffout no guitar's shiny tongue
to sing wiff when de nights got long,
as be de custom wiff a song.

An' dey de songs what sing him too,
an' sing de world, an' me an' you,
wiff parkin' lots an' fields a snow
an' places Robrit's 'fraid to go.

Whoever hear be apt to see
why Robrit be a frien' to me,
despite de fack he awful shy
an' lonesome an' confuse, an' I

don't hardly get his ways a'tall.
Why he forever feelin' fall
when springtime here, de leafs unfurl?
Or why he love dat only girl…

de dark-haired girl who turns away,
dough Robrit shine. It hard to say

how Robrit love her on de day
de story end. It hard to say.

(Beat. He becomes PAP, addresses the audience directly. Through the following, he returns OL' PREACHA's guitar to the stand and raggedy coat to the cart, dons a big ball cap, retrieves an open-back five-string banjo from the cart, and has a seat in the beach chair stage left. We're now on the front porch. It's early morning.)

PAP: I ever tell y'uns 'bout my boy Robert?
Well, they's a lot to tell, an' some you folks
ain't never heard'a him, so, well, I reckon
I'm a'have to start wid basic facks.
Y'uns looky here: see, Robert—that's my boy.
Named for his great-grandaddy John Robert
back in Roanoke, Virginny, who
hisself was named for Robert Wallace that
come over on a boat from Edinburry
back a fair long time ago. Now, Robert,
he's a good kid, I like him. Does ever
what you tell him to, an' don't talk back,
not like some a these young folk nowadays,
act like they brought theirselves up w'out
   no help.
He's a fine boy in his own way, but *dawg my cats* if ever now an' then he don't
git *funny* on ye… I don't mean *funny like that!* He's always moanin' an'
   a'groanin'
'bout some prissy cheerleader. I mean
but just a little *idjo-syncracy*,
like his *idears* is funny. An' the way
he talks is funny. If'n when he talks,
that is. His mom an' me, we knowed
   long since
'at boy was readin' way too much. Ain't natchral,
boy his age. Ain't right. An' not just readin':

drawin' pitchers...I don't mean *pitchers like that!*
Just, you know, differ'nt kinda thangs, like, well...
like barns an' stuff. Why, that there boy done drawed
a hunnert pitchers a the barn on top the hill
up there. Ol' Watson barn. Hain't been repaired
since it was raised in *nineteen ten*, I swarr!
Now, what y'uns make a that? What in the world
possess a feller *take* an' *draw* a broke-down,
sideways, roof-collapsin' ol' tobacky barn a *hunnert*—'Hit don't make a *lick*—
And now he's got this, what, this *skollership*
to some damn place. A art school. Lord have mercy!
Way up there in—y'uns ain't never gonna guess: Rhode Island! *Whoop-de-doodle-do!*
A island wid a road acrosst it! Town they call Pro*vide*-ence. School the name a *Rizzdy*.
Dawg my cats if that don't take the cotton-pickin'—Who the *diggins* ever heard
a *Rizzdy*? Smack-dog-dab in Yankeeland, an' they think—lemme tell you somethin', folks:
they think they gonna *buy my boy off me* with some dang *skollership*, they got another
think coming. No sir-ee. We ain't that kind a family. Robert stays right here.
State College good enough for him, I reckon.
—Ain't that right, now, Momma?... S'right.

(*He sings the traditional "Little Birdie" while accompanying himself on a banjo.*)

LITTLE BIRDIE, LITTLE BIRDIE
WON'T YOU SING TO ME A SONG
I GOT A SHORT TIME TO STAY HERE
AND A LONG TIME TO BE GONE

RUTHER BE IN SOME DARK HOLLER
WHERE THE SUN DON'T NEVER SHINE
THAN FOR YOU TO BE ANOTHER MAN'S DARLIN'
AND TO KNOW THAT YOU'D NEVER BE MINE

LITTLE BIRDIE, LITTLE BIRDIE
WHAT MAKES YOU FLY SO HIGH
WHEN YOU KNOW THAT MY TRUE LOVER
IS A WAITIN' IN THE SKY

(*Beat. He removes his hat, becomes ROBERT. Through the following, he returns the banjo to the stand, hangs the hat on it, rises. We're in a teenage boy's bedroom. It's early morning. A choreographic scene.*)

ROBERT: Today I'll speak to her.
Today I'll ask her to the Prom.
And when the time comes, she
will answer the door in a blue-green dress,
her eyes blue-green and patient
as the rain, and I
will take her hand,
and lead her forth into the listening night
where no more than a breath
ruffles the silver-backed leaves,
where I am strong and courteous
as a pilgrim in my gray tailcoat,
my crisp white collar like a promise
in the dusk, my dress shoes freshly polished,
beading up with dew, and she...
oh, she's more beautiful than moonlight
on the rhododendron leaves,
and she is softer than a sprig of ferns
unfurling by the spring
and she is graceful as a deer
and she is here...

And there is finally a knowing,
and the knowing is itself the known,
a light reflected in her blue-green eyes,
her face, her vulnerable ear a miracle

of whiteness I would save my softest
    song for,
which I do, my cheek so lightly nestled
in her hair, my lips anointed
by the smell of rain on honeysuckle,
simple *here-ness* moving now so ever
slowly next to me and with me,
curvature of spine beneath my dream-
    ing fingers,
slightest brush of heat and thighs
through silk, through finely woven wool,
and later, at the punch bowl,
as she sips her drink,
I'll ask her out beneath the stars,
and ask her which one is ours…

(The sound of a horn honking startles him: the bus is waiting. He grabs his backpack, hurries off and around behind the cart. Beat. He becomes MRS. ANDERSON, who puts on a pearl necklace and rings a small hand bell. She is an imposing African American woman, who stands scowling down at the audience. She holds a well-worn paperback edition of Catcher in the Rye *in her lacquered fingertips. We are now in her 1st Period English class.)*

MRS. ANDERSON: Now what is the
    problem? You people just sit there
like bumps on a desk, and I have to say,
it inclines me to some irritation. In fact,
I begin to suspect—now be honest:
    how many
of you have actually finished the book?
I mean cover to cover, first page to last
    page.
Hands up, now… Um hm. I thought
so. Well that
makes me sad. 'Cause this is your *life*,
    people,
this here is *your* education, and if
you don't put forth some effort and come
    in prepared,
folks, you're wasting your time. And
what's infinitely worse,
you're wasting *my* time. Folks, I don't
    have much left.
And I don't take too kindly to folks who
    go wasting it
for me. And so, I will ask those among you
who seem to respect neither their time
    nor others'
to lay your heads down on your desks
    and do not
even think about raising them till class
    is done.
Because I do not wish to be thereby
    reminded
of your disrespect for yourselves and
    for me.
Now the rest of you. Jamie and Valerie,
    Tom
and Elisha and Josh and… who else was
    it?—Robert:
we shall, as they say, *overcome*, shall
    we not?

So where were we? Oh yes: Holden's
    psychology.
Holden, we saw, is a sensitive boy
underneath. He is also, we saw, not
    untouched
by emotional pain. So I ask you. What
    could be
the sources of Holden's emotional pain?
Ah, yes, Jamie?… Indeed. Well remarked.
    There is evidence
Holden still misses his brother who died,
and thus carries a burden of grief. And
    what else?
Is there—Valerie, yes… Well, now… very
    intriguing.
He's afraid of, you think, *growing up*.
He's afraid
of the *changes*. From Holden's perspec-
    tive, these changes
seem more like a fall off a cliff without
    anyone
waiting to catch him. What else? Can
    we go

any deeper?…Yes, Robert…Um hm…
Um hm hm!
How astute. Did ya'll hear what he said
in the back?
He said—Robert, repeat what you said
for us please…
No, the other thing…yes…Well, okay,
class. So what
do you think? This *Jane Gallagher* per-
sonage
seems to be much on the mind of our
hero.
Although we do not have the honor of
meeting her,
woven throughout the novella is Holden's
remembrance of *Jane*, his desire to call her,
his longing to know if she thinks of him.
Longing.
Now what, class, is *longing*? How does
it arise
in the soul? Is it not rather different
from simple
desire for an object? What meaning
inheres
in this *longing*, whereby a boy's soul is
elongated,
stretched to the *breaking point*, pulled
till it's taut
as a *fresh-tuned guitar-string*: a *touch*, and
at last it would *sing!*

(*Beat. Her gesture morphs into that of a
kid holding a lit joint. We are now in an
obscure corner of the high school parking
lot. A dangerous and angry young man
slouches against a car, smoking a joint.
It is TODD, a dropout who still hangs
around the high school. He keeps a sly
lookout over his shoulder for the Assistant
Principal on Parking Lot Patrol. A pause
while he takes a hit. Then he addresses the
audience directly.*)

TODD: Robert is
a science whiz.
I'd rather not
say the science of what.

Robert are
but seldom far
from dreamy girly
whose hair is dark but not all that curly.

Robert be
a friend to me.
Except that I
can't stand the little guy.

(*He giggles, recovers, looks over his shoulder,
takes a hit.*)

Robert was
covered with fuzz.
They shaved his head.
His ears turned red.

If Robert were
a dog, he'd purr.
And if a cat,
he'd wish he were the opposite of a cat.

(*He takes a hit, has a coughing fit, recovers.*)

Robert am
a partial sham.
I hate to say it,
but that's sorta the way it
is…

(*He considers the remains of his roach,
extinguishes it, pops it in his mouth, turns
upstage, and swallows it. Beat. The piercing sound of a coach's whistle. He turns
around as COACH SLOE, a pot-bellied
man wearing a ball cap and a whistle
around his neck who motions for us to
come closer. We are on the bleachers of a
high school gymnasium. It is late morning.*)

COACH SLOE: All right, now, men.
Let's gather 'round a minute.
Men, I stopped class early 'cause we need
to have ourselves a little talk. That's right.
Now, men, I know we're gettin' toward
the end,

an' Prom an' Gradjiation, all a that.
I know that. An' I know how all this Springtime
weather's like to git a feller's thoughts
to wanderin' a bit. I know all that.
But, men, I tell ye, school ain't over yet.
We got a job to do here, men. We still
got volleyball. That's gonna take some focus,
yes it is. We got to keep our focus,
men, 'cause—
          ...See, now this here's just the thing
I'm talkin' 'bout: while I been standin' here
this whole time they's been couple three a y'uns
that keep a'lookin' way on over there
at Mrs. Pinnick's class. Now, men, I told ye
we was gonna have to share the gym
with them this week, uh, on account a that
the softball field got flooded. They's our guests.
An', men, we need to treat them wimminfolks
like guests. I mean, I know they's purty girls
an' all, an' ever one a them has got
her little shorts on an' what-have-ye, such
that I could understand if some you men
was to, uh, git *dis-tracted*. I know that.
Hell, I was yer age oncet. An' so I know
they's gonna be, from time to time, ye know,
some, *tem-ptations*, to be lookin' over
there instead a here at what we're doin'.

Especially when ye make out amongst
the girly tribe a certain Dark-Haired Presence,
as it were, a certain kind a ripple
in the light, as of a angel's footsteps
on the smooth of ponds at evening...

(He takes a knee, calls us in closer.)

Now, men, this individual may waft
from time to time acrosst yer field of vision
in a somewhat mysterious manner,
an' she may cast about herself a glow
both numinous an' veined with unheard songs,
an' ye may very well begin to feel
y'seff transported to the sacred groves
of ecstasy an' I don't know what 'hall.
Yessir, why ye might even think ye breathe
her holy scent from time to time, the faintest
breath that rustles in yer heartstrings,
drawin' forth a music no one hears,
an' so on. Right?

(He begins rising to his feet again.)

          But, men, now, uh, despite
these, so to speak, divine epiphanies,
ye need to find some way to keep yer mind
on what ye're doing. Right? Ye understand?
'Cause otherwise, ye're liable to git whollop't
on the nose with that there volleyball.
An', men, uh, that ain't gonna feel too good,
an', well, it shore ain't gonna *look* too good.
Why, coupla three minutes, an' yer nose
is gonna swell up like a sweet tater.
An' maybe now ye got that Dark-Haired Girl
to look at ye, but 'hit t'ain't gonna be
a compliment'ry look, I tell ye what.
An' so I'd like to recommend ye fellers
undertake, uh, ever-what evasive
countermeasures ye deem necessary
an' sufficient to, uh, circumvent,
uh, that particular misfortune. Right?

An' 'at brings me to one last thing, here, men.

Now, men, we all has got the same
   equipment.
Might look a little differ'nt, but hit's all
the same. So, men, I *do not* wanna hear
nobody call nobody else a faggit.
Sakes alive, men, seems like ever other
word out some a y'uns's mouth is "faggit."
Tell ye, men, I've had enough a that.
Ain't no one here a faggit, men, so I
don't wanna hear it. I don't even want
to *think* I hear it. I don't even want
to *smell you thinking* it. We straight on
   that?

Besides, men, even if they was a faggit
here amongst us. Don't ye know the Lord
done made him too? An' don't ye know
   the Lord
loves *ever'thang* he made? Now, maybe
   that
there fella feels, uh, *differ'ntly* than you,
but he cain't hepp it, it's the way he is.
An' here you take an' call somebody faggit
like a *insult*, an' it hurts his feelins.
Hell, men, inside it makes him feel…
   ashamed.

All right, it's lunchtime, men. Get in,
   get eat, get out.
—An' oh, I almost done forgot: Mister
Davenport done ast me to announce
that tickets to the Prom will be on sale
in the Guidance Office during lunch.
   If y'uns
ain't got yer tickets, now's yer final chance.

(He removes his hat, tucks his whistle back into his shirt. He is now ROBERT, who begins searching his pockets for his tickets. With a sigh of relief, he finds them in a pocket of his backpack. He proceeds to the chair downstage left. We are now in the school cafeteria. ROBERT sits by himself with his backpack and a sandwich. He begins to plan out how he's going to ask her.)

ROBERT: One day she walks in, takes
   a seat
almost across from me, and I
pretend to eat my Tater Tots
while the maw of my heart gapes
and for terror my thin hands weep:
she finishes her yogurt, leaves.

(He pauses, starts again.)

One day she walks in, takes a seat
almost across from me, and I
fold up my napkin, rise and cough
a little cough to catch her eye
then introduce myself: she smiles,
asks me to sit with her: we talk.

(He pauses, starts again.)

One day she walks in, takes a seat
almost across from me, and I
fold up my napkin, rise and cough
a little cough, then notice she
is smiling at me: I'm about
to speak: she takes my hand: *let's go—*

(He sees her actually walk in.)

One day she walks in, takes a seat
almost across from me, and I
besiege my poor astonished brain
for an excuse: the seconds sting
like bees: she looks: I look away:
that night my bones cry out for love!

(ROBERT is left alone. Beat. He springs up from the chair as JUAN-JORGE JESUS FILIPE PABLO DEL AMOR IMPOSSIBILE, a Latino tough who also happens to be Robert's guardian angel. He pulls out a pack of cigarettes. Through the following, he lights up, smokes. Or maybe he gets so carried away with his story that he forgets to smoke. In any event, he addresses the audience directly.)

JUAN-JORGE: *Olà! Me llamo* Juan-
   Jorge Jesus
Filipe Pablo *del Amor Impossíbile.*

But *you* can call me Juan. Okay, for starters,
I'm an angel. *Si.* In case de *whings*
confuse you. You can see de big whings, right?
You don't see de whings? Okay, ah...dis is very bad for you. We talking later.
What was I about to—? Oh: I'm not just any angel, *mi muchachos*. No.
I have de special privilege to be de one responsible for Don Roberto.
I'm his, how you say, ah, "Guardian Angel."
Basically I keep de kid from getting killed.
But other stuff as well, less serious, like getting pooped on by a passing bluejay.
You ever have dis happen? Well, if not, you're lucky. Wouldn't believe how much a bird
dis size—an' accurate too. So, anyways, de kid was doing fine, apart from bumps
an' scrapes an' every now an' den de flu, until dis so-call "Dark-Haired Girl" show up.
Since den, believe me, you don't want my job.
I started back to smoking. Had to, just to *calm my friggin' nerbes*. All day de kid's on dis, like, cosmic roller coaster, up an' down an' up an' down an' tru de loop-dee-loop an' backwards down a free fall.
Makes me dizzy—an' I can *fly*, okay? Dis girl so much as maybe glance at him in de hall, he's on cloud nine, his eyes glaze over, knees go *pfth*, it's all I can do to keep his stupid self from passing out.
Next time he sees her, what, she's looking down
or up, she's talking to her friend, she's got her textboook out, she's picking her nose, who cares,
point is: she does no *see* him—*O Dios* in Heaven! Principalities an' Powers!

Suddenly de world goes dark, a vale of tears, de valley of the shadow of death,
an' O how Roberto weepeth! O how Roberto
gnasheth all his teeth, yea verily,
an' all the braces thereunto pertaining!
Woe an' Cataclysm! Heckie-Dern an' Phooey! Lawd I got de blues so bad,
I tink I going to die, die, die, die...
Maybe I should kill him? If I was his friend,
I say, *Muchacho*! What are you doing? You got
de *tickets*. All you gotta do is ask her to de *stupid friggin' Prom!* No more goof-offing! Is time for *attacar*!

(*He crushes out his cigarette in disgust. Beat. He takes a step back, becomes OL' PREACHA, who through the following retrieves his coat and shuffles back toward his seat. Once again we're on the dusty street corner. Once again he struggles with the guitar, etc.*)

OL' PREACHA: Dat Robrit, he a funky dude!
—wiffout he mean to be.
I never see him gruff or rude
or huggin' on a tree,

but he got funny ways, fo' sho'!
I's de firse one to admit.
Why, sometime I says, Gret Good Lo'!
let's put a stop to 'hit!

De way he go on, chase dat gal
like she de evenin' star,
den lay an' moan it at de wall
—as if de wall could hear!

Mo' likely she a jackma'lannern,
lead 'im off a gully,
break his neck down in de shaddern
—den he lookin' silly!

But when he sunk down in de earff,
his bones all good an' clean,

I'll pick me out one from de stuff,
a armbone or a shin,

den take my guitar at my side,
an tune up dis ol' thing,
an' wiff de shinbone fo' a slide,
I'll make ol' Robrit sing!

(He breaks into "Farewell Blues.")

WELL I WENT DOWN TO DE STATION
WANTED TO CATCH A RIDE ON DAT EMPIRE
 STATE EXPRESS
SAY I WENT DOWN TO DE STATION
HAD TO CATCH ME A RIDE ON DAT EMPIRE
 STATE EXPRESS
LORD, I DIDN'T HAVE NOTHIN' BUT EMPTY
 POCKETS
AN' A EMPTY FEELIN' WAY DOWN IN MY
 CHES'
SO I WENT UP TO DE DEPOT AGENT
SAID PLEASE WON'T YOU LET ME RIDE
 HER BLIND?
I SAID, PLEASE, MISTER DEPOT AGENT
PLEASE WON'T YOU LET ME RIDE HER
 BLIND?
HE SAID, "YOU KNOW I WOULDN'T MIND
 IT, PREACHA MAN,
BUT THIS EMPIRE STATE, IT AIN'T MINE"

THEN THE ENGINEER HE BLOWED THE
 WHISTLE
AN' THE FIREMAN HE RUNG THE BELL
I SAY THAT MEAN OL' ENGINEER BLOWED
 THE WHISTLE
AN' THAT CRUEL, CRUEL FIREMAN RUNG
 THE BELL
LORD, MY SWEET WOMAN'S ON BOARD
AN' SHE'S WAVIN' BACK FARE-YE-WELL
SAID MY SWEET LITTLE WOMAN'S ON
 BOARD
LORD, SHE'S WAVIN' BACK FARE-YE-WELL

(Beat. He becomes MR. DAVENPORT, dons an awful pair of glasses, and addresses someone in the audience house right. Through the following, he stands, returns the guitar to its place, clips on a tie. Toward the end of the speech, he will whip off his coat, throw it on the ground, and stomp on it. We are in an office in the high school.)

MR. DAVENPORT: Robert. You're a
 smart boy. I assume
you know I didn't call you in to chat
about the pretty flowers all in bloom.
I'd love to, but we haven't time for that.

Need I remind you, Graduation's near.
The final testament to all you've done.
The last accounting of your time spent
 here.
The day we see who's lost and who has
 won.

And, son, I hope you'll make the winning list,
I really do. But lately, I don't know,
your grades, for instance, Robert, I insist
you tell me why they've dropped so low.

The numbers hardly look like you at all!
And I'd be *most reluctant* to report
so poor a showing, I mean, after all,
your *scholarship* depends upon it, sport.

Don't get me wrong, I'd love to see you off
to…Art School. You deserve it. But,
 you see,
you can't go out ass-first, like…Gor-
 bechev!
You gotta finish *strong*, at least a B,

or it'll look to them like you've been *slack*.
And come to think of it, it looks that way
to me as well, I mean—And what's
 this stack
of—Christ!—*detention slips?* I have to say,

it's rather out of character for you.
What's going on here, son? I'd like to
 know.
S'it *senioritis?* Have you got the *flu?*
Too busy playing someone's *Romeo?*

Now, if you've got, you know, a *problem*
 here,

then maybe you should talk to Miss Medula.
Otherwise, I recommend you steer
a straighter course these last few weeks, don't fool a-

round, get first things first. Unless you want
to end up lying face-down in a ditch
somewhere in Idaho. Unshaven. Gaunt.
And wearing nothing but a greasy stitch

or two that used to be a pair of jeans.
Your eyelids crusted shut with yellow snot.
Your lips—your skin like dried-out collard greens.
Your toenails—oh my God!—your toenails—what

the—ugh! The *smell!* The rank, ungodly *stench!*
How is it *possible*, you loathsome lump
of *excrement*, you *filth*, you *turd*, you trench-
foot effigy, you medical waste dump,

you parasitic, verminous, obscene,
Disgusting, toothless, worthless piece of sh—!

Well,
You get the point. Success, my boy! I mean
the means to make ends meet. And that means: Sell

Yourself. If you can't sell yourself, then how
will you sell something else? Do tell me, please.
There's only one way, son, to milk a cow.
You gotta grab that teat, and then you squeeze!

(*He savors the moment. Beat. He becomes MISS MEDULA, who looks up at an audience member house left as she pulls off the glasses and puts the tie in her pocket. She hurries to welcome "Robert" into her office, has a seat downstage right, and adjusts a silk floral-print scarf around her neck while continuing to hold the glasses in her hand.*)

MISS MEDULA: Well, what a pleasure! Here you are again!
I'm flattered, Robert, really. Please, come in
and have a seat. Some pretzels? Here, have all
you want. —Oh, by the way, I've got a call
to make at two, so this'll have to be
a quickie, 'kay? So tell me, Robert, tell me
your concerns. You must be quite excited
for the Prom! I wish you had invited
me, you devil you! —Just kidding. Wow!
It always brings back memories of how
I used to be in high school. You would not
have recognized me, Robert. Quite a lot
has changed. You won't believe it, but I used
to be *so shy!* I always felt confused
around the boys—especially a boy
I liked. One chilly look would just *destroy*
my confidence! Unfortunately, chilly
looks was all I got. It seems so *silly*
now—that I would get myself all twisted up!— He didn't even know that I existed!
What a *loser* I was then. If he
had even just so much as *looked* at me,
I would have melted like a ball of wax!
I swear I would have stopped dead in my tracks
and *fainted!* —*God*, it's so *pathetic*. Who
can blame the guy for shunning me? It's true
he always had some *bimbo* on his arm,
some *suburb slut* whose only source of charm
was twitching in that cutsie little skirt,
the stupid *bitch*. And, oh! she *loved* to *flirt*
with everybody! Even with the *teachers!*

Even with the *coach*, behind the *bleachers!*
God I hated her! I hope she's got
twelve kids all living in a *parking* lot!
I hope she's fat as hell, with sagging
  breasts!
And sells herself for scientific tests!
I hope he *married* her, the stupid *slob!*
I hope he's lost his *hair*, his *car*, his *job!*
I hope they both go rot in Hell with all
those other—! —Oops! It's two! I've got
  that call…

*(An awkward smile. Beat. She becomes
ROBERT, sinks down in the chair, removes
the scarf. We are now in the school courtyard. A choreographic scene.)*

ROBERT: Why am I so alonesome?
Did I bring this with me to the world
to darken it? I weigh a zillion pounds.
I can't stand up. It's sitting on my back.

If listening's not given in the song,
then why the sound? If reaching's just
  the dream
of touch, then why these hands, these
  fingers
curved to light so gently on a cheek?

If I could die an accidental death
I would as soon as it could be arranged!
—Though then it wouldn't be an ac-
  cident.
—Please! just some way to snuff me
  out, so I

won't have to see the mossy rocks and
  sticks
persist and flourish in the springy light,
the leaves outrageous where the birdlife
makes its urgent little sounds, the breezes

turn the pages of the grass, whereon
the scrawl of dead men scripts the story of
my hardscrabble life, its years lived out
  among
the grayish faces. What's the point of
  going

further? If I called out, who would
  hear me
in the houses built of darkness? Who
would know? My voice fills up the little
  spaces
in the homes of insects.

*(Beat. He becomes OL' PREACHA, who
addresses us directly. We're on the dusty
street corner again. Through the following,
he picks his coat up off the ground, dusts it
off, puts it on, makes his way back to his
guitar and chair, etc.)*

OL' PREACHA: Now, how come Robrit
  talk so much,
all 'bout dem cullu'd leaves an' such?
An' how come he so sad an' blue?
Why, bofe his feets dey has a shoe.
An' he got plinny grub to eat.
His deddy love 'im, momma sweet,
an' ebrybody in dis town,
dey treats 'im nice, don't dog 'im roun'.
He talk a little funny, y'all,
what wiff de readin' books an' all,
But he polite in his own way.
—Dough I don't git half what he say!
But dat's all right, I bleeb I know
what Robrit talkin' 'bout, aldough
he git de tongue wrapped in a knot,
I 'dennifies wiff him a lot.
What he be feelin' hard to 'spress!
You sweats an' moans an' tries yo' bes',
an' still de woids don' come out right.
Why? 'Cause de brain put up a fight.
De heart, he want de troof be said;
De brain, dough, rutha drop down dead.
An' den de blues come down like hail,
de world be lookin' like de jail.
Gret Gawd in Heb'm! Lawd above!
It whup you hiney, be in love!

(He breaks into "Discouraged Blues.")

SOMETIMES I GET DISCOURAGED
AN' I HANG MY HEAD AN' CRY
AIN'T NO FOOD UPON DE TABLE

AIN'T NO HEAVEN IN DE SKY

SOMETIMES I FEEL LIKE DYIN'
WHEN DAT LONESOME SUN GO DOWN
'CAUSE I SHO' AIN'T GOT NOBODY
FO' TO THROW MY ARMS AROUN'

SO I SET DOWN BY MY WINDOW
WATCH DE EVENIN' FILL DE TREE
NUTHA MAN DONE GOT MY WOMAN
AN DESE MEAN OL' BLUES GOT ME

SOME DESE DAYS I'M UP AN' LEAVE HERE
I'M A WALK RIGHT OUT DAT DO'
I'M A CROSS DAT MIGHTY RIVER
AN' I WON'T LOOK BACK NO MO'
NO I WON'T LOOK BACK NO MO'

(Beat. He becomes COACH SLOE, who, through the following rises, pulls his whistle out, puts the guitar back in its place, and removes the coat and takes it to the cart, where he retrieves his hat and a basketball. We are now in the school gym at the end of the day.)

COACH SLOE: Now, men, they's just
 a couple three more minutes
'til the busses git back for the rest a y'uns,
to take ye home, so time to clean on
 up now.
—Johnston, you an' Critcher there,
 you fellers,
I done told ye oncet...Don't make me
 hurt ye.
Put the basketballs back in the hopper
 like I said...
All right. Now, men, let's gather 'round
 a minute.
Men, the Prom's tomorry night. I want
to larn ye one last thing before ye go.
So looky here now, men: a *basketball*,
y'uns will have had occasion to observe,
is *round*. The basketball as such, I mean.
It is, as y'uns can see, a thoroughly,
uh, *curved* an' *roundified phenomenon*.
It is, in fact, a *sphere*. You follow me?

It is, a fella might could even say,
a object of exquisite wholeness an' per-
 fection.
Now. It bein' thusly circumscribed,
you might could also see it as the sort
a thing what has a *extry meaning*, like...
symbolical or something. Right? See, men,
the basketball is sorta like a fella's *soul*:
it's round an' perfect, see, an' when you
 take
an' thow that ball up toward the hoop
 up there,
it, uh, describes this *arc of aspiration*,
as it were, this sorta *longing* for
the divine consummation represented
by the basket which receives it, such
that ball an' hoop are, so to speak, *united*
in a *mystical* an' *holy weddin'*.

Which reminds me: if your soul is shaped
for instance like a *football*, men, it shore
ain't gonna fit too good down in the
 basket,
is it now? An' if your soul's the size
of, say, a *tennis ball*, well, men, it's gonna
look, uh, *mighty funny* when you thow it
at that hoop. Same thing if what you got
is blowed up like a, like a big ol' beachball.
Right? The *basket*, men, is made to take
a *basketball*. —An' not no flat one neither.
Men, you want that *dee-vine consummation*
with your soul's, uh, *special counterpart*,
you dern well better see to it your soul
is *round* an' *bouncy*, pumped up good,
 but not
too much. 'Hit cain't be *flat* an' *de-flated*,
'hit cain't be *ob-long*, 'hit cain't be *over-
 inflated*,
'hit cain't have the *pumpin' spike* broke off
an' rattlin' around inside an' all.
'Hit's gotta be like 'hit was meant to be.

(Beat. Through the following, he makes his way back to the cart, replaces the basketball, etc.)

Okay, men. They's bus 55. Who's that?
Uh, Critcher... Perry, Simpson... all
    you fellers
gitchee stuff, don't keep Lurlene a'waitin'.
I'll see you men tomorry at the Prom!
Y'uns all done ast somebody, right?... Do
    what?
...Uh oh. Well, Larry, you an' Robert
    better
make it snappy. I don't reckon they
got dates a'waitin' fer y'uns at the door!

(Beat. He removes his hat and whistle, becomes JENNIE, who picks up the pompoms. We are at JV cheerleading practice. She does her routine. It is very expressive.)

JENNIE: Faith Robert Hope Robert Life
    Robert Love!
Hat Robert Shoe Robert Shirt Robert
    Glove!

Show Robert Tell Robert Truth Robert
    Lie!
P Robert Q Robert X Robert Y!

Angst Robert Doom Robert Fate Robert
    Hell!
Read Robert Write Robert Speak Robert
    Spell!

More Robert Less Robert Big Robert
    Small!
Day Robert Night Robert Spring Robert
    Fall!

(Beat. She retreats to the cart, ditches the pom-poms, dons a gangsta hat, whirls around, and strikes a pose, having become SIR JAMZALOT. He addresses the audience directly, showing off his hip-hop moves. We're at an impromptu performance in the school courtyard.)

SIR JAMZALOT: Hang yo' white hineys
    on de edge a yo' seats,
'cause here come de king a de kick-ass
    beats.

People say dey don't know me, an' I say,
    "Say what?
you be talkin' to de real Sir Jamzalot!"

(He pulls a massive gold chain from beneath his shirt: his personal "signifier.")

An' if dat don't ring a bell, I always got
    plan B:
dat's when I slap you 'side de head wiff
    a rhyme fo' free.

Now if you listen to my words, dey
    gonna blow yo' parameter,
just like dey bustin' out a dis iambic
    pentameter.

An' if you think dat's funky, watch me
    imper-o-vise
a little ditty bout de kid you seen befo'
    yo' eyes.

Say werd...
Say werd...

His daddy call him Robrit, Robrit,
    Robrit,
Daddy call him Robrit on de day he born
His daddy call him Robrit, Robrit,
    Robrit
Runnin' like a rabbit tru de knee-high
    corn

Say werd...
Say werd...

An' if you talks to Robrit, Robrit, Robrit
if you talks to Robrit gonna skiddle wiff
    de scary
'Cause if you talks to Robrit, Robrit,
    Robrit
Robrit gonna hit you wiff de big vo-
    cabulary
say dat Robrit gonna hit you wiff de big
    vocabulary

Break it down...

This next one begins with

This with which this
begins it says Robrit with this
This with which this begins
Oh says Robrit
well let's get on with it!

Here comes Robrit, he's walkin' down de hall,
his brain be bouncin' like a basketball,
he thinks nobody loves him—he's probably right—
but dat hold him back from havin' dreams at night,
an' daydreams too, when he's sittin' on his ass,
tryin' to stay awake in some stupid class,
an' what's he dream about, you peoples wants to know?
If you ain't figured it by now, you honkeys too slow!
He's dreamin' of this girl—I've known her since grade three,
an' she ain't nothin' special, ya'll, take it from me.
I mean, she's nice, makes good grades an' whateva,
but if you aks me would I aks her out, I say, Neva!
Day's way too many hotties, ain't no time to waste
on chilly ones, but hey, dey's no accountin' fo' taste.
But whether hot or cold, you best be giddyin' uppa,
'cause time be runnin' out to aks a girl to suppa,
by which I mean fo' Robrit to aks her to de Prom,
an' if he chickins out, he'll have to go wiff his mom!
Naw, dat ain't funny, ya'll, I takes it back.
But all dat I be sayin', Robrit gots to a-tack,
'cause if he don't, I give him maybe coupla years,
till nothin' left a him but lonesome tears.

(He strikes another hip-hop pose. Beat. He whirls around to face the cart. Sound of the bus horn honking. The cap comes off, chain disappears, a beat-up pair of glasses goes on; he has become LURLENE. *Through the following, she puts on a headscarf, mimes handling the steering wheel, glances up from time to time into the "mirror," and addresses the "passengers" behind her.)*

LURLENE: Ya'll quieten down! Hush up! Don't make me cuss.
Or how am I supposed to drive this bus
with all that racket? I cain't hardly think!
Ya'll keep it up, an' quicker than a wink
I'll turn this bus around an'—Robert? Son?
The heck you standin' over there? Set down!
You young'uns, what's got into y'all today?
I swarr, I'd have more fun with better pay
a gettin' blowed up in Iraq, an' —*ow!*
—That does it.

(She pulls the bus over, slams it into park, gets out of the driver's seat, whirls around, and stares at us furiously.)

Now. Who shot that spit wad?... Well? Who was it?
Swarr this bus ain't movin' half a inch
till someone fesses up. I'm gonna pinch
some arms an' knock some heads together too.
Felicia?... Dudley?... Danny?... Cindy-Lou?
I know it wasn't Robert. Jill?... Maureen?
Wait—who's that hidin' back there?
 ...Sherry Green!
Don't look all innocent, young lady. Shucks!
I know a guilty face! I bet ten bucks
you done it. You or Danny Johnston, one.

...You think you're funny, huh? I'll show
   you fun.
I'll show you fun. What say I drive us off
   the bridge at Vengeance Creek? Sound
   fun enough?
'Cause I ain't got a dad-blame thing to
   lose.
My momma's back in jail for runnin'
   booze,
my car's impounded, husband's hooked
   on meth,
an' if you young'uns think I'm skeered
   of death,
you got a *great big fat surprise a comin'!*
Keep on knockin', people, keep on
   drummin'
Heaven's Door, it's gonna open right
about the time I gun this sumbitch
   straight
on through that guardrail out into the
   blue!
So bring it on, you little turds! I dare you!
Bring it on! It's time to go meet God!
...All right then. Now. Who shot me
   with that spit wad?

*(She glares at us, waiting. Beat. She morphs
into ROBERT, who pulls the scarf off his
head, removes the glasses, and speaks to the
audience directly. He's just been dropped
off at the bus stop in his neighborhood. It's
mid-afternoon. He gradually makes his
way back to the cart.)*

ROBERT: Well, I was gonna ask her
   on the bus.
But then I didn't feel like it. Some kids
got rowdy was the thing. Stupid Danny
   Johnston snapped Felicia Higgins' bra
   strap.
And well it sort of went downhill from
   there.
But that's okay, though, I can call tonight.
I have her number written down. Right
   here.

*(Beat. He becomes OL' PREACHA, who
shuffles back to his chair as he puts on his
coat. Through the following, he picks up
his guitar, is about to attempt to put it on
again, reconsiders, uses it instead as a cane
to lower himself into his seat, then rests it
on his lap and plays softly underneath the
remainder of the speech. He addresses the
audience directly. It's now evening.)*

OL' PREACHA: It always look like
   afternoon
wiff Robrit, always gettin' late.
Sometime a leaf or two come down,
come droppin' tru de copp'ry light,

not in de sky a cloud above,
no robin in de lonesome tree,
ol' Robrit take his hat an' glove,
go walkin', feelin' misery

an' all broke down wiff heavy hurt.
He come by, see me at my shack
an' squat down in de leafy dirt,
de sun sink low behine his back.

I plays a song. Sometime it help:
he lookin' an' a'list'nin' hard,
den stomp his foot an' moan an' yelp—
he scare de chiggins out de yard!

Come time I pats him on de head
an' sends him on his merry way.
(No sense he make his momma mad
not gettin' home till break a day!)

*(The music trails off into the evening. Beat.
He becomes JUAN-JORGE, who pulls out
a cigarette as he addresses the audience
directly. Through the following, he rises,
returns OL' PREACHA's guitar, removes
the coat, pulls up a chair down center,
which he straddles backwards facing us.)*

JUAN-JORGE: *Olá.* It's me again. You
   mind if I...?
If you'll indulge me for a moment here,
while Roberto get his courage up to ask

dis so-call "Dark-Haired Girl" to Prom,
—an' none too soon—I thought I share
   with you
some *observationes*. Well, more like dis ting
dat sort of bothers me. I've been at dis
angelic stuff awhile now, seen a lot
of people come an' go, but one ting always
seem to—I don't know—to make me
   tink.
...I mean, *it must be hard to be alive.*
'Cause, well, 'cause first of all, you're
   stuck in Time.
So all dis *stuff* keeps *happening*, you know?
Like, every moment's *packed* with all
   dis *stuff*!
An' who knows *what's* important an'
   what isn't.
Hell, it's like you're in dis giant *tunnel*,
an' dis *blizzard* blowing past you from
behind, a hundred fifty miles an hour,
an' you're supposed to read a secret
   message
written on a snowflake. *Muy difícil*, no?
An' plus, let's say you even somehow knew
which snowflake had de message. Still,
   you know
what happens when you try to grab a
   snowflake...
Sí. An' dat's de meaning of your life.
Oh, sure, you do your best, you try to
   choose
as wisely as you can from what you know,
but it's all happening so doggone fast.
You're focused on some great big ting
   or other
seems muy importante at de time,
'til thirty-five years later, you discover
someting else off in de corner, someting
you had barely noticed, some slight shift
in tone of voice, a glance, a hunch, de
   briefest
moment of distraction, or a message
left unopen in your Inbox, dat
turns out to have determined who you
   are,

to have laid out your life's direction—not
your constant worrying an' planning, not
your conscious choices, not your constant flailing
after flakes of snow! An' so, before
you know it, you've become precisely
   who
you are. An' you may say den to yourself,
*If only I had known, if only I
had paid attention to dat slightest shifting
in her tone of voice, dat glance I let
slip by, if only I had called him back,
if only I had seen de pattern, seen
de truth of what was happening! I could
have chosen differently! I could have changed
de shape of things! But dat was it: dat single
moment back so many years ago, when I
was just a kid! Dat moment when I blinked,
an' universes trembled into motion...*

(*Beat. The sound of a phone ringing.
He brightens with anticipation, having
become JENNIE. She runs back to the cart,
retrieves a cordless phone along with one of
her pom-poms, comes back downstage. We
are in her room. It is evening. Through the
following, she absentmindedly plays with
her pom-pom, checks her midriff, does some
floor work, etc.*)

JENNIE: Hello?...Okay, so, oh my God,
so, like, my brother? Oh my God.
He's such a *dork*—you won't believe—
He doesn't have a date for Prom?
Like, *duh*, but it's his *senior Prom*,
his only chance to, like, be *normal*?
Right? But so he hasn't even
asked anybody yet!...I know!
And now *tomorrow* is the Prom!
...Huh?...Oh, no, he bought 'em, like,
three months ago, I remember
when he asked Daddy for the money.
He never asks Daddy for, like,
anything, this was a *huge* deal.
...Huh?...Well, so, like, today I tried
to set him up with Melanie,

who's been, like, totally *in love*
with him since *seventh grade*,
I can't imagine *why*, he doesn't
even *look* at her, I mean
he's nice and all, and he's my *brother*
and I *love* him blah blah blah,
but, oh my God, he's such a *retard*!
I mean, his *Senior Prom*, okay?
Like, what's he *waiting* for? And so
I'm thinking, Why not set him up
with Melanie? You know? So, like,
this afternoon? Like, Melanie
comes over for a while, and she's
like, *totally* psyched about it,
'cause it's, like, her *dream come true*,
I can't imagine why, and we're
all set to spring the question on him?
Then, so, here he comes, okay?
He walks in, doesn't even *look*
at us, goes straight up to the *phone*,
like, picks it *up*, okay? He's, like,
about to *dial*—and then he puts it
down again and leaves…Oh it
was quite peculiar…No, but then,
but *then*, so fifteen minutes later,
here he comes *again*, picks up the phone,
dials a number, and I mean,
like, *a* number, then he stops
again and walks away!…I know, I
    know!—
And *then*, another fifteen minutes,
here he comes *again* and *this* time,
what a *hero*, gets through *three*
big numbers. Oh my God, he came back
seven times, and never actually
talked to anybody, right?
So Melanie and I were, like,
Is Robert, like, *insane*? But then
we realized, like, this whole time?
He'd been, like, trying to get his *courage*
up to ask some *girl* to Prom!
…I know, I know! It's so *pathetic*!
So Melanie is, like, You *dork*.
I would *totally* have gone
to *Prom* with you, except that now

she sees what I've been telling her
since *seventh grade*: he's, like, this total
space cadet! He does not have
clue one…I know, it's just so *sad*.
And I'm, like, Oh my God, *why can't
I have a normal brother?* —Hey,
what you get on the Civics test?
No way!…Oh my God, I hate you!

*(She hangs up. Beat. She becomes PAP,
who cleans up his daughter's stuff, slowly
rises to his feet. Through the following, he
returns phone and pom-pom to the cart,
retrieves a can of PBR, drinks, returns to
his chair on the "porch," sits, puts on his
hat. He addresses the audience directly. It
is late evening.)*

PAP: Some things is hard to say.
To say is hard and having said is also hard.

Sometimes it's best to steer clear of the
    thicket,
keep your back to all that's hidin' there.
It ain't pretty.
Not very edifying for the youth of today.

Some days I wonder why do I—why
does anyone do anything?
I could set and sink without I even
move a muscle, feel, or think,
just let the whole thing go to hell.
Or maybe just I go to hell
and let them all be happy and perfect,
their perfect happiness not tugged at,
jostled by my trying to have a place there.

*(He crushes his empty beer can, retrieves
his banjo.)*

So many people born after me!
So many girls and young fellers
who will grow up and do their thing.
Interesting, amazing things they'll do,
overtaking me and moving on,
while I sit in the same spot off in the weeds
year after year, my mind all rust-empty,
my body in its roots like a stump,

as the whole civilization jangles on
without me.

(He plays and sings "Mole in the Ground.")

WELL I WISH I WAS A MOLE IN THE GROUND
YES I WISH I WAS A MOLE IN THE GROUND
IF I'S A MOLE IN THE GROUND, I'D ROOT
  THAT MOUNTAIN DOWN
AND I WISH I WAS A MOLE IN THE GROUND

I WISH I WAS A LIZARD IN THE SPRING
YES I WISH I WAS A LIZARD IN THE SPRING
IF I'S A LIZARD IN THE SPRING, I'D HEAR
  MY DARLIN' SING
AND I WISH I WAS A LIZARD IN THE SPRING

I WISH I WAS A BIRD IN THE SKY
YES I WISH I WAS A BIRD IN THE SKY
IF I'S A BIRD IN THE SKY, AWAY, AWAY I'D FLY
AND I WISH I WAS A BIRD IN THE SKY

(The song has revived his spirits. He's back to his old self. Through the following, he returns the banjo to its place.)

PAP: I ever tell y'uns bout the time that Robert
won the County Science Fair? Well, *should*
  a won. —Oh, Lard! That boy got this
  idear
he could get a radish plant to growin'
bigger radishes by *starin'* at it!
Boy said he was, what, was *meddy-tatin'*.
Thinkin' lovie-dovie thoughts about
a plant! I swarr, that young'un. Has hisself
some funny ways a'doin' things. Sometimes
I get to thinking that I might a raised
a Communist or somethin'! Boy's a
  dreamer,
like I say. Not like his sister here.
She's practical. She knows what's what.
  Like me.
She's got some street smarts like you
  never see.
A girl her age. But Robert, now, well,
  Robert,

he, uh, *booksmarts* 'bout the only kind
a smarts he got. But, boy, he's got 'em too.
I tell ye what. I set him down just now
to talk about this *Rizzdy* type a deal,
this *skollership*. An' dawg my two-bit cats
if Robert didn't lay it out just like a
  lawyer
and a banker all rolled up in one!
Why, he knowed all about the differ'nt
  kinda
costs an' such, tuition, fees, supplies
an' I don't know what 'hall...his *livin'*
  costs.
And, boys, I tell y'uns what, 'hit t'weren't
  no peanuts
neither. Nawsir. Hell, I didn't know
the guvment even *printed* that much
  money!
Then he took an' showed me where it says
these *Rizzdy* folks is gonna pay it all,
an' I mean ever cotton-pickin' cent.
I swarr! I never hear'd a nothin' like it.
Made me sorta proud. Ol' Robert must
be pretty smart, work out a deal like that
with all them big-shot *finance* type a
  Yankees.
Heck, I bet he's gonna make a lawyer
after all! He'll win us back the old place
from his momma's no good brother! Ha!
She tells me not to go an' count my
  chiggins.
Shucks! I tell her, Woman! What's got holt
a you? Ain't you got any faith in Robert's
future as a *ligi-tater?* She says,
"Honey, you can put a cat in the oven,
but that don't make it a biscuit." Folks,
  I deal
with that stuff ever' day. But me, why,
  shucks,
I figger anybody what can git
a radish growin' twicet its normal size
by just a-*settin'* there an *thinkin'* at it
why I say, a—*meddy-tatin'*—why,
a fella what can do a thing like that
has got potential. Leastaways in farmin'.

(Beat. He removes his hat, having become ROBERT, who now considers his hands. Through the following, he returns the hat to its place hanging on the banjo, moves the two chairs together to make his bed, and uses OL' PREACHA's coat as a pillow. We are once again in his bedroom. It is night.)

ROBERT: My hands look funny.
And my feet, which wanted to be hands.
All those little bones in there.
What do they think about all this?
About all these terrible, these—.

Is one of my legs crooked?

If there were more pillows I would make
   a fort.
I would hide there, in the blue stillness.
And no one would touch me.
No one would touch me.

Sometimes a body likes to be alone,
like this, farming its little patch of warmth.

*(Though other times it aches
to feel a shy and lovely nother near it,
hear another voice drift over it,
sink down in it
and sleep.)*

(His head drifts toward the pillow. He falls asleep. Pause. JUAN-JORGE emerges. He addresses us directly and in a whisper. We are in ROBERT's dream.)

JUAN-JORGE: In his dream,
she smiles an' says *Honest: I've walked alone more than a thousand miles.*
Slender her barefoot foot, de nails
atwinkle pinkly on dirt-speckled
toes, empty her handedness, no
foodstuff, no extra clothes—nothing.
He hefts his towered pack... *No kidding! That's more than I could dream to do!*
And den she leads de way, de trail
opens to heathbald, crusted stone,
blue ridge-backs an' de far-off tongues
of smoke an' he says... *Beautiful. One day I'll make it back again!*
Her dark hair whirls. De sunlight sings!

(He retrieves OL' PREACHA's guitar, places it carefully on the floor beside ROBERT's bed. He brushes the strings with his hand, departs. ROBERT wakes, sees the guitar, slowly reaches for it, grasps it gently, lifts it to his lap, and slips the strap over his head. He plays tentatively at first, as if learning, then sings.)

ROBERT: DON'T LOOK NOW, I'M NORTH-
   BOUND, ON THE MOVE,
I'M FLYIN', CRYIN' DOWN THE MOUNTAIN-
   SIDE,
I GOT THE WHEELS, I GOT THE JUICE, I GOT
   THE TITLE, TAX, AND TAGS, I GOT MY STUFF
   STASHED IN THE BACK, I GOT THE PLAN,
   AND MAN,
I'M MOVING OUT, IT'S AUGUST, AND THE SUN
   IS IN ITS PLACE, AND IN ITS PLACE THE
   MOON,
THE SMOKY HILLS, THE HIGHWAY CARV-
   ING THROUGH,
AND DEDDY'S GREEN T-BIRD'S RUST-
   BESPECKLED
HOOD'S BELLICOSE UPSLOPE CUTS MY
   WAKE
DOWN HARVEST-HEAVY MORNING, DOWN
   THROUGH MIST
OF CREEK AND POLLEN-LADEN LAUREL
   COVE,
THE ENGINE PURRING LIKE A PANTHER,
   LAPPING
CLOUDS OF PERFECT SPIN, THE BLUR OF
   MILES
AND LANDSCAPES DISAPPEARING, VIRGIN
   TWIRLING, STAINS
AND PEELING VINYL, HAND SO LIGHTLY
   RESTING
ON THE ROUGH-HAND-SMOOTH-WORN
   STEERING WHEEL,
MY OTHER HAND A WING OUTSIDE THE
   WINDOW,

LIFTING, GATHERING THE SUSTENANCE
OF RUSHING AIR BENEATH IT, FINGERING
THE BURLY GUSTS LIKE GOLDEN RUNGS,
  THE LADDER
I'VE BEEN CLIMBING, SOON TO LEAVE
  THIS GROUND,
STEP FROM IT INTO HEAT-CURLED LIGHT,
  RISE UP,
AND SING A SONG OF LONGINGS LONG
  UNSUNG,
WHERETO I'M UNDER WAY, THE MOMENTARY
MONARCH OF THESE WEEDS AND DITCHES,
  RAIL,
ERODED BANK, RUNAWAY-TRUCK RAMP,
  BOTTLES
AND CANS AND PAPER BAGS AND PLASTIC
  BAGS,
OLD TIRES AND TIRE-PEELINGS, BILL-
  BOARDS, BITS
OF PAPER, POLES AND PILES, AND OTHER
  CARS
SOMETIMES WITH GIRLS, AND ALWAYS
  OUT AHEAD
THE PULSING ARC OF GOLD TO GUIDE
  MY PASSAGE
IN RHYTHM TO THIS DAY'S ALWAYS BEGIN-
  NING,
AS BEHIND, A DEARER THREAD SPINS OUT
OF ME, UNRAVELING FOR MILES AND MILES
INVISIBLY TO WHERE SHE STOOD AND
  TWIRLED,
THE SUNLIGHT SANG, AND I COULD GO
  UNTO
THE ENDS OF EARTH—AND MAYBE I JUST
  WILL—
AND NEVER SEE THE DARK-HAIRED MOON
  AGAIN,
BUT I WILL FEEL HER GRAVITATION TUG ME,
I WILL TEST THE THREAD AND KNOW IT
  STRONG
AND TOUCHING SOMETHING, THRUMMING
  IN THE WIND
OF YEARS TOWARD THAT HOLY CITADEL
OF MOMENTS WHEN SHE ALWAYS SET
  ME FREE.

FOR THERE IS THAT VASTNESS DEEP IN ME.

(Pause. He morphs into OL' PREACHA. Through the following, he places the guitar, banjo, and other remaining props back in the cart, and puts on his coat.)

OL' PREACHA: Now Robrit's songs be
  right near done.
An' some a dem was kinda fun
to hear. Dough I cain't get holt on
de half a 'hit. An' now he's gone.

Growed up I guess. Or moved away
like young'uns do, some brisky day,
when autumn flecks de black-stemmed
  tree
wiff gold. I has to let it be.

But still I likes to think a him
a settin' dere, full to de brim
wid love, an wonder what became
a all dem hurts wiffout no name.

You aks about de Dark-Haired Girl?
His lovely one, his priceless pearl?...

(He remembers his hat on the floor, notices it contains only the change he put there. He's been at this too long to make much fuss. He reaches down, picks it up, empties the change once again into his pocket, folds down the "$" sign, puts the hat on. This takes no more than a few seconds.)

De feeling wadn't mutual,
you know.

(He returns to his cart, preparing to leave. He pauses, turns back to the audience one last time.)

> Someday it will be, though.
> Dat's all.

(He nods in farewell, pushes the cart out as the lights fade. Maybe he hums the old gospel blues tune, "I'm Goin' Home.")

(END OF PLAY)

MILKMILKLEMONADE

Joshua Conkel

JOSHUA CONKEL was born in 1980 in Lexington, Kentucky, and was raised principally in Hansville, Washington, a small town north of Seattle. He has a BFA in theater from Cornish College of the Arts in Seattle (which he attended at the same time as fellow *Plays and Playwrights 2010* contributor Will Le Vasseur). After moving to New York, he joined The Management theatre company, for which he now serves as artistic director. The Management produced his play *The Chalk Boy* in 2008 in New York City. Other productions of his include *The Chalk Boy* (Company of Angels, Los Angeles, 2008) and the forthcoming West Coast premiere of *MilkMilkLemonade* at Impact Theatre in Berkeley, California. Conkel's short plays have been produced by Youngblood/Ensemble Studio Theatre in New York and around the United States; *Up With (Some) People* was a finalist at the 2009 Samuel French Off-Off Broadway Festival. Conkel also works as a director; some notable credits include assistant direction of the original production of *The Light in the Piazza* at the Intiman Theatre in Seattle, and assisting Craig Lucas with preproduction of the film *The Dying Gaul*. Conkel is currently working on a dark comedy about housewives who huff, a soap opera inspired in part by Franz Kafka's "The Metamorphosis," a web series with playwright/actress Nikole Beckwith, and a graphic novel. He lives in Williamsburg, Brooklyn, with his soon-to-be husband, Keith, and a cat named Gus.

MilkMilkLemonade was developed by Pavement Group of Chicago, Illinois. It was subsequently presented in New York by The Management in association with Horse Trade Theater Group (Erez Ziv, Executive Director) at Under St. Marks on September 10, 2010, with the following cast and credits:

Emory	Andy Phelan
Elliot	Jess Barbagallo
Nanna	Michael Cyril Creighton
Linda	Jennifer Harder
Lady in a Leotard	Nikole Beckwith

Directed by: Isaac Butler
Sets by: Jason Simms
Lighting by: Sabrina Braswell
Costumes by: Sydney Maresca
Sound by: Isaac Butler
Stage Managed by: Kelsi Welter
Publicity by: Emily Owens PR
Graphic Design by: John Alexander
Choreography by: Meredith Steinberg

For Keith Aaron Rohn and queer kids everywhere. Keep reaching for those stars!

CAST OF CHARACTERS

EMORY: An effeminate eleven-year-old boy.

ELLIOT: The little boy from down the road. Has a parasitic twin living in his enormous thigh.

NANNA: An elderly cancer patient and Emory's grandmother. Bald, with an oxygen tank.

LINDA: A depressed chicken with a Brooklyn accent. Emory's best friend and confidante.

LADY IN A LEOTARD: A narrator in a black leotard. Suffers from performance anxiety.

SETTING

A farm near Mall Town, USA. The set should look as if it were designed and built by second graders for their school play: slightly retarded-looking, but charming just the same. A farmhouse, a big red barn, etc. There should be several bales of hay for the actors to sit on. Surrounding the playing space are many inanimate chickens who are alive but too lethargic to move. Important: a cassette player. Important also: a lemon yellow sun that passes from sun up to sun down over the course of the play. One corner of the stage is the domain of the Lady in a Leotard, who has a microphone, claves, a toy xylophone, etc., and provides foley art during the show. She never leaves the stage.

TIME

Whenever. Now-ish.

A NOTE ON CASTING

The characters may be played by actors of any physical description, across gender or ethnicity. I want to especially encourage directors to cast actors who are transgender or gender queer. Don't be a pussy. BE BOLD.

Chickens clucking in darkness. A LADY IN A LEOTARD appears in a bubble of light. She has a dumpy butt which, when shoved into spandex, gives her a pitiable air. She surveys the audience but says nothing. She seems nervous. Actually, she is terrified. She is about to cry or throw up from nerves. It becomes awkward. Not knowing what to do, she sings.

LADY IN A LEOTARD: *(Singing with gestures.)* Head, shoulders, knees, and toes, knees and toes. Head, shoulders, knees, and toes, knees and toes. Eyes and ears and mouth and nose. Head, shoulders, knees, and toes, knees and toes. *(Speaking, but nervously and flatly. She asks questions but doesn't wait for an answer.)* Hooray. That was fun. That was a song about your body. This is my body here. Can you point to your body? Good work. Morrissey asked, does the body rule the mind or does the mind rule the body? He was super wise. And what is the body? Is it us? Are we our bodies? Or are we inside our bodies looking out as if through a window? Don't think too hard. Is your noodle warmed up? It is? Okay. Then follow me and we'll see a play, *MilkMilkLemonade*, and use our imaginations. Yay. You should know that when I'm not onstage playing a parasitic twin, giving voice to the inanimate, or translating chicken clucking into common English, I will attempt to remain as neutral as possible. Neutral means boring. To that end, I've decided to wear this simple black leotard and these sensible flats. You're welcome. Follow me now, if you will, and the play will begin. *(She tiptoes to another part of the stage.)* Oh! This is the set. Ta da. Mall Town, USA, with its Radio Shacks and Taco Bells, is just thirty minutes west. But here, on the farm, there is clean air, green grass, and space. Lots of space. Smell that air! *(She takes in a deep breath.)* What a beautiful day. *(She crosses to the inanimate chickens.)* These represent the chickens on the farm. They're important.

(The sun rises. Dawn. She crows like a rooster.)

LADY IN A LEOTARD: PROLOGUE! Emory and Linda.

(EMORY, a little boy, and LINDA, a chicken, appear in a bubble of light. LADY IN A LEOTARD translates LINDA's clucking into common English.)

EMORY: Linda!

LINDA: Bawk!

LADY IN A LEOTARD: Emory.

EMORY: Are you okay, girl?

LINDA: Bawk bawk bawk bawk.

LADY IN A LEOTARD: I'm extremely depressed. I'm in my dark place again.

EMORY: You need to cheer up, Linda. It's a beautiful day!

LINDA: Bawk bawk bawk bawk bawk.

LADY IN A LEOTARD: I know I should be happy…but I just can't help it.

EMORY: Oh, Linda. You just need to find some self-confidence.

LINDA: Bawk bawk bawk P-KAW.

LADY IN A LEOTARD: I have a terrible sense of foreboding.

EMORY: Don't be afraid, Linda. You've got me. I'm here, and I won't let anything happen to you.

LINDA: Bawk bawk bawk bawk.

LADY IN A LEOTARD: Thanks. You're a real pal, Emory. A real pal.

EMORY: You too. Wanna practice for our dance routine?

LINDA: P-KAW!

(EMORY pushes "play" on the cassette player: "Anything Goes" by Harpers Bizarre, the '70s version from The Boys in the Band*. They begin a highly choreographed dance routine. What follows is a full-fledged dance number. Perhaps the LADY*

IN A LEOTARD joins in. It ends in a tableau. The ACTORS are panting as if they've just done something spectacular. And... break—)

NANNA: *(From offstage.)* Emory! Oh, Emory! Stop dancing with that big old chicken!

EMORY: Shoot. It's Nanna. Go, Linda, go!

LINDA: P-KAW! *(Exits.)*

LADY IN A LEOTARD: That was the prologue. Now the play begins...

(NANNA appears seated on a bale of hay. She is attached to an oxygen tank by way of tubes coming from her nostrils and has a shaved head. She is dressed in denim knee-length shorts and the type of shirt that depicts either (a) a wolf howling at the moon, or (b) a majestic Native American woman. EMORY, doll in hand, sulks at her feet. They are frozen.)

LADY IN A LEOTARD: Emory and his grandmother. A sturdy, Christian woman. Her name is Nanna. Emory is receiving a lecture. He sulks.

(She recedes into the shadows and the play begins.)

NANNA: Where was I? Oh, yes. I think it was Jesus or god who said, "Thou shalt not lie with another man as with a woman. It is an abomination." Now, that's in Leviticus. And that's why fags are nasty.

EMORY: I still don't see why I can't keep Starlene.

NANNA: See, we've all got roles in Life, Emory. And it's these roles that keep order. Like you're my grandson and I'm your Nanna. That's how we know each other. Now, if people didn't play the roles that god gave 'em, then what would happen?

EMORY: I don't know.

NANNA: What's that?

EMORY: I said I don't know, Nanna.

NANNA: We'd have chaos, is what.

EMORY: I guess.

NANNA: You guess? Let me ask you this: what would happen if we stopped farming chickens?

EMORY: I don't know. Somebody else would, I guess.

NANNA: But what if everybody stopped farming chickens?

EMORY: Then there'd be no chickens to eat.

NANNA: That's right. There'd be no chickens to eat. So "chicken farmer" is one of our roles, and an important one.

EMORY: But people could just eat cereal or strawberries or something.

NANNA: Ah, but suppose people stopped showing up to work at the cereal factory? Suppose the Mexicans went back to Mexico? What then?

EMORY: I get it.

NANNA: Good. Now. Let's come up with some other roles you play. Can you think of any?

EMORY: I'm a grandson.

NANNA: Okay, we covered that one. Any others?

EMORY: I'm a fifth grader.

NANNA: Good, good...

EMORY: I'm a singer and a dancer!

NANNA: Let's not get carried away, now. What else are you?

(Pause. EMORY is stumped.)

NANNA: You're a boy.

EMORY: Oh!

NANNA: And boys have got to be boys. Because our gender is one of the many roles we play. We gotta follow the plan that god gives us. You have a pee-pee between your legs and so that is who you are. A boy!

EMORY: But can't some boys, just some, why can't they do girl stuff?

NANNA: No. Now I think it's time you handed her over.

EMORY: *(He does. Slowly and sadly.)* Bye, Starlene. I'll miss your hair.

NANNA: That's my little man.

EMORY: Nanna?

NANNA: Yes, Emory?

EMORY: I miss her. I miss her already.

NANNA: Well, I know it's rough, but Starlene was impeding your potential.

EMORY: I guess.

NANNA: Now you can grow up to be a big strong man like your daddy. Now he's a real man. Thick as a barrel and hairy as a wookie!

EMORY: Who?

NANNA: You know who I'm talking about. My Chuck. He's tall? Has a beard? Wears a lot of plaid?

EMORY: Oh, right. Where is he again?

NANNA: I wish I knew, darlin'.

EMORY: He must be with Mother.

NANNA: It barely matters.

EMORY: Nanna?

NANNA: Mm-hmm?

EMORY: Did you always wanna be a chicken farmer?

NANNA: I suppose I never thought about it much. I just always was one.

EMORY: You never wanted to live in Mall Town?

NANNA: Oh, I don't know. I like it here.

EMORY: You don't like Mall Town?

NANNA: Sure I do. They have a Home Depot there and I enjoy that very much.

EMORY: I like Cinnabon.

NANNA: Oh, me too.

EMORY: I feel bad for them. The chickens.

NANNA: Don't feel bad, Emory. These chickens here, they have a nice life.

EMORY: But they get killed and eaten up.

NANNA: But that's their role, see? Chickens are born to be eaten. And besides, here on our farm, everything before then is pretty nice. Our chickens here, they get to stretch their legs and feel the sunlight on their backs. That's what you call your "free range." The end part, the frightening part, is quick. They don't feel a thing.

EMORY: How do you know?

NANNA: Because I've seen pain before, and plenty of it. On some farms the chickens are put in tiny little cages and stacked eight or nine high. The farmer gives 'em drugs so they get fat and stupid like. Oh, it's a terrible life for an animal.

EMORY: Gross.

NANNA: You better believe it. But still...that's better than a... *(Leaning in to whisper.)* ...Boneless, skinless chicken farm.

EMORY: There's no such thing!

NANNA: There most certainly is. Where do you think boneless, skinless chicken comes from? You wanna know something? I went to one up north of Mall Town once.

EMORY: You lie!

NANNA: Hand to god! I'll never forget it.

EMORY: What were they like?

NANNA: Funny little birds. They're bred so they don't got any bones or skin whatsoever. They're just fleshy pink things, really. Not much more than blobs.

EMORY: Stop.

NANNA: They can't move a muscle because they don't got none. The farmer has to come around with a spray bottle to keep their flesh moist else they dry up.

EMORY: Nuh-huh.

NANNA: And their eyes, Emory. God, their eyes! I never seen such hollow eyes.

EMORY: Stop talking, Nanna!

NANNA: Oh, don't be such a little girl.

EMORY: You must be lying. How do they eat if they can't move?

NANNA: The farmer sticks a funnel down their beaks and pours the scraps in, of course. The noise they make. I'll never forget that noise. It was like...

(She throws her head back and makes a disgusting gargling sound. EMORY screams and NANNA laughs.)

EMORY: Are there really boneless, skinless chicken farms?

NANNA: I said there were, didn't I?

EMORY: I'm never eating a chicken again.

NANNA: Sure you will. Because chickens are delicious. And just like they were born to be eaten, we were born to eat 'em.

EMORY: Nope. I'm a vegan now.

NANNA: I wonder how long that'll last.

EMORY: I hate this farm. I wanna move to Mall Town.

NANNA: Well, fortunately for you by the time you're old enough to make a decision like that, Mall Town will have already come here to us. That's what you call "sprawl."

EMORY: I could have Cinnabon every day.

NANNA: Yes, indeed.

EMORY: Nanna?

NANNA: Yes, Emory?

EMORY: I wanna go to Mall Town and audition for *Reach for the Stars*.

NANNA: Reach for the what now?

EMORY: It's a TV show, a talent competition, and you can sing or dance or do comedy and they rate you on a scale of one to ten. I think I could win it. I've been practicing really hard.

NANNA: Yes, well. Best give up on that dream before it gets out of hand. You are so thin skinned, after all. Remember when you didn't win that design contest in *Homes and Gardens Magazine*?

EMORY: My zen room was fantastic! The Far East meets the Midwest!

NANNA: Get ahold of yourself. My stars! Just imagine how you would feel if you went on the boob tube and made a fool of yourself in front of god and America and everybody.

EMORY: But I would win!

NANNA: But what if you didn't?

EMORY: But I would.

NANNA: No, no, no, no. Best to stay here with your Nanna where it's nice and safe.

EMORY: I don't ever feel safe.

NANNA: Now I'm all worn out. Emory, I don't feel so good. I think I better go and lie down. Will you finish feeding the chickens?

EMORY: Sure.

NANNA: They gotta go in the machine today.

EMORY: Today?

NANNA: Yes, sir. We gotta put them chickens in today or else…

EMORY: Can't we wait?

NANNA: You know we can't. And after you finish feeding the chickens you may play for a while, but make sure it's something that isn't too girly. Why don't you invite your friend over?

EMORY: Linda?

NANNA: Who? No, I was talking about that little boy from down the road. The one whose family is always burning garbage in their yard.

EMORY: Elliot. He's not my friend. He's a creep.

LADY IN A LEOTARD: *(Interjects.)* This is Elliot, the little boy from down the road.

(ELLIOT appears in a bubble of light. He has a black eye. He pulls pages from a textbook one by one, lights them on fire, and drops them into a wastebasket.)

ELLIOT: *(Singing to the tune of the "Battle Hymn of the Republic.")* My eyes have seen the glory of the burning of the school. We have tortured every teacher, we have broken every rule. We have barbecued the principal, destroyed the PTA, our school keeps burning on. *(He disappears.)*

LADY IN A LEOTARD: He's important.

(LADY IN A LEOTARD retreats into the shadows and the previous scene continues.)

NANNA: I said, dinner will be ready by six o'clock. You gotta stop your brain from wandering so.

EMORY: Sorry.

NANNA: My sweet prince. *(As she exits.)* Next time I got into town I'm gonna buy you a brand-new baseball. *(She is gone.)*

EMORY: *(To himself.)* I hate baseball. *(Gets up and begins to feed scraps to the motionless chickens.)* Here chick-chick-chick-chick. Here chick-chick-chick-chick. *(He stops. He throws his head back and makes a gargling noise, pretending to be a boneless, skinless chicken. He does this for a while. He looks to see if anybody is around and, satisfied they are not, he nods to LADY IN A LEOTARD as if to say, "Let's begin." He exits. He renters with a ribbon stick. He presses "play" on the cassette player.)*

LADY IN A LEOTARD: Ladies and gentlemen, please give a warm *Reach for the Stars* welcome for Emory and his amazing ribbon stick!

(Applause. Spotlight. EMORY begins a highly choreographed and expertly lip-synched ribbon stick number to Nina Simone's "Ain't Got No/I Got Life." He's talented. Shortly into the number he loses his place. He pushes "stop" and then "rewind." NANNA, ELLIOT, and LINDA appear in a bubble of light. They are the judges. They hold up their scores. NANNA: 2. ELLIOT: 6. LINDA: 10. The light returns to normal and all are gone but EMORY and LINDA.)

EMORY: Wait. There's a turn I missed there! *(To himself.)* If you wanna be famous it's time you start paying. In sweat!

(LINDA approaches EMORY affectionately. LADY IN A LEOTARD translates her clucking into common English. It's okay if their lines overlap just slightly.)

LINDA: P-KAW!

LADY IN A LEOTARD: Bravo. Encore. Encore.

EMORY: Oh, it's you, Linda. I was just practicing my passion speech for school. It's about *Reach for the Stars*.

LINDA: Bawk bawk bawk cluck cluck cluck.

LADY IN A LEOTARD: You are so freakin' talented, Emory. Your dancing makes me feel as if the farm is a lovely place to be instead of a pit of loneliness and despair.

EMORY: Thank you, Linda. That's very sweet of you. You're my favorite of all the chickens on the farm.

LINDA: P-KAW cluck cluck cluck.

LADY IN A LEOTARD: I don't know why. I can't stand myself.

EMORY: That's hysterical. You're so crazy.

LINDA: Bawk bawk bawk.

LADY IN A LEOTARD: I'll be here all week. Hey. What was that song?

EMORY: Oh, that was "Ain't Got No/I Got Life" by Nina Simone, may god rest her soul. You might recognize it from the musical *Hair*?

LINDA: Bawk bawk bawk bawk.

LADY IN A LEOTARD: Oh. I felt the film version was too disco.

EMORY: The movie wasn't as good as the stage show, no. It's a great song though. *(EMORY deflates.)*

LINDA: Cluck cluck.

LADY IN A LEOTARD: Hey. What's eating you?

EMORY: Oh, Linda. You can always read right through me. I've got bad news and I've got worse news.

LINDA: Bawk bawk bawk.

LADY IN A LEOTARD: I'll have the bad news and then the worse news.

EMORY: Nanna won't let me keep Starlene. She says dolls are for girls and fags.

LINDA: P-KAW!

LADY IN A LEOTARD: Say what!

EMORY: That's what I said. I tried to tell her that you and I and Starlene were gonna go on *Reach for the Stars*, but she didn't want to hear it.

LINDA: Bawk bawk bawk.

LADY IN A LEOTARD: Oh no.

EMORY: And now the worse news... today is processing day.

LINDA: Cluck cluck cluck.

LADY IN A LEOTARD: Should I worry?

EMORY: No. No, of course not. I always help you get out of it, don't I?

LINDA: Bawk bawk bawk.

LADY IN A LEOTARD: So you'll take care of me?

EMORY: Of course. Maybe I can sneak you into my room in my backpack again.

LINDA: Bawk bawk cluck. Cluck cluck cluck.

LADY IN A LEOTARD: I think the feed has made me too big for that now. Look at me, I'm enormous.

EMORY: You're not so big.

LINDA: Cluck cluck bawk bawk.

LADY IN A LEOTARD: Something is definitely happening to my body.

EMORY: I know what you mean. Hey! I know what we can do. You can stand on my shoulders with a wig and a mustache on and we'll wear a big trench coat over us.

LINDA: Bawk bawk bawk bawk.

LADY IN A LEOTARD: I don't think that would fool anybody.

EMORY: No, you're right. Think, Emory, think. We've got to get you out of here. But how?

LINDA: Cluck cluck.

LADY IN A LEOTARD: But—

EMORY: Ssh! Let me think. If you go into that machine you'll never come out again. Linda, do you know what happens in there?

LINDA: Bawk.

LADY IN A LEOTARD: No.

EMORY: *(Whispers into her ear.)* ...And then... *(He whispers more.)*

LINDA: P-KAW! P-KAW! P-KAW!

LADY IN A LEOTARD: Wh-Wh-What!?

EMORY: Quiet! Don't draw attention to yourself. I'm working on a plan to get us out of here. You, me, and Starlene.

LINDA: Cluck cluck cluck cluck.

LADY IN A LEOTARD: You'll help me?

EMORY: What did you expect? You're my best friend.

(A baseball rolls onto the stage.)

LINDA: P-Kaw!

LADY IN A LEOTARD: Dang!

EMORY: Shoot. Here comes Elliot.

LINDA: Bawk bawk bawk.

LADY IN A LEOTARD: He'll ruin everything.

EMORY: Go. I'll get rid of him.

LINDA: Bawk.

LADY IN A LEOTARD: I love you.

EMORY: I love you too. Now go! I'll find you.

(ELLIOT enters with a lit Virginia Slim in his mouth.)

ELLIOT: *(With appropriate gestures.)* Chinese, Japanese, dirty knees, look at THESE. *(He finds himself hysterical and laughs.)*

EMORY: That's so funny I forgot to laugh.

ELLIOT: What's going on, sissy?

EMORY: Elliot, leave me alone.

ELLIOT: No.

EMORY: Go away.

ELLIOT: No.

EMORY: Get off my property.

ELLIOT: It's not your property. This farm is your Nanna's.

EMORY: Get off my Nanna's farm.

ELLIOT: I said no.

EMORY: Where'd you get that black eye?

ELLIOT: My brother Danny hit me.

EMORY: Why?

ELLIOT: Because he's a dick.

EMORY: Oh.

ELLIOT: No, I set his health book on fire.

EMORY: Why?

ELLIOT: Because I felt like it. I like setting stuff on fire. Fire is cool.

EMORY: Oh.

ELLIOT: You're a faggot.

EMORY: I'll tell you smoke.

ELLIOT: Go ahead.

EMORY: I will.

ELLIOT: I said go ahead. I stole this one here from your Nanna. She's passed out on your porch again. Took it right out of the pack.

EMORY: I'll tell her.

ELLIOT: So tell her. She doesn't even know her ass from a hole in the ground.

EMORY: She's sick.

ELLIOT: You're sick. You're a faggot.

EMORY: Am not.

ELLIOT: Yes huh.

EMORY: Nuh-huh.

ELLIOT: Your Nanna has no hair. And the veins on her legs look like roads on a map. Take a drag of this cigarette.

EMORY: No.

ELLIOT: Yes.

EMORY: I said no.

ELLIOT: Emory has a vagina! Emory has a vagina!

EMORY: Do not.

ELLIOT: Then take a puff of this Virginia Slim.

(*EMORY doesn't move.*)

ELLIOT: Pussy.

EMORY: I'll do it.

(*EMORY timidly crosses to ELLIOT and takes a drag from his cigarette. He explodes into a coughing fit.*)

ELLIOT: You're a girl.

EMORY: Shut up.

ELLIOT: I wanna stick my dick in you.

EMORY: Leave me alone.

ELLIOT: I'm only teasing. Don't have a cow.

EMORY: Jerk.

ELLIOT: I said I was only joking. Don't be such a faggot.

EMORY: If my Nanna hears you curse she'll skin you alive.

ELLIOT: I'm not afraid of your Nanna. If she tries anything I'll punch her in her front butt.

EMORY: She will. She'll skin you alive.

ELLIOT: Listen, Emory. I came to see the chicken.

EMORY: No.

ELLIOT: YES.

EMORY: No.

ELLIOT: I'll punch you in the eye.

EMORY: I don't believe you.

(ELLIOT punches EMORY in the eye. EMORY screams.)

ELLIOT: You made me.

EMORY: Ouch. You jerk!

ELLIOT: You made me do it.

EMORY: I'm gonna tell.

ELLIOT: Don't.

(Punches him again.)

EMORY: Ouch.

ELLIOT: What were you doing when I came?

EMORY: What? Nothing.

ELLIOT: Tell.

EMORY: I was practicing my passion speech.

ELLIOT: Nuh-huh.

EMORY: I was. It's about *Reach for the Stars*.

ELLIOT: You can't do a passion speech like that. Everybody will think you're a homo.

EMORY: I'm not.

ELLIOT: A butt pirate!

EMORY: Stop.

ELLIOT: A fudge packer!

EMORY: Stop saying that stuff.

ELLIOT: Okay.

EMORY: I'm gonna be on *Reach for the Stars* and then move to New York and then everybody will see me and I'm famous and I'm on a red carpet and I'm tan and they'll be jealous because I'm so tan and my teeth are so white. But first, *Reach for the Stars*. And then maybe— (With jazz hands and singsong Ethel Merman voice.) Broadway! (Beat.) What's your passion speech about?

ELLIOT: Trucks.

EMORY: Oh.

ELLIOT: Emory? I'm sorry.

EMORY: For what?

ELLIOT: (Observing a feeling coldly and clinically.) I have a feeling. Here. (Points at his heart.) It feels bad.

EMORY: That's guilt.

(ELLIOT explodes into a rage out of nowhere, kicking and punching at air.)

EMORY: What is wrong with you?

ELLIOT: There's all this stuff inside of me, all these feelings, these things I want to say, but I don't know how to get them out of my skull. It's like they get stuck. I hate it.

EMORY: Use your words.

ELLIOT: I just wish that you didn't act like a girl all the time.

EMORY: I try to act like a boy. I kissed Ayesha Mitchell on the four square court so everybody would see.

ELLIOT: I know.

EMORY: She kicked me in the balls.

ELLIOT: I saw.

EMORY: I'll never double dutch with her again.

ELLIOT: See, that's an example of something that would make me punch you. Boys don't play jump rope.

EMORY: But I like it.

ELLIOT: I know.

EMORY: I'm good at it.

ELLIOT: I know. Want me to teach you how to throw? The guys would like you better.

EMORY: I don't care if they like me.

ELLIOT: But they always beat you up.

EMORY: Not always. Just sometimes.

ELLIOT: I hate that. I saw this show on cable. A science show. There was this guy who had all these aches and stuff and so the doctor cut him open and there was another little person inside.

EMORY: Like a baby?

ELLIOT: Like a twin. Like a dead little twin he absorbed before he was born.

EMORY: Oh.

ELLIOT: It had hair and a face and little arms and stuff.

EMORY: Gross.

ELLIOT: Yeah. But, like, what if I have one in me? And it's alive and it's my evil twin and it makes me do awful things like hit you? And what if it's just getting bigger and bigger until it's a teenager and it steals my date for the prom!

EMORY: You're so weird about the prom.

ELLIOT: I like tuxedos is all!

EMORY: Anyway, there's nothing living inside of you.

ELLIOT: But I can feel it. Growing. I can feel things shifting inside.

EMORY: You're just growing.

ELLIOT: Or IT's growing. Getting bigger and bigger like your Nanna's cancer and it's just waiting to rip me open and run free.

(*LADY IN A LEOTARD interjects. She wraps herself around ELLIOT's leg, like a parasite.*)

LADY IN A LEOTARD: In truth, Elliot does have a parasitic twin living inside of him. A tiny little person inside his thigh. A conscience is defined as an inner sense of what is right or wrong in one's conduct. That's just a fancy way of saying "your brain." If this is so then Elliot's twin serves as a sort of anti-conscience, making him do awful things. (*She transforms into ELLIOT's parasitic twin. Raspy voice.*) Hit that faggot in the face, Elliot! He's asking for it. Smear the queer. Smear the queer. SMEAR THE QUEER.

(*ELLIOT raises his fist to punch EMORY, who winces. LADY IN A LEOTARD transforms back into herself and begins to recede.*)

LADY IN A LEOTARD: That part is scary.

ELLIOT: Now let's go look at that chicken.

EMORY: No.

ELLIOT: I want to.

EMORY: Tough titty.

ELLIOT: You cursed.

EMORY: No, I didn't.

ELLIOT: Why won't you let me look at that chicken?

EMORY: You chase her.

ELLIOT: I just like her is all.

EMORY: Look at *these* chickens.

ELLIOT: These chickens are dumb.

(They survey the motionless chickens.)

ELLIOT: They sure don't move much.

EMORY: No.

ELLIOT: I wanna see that gigantic chicken you always talk to.

EMORY: Nope.

ELLIOT: YES!

EMORY: She's supposed to go into the machine today.

ELLIOT: Are you sad?

EMORY: Yes.

ELLIOT: Can I watch?

EMORY: No.

ELLIOT: Do you think it hurts 'em in there?

EMORY: Nanna used to kill 'em by hand. Did you know that? I woke up once and looked out the window and there was Nanna—swinging some chickens around in the air by their necks. Maybe that was better.

ELLIOT: Awesome.

EMORY: Now we have the machine. You just throw 'em in and—pop!—they come out food.

ELLIOT: If you let me play with the chickens I'll let you hold my hand.

EMORY: I don't wanna hold your dumb old hand. I've gotta go anyway.

ELLIOT: Go where?

EMORY: I've got chores.

ELLIOT: You don't got chores. This is the shittiest most rotten old farm ever. What chores are there?

EMORY: Just chores.

ELLIOT: What happens to them? In the machine?

EMORY: *(Whispers into ELLIOT's ear.)* ...And then... *(He whispers some more.)*

ELLIOT: Wow! I gotta see that!

EMORY: You can't. I'm gonna stop it from happening.

ELLIOT: I'll kiss you on the mouth.

EMORY: Go away.

ELLIOT: You know you want to.

EMORY: Quiet!

(EMORY places his hand over ELLIOT's mouth as NANNA passes by in the distance, oxygen tank in tow. She is having trouble breathing. She exits.)

ELLIOT: Your Nanna is weird.

EMORY: She's dying. She has been for a long time.

ELLIOT: I know.

EMORY: The doctor's say any day now.

ELLIOT: That sucks.

EMORY: Yep.

ELLIOT: So, like, what about you?

EMORY: I suppose I'll go to an orphanage. Like Annie. *(He sings a few lines of "Tomorrow.")*

ELLIOT: Oh.

EMORY: Or Nanna will leave the farm to me and I can finally stop processing meat and turn it into a vegan food co-op.

ELLIOT: You can't live here by yourself.

EMORY: Why not?

ELLIOT: They won't let you.

EMORY: Who won't?

ELLIOT: Them.

EMORY: I can if I want to. It'll finally be all mine. I'll tear out the living room and put in a little stage where me and Linda can put on a variety show. Then we'll get famous. Then rich! Then I'll level the barn and put in a swimming pool in the shape of a dollar sign.

ELLIOT: Who is Linda?

EMORY: That big chicken that talks.

ELLIOT: Oh. Well, that won't happen. They'll come and get you and force you to live with a foster family in a mobile home where the dad wears dirty tank tops and beats you with a belt when you spill his beer. Hey, let's go into the barn.

EMORY: I can't play. I have to go.

ELLIOT: Yes.

EMORY: I have to go.

ELLIOT: You know you want to.

EMORY: No, I don't.

ELLIOT: Come on.

EMORY: No.

ELLIOT: I said YES. I wanna play.

EMORY: You play too rough. I don't like it.

ELLIOT: Do too.

EMORY: Nuh-huh.

ELLIOT: Yeah huh. You moaned last time. You said you climaxed.

EMORY: I was only make believing.

ELLIOT: Emory. Come into the barn right now.

EMORY: I don't want to.

ELLIOT: How come?

EMORY: I'm not supposed to like it.

ELLIOT: No one will know.

EMORY: God will.

ELLIOT: Oh, shut up. Let's go.

EMORY: Okay. But not so hard. Don't leave any marks. And make it quick so I can go.

ELLIOT: *(Crosses his fingers behind his back.)* I promise.

(ELLIOT shoves EMORY offstage following closely behind. Elsewhere on the farm... NANNA is walking with her oxygen tank. She is holding Starlene.)

NANNA: You sure are one ugly-looking thing. Look at that hair. Tsk, tsk, tsk. And with a face like that you'd have to sneak up on a glass of water. I'm just gonna throw you in the fire pit so nobody will miss you anymore. Out of sight, out of mind. *(She feels flushed.)* Oh balls. I'm gonna have to sit down and rest a moment. *(She sits on a bale of hay.)* No doubt about it. This old body is going now. Anywhoodle...

(She falls asleep sitting up and drops Starlene at her feet. LINDA sneaks on, sees

Starlene, picks her up, and exits. Lights and music and applause...)*

LADY IN A LEOTARD: Ladies and gentlemen, our next act hails from somewhere deep in the heartland. Please give a warm *Reach for the Stars* welcome to shock comedian, Linda the Chicken!

(Meager applause as LINDA appears in a bubble of light. She has a mic. Nearby, a lonely stool with a glass of water on it. She is a terrible stand-up comedian. She's like a female Andrew Dice Clay except, you know, a chicken. She speaks perfect English, but with a thick Brooklyn accent.)

LINDA: Wow. Thank you. Thank you so much. That's really nice. You bitches are really beautiful. Oh! I know what you're thinking and the answer is yes. I am better than the chicken they serve in this joint. Seriously, what's that on your plate, it looks like chicken cordon *blech*. Oh! No, but seriously...I just flew in from the heartland. On a plane, bitches! You were expecting the old "and boy are my arms tired" bit? Hell no! I took friggin' Jet Blue and my ass is tired. Oh! My liver's tired too. I had four rum and Cokes before I came up here. Fine, you got me. Seven. Oh! No, I know chickens can't fly. I'm not delusional. Now some of you are probably thinking, *not delusional? This chicken is doing stand-up instead of laying on my god damn plate. Who does she think she is, the friggin' Paula Poundstone of poultry?* No, bitches! I'm not standing up here in some busted-ass Wranglers and a bolo tie talking about cats or my thighs or some shit. Although my thighs are delicious. Oh! I'm not the Elaine Boosler of chickens, bitches. I'm the friggin' Andrew Dice Clay! Oh! *(She crosses her wings across her chest and purses her beak, à la Andrew Dice Clay.)*

LADY IN A LEOTARD: *(As a heckler.)* You suck!

LINDA: No, you suck you hatchet-faced bitch. Now shut your face before I peck at your ankles.

LADY IN A LEOTARD: Boo!

LINDA: Boo you, slut!

LADY IN A LEOTARD: Boo! You suck!

(Boos from all around. The lights come up and LADY IN A LEOTARD encourages the audience to boo LINDA, who doesn't know what to do. She drops the microphone and begins to leave. She gets mad and comes back.)

LINDA: Nah. I ain't going out like that. Stop friggin' booing me.

(The boos continue.)

LINDA: I said stop it.

(They continue.)

LINDA: I ONLY WANTED TO ENTERTAIN YOU!

(The boos stop.)

LINDA: See, you made me go and freak out. I hate that. I work really hard on my act, folks. I deserve a little common courtesy. Do any of yous know how hard it is to get up here and take a chance on something? To be your authentic self in front of god and America and all you carnivores?

(Sympathetic "aws." NANNA, ELLIOT, and EMORY appear with signs. NANNA: 4. ELLIOT: -1. EMORY: 111.)

LINDA: No. I don't need your pity. I'm gonna be all right. Come on, Starlene. *(To audience.)* Peace. I'm out.

(Lights go back to normal, the stool is gone, and... LINDA begins to exit. EMORY tiptoes on.)

EMORY: Psst! Linda!

(LINDA tiptoes over to EMORY.)

EMORY: I'm sorry. I'm stuck at the moment. Elliot is forcing me to play house again.

LINDA: Bawk bawk bawk bawk.

LADY IN A LEOTARD: *(Translating.)* We don't have much time.

EMORY: I know, I know. Listen, go hide under the porch. I'll come and find you when I can get away.

LINDA: P-KAW! Cluck cluck!

LADY IN A LEOTARD: Under the porch? Are you friggin' nuts? The spider!

EMORY: I know a spider lives down there, but it's safer than the coop right now. Just trust me.

LINDA: Cluck cluck cluck.

LADY IN A LEOTARD: I trust you, Emory.

EMORY: Super. See you soon. *(Begins to exit.)*

LINDA: P-Kaw!

LADY IN A LEOTARD: Wait!

EMORY: What is it?

(She holds out Starlene, sweetly.)

EMORY: Linda, you're amazing! *(Takes Starlene and hugs LINDA.)* I love you, Linda. I really, really do.

ELLIOT: *(From offstage.)* Emory. Oh, Emory!

EMORY: *(To LINDA.)* Go!

(LINDA exits and EMORY hides Starlene just as ELLIOT enters. ELLIOT is wearing a trucker's cap and has a can of beer. He holds out a woman's slip or a silky kimono for EMORY, who takes it.)

ELLIOT: You ready?

EMORY: Yeah. Okay.

ELLIOT: You be the mom and I'll be the dad. Go!

(They hurriedly ready themselves to perform some kind of kitchen-sink drama from their own imaginations. The space is transformed into a darling little house complete with windows, one of which EMORY stares longingly through at the top of the scene.)

ELLIOT: The god damn fan belt went out on the god damn Honda again. I don't know what Eddie does to fix it but it always craps out again after a week or two. What's with you?

EMORY: Hmm? Oh, sorry. I was miles away. I like to look out this window on hot nights like this. You wanna go for a walk in a bit?

ELLIOT: Why would I want to do that?

EMORY: It's nice out.

ELLIOT: I'm tired, woman. I just wanna watch the boob tube and drink my tall boy.

EMORY: Suit yourself. I just thought it would be nice is all. I'll just sit here and watch the bugs fly into the Zapper.

ELLIOT: What's eating you?

EMORY: Nothing, honey.

ELLIOT: Out with it.

EMORY: Nothing. Funny how I always root for the moths. Don't go into that light, I think, don't do it! And just for a second I think they won't. Then ZAP.

ELLIOT: I can take the Zapper down if you want me to. Though it hardly seems worth it. Moths die, you know.

EMORY: Moths die. Too true.

(LADY IN A LEOTARD hoots like an owl.)

EMORY: You hear that owl? *(He calls back.)* Who! Who! Oh, Elliot, let's go for a stroll.

ELLIOT: Oh, all right. Let me get the flashlight. We can go for a walk.

EMORY: You don't want to.

ELLIOT: It's okay. Let's go.

EMORY: No, really. It's fine. Drink your beer. Watch your stories.

ELLIOT: Well, which is it?

EMORY: We don't have to go out for a walk. I was just pointing out that it would be nice is all. It would be nice if you felt like it, but you don't, so it's fine. We needn't bother.

ELLIOT: Okay. I won't bother. So. What's for dinner?

EMORY: Sorry? I was lost again.

ELLIOT: Dinner, woman.

EMORY: You catch it, you eat it. Boil a hot dog or something. Microwave a Hot Pocket.

ELLIOT: Fuck your hot pocket!

EMORY: I'm tired, honey.

ELLIOT: From what? All you did was sit on your ass and watch Oprah all day while I worked my hands to the bone.

EMORY: Hands to the—you're a landscaper for god's sake. What? You planted too many flowers today? Drank too much lemonade?

ELLIOT: Shut it.

EMORY: I'm sorry. I don't feel right. If you must know I did the grocery shopping, washed and ironed your shirts, and scrubbed the bathroom floor.

ELLIOT: That all?

EMORY: No. I went to see the doctor today.

ELLIOT: You feeling sick or something?

EMORY: I just said I didn't feel right, didn't I?

ELLIOT: Sorry.

EMORY: I'm gonna have another baby, Elliot.

ELLIOT: You what?

EMORY: Another baby.

ELLIOT: God damn it, woman!

EMORY: I'm sorry.

ELLIOT: We can't afford another baby.

EMORY: I know, Elliot.

ELLIOT: We gotta do something.

EMORY: I know. I got that planned. It's gonna cost four hundred dollars.

ELLIOT: FOUR HUNDRED DOLLARS?

EMORY: Well? What else are we gonna do?

ELLIOT: I'm sorry. So when do they do it?

EMORY: I have an appointment in two weeks.

ELLIOT: Two weeks.

(Long pause.)

EMORY: It's a sin, you know.

ELLIOT: Yep.

EMORY: Should we keep it?

ELLIOT: Nope.

EMORY: I'm gonna go lie down.

ELLIOT: We got too many kids already.

EMORY: I know.

(EMORY begins to exits but ELLIOT stops him. ELLIOT wraps his arms around EMORY and kisses his neck.)

ELLIOT: Hey. I'm sorry.

EMORY: I know.

ELLIOT: I'm a jerk.

(ELLIOT spins EMORY around and begins to dance with him.)

ELLIOT: Another baby. That's great news.

EMORY: You really think so?

ELLIOT: Sure I do.

(Long pause.)

ELLIOT: Jesus, what happened to us?

EMORY: Nothing. Just tired, I guess. Overworked.

ELLIOT: You're beautiful. You know that?

EMORY: Stop it.

ELLIOT: I mean it. You are.

EMORY: I'm all sweaty and red.

ELLIOT: I think you're gorgeous.

EMORY: Well, thank you.

ELLIOT: You remember the prom?

EMORY: Mm-hmm.

ELLIOT: I was thinking about that today.

EMORY: You were?

ELLIOT: It was the first time I ever got to wear a tuxedo. I was so nervous sitting there in your brown and mustard living room. With your pop just in his boxer shorts giving me the fish eye. That gun rack behind him. And then you came down those stairs. A vision in pink, walking in slow motion.

EMORY: I wore stiletto heels for the first time and I was afraid I'd fall face forward down those stairs.

ELLIOT: I remember you couldn't dance because of those shoes. Remember? We just sat there because your feet hurt too bad and finally you turned to me and said—

EMORY: Would you be embarrassed if I took my shoes off?

ELLIOT and EMORY: —I feel like dancing.

ELLIOT: And dance we did. I thought, I'm gonna marry that girl. And I did.

EMORY: I still have that dress.

ELLIOT: You do?

EMORY: It's in a plastic storage box under the bed. Still fit the last time I tried it on.

ELLIOT: After all them kids?

EMORY: Mm-hmm.

ELLIOT: Damn, woman. You still got it.

(ELLIOT kisses EMORY passionately and begins removing his clothes.)

ELLIOT: Get in that bedroom, girl. I feel like making love.

EMORY: Again? Elliot, I've got something I've gotta do.

ELLIOT: Stop your yapping.

EMORY: Seriously, I can't play anymore. There's something I gotta do.

ELLIOT: Sometimes I think you like that chicken more than me.

EMORY: Elliot...

ELLIOT: I said go. Now.

(EMORY exits. ELLIOT's giant thigh is hurting. He crosses to a bale of hay, sits, and rubs it. He finds Starlene.)

ELLIOT: What the—

(He picks her up. Music. Magic. He is in love with her. NANNA enters. Sees ELLIOT. Music stops and ELLIOT hides Starlene.)

NANNA: Who the hell are you?

ELLIOT: Name's Elliot. I live down the road.

NANNA: I seen your place before. Your family's got all them trucks in the yard.

ELLIOT: Yeah.

NANNA: And your mama's got Mountain Dew mouth. I can smell it clear down the road. My, it lets off such a stink. What's your name again?

ELLIOT: Elliot.

NANNA: Mm-hmm. And what are you doing on my property?

ELLIOT: I was playing catch with Emory.

NANNA: You wouldn't lie to a gal, would you?

ELLIOT: No.

NANNA: Well, that's nice. You teach him to throw like a boy, would you?

ELLIOT: Okay.

NANNA: That's a good man. You good to my Emory?

ELLIOT: Yes.

NANNA: He's real soft. Gotta wear kiddie gloves with that one.

(Quiet as they stare at one another. LADY IN A LEOTARD wraps herself around ELLIOT's leg and becomes his parasitic twin.)

LADY IN A LEOTARD: She wants something from us.

ELLIOT: What are you staring at?

NANNA: Where did you get that doll?

ELLIOT: I found it.

NANNA: Hand it over.

LADY IN A LEOTARD: Give it to her!

(ELLIOT crosses to NANNA and hands her the doll. It is difficult for him to move with LADY IN A LEOTARD attached to his leg.)

NANNA: What's the matter with your leg?

ELLIOT and LADY IN A LEOTARD: Nothing.

NANNA: How would you like to make some money today?

LADY IN A LEOTARD: Ask her what we have to do.

ELLIOT: What do I have to do?

NANNA: Well...today is processing day.

(Elsewhere...LINDA appears seated in a tight, dark place beneath the porch. She has a suitcase with her. There are spider webs all around her. Beams of light sneak *through the floorboards overhead and cast eerie shadows on her face. She talks to herself.)*

LINDA: Sure is friggin' creepy here beneath the porch. I don't like all these spider webs. *(Beat.)* I wonder if I'm feeding into the stereotype of chickens being cowardly, or do you think it's simply normal to be frightened in a situation like the one I currently find myself in? I mean, the thing about being a chicken is that there's very little in the way of spontaneity. Mostly things just trudge on in the same way. No surprises. You kind of get used to it after some time, and you think, this is how my life will proceed. On a straight line, in measurable increments, until I die. Until I go into the machine, which is my manifest destiny. And then something happens, and it's like, "Oh. There's all these other things I can do." And it's strange and sort of scary, but for the first time you feel sort of hopeful. For the first time you feel something that's not just a sort of dull contentment. And it's nice. Scary and nice. *(Something comes over her and she clucks loudly. She reaches beneath her and pulls out an egg.)* I just laid an egg!

(LADY IN A LEOTARD becomes a spider—I think a puppet or some sort of eight-legged, eight-eyed costume piece is in order. LINDA doesn't see her at first.)

LADY IN A LEOTARD: Girl, I'm gonna bite you.

LINDA: Who said that?

LADY IN A LEOTARD: I did. Me. The spider. I'm gonna bite you.

LINDA: Why?

LADY IN A LEOTARD: For straight up wrecking my web!

LINDA: I'm sorry. I didn't mean to.

LADY IN A LEOTARD: It took me forever to make that web.

LINDA: Like I said, I'm really sorry.

LADY IN A LEOTARD: You're a chicken.

LINDA: Yeah.

LADY IN A LEOTARD: Ima bite you.

LINDA: WAIT.

LADY IN A LEOTARD: What?

LINDA: Why bite me? I'm too big for you to eat.

LADY IN A LEOTARD: True, true.

LINDA: And it was an accident.

LADY IN A LEOTARD: Mm-hmm.

LINDA: And I said I was sorry.

LADY IN A LEOTARD: True, true.

LINDA: So it wouldn't do much good to bite me.

LADY IN A LEOTARD: I guess not.

LINDA: What's your name?

LADY IN A LEOTARD: Rochelle.

LINDA: It's nice to meet you.

LADY IN A LEOTARD: It's nice to meet you too—

LINDA: Linda.

LADY IN A LEOTARD: It's nice to meet you, Linda. Listen, you really could have fucked up my egg sacks just then.

LINDA: I'm sorry.

LADY IN A LEOTARD: I don't like people fucking with my eggs.

LINDA: I get it, really. I don't like people messing with my eggs either.

LADY IN A LEOTARD: It makes Rochelle mad.

LINDA: It makes Linda mad too.

LADY IN A LEOTARD: 'Cause I'm gonna straight up eat me some of them babies when they come…

LINDA: Oh—

LADY IN A LEOTARD: Just like I ate their daddy.

LINDA: I should probably go.

LADY IN A LEOTARD: Don't judge me. You come up here under my porch, mess up my web, and now you're gonna judge me for having a little snack? Shit, there's gonna be like a thousand of 'em. Why can't Rochelle have a little taste after a hard day's work? Babies are delicious.

LINDA: Of course Rochelle can have a snack.

LADY IN A LEOTARD: You scared of me? I know, I know. Look it, I got eight eyes! That's crazy, right?

LINDA: Crazy.

LADY IN A LEOTARD: *(Laughing to herself, pleased.)* Everybody's scared of Rochelle.

LINDA: Do you like that?

LADY IN A LEOTARD: What do you mean, do I like it? Of course I like it! I get to straight up do whatever I want. Eat whatever I want. Rochelle likes to eat stuff.

LINDA: Like what?

LADY IN A LEOTARD: I don't know. Whatever is smaller and slower than me.

LINDA: Oh.

LADY IN A LEOTARD: I like killing pathetic things.

LINDA: I eat worms.

LADY IN A LEOTARD: Exactly. Say, all this talk about food makes me hungry. Maybe I'll eat you after all.

LINDA: I'm like forty times bigger than you.

LADY IN A LEOTARD: That's it, chicken bitch. Ima bite you.

(LINDA gets bitten.)

LINDA: Ouch!

LADY IN A LEOTARD: Ha!

LINDA: What did you do that for?

LADY IN A LEOTARD: 'Cause I can. 'Cause I felt like it!

LINDA: You're such a friggin' jerk!

LADY IN A LEOTARD: You're gonna get wicked stomach cramps now.

LINDA: I don't feel— *(She goes stiff as a board.)* Ow. Ow. Ow.

LADY IN A LEOTARD: Told you. Now you're gonna foam up at the beak. Wait for it…

(LINDA does.)

LADY IN A LEOTARD: Pow! That's what you get for coming up under my porch! *(She laughs.)*

(NANNA enters.)

NANNA: What's going on down here?

LADY IN A LEOTARD: Oh snap! Gotta go! *(Scurries off into the shadows.)*

NANNA: What are you doing under here, little chicken? *(To herself.)* Lord have mercy, it's like they got a sixth sense on processing day. *(To LINDA.)* Come on now…

(She grabs LINDA by the neck, who is paralyzed by spider poison.)

NANNA: Got bit by that spider, huh? Yep. Happens to the best of 'em.

(LINDA works up the strength to move and pecks NANNA's hand. She runs off.)

NANNA: Damn it. I'll get that giant chicken if it's the last thing I do.

(Meanwhile, elsewhere... EMORY and ELLIOT sit cross-legged facing one another. They are naked. If one or both characters is played by a female, it might be funny to put them in flesh-colored nude suits with tiny penises and testicles. In fact, that might be funny even if both characters are played by men.)

ELLIOT: *(With corresponding gestures.)* Milk, milk, lemonade. Around the corner fudge is made.

(EMORY laughs.)

ELLIOT: *(With corresponding gestures.)* Chinese, Japanese, dirty knees, look at these!

(Laughter.)

ELLIOT: Lady, lady, in the tub. How many titties did you scrub?

EMORY: Stop it! My stomach hurts.

ELLIOT: You laugh like a girl.

EMORY: No, I don't.

ELLIOT: You act like one.

EMORY: I like acting like a girl.

ELLIOT: I know, but—

EMORY: I mean, to me I'm not acting like a girl. I'm just acting like myself. So if this is how girls act then I like it.

ELLIOT: What are you even talking about, Emory?

EMORY: I'm talking about my feelings.

ELLIOT: Great.

EMORY: See, no matter how much people call me faggot or sissy or fudge packer or butt pirate, I really like being me. You wanna know a secret?

ELLIOT: No.

EMORY: Come on.

ELLIOT: It's not right, what we did.

EMORY: Not again. You do this every time.

ELLIOT: You're not a girl.

EMORY: I kind of am.

ELLIOT: No, you're not. It's gross.

EMORY: It's not gross.

ELLIOT: What's your secret?

EMORY: Okay. Every time you or one of the other boys beats me up, I come here to the barn and I choreograph a new dance routine. And I think about how awesome I am. And how someday other people will see it too.

ELLIOT: Emory?

EMORY: Yeah?

ELLIOT: You are awesome.

EMORY: I know. Elliot?

ELLIOT: Yeah.

EMORY: Do you think you could stop calling me names in front of the other kids at school?

ELLIOT: I can't.

EMORY: How come?

ELLIOT: Because.

EMORY: Because why?

ELLIOT: Because people might see that I like you.

EMORY: Oh. Okay.

ELLIOT: Does that make you sad?

EMORY: It's okay. I'm used to it.

ELLIOT: I do think you're awesome though. Secretly.

EMORY: I know.

ELLIOT: And I do wanna keep doing this. Even though I know it's wrong. It's good practice until middle school when I'll have a girlfriend.

EMORY: Things would be a lot easier if I really was a girl. Sometimes I wish god would take my privates away so that things would go more smoothly. Everybody's so obsessed with them.

ELLIOT: Does that make you sad?

EMORY: Sometimes. A lot. But I'll get used to it.

ELLIOT: You can get used to anything.

EMORY: Can I get dressed now?

ELLIOT: Yeah. Okay.

(They begin to dress.)

ELLIOT: Yup. I guess we can get used to anything.

EMORY: Hey...

ELLIOT: What?

EMORY: I have an idea for a game.

(He procures a spray bottle, which he hands to ELLIOT.)

EMORY: I'll pretend to be a boneless, skinless chicken and you'll be the farmer. Okay?

ELLIOT: What do I do?

EMORY: I am totally defenseless so you have to nurse me. Spray me with water so I don't dry up.

(ELLIOT begins to spray EMORY, lovingly. EMORY throws his head back and makes the same gargling noise that NANNA made earlier. Music. What begins is a sort of dreamy ballet happening all over the farm at once. And... NANNA is setting fire to Starlene over a trash heap.)

LADY IN A LEOTARD: Ladies and gentlemen, this is a very special *Reach for the Stars*. This is the final performance of of the one, the only, Starlene.

(LADY IN A LEOTARD puts on a wig and a small costume piece so that she is twinsies with Starlene. She has a microphone. She begins to sing "I've Been to Paradise" by Charlene. And... ELLIOT is spraying EMORY with the water. EMORY gurgles softly.)

ELLIOT: Here chick, chick, chick...

(And... LINDA is crossing in the distance with foam coming from her beak. She is tired and confused. She exits. And... The sun has reached its peak and is now descending. And... NANNA drops the doll into the fire.)

NANNA: Goodbye, ugly. *(She exits.)*

(LADY IN A LEOTARD finishes the song but the music continues.)

LADY IN A LEOTARD: Good-night, everybody! I love you all! *(She removes Starlene's wig and throws it into the fire. She crawls over to ELLIOT as the music ends and becomes his parasitic twin.)*

LADY IN A LEOTARD: Psst. That chicken is nearby. You could get her. She's sick anyway.

ELLIOT: Leave me alone.

EMORY: I'm just playing.

ELLIOT: Not you.

LADY IN A LEOTARD: Do what I say! Here she comes.

(LINDA enters and sits on a bale of hay. She is foaming at the beak and her feathers are ruffled. She is exhausted and delirious.)

EMORY: Linda, what happened?

LINDA: Bawk...bawk bawk cluck cluck cluck.

LADY IN A LEOTARD: Well...it started in my neck and then traveled into my left wing.

LINDA: Bawk bawk bawk bawk bawk bawk.

LADY IN A LEOTARD: And then it sort of eased on over to my breast. My heart is beating so fast, Emory. It's throbbing. Also, my legs are all tingly. Do I look all right?

EMORY: I have to be honest. You don't look so good.

ELLIOT: What is she saying?

EMORY: Nothing.

ELLIOT: She looks like she woke up in a flop house.

EMORY: Shut up.

ELLIOT: Well, she's dying, Emory. Just look at her!

EMORY: What happened to you, Linda?

LINDA: Bawk bawk P-KAW.

LADY IN A LEOTARD: I got bit by the spider. Right in the neck.

EMORY: I'm so sorry. Are you in pain?

ELLIOT: Of course she's in pain, just look at her!

LINDA: Cluck cluck cluck cluck.

LADY IN A LEOTARD: It doesn't hurt so bad. Is my beak foamy? It feels foamy and there's a funny taste.

EMORY: Yes. It's foamy.

LINDA: Bawk bawk bawk.

LADY IN A LEOTARD: I think I'm dying, Emory.

(Beat.)

ELLIOT: I think we should break her neck, Emory.

EMORY: No!

ELLIOT: She's in pain!

EMORY: If you touch her I swear I'll never touch you again.

ELLIOT: Can't you see it's hurting her?

EMORY: YOU wanna hurt her. You're sick.

ELLIOT: Am not.

EMORY: Are too. You're always punching people and setting stuff on fire.

ELLIOT: I just get mad is all. You don't know how it is for me.

EMORY: Don't come near us.

ELLIOT: We have to put her out of her misery, Emory. I can't watch her like this. Let's put her in the machine.

EMORY: Why don't you go back to your filthy house and leave us alone?

ELLIOT: No. I hate it there. Everybody is ugly and mean.

EMORY: YOU'RE ugly and mean.

ELLIOT: I WANNA BE NICE. I do. I wanna dress up and say things like "cool haircut" or "I like your dress." *(He has a spastic fit. He punches and kicks at the air, screaming, until he is utterly exhausted.)* My sisters watch this movie all the time. About some redhead who's supposed to go to the prom with some douche bag, but the douche bag ditches her. Then this redhead, she works up her inner strength and she goes to the prom anyway. They end up falling in love or whatever. This redhead, she's in a lot of movies about prom. I love them. Everybody gets dressed up and there's this excitement. Everybody's excited about whatever, like who they'll become. You know? And everybody's slow dancing with their best girl and you know that everything will be okay. *(Gets lost in his imaginary prom. He closes his eyes and begins to slow dance with an invisible partner whilst singing a few bars of Spandau Ballet's "True.")*

EMORY: *(Interrupts.)* Well, you can't be nice! Your heart is made of tar and it looks like a craisin! Now go home!

ELLIOT: I like it here. I like being with you.

EMORY: Please? Linda is sick.

ELLIOT: She's dying, Emory. Let me help her.

EMORY: We just have to get rid of the poison is all. Hold on, Linda! I'll save you!

(EMORY runs to her and begins to suck the poison out. It tastes awful. NANNA enters with The Machine, a giant steel monstrosity that looks very much like an enormous meat grinder. One end is marked "IN." The other, "OUT.")

NANNA: Grab that chicken.

LADY IN A LEOTARD: *(As the parasitic twin.)* Do it. NOW.

(ELLIOT grabs LINDA. NANNA begins to throw inanimate chickens into the machine, one by one. With each one there is a buzz-saw sound, a blast of feathers from one side. On the other side, a perfect packaged chicken is produced. Clucking.)

NANNA: Quiet down, you chickens. You won't feel a thing.

EMORY: Nanna, stop!

NANNA: Oh, don't make such a fuss, Emory. *(She throws a chicken in.)* We gotta make a living. *(And another one.)* We gotta eat, don't we?

EMORY: Nanna, I'm leaving here. You hear me?

NANNA: What are you talking about?

EMORY: I'm taking Linda and I'm going.

NANNA: Who is Linda? That big chicken there?

EMORY: Yes, that chicken. She's my friend.

NANNA: You can't be friends with a chicken.

EMORY: Well, I am. Nanna, I'm not like you. I'm different. I'm different and I'm dying here.

NANNA: No, that chicken is dying. Can't you see she got bit by a spider? She's dying, Emory. Might as well throw her in. *(Throws another chicken in.)*

EMORY: Stop it!

NANNA: This is why I'm so tough on you. Life is hard, Emory. If you're too soft it just chews you up and spits you out again. That's what separates these chickens from us. See? *(Throws a chicken in.)* Bawk bawk bawk! *(And another.)*

They're too stupid to do anything and that's why I get to eat 'em. Now quit buggin' me and let me work!

(She throws another chicken in. EMORY rushes to her and grabs her. She pushes him down and throws another chicken in. She continues to throw chickens in during the following speech. The sound and feathers serve as punctuation.)

NANNA: I know I should use this opportunity to teach you a thing or two. Now that I'm in my last days and all. I know I should impart some kind of wisdom about the nature of life and death. I could use metaphors, farming metaphors, about harvests and the changing of seasons, and burning the crops to prepare for a rebirth. But I don't feel like it. *(Throws a chicken in.)* I'm too sick. Emory, there might come a time when you feel so bad it's in every part of you. It's crawling inside of you like ants marching up a tree. That's how I feel today. Like ants are in my veins taking every good feeling I have and toting them off to some hidden place I can't see. This is what I wish somebody would have told me: that some days it hurts so bad to be alive you just wish it would end. People always say that one day you wake up old, wondering where all the years went. But I felt myself getting older. In increments large and small, I felt my body getting rickety. Stiff. My brain getting tired and confused. I wish it had happened in one moment. But it didn't. It took my whole life and it hurt like hell. Now bring me that chicken.

(ELLIOT crosses to her with LINDA. LINDA is on the threshold of the machine. Long silence.)

EMORY: Linda.

LINDA: Bawk bawk bawk.

LADY IN A LEOTARD: *(Has removed herself from ELLIOT's leg and translates as usual.)* It's okay, Emory.

EMORY: Don't say that.

LINDA: Bawk bawk bawk.

LADY IN A LEOTARD: I know you tried. Thanks. But I couldn't have lived anyway.

NANNA: It's just a chicken, Emory.

EMORY: She's my friend.

NANNA: You'll live. Kid, put her in.

(ELLIOT starts to put LINDA in.)

EMORY: Fight back!

LINDA: Cluck cluck cluck cluck.

LADY IN A LEOTARD: There's no point.

LINDA: Bawk bawk bawk.

LADY IN A LEOTARD: It's too late.

EMORY: Linda…

LINDA: P-Kaw! P-Kaw! P-P-P—P

(Suddenly LINDA is in a bubble of light whilst on the threshold. She speaks perfect English.)

LINDA: Please, Emory. Don't be sad for me. I'm not something alive. I mean, I am alive, but it's not my place to make waves, you know? I was born to go into the machine. If you think about it, I'm really just a function. Something to be used. That's why I don't feel so sad. I'm fulfilling my friggin' destiny.

EMORY: I'm sorry, Linda.

LINDA: Don't worry. Everything is gonna be a-okay. Bye now!

EMORY: Bye.

ELLIOT: I'm sorry, Emory. I can't help it.

(He shoves LINDA in.)

LINDA: P-KAAAAAAAWWWWWW!

(Light shift. Music. Something throbbing and dirty. "Chicken Walk" by Hasil Adkins works well. We are inside of the machine. LINDA appears falling, falling, falling. She lands with a thump and looks around. The rest of the cast becomes cogs, and blades, and mechanical arms that take LINDA through the machine in an elaborate dance. Her beak is shaved off, feathers plucked out, legs sawed off, etc. Lastly, she is decapitated. She runs around without a head for a moment but is scooped up and carried off. Music out. Lights back to normal and... We are back in the barn as before. EMORY has his head in the machine. When he comes away he has LINDA's blood on his face. NANNA has crossed to ELLIOT and handed him a ten-dollar bill.)

ELLIOT: I'm sorry, Emory. *(He exits.)*

NANNA: *(Sitting.)* I don't feel well.

(EMORY runs to her and hits her over and over again. He tries to pull the tubes from her nose.)

EMORY: I hate you!

NANNA: *(Grabbing his hands.)* After everything I did for you? Raised you like my own? Fed and clothed you? You're breaking my heart. Yep. My heart's broken. Oh, who cares? I'm a goner anyway. Might as well just jump into that machine too. *(She begins to walk toward the machine.)*

EMORY: I don't care.

NANNA: Oh, my heart! My heart can't take it! *(Grabs at her heart and begins to stumble forward.)* I'm having a heart attack.

(She falls onto a bale of hay and sits motionless, eyes closed. EMORY steps very, very close to her for a good look. Her eyes pop open, scaring EMORY. She laughs hysterically.)

NANNA: Ha! You think I was a goner? Please. I'll outlive you all. I'm gonna go up to the house. The *Wheel* is starting. Dinner will be at seven o'clock sharp. *(Wanders over to the machine and picks up a package of chicken. She sees EMORY.)* Don't worry. I'll fix you some oatmeal.

(She exits. EMORY is alone. He wipes the blood and feathers from his face. The sun is setting. It is practically night. ELLIOT enters.)

ELLIOT: Hi.

EMORY: Go away.

ELLIOT: Are you mad?

EMORY: Yes.

ELLIOT: Do you hate me?

EMORY: Yes.

ELLIOT: I hate me too.

EMORY: Good.

ELLIOT: I'm sorry.

EMORY: No you aren't.

ELLIOT: Am too.

EMORY: Well, I don't care.

ELLIOT: If you still want to run away I'll go with you. If you want. I don't wanna be how I am anymore.

EMORY: I don't want to.

ELLIOT: Oh. *(Pulls out his lighter and begins to play with it.)*

EMORY: I hate you.

ELLIOT: No you don't.

EMORY: Do too.

ELLIOT: Nuh-huh.

EMORY: Leave me alone. Why don't you ever just leave me alone?

ELLIOT: Because I like you.

EMORY: You do?

ELLIOT: Sure.

EMORY: I need to be alone.

ELLIOT: Play with me.

EMORY: No.

ELLIOT: Yes.

(ELLIOT crosses to cassette player and pushes "play." A slow song. Maybe "Forever Young" by Alphaville.)

ELLIOT: Dance with me.

EMORY: What?

ELLIOT: Come dance with me.

EMORY: I don't feel like it.

ELLIOT: Come on.

(EMORY crosses to ELLIOT, who puts a corsage around his wrist. They slow dance.)

EMORY: I really, really hate you.

ELLIOT: No, you don't. You're too soft to hate people.

EMORY: Maybe.

ELLIOT: Isn't it amazing. It's finally Prom Night.

EMORY: *(Begrudgingly plays along.)* The end of an era. Our lives will never be the same.

ELLIOT: I wonder what will become of us.

EMORY: Nothin' much.

ELLIOT: You're my best girl. You know that, don't you?

EMORY: Yep.

ELLIOT: I rented a hotel room.

EMORY: Fresh.

ELLIOT: You want to?

EMORY: I'm scared.

ELLIOT: Me too.

EMORY: You mind if I take my shoes off? I can't dance in these.

ELLIOT: Feel free.

EMORY: Elliot?

ELLIOT: Yeah, babe?

EMORY: Let's burn the whole thing down.

ELLIOT: Way ahead of you, babe. Way ahead of you.

(The farm is burning. LINDA appears as a chicken angel. EMORY stares at her. She flies toward him and lands. She shrugs at him slowly. She holds ups a sign that reads "10.")

ELLIOT: Don't worry, girl. I've got you now. I got you.

(Both BOYS throw their heads back and begin to gurgle. They are boneless, skinless chickens.)

LADY IN A LEOTARD: *(Spraying them with water from a spray bottle.)* Hooray.

(The farm continues to burn all around them as the BOYS continue to dance.)

(END OF PLAY.)

ABOUT THE EDITOR

MARTIN DENTON is the founder and Executive Director of The New York Theatre Experience, Inc., (NYTE) and editor and chief theatre reviewer for NYTE's website nytheatre.com. He has edited all the play anthologies published by NYTE Small Press featuring, to date, the work of 156 emerging playwrights. He is, also, the creator of the nytheatrecast (www.nytheatrecast.com) New York City's first theatre podcast offering original content.

ABOUT THE PUBLISHER

THE NEW YORK THEATRE EXPERIENCE, INC. (NYTE), is a nonprofit New York State corporation. Its mission is to use traditional and new media to foster interest, engagement and participation in theatre and drama and to provide tangible support to theatre artists and dramatists, especially emerging artists and artists in the nonprofit sector. The principal activity of The New York Theatre Experience is the operation of a free website (www.nytheatre.com) that comprehensively covers the New York theatre scene – on, off-, and off-off-Broadway. An ongoing program is NYTE Small Press which publishes yearly anthologies of new plays by emerging playwrights. Information about NYTE can be found on the Internet at www.nyte.org. Contact NYTE online at info@nyte.org or by mail at: The New York Theatre Experience, Inc., P.O. Box 1606, Murray Hill Station, New York, NY 10156.

ABOUT THE SERIES

The *Plays and Playwrights* series is a yearly anthology of plays by emerging playwrights whose work received a production in NYC in the previous theatre season. Since 2000, The New York Theatre Experience, Inc. (NYTE) has published these anthologies which include complete scripts, biographical sketches, and a detailed introduction by the editor, Martin Denton. In 2004, the Library of Congress designated these anthologies a series. NYTE is a nonprofit corporation that utilizes its small press to promote the works of emerging playwrights so as to reach a wide audience to show the diverse spirit of contemporary theatre, in terms of genre, form, and subject matter. For complete information about these volumes, please visit www.nytesmallpress.com.

E-BOOK FOR THE KINDLE

Plays and Playwrights for the New Millennium – the e-book was released in February 2010 purchasable through Amazon.com's Kindle Store. This new updated version of NYTE's first publication includes the complete scripts of seven plays plus bonus material, new short works from six of the authors. Information about the e-book is available online at www.amazon.com/dp/B00378L6LO.